THE SPIRIT OF RUSSIA

BY T. G. MASARYK
THE IDEALS OF HUMANITY AND HOW TO WORK
MODERN MAN AND RELIGION

BY KAREL ČAPEK
MASARYK ON THOUGHT AND LIFE

THOMAS GARRIGUE MASARYK

The Spirit of Russia

STUDIES IN HISTORY, LITERATURE AND PHILOSOPHY

translated from the German original by
Eden and Cedar Paul

with additional chapters and
bibliographies by
Jan Slavik

the former translated and the latter
condensed and translated by
W. R. & Z. Lee

VOLUME ONE

LONDON: GEORGE ALLEN & UNWIN LTD
NEW YORK: THE MACMILLAN COMPANY

FIRST IMPRESSION 1919
SECOND EDITION 1955
THIRD IMPRESSION 1961

PRINTED IN GREAT BRITAIN BY
BRADFORD AND DICKENS
DRAYTON HOUSE, LONDON, W.C.1

TRANSLATORS' FOREWORD
TO THE FIRST EDITION

THOMAS GARRIGUE MASARYK was born at Göding,
Moravia, in the year 1850. The child of poor parents,
after passing through the primary school he was apprenticed
to a blacksmith and worked at this trade for some time. He
studied in Vienna and in Leipzig, and at the age of
twenty-nine he became lecturer on philosophy at the university of Vienna. His first publication was a work on
suicide, which he regarded as a morbid symptom of the
condition of contemporary Europe, declaring its chief cause
to be the decay in religious sentiment. In 1882 he was
appointed professor of philosophy at the newly founded Czech
university of Prague. Extremely well versed in English philosophy, and a critical student of Hume, John Stuart Mill, and
Herbert Spencer, he has published a monograph on the first-
named writer. Comte and modern French philosophy, Kant
and modern German philosophy, have likewise been two of
the main factors in his mental development, so that his whole
reading of history is based upon a philosophical and humanist
foundation. Prior to the war, it was perhaps among Marxist
students that his name was most widely known in this country
and the United States, for he is the author of a detailed study
of Marxism, and is an opponent of the famous doctrine of
historical materialism.

From the opening of his career, Masaryk's influence in
Bohemia has been extraordinary, his leadership being accepted
in all branches of public life, political, scientific, and philosophical. Apart from his popularisation, always more or less critical,
of the teaching of the French and British positivists, he has
been a close student of French, English, and Russian literature,

▼

and has been instrumental in promoting the issue of Czech translations of standard works, and in the establishment of a library of French, English, and Russian authors.

A Czech nationalist at a time when the present expansion of Czecho-Slovak power and the sudden collapse of German dominion in Bohemia could not possibly be foreseen, his idea was that the Czechs must be under no illusions as to their strength. He considered that a population of ten million Bohemians face to face with seventy million Germans, must look to cultural and economic forces for the maintenance of a substantial independence. Owing to his unflagging insistence upon these considerations, his party was termed the Realist Party, and the movement of which he became the head was known as " the realist movement." For some years before the war, his moral influence in the Czech lands had been unrivalled. He was considered to be the one man who could speak to Europe on behalf of his nation, was looked upon as the prime initiator of his country's national rebirth.

In Austro-Hungarian politics he was a federalist, believing that reorganisation on democratic lines could secure peace and satisfactory development for all the nations under Austro-Hungarian rule. Elected to the Reichsrat in 1891, he was a consistent opponent of the Germanisation of Bohemia and of the antinationalist activities of the Austrian bureaucracy in that country. No less zealously and acutely did he criticise Austro-Hungarian policy in Bosnia-Herzegovina. During the first years of his parliamentary activities he wrote *The Czech Question*, a political catechism expounding the role of the Czech nation in European history. The Czech question seemed to him an international one, but at the same time he regarded it as the very kernel of the Austro-Hungarian problem. The key-note of his political outlook may perhaps be formulated in a single phrase, in a prophecy more than once enunciated, a peculiarly fortunate venture in the prophetic field. " Austria must completely modify her internal structure, or she will be erased from the map of Europe."

Definitely espousing the Allied cause in the summer of 1914, Masaryk necessarily became an exile from his own land, and was for a time a refugee in London. This is not the place for an account of his recent activities in connection with the Czecho-Slovak movement, but we may fittingly record that as we write these lines news comes to hand that the author of

The Spirit of Russia has been elected first president of the Czecho-Slovak republic.

An account of the origin of the study of Russia now presented to the English-speaking world may best be given in the author's own words.

" When the Russo-Japanese War and the revolution of 1905 increased the general interest in Russia, acquaintances of mine who knew that I had made a special study of that country suggested that I should write on the subject. I therefore published in the ' Oesterreichische Rundschau ' an article giving a detailed account of the intimate connection between the revolution and Russian literature ; and I also wrote reviews of the books then recently published by Mackenzie Wallace, Ular, Konni, Kropotkin, Petrov, Reissner, and Brückner. When reading these works I conceived the idea of elucidating the nature of the Russian revolution, and of discussing the Russian problem as a whole, in a study of Dostoevskii. The attempt, however, proved unsuccessful, for while making it I came to realize that it would be impossible to do justice to Dostoevskii without discussing his predecessors and successors, and that this would involve the consideration of the chief problems of the history of Russian literature, of the religious and philosophical thought of that country, indeed, of Russian literature in general.

" From youth onwards I had been greatly interested in Russia, my study of the country having begun with its literature. Contenting myself first with translations and subsequently learning Russian, from the study of Russian authors I acquired a knowledge of the country which I then endeavoured to amplify by reading history, etc., and by visits to the Russian empire.

" The aim of the present work is to furnish an understanding of Russia from the inside, through the instrumentality of Russian literature ; and since I have long paid especial attention to Dostoevskii and to his analysis of Russia, what I write about Dostoevskii is the core of the undertaking.

" Properly speaking, the entire study is devoted to Dostoevskii, but I lacked the literary skill requisite for the interweaving of all I wanted to say into an account of that author. The work has therefore been subdivided. The first part, that which I now publish, contains an account of the philosophy of history and the philosophy of religion of Dostoevskii's predecessors and successors, and this is compiled in such a fashion as to present something approaching a history of the evolution of these ideas.

" The introductory section dealing with the history of Russia has been prefixed because in my account of the individual writers under consideration various historical references are requisite, and instead of complicating the exposition by notes and interpolations it seemed preferable to undertake a systematic survey of historical development, and to utilise this opportunity to direct the reader's attention to the problems subsequently to be discussed.

" The first half of the second portion will deal with Dostoevskii's philosophy of history and philosophy of religion (A Struggle for God—Dostoevskii and Nihilism) ; the second half will expound the relationship of Dostoevskii to Russian literature since Puškin, and his relationship to European literature (Titanism or Humanism ? From Puškin to Gor'kii).

" The work will afford proof that an analysis of Dostoevskii is a sound method of studying Russia, though some might doubt this at first sight. By word of mouth certain experts have expressed such a doubt, but I hope to show that I have been right in choosing Dostoevskii as my main text—and this although, or for the very reason that, I differ profoundly from Dostoevskii's outlook.

" Whilst writing I have had in mind the interests of two distinct reading publics, that of Europe and that of Russia. This has involved a peculiar duplex position. For Europe, it was necessary to explain much that would be unknown to my readers. For Russia, I have often had to formulate the known in some fresh way, and to present the whole object of vision in an unfamiliar light.

" The result has been a certain lack of symmetry. The reader will have to forgive me for dealing with matters unknown or comparatively unknown in Europe at greater length than is consistent with the usual canons of literary composition.

" Had I written the book for Russia alone it would have been more concisely expressed. But even as it is, I have assumed a great deal as familiar. This applies above all to descriptive detail, statistics, and the like ; but I devote an appendix to the bibliography of the study of Russia.

" I may add that in the year 1902, in a course of lectures

delivered at the university of Chicago under the auspices of the Crane foundation, I produced the pith of the present book.

" In any work on Russia it is necessary to decide certain special questions of literary style.

" After prolonged hesitation I determined not to give chapter and verse references to Russian literature. In Europe, Russian books are accessible to very few readers, and it seemed to me undesirable to load my text with citations which would have a meaning for Russia alone. For the same reason, I have omitted bibliographical references in the case of such passages as I have quoted textually. There are no critical editions of the works of Russian authors, editions generally recognised as standard, and it would therefore be useless to refer to particular editions.

" Further, seeing that Russian books are so inaccessible and so little known, I have avoided as far as possible any polemic discussion, any detailed reference to conflicting criticisms of Russian authors.

" I have followed the evolution of Russian literature with considerable care, this statement applying also to writings on political subjects, both licit and clandestine. I have to thank my friends and acquaintances for keeping me up to date in these matters.

" Nevertheless the lack of an adequate Russian library has been a serious drawback, especially seeing that a large proportion of Russian literature, alike scientific, philosophical, and belletristic, is buried in periodicals. It is really impossible for one living outside Russia to compose a work upon that country which shall be definitive and complete from the literary point of view. In certain urgent cases, for example, I had to procure manuscript copies of entire articles—a fact that I mention merely in order to show that I have done all that is possible to one who does not live in Russia. I am perfectly serious when I declare that I am presenting nothing more than a sketch."

The translators have little to add to the above quoted exposition. It seems expedient to draw attention to the date of the work. The German edition from which the translation is made was published at Jena in 1913, and the reader must bear in mind that Masaryk's references to contemporary Russian events all refer to a period before the war, and several years before the fall of tsarism. On two or three occasions, in addition to this general reminder, we have deemed it advisable to introduce a special reminder into the text. In view of the date when the work was compiled, we have followed Masaryk throughout in speaking of " St. Petersburg " instead of using the now accepted name of " Petrograd." In certain respects, as far as philosophical discussions are concerned, the author breaks new ground, and it has therefore been difficult at times to render his meaning into intelligible English. There are difficulties even in the German original, and on one occasion, when Masaryk coins the term " solomnism," he writes in a parenthesis " I really must ask pardon of the philologists ! " For the use of this and many similar barbarous terms, such as historism, historicism, and the like, the translators, for their part, must claim the reader's indulgence.

Cordial acknowledgments are due to R. W. Seton-Watson, R. A. Leeper, and L. C. Wharton, who have rendered help of inestimable value in the elucidation of various difficult points.

A final word is requisite concerning personal names, the names of places, and the thorny problem of transliteration. Following the usual convention, the names of royalties have been anglicised. As regards the Russians this has not been applied to the grand princes, but only to the tsars and their successors. This is why we speak of " Ivan Kalita " and of " Ivan III," whereas the ruler who is most frequently spoken of in England as " Ivan the Terrible " is termed " John IV," just as " Petr Velikii " becomes " Peter the Great," or in most cases simply " Peter."

With regard to personal names in general, we have not followed the author strictly, but, acting on the advice of L. C. Wharton of the British Museum Library staff, have adopted, with a few trifling modifications, the Bohemian transliteration as used in the Slavonic library at King's College, London. It is possible that this system will be adopted some day in the British Museum Library catalogue, but for the present in that catalogue a more complicated system is used, whose chief merit is that it provides uninstructed English readers with more obvious clues to Russian pronunciation. In the subjoined table, the Russian alphabet is given in the first column, the British Museum transliteration in the second, and the Slavonic library transliteration (the one we have adopted) in the third :

а	a	a	с	s	s
б	b	b	т	t	t
в	v	v	у	u	u
г	g	g	ф	f	f
д	d	d	х	kh	h
е	e	e	ц	ts	c
ж	zh	ž	ч	ch	č
з	z	z	ш	sh	š
и	i	i	щ	shch	šč
i	i	i	ъ	' (medial only)	' (medial only)
й	i	i	ы	ui	y
к	k	k	ь	' (medial and final)	' (medial and final)
л	l	l	ѣ	ye	ě
м	m	m	э	e	e
н	n	n	ю	yu	ju
о	o	o	я	ya	ja
п	p	p	ѳ	th	f
р	r	r	ѵ	i	i

Our only divergences from the Slavonic Library transliteration are that we completely ignore the ъ or "hard sign," whilst in the case of the ь or "soft sign" we ignore it as a terminal letter as far as personal names are concerned. Thus we write Gor'kii, where the soft sign is medial, but Pestel, though in the Russian there is a soft sign at the end of this name. In the transliteration of Russian words other than personal names we similarly ignore the hard sign, but reproduce the soft sign, both medial and final, writing "krest'-janin" (peasant) and "knjaz'" (prince). Certain Russian words used repeatedly in the text, words with which many English readers are already familiar, such as "volost" and "artel," are treated as English words, the terminal soft sign being dropped, at any rate after their first use. Finally, we have preferred to retain "th" for the transliteration of θ (thus distinguishing that letter from φ), though in the most recent form of the Slavonic Library transliteration θ, like φ, is rendered by "f."

Even an elaborate treatise can hardly convey to English readers the niceties of Russian pronunciation, and it must suffice to give the following hints :—the Russian "g" is always hard, as in "gander"; "r" is strongly trilled; "ž" is pronounced like z in "azure;" "h" is strongly aspirated even in the middle or at the end of a word, and has a guttural sound, somewhat resembling the ch of the Scottish "loch"; "c" = ts; "č" = ch (as in "church"); "š" = sh; "šč" = shch; "y" sounds like the final y in "dirty," but is rather more guttural; "e" and "ě" are usually pronounced ye as in "yet"; "ju," as in "you" and "ja" as in "yah." Substantially, with the exception of e and ě (see above) the vowels are pronounced as in Italian.

It has not been thought expedient to apply this system of transliteration to geographical names, except in the case of minor places practically unknown in England. For all well-known geographical names, such as "Dnieper," the conventional English spelling has been used. Where rival spellings occupy the field, Longman's *Gazeteer* has been followed. The native spelling of nonrussian names of Slav origin has been retained.

The bibliography has been transferred from § 47 to an appendix, this accounting for the inconsecutiveness in the numbering of the sections. It will be noted that the leading authorities are German.*

EDEN AND CEDAR PAUL

LONDON, *November* 17, 1918.

---

*In the second edition this Bibliography has been entirely replaced. Throughout the additions to the second edition, the translators have endeavoured to follow, as nearly as seems practicable, the conventions laid down by their predecessors in the treatment of proper names.

CONTENTS

PAGE

TRANSLATORS' FOREWORD TO THE FIRST EDITION   V

NOTE ON THE SECOND EDITION   XII

INTRODUCTORY CHAPTER   I

PART ONE.

THE PROBLEMS OF RUSSIAN PHILOSOPHY OF HISTORY AND PHILOSOPHY OF RELIGION

CHAPTER ONE: "HOLY RUSSIA." MOSCOW AS THIRD ROME.

§ 1. Kievic Old Russia.

  i. Geographical Preliminaries.—The Russian Slavs and their Neighbours.—Racial Fusions.—Slavs and Russians, Great Russia and Little Russia.—Was the Russian State of Norse Origin ?   9

  ii. Alleged unwarlike Character of the Slavs.—Negative Democracy.—The Village Community (Mir) and the Family Community (Zadruga)   13

  iii. Effect of Soil and Climate   16

  iv. Significance of Commerce to Kiev   17

  v. Evolution of Law.—Defective Sense of the State (Anarchism ?)   17

  vi. Political Position of the Grand Princes.—Absolutism.—The Duma of Boyars and the Věče   18

  vii. Kiev breaks up into petty Principalities.—The Country is centralised by Moscow.—Sociological Appraisement of the centralising Forces: the Power of Religion and of the Church   19

  viii. Centralisation : the Boyars become subordinate to the Tsar.—The Duma of Boyars and the Věče.—The Zemskii Sobor of Moscow.—The Muscovite administrative State   25

  ix. The Peasant, too, becomes Subject to the State : Serfdom.—Agrarian Communism in Moscow —The Towns.—Aristocratic Subdivision of Society.—Social Significance of the new Dynasty of the Romanovs   30

CONTENTS

PAGE

§ 2. Origin and Development of the Russian Church; Christianisation of Kiev from Byzantium and Foundation of the Russian Theocracy (Caesaropapism).—Old Russian Civilisation; Church Religion and Folk-Morality.—The Cleavage in Old Russia; Byzantium and Old Russia   35

§ 3. Moscow as Third Rome; the Muscovite Theocracy religious and ethical.—The Tsar as Vicegerent of God and religious Instructor of the People   41

§ 4. Orthodox Moscow seeks Help in Civilisation from Catholic and Protestant Europe.—Ecclesiastical Reform in Russia and the Development of the Raskol   44

§ 5. Practical Needs likewise impel Moscow towards Reform and towards Europeanisation.—The Concept of Europeanisation   49

CHAPTER TWO: PETER'S REFORMS. THE LINKING UP OF RUSSIA WITH EUROPE.

§ 6. Peter's Reforms mainly practical in Character   53

§ 7. Scientific and social Reforms   55

§ 8. Russia becomes a European great Power and a World Power, the Muscovite State being transformed into an absolutist State upon the European Model   57

§ 9. Peter's ecclesiastical Reforms; the Patriarchate is replaced by the Synod.—The Synod uncanonical.—Definitive Subordination of the Church to the State.—Influence of Protestantism and Catholicism during Peter's Reign.—The Raskolniki   61

§ 10. Theocratic Muscovy secularised by Peter   64

§ 11. Consolidation of tsarist Absolutism.—Progressive Europeanisation and Asiatisation   65

§ 12. Catherine II's enlightened Despotism   69

§ 13. The Philosophy of the Enlightenment and humanitarian Ideals in Russia.—Preponderant Influence of France; Voltairism and Mysticism.—Freemasonry.—The Problem of Serfdom   72

§ 14. First Formulation of the historical and philosophical Contrast between Old and New Russia   79

CHAPTER THREE: THEOCRATIC REACTION AFTER THE FRENCH REVOLUTION; ITS DEFEAT BEFORE SEVASTOPOL. OPENING OF THE POLITICAL AND PHILOSOPHICAL REVOLUTION (CATHERINE II—NICHOLAS I).

§ 15. Reaction against the French Revolution under Paul I and Alexander I.—Futile Attempts to establish constitutional Government; Speranskii and Karamzin.—Movement for and against the Liberation of the Peasantry.—Alexander as Head of the Holy Alliance; theocratic Reaction; the Regime of Arakčeev and Photius   82

§ 16. Organisation of the political Opposition in secret Societies; the decabrist Rising; Pestel   95

PAGE

§ 17. Nicholas' Reaction against the Revolution.—Uvarov's theocratic Trinitarianism ; Orthodoxy, Autocracy, and Patriotism.—Caadaev's Renouncement of this Doctrine   104

§ 18. Oppression of Universities, Schools, and Literature.—" The Word Progress must be erased from official Terminology "   111

§ 19. Strengthening of national Sentiment under Alexander and Nicholas   114

§ 20. Growth of manufacturing Industry ; its Europeanising Influence   117

§ 21. Modern Russian Literature originates in the Epoch of theocratic Reaction.—Its essential Tendency is that of a Literature of Opposition   120

§ 22. Influence of German Philosophy and Literature.—Hegel and the Hegelian Left ; Feuerbach.—French Socialism and English Thought.—Beginnings of Russian Socialism ; the Petraševcy Group.—The Intelligentsia and the Democratisation of Literature (the Raznočincy)   122

§ 23. Organisation of the literary Movement of Opposition and Revolution.—Clandestine Literature and Emigration.—N. Turgenev as typical Representative of constitutionalist Refugees under Nicholas.—I. G. Golovin   125

§ 24. Autocracy, Aristocracy, and Serfdom.—Social Disorders.   128

§ 25. Collapse of theocratic Obscurantism before Sevastopol   132

CHAPTER FOUR : LIBERATION OF THE PEASANTRY IN 1861. ADMINISTRATIVE REFORMS.

§ 26. Abolition of Serfdom.—Moral and legal Significance of Slavery. —Slavery and Aristocracy   134

§ 27. Economic Significance of the Liberation of the Peasantry.—An agrarian Crisis ensues notwithstanding Enfranchisement   138

§ 28. The " Great Reforms " of the Administration   142

CHAPTER FIVE : RENEWAL AND CONTINUATION OF THE NICOLAITAN REGIME AFTER A BRIEF LIBERAL INTERLUDE. GROWTH OF THE TERRORIST GUERILLA-REVOLUTION ; ALEXANDER II BECOMES ITS VICTIM. ACCENTUATION OF THE THEOCRATIC REACTION ; COUNTER-TERRORISM. ITS DEFEAT IN THE WAR AGAINST JAPAN.

§ 29. Uncensored Journalism and Literature in Association with Alexandrine Reforms.—Criticism in Literature.—The Slavophils and the Westernisers ; the Počvenniki and the Narodniki ; Socialism and Anarchism.—The philosophic Reaction, Katkov and Pobědonoscev.—Nihilism as a Manifestation of New Russia ; Dostoevskii's Contest with Nihilism.—The liberal Movement in Theology.—Influence of recent German, French, and English Philosophy ; Positivism and Socialism.—Lassalle

PAGE

and Marx.—The Internàtional and German socialist Organisation.—Philosophic and Religious Rationalism of the Mužik (Stundism) 146

§ 30. The Opposition aims at a Constitution.—Political secret Societies (Zemlja i Volja) and the Polish Revolt.—The Reaction (Katkov) and the first Attempt on the Tsar in 1866 (Karakozov).—Propaganda among Operatives and Peasants in the early Seventies, and the Development of individual Efforts at Terrorism; Věra Zasulič and Stepniak (1878).—The Zemlja i Volja splits into the terroristic Narodnaja Volja and the socialistic Cernyi Pereděl.—The Tsar's Appeal for a Campaign against the Terror, and his Assassination on March 1/13, 1881. —Loris-Melikov's " Constitution " 151

§ 31. Reaction in Revenge for the Assassination of Alexander II; Pobědonoscev's Regime.—Protection (Ohrana).—Marxism and the first socialist Party (1883).—Literary Disputes concerning the Problem of capitalist Development in Russia; Marxism and the Narodniki.—Revisionism (Struve) and the Revulsion from Materialism.—Influence of Dostoevskii, of Solov'ev, and of Leont'ev; religious Mysticism.—The Decadents (Neo-Idealism, Neo-Romanticism); Čehov 156

§ 32. The Reaction aims at improving economic Conditions.—Foreign Capital and foreign Policy; Tsarism and French Republicanism.—Care for the Aristocracy.—The Agrarian Crisis; Land Hunger and Famine.—Growth of manufacturing Industry; the labour Question 161

§ 33. Orthodox Caesaropapism culminates in the Program of imperialistic Panasiatism.—Russia's Defeat by Japan 167

CHAPTER SIX: THE FIRST GENERAL REVOLUTIONARY MOVEMENT AMONG THE MASSES; THE BEGINNINGS OF THE CONSTITUTION. THE COUNTER-REVOLUTION.

§ 34. Union of all Classes and all Schools of progressive Thought in the Mass Revolution.—Significance of the Year 1905.—Gor'kii as the literary Spokesman of the Revolution 170

§ 35. Attack by the Reaction upon the solemnly proclaimed Constitution and upon the new Duma 178

§ 36. The Counter-Revolution and the White Terror.—The reactionary Intelligentsia; the Union of the Russian People (the " Black Hundred ").—Tsarism and provocative Agents (Azev and Sudeikin).—The White Terror refutes the alleged religious and moral Foundations of theocratic Caesaropapism and the alleged Divinity of the Church; the Church and the Elections to the fourth Duma.—Reform of the Church Schools; back to Muscovite Russia! 186

§ 37. The postrevolutionary Crisis.—Discussion concerning the Revolution.—Revolutionary Sentiment is increased by the Reaction.—Spiritual Crisis in Literature and Philosophy.—Mysticism and religious Revival.—Influence of Dostoevskii and Solov'ev.—Decadence and Sexuality (" Saninism ").—Pessimism and suicidal Tendencies.—Symptoms of Renovation 196

PAGE

CHAPTER SEVEN: PROBLEMS OF THE PHILOSOPHY OF HISTORY AND OF RELIGION IN RUSSIA. A SUMMARY STATEMENT.

I

§ 38. Character of Russian Philosophy.—The ethical Problem: Politics; Socialism; Revolution.—The sociological Problem: History of Philosophy; Russia and Europe.—The religious Problem: Mysticism.—The epistemological Problem: Literary Criticism 199

II

§ 39. Character of recent European Philosophy.—Growth of the historic Sense during the eighteenth Century; Beginnings of scientific Historiography, of the Philosophy of History, and of Sociology.—Evolutionary Science considered as a Reinforcement of the historic Sense 201

§ 40. The historic Sense and the Idea of Progress; Philoneism and the Desire for Reform.—Revolution in general and Revolutions in particular; the old Regime or the new.—The Problem of Revolution 204

§ 41. The eighteenth Century as the Epoch of Enlightenment and of Rationalism.—The Kantian Criticism and its historical Significance.—The new Philosophy as Philosophy of Religion.—Opposition to Theology determined by the theocratic Unity of Church and State becomes an Opposition to official Doctrine, Morality, and Politics 205

§ 41A. Hume's Rejection of Religion as Anthropomorphism.—Analysis of this Concept by Kant, Comte, Vico, Feuerbach, Spencer, and Tylor.—Anthropomorphism is equivalent to Myth.—Criticism versus Mythopoiesis.—The old Opposition between Philosophy and Mythology; Theology as Christian Mythology.—Modern Philosophy in Opposition to Theology.—Theology as the Instrument of Myth, Philosophy as the Instrument of Science.—Religion and Myth.—Theism and Belief in Revelation; believing Catholicity.—Faith and Priests; Church and Theocracy.—Philosophy versus Theology; Anthropism versus Theism.—The Problem of Individualism and Subjectivism; Unfaith and Criticism; Empirical Thought versus Authority and Tradition; Science and Philosophy, not Priests and Church; Anthropocracy or Democracy, versus Theocracy; critical Catholicity.—The Question, Can an unrevealed Religion exist?—The Religion of the scientific and critical Thinker 206

§ 42. The Enlightenment and Humanitarianism.—Kant and Hume render Philosophy predominantly practical and ethical; the Ideal of Naturalness.—During the nineteenth Century, Emotionalism and Voluntarism are opposed to Rationalism (Intellectualism).—Democracy versus Theocracy 210

§ 43. The Enlightenment and Humanitarian Philosophy lead to
political Reforms ; the Proclamation of the Rights of Man.—
The Proclamation of the Rights of Man necessitates social
Reforms.—Socialism and Sociology ; German Idealism likewise leads to Socialism.—Humanitarianism and Nationality ;
The Principle of Nationality is at once philosophical and
political   211

§ 44. Individualism and Subjectivism.—Subjectivism as Activism.—
Subjectivism as Solipsism ; Kant, Fichte, Schelling, Hegel,
Stirner, Schopenhauer, Feuerbach, Marx ; History and
Society versus the Ego.—The Problem of Subjectivism in
Russian Philosophy   212

§ 45. The three Antitheses : Philosophy and Theology ; Anthropism
and Theism ; Democracy and Theocracy (theocratic Aris-
tocracy)   213

III

§ 46. Russian Historiography in association with the Reforms of
Peter and with Nestor the Chronicler.—Tatiščev's Formula
concerning the Evolution of the Russian State ; supreme
Value of monarchist Absolutism.—Russian Historians down
to Karamzin.—German Historians in Russia.—Expansion of
Historiography by the Inclusion of administrative, legal, and
economic History.—Influence of the History of Literature.—
Political History and the History of Civilisation.—The new
historical Outlook resulting from Experiences of the Revolution in Europe and in Russia ; Influence of German Philo-
sophy under Nicholas I   213

§ 47. See Translators' Foreword, page xii.

PART TWO.

SKETCHES OF RUSSIAN PHILOSOPHY OF HISTORY AND PHILOSOPHY OF RELIGION

CHAPTER EIGHT : P. J. ČAADAEV. CATHOLIC VERSUS
ORTHODOX THEOCRACY.

§ 48. Čaadaev's Philosophic Writing as a Denial of Uvarov's Trinity
and an Assertion that Byzantine Russia is a cultural Nonen-
tity.—Catholicism is true Christianity and the true Church   221

§ 49. Was Čaadaev a Mystic ?—His Attitude towards Catholicism;
in Russia as elsewhere there took place a romanticist Reversion towards Catholicism   225

§ 50. Čaadaev's *Apology*   229

§ 51. The basic Ideas of Čaadaev's Philosophy of History.—Čaadaev
as the first Russian Philosopher of History   232

PAGE

Chapter Nine : Slavophilism. The Messianism of Orthodox Theocracy. Slavophilism and Pan-slavism.

I

§ 52. Ivan Vasilievič Kirčevskii, the Founder of Slavophilism.—His first cultural Ideal based upon the Philosophy of Schelling : Europeanisation   237

§ 53. Kirčevskii's second Stage ; Evolution towards Pietism.— Slavophil Philosophy of History and of Religion.—Disintegration of the modern European Mind (including the Russian) and of the human Mind in general ; Rationalism versus Faith, Europe versus Russia.—Russia as the Old Russia of the Mužik.—Russia's messianic Mission, to reorganise Humanity as a unitary Whole upon the Foundation of the Old Russian religious Spirit, and thus to save Mankind from Decay.—Schelling as Saviour versus Kant and Hegel   241

§ 54. Critique of Kirčevskii   247

§ 55. Continuation and Fortification of Kirčevskii's Doctrine by Homjakov.—Homjakov as an orthodox religious Teacher : his Doctrine of the Church and of Belief.—Stirner as the summary Expression of Protestant Philosophy   254

§ 56. Homjakov upon the Relationship between Church and State ; Theocracy in Catholicism, Protestantism, and the Orthodox Church   261

§ 57. The theocratic political Doctrine of Aksakov : the primitive Russian State conceived as " inner Truth " in Contrast with the European State as " outer Truth "   266

§ 58. Homjakov's Philosophy of the State and of Nationality   270

§ 59. Excursus concerning the chief Problems of the Philosophy of Nationality.—The slavophil Doctrine of Nationality is inadequate   274

§ 59A. Homjakov upon the Slav national Character   282

§ 60. Jurii F. Samarin, and his Polemic against Catholicism and Jesuitism.—The Polish Question   285

§ 61. Ivan Aksakov, nihilistic Terrorism as a form of Atheism   287

§ 62. N. Danilevskii, racial Nationalism   291

II

§ 63. The national Renaissance of the eastern Nations, and in particular of the Slavs, from the eighteenth Century onwards.— The Program of this Renaissance considered from the Outlooks of the Philosophy of History and the Philosophy of Nationality (Slavistic Movement).—Panslavism   293

§ 64. The humanitarian Panslavism of the Czechs and the Slovaks   296

§ 65. The southern Slavs ; Serbo-Croats and Bulgarians.—Ecclesiastical and religious Divisions. (Illyrism). The Slovenes   299

PAGE

§ 66. The Little Russian Problem
301

§ 67. Polish Messianism
304

§ 68. Russian Panslavism.—The Russian slavistic Movement ; Pogodin and Ševyrev.—Panslavism replaced by Panasiatism.—Importance of the nonslav Peoples of Russia
307

§ 69. Historical Explanation of slavophil Messianism as an Outcome of the social and philosophical Situation during the postrevolutionary Epoch of Restoration and Reaction
316

III

§ 70. Concluding and amplificatory Discussion of the Nature and Development of Slavophilism
321

CHAPTER TEN : WESTERNISM. V. G. BĚLINSKII.

I

§ 71. Westernism in its wider Sense of Europeanisation, and in its narrower Sense of Opposition to Slavophilism.—Westernism is religious, ecclesiastical, and metaphysical.—The Westernisers, too, are opposed to Scepticism.—Through Young Hegelian, Feuerbachian and French socialist Influences, the Socialists (Radicals) and Revolutionaries have been segregated from the Liberals, Herzen entering a different Camp from Granovskii.—Theocracy, by Contre-coup, gives rise to Opposition and Revolution : Atheism, Materialism, and Positivism
336

§ 72. The Westernisers' Teaching concerning State and Laws, their Esteem for Peter ; the Relationship between Church and State ; the Mir, Nationality, the Slav (Polish) Question
342

§ 72A. Some of the chief Representatives of Westernism
347

II.

§ 73. Bělinskii as Westerniser.—His literary and philosophical Development.—His slavophil Phase
350

§ 74. Philosophical Significance of the Essay on Borodino ; Hegel versus Fichte.—Hegel's rational Reality.—Bělinskii's Opposition to the Extremes of Subjectivism and Objectivism ; neither Crime nor Superstition !
356

§ 75. Bělinskii versus Hegel's Sense of Reality.—Feuerbach's Anthropologism ; Materialism and Atheism versus Theism, Man versus God.—Bělinskii and French Socialism ; Approval of Terrorism and Revolution.—The Intelligentsia as a Class, the Bourgeoisie.—Bělinskii versus Gogol ; the Struggle against Theocracy.—Bělinskii versus extreme Historism and Positivism (Stirner, Marx, Comte).—The Struggle against Scepticism and Mysticism.—Faith in Europe and in New Russia
359

§ 76. Bělinskii as Critic and Aestheticist.—His Influence.—Creative Scepticism
370

CHAPTER ELEVEN : THE SYNTHESIS OF WESTERNISM AND
    SLAVOPHILISM. APOLLON GRIGOR'EV.

§ 77. Grigor'ev's Synthesis of Slavophilism and Westernism.—
    Grigor'ev as Počvennik ; Puškin's organic Synthesis of
    Europeanism and Russism.—Art as Instrument of Nationality.
    —Organic Criticism.—Idea versus Development.—Roman-
    ticist Campaign against Romanticism.—Grigor'ev versus
    Nihilism.—Grigor'ev and Dostoevskii. (N. Strahov)   379

CHAPTER TWELVE : ALEKSANDR HERZEN. PHILOSOPHICAL
    AND POLITICAL RADICALISM.

§ 78. Herzen continues Bělinskii's literary Revolution.—Herzen
    before and after 1848 ; Radicalism ; Curses upon the Year
    1848.—Positivist Convalescence from religious Illusion ; to
    atheistic Materialism the French Revolution seems inade-
    quate.—Christianity tantamount to Monarchy.—The only
    Path of Salvation—not Goethe's *Faust* but Byron's Lucifer ;
    Crime   384

§ 79. Was Herzen an Eclectic ?—Positivism and Materialism versus
    Religion.—Herzen upon Christianity and the three leading
    Christian Churches. (Old Believers)   392

§ 80. Herzen's Analysis of positivist Disillusionment.—His Explana-
    tion of Turgenev's Bazarov as Science conjoined with Love.—
    Byron's Lucifer overcome ; Vindication of the " superfluous
    Person "   395

§ 81. The Problem of Crime as Subjectivism and Objectivism.—
    Crime and Revolution.—How Herzen came to terms with
    Bakunin and Revolutionism ; the Galilean in the End gains
    the Victory over Byron   400

§ 82. Herzen's Philosophy of History.—At first he assumes that there
    is Progress.—In 1850 he denies Progress, denies that there is
    Teleology.—Later still he is again willing to admit the Occur-
    rence of historical Progress   407

§ 83. Herzen's Conversion to slavophil Messianism.—Will Russian
    social Evolution follow a different Course from that of
    Europe ?—Herzen as Narodnik.—Herzen's Panslavism   410

§ 84. Herzen's " Russian " Socialism and Communism.—Herzen
    versus Marx and political Economy.—Herzen, like Proudhon,
    is Individualist, Federalist, and Anarchist.—The social Revo-
    lution in the Form of the Liberation of the Peasantry in the
    Year 1861.—Herzen in Favour of Parliamentarism.—Herzen's
    Doubts concerning messianic Schemes   417

§ 85. Herzen's Influence in all Directions.—This Influence weakened
    after the Polish Rising of 1863.—Herzen and Černyševskii.—
    The Radicals versus Herzen.—Cause of Herzen's Change of
    Views.—Herzen's Defects.—Anarchism as Unpracticality ;
    social Isolation of the Refugee.—Herzen's aristocratic Trend ;
    Sympathy with the Bourgeois.—Scepticism and Dilettantism.
    —Analysis of the " superfluous Person "   422

PAGE

CHAPTER THIRTEEN : M. A. BAKUNIN. REVOLUTIONARY
    ANARCHISM.

§ 86. Bakunin's philosophical Evolution towards the Hegelian Left   430

§ 87. Bakunin versus Subjectivism ; Suicide   434

§ 88. Bakunin's first Program of 1882 ; the Destruction of the existing
    Order by religio-political Democracy ; the old World is perish-
    .ing from Scepticism   436

§ 89. Antitheology upon a Feuerbachian Basis as the Foundation of
    true Democracy.—The ontological Proof of Atheism   446

§ 90. Absolute Equality in the Absence of all Authority the Goal of
    the Future.—Anarchy as a stateless Amorphism the Precon-
    dition of the future Federation.—Pandestruction and partial
    Destruction.—Atheism and political Revolution   448

§ 91. Bakunin's " new Morality " as a Theory of Revolution.—The
    Right to kill.—Jesuitism and Machiavellianism.—The Aris-
    tocracy of the secret Society   450

§ 92. Did Bakunin recant ?   457

§ 93. Bakunin and Slav Messianism   458

§ 94. The Light thrown on Anarchism by the Struggle between Baku-
    nin and Marx.—Bakunin's Influence in Europe and Russia   461

INDEX OF NAMES   472

THE SPIRIT OF RUSSIA

INTRODUCTORY CHAPTER

RUSSIA AND EUROPE. THE RUSSIAN MONK

A GENERAL survey of Russian development since the days of Peter the Great shows the country divided into two halves, consisting respectively of an Old Russia with a prepetrine civilisation, and a New, European Russia.

An alert observer travelling through Russia will gain a vivid perception of the nature and evolution of this cultural divergence. One entering Russia from Europe (it must be remembered that the Russian crossing the western frontier speaks always of " going to Europe ") has first to traverse a nonrussian province or territory. He must pass through Poland, the Baltic provinces, or Finland, through lands annexed from Europe, whose inhabitants are Catholic or Protestant, and who have a European civilisation of old date. The connection of these regions with Orthodox Russia is still comparatively superficial. But the further eastward we go, the further do we find ourselves from Europe, until at length Europe is represented only by the railway, the refreshment rooms at the stations, and isolated hotels furnished and managed in European style. The same contrast strikes us between Petrograd and Moscow. In Moscow, and also in Petrograd, it strikes us between the modern portions of the city and the old town which is purely Russian. Odessa, on the other hand, is a new town, quite European.

When compared with the two capitals, and especially when compared with Petrograd, the rural districts, the villages, are Russian. The great landowners, aristocrats, furnish their country-seats in European style. Similarly, many factories

2

in country districts are European oases. Things technical, things practical, are for the most part European : railways, factories, and banks ; commerce to some extent (including internal trade) ; army and navy ; in part, also, the bureaucratic machine of state. It is true that any one whose first impression of this machine is derived from the Warsaw post office will find it extremely disagreeable. I need hardly say that European elements are everywhere intermingled with Russian, and after a little practice we learn to distinguish the transitional stages and the manifold combinations. Close observation and increasing knowledge enable us to detect the difference between that which has been directly imported from Europe and the native imitation or adaptation, so that we come to recognise how Russia and Europe merge in great things and in small.

After a time we shall obviously learn to detect the same contrasts in men as well as in things. European and Russian thought and feeling present themselves in the most diversified combinations. Before long the conviction is forced upon us that the Europeanisation of Russia does not consist solely in the adoption of isolated ideas and isolated practical institutions, but that we have to do with a characteristic historical process in virtue of which the Old Russian essence, civilisation, and modes of life are being transformed and destroyed by the inroad of the European essence, civilisation, and modes of life. The individual Russian undergoing Europeanisation experiences this contrast in his own intimate personality. Since the human being cannot live disintegrated, there is forced upon him the attempt to secure an organic connection between the Russian that he is by inheritance and the European that he is by acquirement, to secure as far as possible a unification of the two. The task is difficult ! Try to picture to yourself vividly the contrast between the Russian peasant (and the peasant is still Russia), on the one hand, and the writer, the officer, the landowner, or the skilled technician, on the other— men who have been educated in Paris, Berlin, or Zurich, and who are familiar with the life of these cities. People differing thus widely have not merely to live side by side, but must think and work with one another and for one another !

The spiritual contrast between Russia and Europe is displayed in its fullest significance in the Russian monastery. Here we find the most genuine and the oldest Russian life, the feeling and thought of Old Russia. We see this already in the monasteries of Petrograd, but we see it yet more clearly in remoter monasteries and hermitages. Russia, Old Russia, is the Russian monk. During my first visit to Russia I had a vivid experience of this. In Moscow I was moving in circles where intellectual development was most advanced, but withdrawing one day from this Europeanised environment, I paid a visit to the Troicko-Sergievskaja monastery. With its institutions, its treasures, and its relics, this monastery takes us back into fourteenth-century Russia; but in the dependent monastery Bethany, and yet more in the hermitage of Gethsemane, we find ourselves in an even remoter historical epoch. In the centre of the forest stands the hermitage, with an ancient wooden church—a veritable Gethsemane! The contrast was all the more striking seeing that the previous day I had been debating religious problems with Tolstoi and his friends. Brandes, too, chanced to be visiting Moscow at the time, to expound his literary views in lectures delivered in the French tongue. Now I found myself at the hermitage of Gethsemane, with its catacombs, its wonder-working relics, and its icons! One of Tolstoi's friends, a man of position, had given me a letter of introduction to the head of the monastery, so that I was able to see everything. Never shall I forget the man who showed me round the hermitage. This monk was about twenty-five years old. He had grown up in and for the monastery, and his mind was entirely dominated by its Orthodox ideas. To him the world seemed something altogether foreign, whilst I was an emissary from, a part of, the outer world, from which he was a refugee. Now he was to accompany me through the catacombs and to explain what I saw. The things which to him were objects of the most devout contemplation were to be elucidated to the nonrussian, the European, the heretic, the mere sightseer! I could not fail to note and to be sorry for my guide's distress, but I must admit that his uneasiness was a trifle irritating to the European in me. He genuflected before every relic and every icon, at least before the principal ones; he was continually crossing himself; kneeling down he touched the holy precincts with forehead and lips. As I watched him closely I perceived that alarm was gaining on him, that he was obviously terrified, momentarily expecting that Heaven would punish me for my wickedness and unbelief. But punishment was withheld, and almost without his knowledge and understanding, into the depths of his soul there crept a shadow of doubt. This was obvious in his earnest request that I would at least bow before the chief relic. It was plain that he was no longer anxious about the safety of the heretic, but that the Almighty's failure to send due punishment was troubling him. . . . After we had finished with the catacombs I wished to return alone, but my guide would not leave me. Before long I realised that the monk on his side wanted to acquire knowledge. He gave free rein to his curiosity, to his eager desire to learn something of the world, of Europe. His world-hunger sparkled in his eyes, and I could not satisfy his appetite for narrative and explanation. At length he, a Russian, began to ask me, a nonrussian, about Moscow, Petrograd, Russia. Several times we paced the distance between the hermitage and the margin of the forest. My companion never wearied in his interrogations. Hitherto he had known the world in the light of the Bible and the legends of the saints, but now he was listening to the unheard of and unsuspected. At length I had to make my way back to the principal monastery. Despite my repeated and cordial thanks, the monk accompanied me to the very gate ; there he continued to stand, and would not take his homeward path after my last words of farewell had been uttered—what on earth did the man want ? Did he expect a gratuity ? The thought had been worrying me for some little time. I was ashamed of it ; it hurt me to entertain it ; but in the end I found it impossible to doubt that this strictly religious contemner of the world was accustomed to receive tips ! My head was whirling with thoughts about Russia and Europe, belief and unbelief; and I blushed as I slipped a note into the extended palm of the guardian of Gethsemane. . . .

This experience and many similar ones, especially those gained during a pilgrimage to another leading monastery, and during my intercourse with the " old believers " and the sectaries —in a word, the observation and study of the religious life of the churches, afford ample insight into Old Russia of the days before Peter the Great. To understand European and Europeanised Russia, it is necessary to know what Moscow, the third Rome, has been and still is for Russia in matters of civilisation.

I owe to Tolstoi my introduction to the old believer wonderland. One of the best old believer curio dealers in

Moscow gave me his personal guidance through the length and breadth of this Old Russia.[1]

Old Russia, Russia in contrast to Europe! Yet the monk in Gethsemane, the pilgrims, the Orthodox, the peasantry— they all carried me back in memory to childhood, when my primitive faith was undisturbed. Such were my own beliefs and such were my own actions when I went on pilgrimage in boyhood; such are still the beliefs and actions of the children and the wives of our Slovak peasants when they visit the shrine of the miracle-working virgin on Mt. Hostein; such were the beliefs and such was the teaching of my own mother. But this childhood has passed away for ever, simply because childhood must yield place to maturity. . . .

Russia has preserved the childhood of Europe; in the over-whelming mass of its peasant population it represents Christian medievalism and, in particular, Byzantine medievalism. It was but a question of time when this middle age would awaken to modernity, and the awakening was in large part due to Peter and his successors.

I am acquainted with a fair proportion of the civilised and uncivilised world, and I have no hesitation in saying that Russia was and is the most interesting country known to me. Slav as I am, a visit to Russia has involved many more surprises than a visit to any other land. In England and America, for example, I had no feeling of surprise. The latest novelty seemed to me nothing more than an obvious development of something with which I was already familiar at home. Yet in Russia, although as a Slav I am competent, I believe, to grasp in Russian literature what is termed the spirit of the language and of the nation; although Russian life, as revealed in the creative works of Russian authors, is intimately congenial to my own moods, in so far as these are Slav, and arouses harmonious echoes in my own Slav nature—yet in Russia I ever and anon feel surprise! The European, one who lives in the present, has the current of his thought involuntarily directed towards the future, and anticipates the conclusions that will follow from the given historic premises. But in Russia he finds himself back in the past, often in the middle ages, finds

---

[1] The novels of Mel'nikov (whose pen-name is Pečerskii) entitled "In the Forests," and "On the Mountains," give an excellent description of old believer life as far as details are concerned, but the general picture is marred by a modern, decadent, subflavour.

himself in a life utterly different from that of the modern and progressive west. In the nonchristian lands of Asia and Africa we do not receive this general impression in anything like the same strength, because the customs differ so utterly from ours ; but Russia is of our own kind, exhibits our own quality, is what Europe has been. . . .

Russia is—Europe as well. When, therefore, I contrast Russia and Europe, I contrast two epochs. Russia does not differ essentially from Europe ; but Russia is not yet essentially one with Europe.

PART ONE

THE PROBLEMS OF RUSSIAN PHILOSOPHY OF HISTORY AND PHILOSOPHY OF RELIGION

CHAPTER ONE

" HOLY RUSSIA." MOSCOW AS THIRD ROME

§ I.

RUSSIAN historians have as yet thrown little light upon the origin and development of the Russian state. In the first place, a number of extremely important facts have not been established with incontestable certainty, while secondly the attempts that have been made to explain the historical evolution of Russia are far from satisfactory.

We need for our purposes a sketch of Russian history, on the one hand because we have to make acquaintance with the problems with which the philosophers of history deal, while on the other hand this historical sketch will form the background for the studies here offered.

Our most direct interest is with recent Russian history, that of the nineteenth century ; but to understand this we have to discuss the history of an earlier epoch, from the days of Peter the Great onwards. In especial, we shall give a detailed account of Peter's reforms, since this will furnish the reader with an impression of the characteristics of the pre-reform period, above all in Moscow. The early history of Moscow, and that of the earlier epochs of the petty princi-palities and Kiev, will be dealt with very briefly.

i. The Russian state took its rise in the wide area between the site of the modern Novgorod (on Lake Ilmen) and Kiev, between the two seas, the Baltic in the north and the Black Sea in the south. This region, traversed by the rivers Vistula, Dnieper, Don, and Volga, was considerably larger than the middle Europe of the ninth century inhabited by the Germans and the Latins.

The political organisation of the Russians spread from two centres, a northern on the Baltic and a southern on the

Black Sea. In the north, along their native shores, the Swedes, Norwegians, and Danes had attained a notable degree of political development and a high level of civilisation. On the Black Sea lay the outposts of the Byzantine empire; all the great rivers of Russia led southward, and across the Black Sea was the route to Constantinople.

The political organisation of Novgorod dates from the ninth century, but at the close of this century Kiev became the capital of the Russian realm. The subsequent development of Novgorod was comparatively independent, and it later became a powerful northern republic, whose territories in the twelfth century, when Kiev grew weak, extended to the White Sea and across the Urals.

From Kiev the Russians were in touch with the Greeks, while across the Caspian they came in contact with the advancing Arabs. Further, and in especial, they had to contend with nomadic tribes, the Khazars, the Pechenegs,. and the Polovzians. Kiev was able to defend itself against these peoples, but it succumbed to the Tatars, in whose onslaught against the Russians the nomad tribes were broken up.

In addition to these Asiatics, the Russians of Novgorod and Kiev had the Finns as neighbours. Before long, too, they had to maintain themselves against the Lithuanians, and ultimately against the Slavonian Poles.

The first princes of Novgorod and Kiev whose names appear in the ninth-century chronicles are stated by the "Normanists" (basing their views upon Nestor's chronicle and other data) to have been Norsemen—Varangians. The "Slavists," on the other hand, contend that these princes were Slavs. It is certain that the state of Novgorod existed before the arrival of the three Variag brothers Rjurik, Sineus, and Truvor; but it is uncertain how this state originated, whether these princes were the first, whether they had a numerous following, and how soon they became Russified.

Other Russian towns besides Novgorod appear to have been occupied by Swedish Varangians. Among these was Kiev, which was occupied twice at least, for Oleg, a successor of Rjurik, seized Kiev from the Norse princes Askold and Dir. Subsequently we are told that princes who were established in Kiev summoned Norse followers. In this connection, too, the question arises when and how the dominion of Kiev was founded in the south, whether there was a Russian realm in the south before Oleg's occupation of Kiev, and if so, where that realm was and how long it endured.

There is no apriori improbability in the contention that during the ninth century Russian regions peopled by Slavs and Finns were ravaged by Swedish vikings. During this same period, the Norsemen conquered Paris (for the first time in 845), invaded England (836), and occupied numerous places on the coasts of the North Sea and the Mediterranean, establishing their dominions in Frisia, Italy, and Spain. Novgorod and Kiev were equally accessible.

It is possible, however, that the first Norsemen to enter Kiev came, not from the north, but from the south. In the fifth and sixth centuries, the Herulians, a Teuton tribe, were settled on the sea of Azov, and may have made their way thence to Kiev. Further, it may be that these southland Teutons bore the name of Rōs, and that " Russia " originated on the sea of Azov. All these things, and many others, are possible. But hitherto neither the interpretation of the scanty historical records nor the etymological study of such descriptions as have come down to us, can warrant any definite conclusions.[1] The Varangian problem would have been ignored here were it not that it bulks so largely in the historical disputes between the slavophils and their opponents. The mingling of nations

[1] Vikings = warriors, de facto pirates. The Russian *varjagi* is derived from the western Norse *vaeringi* in the plural *vaeringjar*, and is supposed to denote a stranger or foreigner who puts himself under the king's protection and petitions for a pledge of safety (*uāra*) ; the *vaeringjar* enjoyed a privileged position on account of this pledge of protection. By the " Normanists," *Rus'*, the Russian name for the country, is derived from *Ruotsi*, a name which the Finns applied to the Swedes ; this word is itself Norse, and signifies " rowers," but the Finns imagined it to be a national name. This name was also given to the Swedish Norsemen, the Varangians, and had remained as the name of the Russians after the amalgamation of these Norsemen with the Russian Slavs (and Finns). According to this view the denomination *Rus'* was originally applied to the Norse Varangians ; was subsequently used to denote the higher aristocratic stratum of Kiev (the prince and his immediate following), of Norse descent ; and was ultimately transferred to the territory of Kiev and to the expanding realm. I do not know how or whether the word *Rōs* used by the Byzantines has any connection with this word *Rus'*. I have no expert judgment to offer upon these etymological problems, but the contention of the " Slavists " that the name *Rus'* is of Slav origin appears to me ill supported. Readers desiring further information regarding the uncertain ethnological and linguistic conditions of the Kievic epoch, and wishing to make acquaintance with the history of this period and the difficulties of the etymological problems, should consult the instructive work of Marquart, the orientalist, " Osteuropäische und ostasiatische Streifzüge. Ethnologische und historisch topographische Studien zur Geschichte des ix und x Jahrhunderts " (circa 840-940), 1903, pp. 346 353, and 382.

and races has important bearings upon the origins of Kiev and Novgorod. It is unquestionable that Finnish and other European and Asiatic racial elements enter into the composition of the Russian people, but it is to-day impossible to ascertain with anything approaching precision, when, whence, and how these interminglings and Russifications occurred. In the present state of research it is extremely hazardous to make extensive use of theories of race and nationality to explain the characteristics of Kievic Old Russia.

As far as the epoch we have been considering is concerned, no clear light has hitherto been thrown upon the distinction between Great and Little Russia. The term " Little Russia " makes its first appearance in fourteenth-century documents. It is uncertain when and how the linguistic separation of the Little Russians occurred ; and we are quite unable to determine when, how, and to what extent the Little Russians underwent anthropological and ethnological differentiation from the Great Russians. It is possible that the Lithuanians, the Poles, and some of the Czechs (Aryan and direct Slavic stocks), have had a racial influence upon the Little Russians—but these are mere speculations. The differences in character between the Great Russians and the Little Russians are an actual fact, like the analogous differences between northerners and southerners in many nations occupying extensive tracts of territory ; but it remains uncertain whether climatic influences, the character of the soil, and the methods of agriculture, have had more to do or less to do with the differentiation of the two stocks than a hypothetical racial divergence.

It is certainly possible that the distinction between Kiev and Novgorod in these earliest days was in some way related to the distinction between Little Russians and Great Russians. Gruševskii, the historian of Little Russia, regards the Antes as the ancestors of the Little Russians.

This indefiniteness is manifest in another direction. In speaking of the earliest epochs, the terms Slav and Russian are apt to be used as if they were interchangeable. It is generally assumed, in the case of the Russians as in the case of the other Slav nations of to-day, that in this remote period no notable differentiation had taken place among the Slavs. For the nonce the assertion is unproved. It may be true that in prehistoric times the Slavs, like the Teutons, etc., were a unitary race with an integral type of civilisation ; but we do not know how long ago this may have been, or when and how the differentiation between the various Slavic stocks began. This much seems clear, that in the ninth century differentiation was already far advanced.

In this connection it is unfortunately essential to touch upon the question of the so-called primitive home and primitive condition of the Slavs, it being premised that by the term " primitive home " we are to understand the last region in which the Slavs existed as a unified stock. The latest researches suggest that this region lay northward of the Carpathians, between Warsaw and Cracow on the one hand and Chernigov and Kiev on the other. From this region, migrations may be supposed to have started in the second century of the Christian era.

If this view be correct, if the alternative view that the unified Slavs had their home on the lower Danube or elsewhere be dismissed, it is clear that the Kievic realm may have contained the primitive Slav population ; but it is also possible that the Slavs, starting their migrations from Kiev or its neighbourhood, may have returned to occupy or to reoccupy Kiev after numerous wanderings and when many centuries had elapsed.

Nothing can be said here regarding the civilisation of the primitive Slavs, or regarding the influence exercised on them by the Celts, the Baltic peoples, etc., for these are matters concerning which hypotheses are only now being formulated.

ii. Many Slav and Russian historians have described the Russians and Slavs of earlier days (contrasting them with the Teutons and the Latins) as unwarlike, as people of pacific and dovelike nature, and as democratic lovers of freedom. It is true that early German and Byzantine writers who made acquaintance with the Slavs and the Russians bear witness to their love of liberty and to the gentleness of their disposition. It is necessary to discriminate. Unwarlike, liberty loving, pacific, and democratic, are not interchangeable terms. As far as concerns the idea democratic, we must remember that when used by a Byzantine writer of the sixth century (Procopius) or even of the tenth century (Constantine Porphyrogenitus) the word has an anarchistic flavour—and we actually find that a tendency to anarchism has been ascribed alike to the ancient and to the modern Slavs.

For the remote epoch we are discussing I shall make use of the term " negative democracy." By this I understand the

condition associated with the absence of a well-contrived
political regulation of social life (this is not to say that ideas
as to such regulation had never been considered) ; those associated with the impossibility of efficient centralisation, if only
because the ruler has not sufficient servants, a modern might
say not sufficient policemen, at his disposal ; the conditions
associated with the absence of suitable and firmly established
traditions. The resulting freedom was that of the so-called
state of nature, and it was characterised by the absence of the
evil institutions, but likewise by the absence of the good
institutions, of a more finished type of political governance.

On the whole, however, the development of the Old Russians
and that of the Old Slavs in general may have been more
closely akin to the development of the Teutons than many
Slav authors are willing to admit.

In Kiev and in the oldest Russian cities we find, in addition
to a free population, a servile and a semi-free population, both
the last-named elements being likewise Slavic. In Kiev the
peasantry was free.[1]

The existence of Old Slav and Old Russian democracy is
by some deduced as an outcome of agrarian communism,
being considered a corollary of the Russian institution known
as the *mir*, the village community, and of the occasional existence
of the family community (known among the Serbs as *zadruga*).
This theory has been advanced by the slavophils and the
narodniki.

The earliest historical data regarding Old Russia may be
interpreted by the analogy of the primitive institutions obtaining
among other Slav and Aryan nations, and by the analogy of
the primitive conditions contemporarily existing in certain
regions of Russia (Siberia, for instance) and among the so-called
primitive peoples inhabiting various regions and belonging
to divers races. By these considerations we are led to suppose
that agrarian communism prevailed in Kievic Russia.

This communism was of a negative character. It must
not be regarded as representing the communism demanded

---

[1] The semi-freeman (*zakup*), the man who offered himself for purchase or
hire) was one who worked for a peculium or for some service extended to him ;
the bondsman (*holop*) worked for his lord as a servile dependent. In the
remoter ages of history the state of bondage originated mainly through capture
in war, but the commission of certain crimes on the part of a freeman might
lead to his becoming a bondsman ; later, indebtedness became a cause. It
need hardly be said that the condition was hereditary.

by modern socialists to contrast with and to supersede private ownership and capitalism. It is not a higher and better stage of economic and social development, but the primitive stage (I by no means suggest the first of all stages) of fallowing, the primitive stage of landholding in accordance with which land having little or no value could be occupied and held at will as *res nullius*.

Like the soil, the dwellings in Old Russia were of little value, consisting merely of wooden shanties and wattle-and-dab huts, such as were practicable in the forest-clad plains. The extensive Russian lowlands were therefore defenceless against hostile inroads, all the permanent possessions being easily destroyed by fire. It is true that the attacking parties, and especially the inhabitants of the steppes, were likewise poorly equipped. The European who to-day sees the Kremlin for the first time is impressed by the positively childish mode of fortification against the Tatar hordes of cavalry.

Owing to sparseness of population and continuous danger of hostile attack from robber horsemen, it was absolutely indispensable that the various members of the family and of the tribe should co-operate for labour and for defence. The family grew to become a tribe, the members of the latter remaining for a time aware of mutual dependence. Moreover, the family was often large, for the pagan Russians, the well-to-do at least, practised polygamy.

The soil and the house had little value ; but for strategic reasons the family had to hold rigidly together ; and the primitive Russian, work-shy like the members of all other races at this stage, had to be constrained to labour. Consequently the so-called patriarchalism was anything but a moral and democratic institution. On the contrary, it was a means of coercion, consecrated mainly by religious ties—by ancestor-worship which was already firmly established among the Slavs of that day.

Thus originated agrarian communism. Such objects as had value (weapons, for example) and *pretia affectionis* were private property ; so were the dwellings ; so was everything except the soil.

This communism, therefore, had no dominant or notable significance for the society of that day. To the Old Russians, the prince, the boyar, and the monastery, with the private possessions of these. seemed far more important than their own inconspicuous doings. To the tiller of the soil, the prince, the boyar, and the monastery were an example and an ideal. In Kievic Russia, therefore, as in the west, the palace of the prince (above all, of the grand prince) and the city were of preponderant importance, strategically and politically, administratively and economically, in respect alike of craftsmanship, industry, and commerce. It is therefore erroneous to ascribe to agrarian communism, and to ancient social institutions in general, a notable moral significance, as if family ties and other bonds of kinship had predominantly, or even exclusively, determined the organisation of society.

The development of Russian law, of civil law above all, affords unambiguous proof of what has just been said. During the Kievic epoch, commercial interests became so outstanding as to secure legal formulation to a far greater extent than did agricultural interests. It was not until towards the close of the Kievic regime, and subsequently in Moscow, that legal specifications in the interests of agriculture came to occupy the premier place.[1]

iii. Economic relationships are, of course, largely dependent upon the qualities of the soil and upon climatic conditions. Primitive agriculture and primitive forestry seem prescribed by nature upon the boundless, thinly inhabited, beforested plains, whilst fishery is similarly prescribed by the existence of numerous large rivers and lakes. Trustworthy descriptions of Old Russian agriculture and stock-farming are, however, not forthcoming.

The direct and indirect influence, the economic and strategic

[1] The latest researches into primitive times have shown that the mir and the zadruga existed and still exist in the most varied forms and among the most divers people—among the Germans, the English, and the French, but also in India and Africa. There is nothing specifically Slavic about the mir. The only points remaining for enquiry in this connection are wherein the Russian mir and the zadruga may have differed from similar institutions elsewhere. Moreover if our ideas concerning the origin of the state and other institutions were to become more precise, we should less readily content ourselves with such schematic and unduly generalised concepts as "patriarchalism" etc., and we should undertake a more accurate analysis of the individual social and historical forces that were operative. The inaccuracy of the Slavic theory is further shown by a closer analysis of the mir. We cannot point out too often that the mir is not identical throughout Russia. It exhibits manifold modifications, which present its economic administrative, and legal functions in a light very different from that favoured by the slavophils and by Haxthausen. In North Russia, for example, and in Siberia we see the mir in its older and more primitive form.

influence, of soil and climate upon the character of the inhabitants was considerable, and remains considerable to-day. Much of interest from this outlook can be gleaned from descriptions in Russian literature and from the accounts of Russia given by such nonrussian writers as Leroy-Beaulieu.[1]

iv. As early as the ninth century, commerce was active with the Teutonic north, with Byzantium, and with certain other neighbour nations. Kiev and Novgorod, situate between the developed commercial peoples on the Baltic and the Black Sea, likewise became important centres of transit trade.

In Kiev, therefore, there was a conspicuous growth of a monetary economy, though subsequently in Moscow this economy was greatly restricted.

Oldtime commerce, that of Russia at any rate, must not be thought of as sharply contrasted with militarism. Trade, or to be concrete, the traders, proceeding by land in caravans and by water in fleets of river-going or seaworthy vessels, travelled on a warlike footing, and were organised for war. The trader was also a conqueror, and on occasions a robber or a pirate. Kiev was certainly occupied by such warlike " traders " from Novgorod, and thus became the capital of the realm.

The first development of the state and of civilisation in general took place in fortified towns.[2]

v. We may say, in conclusion, that political, social, and economic conditions in Kiev were somewhat unstable, and that correspondingly the evolution of Russian law, both of public law and of civil law, displayed a certain indefiniteness.

[1] A closer criticism of the various theories is requisite : o the opinion, for example, that the qualities of the soil (as in the marshy flats of the primitive home) or the peculiarities of occupation (agriculture) rendered the Old Russians unwarlike, etc., whereas the Teutons and the Turco-Tatars, the latter as horse-riding nomads of the deserts and the steppes, and the former as cattle breeders and consequently milk consumers, were in respect of social and political development superior to the Slav vegetarians. Not the explanation merely, but the alleged fact, appear to lack adequate proof. It is possible, for example, in relation to Old Russian economic history, to point to the significance of the chase in the forest rich in wild animal life, and of fishery in waters well stocked with fish. It is beyond question that a notable proportion of Old Russians lived by the chase, and that this occupation must have had an influence upon character. For a considerable period the trapping of beavers was widely practised. Many men, again, procured honey and wax from the nests of wild bees. Doubtless these occupations influenced the character of those engaged in them —but how, and to what extent ?

[2] *Gorod* (town) primarily signified a fenced or fortified place, fortifications in Old Russia being constructed principally of wood.

The importance attached in earlier times, and even to-day, to custom, affords additional proof of this. In the west, conditions were different. Russia had no legal evolution corresponding to that of Rome and of the western states which carried on the development of the Roman realm and adopted the idea of the Roman imperium. Kiev was not so directly connected with Byzantium and the Byzantine empire as France and Germany were connected with Rome. Russia was not conquered by Byzantium, nor was Russia colonised by Byzantium. In the west, as early as the close of the eighth century, with the aid of the pope and the hierarchy, Charlemagne established the Roman theocracy ; but the adoption of Christianity by Russia did not occur until a century later. At the end of the tenth century there was a school of law at Bologna where year after year during the middle ages jurists were trained to the number of many thousand ; but in the Russia of that day there were only the Greek hierarchs and monks to exercise a trifling and indirect influence upon the development of legal institutions. There was in Europe a legal continuity which was lacking in Russia.

Owing to the comparative indefiniteness of their juristic concepts, the Russians have often been undeservedly reproached with anarchism and with incapacity for the founding and maintaining of states.

vi. The prince with his retainers constituted the political centre, and administration was predominantly militarist at the outset. This was brought about by the foreign origin of the rulers, by the warlike character of the neighbouring peoples, and by the hostile inroads of the barbarians.

The prince was not a solitary personality ; he had brothers, a numerous family, and in accordance with ancient Russian custom all male children ranked equally as heirs. In conformity with this custom, we find, in the sphere of political power, either a temporary regime of all the brothers and of the more closely related agnates and cognates, or else a partition of the realm into minor princedoms. In either case there resulted an evolution of the idea and the institution of supreme sovereignty—grand princedom. Despite the equality of prestige which is characteristic of equality of inheritance, here, as universally, age and experience claimed their rights. To put the matter in legal terminology, seniority developed, not at this stage precisely distinguished as majorat and primogeniture.

The grand prince of Kiev was an absolute monarch. His throne was supported by the boyars, the aristocratic caste, from among whom he formed a council, the duma of boyars.[1] After their conversion to Christianity, the princes took the hierarchy into their counsel as well. In the towns, which in Old Russia as in the west were the strategic centres, there existed in addition a popular assembly, the *věče* (folkmote). In Novgorod alone did this body flourish ; elsewhere the institution proved incapable of development and ceased to exercise any influence.

vii. Moscow replaced Kiev. From the twelfth century onwards the Kievic realm was threatened more and more seriously by external enemies. Inadequately consolidated, it was attacked from the south and the east by Mongol and Turanian nomadic tribes ; Poles, Lithuanians, and Germans pressed in upon the west and the north ; the Finns constituted a hostile element against the Russians. Kiev ceased to be the capital of the grand princedom (1169). After the middle of the twelfth century the realm broke up into a number of principalities, whose mutual struggles for supremacy so greatly lessened the resisting power of the loose Russian federation that it proved unable to withstand the Tatar onslaught. In 1223 Russia passed under Tatar suzerainty, which endured for two and a half centuries, till 1480. In 1240 Kiev was destroyed by the Tatars.

From the north and the north-west, Russia was hard pressed by the Swedes, and also by the Livonian order of the Brethren of the Sword (founded 1202) ; and soon afterwards by the Teutonic Knights, who in 1225, proceeding from Transylvania, had settled on the Vistula and in 1237 absorbed the Livonian order. Lithuania likewise underwent centralisation towards the middle of the thirteenth century, threatened Russia, and conquered certain Russian territories. In 1386 Lithuania was united with Poland ; South Russia and West Russia were annexed by Lithuania.

---

[1] *Bojarin* originally signified " warrior," the boyars being military retainers of the prince. At a later date the word came to denote the landowning subjects of the prince, the members of the aristocracy, who monopolised the highest offices of state. The derivation of the word from *boljarin*, itself a derivative of *bol'*, meaning " more " or " better," *boljarin* thus signifying " optimate," is in my opinion the fruit of an over-ingenious attempt to assimilate the boyars to the European aristocracy. The Russian term for " prince " is *knjaz'*, that for " grand prince " is *velikii knjaz'*. In certain Slav tongues *knjaz'* signifies " priest."

At the end of the thirteenth century the principality of Moscow was founded by Daniel Aleksandrovič (ob. 1303). His son Jurii, who was married to the khan's sister, became grand prince. Jurii's successors outsoared the other princes, and Moscow was able to centralise the Russian petty realms. Ivan Kalita (1328–1341) "gathered together the Russian territories," and Moscow became the metropolitanate ; Dmitrii Donskoi (1363–1389) established primogeniture, and his son Vasilii (1389–1425) reigned as first hereditary prince. After the death of Vasilii there occurred the final struggle between the advocates of primogeniture and those of seniority, and from 1450 the rule was established that the succession should be willed to the eldest son. Moscow became a hereditary monarchy, absorbed the princedoms, threw off the Tatar yoke in 1480 and at length, in 1523, united Russian territories into a powerful realm. Muscovy was better able to resist the newly established Mongolian khanates of Kazan and Crimea than she had been able in earlier days to withstand the great Golden Horde.

At the opening of the fifteenth century the primitively patriarchal regime, which as the dynasties had grown had taken the form of petty principalities, finally gave place to a centralised state consciously based upon public law. This development secured political expression in the legal fiction that Grand Prince Ivan III, on his marriage in 1472 with the daughter of the last Palæologus, had received from Constantinople the headship of the Byzantine empire. Muscovy now adopted the two-headed Byzantine eagle as its escutcheon, but not until the following century, in the year 1547, did John IV, the Terrible, assuming the title of tsar, have himself crowned as successor of the Cæsars.

In such brief outline may be recorded the historic fact that in three centuries the realm of Kiev had been replaced by the realm of Muscovy. Russian historians and historical philosophers have propounded the most manifold theories to explain the centralisation of Russia by Moscow.

The centralisation of Muscovy is made more comprehensible by reference to the parallel development of all European states. What has to be explained is how, and by the application of what energies, Moscow was able to carry out the work of centralisation.

In the first place it remains problematical how the mutual

relationships of the petty principalities and how the relationships of these to the grand prince could be formulated from the outlook of constitutional law. Had the minor princes a sense of association ; did this sentiment arise out of racial or out of family considerations ; what were the motives of union ? It is asserted that the territories became united upon a federative basis. As far, however, as I am able to judge, no constitutionally organised federation ever existed. The sense of racial kinship was not strong enough. The princes regarded themselves as independent, but the general danger and the common need led from time to time to a loose unification based upon treaties.

Nor can it be said that the relationship of the grand prince to the minor princes was analogous to European feudalism ; even the relationship of the princes to the boyars was not feudal. The Tatar yoke (the phrase has become current) is still frequently invoked as an explanation, and was unquestionably a co-operative factor, although to a less notable extent than many historians assume. It is asserted that in face of the khans the minor princes were all reduced to an equally low level, and that this contributed to unification. We are told that the military importance of the princes was increased by the struggle with the Tatars, the boyars and the věče (folkmote) being correspondingly weakened, and the way being thus paved for a centralising absolutism. The khan is supposed to have allotted the title of grand prince to whomsoever he pleased (in actual fact this title was assumed by many of the minor princes), until it ultimately remained with the Moscow ruler. It is further contended that the Russians learned much from the Tatars in respect alike of military and administrative matters, and that the " soft " Russian character was " hardened " by Tatar influence—an explanation that overlooks the question why centralisation was effected by Moscow in especial.

Indubitably the Tatar supremacy exerted a notable influence, but this influence was not decisive in the spheres of politics, administration, or civilisation. There is no direction in which Tatar rule can be said to have initiated a new epoch. It was impossible that the influence of the Tatars could be profound, for the Russian states or peoples were at this time widely separated, and the northern territories, that of Novgorod for instance, were almost untouched by the Tatars. In respect of culture and economic development the Tatars were by no means in advance of the Russians. It was therefore impossible for them to exercise a strong positive influence upon the Russians, and it may rather be considered probable that Russia exercised a civilising influence upon the Tatars. We must not forget that the Tatars, at the time when they first came into conflict with the Russians, were not as yet Mohammedans, but were pagans who showed no disinclination to accept Christianity. Their Mohammedanisation came later. It is probable that the racial and national influence of the Russians upon the Tatars was considerable, and among the Tatars there were more Tatarised Slavs than there were Tatars living among the Russians of that day.

None the less, Tatar influence is undeniable. We trace it in court ceremonial, as in prostration before the tsars ; in administrative life, for in territories taken from the Tatars slaves were not freed ; in the conduct of warfare ; in many barbarous manners and customs (Tatar punishments, such as the branding of criminals) ; and in the adoption of Tatar words into the Russian language. The general effect of Tatar rule was to arrest or to retard Russian development. In my opinion, Polish and Lithuanian influence and Swedish and German influence were of greater importance than Tatar. The pressure upon Russia from the north and the north-west was no less severe than the pressure from the east and the south-east. Apart from the strategic reasons rendering unification against these enemies advisable, civilising influences came into play. In respect of military and administrative concerns there was far more to learn from the Teutonic Knights, from the Swedes, and from the Poles, than from the Tatars.

When this pressure from the north was superadded to the pressure from the south and the south-east, the political attention of the Russians was directed towards the north, towards the sea. Colonisation moved northwards from Kiev, and to-day Russian colonisation continues to move towards the north and the north-east (Siberia). Frequently conquest and colonisation have moved from north to south, the northlander being attracted towards the wealthier and warmer southern territories. In Russia, too, this rule was exemplified but with modifications. Norsemen founded Kiev, or at least participated in its foundation ; but Kiev was subse-

quently threatened from the south and south-east (by the
Pechenegs, etc.), and thus the outflow of Russian energies
was directed towards the north. Northward and north-
eastward lay unoccupied land, and this therefore was the
direction of voluntary and involuntary colonisation. It was
not merely the pressure of the Pechenegs and later of the
Tatars, but perhaps even more the oppression of the petty
princely tyrants, which induced the Russian population to
seek refuge in the north and the north-east and to found
colonies in these regions.

Just as sovereignty passed from Kiev to the more northerly
situated Moscow, so at a later date did sovereignty pass yet
further northward to St. Petersburg, thence to centralise
the southern regions and the entire land.

We have to remember that at this epoch the land to the
south and east of Kiev was not Slav or Russian, so that here
Tatar rule could more readily be established.

Some historians draw attention to the distinction between
Little Russia and Great Russia, suggesting that the Great
Russians of Moscow were more energetic, more warlike, and
ruder in character, when compared with the inhabitants of
Little Russia, who were of gentler disposition. But national
characteristics have not as yet been defined with sufficient
precision. Nor must we forget that such qualities change,
and that they themselves stand in need of explanation. It
is questionable whether the Kievic Russians already exhibited
the characteristics of the Little Russians of to-day, and whether
the Muscovites proper then possessed the qualities they now
exhibit. It is obvious, moreover, that energy, courage in
war, and roughness of disposition, do not suffice per se to lead
to the centralisation of a great realm, and that a certain
amount of administrative capacity is requisite in addition.
We have to remember that the main topic of consideration
at the moment is not the Russian people but the Russian
state.

This much is certain, that attempts at centralisation were
made by the princes of Kiev. Vladimir Monomachus (1113–
1125) united a considerable portion of the minor principalities,
whilst in Andrei Bogoljubskii (ob. 1174) we have an absolutist
tsar before the Moscow tsars.

Commerce likewise contributed greatly towards the unification of Russia. For Kiev, trade with economically more

developed foreign regions was already of great moment. In Muscovy the importance of trade increased in proportion as forests were cleared, and in proportion as all departments of agriculture experienced a comparatively equable development. The existence of the minor principalities was favourable to the general spread of agriculture, for in their individual territories the princes zealously promoted the cultivation of the soil and the settlement of peasants. The import of manufactured articles became more and more essential, and alike for the importing country and for the exporting countries trade was more lucrative in a large area with a centralised and unified administration, freed from tariff hindrances imposed by petty states. Just as in Germany the customs union was established before the political unification of the country, so also under primitive conditions in Russia was a " customs union " aimed at and secured. Trade strengthened centralisation and centralisation fostered trade. The capital and the other fortified towns promoted commerce, while commerce in its turn required security and unity in matters of administration and legislation. In particular, military and strategical needs were satisfied by trade, and the development of manufacture began. Commerce had likewise to satisfy the numerous courts, with their demand for luxuries.

A notable contributory economic cause and a prerequisite to centralisation was the diffusion and perfectionment of agriculture, which in Russia more than in other countries signified settlement. Herberstein, writing as late as the beginning of the sixteenth century, observed that in the realm of Muscovy cereals were less grown than elsewhere in Europe.[1]

It would be an error to assume at the outset that the growth of the realm of Muscovy was promoted by the co-operation of all the factors that have been named. To prove such a contention it would be necessary to undertake a more comprehensive analysis of individual factors, to study the varieties of agriculture, and to take into account the nature of the soil, its fertility, its water supply, etc.

In my view, the decisive centralising force of Moscow was to be found in the dependence of the grand princes upon the church. Grand princely absolutism received a religious

[1] For a long period the south remained uncultivated or almost uncultivated steppe. As late as 1690 the Don Cossacks determined to slay those who desired to cultivate the soil.

sanction from the church, and from the patriarch, the head of the church.

It was the opposition of creed against the Asiatic east, and still more the opposition of creed against the west and the north-west, Catholic at first and subsequently Protestant, which developed so effectively the religious and ecclesiastical strength of Moscow, and concurrently its political strength. Ecclesiastical centralisation began with the establishment of the Kievic metropolitanate, and the centralising process was continued by Moscow when the metropolitanate was removed to that city.

viii. Centralisation against the foreign world signified at the same time a rigid centralisation at home. The grand princes became absolute monarchs, tsars. John the Terrible's new title denoted from the outlook of constitutional law that the state had been modified. This is shown by the fact that on the extinction of the Vladimir dynasty (1598) the new tsar was not chosen from the distinguished house of Rjurik, but was none the less readily able to acquire absolute power.

The minor princes had already weakened the strength of their boyars. In the petty state the ruler was able to take more energetic action, could have recourse to more directly forcible means, than could the grand prince, typical in this respect being the weakening of the boyars in Halicz. Moscow carried this process to its term. But even during the reign of John the Terrible the struggle between the two powers had not yet come to a close, as is indicated by the division of the state into boyarsland and tsarsland (*zemščina* and *opričina*). Kurbskii's revolt against John shows how the descendants of the princely families were inclined to regard themselves as the equals of the tsar. The final victory of the tsar over the boyars was due to the evolution of the great state and of its administrative needs. As long as the boyars still retained their old military importance, the prince, the grand prince, even the tsar, was no more than par inter pares. Owing to centralisation, the princely families in Moscow, as members of the dynasty, secured a position superior to that of the boyars. More stress was laid upon the boyars' obligation to service ; and since it was no longer possible, as in the days of the petty princes, for a boyar to transfer his allegiance from one sovereign to another, service became less free. Primitively, the boyars not in service enjoyed higher prestige

than those in service (*bojarin* signifying free landowner) ; but
as time passed the power of the serving boyars increased, and
therewith their prestige. In the sixteenth century the boyar
had already become a greater man than the prince. It was
in the tsar's interest to restrict the princes to a purely honorary
position, whereas those who directly served the court secured
henceforward higher respect, so that the Russian term for
nobleman was *dvorjanin,* " courtier."

It was impossible that the centralised great state should
be administered by the monarch alone, and the sovereign
therefore sought councillors and assistants in the duma of
boyars. The ancient council of boyars, the composition of
which had been subject to frequent changes, became transformed in Moscow into a species of permanent council of state.[1]

Owing to the increase in business it became necessary
to appoint governmental departments ; while scriveners, ready
writers and experts in customary law, were also essential,
and bore the title of *dumnyi djak,* secretary to the council.
The secretaries, whose numbers varied from four to fourteen,
occupied subordinate positions at first ; but since they had
continuously to work as delegates to the duma, they became
ministers, as it were, holding important posts. Simultaneously
the membership of the duma increased, and a differentiation
of official duties occurred. Under John there were at the
outset twenty-one members, whilst under Theodore Alekséevič
there were one hundred and sixty-seven. During the seventeenth century the department of justice, in especial, underwent separate development, and a foreign office was also
established, these changes affording satisfactory proof of the
manner in which the position of the tsars had become constitutionally established. The prestige and importance of the
Moscow duma is indicated by the fact that the aforesaid Theodore, in the year 1681, abolished the old system in accordance
with which the leading posts in the public service had been
filled by boyars and princes in conformity with the dictates
of genealogical trees—to the great detriment of the administration in general and of military affairs in particular. Thus
did the first Romanovs found the bureaucracy.

[1] It has not yet been ascertained whether and to what extent members
of the duma were regularly summoned from other towns and from ex-
principalities. We must on no account in this connection think of a system
of popular representation, nor had the duma any resemblance to a general
assembly of the people

In Moscow the legislative authority was entirely in the hands of the absolute tsar, but the work of the executive (when the tsar was absent, and so on) necessitated the taking of many decisions by the duma independently of the tsar, the boyars being commissioned for such purposes either in perpetuity or for long periods.

In the year 1700 Peter dissolved the duma of boyars, but the institution persisted in fact, for Peter had to make use of a council. It consisted at first of members directly appointed by himself, but owing to his frequent absences the bureaucracy was strengthened, the duma and its departments living on in the senate and in the governmental colleges.

The centralisation and bureaucratisation of the Muscovite state led to the development of a species of feudalism. Owing to the prevalence of a natural economy the Moscow sovereign could more frequently bestow land as a reward than had been possible to the petty princes and the Kievic grand prince. Centralisation was perfected by confiscating the estates of refractory and obnoxious princes and their boyars, the serving boyars and princes being rewarded with gifts of land. Thus side by side with the inherited family estates (*votčina*), analogous to the western allodia, there grew up the benefices granted in fief by the monarch.[1]

In Russia, enfeoffment had a different signification from what it had in Europe, for the simple reason that the land was here less cultivated than in Germany for instance. In the west the Teutons found cultivated lands, already prepared by tillers of the soil, but the Russians had to undertake the first tasks of cultivation, those which the Romans, the Celts, and the western Slavs had effected before the Franks appeared upon the scene. In Russia the soil was therefore of far less value, and was indeed practically worthless. Subsequently, too, enfeoffment in Russia remained different from the similar institution in the west. The position was comparatively independent of scutage. The prince's retainer was freer and could transfer his services from one prince to another, for this necessarily followed from the subdivision of sovereignty and of territory, the petty princes occupying mutual

---

[1] *Poměstie* signifies land, estate, domain, with a connotation of high social position; from this is derived the contemporary term *pomĕščik*, landed proprietor which lacks the connotation the word had in Moscow.

relationships very different from those which obtained between the European vassals and their feudal lords.

The development of the executive in the Muscovite great state led to the abolition of that general assembly of the people which in earlier days had been necessary not in Moscow alone but in other towns as well. In Moscow the function of the věče lapsed in the fourteenth century, and in the other towns the věče was abolished by the grand princes of Moscow, notably in Novgorod in the year 1478, and in Pskov in the year 1510—the work of centralisation being thus carried through deliberately and with foresight.

Nevertheless the people of the capital possessed here, as everywhere, certain prerogatives, especially in troublous times. For example, as late as the year 1682 Peter and his brother John were elected by the (unorganised !) " people " under the leadership of the patriarch.

The new and difficult administrative tasks of the centralised great state called into existence, side by side with the duma, the peculiar institution of the territorial assembly or provincial council (*zemskii sobor*). The first zemskii sobor was summoned by John the Terrible in 1566 ; the earlier assemblies established by this ruler having, it may be presumed, been purely deliberative. The institution persisted only until 1653.

This territorial assembly had no political significance. It met purely for administrative deliberations on the part of the government and of the monarch. It had no legislative powers, and was not popularly representative. The members of the assembly came together as private persons, so that the sobor was not a continuation of the věče. The outcome of the consultation was definitely and legally formulated by the duma and the monarch, the sovereign deciding for himself whether and to what extent he would be guided by the decisions of the provincial council. Even the enlarged duma, being a central organism, proved inadequate for the needs of the great state. Moscow had to deal with matters of local administration, and this was the origin of the sobor. The councillors, on their return home, became as it were inspectors of local administration or local instruments of the executive. In many cases the territorial assembly had to support the duma, or even to supersede the duma when that body was out of its depth, the functions varying according to circumstances. Ključevskii maintains that the sobor consisted of the duma, the hierarchy, and the higher executive officials of Moscow, together with the serving nobles and the mercantile class. On one occasion only, in 1613, did peasants become members of the sobor.[1]

We cannot here discuss the development of the zemskii sobor, but light is thrown on its significance by the circumstance that its prestige declined with the increasing bureaucratisation and Europeanisation of the executive. Under Tsar Alexis Mihailovič, who favoured Europeanisation, the importance of the sobor sank to zero, and by this ruler the assembly was summoned for the last time in order to confirm the annexation of Little Russia.[2]

It remains uncertain whether the members of the sobor were nominated by the monarch or whether they were elected. It is probable that they were nominated or invited to attend, and that when elections took place it was not for the choice of representatives but in occasional response to some local need. Attendance at the sobor was not an honour but a duty, and was felt to be a disagreeable one, seeing that the members had to maintain themselves at their own expense with no more than occasional assistance from the government.

If some of the successive sobors had exceptional political significance, this arose from the circumstances of the time when they were summoned, and was frequently dependent upon a state of indecision and perplexity. For example, the sobor of 1584 elected Theodore Ivanovič to the throne, and the first Romanov was elected by the sobor of 1613.

Apart from the consideration that the sobor did not meet regularly year by year, but was summoned merely on exceptional occasions, it had just as little in common with constitutionalist assemblies as had the European estates, and each individual sobor varied in its organisation in accordance with the tasks with which it had to deal and the circumstances

---

[1] Certain historians contend, erroneously, that at all the assemblies the peasants were represented by the urban members.

[2] Theodore Aleksčevič, Peter's brother, summoned a kind of sobor on two occasions, but these assemblies were no more than deliberative committees for the discussion of special questions. Their members were drawn from those classes only which could supply persons with expert knowledge, so that, for example, peasants were among those summoned to deliberate concerning the reform of taxation. In the year 1698 Peter the Great, desiring the condemnation of his sister Sophia, but wishing to evade personal responsibility, convoked an assembly whose members were drawn from all classes. This sobor was the last of its kind.

under which it was convened. Thus, though the sobor of 1648 was organised bicamerally, the resemblance to the constitutionalist bicameral system was purely superficial.

ix. Concurrently with the increase in power of the grand princes of Moscow and with the centralisation of the great state, there occurred a change in the position, not of the aristocracy alone, but also of the rest of the population, and in especial of the peasants.

At first, in Moscow as in Kiev, the peasant was for the most part free ; but in comparison with the aristocrat he was the disregarded " little man," or " manling," this being the literal signification of the word *mužik*. " Black people " is the other characteristic term used already in early days at Moscow to denote the peasantry or special classes of that order. The official designation for the peasant is *krest'janin*, meaning literally the anointed or christened person.

In Moscow, too, as in Kiev, in addition to free peasants, there existed serfs and semi-free peasants ; · but with the centralisation of the princedoms the social status of the serfs underwent a change. Capture in war no longer provided so many bondsmen as in the days when the principalities were perpetually at feud. Economic need now became the most potent and decisive cause of serfdom, the indebted peasant, voluntarily in many cases, accepting a state of bondage vis-à-vis the wealthy lord. From the end of the fifteenth century onwards there came into existence in Muscovy what was known as kabal-serfdom (*kabalnoje holopstvo*), *kabala* being the Tatar word for indebtedness. The debtor worked in order to pay the interest, but, the capital charge remaining unreduced, the debtor was bond for life, and so were his children. Towards the middle of the seventeenth century, when repeated scarcity of food had much degraded the peasants of Muscovy, it frequently happened that impoverished and hungry peasants voluntarily renounced the status of freedom.

Centralised administration completed what economic conditions had begun, the influences of national economics being superadded to those of domestic economics. The new state needed money, the thinly peopled land required labour, the army demanded soldiers, and thus it was that the peasant who had hitherto been privileged to change his lord, became " bound " to the soil. *Prikrěplenie*, the state of being bound, is the Russian term for villeinage and bondage to the soil, but also for serfdom, the fuller development of villeinage.

In 1597, Boris Godunov finally established villeinage as a legal institution. As regent, the clever boyar was keenly alive to the economic interests of his order and of the church (the monasteries). The peasant must be more efficiently exploited by his lord and by the state, and he was therefore deprived of the right to transfer his services.

The question how and when serfdom, strictly speaking, was introduced has not been fully answered by Russian historians and jurists. I do not believe that the institution originated through direct legislative procedure, and in consequence of state intervention. It was a gradual development. Codification served merely to give a legal warrant to what already existed, though doubtless thenceforward evolution, having become deliberate, advanced with more rapid strides. Among numerous explanations, I would lay especial stress upon the political and administrative centralisation of the new state, and would point to the parallel evolution of the nobility and the peasantry. In Kiev the nobleman was a free servant of the prince, just as the peasant was a freeman ; both had the right of free movement ; the nobleman could leave his prince to take service with another ; the peasant could transfer himself at will to work for another lord, or to become a colonist. In Muscovy free service came to an end ; the nobleman was gradually " bound " to service, until at length he became transformed into the bureaucrat. Simultaneously the free peasant was tied to the soil. The prince and his descendants became bureaucrats, the peasant and his children became villeins. This peculiar political process did not come to an end with the year 1597. Under the second Romanov, contracts between peasants and their lords received national recognition in that the duties of the peasant were inscribed on the public rolls and were officially regulated.

The consequences of the new situation soon became clear to the peasantry. Under the leadership of the bold Sten'ka Razin, a Cossack and proletarian revolution was organised in 1670. Peter and his descendants increased the bondage of the peasants to actual serfdom, the peasant becoming personally dependent upon his lord. It is true that simultaneously Peter bureaucratised the nobility more thoroughly than before, making service obligatory upon the nobles.

Serfdom and the disappearance of free service give expression to the fact that the Russians in Muscovy had become a settled population, this being itself connected with their absolute and relative increase in numbers. The peasant's lack of freedom was not everywhere the same either in fact or legally. The state of Moscow owned enormous areas of land, both tilled and untilled. The peasants upon the state or crown lands and upon the private property of the tsars had a position which naturally differed in some respects from that of the peasants upon the boyar's estates, for the relationship of the tsar to the boyars was reflected in the relationship between the boyars and the peasants. Legislation was more directly concerned with the peasants on the crown lands. As time passed, the distinction between the two categories was legally formulated, the main difference being that the peasants on the crown lands were comparatively well to do. Similarly, the peasants upon large estates were better off economically speaking than those on small estates, for the small landlord tended to satisfy his aristocratic needs by means of the more vigorous oppression of a restricted number of peasants.

The differences found expression also in the nature of the burdens imposed. The corvée (*barščina*, from *bojarščina*, boyar service), perhaps chronologically the primitive form of service, was harsher than the natural or monetary burden (*obrok*, rent), which was general upon the crown lands. The latter form permitted a certain freedom of movement. The serf could go to the town to seek work there, and could engage in various occupations, becoming a craftsman, a trader, etc. Not infrequently such a serf was better off than his lord.

In addition to the serfs there were semi-free and free peasants. The peasants on the crown lands, as already explained, were freer than the others. Peasants who had done well in service or who had acquired means were free in actual fact, and in many cases in point of law also. From the sixteenth century onwards, that is from the time when serfdom was definitively established, there existed a special category of frontier peasants in the southern and eastern parts of the realm. These were enfeoffed with land in order that they might guard the frontier, their feoffs being given as a reward for zealous service, and their holdings of land becoming in course of time hereditary private property, increasing in extent. These free peasants, constituting a species of lesser gentry (they were entitled to keep serfs), were known as *odnodvorcy*, one-farm-men, that is individual farm men, those who owned their farm buildings and land individually and not communally. When the realm extended its frontiers, the military duties of the odnodvorcy lapsed. In Ukraine the Cossacks had similar functions.[1]

Russian serfdom differed from European serfdom in that the earlier mir constitution was retained, but under serfdom the mir and its agrarian communism acquired a different legal and economic significance. Owing to the increasing power of the grand princes and the tsars, the idea became current that the land in its entirety was the property of the sovereign, the usufruct merely being ceded to the landowners and through these to the peasants. In actual fact, however, the land-owner possessed the soil jointly with the grand prince, the landowner being the real possessor, not merely of his family estate, but also of the farms of his peasants. Thus the land-lord could withdraw a peasant from the community or intro-duce a peasant into the community at his own will and pleasure.

The centralised state turned the mir to account in fiscal matters by raising taxes from the village community as a whole and not from the individual peasant. Through this joint responsibility the mir became more firmly established and was endowed with a certain power over the individual; but it is an error to hold that the mir really originated out of such joint responsibility. Changes in agriculture likewise promoted an increase in the power and prestige of the mir. With the steady growth of a settled population there resulted an increase in the value of land, although there was not as yet any scarcity of land. In the sixteenth century, fallowing was replaced by the more lucrative triennial rotation of crops, whereby the economic value of the soil was enhanced.

Settlement on the land naturally involved numerous disputes, and these had to be settled by the village community. The tsar was remote, and his servants were by no means close at hand. Disputes concerning the soil could be most

---

[1] The odnodvorcy villages have here and there in course of time undergone partial or complete conversion into village communities. In the Kursk ad-ministrative district the odnodvorcy have continued, for the most part, to exist as such to the present day. During the sixteenth century this district, in conjunction with those of Voronezh Tambov, Orlov, etc , constituted the frontier region.

conveniently arranged by redistribution, for in the case of illiterates left to their own devices there were no court rolls or cadasters.

Centralised administration brought order and stability into all relationships. The earlier freedom was at an end. From the fourteenth century onward the *volost'*, the amalgamation of several village communities, replaced the individual community as the administrative unit, for Moscow had not servants enough or means enough to deal directly with each village. The volosts in their turn were united in a larger unit called the circle, which was placed under the supervision, and properly speaking under the rule of the *voevoda* or waywode (literally "army leader"), who for practical purposes concentrated in his person the entire administration. In essence the administration was fiscal, but order had also to be maintained by force of arms.

It need hardly be said that the towns and their inhabitants remained exempt from serfdom, except that the serf might seek work in the town; but the town could be more readily supervised by the treasury and the executive in general, for it was often the seat of the circle authority. The definite segregation of the peasants as serfs involved as a corollary the segregation of the other estates. The realm of Muscovy was organised in separate estates with distinct rights and privileges. There were four principal estates, the nobility, the church, the burghers, and the peasants. Each of these became subdivided in course of time into classes or sub-estates. In especial did this subdivision take place in the case of the burghership, the mercantile class coming here to play a dominant role, above all in the capital. Owing to administrative centralisation, Moscow became the principal focus of commerce and industry, the latter being still extremely primitive; but there were certain lesser commercial centres, such as Jaroslav, Tula, Smolensk, etc.

In proportion as commerce prospered at home and abroad, and in proportion as the agricultural development of the country matured, the natural economy was replaced by a monetary economy, and the ancient feudalist state became transformed, the numerous lesser landowners and the mercantile class gaining power and prestige alongside the bureaucracy, the military officers, and the hierarchy. The old feudal subdivisions were transformed into a new gradation of classes.

This process of internal development coincides with the period of persistent confusions and revolutions which ensued upon the dying out of the successors of Vladimir, disorders lasting more than a decade, and terminating mainly in the victory of the minor aristocracy and the wealthier bourgeoisie. In 1613, Michael Theodorovič Romanov, chosen from the aristocracy, was elected by the people, that is to say by the aristocratic sobor, with some assistance from the discontented Cossacks. His father Filaret, the patriarch, ruled for fourteen years (1619–33) jointly with his son as co-tsar, and the position of the new dynasty was thus consolidated by the full authority of the church.

§ 2.

THE Russian church was organised from Byzantium and it was from Byzantium that the preponderant majority of the Russian people received Christianity. Socially and politically and in respect of general civilisation the Greek priesthood and hierarchy were considerably in advance of the Russians, and in Old Russia therefore the social institutions and civilisation which the Greeks introduced exercised a notable influence. The church assumed the spiritual leadership of the nation and became the educator of the people. The prince remained in supreme command, but the pupils he was to command were prepared by religious education.

From the ninth century onwards, Byzantium was threatened, at first by the Slav peoples, but before long also by Arabs and Turks, and the danger was a spur to a Christianising policy, though not always to Christianisation. In Russia, the Byzantine hierarchy, which led the Russian mission, was concerned from the very outset, not with religion alone, but with ecclesiasticism as well. The Byzantine church was a mighty social organisation, and consequently acquired in Russia, too, great political and social influence. Sociological explanations of Old Russia are apt to pay far too little attention to the direct and indirect influence exercised upon society by the church. This influence is far from inconsiderable if we contemplate merely the suggestive existence of the firmly established hierarchy with its churches and monasteries. In addition, however, it was not long before the church in Russia, like the Roman church among western nations, came to exercise a conscious and carefully planned political and social influence, for it was introduced into Russia as a state church and operated throughout in this capacity. After their conversion the Russians were educated by Greeks who had deliberately severed themselves from Rome. Byzantium had been ravaged on several occasions by the pagan Russians, and for this reason the Christianisation of these Slav enemies was politically important, all the more because the Arabs and the Turks had begun to encroach upon the Byzantine dominions. The positively draconian subjugation of the Bulgars gave a striking demonstration of Byzantium's attitude towards the Slavs. We must not forget that Byzantium never ceased to aim at the expansion of its power. It is sometimes ignored that at the time of the Russian conversion the eastern Roman empire embraced, not merely Asia Minor and the Black Sea region, but in addition considerable domains in Italy and even in Africa. Down to the day of destruction, this imperialist policy was never abandoned by Byzantium, and it was a policy in which the patriarchate of Constantinople collaborated.

In Kiev the Byzantine princes of the church constituted a state within the state. The metropolitan of Kiev was appointed by the patriarch of Constantinople, whereas in Byzantium the bishops were elected by their own colleagues. Kiev was no more than a dependency of Byzantium, and among the Greek bishops the Kievic metropolitan occupied the seventy-first place. The Russian hierarchy always remained Greek. Among the three-and-twenty metropolitans of Kiev in the days before the Tatar dominion, three only were Russians, and three southern Slavs, the remaining seventeen being Byzantines. Many of the priests and monks were likewise Greeks.

Nor must we underestimate the influence of the chroniclers and of all those who were able to write, most of whom, having had a Greek education, diffused and confirmed the ideas and ideals of Byzantium.

Guided by cultured hierarchs, the church and its organisation soon became a model which princely administration strove to imitate. The Byzantines brought to Russia the idea and the practice of law and the legal code ; they introduced a regular system of legal procedure ; and, above all, ecclesiastical centralisation set an example to princely policy. From early days the church was the ally of the grand prince. In many cases the grand prince was a tool of the metropolitans who, for all their cunning, found the princes too stiff-necked to drive. The metropolitans were themselves pliable enough provided only they could send plenty of money to Byzantium, for in Russia, as in the west, the church was also a financial institution, and this redounded in turn to its political power. Such was the case although the Russians had no particular affection for the Greek priests and hierarchs, so that as early as the twelfth century, in the Russian tongue the word Greek (Grek) became synonymous with rapscallion.

It is necessary to conceive and appraise the medieval churches of Rome and Byzantium as constituting social and political organisms side by side with the imperial power. Medievalism is characterised by the development of theocracy, the Roman in the west and the Byzantine in the east. Emperor and pope, emperor and patriarch, church and state, are the organs of political organisation. Theology is the basis and the associative link of social order. The throne rests upon the altar, and the altar supports the throne ; state and church are one. Down to the present day, almost all states are theocratic. Theology, the doctrine of the church, is the official and political outlook on the world ; ecclesiastical morality is official and political morality. In so far as society is organised upon a basis of ideas, the middle ages brought theocracy to maturity, and this theocratic social order has maintained itself in manifold forms and degrees down to the present day.

In the east, the emperor maintained the primacy in theocracy. Constantius II was able to say, " My will is law for the church." This is the practical significance of the theological doctrine of the " symphony " of soul and body, of patriarch and emperor. This symphony materialises in perfected cæsaropapism. Russian theocracy developed in a similar direction. In the east, therefore, the power of the church vis-à-vis the state was for the most part inferior to that possessed by the western church, of which the pope maintained the primacy. The power and the influence of the church depended upon the faith and the credulity of all, emperor, pope, and patriarch.

When the subdivision of the realm among the petty princes began, the metropolitan was able to wield great political power, doing this precisely in virtue of his office, for the local churches were subject to him, and the church was so far independent of the princes inasmuch as it was subject to the patriarch and therefore to the emperor of Constantinople, as supreme head of the Orthodox church. The centralisation of Russian territory began ecclesiastically. In individual princedoms the princes had gained control over the church. In Novgorod the folkmote elected the archbishop.

A perspicacious prince, one with far-reaching political ideals, seizes every opportunity of extending his power, of promoting centralisation, by availing himself of any extraneous help that may offer. The grand princes were not slow to turn the church to political account in this manner.

If we are to think, not merely of ecclesiastical development in Russia, but of the actual Christianisation of the country, it must be pointed out at once that the latter process was by no means intensive, if only for the reason that the church was a Greek church, that its chiefs were foreigners. Slav polytheism continued to live side by side with and beneath official Christianity, which about the year 988 was by St. Vladimir made the religion of the state. Russia long remained, and perhaps is still to-day, the country and the nation of the " twin-faith " (*dvoevěrie*).

The Christianisation of Russia was effected a hundred years later than that of the southern Slavs, and much later than the Christianisation of the west.

It was impossible that the Russians should have a spiritual conception of Christianity, for they lacked the requisite culture. In Byzantium and in Rome it was a cultured and philosophically trained people that was converted to Christianity, and the western nations that were Christianised at a later date had shared in Roman culture. But the Russians were entirely unprepared, and what could the learned divinity of Byzantium signify to them, what could they be expected to make of its theological philosophy of religion ? The Russians, therefore, absorbed from Byzantium chiefly the ritual and the discipline of the church. The morality of these Christians was mainly limited to externals, and was diffused and strengthened by outward constraint. The punishments which, with its independent judicature, the church was able to inflict were more influential than the " word." Most potent of all was the working of monkish morality, of asceticism, and of monastic life. The monk was the living example, the example which as time passed proved most efficacious. The Byzantines did not import any excess of humaneness with the gospel of love.

The newly introduced punishments displayed their Byzantine origin—blinding, chopping off of hands, and similar brutalities—punishments whose atrocity was subsequently reinforced by Tatar influence.

It was natural to the Byzantines to cultivate theology and theological literature. Such literature remained Byzantine when couched in the Slavic ecclesiastical tongue. The Greeks learned Russian, indeed, but their views and their habits remained Byzantine. At the court of the metropolitan and in many of the monasteries there were Byzantine colonies, continually replenished from Byzantium.

Byzantium, less powerful than Rome, was unable to impose its speech upon the daughter churches. The Russians, like the southern Slavs, preserved the Old Slavic ecclesiastical tongue. For this reason the southern Slavs, and especially the Bulgars, who were more directly influenced by Byzantium, took an active part in the Christianisation and civilisation of the Russians.

It will readily be understood that Russian opposition to Byzantine influence in the church sprang to life. This opposition seems to have been active as early as the eleventh century, and was certainly active in the twelfth century, focusing in Kiev, the capital, and above all in the Pečerskii Monastyr (Monastery of the Caves). The grand princes endeavoured to compromise between the metropolitans and the Monastery of the Caves, but favoured the latter.

Novgorod exercised an influence as well as Byzantium, and in Kiev western civilising forces were also at work. St. Vladimir entered into relationships with Germany, Rome, Poland, and Bohemia. It is by no means improbable that the first Christianity in Russia, in Novgorod and Kiev, was Roman, and that the Norsemen who founded the Kievic state were Roman Christians. But history has as yet no definite information how and to what extent western Europe influenced Old Russia.

Russian civilisation, Russian views of the world and of life, were lower than Byzantine. Russia was at a lower level of civilisation. The Russians were not simply uncultured, not merely, as we should say to-day, illiterate ; but their morality was crude ; they were polygamists ; but they were natural, simple, and frank, and despite their roughness they were more humane than most of the Byzantines. This Old

Russian roughness was no worse than the roughness of the Old Teutons. In ancient monuments and other memorials of antique civilisation, the attentive observer can discern Teutonic and Russian elements side by side with Latin and Greek, and can trace how foreign influence was accepted and elaborated, but was also on occasions repelled.

The literary memorials of the Kievic epoch display to us Russian Old Russia in a more favourable light than Byzantine Old Russia. We see this, for example, in Vladimir's *Instruction*, compiled for the use of his sons. It is true that Monomachus's writing (Vladimir Monomachus, 1113-1125) betrays Byzantine influence, but his Christianity is comparatively humane, his morality is comparatively unascetic and natural, and the princely author recommends love and sympathy towards fellow men, especially towards the poor and lowly. The writer's own actions did not, indeed, always square with his words, but this is by no means an infrequent experience, whether we have to do with crowned or uncrowned heads.

Nestor the chronicler, who flourished in the beginning of the twelfth century, gives the same impression of naturalness and freshness. As author he was the first Russian realist. He had a thorough knowledge of peoples and places, and his outlook on life and on historical events was anything but monastic. If he was indeed a monk, as some maintain, this gives us additional proof that even in monasteries at that date Christianity existed solely in externals. To the same period and to the same category belong the epic *The Lay of Igor's Raid*, the vestiges of numerous sagas (*byliny*, etc.), and folk poetry in general collected during the nineteenth century. All these memorials serve to show that the education and transformation of ancient Russia by Byzantine influence was effected very gradually and encountered considerable opposition. The Muscovite realm was the first to become definitely Byzantine, and this only under Tatar auspices.

Kievic territory, however, was detached from Muscovite Great Russia, and was not reunited until the seventeenth century. Thenceforward the south again made its influence felt, politically, socially, and nationally.

§ 3.

" TWO Romes have fallen and have passed away, the western and the eastern ; destiny has prescribed for Moscow the position of the third Rome ; there will never be a fourth." Such were the words wherein, after the fall of Constantinople, the Russian monk glorified and characterised the historical position of Moscow, which had now replaced Kiev as mistress of Russia.

In proportion as Constantinople lost prestige, power, and influence through the continual onslaughts of the Turks, did there ensue an increase in the prestige and power of Moscow, all the more since the enemy who conquered Constantinople was himself conquered by Moscow. The ultimate victory of Moscow over the Tatar Mohammedans seemed especially impressive to the Christian east inasmuch as it was effected soon after the fall of Byzantium.

The political centralisation of Russian territory and the power of the grand princes of Moscow were furthered by ecclesiastical centralisation. The crowning of the grand prince as tsar (Cæsar) followed the establishment of the Moscow patriarchate (1589).

The continuous struggle of Moscow against the east and the west, against the pagan and Mohammedan Tatars, and against the Catholic and Protestant nations, greatly enhanced the ecclesiastical and religious consciousness of the Russians. It is possible that the victory of the Byzantine church over the western Christianity of the Varangians was here a contributory cause. The third Rome took over from Constantinople the idea of the Roman imperium, which Byzantium first of all and subsequently Rome had carried out in theocratic guise. The cæsaropapism of Byzantium was revived by Moscow, and the third Rome became a perfected theocracy.

In Moscow as in the west the outlook on life and the universe upon which Russian cæsaropapism was founded was rigidly orthodox and theological ; but in the east, and above all in Moscow, the dominance of ecclesiastical doctrine was more exclusive. In Moscow there was no classical tradition, no rivalry between different nations. Learned men were few in number, and were characteristically styled men learned in writing, book-learned. The sum total of knowledge was theology and theosophy. This ecclesiastical culture attained its climax at the close of the fourteenth century and the opening of the fifteenth, at the time when in Europe the splendid religious revolution of Bohemia was inaugurating the new age, and when Rome was beginning to give way upon all fronts.

The Byzantine church became petrified, although it was the Greeks who had elaborated its doctrines and its morality. The Byzantines contented themselves with an almost mechanical tradition, their religion consisting mainly of ritual observances. The Russians took over dogmas, ritual, morality, and ecclesiastical organisation ready made from Byzantium. Since they did nothing further for the development of ecclesiastical and religious life, in Russia petrifaction was if possible more marked.

This applies to the clergy, for the laity was content with the passive acceptance of eccclesiastical discipline, and with a blind belief in miracles such as is characteristic of the earlier stages of the mythical outlook on the world.

The Byzantines were scholastically trained, the philosophical tradition of the Greeks being preserved in a sort of theosophical gnosis. The Russians endeavoured to follow their teachers in this respect also, but found fuller satisfaction for their religious needs in ritual. In Moscow, mysticism was not so much theosophical contemplation as practical mystagogy.

This religiosity must be sharply distinguished from morality. Morality is a subordinate element of religion. The ideas of holiness and righteousness are by no means coincident. Ritual, and individual ritual practices, rather than the moral relationships between man and man, are the primary constituents of religion. John the Terrible, an assassin already in his thirteenth year, was a religious man.

Owing to a lack of critical faculty and a deficiency of culture, among the Russians as among most primitive peoples, it was possible for pathological states of nerve and mind to be regarded as manifestations of a religious inner life, to be accepted as divine revelations, and this not solely by isolated sects condemned by the church, but generally. Even to-day in Russia, and not by peasants alone, *jurodivye* (psychopaths—idiots and imbeciles) are regarded as God-inspired individuals.

The history of many of the Russian sects manifests to us this low level of religious sensibility, and displays at the same time the defects of the official church. Europeans were apt to regard the Muscovites as polytheists rather than as Christians, whereas the Russians themselves extolled their land as " Holy Russia."

The church established monastic ethics, monastic asceticism. The most harmless pleasures, even laughter, were penalised by the zealots, and non-theological poetry was banned. The nature of the prevalent morality can be estimated from the views that were current regarding woman and the family. We need only compare the teachings of the *Domostroi* (the book on household management by Silvester, who was banished to a monastery in 1560) or of the *Stoglav* (the code of ecclesiastical law containing one hundred chapters, issued in 1551) with Monomachus' *Instruction*, to learn how unnatural Moscow had become under the rigid discipline of the church. In Tatar fashion women are to be relegated to the harem (*terem*, the Tatar word for palace and in especial for the women's quarters). The family is subordinated to the father, the " patriarch," just as peasants are subordinated to their lords and as lords are subordinated to the tsar. Social and political slavery found its strongest prop in the moral slavery of family life. Intellectually Russia was ruled by the monastery. The hierarchy was chosen from among the monastic clergy, and the secular or " white " clergy was completely subject to the monastic or " black " clergy, the result being that the ethics of the monkish celibates triumphed over the ethics of the married secular priests.

The monastery, shunning the world but dominating men, was wealthy in spite or perhaps because of its asceticism ; and through its extensive ownership of land it was able to wield great political and social power. The monks not infrequently gave a conspicuous example of a mode of life that was far from ascetic.

Those whose views on the world and life were of this character had thoroughly anthropomorphic and sociomorphic conceptions of God and the divine. To the uncultured people and to the uncultured priests it was inevitable that the power of the tsar who had conquered the enemies of the church and had overthrown the domestic opponents of his autocracy, should seem to typify the power of God.

In the fifteenth century, Iosif, the rough and harsh renovator of the monkish ideal, formulated this widely held view of the tsar's theocratic position by saying that while by nature the tsar resembled all other men, in power he resembled the supra-mundane God.

The opponents of Iosif and his party, led by Nil Sorskii, regarded the priestly dignity as higher than the imperial dignity, and denied the emperor's right to interfere in spiritual and ecclesiastical affairs, but this view did not prevail. To protect the church and to maintain the purity of religious dogma were regarded as the principal duties of the grand princes and the tsars. Protection was to be afforded, not merely against foreign enemies holding other creeds, but also against heretics and sectaries at home. Gennadii, archbishop of Novgorod (1485–1504), another harsh ecclesiastic, fulminating against the rationalistic sect of the Judaisers whose doctrines may be regarded as a protest against monkish rule, quoted with approval the example of the king of Spain, and demanded a radical purification of Orthodox Russia. To his opponent Kurbskii, John the Terrible enunciated the doctrine that the tsar's chief duty was to educate his subjects to be religious, so that they might acknowledge the one true triune God, and the tsars given them by God. In the *Stoglav*, the protocol of the Old Russian council of 1551 (wherein the adherents of Iosif maintained a majority), the theocratic position of the tsar and the theological foundation of the Russian theocracy were definitively codified. An outward manifestation of its true nature was furnished by the theocracy in the nomination of the patriarch Filaret to be co-emperor with his son Michael, the first of the Romanovs.

§ 4.

THE weakening and the ultimate fall of the Byzantine empire exercised important effects upon the spiritual life of the third Rome, for the civilising influence of Byzantium was thereby reduced, and Moscow was left to her own resources. The Old Russia of Novgorod and Kiev had been in relationship with Europe as well as with Byzantium. By Byzantine influences Moscow was estranged from Europe, but after the fall of Constantinople became necessarily all the more dependent upon Europe.

Muscovy's need of Europe's spiritual help was shown by the participation of the Russians in the attempts at the union of the eastern and western churches made at Florence in the year 1439. The first complete Russian Bible (the work of the aforesaid Gennadii) was in part translated from the Vulgate. When Kiev and south-western Russia were annexed by Lithuania and Poland, the Polonisation of Russian territory led to a partial, and to a considerable extent forcible, union of the churches, the union of Brest (Brest-Litovsk), effected in the year 1596. The Jesuits summoned to Poland and Lithuania to counteract Protestantism, had likewise a certain influence upon Moscow. Polish Catholic scholasticism exercised a civilising pressure upon the Russians under the rule of Lithuania and Poland. They experienced a spiritual awakening, and their Orthodox brotherhoods founded a number of comparatively flourishing schools in Ostrog and elsewhere. In Kiev, also under Polish auspices, there was founded in the year 1615 the religious academy which was to serve Russian Orthodoxy with the aid of Catholic and Jesuit scholasticism. In 1685 pupils and teachers from the Kievic academy established in Moscow a daughter institution, the Slav-Greek-Latin academy, which at first bore the tautological name of Hellenic-Greek academy because the instruction given there was Greek, not Latin merely. According to the plans of the tsar Theodore Alekséevič, the school was to strengthen and diffuse Orthodoxy, and it did to some extent succeed in these aims, but with the help of the Latin tongue and of Roman scholasticism.

With the utmost of her energies and with all possible severity, though not always with success, Moscow endeavoured to resist the Roman Catholic tendencies of the Kievic scholastics, among whom Medvěděv was the most notable. Turning away from Catholicism, Moscow tended towards Protestantism.

The Czech reformation, Hussitism, and still more the Moravian Brotherhood, secured adherents in Poland and Lithuania. In addition, the German reformation began to make headway in Lithuania as early as the year 1538. From Lithuania and Poland, Protestantism and the Germans penetrated the very heart of Russia. Yet stronger and more persistent was the influence exercised by Protestantism from Sweden and the Baltic provinces.

Under Michael Theodorovič (1613–1645) numerous foreigners resided in all the larger Russian towns. In Moscow, towards the close of the seventeenth century, there came into existence a populous and practically independent German suburb (*sloboda*). The influence of these foreigners, most of whom were Protestants, was considerable. In the main it was civilising and social, but Protestant ideas and Protestant piety aroused imitation and thought throughout wide circles. Before long, Protestant influence was displayed in ecclesiastical and religious fields, Russian theologians undertaking the study of Protestant theology. This trend, which soon made itself felt in the domains of literature and art as well (a German pastor founded the first European theatre in Moscow), was all the more decisive inasmuch as Protestants were considered less dangerous than Catholics. In 1631, when teachers were summoned from Europe for the reorganisation of the army, the tsar expressly commanded that no Frenchmen, and above all no Catholics, were to be engaged; but Swedes, Dutchmen, Englishmen, and Danes were employed.

The European influence of the great movement of the reformation and the renaissance naturally made itself felt first of all in the ecclesiastical domain. Maxim the Greek, who had listened in Italy to the sermons of Savonarola and was in touch with the humanists Lascaris and Manutius, was sent from Athos to Moscow in the year 1515, at the desire of the grand prince, to supervise translations. In Moscow Maxim worked, not merely as translator and reviser of liturgical books, but also as reformer. His religious ideals and his life were a reproach to the ecclesiastical and social life of the Russians. Consequently the metropolitans and grand princes of Moscow sacrificed him to his enemies, and he, an opponent of monasticism, was relegated to various monasteries successively. For thirty-one years, from 1525 to 1556, this man trained in all the learning of Europe could make no use of his powers, for the council that sentenced him forbade him to write.

The criticism of the Russian liturgical books initiated by Maxim was vigorously pursued in the following century by the patriarch Nikon. In view of the great importance of liturgy in the Russian church, it will readily be understood that as time passed the more cultured clerics and laymen found it impossible to tolerate the errors with which the text had been so freely interspersed by inefficient translators and mechanical copyists. Besides Maxim there were still a number of Greeks in the church, men who could not fail to note these errors, and in the seventeenth century the matter of revising the texts became an important ecclesiastical question. In the year 1654, during the patriarchate of Nikon, a council determined that the revision should be undertaken.

Nikon, supported by the power of the tsar, set about the task, introducing simultaneously additional liturgical innovations and improvements in hymnology, etc. His reforms, however, encountered opposition from the clergy and the laity, leading in the end to a schism, that of the *raskol'niki* (dissenters). Nikon introduced a number of reforms from the Greek church, thus increasing the hostility of the Old Russians, who distrusted the orthodoxy of the Greeks ; whilst, since a number of Kiev scholars participated in the work of correction, the reforms came to be regarded as Roman Catholic in tendency. Nikon, in contrast with his predecessor Maxim, was church politician rather than reformer. A man of autocratic temperament, he made many enemies, so that he ultimately lost the favour of the tsar, who had hitherto followed him blindly. Nikon endeavoured to transform the patriarchate into a kind of " national papacy "—the phrase is used by Samarin. In the year 1660 occurred the patriarch's first condemnation by a council, whilst in 1666 came a second and severer sentence. He died in 1681. Ultimately, therefore, the papistical tenets which, in accordance with Nikon's theory, would deduce priesthood directly from God, and tsardom from priesthood, thus making tsardom subordinate to the patriarchate, were confined to an inconsiderable minority.

In these circumstances conservative " old belief," which was properly speaking " old custom " or " old ritual," became ecclesiastical and political schisms (*raskol*).[1] In contradistinction to what happened in the reformation of the west, in Moscow it was the dominant church which carried out reforms, whilst the minority clung to tradition. Only in the subsequent course of development did the schismatic minority come to adopt heretical views, which did not always take the direction of reform.

It is characteristic of the moral and social condition of Moscow that at the opening of the seventeenth century

---

[1] The raskolniki are not identical with the ' old believers " known as *staroobrjadcy* (literally, " old ritualists "), for not all the old believers are definitely opposed to the state church. The old believers clung to the liturgy and prayer-books of the days before Nikon, and diverged in respect of certain ceremonial practices, making the sign of the cross with two fingers, whereas the Orthodox use three, singing two hallelujahs in place of the three sung by the Orthodox, and so on.

millenarian utopianism was widely diffused. In the *Book of Faith* (*Kniga o Věrě*), published in 1648, the year of the peace of Westphalia, the end of the world is announced and the coming of antichrist is anticipated. An apocalyptic interpretation is given to the spread of Jesuit Catholicism (the union). The pope is represented as the precursor of antichrist, and it is indicated that antichrist himself will appear in the person of a pope. Nikon's reforms led to a revolution in this apocalyptic philosophy of history. Hitherto the coming of antichrist had been looked for in the west, but the expectation was now transferred to Holy Russia, conservatives regarding Nikon as the impersonation of antichrist. Should Russia, should the Russian church, become a stage for the activities of antichrist, there would no longer exist an Orthodox church, there would be no hierarchy and no priests—this apocalyptic logic corresponds to the fact that by the dying out of its priests the schism was compelled to dispense with priests. We have here a striking contrast with the Protestant reformation. In the west priesthood was overthrown, but in Russia the institution died out physically, certain sections of the raskolniki becoming a sect of the priestless (*bezpopovcy*). Simultaneously the priestless raskolniki were forced into opposition with the authority of the state. The tsar was described as tool and servant of the antichrist; the raskolnik was forbidden participation in the life of the state, laws and lawcourts being banned as the work of the devil. These anti-political tendencies of the schismatics became accentuated in the reign of Peter, who was denounced as antichrist in person, and the raskolniki took an active part in Pugačev's revolt.

The anti-state tendency of the raskol found its most radical expression in the protopope Avakkum (Habakkuk), Nikon's personal opponent. In fearless and vigorous terms he apostrophised Nikon's patron Alexis, declaring that the tsar, like Nebuchadnezzar, regarded himself as God. In the year of Nikon's death the religious father of the raskol had to pay for his boldness at the stake.

Such uncompromising dissent was soon restricted to a small and dwindling minority of raskolniki. Raskol philosophy was not properly speaking radical. If we are living in the closing days of the world, let us give to the emperor, let us give to every one, that which he demands—such was the conclusion actually drawn by the teachers of the raskolniki.

The force of the conclusion was not weakened by the need for postponing the end of the world, for recalculating the tale of the apocalyptic years. Moreover, the schismatics found it difficult to dispense with priests, and the more moderate among them urged compromise with the state church. After the defeat of Pugačev, no further active revolt was initiated by the raskolniki, the utmost they attempted being passive resistance. In the year 1788 ecclesiastical dioceses were established by the *popovcy* (the raskol communities with priests), and these were sanctioned by the state church, whose supremacy was recognised by the schismatics. In the year 1800 *edinovĕrie* (literally, "unity of faith," the name given in Russia to the religious sect originating in a compromise between the state church and the old believers) was regulated by law, but the schism in the church persists in fact to the present day.[1]

§ 5.

WHILST the religious and ecclesiastical interests of Holy Russia necessitated the borrowing of civilisation from Europe, the practical needs of the state and of its foreign and domestic policy likewise impelled recourse to Europe. The development and equipment of the army upon the European model was essential if Russia were to meet her European opponents victoriously. New barracks and fortresses were requisite for the military arm, and Russia must also have

[1] The Russian raskol has from 1850 onwards been the subject of earnest and diversified studies, initiated by Ščapov the historian. Ščapov contended that the raskol had not simply a religious and ceremonial significance, but that, in its later developments at least (from 1666 onwards, the date of Nikon's condemnation and banishment to a monastery), it had in addition extensive social and political bearings, and that these elements had been especially conspicuous since the days of Peter's reforms. According to this view the raskól was an uprising of the lesser clergy against the hierarchy and the Europeanising state, a popular movement of a nationalist and democratic character, aiming at ocal self-government, and adverse to the centralisation of the state authority. Ščapov and his school took an erroneous view of the political significance of the raskol. They forgot that the Russian state and the Russian church constituted a theocracy, and that opposition to the church necessarily became political because church and state persecuted the old believers. The raskolniki were always religious, but their religion had its associated ethics which led logically to action in the political field. The opposition of the raskolniki to the state church was conservative and reactionary, but *qua* opposition the raskol was often a school for individual firmness of character. Representatives of the modern revolutionary parties go too far however, when they discover their prototypes i.. the raskolniki.

a fleet. These ends could not be secured without more extensive knowledge. Even had it been possible for the Russians to
obtain everything ready made from the Europeans, the simple
upkeep of these material elements of civilisation would have
been impossible without the aid of skilled workmen from
Europe and without the assistance of European architects,
engineers, and the like. Trained Europeans had to be transplanted to Russia.

The Russians had to keep in view the gradual acquirement
of competence to maintain these necessary reforms for themselves, and they therefore visited Europe to study, whilst at
home they established schools and translated books. Cannon,
ships, bastions, etc., cannot be made without knowledge of
mathematics, mechanics. physics, and chemistry, or in default
of technical as well as scientific knowledge. As early, therefore, as the sixteenth century positive science was studied in
Moscow with the encouragement of the state, the movement
becoming still more vigorous in the seventeenth century.

But for all these material and intellectual reforms money
was requisite. It was necessary that the primitive industries
should be perfected, an essential prerequisite being a radical
reform of the administration. Agriculture and the domestic
handicrafts had to be remodelled and furnished with better
implements, and in addition new channels for trade and
new commercial associations must be secured. John the
Terrible opened commercial relationships with the English.
It was John who pushed out into the Baltic; the northern
seas were under Russian control, but it was a long voyage to
Europe from Archangel round North Cape, whilst to communicate with Europe by land the Russians had to cross the hostile
territories of their western neighbours.

Finally, the court and the nobility required articles of
luxury, and a taste for art was arising. In all domains
of practical and theoretical activity the third Rome had to
learn from European civilisation.

Thus, long before the days of Peter, the German Sloboda
of Moscow came into existence. Nevertheless, the entry of
foreigners into Muscovite Russia seems to have been comparatively difficult when we remember that there had been
almost no obstacle to their influx into the petty principalities
of earlier days.

During the sixteenth century, thoughtful Russians gave

frank expression to the need for far-reaching reforms. Prince Kurbskii, with good reason denominated the first " westerner," was one of the earliest to give a clear demonstration of Moscow's poverty in point of morals and civilisation. Kurbskii was a pupil of Maxim, and his correspondence with John IV (see the first letter of 1563) gives eloquent testimony to the pitiful condition of Moscow, but manifests in addition how outstanding was Russian intellectual capacity.

We have similar documents from the seventeenth century. In order to stress the need for reform, Kotošihin gives an admirable description of the Muscovite realm. In personal character this writer was thoroughly a child of his age. In 1667 he was beheaded in Stockholm for a murder committed when in a state of intoxication.

The testimony of Križanič, the Croat, may also be cited. A Catholic priest educated in Italy, he had had personal experience of contemporary Europe, in Constantinople, Rome, Vienna, and elsewhere. He was the first of the panslavists. Through contact with the Russian embassy in Florence he was in 1657 inspired with the idea of emigrating to Moscow. On the way thither he made intimate acquaintance with Poland and Little Russia. His frank writings concerning Little Russia smoothed his path to—Siberia ! In the year 1661, almost immediately after his arrival in Moscow, he was sent to Tobolsk, but there he appears to have been permitted freedom of movement. In Tobolsk he wrote a number of works, including his *Politics*, in which he subjected Muscovite civilisation to severe criticism and advocated European reforms. Križanič was permitted to return to Moscow in 1676 ; it seems probable that he died in Europe.[1]

Notwithstanding its religious and ecclesiastical isolation, there was in Moscow (and it is important to bear the fact in mind) a spontaneous impulse towards reform and towards Europeanisation. By the term Europeanisation we have to understand something more than the mere imitation of Europe or borrowing from Europe. From the first, the Russian state evolved in accordance with its own principles, but this evolution ran on parallel lines with that of Europe, being not merely similar but in many respects positively identical. The Russians were Indo-Europeans just as were the Teutons and the Latins ;

[1] Concerning Muscovite Russia consult also the works of Herberstein, Fletcher, and Horsey, to which reference is made in the sequel.

they learned from the Byzantines as the Teutons and the Latins learned from the Romans; finally, it must be remembered that, despite all mutual segregation, a certain interchange of civilising forces never ceased.

Thus by domestic and by foreign influences alike was the way opened for the reforms of Peter. Alexis, Peter's father, had already engaged in general reforming activities; Michael Theodorovič, his grandfather, had imported foreign craftsmen and manufacturers to Moscow; yet earlier rulers had endeavoured to establish cultural and commercial relationships with Europe.

CHAPTER TWO

PETER'S REFORMS. THE LINKING UP OF RUSSIA WITH EUROPE

§ 6.

IF as a prelude to our account of Russian philosophy of history and philosophy of religion we are to give a summary of leading historical facts, we must examine the reforms of Peter the Great somewhat fully, for these reforms constitute a notable element in any philosophical contemplation of Russia.

Peter the Great and his reforms ! I remember reading in an early history of Peter how the Tsar was on one occasion conversing with Menšikov. Seating themselves at a table and drawing a line across the centre of it, each of them took a louse (his own) and, having placed the insects on the table, they laid bets with one another which louse would first crawl as far as the line. . . .

Peter had merely to continue the reforms initiated by his predecessors. More than one " window towards Europe " had already been opened ; but Peter threw open and kept open the other windows and doors of the Muscovite edifice.

He systematised reform. This is not to say that he did not often enough work without a definite plan ; but in the course of a long epoch (Peter reigned for thirty-six years, from 1689 to 1725), an epoch wherein a new generation grew up and the education of yet another was begun, he raised his very self into a system. Profoundly impressed by the need for civilisation, he gained culture for himself as well as for others. He realised that Russia needed new men in addition to new institutions.

In 1696 Peter granted free entry to all foreigners, and in addition he was able to find suitable assistants among his own subjects. Besides Nikon and other predecessors who had marched in the same direction, there were plenty of contemporary enthusiasts for reform. Excellent helpers were secured from the Kiev academy, and from the Moscow academy which had been founded shortly before Peter ascended the throne. Pososkov, an original thinker sprung from the people, gave expression to the strong need for extensive "renovation." Among Peter's numerous collaborators, there were some who in certain domains were more notable and more far-seeing than the autocrat ; but where he himself lacked competence, far from imposing obstacles to reform, he favoured innovation.

His first and constant care was to provide for the needs of the army and the fleet. The " herd of cattle " (this was Pososkov's critical term for the old Muscovite army) had to be transformed into European regiments. Seamen must be trained ; new weapons must be provided for army and navy. For these changes it was essential to acquire knowledge, alike practical and theoretical. Setting a personal example, Peter visited Europe to study as a simple workman, making his first journey for this purpose in 1697.

Notwithstanding initial defeats, his realm soon began to extend, for it was not long before Peter gained victories over Europeans. In 1696 the Russians reached Azov and built their first navy. In 1703 they secured a firm footing on the Baltic. St. Petersburg was founded. By the victory of Poltava, Sweden was weakened and free access was secured for Russia to the more civilized lands on the shores of the Baltic. In Poland, Peter's influence became decisive, and he had ideas of occupying the country for his son. Henceforward Turkey was menaced by Russia. Peter was unable to extend his sway as far as the southern seas, and Azov was regained by the Turks, but in northern waters his dominion was secured, and Russia was permanently linked with Europe.

Money was needed for the new army and navy, and to this end a suitable reform of the entire administration was essential.

The realm was divided into administrative districts (ultimately eleven in number), and was subdivided into forty-three provinces. The governors were assisted by Landrats chosen from the nobility (the German term Landrat was retained). A kind of ministry of state was established to control the administration, but among the ten departments a ministry for education was lacking, for Peter was his own minister for education. In the year 1711 a senate was created which replaced the old crown council of boyars. Notable was the attempt to separate the judiciary from the executive. The police was Europeanised.

The bureaucracy became more numerous, the position of its members and the utilisation of their powers being regulated. During the reign of Peter's father, in the years 1681 and 1682, occurred the abolition of the *městničestvo*, the system by which officials were appointed by right of birth and in accordance with rank. A new nobility of service was introduced. Peter granted to every official personal rank as a noble, so that increasingly the prestige of the hereditary nobility became purely social. Officials were given regular salaries; enfeoffment (*kormlenie*, " feeding " or " nourishing ") ceased. Fourteen grades of officials were established.

From 1719 onwards statistics of population were kept.

New rules of self-government and jurisdiction came into force for the towns. St. Petersburg, in especial, entirely new and in a sense the leading town of Russia, exercised great influence in the matter of urban administration. The town council of St. Petersburg was placed under the direct control of the senate. Russian towns were enriched by a new element, manufacturing industry, in some cases directly managed by the state, but sometimes carried on in factories favoured by the state. Connected with this development was the transformation of the mercantile community into a distinct class, organised in guilds, and possessing legal jurisdiction of its own.

§ 7.

THE institution of these practical reforms made it necessary for the Russians to acquire theoretical principles as well. Peter's second journey to Europe, in the year 1716, nineteen years after the first, was chiefly devoted to science and art. At this time was conceived the plan advocated by Leibnitz of founding an academy. Oxford University conferred upon Peter an honorary doctor's degree, and the Paris academy nominated him one of its members; this recognition from the official representatives of science was fully deserved.

Peter vigorously furthered the progress of science and the arts, by summoning foreigners to his court, by commanding the translation of important books, and by similar measures. He introduced a more practical alphabet—to Peter himself correct spelling remained a difficulty throughout life. Russian chronology had hitherto dated from the creation, but Peter decided in favour of reckoning from the Christian era, introduced the Julian calendar, and transferred the new year from September to January 1st. Under his auspices, art collections and museums were inaugurated, schools were founded, and the first newspaper came into existence in 1703. Co-ordinated efforts at reform were simultaneously made in all domains. The tsar's earnestness as a reformer was manifested above all by the methodical nature of his efforts.

Nor did Peter forget to institute far-reaching reforms in the ethical domain. His chief desire in this direction was to remodel the Old Russian family. Women were to secure the liberty they possessed in Europe; they were to be restored to social life, and therewith in truth restored also to the family; the Asiatic system of seclusion was to be broken down. The Old Russian law of inheritance was likewise modified, the western system of primogeniture replacing the equality of all the children, and the younger members of the family being left to fend for themselves.

The lot of the serf was to be mitigated to this extent, that the sale of individual " slaves " was forbidden henceforward; the family must be disposed of as a whole.

On one occasion, in conversation with the Danish envoy, Peter summed up his own work of reform by saying that it was his desire to make beasts into men. In actual fact, his reform was a revolution, one which dictated a program to the commencing epoch of enlightenment and humanity. Peter had had personal experience of the need for humanisation in the ethical direction, for his own education had been Old Russian. His private and domestic life was revolutionary to a notable extent, and was a stumbling-block to the sanctimonious. It must, however, be conceded to severe critics that Peter's actions were often unbridled, and that his reformatory revolution was characterised by numerous defects. Much that was needless and much that was hastily conceived was introduced by Peter. On many occasions he insisted upon external trifles (clothing, and the like) in a manner that was despotic rather than reformatory; and in other instances his choice of means was open to criticism, as, for example,

when he decreed that from thirty to a hundred roubles should
be paid for the privilege of wearing a beard.

Peter himself remained the barbarian. Still strong in him
was the Old Russian Adam, the man who desired to become
and was to become the new Adam of enlightenment and
humaneness. Peter was the archetype of the transitional
Russian of his time. Consider him in his later days as imperator, when, after conquering the Swedes, he publicly danced
for joy upon the table, and was hailed by the applause of his
people—was not this the act of a barbarian? But was the.
triumph of the Roman imperators or of the modern European
conquerors one whit less barbaric, or in any essential greater,
than Peter's frank display of jubilation? Peter, insists the
modern European, was barbarian pure and simple. Look at
the way in which he personally applied the rack to those
sentenced by him; look at the way in which he played
the executioner upon his victims! Consider his treatment of
his first wife and his dealings with his son Alexis! Agreed,
Peter was a barbarian. I make no excuses for him, and apply
the term to him in its most literal signification. But I do
not for that reason esteem more highly the French or Spanish
" culture " of a Ferdinand or a Louis, of the men whose nerves
were not strong enough to undertake the immediate supervision of the dragonnades, the inquisitional barbarities, and
the various other acts of inhumanity, for which they were
none the less personally responsible. These refined barbarians
kept hired consciences and executants to do their dirty work.

The follies and base frivolities of his drunken assemblies,
wherein Peter would make fun of the papacy with an oblique
aim at the patriarchate, were in part connected with his work
as reformer, for the frank barbarian was in truth ingenious
in such arts. Peter displayed something stronger than cunning,
both in his doings at home and in his relationships with the
foreign world. To cite but one instance among many, how
keen was the calculation with which he appointed his ecclesiastical opponent Javorskii to be president of the synod.

§ 8.

POLITICALLY and socially, Peter's reforms, taken
in conjunction with the success of his policy of conquest, signified the strengthening of absolutism. When at

length, in the year 1721, Peter assumed the Byzantine title of Imperator, the fullness of power of his reformed absolutism was thereby well characterised. The Moscow tsars, such rulers as John the Terrible, had been absolute or quasi-absolute, but the absolutism of Peter was qualitatively higher. Peter was recognised by Europe; he co-ordinated Russia with the European powers; he made Russia one of the great powers of Europe. At Poltava, Peter broke the might of Sweden. At the very time when Russia was thus becoming predominant in the east, Spain was definitively ceasing to be a world power in the west. Following France, England, and Austria, Russia now took fourth place among the powers of the world, Poland ceasing to count as one of the Slav forces of the east.

In the domestic sphere, too, Peter and his state took a position higher than that which had been occupied by Muscovy.

Peter bureaucratised the organism of state, basing the administration upon the work of expert officials. His father, the second Romanov, had begun this process, but the fuller development and the perfectionment of the bureaucratic machine was the work of Peter.

The duma of boyars was abolished, its place being taken by an advisory council (*bližnaja kanceljarija*), whose relationship to the emperor was a personal one. The institution was not maintained, and the senate was therefore founded as supreme administrative authority.

In the course of years, administrative reform created a better organism of state, but the backbone of the state was the newly established military system, for in this domain was found the core of Peter's reforms; it was by the militarisation of the state and by military successes that Peter's prestige was sustained at home and abroad.

In the plenitude of his power, Peter had even less thought than his two predecessors of summoning the zemskii sobor. It was his aim, not merely to carry on the administration, but to bring new institutions into being, and the sobor would have been unfitted for this work. The effect of Europeanisation in Russia was to strengthen absolutism. It is true that in the year 1698 a species of sobor was summoned from all classes for the condemnation of the tsarevna Sophia, but the sole aim of this was to shift the tsar's responsibility to other shoulders. The failure to summon the sobor and the abolition of the duma characterise the enlightened despotism of Peter in contrast with the earlier Muscovite despotism. Peter understood the situation thoroughly, remaining suspicious throughout life, and not hesitating to avail himself of police help.

Peter Europeanised Muscovite absolutism. He was, we must remember, a contemporary of Louis XIV. We cannot doubt that he had the French ruler's example before his eyes. Both his domestic and his foreign policy display more than one analogy to those of Louis.

His absolutism is manifest in his relationship to the nobility. Obviously he had to work through the nobility, and he therefore imposed new duties on the nobles. The nobleman must serve the new state, and in addition he must learn. In Moscow, office was secured to him by right of birth, rank by his family tree, and there he enjoyed the privilege of free service.[1] Peter endeavoured to raise the nobility to a higher level, and he therefore associated it with the bureaucracy; the bureaucracy was ennobled, the nobility bureaucratised. Unlike his predecessors, he did not aim at weakening the nobility, desiring rather to strengthen it. It was with this end in view that in the year 1714 he introduced majorat upon the western model. The far-reaching significance of the ukase relating to majorat or primogeniture depended upon this, that it spoke of the land as the owner's property independently of service. The result was to enhance the prestige of the nobility.

For these reasons, too, Peter introduced a new, European, order of nobility. The first Russian title of count (*graf*) was bestowed upon Šeremetev, in the year 1706. At the outset the tsar even endeavoured to have the count's title confirmed by the Holy Roman emperor, but the idea was subsequently abandoned.

Peter was the first Russian ruler to bestow the old princely rank as a title, and this title too was made European. Menšikov, the first of the new princes, who received the title in 1705, was prince of the Holy Roman empire, and several princely titles were bestowed upon Russians by the Holy

---

[1] In Peter's reign a new designation was found for the nobility. The old names *dvorjanin* (literally, courtier) and *bojar* were replaced by *caredvorec* (approximately, tsar's man) and by the Polish *szlachta* (nobleman).

Roman emperor.[1] With the newly conquered territories the baronage was taken over as a working institution.

Peter's absolutism was likewise displayed in the tsar's relationship to the peasantry. By the introduction of the poll tax and of other dues based thereon in place of the land tax the peasant was grievously affected. The entire burden of taxation was laid upon him, the new and oppressive element in the poll tax consisting in its imposition upon all peasants. The nobility, the state clergy, and the ennobled officials, together with persons of academic status and certain special classes, were exempt from taxation.

The introduction of this imperfect and ill-considered system of direct individual taxation was characteristic of the defects of Petrine financial policy. The tsar himself was interested in commerce alone. He had adopted the principles of the mercantile system ; his policy of conquest, and above all his desire to make use of the sea, were closely connected with these principles. He initiated the construction of the Ladoga canal, completed in 1732, to connect the Baltic with the Caspian. The desire to favour commerce and manufacture (the time for the export of grain had not yet come) led to the institution of the system of privileges for the benefit of the upper classes and the mercantile community.

Before Peter's reign the state revenue had been about one and a half million roubles. The revenue for the year 1715 was eight and a half million roubles.

Pososkov, a self-taught economist, was profoundly touched by the tragical situation of the peasantry in the days of Peter. Despite his espousal of the cause of the autocrat as against the nobility, he recognised the severities of Peter's absolutism, and desired the establishment of a people's council (*narodosovětie*). He atoned for his opinions by lifelong imprisonment in the fortress of St. Peter and St. Paul.

At the close of Peter's reign the inhabitants of Russia numbered thirteen millions.

---

[1] In Muscovy the descendants of the princes had naturally become very numerous, and had consequently lost prestige · before the days of Peter, princes were noble by race merely, not titular princes. The princely families were the offspring of Rjurik, and also of Lithuanian, Tatar, and other princes. In contemporary Russia a prince without office or wealth is less regarded than a count or even a baron.

§ 9.

PETER'S absolutism found its most momentous expression in the reform of ecclesiastical administration. In religious matters Peter was moderately enlightened. He had grasped the weak side of the theological belief in miracle, and aimed at the diminution of its potency, for his work of reform was necessarily founded upon the scientific conception of the universe, a conception diametrically opposed to that of the theologians, although his own views were not so much derived from the philosophers and thinkers of the west as based upon the practical acquirements of Europe.

In the Moscow Sloboda, among Russia's western neighbours, and in Europe in general, he had had practical experience of Protestant influences; his advisers, friends, and teachers were almost exclusively Protestants. The influence of Protestantism was especially manifested among the cultured classes, but it was strong also among the masses. This is conspicuous in the field of theology, being represented, for instance, by Theophan Prokopovič, and being shown also in Tveritinov's popular movement towards Protestantism.

Theophan Prokopovič, at first pupil and subsequently teacher at the Kiev academy, studied theology and philosophy in Europe as well. Having espoused the views of Bacon and Descartes, he tended in theology in the direction of Protestantism, expounding his views from the pulpit and in writing. Peter summoned him to St. Petersburg, establishing under his leadership the holy synod, the supreme ecclesiastical authority. It is important to note that Theophan's transference to St. Petersburg did not take place until 1716. Prior to that date, and after his return from Europe in the year 1704, his influence was exercised in the same direction as that of Peter, but outside the monarch's direct sphere of operation.

It was the aim of Peter's ecclesiastical policy to abate the prestige of the hierarchy, which was to be conspicuously subordinated and made serviceable to the imperial power. Peter attained to a clear view upon this matter at a comparatively early date. When the patriarch Adrian died in the year 1700, no successor was appointed. Adrian had been Peter's opponent. For more than two decades the tsar left matters in an interim condition, for the synod was not established until 1721. The ecclesiastical regulations (*duhovnyi reglament*) upon which the synodal constitution and the other church reforms were based, were drawn up by Theophan and revised by Peter in person.

The constitution of the synod was in conformity, not with monarchical patriarchalism, but with the secular system of government by committee. In the regulations a definite reference was made to the papacy, pointing out how this had wrongfully outgrown the control of the temporal power. The analogous usurpation of power by the Moscow patriarchate was censured, and it was decreed that there must be no place for such an evil in the administration of the ecclesiastical committee. The members of the synod had to take oath as follows : " I testify and swear that the monarch of all the Russias is the supreme authority of this ecclesiastical committee." [1]

Peter, supported by Theophan, interpreted the term autocracy in its most literal sense, holding that the church and the hierarchy which governed it were subject to the emperor. " Here is your patriarch," said Peter, tapping his breast, when a deputation of spiritual dignitaries besought him to appoint an incumbent to the patriarchal see. Theophan spoke of his imperial patron as " the anointed " (using the Greek term χριστός). It is unquestionable that electoral powers within the church were greater before than after the days of Peter.

The committee constitution of the synod, in which the lay representative of the emperor, the chief procurator, sat beside the ecclesiastical members, has been commonly regarded as a Protestant institution, but this view is not altogether correct.

The synod corresponded to the ancient episcopal organisation of the church, but the introduction of a lay element into church administration and the inauguration of the office of chief procurator were Protestant. It is possible that Peter and his contemporaries were influenced by the example of the Protestant national or state churches.

Peter did not venture upon any innovations in the matter of religious doctrine. Although in other respects he was

---

[1] This oath was abolished in 1901, but section 65 of the state fundamental law runs as follows : " In the government of the church, autocratic author ty works through the instrumentality of the holy directing synod, constituted by that authority."

tolerant, he supported with his authority Mogila's *Orthodox Confession*. But the tsar's general outlook in religious matters found expression in the words : " The human conscience is subject to God alone, and no ruler is entitled to constrain any man to change his creed."

Whereas Peter in conjunction with Theophan tended towards Protestantism, Javorskii, the other most notable ecclesiastic of those days, represented the Romanising inclinations of conservative theologians and church politicians. Theophan learned in Jesuit schools and academies to hate Catholicism, but it was there conversely that Javorskii learned to detest Protestantism.[1] Owing to his European education, however, as representative of the patriarchate he was from 1700 onwards an adherent of the Petrine policy, though only in temporal matters, for in religious and ecclesiastical affairs Javorskii was a Romaniser. His principal work (*Kamen' Věry—The Stone of Faith*), directed against Protestantism, was written during the years 1713 to 1718, but could not be printed until 1728, after Peter's death.   Javorskii taught the primacy of the church over the state, and accepted the doctrine of Boniface VIII concerning the two sisters of the church, but without avail.   Peter made an adroit use of the refractory churchman on behalf of his own ecclesiastical policy, compelling Javorskii to subscribe the new regulations (which were signed by all the hierarchs in the realm), and actually appointing him first president of the synod.

The significance of Peter's reforms in ecclesiastical administration was underlined by the profound disturbance which affected the raskolniki.   They stigmatised Peter as antichrist, and in their hearts the conservatives and the reactionaries were in agreement with this designation, not excepting Javorskii, who compiled a writing upon the coming of antichrist.   The conservatives' view of Peter was vividly displayed in a work upon the beard from the pen of Adrian, the last patriarch, wherein to shave the beard was described as a deadly sin.   The expectations of the end of the world in 1666 having remained unfulfilled, the apocalyptic chronologers

---

[1] The way in which the Russians obtained admittance into the Catholic schools of Poland and of Europe is worthy of mention. To secure an entry they had to make outward profession of Catholicism, returning to the Orthodox faith when they went back to Russia.   Both Theophan and Javorskii had constrained their consciences to this hypocrisy.

revised their calculations, and fixed upon the year 1699. The final destruction was to take place in 1702. Peter returned from his first great journey to Europe a few days before the anticipated coming of antichrist, to be hailed as the expected one.

Peter, were it simply as guardian of Muscovite tradition, was anything but tolerant vis-à-vis the raskolniki. Their propaganda was made a capital offence. It was decreed that they must attend Orthodox churches and must have their children baptized in the Orthodox manner. They were excluded from all public offices, and were not allowed to take oaths. They were compelled to pay double taxes, had extra taxation for wearing a beard, and were forced to assume distinctive dress.

In one respect, a matter of form, Peter's conservative opponents were right. The establishment of the synod was uncanonical and autocratic. It was true that this body was composed of clergy, and that Peter had his ecclesiastical reforms confirmed by the Russian and the Greek hierarchs ; but it is demonstrable that, as far as the Russians were concerned, the confirmation was the fruit of compulsion, whilst in the case of the eastern patriarchs, no more than two visited St. Petersburg, and this was subsequently, when the synod had already exercised its functions.

§ 10.

THE reforms of Peter and his collaborators secularised theocratic Russia to a considerable extent, so that it is permissible to speak of a contrast between the Russia of St. Petersburg and the Russia of Moscow. Moscow's civilisation and outlook were thoroughly clericalised and ecclesiasticised ; Peter made the state the determinative organ of politics and civilisation. When Peter extolled army reform in the words, " We have emerged into light from darkness," he gave a fairly accurate characterisation of the significance of the new Russia. The medieval Russian theocracy acquired a new head, the state a new centre ; St. Petersburg, the seaport capital, replacing Moscow, the midland capital.

A secular and non-theological character was likewise manifest in seventeenth-century literature, even theological literature. Peter had little time to spare for Russian literature, but his reforms initiated the tendency which literature followed.[1]

In this connection it is above all necessary to make further reference to Pososkov, an unschooled peasant. A convert from the raskol to the state church, his writings have, indeed, a certain theological flavour, but his interests are in secular reforms of the army and of the administration. *Paternal Inheritance* was written to promote the better moralisation of family life. *Concerning Poverty and Riches* (1721–1724) was a practical work by a keen observer, furnishing penetrating criticism of contemporary conditions and advocating a sound program of reforms in all departments of public life.

Considered as a whole, Peter's reforms were of great value to Russia, constituting a natural advance along the lines indicated by previous development. Lomonosov went too far in the deification of Peter (" He is thy god, thy god, O Russia ! "), in his personification of the entire evolution of Russia in the figure of the autocrat ; but the reforms effected by Peter and his circle were imposing for all their defects.

At a later date, the slavophils spoke of Peter and his reforms as unpatriotic, unrussian, Moscow and Muscovite Russia being contrasted with St. Petersburg and Europe, but this was unhistorical exaggeration. Europe, too, had to experience revolutionary reforms, more far-reaching than the reforms of Peter. Accurate historical analysis will increasingly show that the reform movements at the close of the seventeenth century were logically determined by the previous course of evolution.

§ 11.

THE need for Peter's reforms is sufficiently proved by the continuance, or rather the consolidation, of these reforms by his successors, for the changes subsequently attempted in this or that branch of the administration were built upon the foundations laid by Peter.

Under the rule of the empresses and the shadow emperors we observe a continuous oscillation in the constitution of the council of state essential to the renovated absolutism.

[1] I think, for example, of *Jers Sčetinnikov* (a popular satire upon Moscow judicial procedure during the fifteenth, sixteenth, and seventeenth centuries), and of the writings of Frol Skoběev and others, wherein a natural outlook and a natural style, unaffected by theology, find expression.

Catherine I established a " supreme privy council "; under Anne, a " cabinet " came into existence; under Elizabeth, this body yielded before the Petrine " senate."

These changes were dependent upon the instability in the relationships between the autocrat and the aristocracy. Given a higher position by Peter, but constrained to service and subordinated to the tsar, the aristocracy endeavoured to consolidate its dominion. In the year 1730 Anne adopted the " magna charta " of the Dolgorukis and their associates, the real power passing into the hands of the supreme privy council. Theophan, however, organised the party of the " people of intermediate rank " against the *verhovniki* (magnates), and petitioned for the re-establishment of the aristocracy— the Orthodox prince of the church becoming the mouthpiece of the absolutists and the tool of the Lutheran favourites. Dissension was sown between the Russian magnates and the German, and autocracy was reinstated by the violent deeds of Biron and his confederates. The example of Sweden had great influence in St. Petersburg during the eighteenth century, and the Swedish oligarchy had triumphed in the year 1726.

The autocracy was maintained. Although the new dynasty of the Romanovs had become extinct in the male line, the foreign sovereigns who were now raised to the throne were able to exercise unrestricted sway. Women of notoriously loose character could reign without opposition, and those only among the tyrants who were mentally disordered were suppressed after the Asiatic manner by family conspiracies and palace revolts.

The example set by Peter in the case of his son Alexis found imitators. John VI was imprisoned in Schlüsselburg, and was ultimately murdered, although a lunatic. No better was the fate of Peter III, likewise mentally disordered, who was deposed by his consort Catherine II, and died four days later, the cause being officially announced as hæmorrhage from the bowel and brain disorder. A similar destiny awaited Catherine's son, Paul I, who had also become insane. The terrorist assassins of Alexander II had a whole series of illustrious teachers. In the eighteenth century even such men as Voltaire considered the doings of Catherine purely " domestic affairs."

Autocracy had been consolidated, but aristocracy, too,

Boyar Roman Jur'evič Zahar'in

- Anastasia
  m John IV (Ivan the Terrible)

- Nikita
  - FILARET 1619–1633
    - MICHAEL 1633–1645
      - ALEXIS 1645–1676
        - THEODORE 1676–1682
        - Sophia
        - JOHN V 1682–1689 († 1696)
          - Catherine
            m Leopold of Mecklenburg
            - ANNE 1730–1740
              - Anne
                m Antony of Brunswick
                - JOHN VI 1740–1741
        - PETER I, THE GREAT 1689–1725
          m CATHERINE I 1725–1727
          - Anne
            m Charles Frederick of Holstein-Gottorp
            - PETER III 1761–1762
              m CATHERINE II of Anhalt-Zerbst 1762–1796
              - PAUL I 1796–1801
                m Sophia Dorothea Augusta of Würtemberg (Maria Theodorovna)
                - ALEXANDER I 1801–1825
                - Constantine
                - NICHOLAS I 1825–1854
                  - ALEXANDER II 1855–1881
                    - ALEXANDER III 1881–1894
                      - NICHOLAS II.
          - Alexis (by Evdokija Lopuhin)
            - PETER II 1727–1730
          - ELIZABETH 1741–1761

could consolidate its forces; in the reign of Peter III the obligation to service was abolished.

The Europeanisation of Russia in respect of civilisation and of political and military concerns, was continued by Peter's successors. In the reign of Anne, Russian armies entered Europe for the first time, besieging Dantzig in 1734. Under Elizabeth these European campaigns were continued during the Seven Years War, whilst subsequently Russia fought against France. In Elizabeth's reign Finland was occupied as far as the river Kymene (1743). Of especial importance for Russia was the annexation of Poland (first partition 1772, second partition 1793, third partition 1795).

At the end of Catherine's reign the population of Russia numbered 36,000,000.

In matters of civilisation and diplomatic intercourse Russia became closely associated with her neighbours Prussia and Austria, relationships with the two chief powers of the weakly German realm being promoted by Russia's hostility to Sweden on the one hand and Turkey on the other. Prussia, in particular, exercised an attractive influence upon Russia. From early days, eastern Prussia had had common interests with Russia against Poland and Lithuania. The policy of Peter III, " the monkey imitator of Frederick the Great," was no more than a temporary accentuation of a normal tendency, which persisted for a century after the two states had become contiguous in the reign of Catherine II. It was Prussia and the lesser princely houses of the German north which provided the Russians with emperors and empresses after the dying out of the Romanovs in the male line.

In home affairs Europeanisation was promoted by the further annexation of European territories. Poland was European, was Catholic, so that the contrast between Europe and Russia was transported into Russia, was incorporated into Russian absolutist administration. This, too, was merely a reinforcement of a previous trend, for heretofore the Lutheran Baltic provinces had already supplied higher officials, soldiers, and politicians tinctured by European culture.

The influence of the European territories was extremely noticeable in social institutions and legislation, especially in the laws for the administration of the towns, those dealing with the mercantile classes, and the like.

Asiatisation advanced pari passu with Europeanisation.

The occupation of Siberia involved close relationships with China, a commercial treaty with that country being signed in the reign of Peter II. In 1783 Crimea was annexed, the movement towards the Black Sea involving Russia in wars and alliances with the Turks. Before long, contact with Persia began. It will readily be understood that these extensive Asiatic developments affected Russian civilisation. Asiatic influences similar to those which had acted upon Muscovy during the Mongol regime, had their place also in the development of the Russia of St. Petersburg.

§ 12.

CATHERINE II took a lively part in the cultural development of Russia, by promoting the growth of science and literature. She herself was an author and a protagonist in literary feuds. Catherine endeavoured to improve the educational system, favouring in especial the education of women. She actually appointed her friend Princess Daškova president of the academy, an appointment justified by success.

When a princess of no more than fifteen years old, Catherine had read Cicero and Plato. Voltaire and Diderot were her friends ; Montesquieu's works, " the breviary of sovereigns " (" Were I pope, I would canonise him ! ") were her literary and philosophical favourites ; Locke and other revolutionary thinkers were not unknown to her. " Liberty, thou soul of all things " is but one of the many sayings with which this despot charmed her subjects and her European admirers. She did not hesitate at times to describe herself as a republican.

During Catherine's reign the aristocracy was continually thinking of a constitution or of some form of representation by estates. As early as 1762, Count Panin, envoy in Sweden, submitted a plan based upon the Swedish model, which was, however, practically ignored. Later, from 1780 onwards, Panin elaborated a new design, drafted by D. I. Fonvizin, his secretary, and received with approval by Paul and certain leading members of the nobility. It was based upon the theories of natural law and the social contract, and foreshadowed the liberation of the peasants. For the time being the " fundamental laws " were to concern the aristocracy, who were to have joint powers of government exercised through an elected senate with legislative faculty. The tendency of the scheme was to restrict absolutism.

Publicist literature of the years preceding the French revolution was full of ideas about liberty and plans for realising it ; it displayed an acquaintance with European affairs and political writings, and was obviously inspired by a dislike to the native despotism. Catherine had a keen in-telligence, and was far-seeing enough to recognise that adminis-trative reforms were essential to the security of a Russia continually enlarged by fresh annexations in Europe and Asia. In order to regulate the entire realm in a homogeneous manner, in 1767 the celebrated "commission of deputies" was sum-moned from all parts, including Siberia. The deputies, num-bering five hundred and sixty-four, held two hundred sittings, and did much good work, while perpetrating some absurdities. In the *Book of Instructions*, which the empress compiled for the commission from the works of Montesquieu, Beccaria, and others, we are told that "Russia is a European state." In 1768 the commission was prorogued, and was never resummoned, notwithstanding Diderot's recommenda-tion. In actual experience Catherine could not put up with even a consultative parliament, although its members were chosen exclusively from the aristocracy.

In 1768, Desnickii, professor at Moscow, who had attended the lectures of Adam Smith, submitted to the empress a plan for reorganising the senate to constitute of it an elected body, with consultative powers and a certain voice in legislation. Associated with this change, there was to be a reform of the entire administration. For years the empress had enter-tained thoughts of some such reform of the senate, having studied the English constitution and read Blackstone and other English authors, but the plan was never realised. The historian Ščerbatov likewise wrote in favour of the English constitution.

In order to appease the aristocracy, the empress granted the charter of 1785. As a class the aristocracy was accorded a considerable degree of autonomy (the right to hold assem-blies of the nobles, the right to elect marshals, etc.) ; aris-tocrats were freed from state service and from taxation; corporal punishment was abolished ; the peasant was made exclusively subject to his lord. Thus did enlightened despotism seek support from the nobility at the cost of the peasantry.

Pugačev's revolt (1772–1775) showed that the peasantry suffered from a sense of oppression. Nor did the peasants stand alone in their discontent. General Bibikov, who suppressed the rising, declared that it was not Pugačev that mattered but the dissatisfaction that was widespread throughout Russia.[1] Catherine herself had an uneasy conscience. Upon her initiative there was founded in the year 1765 the " Free Economic Society " which, in understanding with the empress, immediately began to study the question of liberating the peasants, published prize essays, etc.

On the other hand the empress did not forget to regulate the administration. Russia was divided into fifty administrative districts ; political and legal organisation was perfected ; the towns were granted charters giving them a certain administrative and judicial autonomy.

Commerce and industry were vigorously promoted.

Catherine, like the enlightened absolutists in Europe, was a thorough-going utilitarian. In the year 1764, when need was pressing, church property was confiscated,[2] although now and at all times the rights of the church, of the hierarchy, were preserved. The raskolniki, who under Peter II, Anne, and Elizabeth, had been oppressed in Petrine fashion, were more gently handled, notwithstanding their share in Pugačev's rising, for the semblance of provocative measures had to be avoided. Schismatics were admitted to public office.

In Europe, Catherine was greatly admired. Voltaire wrote a panegyric history of Peter, and extolled Catherine as " benefactress of the human race " and as " saint," even comparing her to the mother of God. The flatterer went so far as to declare that her autocracy was the ne plus ultra of statecraft. Herder, who had had opportunity in Riga of studying the empress and Russia, was full of admiration for

---

[1] The social significance of the rising is incontestable. At the outset it was directed against the officials, and during the rebellion 1,572 landlords were killed. The Cossacks participated in the leadership, and it may be remembered that the southern Cossacks had already rebelled against Peter. In their campaigns under Hmelnickii the Cossacks symbolised their program by three gallows, upon which a noble, a Jew, and a dog had respectively been hanged. The hetmanship of the Cossacks was abolished by Catherine in 1764.

[2] That is to say, peasants male and female to the number of about 2,000,000 were transferred from the church to the state, their lot being alleviated thereby.

Catherine's reforms.   I may recall his enthusiasm for Russia's great civilising task, an enthusiasm to which he gave free expression in his diary when journeying from Riga to Europe in 1769.   He looked forward to a rejuvenescence of the hoary civilisation of Europe.   Russia was to become the leader of culture and to make Europe happy with a second renaissance. Ukraine would become a new Greece.   Herder was by no means blind to the errors and defects of the Russians, but he considered that they were animated by a sense of the good, which was notably manifest in their imitative capacity. Peter the Great and Catherine II were to him ideal figures ; they were predestined to make a nation of elemental greatness out of the Russian barbarians—of course in accordance with the prescriptions of the works on political education which Herder intended to write in order to win the empress' favour.

Such flatteries, and others yet more gross, were customary at that epoch ; but Catherine could make a very adroit use of fulsome praise, and was glad to pay for advertisements of the kind.[1]

§ 13.

PETER'S reforms were mainly of a practical character, but, since practice must be based on theory, practical needs necessitated a theoretical foundation.   Nor was it sufficient to transplant individual Europeans to Russia and to send Russians to study in Europe ; it was essential ·that schools and other means of culture should be provided at home.   The plan for the foundation of the academy originated with Peter ; and in the year 1726, shortly after his death, it was carried out by his widow.   The Livonian peasant girl, unable to read or write, was a faithful patron of the new institution.   The initial aims of the academy were of a practical nature, for it had a printing establishment and other workshops, but it tended more and more towards theoretical activities.   The first university (1747), somewhat primitive, was an offshoot of the academy ; the first academic *gimnazija* (higher school) was founded as early as 1726.   The university

---

[1] The view of certain Russian historians that the modern history of Russia begins with Catherine is, in my opinion, erroneous.

of Moscow came into being in 1775.[1] The first students and professors at the universities and *gimnazijas* were Germans.

But the higher schools in the capitals were not the only nurseries of culture. Society, too, promoted its diffusion, and this not in the capital alone, for during the second half of the eighteenth century there rapidly developed a cultured society in the provinces, which was of the first importance to Russian civilisation of that date.

In conformity with the aristocratic character of eighteenth-century Russia, the work of education was likewise aristocratic. Higher and middle schools only were founded. Even now, public elementary schools can hardly be said to exist, although Peter had thoughts of reform in this direction also.[2]

The Russians, like their sovereign, energetically furthered the spread of western culture, and after Peter's death a number of notable men carried forward the work. Lomonosov and Kantemir, the former of whom may be termed the Peter of Russian literature, sprang from the Moscow academy. Natural science, technology, and history, were the leading subjects of original study ; legal and political enlightenment was sought ready made in Germany.

The influences encouraged by Peter were mainly Dutch and German, and Lomonosov drew inspiration from the same sources. But already during the reign of Elizabeth, the court and the aristocracy became French in spirit through the cultural and political primacy of France ; the common people were excluded from all share in higher civilisation. The spread of the French tongue was so general that as late as the first half of the nineteenth century many Russians spoke better French than Russian, and there were some who never learned Russian at all. Puškin, for example, was an accomplished French scholar, and wrote at first in French. This is true also of Lermontov. We find Gallicisms in the earlier works of Tolstoi. Quite a number of writers made use of French as well as Russian—Herzen, for instance.

This predominance of French influences among the Russian aristocracy runs parallel with the spread of the same influences

[1] The juristic faculty of Moscow university had at first but one professor, the number being subsequently increased to three. On several occasions the number of students sank to one.

[2] In 1724 there were 110 secular elementary schools and 46 church schools, from which ecclesiastical seminaries developed in the course of the eighteenth century.

among the Polish and European aristocracies. At the same epoch Frederick the Great had his French academy in Berlin, and wrote in the tongue of Voltaire. At the court of Vienna, German poets had to be translated into French.

French exercised its influence mainly in the social and political spheres, and above all in the field of diplomacy. German was the language of culture. It was not spoken, but German authors were thoroughly studied in the original.

We cannot do justice to the effect of these two European tongues without taking into account the personal influence of Frenchmen and Germans in Russia. The annexation of the Baltic provinces was followed by the entry of German barons into the administration, and subsequently by the entry of Swedes, Finns, and Poles. From France came the persons needed by the court and the aristocracy—physicians, actors, teachers of language, of dancing, etc. During the revolution, some of the émigrés came to Russia. From German sources were mainly derived professors, tutors, craftsmen, and merchants. Thus in one way and another, during the eighteenth century, Russia, official and socially decisive Russia, became Europeanised in speech. Europe and the Frenchified court and nobility of Russia grew aloof from and became contrasted with the Russian peasant and the Russian clergy. It was in the academies and the schools that German influence was predominant.

Owing to this Gallicising movement, prerevolutionary and revolutionary French literature made its way into Russian drawing-rooms and studies (of these latter, there were few). Voltaire, Rousseau, Montesquieu, Diderot, Holbach, Morelly, Mably, etc., were as much read in St. Petersburg as in France, and the political sentiment of St. Petersburg was almost identical with that of Paris. It must not be forgotten that in France the revolution was initiated by the aristocracy and the middle classes, and it was only when the movement was well advanced that the rural population, the peasantry, came to participate in it. The course of development in Russia was analogous. The aristocracy became imbued with the French and German philosophy of enlightenment. Popular revolt was the outcome of poverty and distress (Pugačev), but the life and general outlook of the common people made them hostile to the apostles of the enlightenment. Similar were conditions in France, and they are similar everywhere even to-day, above all in Russia.

Taking a broad view of the history of civilisation, we are concerned here with the great movement of the eighteenth century, the endeavours towards rebirth which affected all the nations of Europe, endeavours whose insignia were enlightenment and humanitarianism. This movement, the natural continuation of the humanist renaissance and the religious reformation, permeated Russia as well, and it was during the reign of Catherine II that French and German enlightenment became naturalised in Russia.

To Petrine New Russia, freemasonry was of especial importance as organiser of European civilisation and as zealous propagator of humanitarian ideals. From about 1731 onwards lodges were established in St. Petersburg, and subsequently in Moscow and the provinces. In 1747 they began to receive attention from the governmental police department, but they were tolerated and even favoured, and there was no mystery about their meetings. Novikov was a leading freemason, and in his *Lexicon of Russian Authors* we can study the history of the Russian enlightenment.[1]

Freemasonry and the freemasons, Novikov in especial, are of great importance in relation to the development of Russian civilization. The ideas of the enlightenment were deliberately and unceasingly propagated in the lodges. Participation in the ritual of the churches was natural to the Russians, and for those among them who had been spiritually estranged from the church by the study of Voltaire and other French philosophers, the ritual of freemasonry provided a welcome substitute. We must remember that the Russian freemasons were not properly speaking freethinkers either in religion or philosophy. They inclined rather to regard Voltairism with horror, and in political views were conservative. Lopuhin, in especial, was not merely hostile to the revolution, but was opposed to the French and to French civilisation in general, and favoured the maintenance of serfdom.[2]

There was another direction in which the masonic lodges

---

[1] Novikov was imprisoned in 1792, and the lodges were threatened. Emperor Paul set Novikov at liberty. As crown prince he had been on intimate terms with the freemasons, and it is probable that Catherine looked askance at the friendship. Toleration was re-extended to freemasonry by Alexander I in the year 1805.

[2] Catherine sent Novikov to be examined by the archbishop of Moscow, who reported to the empress that it was his prayer that the Russian church and the world at large might contain such Christians.

affected Russian life, namely by paving the way for the development of political secret societies. These had at first unmistakable resemblances to lodges, and among the decabrists were a number of ex-members of lodges and sons of freemasons.

It was inevitable that the spread of the ideals of enlightenment and humanitarianism, as preached not by the freemasons alone but by eighteenth - century philosophy and literature in general, should lead in Russia to the question of serfdom becoming foremost in all theoretical and practical thought. It was impossible that Pugačev's revolt should pass without notice. Catherine said that it would be better to grant freedom to the serfs than to leave them to secure freedom by force.

In Russia as in the west there were practical no less than humanitarian grounds for the liberation of the peasantry. Russia needed more intensive agriculture; for the enhanced national expenditure and for the more refined tastes of the Gallicised nobility, more and more money was requisite. For fiscal reasons, therefore, the peasants must be freed, and must be trained so that their labours might be more productive. Europe set the example to Russia. In Austria, serfdom was abolished in the royal domains under Maria Theresa and Joseph II; Frederick the Great aimed at similar reforms in Prussia, though with little result; in France, enfranchisement was effected in 1789 (the work was actually begun in 1779) by an extremely radical measure, the landowners being dispossessed without compensation.

Radiščev was a typical representative of advanced Russian thought in the days of the French revolution. His education had been mainly German, for he was at Leipzig university from 1766 to 1771, but his political ideals were derived from those of French thinkers. In addition to Herder and Leibnitz, his teachers had been Rousseau, Mably, Raynal, the encyclopædists, and Voltaire. The form of his most notable work, *Journey from St. Petersburg to Moscow*, was borrowed from Sterne. The contents are thoroughly Russian, splendid realistic descriptions of men and things, with enthusiastic propaganda on behalf of French ideals of freedom. The book was published in 1790. Catherine promptly had the author haled before the courts and sentenced to death—the same Catherine whose *Book of Instructions* of the year 1766 had been interdicted in the France of Louis XV. Radiščev's sentence was commuted to banishment, and he remained in Siberia until the accession of Paul I.

The *Journey* is unquestionably a bold work, and above all it is the political credo of a thoroughly cultured man, of one who in thought and feeling had attained to an exceptional grasp of the significance of the eighteenth century. In a brilliant ode, *The Giant*, Radiščev apostrophises the eighteenth century, blood-stained, mad, and yet wise. With reasoning based upon natural law he proves the bloody and mad doctrine of wisdom, the right of revolution. To Catherine in her passion it seemed that Radiščev was a more dangerous revolutionary than Pugačev, for the former aimed not merely at the abolition of serfdom (writing " the peasant is dead in law "), but demanded a representative constitution and far-reaching liberties (freedom of the press, etc.).

In Siberia, Radiščev, an enlightened opponent of mysticism, wrote an essay upon immortality, maintaining, in opposition to Helvetius, Holbach, and Lamettrie, the possibility and probability of immortality.

Under Alexander I, Radiščev was again given an appointment ; but in 1802, when no more than fifty-three years old, suffering from nervous breakdown, he committed suicide by taking poison.

Next to Radiščev, Pnin, poet and prose writer, was in that day the most zealous and notable opponent of serfdom. While Radiščev, following Rousseau, regards slavery as essentially a form of theft, Pnin, taught by the French constitution, dwells rather upon the favourable aspects of private property, desiring that the Russian peasant shall become a proprietor. Excellent is Pnin's demonstration that the liberation of the peasantry is a logical consequence of the generally acclaimed enlightenment.

The poet Sumarokov was the leader of the social reactionaries. In the year 1766, the empress, anonymously and through the instrumentality of the Free Economic Society, offered a prize for an essay upon the question whether it was more advantageous to society that the peasant should own land or should own nothing but personal property, and how far in either case it was desirable that his rights should extend. Sumarokov responded in a vigorous writing that there could be absolutely no doubt as to the nobleman's exclusive ownership of the soil. " The canary bird would be better pleased to have no cage, and the dog would prefer to be without a chain. But the bird would fly away, and the dog would bite. One is therefore necessary for the peasant, the other for the noble."

The political ideals of constitutionalism, or at least of a restriction of absolutism, prevailed throughout society, and even flatteries of the good autocrat, Byzantine in their servility and couched in the style of Fénelon's *Télémaque* (first translated in 1747), furthered criticism and endeavours towards liberty, for the adulation of autocratic ideals and virtues challenged rejoinder. Among Fénelon's numerous imitators, Heraskov the novelist may be mentioned. Until Catherine II took to suppressing tendencies towards freedom, this writer had displayed liberal sentiments ; but when reaction followed upon the French revolution, Heraskov, too, became an opponent of the republic and of French philosophy.

Condorcet tells us that " reason and tolerance " was the device of Voltaire. The spirit of Voltaire, the spirit of the encyclopædists and the philosophers of the enlightenment in general, had in Russia as in Europe been directed against the church and ecclesiasticism. Many translations from Voltaire were published during the decade 1760 to 1770. Four editions of *Candide* appeared between 1769 and 1798. In St. Petersburg, Moscow, and provincial towns, this author's writings were not read merely, but positively devoured. His criticism of superstition, priestly dominion, monasticism, the perversities of official morals and politics, set Russia ablaze. The Russian imitators of Voltaire and the French devoted most of their energies to invectives against the church, the priests, and the monks ; they renounced belief in miracle ; and mostly advocated natural religion in the sense of deism and free-thought.[1]

The Russian enlightenment was not exclusively rationalistic. As in the west, so here, there was a vigorous mystical movement, directed primarily against Voltairism, but also against official ecclesiasticism. This tendency dominated the freemasons (Martinism) and wide circles among the cultured. Rousseau and his religious ideas found many adherents, in addition to those who followed Voltaire and the encyclopædists, as we have learned already in the case of Radiščev.

---

[1] I may mention in this connection Heraskov (the earlier works), the brothers Eminov, Rahmanin, Dmitriev-Mamonov, Čulkov, Popov, the brothers Izmailov, L'vov, and Zahar'in—and, of course, Radiščev.

§ 14.

IT was inevitable that the spread of European ideas of freedom should have evil consequences as well as good. Deplorable half culture and moral laxity soon became general, and earlier and rougher customs came to be regarded in an ideal light. There were excellent men enough, of outstanding intelligence and honourable character, like Radiščev; but the bulk of the aristocracy was half educated, whilst the court was immoral, a compost of unbridled sexuality, boorishness, and cruelty, and its example was contagious (cf. Herzen's *A Brothel Tragedy*).[1] Fonvizin's comedies (*Brigadier*, 1766, *The Minor*, 1782), and their satire upon half culture, are descriptions far from exaggerated of the state of so-called good society in the days of Catherine.

It was inevitable that these cultural contrasts should be manifested in the work of administration. For example, Elizabeth abolished capital punishment, but introduced the knout. Publicists and historians, no less than Fonvizin and the politicians, noted the imperfections of contemporary Russian civilisation, for the contrast between the old Russia and the new, between the peasantry and the nobility, was too glaring to escape observation.

[1] A few instances only need be given from the days following Peter. Consider Anne's relationship with Biron. Elizabeth was properly speaking illegitimate, and was secretly married to Razumovskii. Catherine I and Elizabeth were addicted to drink. Catherine II, whose grandson Nicholas I described her as a "crowned whore," from early in her reign made a male harem of the court, and this naturally involved enormous expenditure. During the years from 1762 to 1783, the family of Orlov received from Catherine "the Great" (as she was named by the Prince de Ligne) 17,000,000 roubles and 45,000 "souls." The moral corruption issuing from Catherine and her lovers can be readily imagined. A few figures will suffice. During the twenty-two months in which he was the favourite, Vasilčikov, lieutenant in the guards, received 100,000 roubles in cash, presents valued at 50,000 roubles, a palace costing 100,000 roubles and furnished for 50,000 roubles, 7,000 souls, and an allowance of 20,000 roubles. In the course of two years Potemkin was given 37,000 souls, and the money value of his other gifts was 9,000,000 roubles. To Zavodskii, during eighteen months, were given 9,800 souls, 15,000 roubles in cash, presents worth 80,000 roubles, furniture to the value of 30,000 roubles, and an allowance of 10,000 roubles. Zorin, a Serb, received in one year an estate valued at 600,000 roubles, 500,000 roubles in cash, presents worth 200,000 roubles, a post in Poland with a salary of 12,000 roubles. Korsakov, an officer in the army, was given during sixteen months presents to the value of 150,000 roubles, 4,000 souls, 100,000 roubles to pay off his debts, a further sum of 100,000 roubles, 2,000 roubles a month as travelling allowance, and a palace. Upon Lanskoi were bestowed jewelled breast-pins costing 80,000 roubles, and 30,000 roubles for the discharge of his debts.

The first historians after the close of Peter's reign were foreigners, Germans for the most part. This was advantageous on the whole, for as Europeans they could display in a strong light the foreign elements in Russian development. It is true that their treatment of the subject was by no means impartial; and their comparison between Russia and Europe from the outlook of eighteenth-century history and philosophy was of little value. Writing as German patriots, they tended to lay especial stress upon the barbarism of the Old Slavs and Old Russians, and to extol the civilising influence and the state-constructive talent of the Teutonic Varangians.

The publication of these German theories aroused a spirit of contradiction among the Russians, who inclined to insist upon the moral value of Old Russian life and institutions.

Prince Ščerbatov was not troubled because the first Russian princes were foreigners, perhaps Germans; but he championed Old Russian simplicity. One of his writings was devoted to the criticism of the reforms of Peter and his successors. This work, *The Corruption of Russian Morals,* is all the more interesting seeing that its author was an aristocrat and conservative, but had had a European education, and exhibited strong leanings towards rationalist liberalism. Ščerbatov was among the most zealous advocates of representative government and the restriction of absolutism. He recognised that since the days of Peter, the Russians had made social and political advances, but held that their progress had been achieved at the cost of moral backsliding. He was sufficiently logical to blame Catherine and her life as well as Peter's reforms. In contrast with the innovations, he extolled as an ideal to which the Russians should return the morals of prepetrine Old Russia.[1]

Ščerbatov did not stand alone as critic. His noted opponent Boltin the historian and general, criticising the *Histoire de la Russie ancienne et moderne* issued in 1783 by Le Clerc, a French physician in Russia, was the first to attempt a logical and detailed demonstration that the defects which foreigners, and above all the French, were accustomed to point out in the

---

[1] It is characteristic of the conditions of the day, conditions still prevailing, that Radiščev's book was seized in the year 1790, and that Ščerbatov did not venture to have his work printed. Both were first published in London in 1858. Radiščev's Journey could not be circulated by the Russian book trade until 1905. Tatiščev, promoter of culture and champion of autocracy, had a similar fate with the work he wrote in 1733, entitled Discussion Concerning the Value of Science, and it was not published until 1887.

Russians, existed also among these foreigners, and often in greater degree. In the history of Europe, Boltin was able to point to not a few indications of barbarism. Urging his countrymen not to be too ready to esteem the foreign and the new, he insisted upon the superiority of prepetrine morals and institutions. Like Ščerbatov, Boltin was a conservative. He defended autocracy (an institution not unknown in the Europe of that day!). He displayed no enthusiasm for the humanitarians' demand that the peasantry should be enfranchised. It seemed enough to him that the power of the landlords should be maintained, a power to be benevolently exercised and strictly limited by law.

Both these adulators of Old Russia, Ščerbatov and Boltin, were Voltairians, and this is an instructive instance of the perplexing contrasts between Old and New Russia. The raskolniki had defended Old Russia against Peter. At the close of the eighteenth century, in the camp of the liberal friends to reform, the contrast between the old and the new was philosophically formulated, preference being given to the new. Catherine's morals were too loose for the taste of prince and general, but they supported her reactionary tendencies in politics.

CHAPTER THREE

THEOCRATIC REACTION AFTER THE FRENCH REVOLUTION ; ITS DEFEAT BEFORE SEVASTOPOL. OPENING OF THE POLITICAL AND PHILOSOPHICAL REVOLUTION (CATHERINE II—NICHOLAS I)

§ 15.

IN Russia, as in Europe, the revolution, and above all the jacobin terror, were followed by a notable decline in aspirations towards enlightenment and liberty. It was not in France alone that reaction occurred, but in Prussia and Austria as well, Frederick and Joseph being replaced by Frederick William and Francis. England exploited the antifrench alliance of the continent for the furtherance of her conservative policy.

In Russia, the aristocrats and the court, speaking French and having enjoyed a French education, made common cause with the reactionary aristocrats of France. Catherine temporarily forbade the printing of Russian translations from Voltaire ; the masonic lodges were closed ; Radiščev was sent to Siberia. Emperor Paul I, accentuating the reactionary movement initiated by Catherine, went so far as to refuse to tolerate anything French that did not bear the royalist and Bourbon stamp. Unofficial printing establishments were suppressed ; the import of foreign books was prohibited ; in 1797 the censorship was reorganized ; and in addition a religious censorship, which had been unknown throughout the eighteenth century, was introduced in Moscow in 1796 and was subsequently extended throughout the realm. The religious censorship was regulated in accordance with the principles of " the divine law [holy writ], the rules of the state, good morals and literature." It is not difficult to imagine how these principles were applied in practice. The use of the words "citoyen" and "société" was forbidden. It need hardly be said that Russia participated in the second coalition against France (1799). In 1798 and 1800, Tsar Paul issued a decree to the following effect : " The supreme power of the autocrat, bestowed on him by God, extends over the church. It is the duty of the entire clergy to comply with the commands of the tsar as divinely appointed head of the church, and to do this in all things, in religious matters as well as in civil."

It is true that Paul was already mentally disordered. Reaction, legitimism, and the censorship did not suffice to protect the tsar against the palace revolution, a revolution which his own son made no attempt to hinder ! Alexander I, who was born in 1777 and reigned from 1801 to 1825, had been educated by his grandmother Catherine upon Rousseauist principles. Laharpe, the republican, subsequently one of the leading spirits in the Helvetian republic, was from 1782 to 1795 tutor to the princes Alexander and Constantine. The education given to the brothers was characteristic of the half culture which then prevailed at court, the influence exercised by Laharpe and by the entourage in general being superficial and desultory.

As crown prince this pupil of Laharpe the humanist and philosopher of enlightenment promised himself to effect far-reaching reforms. He was an enthusiast for the abolition of serfdom. In 1796, writing to his friend Kočubei, he said : " Incredible disorder prevails in the administration ; robbery goes on everywhere ; all departments are ill-managed ; order seems to have been banished, but the empire recks nothing, striving only after expansion." In the same year, Alexander assured Prince Czartoryski that though he disapproved the excesses of the revolution he wished all success to the French republic. When he ascended the throne, he gave a public pledge to abide by the liberal traditions of his grandmother, saying that it was a sacred obligation to maintain one law for all, and promising to rule " in accordance with the laws and spirit of Catherine."

Russia overflowed with joy and enthusiasm. Certain steps taken by the tsar encouraged hope. Radiščev was given legislative employment. Alexander furthered the translation of the works of Adam Smith, Bentham, Beccaria, Montesquieu, and similar writers. He was an enthusiast for Pestalozzi, and provided money on behalf of the socialistic experiments of Robert Owen. None the less, after a period of vacillation (1801–1811), reaction set in, although down to the year 1820 the emperor continued on occasions to give expression to liberal views, especially before foreigners.

In Alexander's day occurred the restoration in France and the reaction in the other European states, and these experiences exercised a more decisive effect upon his mind than the direct teaching of his tutor. The influence of such men as Owen, Fourier, and Saint-Simon was replaced by that of such men as Burke, de Bonald, and Gentz. De Maistre visited St. Petersburg and was able to wield immediate influence over Alexander. Chateaubriand likewise inspired St. Petersburg drawing-rooms with a taste for romanticist Christianity. During the reign of Alexander I religious mysticism became widely diffused among the upper circles of society. The mystical writings of Eckartshausen were made known by Lopuhin, and most of them were translated. Translated also were the works of Jung-Stilling and of earlier mystics, such as Madame de Guyon, Swedenborg, Tauler, etc., etc. The main interest of these mystics was in the spirit world, and they displayed full understanding of the various grades of occultism.

The fate of Radiščev was typical of Alexander's mental development. He had Radiščev recalled from exile, but the tragic end of this notable writer and man of fine character offers the severest criticism of the reign that was now opening. Radiščev despaired of the realisation of his ideals.

Ten days after ascending the throne Alexander found on his writing table Karazin's plan for a constitutional monarchy. In fact, the design was extremely unconstitutional, for the constitution was to come into existence through a -kind of constitutionalist conspiracy. Karazin was for a time a personal friend of the young tsar, but before long he fell into disfavour. Similar was the fate of constitutionalism.

Throughout the reigns of Alexander and his successors we may say that the question of the constitutionalisation of Russia remained on the agenda. Europe's example in this respect could not fail to produce in all Russians a lively sense of oppression. Nor was the sentiment weakened when the absolutists referred to the horrors of the revolution. None the less, constitutional government was successively established in other European countries, whilst the example of England could always be quoted in favour of the thesis that constitutionalism was prophylactic of revolution.

In Russia under Alexander, as everywhere else, the English example exercised notable influence. Alexander's friend Kočubei had been educated in London; Novosilcev, who played an important part in this connection immediately after Alexander became tsar, had lived in London for a considerable time; Speranskii was a friend of Bentham's brother and had an English wife. Many other members of the official circle were admirers of England.

In the early days of his reign Alexander appointed an unofficial committee to draft plans for a thorough reform of the administration. The labours of the committee were continued for two years, and the tsar took personal part in its deliberations.

In 1804 Alexander commissioned Baron Rosenkampf to formulate a constitution for Russia, while in the following year he established a privy cabinet to supervise liberalising endeavours. In 1807 this cabinet was made a permanent institution, and it lasted until 1829.

Repeatedly and with indefatigable energy Speranskii brought forward constitutionalist plans during the years 1803, 1808, 1809, and 1813. From 1806 to 1812 this statesman was in close personal touch with the tsar. Alexander gave special approval to the mature *Introduction to the Code of National Laws*, written in the year 1809; but the admirer of Napoleon, infirm of will, could not make up his mind to carry out the scheme. The views of the historian Karamzin, brought forward in 1811 in the form then customary of a memorial (*Old and New Russia in Political and Civil Relationships*), gained the upper hand.

Speranskii was an able administrator and a philosophically trained publicist. His plans for constitutionalist reform show him to have been a practical politician, one whose aims were realisable in the given conditions. From the position of mathematical teacher at the seminary he rose to that of the most powerful of Alexander's councillors. His sympathies were with the eighteenth‑century enlightenment, with Voltaire, Diderot, Montesquieu, and Rousseau; with Blackstone and the English constitutionalists; and with the philosopher Locke. Through and through a man of the progressive eighteenth century, the Russian influences that moulded him were those of Radiščev and his school,

From early days it was Speranskii's aim to adapt to Russian conditions the teachings of his French and English exemplars. His demands, far from being revolutionary, were extremely moderate. A gradual development can be noted. In the first plans, those expounded in the memorial of 1802, the effect of foreign influences is more conspicuous than in the later designs ; we trace the hand of Rousseau, Montesquieu, and English writers. Rousseau's "general will" becomes the will of the aristocracy. After the English manner, aristocratic privilege is to be transmitted to the first-born son alone ; the younger sons are to belong to the people. Speranskii had no thought of a complete liberation of the peasantry. No such liberation was recommended in the plan of 1809. Domestic servants, day-labourers, workmen, and handicraftsmen were to have civil rights ; but political rights were to be the exclusive privilege of the two upper orders, of the aristocrats and of the middle class, the latter comprising merchants, burghers, peasant proprietors, and other property owners.

The most characteristic point of Speranskii's proposals, and the one most important to Russia, was his suggestion for the establishment of a "real monarchy," by which he meant a constitutional monarchy, to replace the existing despotism, this change being part of a radical reform of the machine of state. The changes in the administration made by Peter, Catherine, and other rulers, needed, according to Speranskii, to be unified and organically developed ; above all, the functions of each office should, he contended, be clearly defined. Speranskii's leading principle was that political power proceeds from the people ; but "the people," as he used the term, meant only the upper classes. The monarch was irresponsible, but, like the responsible ministers and all the citizens of the state, he was bound by the basic laws of the community. Speranskii laid great stress upon the maintenance of these fundamental laws which, in accordance with his Rousseauist outlook, seemed to him the essential bulwark of the constitution. A point of special importance was that Speranskii proposed the creation of a parliament which was to be organically associated with the other autonomous representative bodies. The volost (vide supra, p. 34) and its elected council, the volost duma, were to constitute, as it were, the elementary cell of constitutionalism. The electoral councils of the next grade, the circle dumas, were to be elected by the volost dumas; the circle dumas were to elect the dumas of the administrative districts; these last, finally, were to elect the state duma. The state duma was to have no legislative power, but it alone could promulgate laws, the government being merely entitled to issue ordinances. The duma could take the initiative in exceptional cases only, when the fundamental law had been infringed by the government. Speranskii's scheme provided for but one chamber. It was the function of the council of state to discuss the affairs of the legislature, the judiciary, and the executive, and above all to discuss proposals emanating from these three branches of the political organism; personal report to the monarch was to be done away with.

A mere outline has been given of Sperenskii's design, but enough has been said to show that it was thought out in all its details and planned to put an end imperceptibly to absolutist despotism. Alexander approved the scheme, but it was never carried out. On the contrary, the tsar's advisers accused Speranskii of a secret understanding with foreign embassies and agents, and of direct treason. Alexander, though he did not believe the accusation, failed to protect Speranskii, who was sent to Siberia.

From time to time in his earlier works Speranskii criticised Russian despotism, but a far more eloquent criticism of this despotism was voiced by his demands for reform, for these all aimed at educating the Russian people so that it might become competent to exercise political initiative in the entire domain of public activity. He knew that there were in reality only two classes in Russia—to quote his own phraseology, the slaves of the tsar and the slaves of the landowners. Although there was a lack of definiteness about his proposals concerning the legislative organism (tsar, council of state, and duma) and its initiative, we must remember that the initiative of the volost was very definitely formulated, and that all his suggestions culminated in a restriction of the imperial initiative. Completed deliberations merely were to be laid before the tsar; the lawcourts were to be placed on an elective basis; foreign policy was to be in the hands of the executive; the aristocracy was to be independent of the crown. Speranskii made a far-reaching distinction between state and people, and he was convinced that the state is in an unhealthy condition when its development either lags behind the political sense of the people or runs unduly in advance of that sense.

Speranskii's constitution was a plan for a political elementary school, finished in all its details. His reward, like that of his predecessor Radiščev, was banishment to Siberia. After two years he was permitted to return, and subsequently held various offices in the state service. From 1819 to 1821 he was governor-general of Siberia. In the reign of Nicholas I he was in charge of the work of legal codification. During these later years Speranskii's views underwent modification, so that he drew nearer to his sometime opponents.

Karamzin, in opposition to Speranskii's broadly conceived scheme for representative government, recommended the appointment of fifty benevolent governors with despotic powers. Karamzin went so far as to contend that the tsar had no right to restrict the absolutist privileges inherited from his ancestors. Speranskii, however, was in harmony with Karamzin on one point, for he too had grasped how the institution of serfdom contributes to the strength of absolutism.

In the year 1815, Alexander granted a constitution to Poland, and his regime there as constitutionalist absolutist gave him continued occasion to consider the question of constitutional government for Russia. At the opening of the Polish diet in 1818, the tsar even gave a half promise to establish constitutional government throughout Russia, saying : " You have provided me with an opportunity of announcing to my fatherland what I have been preparing for it for many years, and what it will make a good use of, as soon as the preliminaries for so important a change shall have sufficiently matured." This speech aroused high hopes in Russia, for the Russians had no wish to be less privileged than the Poles ; and the tsar commissioned Novosilcev to draft a new scheme. It was commented on and approved by Alexander, presumably in the year 1821, but was still-born like that of Speranskii, which it closely resembled. The tsar's reluctance to initiate these reforms was probably stimulated by the discovery of plots, aiming in 1817 at his assassination, and in 1818 at his imprisonment.

Notwithstanding the example set by European states, the majority of the aristocracy, like the tsar, had no faith in constitutionalism. Typical of these doubts was the previously mentioned Karazin. In an address delivered in 1816, and again later, after Alexander's Warsaw speech, he energetically opposed the introduction of a constitution. His contention was that

an autocrat was absolutely indispensable to a great realm, but
that a national convention was not requisite. " Our tsars,"
he wrote, " are not representatives of the peoples, but representatives of Him who rules empires." Thus logically did
Karazin formulate the theocratic doctrine of cæsaropapism.
In another lecture he publicly denounced the constitutionalists
as republicans, and expressed his opposition to the theories
of the rights of man and of civil rights.

Whilst Alexander thus failed to fulfil his pledges for the
establishment of constitutionalism, he showed himself no less
feeble and reactionary in the matter of liberating the peasantry.
In 1806 he accepted the dedication of Kaisarov's Göttingen
dissertation against serfdom, a question which through the writings of Radiščev, Pnin, Novikov, Polěnov, and other opponents,
had become more and more acute. The tsar could, indeed,
appeal to notable names upon the other side, to Sumarokov,
Ščerbatov, and Boltin, for instance. Alexander was urged
towards reform, not by Russian theorists alone, but by the
example of Europe and of his own European territories. In
the Baltic provinces the peasants were liberated during the
years 1816 to 1819. Among the Russian aristocracy, warm
advocates of this humane (and practical) reform were invariably
to be found. Prince Vjazemskii, a noted writer who had
translated Novosilcev's draft from French into Russian, conceived the idea of founding a society for the liberation of the
peasants. In 1820 he sent the tsar a memorial wherein the
liberation of the peasants and the domestic serfs was advocated
by himself and his friends on grounds of justice and expediency.
In 1818, Kankrin, minister for finance, favoured this reform,
but without avail.

The opposing views were voiced by Karazin. In the address
to which reference has previously been made, the one in which
his opposition to constitutionalism was definitely formulated, he
expounded also the divine and ethical justification for serfdom.
The great landed proprietors, he said, were " almost " as
indispensable to the wellbeing of the peasant villagers as was
the monarch to that of his subjects in general. The landlord
was a hereditary official to whose care the peasants had been
entrusted by the supreme authority; vis-à-vis the state,
the relationship of landlord to peasant was that of " governor-
general in miniature." He wrote: " Russian landlords are
nothing other than vice-gerents of their great tsar, each in the

domain hereditarily entrusted to him." . Karazin remained animated by a kindly spirit. His "governor-general in miniature" was likewise to be the father of the serfs. It was his aim to discover a middle course between the behaviour of the capitalists with their "ubi bene ibi patria," and the maltreatment of the serfs as slaves.

Be it noted, the tsar is the representative of God, and the landlord is the vice-gerent of the tsar. The landlord, therefore, is co-representative of God, and the holder of this aristocratic doctrine is, consequently, perfectly logical when he defends serfdom. Men whose views were in other respects extremely liberal, were to be found on the side of Karazin. I may mention Mordvinov, friend and pupil of Speranskii, a cultured statesman who as minister and official in various departments exercised for a time considerable influence upon the tsar. An enthusiastic adherent of Adam Smith, he was a warm advocate of political reforms after the English model. In social matters, however, he was ever the Old Russian reactionary, willing only to enfranchise his peasants at a high price and without granting them any rights in the soil.

Deržavin wrote an inflated *Ode to God* which is to be found in all the reading books put into the hands of young people in Russia. Here we are told that in poesy we are to be for God, and in politics for serfdom.

Karazin expressed the views of the hardshelled agrarian aristocrat, the man who exploited European constitutionalist doctrines for the benefit of feudalism. In essence his views were shared by many others, liberals not excepted, although these might employ different arguments. Karamzin, for example, maintained the natural necessity of serfdom. "Serfs," he wrote, "can be liberated as soon as it is possible for wolves to be full fed while sheep remain uninjured." In the memorial previously mentioned, the adulator of Russian monarchical absolutism took it upon himself to say that it was less dangerous to the state that men should be enslaved than that they should be granted freedom at an inappropriate time. If enfranchisement should prove necessary, it should be effected without the partition of the soil.

Karamzin is typical, and represents an entire school. In youth he was an enthusiastic admirer of Europe and of European ideas of progress, as we may see in his *Letters of a Russian Traveller*. He had an ardent appreciation of Robespierre, and

profoundly deplored his death. But the romanticist senti-
mentality to which he gave expression in his poetic works,
evaporated. He abandoned the ideals of Plato's republic.
When he came to write *The History of Russia*, by Russia he
meant the state, and by the state he understood the absolute
monarchy. He did not, indeed, go so far as to oppose European
influences, but he preferred Muscovite Russia to the Russia
of Peter the Great, considering Ivan III a greater man than
Peter. " The strength of the state is to be found in the strength
of the sentiment of obedience displayed by the people "—
such was the political doctrine of the leading historian of the
restoration epoch.

Nevertheless, a few reforms were carried out in the earlier
years of Alexander's reign. Corporal punishment was mitigated,
and torture was abolished. Somewhat later (1817), when the
clericalist reaction was already in full swing, slitting of the
nostrils was done away with.[1] For a few years the censorship
was less severe. Middle and elementary schools were founded,
and four universities were created (Dorpat, St. Petersburg,
Kharkov, and Kazan). In 1803 the lot of the peasantry was
somewhat alleviated. The principal aim of the reforms of
Alexander's reign was, however, the improvement of the
administration and of the army, in order to increase the func-
tional efficiency of absolutist government. In this connection
may be mentioned the establishment of separate ministries,
among them a ministry of education (officially known as the
ministry of public instruction), in 1802 ; the foundation of the
council of state in 1810 ; and the formation of the military
colonies on the frontier.

By the French revolution, and subsequently by Napoleon,
the great power whose bases had been established by Peter was
drawn into the field of European politics. The reaction in
Europe looked upon Alexander as the guardian of monarchy,
and the overthrow of Napoleon in Russia confirmed Alexander's
faith in absolutism.[2] Attention to European concerns and to

[1] This punishment had no longer been applicable to women since 1757.
[2] In judging the relative power of the various states we must recall the
statistics of population. In 1798, when the armies of Tsar Paul under the
command of Suvarov were being equipped for the campaign in Europe,
the inhabitants of European Russia numbered 38,000,000, and of Asiatic
Russia 5,000,000. At this time the population of France was 26,000,000, of
Great Britain and Ireland 11,000,000, of Prussia 6,000,000, of Poland 9,000,000,
of Austria 16,500,000 (or with the Netherlands and Lombardy 19,500,000),
and of Turkey 23,000,000,

foreign policy, and the laurels gained by the Russian generals on the battlefields of Russia and of Europe, diverted Alexander's attention from domestic weaknesses. It may almost be said that the tsar was more at home in Europe than in Russia. Again and again, a strange restlessness drove him from St. Petersburg to Europe. Reactionary Europe, and Metternich above all, acquired a momentous influence over him. Thus it was that Alexander came to inaugurate the reactionary system which inevitably culminated in catastrophe.

In perfect accord with the reactionary spirit of the restoration epoch, Alexander became increasingly affected with religious sentimentalism, and inclined more and more towards clericalism. The fact might seem to be sufficiently explained by the diffusion throughout Europe of medieval religious romanticism, but to this strong factor there was superadded in Alexander's case a yet more powerful personal motive. The tsar had had prior knowledge of the conspiracy that culminated in his father's death, and had tacitly assented to the crime. His uneasy conscience urged him ever further along the path of religious reaction. It has been asserted, and was maintained even during his lifetime, that he wished to turn Catholic. The assertion is erroneous, but it is true that he hoped to secure absolution from the pope—this Orthodox imperator of the third Rome longed for the absolution of the Roman pope.

Alexander's young wife, Elizabeth Alekséevna, was bold enough to approve the death of Paul. Three days after the murder the empress wrote : " I preached the revolution like a madwoman, for I had but one wish, that happiness should be restored to unhappy Russia, at any cost." We can imagine the conditions prevailing at the court of St. Petersburg when the empress could see no hope of her husband's delivery from his father's tyranny except by political crime. But liberation was not effected nor was happiness restored to Russia. The crime committed against his father separated Alexander from his wife, and he died without legitimate heirs.

Access to Alexander was secured, not only by serious and religiously inclined philosophers, authors, and politicians, but also by all kinds of religious fanatics. He consorted with sectaries and zealots, Protestant as well as Catholic. Baader, the Catholic romanticist, built his hopes upon Alexander. Jung-Stilling, Quakers, and Moravian Brethren, were among his acquaintances. The outlines of the plan for the holy alliance of which he became the head were furnished him by Baroness Krüdener.[1] In courtly and noble circles mysticism of the most varied kinds was at that time prevalent. Some were adherents of Irvingism, advocating a spiritual imitation of Christ ; others followed Selivanov of the skoptsy sect (before the war with Napoleon, Alexander had made a pilgrimage to this pope of the skoptsy) ; Baroness Krüdener, Tatarinova, and others, had adherents. The Bible Society had flourished since 1812. Religious fanaticism was cultivated in many masonic lodges. Notable churchmen, Filaret, for example, participated in this movement ; but the official guardians of the church speedily awoke to the danger. Fotii (Photius) Spasskii, a typical religious fanatic, took the field against all these romanticists.

Reaction towards superstition became more and more frequently manifest. From time to time Alexander saw through its pretensions, but he looked on passively, as in the case of the other excesses of his subordinates. It was owing to his weakness in this respect that the real work of government passed into the hands of such men as the war minister Arakcěev, Benckendorff, the censors Magnickii and Runič, etc., etc.

It is psychologically instructive to note that despite his infirmity of will Alexander was strong enough to carry out the most draconian measures. As previously recorded, he had agreed to mitigate the lot of the peasantry, but he subsequently established the notorious military colonies by which he hoped to secure a large army at low cost and to regulate agricultural production with military precision. His detestation of Speranskii became so acute that he would gladly have shot his faithful adviser with his own hand.

The spirit of this reaction is characterised by the fact that Magnickii had pathological specimens taken from the museums and buried in the churchyard. During the years 1821 to 1824

[1] The alliance personally entered into by the three monarchs of Russia, Prussia, and Austria, has its objects defined in the pact of September 26, 1815. We are told that the three sovereigns will be guided solely by the prescriptions of the Christian religion, namely by the principles of justice, Christian love, and peace. Since we learn from Holy Writ that all men are brothers, the monarchs will in future behave as brothers, and will regard their subjects as members of a single nation. " The monarchs consider themselves to be no more than plenipotentiaries of divine providence, privileged to rule three branches of the same family, and they recognize no other sovereign than God, Christ, the living word of the Almighty."

liberal professors were dismissed from St. Petersburg university ; university students and even the pupils of the higher schools were sent to Siberia ; masonic lodges were closed (the lodges closed in 1822 had 2,000 members). The protector of the holy alliance, of Baroness Krüdener, and of all the reactionary mystics, passed in the end beneath the spiritual sway of Photius.

Photius, an uncultured man sprung from the peasantry, rough and selfish, became ruler of the court, the vigorous will of the fanatic and ascetic gaining the upper hand over the aimless romanticism of the religious enthusiast. Even Prince Golicyn, chief procurator to the synod, a man of great influence and for many years one of Alexander's intimates, had to yield to the power of Photius. Golicyn, Alexander's " postillon d'amour," a man who read the gospels for the first time subsequently to his appointment as chief procurator, was deprived of his office ; and the sub-department of the ministry of education to deal with religious affairs, established in 1817 and entrusted to Golicyn, was abolished, the work being transferred to the synod. " The only minister we have is the Lord Jesus Christ," wrote Photius to a friend. In reality the minister for religion was Count Arakcĕev, the lay Photius, as Photius was the spiritual Arakcĕev. Arakcĕev and Photius represent theocratic cæsaropapism at the close of Alexander's reign ; they are the throne and the altar which Photius defended against the revolution. Photius never wearied of prophesying the coming of antichrist. He announced the final revolution in Russia and the world at large, the onset of " universal destruction," for the year 1836, this being his interpretation of the apocalyptic number. Photius himself died in that year. It was characteristic of this fanatic of the Orthodox letter that he should condemn the moral laxity of the emperor but should condone Arakcĕev's weaknesses because Arakcĕev was friendly to his own lust for power. When Arakcĕev's mistress was murdered on account of her cruelty, Photius celebrated a funeral service on her behalf although she was a Lutheran. In a word, Photius' minister was not Christ, but Arakcĕev-Photius at the court of Alexander—an eloquent demonstration that morality and fanatical religious faith are two utterly different things.

§ 16.

ALEXANDER'S reaction called into life an opposition which ultimately increased to become a definitely revolutionary movement.

The tradition of the eighteenth century and the example of progressive and democratic Europe produced in the best and noblest minds an inclination towards an opposition standpoint ; the tsar's weakness and vacillation increased the revolutionary tendency. In France the reaction had not ventured upon an attempt to restore absolutism, and was content to achieve constitutional monarchy. Prussia carried out the far-reaching reforms of Stein and Hardenberg, adopted the towns' ordinance, and liberated the peasantry and manufacturing industry. Representative constitutions were introduced in several German states. Norway received a thoroughly democratic constitution ; absolutism disappeared in Portugal ; the Swiss constitution was revised. It was in Austria and Prussia alone — and in Turkey — that absolutist methods in politics were stubbornly maintained. The Russians of Alexander's day could not fail to note all these changes, and it was inevitable that discontent with reaction should be greatly accentuated because for so long a period the tsar had cherished constitutionalist designs and had given public pledges of reform. Moreover, Poland and Finland were granted constitutions, and in view of their own condition it was natural that the Russians should feel that this implied a slight to themselves. Progressive philosophy, opposition ideas, sociological and political journalism and literature, were widely circulated. The writings of Constant and Bentham, Destutt de Tracy's *Commentary on Montesquieu*, Montesquieu himself and the eighteenth-century philosophers, were continually read. Works explaining the English and American constitutions were by now accessible ; and as a matter of course many Russians were acquainted with European countries and institutions. In conjunction with European literature, Russian eighteenth-century literature, and yet more the newer Russian literature, the early works of Puškin, and Griboedov's comedies (circulated in manuscript), nourished the spirit of opposition. The writings of Görres, de Bonald, etc., the politicians and sociologists who championed the restoration and the reaction, were likewise known to the Russians, but it will readily be understood that they worked by contraries and served to strengthen the opposition tendency.

Everywhere the advanced parties endeavoured to countermine reaction by working for a new revolution; and after the days of the great revolution France remained the classic land and prototype of revolution. The French movement was joined by that of Young Italy, of Young Germany, of Young Europe, and consequently by that of Young Russia as well. Profound was the impression made in Russia by the revolt of the Greeks. In part the interest was in the country which Byron had sung, but in part it was due to the community of creed. Metternich was, however, successful in inducing Russia to withhold any official expression of sympathy with the insurgents. The influence of the Serbian rising was less conspicuous.

It was from Europe, too, that the Russians acquired their knowledge of political secret societies. The way for these had been prepared by the masonic lodges, and several of the most notable leaders in the secret societies were freemasons. The first secret political society was constituted towards the close of 1816 or the beginning of 1817. Known at first as the Union of Rescue or as the True and Faithful Sons of the Fatherland, in 1818 it was rechristened the Welfare Society. Its organization was modelled on that of the Tugendbund. Some of the decabrists were intimately acquainted with this German society; others had been adepts in the carbonari leagues and in the illuminate orders. The tsar knew of the existence of the secret societies and was familiar with their rules, but he contented himself with prohibiting all secret societies, and with arranging for more vigorous police supervision. His own uneasy conscience rendered it impossible for him to follow the energetic counsels of Benckendorff and other advisers. After the Welfare Society had been dissolved, a new society was constituted in 1821 consisting of Northern and Southern Sections. In 1825 there came into existence the secret society of United Slavs, which aimed at liberating and federating the Slavs; this body joined the Southern Section. Close relationships were likewise entered into with the Polish secret society known as the Patriotic League. A number of lesser societies whose aims were literary rather than political likewise existed in various towns.

The members of all these societies were aristocrats and

belonged to distinguished families. Most of them were military officers, chiefly guardsmen. From the nature of the case, the army and the fleet were more Europeanised and more progressive in point of organisation than any other Russian institution. The officers were the most highly cultured members of the population, especially in the field of natural science, and they therefore were the first to come into conflict with the reaction. Many of them, too, were men who during the Napoleonic wars had had personal experience of Europe and of European acquirements in all domains, men who had faced European armies. The first secret society came into existence when the officers returned to Russia after spending a year and a half in Europe.

At the outset, the aims of all these societies were ill-defined, comprising a mingling of humanitarian philanthropy, the philosophy of the enlightenment, and literary ideas, with designs to work for political and social freedom. By degrees, their aims became clearer ; with increasing resolution they looked forward to tyrannicide and armed rising ; and at length the revolution broke out in December 1825. The Russian for December being *dekabr*, these revolutionaries are known as decabrists. It was the initial attempt at a mass revolution in New Russia, though at first a revolution of the aristocracy. The struggle against Napoleon had served to fortify a senti-ment of strength and independence, and this culminated in the rising which immediately succeeded the death of Alex-ander. The political and social ideals of the decabrists are not yet fully known, for it is but quite recently that the issue of their writings and memoirs has begun, that a literary revision has been made of the legal proceedings against them, and that their biographies have been written. The decabrists were aristocrats, men who could not readily escape the prejudices and habits of their caste. Most of them, doubtless, aimed at the establishment of a constitution which should give some form of representative government such as existed in western countries ; they desired that electors should have a property qualification ; the representatives were to be drawn from the nobility and the bourgeoisie. Some of them made no demand for the liberation of the peasantry ; whilst others, if they desired liberation, did not wish the peasants to be assigned any land. Speaking generally, the decabrists favoured political reform, but had no enthusiasm for social reform.

With the introduction of constitutional government must naturally be associated suitable administrative reforms, and above all reform in judicial and criminal procedure (publicity, trial by jury, the appointment of official counsel for the defence, and so on). Other important requirements were a restriction of the censorship and a remodelling of the conditions of military service. All the decabrists were opposed to the military colonies; the term of service was to be reduced from the twenty-five years then prevalent; corporal punishment was to be mitigated —not abolished.

Most of the political labours of the decabrists, so far as we can judge to-day, remained unfinished, being mere sketches, intended to form the basis of discussion in their meetings. Alexander's death and the peculiar interregnum that followed induced the revolt of December 14, 1825, and by this revolt and its consequences the literary elaboration of their ideas was prevented. When the materials furnished by the evidence given at their trial and the works they subsequently wrote in prison and in Siberia have been sufficiently examined, it may become possible to combine the decabrist fragments to constitute an organic whole.

We possess certain decabrist projects for a constitution. Nikolai Novikov, nephew of the freemason, drafted a republican constitution, but in outline merely. A more finished work is that by Nikita Murav'ev (there were no fewer than seven Murav'evs among the decabrists), of which two separate drafts exist; this is of especial importance because it was known to many of the decabrists and was eagerly discussed. Moreover, Murav'ev's constitution is genuinely republican, or at least the monarch's rôle is reduced to that of president of the republic. Should the tsar fail to approve the scheme he and his family were to be expelled and a republic was to be proclaimed. Murav'ev's plan was based upon the constitution of the United States. Russia was to be subdivided into thirteen states (thirteen was the original number of the states of the American union) and two territories; these were to be federated to constitute a realm known as the Slavo-Russian empire; four governmental departments only were to be common to all the states, foreign affairs, army, navy, and finance. Moscow was to be the capital. The property qualification of an elector was to be very high; in fact, in Murav'ev's constitution the electors were to be Crœsuses. Serfdom was to be abolished, but no land was to be assigned to the enfranchised peasantry, so that the enormous majority of the population would have no electoral rights.

The strongest intelligence among the decabrists and the man with the fullest political culture was Pestel, and his program was the most advanced and the most democratic. The force of Pestel's personality and his influence upon the opposition movement were recognised by the government through the imposition of a death sentence, although Pestel had neither led nor directly prepared the revolt.

Of German descent, Pestel was educated in Dresden, and subsequently had a distinguished military career, not merely showing his bravery in numerous actions (he was wounded at Vilna), but proving himself an energetic and efficient army organiser. Pestel was one of the founders of the Welfare Union, and was subsequently the soul of the Southern Section. He expounded his views in the comprehensive work *Russkaja Pravda* (Russian Truth, the title of the old collection of laws) and in various lesser writings. His magnum opus remained incomplete, but was designed to furnish guidance for the provisional government during the reconstruction period. It is significant of the decabrist political outlook that in Pestel's view this reconstruction period was to last ten years.

In opposition to the reactionary judgments of the revolution that were then current, Pestel proved from a study of the Bourbon restoration that the revolution had been beneficial and necessary, for the restored monarchy had left intact the institutions created by the revolution. On the other hand, as Pestel pointed out, in states where no revolution had taken place the old evils persisted. The existence of Russian absolutism made him a convinced revolutionary and republican. Pestel's analysis of political evolution had led him to the view that constitutionalism is a mere half-measure, a mask for absolutism. Frank autocracy seemed to him preferable to parliamentary government, because absolutism, with its open use of force, leads by the reaction it provokes to speedier and more radical reforms, whereas under constitutional parliamentary government evils are more enduring. It was therefore Pestel's opinion that constitutional monarchy would be a temporary affair, and he considered that the political task of the day was not the constitutionalisation but the democratisation of the state. " The leading endeavour of our time is to be found in the struggle between the masses of the population and aristocracies of every kind, whether based on wealth or birth." For this reason Pestel ardently advocated the liberation of the peasantry, desiring to destroy the aristocracy, the barrier between tsar and people. He was a sympathiser with socialist doctrine, and Herzen speaks of him as " a socialist before socialism."

It is noteworthy that Pestel desired that the enfranchised land of the peasants should become communal property, even where communal property had not previously existed ; but half of the land was to be privately held by the peasants.

There is a socialistic ring about Pestel's idea that the poor man's work is his capital. The rich man can live upon capital, can live without labour, and can wait for better times ; the poor man cannot wait, but must accept whatever conditions are offered him. The fewer persons there are who live solely by work, that is to say the fewer wage earners there are, the fewer will be unhappy. " But since, however good laws and institutions may be, wage earners will continue to exist, the government must protect them against the arbitrary exactions of the wealthy, and must not forget that the unhappy poor fall sick, grow old, and become unfitted for work, being then unable to earn even their pitiful maintenance."

In Pestel's view the epoch in which he lived was characterised by the opening of the struggle waged by the people against the feudal aristocracy. During this struggle an " aristocracy of wealth " came into existence, and from the social outlook the new aristocracy was worse than the old, for the feudal aristocracy, after all, was dependent upon public opinion, whereas the wealthy were enabled by their wealth, in defiance of public opinion, to enslave the entire population.

Pestel's opinions underwent gradual development towards a more logically libertarian and democratic outlook. At the outset, for example, he advocated a mitigation of the censorship and a reduced property qualification ; but in his later writings he was opposed to any property qualification, or to any unequal property qualification, seeing that every Russian should, if the worst came to the worst, be at least able to find a piece of land to till. At first favouring monarchy, Pestel later became a declared republican. In certain respects he was unable to overcome the influence of aristocratic and absolutist education. For example, he proposed to retain corporal punishment in the army, to preserve the indirect system of election, and so on. The sources available to me have not enabled me to ascertain how far Pestel, as member of a secret society, shared the conclusions and views of his associates.

Enough has been said to show that Pestel had given detailed consideration to the chief political and social problems of his day, and that he desired Russian reform to be carried out as an organic whole. He was not satisfied with a constitution, but aimed at a far-reaching internal transformation of men as well as of institutions. His plans, therefore, were something more than constitutionalist and republican ; they were democratic and socialist. His socialism was carried to its logical conclusions as we see in his views regarding inheritance and various other matters.

Nevertheless, Pestel shared many of the prejudices of his time. Noteworthy was his preference for political centralisation, which he advocated in opposition to those who favoured federative schemes. Pestel lays great stress upon the state, upon its unity and indivisibility. Unity is to be secured by the linguistic unification of the entire realm. With the exception of the Poles, all the races and tribes inhabiting Russia are, to use his own expression, " to be amalgamated to form a single people." This amalgamation is to involve civilisation as well as language. Complete Russification is essential. Not merely is the Russian tongue to be used exclusively throughout the realm, but the very names hitherto used by the separate nationalities are to be abolished.

This scheme for Russification is to be applied above all to the civilised national sections under Russian rule, to the Finns and to the Germans ; the Poles, as already stated, are to constitute the solitary exception. Pestel's attitude towards Poland is politically significant for his own and for subsequent days.

In Alexander's time, Russian Poland was entirely distinct from Russia at once politically and in point of civilisation. Not only did the tsar respect the political constitution of Poland, but he even had thoughts of restoring to .that country the provinces that had formerly been Polish. Influential statesmen and publicists were, however, opposed to this plan—such men as Karamzin, and the decabrist Nikolai Turgenev, of whom we shall shortly have to speak as constitutionalist. Prince Orlov, the decabrist, and his friend Dmitriev-Mamonov demanded the suppression of the name Poland ; Prussian and Austrian Poland were likewise to be annexed to Russia.

Pestel, on the other hand, was in agreement with Alexander upon the Polish question. He was willing to accord the rights of nationality to those peoples alone that were numerous enough to exist as independent states ; lesser peoples must be content to sacrifice their national rights to the demands of political utility. Russia, therefore, was to recognise Poland as an independent state, but Russia and Poland were to enter into an " intimate league," and Poland was to have identical forms of government and administration with Russia, all aristocracy, whether feudal or plutocratic, being abolished.

Pestel does not discuss the position of the other Slavs, although the amalgamation of the Society of the United Slavs with the Southern Section might have offered him a text for such discussion. He gives the name of Slav to Muscovite territory and to the Russian people alone, distinguishing five dialects and five " shades " of nationality, namely, Russian, Little Russian, Ukrainian, Ruthenian, and White Russian. The program of the Society of United Slavs aspired to a federal union of the Slav peoples, recognising eight of these, Russians, Serbo-Croats, Bulgarians, Czechs, Slovaks, Lusatian Wends, Slovenes, and Poles. Orlov and Dmitriev-Mamonov designed to effect, not merely the complete reunion of Poland, but a union of the other Slavs with Russia, " the Union of Hungary, Serbia, and all the Slav nations."

Pestel gave the Jewish problem careful consideration. He considered that in Russia and in Poland the Jews constituted a state within the state, and desired therefore to break down the peculiarly powerful cohesion of the Jews. To this end, the most learned rabbis and other Jews of exceptional ability were to elaborate a plan in conjunction with the government. Pestel was likewise a pioneer in the " gigantic " design of Zionism. To carry it through, he said, " positive genius for the enterprise " would be essential. The two millions of Russian and Polish Jews were to found an independent state in some part of Asia Minor. " So large a number of men desiring a fatherland ought not to find much difficulty in overcoming all hindrances which might be placed in their way by the Turks."

Other somewhat utopian suggestions are to be found in Pestel's writings, such as his notion that Nizhni Novgorod should become the capital. On the whole Pestel's ideas were remarkable, and were distinguished especially by the way in which all the important institutions of a well-ordered democratic state were conceived as comprising an organically united whole. Apart from the exceptions indicated, Pestel's mind was liberal and progressive, this being clearly shown by his views regarding the futility of punishing attempted suicides, regarding the equality of status for illegitimate children, etc. Yet the governmental centralisation to which he aspired would have been no less absolutist than was the "enlightened" tsarism of the preceding epoch. This is especially plain in his views upon religion and the church. Here Pestel is wholly at one with Peter the Great. The clergy are not to form a distinct order, being merely entitled to the exercise of a specific profession ; and they must do their work as constituents of the governmental machine. The remodelling of their status in this direction was the aim of his proposed ecclesiastical reforms. Besides demanding that the clergy should be better educated and better paid, Pestel insisted that they ought to lead a truly Christian life, and desired the abolition of monasticism and of monastic control of the white or secular clergy. He prudently recognised that this aim must be secured by a process of gradual change. One of his recommendations was that no one should be allowed to take monastic vows before the age of sixty, or to become a secular priest before the age of forty. In the matter of alien creeds, Pestel held that no member of the clergy ought to be subject to any foreign authority, seeing that the clergy are state servants. Foreign monastic orders, being contrary to the spirit of the Orthodox church, could not be tolerated in Russia.

Of course the proposals were mainly directed against the pope and the Catholics. Pestel's attitude towards the church serves also to explain why he desired that Poland and the Polish provinces should be separated from Russia.

Pestel's religious ideas require further study. It was natural that as a Lutheran he should take a progressive attitude vis-à-vis Orthodoxy. Puškin records that Pestel once said, " Mon cœur est matérialiste, mais ma raison s'y refuse."

A more detailed analysis of Pestel's political conceptions would here be out of place, and it is impossible to refer to the writings and sketches of the other decabrists. The only one with whom we shall have occasion to deal at some length is Nikolai Turgenev.[1]

It is hardly possible to overestimate the political importance of decabrism. The movement was widespread. After December 14 (old style), 1825, more than a thousand arrests were made, and one hundred and twenty sentences were passed by the supreme criminal court. Among notable writers of the twenties, Rylčev, Bestužev (Marlinskii), Küchelberg, and Prince Odoevskii were decabrists, and Griboedov was closely related to the movement. Puškin, too, for a time displayed decabrist leanings. Spiritually and morally the decabrists constituted an élite in Russian society of that day. This is proved by the literature now becoming known, describing the sorrows, the studies, and the labours of the Siberian exiles. There were brave women among them, who shared their fate.

Almost all the political tendencies of subsequent years, alike theoretical and practical, are foreshadowed among the decabrists. Even the most revolutionary of these conceptions, and above all those of Herzen, may be directly deduced from decabrist political ideals.

Although in later days some of the decabrists (a few of whom lived on into the reform epoch of Alexander II) expressed extremely conservative views, we have to take into account the effects of banishment. From the decabrist memoirs, those of Jakuškin, for example, we learn what a martyrdom the banished men had to endure.

§ 17.

THE leaders of the revolt of December 14th were punished by the new tsar with extreme rigour. Of the one hundred and twenty-one accused, five were to be quartered, among them Pestel and the poet Rylěev, thirty-one guillotined, and the remainder exiled to Siberia, the officers being degraded. The tsar, however, exercised his clemency—and the five principal offenders were merely hanged.

Hardly had the revolution been suppressed in the capital and subsequently in the army, when further revolutionary

---

[1] Sergii Murav'ev-Apostol wrote an Orthodox Catechism. His brother, Nikita Murav'ev, outlined a Freeman's Catechism.. Several of the decabrists wrote memoirs, and some compiled historical and other studies. Their correspondence is of considerable interest.

disturbances broke out at home and abroad. Throughout life Nicholas trembled at the spectre of revolution. In his own family he had before him the example of his sister-in-law, the unhappy wife of Alexander I ; after her death (1826) he burned her diary with his own hand. The hanging of Pestel did not suffice to erase the memory of his father's death and his brother's guilt. Not many years before Nicholas ascended the throne occurred the rising in Spain in 1820 and that in Piedmont in 1821 ; during his reign came the July revolution, the Polish revolt, lesser risings in France, and at length the revolutions of 1848. After the Polish rebellion, not merely were the Polish constitution, diet, and national army abolished, but pitiless confiscations of property were carried out, and the university of Vilna was closed.

Tsar Nicholas had a very different education from his two elder brothers. Born in 1796, he was nearly twenty years younger than Alexander, and he was not yet five years old when the latter began to reign. There seemed no probability that he would ever be tsar. Not until it became clear that Alexander would have no legitimate offspring was Constantine induced to renounce the succession. Nicholas' tutor was General Lamsdorf, a rough man who made use of corporal punishment as one of the principal means of education. The prince's only keen interest was in the army. Strict subordination, unquestioning obedience, were Nicholas' system. In his psychology men were mere machines, or at most, animated slaves. " I regard the whole of human life as service," he said on one occasion. The anti-revolutionary mission of Russia therefore began with the reign of this " supreme lord of the narrow world," as Frederick William IV termed him. Žukovskii the poet, tutor to the next tsar, who was in Paris during the February revolution, in his letters to the heir to the throne eloquently pointed the moral that in the universal deluge Russia was the ark of salvation, not for herself alone, but for the rest of the world. Žukovskii hoped that the reigning tsar would keep his country remote from the European plague, would isolate it from the infection by building a Chinese wall. It was the unmistakable design of Providence that Russia should continue to constitute a separate and entirely independent world.

In European policy, Nicholas, like Alexander, was, therefore, protector of legitimism. He was the declared opponent of Louis Philippe, condemning as unlawful the French monarch's election and investiture by the bourgeoisie. It was in this spirit that in the year 1849 he sent troops to assist in suppressing the revolution in Hungary. In 1853 he ordered Serbia to dismiss the premier Garašanin (senior) because that statesman had been a pupil of Kossuth and Mazzini. Metternich's policy in Austria and Germany was a delight to Nicholas. He was not without objections to Napoleon III, but he accepted the coup d'état. Metternich, in turn, sought and found in Nicholas a protector against the revolution, of which he had himself been regarded as the chief opponent, and the Austrian chancellor came to terms with Russia in order to keep Germany and Italy dependent. In Europe Nicholas was admired by all conservatives and reactionaries, and by some actually worshipped, as for example by his brother-in-law Frederick William IV, who said : " I thank God upon my knees for having vouchsafed to me the profound grief I experience at the death of Tsar Nicholas, for having vouchsafed to me to be the tsar's faithful friend in the best sense of the word." Nicholas, for his part, was devoted to the kings of Prussia, highly esteeming Prussian accuracy and orderliness. He preferred Germans in the army and in the administration.

With Nicholas began the " plague zone which extended from 1825 to 1855 " (Herzen). Reaction became a carefully considered police system, the tsar in person assuming the office of chief superintendent of police, for this was the literal significance of the foundation in 1826 of the famous " third section of the departments under his majesty's immediate supervision," which down to the year 1880 was devoted to the attempt to gag Russia intellectually. The notorious Benckendorff, who had secured the tsar's favour through his zeal in the suppression of decabrism, was appointed chief of this institution. Later he also became chief of the gendarmerie, consecrating all his energies to the work of repression.

In this sketch it would be difficult to give an adequate idea of the abominable stupidity and provocative brutality that characterised reaction under Nicholas. For the utterance of liberal ideas conflicting with the official program, leading men were simply declared insane. This happened to Čaadaev and to a number of officers inclined towards revolutionary notions. In one case Nicholas had the death announced of a certain Engelhardt whose sentence had in reality been commuted to imprisonment for life ; his wife was compelled to

wear mourning ; and the very number of his grave in the
churchyard was entered in the records. When the poet Ševčenko
and his associates were sentenced in 1847 as members of the
slavophil Cyrillo-Methodian Union, the tsar aggravated the
punishment in the case of Ševčenko, to whom the use of writing
materials was denied. In his diary the poet complains that
while the pagan Augustus permitted Ovid to write, this indulgence was forbidden to himself by the Christian ruler. Not
merely was the tsar chief officer of police, but in his own exalted
person he revised the sentences of the courts. In the year
1837 two Jews were condemned to death in Odessa because,
from fear of the plague, they had attempted to escape across
the frontier. Nicholas commuted the death penalty as follows :
" The convicts are to run the gauntlet—a thousand men—twelve
times. God be thanked, with us the death penalty has been
abolished, and I will not reintroduce it." This is but one
among numerous instances of the theocratic sovereign's power
of self-deception and of his cruelty—for who had proposed that
the decabrists should be quartered, and who had commuted
their punishment to hanging ? In the year 1838 a student
named Sočinskii gave the director of the surgical academy a
box on the ear. He was sentenced to run the gauntlet—five
hundred men—three times. Nicholas revised the sentence
thus : " To be carried out in the presence of all the students
of the academy. Subsequently the offender, instead of being
sent to Siberia, is to spend ten years, wearing fetters, in the
disciplinary battalion at Kronstadt." It is hardly necessary
to add that though there was no capital punishment, the men
thus sentenced died under the blows of the soldiers.

The severities of Nicholas were hardly credible. The wives
of the decabrists who followed their husbands to Siberia were
not permitted to return to Russia after the death of these ; those
among the decabrists who lived on into the reign of Alexander
II received amnesty from that ruler. Only to one like Nicholas
was it possible to have sane men declared insane, or to inflict
upon Dostoevskii and the Petraševcy the tortures of a death
sentence. Herzen, too, and some of his acquaintances, sus-
pected of Saint-Simonism, were arrested. They were condemned to death in the first instance, but by the tsar's clemency
the sentences were commuted, first to imprisonment and subsequently to exile.

Here is an additional contribution to the psychology,

perhaps it would be better to say the psychopathology, of Tsar Nicholas. A young man named Poležaev wrote a satire upon contemporary student life. The work was circulated in manuscript, and a copy fell into the hands of the emperor, who was especially incensed at the strictures upon the church and political institutions. He sent for the author and compelled him to read the composition aloud to himself and the minister for education. After a severe reprimand, wherein the writing was stigmatised as a product of decabrist sentiment, Nicholas kissed his victim upon the forehead and dismissed him with the sentence that he was to serve at the front, the minister's advocacy averting a worse issue. The tsar granted the offender the privilege of writing to his sovereign in order to recount progress on the right path. Poležaev availed himself of this privilege to beg for pardon, or at least for a mitigation of punishment, but his petitions were disregarded, and his biographers tell us how the unhappy man was tantalised, how in his despair he took to drink, and how finally in 1837 he died of consumption, at the age of two and thirty years. We learn from Poležaev's verses what the age of Nicholas seemed to reflective minds.

Reforms, properly speaking, were unknown in the reign of Nicholas. Much was done to safeguard order, and especial attention was devoted to the army. Under the guidance of Speranskii, legislation was codified in 1833, a new criminal code was issued (1845), and the ministry of the state domains was founded (1837). In 1839, in order to promote the efficiency of centralisation, the village replaced the volost as the administrative unit.

I must not omit to mention that under Nicholas the use of the rod in punishment was abolished, the lash taking its place (1845). Humanitarian considerations, however, were not solely determinative, for those chastised with the rod were no longer fit for military service.[1]

Some of the changes introduced in this reign were beneficial. For example, educational reform was forced upon the Jews, and thereby some of the Jews had opened to them the path to general culture.

Naturally, the reaction under Nicholas was based upon the state church, just as happened in Austria and Prussia, and quite in accordance with the teachings of de Maistre, de Bonald,

---

[1] We find that as early as 1730 offenders fit for military service were sentenced to the lash, the unfit to the rod !

Görres, Gentz, and the various other theorists of the anti-revolutionary restoration and reaction.

All independent thought was to be inexorably suppressed; higher education was to be reduced to the minimum of essential knowledge; philosophy and literature, attempts at general culture and at the attainment of a philosophic outlook upon the universe, were to be stifled in the germ. Count Uvarov, minister for education from 1833 to 1849, addressing the governing committees of the schools, announced his advent to office in the following terms: " It is our joint task to secure that the culture of the nation shall be carried on in the unified spirit of Orthodoxy, autocracy and patriotism." Yet more thoroughly did Uvarov, in the course of the same year, formulate this trinitarian doctrine as " the main principle of the social system of education," writing as follows: " Amid the rapid decay of religious and civil institutions in Europe, amid the widespread diffusion of revolutionary ideas, it becomes our duty to establish the foundations of the fatherland so firmly that they cannot be shaken. We must find a basis from which right conduct can spring; we must discover energies which will develop the distinctive characteristics of Russia, and will ultimately enable our country to assemble the sacred heritage of nationality into a compact whole, to which we must anchor our salvation. How fortunate is it that Russia has preserved ardent faith in those saving principles in default of which right conduct is impossible, without which an energetic and worthy life is unknown. A Russian devoted to his fatherland is as little willing to permit the subtraction of a single dogma from our Orthodox faith as he would be to allow the theft of a pearl from the crown of Monomachus. Autocracy is the main condition of Russia's political existence. In conformity with these two national bases is the third basis, equally important and equally strong—patriotism."

The official program of reaction—Orthodoxy, autocracy, and patriotism—had thus been formulated. To the present day this program constitutes the alpha and omega of official political wisdom; it is the program of the Russian theocracy, which declares the tsar's will a divine revelation, and deduces bureaucratic politics and administration from God's will thus revealed. In the first section of the fundamental law of 1832 (it became section 4 when the law was re-edited in 1906), autocracy is defined in the following terms: " The tsar of all the

Russias is an autocratic and absolute monarch. God himself commands us to obey the tsar's supreme authority, not from fear alone, but as a point of conscience." The theocratic relationship of the tsar to the church is thus defined : " The Russian tsar, as a Christian sovereign, is supreme protector and defender of the dogmas of the Greco-Russian faith and supervisor of Orthodoxy and of good order in general throughout holy church. In this sense he is spoken of as the head of the church " (Fundamental Law of 1906, Section 64).

Similarly Filaret, authoritative exponent of church doctrine under Alexander II, redefined the divine mission of the tsar in the sense of the *Stoglav*, saying : " God has given us the autocratic tsar after the image of His own universal dominion."

Peter the Great had proposed to establish at the academy a chair of natural law. Under Nicholas, in the year 1849, legal proceedings were taken against Solncev, professor at the university of Kazan, because he had deduced the principles of law from the healthy human reason instead of from the gospels.

To Peter, the church was no more than means to an end, and he was little concerned about his subjects' inner convictions. The same may be said of the empresses who succeeded Peter, for even under Catherine II reaction remained incomplete. In the reign of Alexander I closer supervision of the schools and of literature had begun ; and attempts had been made at the radical extirpation of Voltairism. Nicholas, however, was the first tsar to adapt his mentality to religion (though not indeed in every respect !) that he might be enabled to exploit the church effectively for his own ends. At his court there was no place for Krüdener and other prophets ; Photius was to rule men's minds. Even Photius was not a persona grata to Nicholas, and no long time elapsed before the tsar dismissed Arakčeev. The autocrat was strong enough to assume for himself the rôles of Photius and Arakčeev. There can be no doubt that his firmness of will contributed to make him appear the born autocrat.

By religion Nicholas chiefly understood fear of the Lord ; the Lord was conceived by him as an anthropomorphic being, simultaneously God and tsar. In the training colleges for cadets the priests were to suggest to their pupils that the greatness of Christ had been displayed above all in His submission to the government, in the way in which He had shown Himself

to be " an example of obedience and discipline." To the army
recruits, who had to look forward to a term of service lasting
twenty-five years, the chaplains preached : " God chooses men
for all professions as He wills. You are chosen and destined
for the military career by the will of God. . . . God wills that
you shall serve God and the great tsar as soldiers. . . . Before
you were born, it was God's determination that you should
become warriors."

Military discipline prevailed in the schools. Count Protasov,
a cavalry general, was appointed chief procurator of the synod
in 1836 and held office until 1855. Army discipline was introduced into the seminaries. " I know only the tsar," was his
favourite saying. Nevertheless he found place in the curriculum for the " revolutionary " natural sciences, since as a
soldier he recognised their value.

Nicholas desired in good earnest to realise Uvarov's formula.
Russia had the advantage over Europe of possessing the only
true faith, and uniformity of religious belief was to prevail.
The outcome of this ecclesiastical policy was the adoption of
harsh police measures against the raskolniki and other sectaries,
such as the dukhobors ; and it was the same policy which
induced the enforcement of religious uniformity.[1]

Enough has been said to show how Nicholas and his devoted
assistants were likely to receive the fierce protest which Čaadaev
issued in his *Philosophic Essay* (1836), renouncing, in the name
of religion, Uvarov's formula and Russian theocracy in its
entirety.

§ 18.

HARDLY had Nicholas become tsar when he abolished
the chair of philosophy at Moscow university. Driving
past the university on one occasion, looking very serious, he
pointed to the building and said, " There is the wolf's den."
The less developed universities were dealt with in accordance
with this estimate. A fuller activity had begun at the universities during the liberal epoch of Alexander I, with the issue
of the studies' ordinance of 1804, although even then the police
outlook towards these institutions was not abandoned. In
1835 Uvarov reorganised the universities in conformity with
his general program, making the study of theology and ecclesias-

---

[1] It may be recalled in comparison, that in Austria under Metternich the
Zillertal Protestants were driven from their homes.

tical history obligatory in all faculties. In 1850, owing to the alarm inspired by the revolution of 1848, certain disciplines, and notably the study of European constitutional law, were banished from the university as deleterious.; whilst philosophy was reduced to courses upon logic and psychology which had in future to be delivered by theologians, the pretext given for the change being "the blameworthy development of this science by German professors." The historian Granovskii was not permitted to lecture on the reformation. The number of students was restricted to three hundred. The object of universities was announced to be, "the education of loyal sons for the Orthodox church, of loyal subjects for the tsar, and of good and useful citizens for the fatherland." Not until the days of Alexander II. were these and other reactionary measures abrogated. Nevertheless, even during the reign of Nicholas one new university was founded, at Kiev in 1833, for these "wolves' dens" were indispensable to the civil administration and the army.

Reform of the higher schools (1847) was effected in conformity with the restrictions imposed on the universities. The study of classical tongues was discontinued lest youth should be corrupted by the reading of Greek authors who had written in republics. In this connection we may refer to a European example of the same way of thinking. Napoleon III held the like view of Greek authors, and Nicholas might have appealed to the French emperor for support. But reaction in Russia works and thinks from day to day only. In 1854 classical studies were partially reintroduced, the idea being that Greek and Latin fathers of the church would inspire refractory youths with due veneration for the official program.

The history of recent Russian literature is filled with stories of the oppression which great writers had to suffer under Alexander and still more under Nicholas. The work of Griboedov, Puškin, Lermontov, and Gogol was hindered in every possible way. Banishment was a frequent penalty. Books were mutilated by the censorship. Newspapers were suppressed, among them an opposition journal edited by Ryléev and Marlinskii, and entitled "Poljarnaja Zvězda" (Polar Star, a name chosen later by Herzen for his organ). In the "Moskovskii Telegraf," Polevoi adopted an opposition standpoint from 1825 onwards, and was able to continue his journalistic advocacy of liberal ideas down to 1834, but this

" Revue des décabristes " was in the end suppressed by Uvarov.
I record, not in jest but in earnest, that this minister for edu-
cation and president of the academy of sciences expressed a
strong desire that Russian literature should cease to exist.
Almost all notable authors suffered during the reign of
Nicholas. I have previously referred to Čaadaev and Ševčenko.
Bělinskii was unable to print his first drama. Puškin was
informed of the tsar's exalted disapproval.

Puškin's aristocratic inclinations led him astray not infrequently, and he experienced a shortsighted pleasure when
Polevoi's newspaper was suppressed, for he regarded the Moscow
journalist as " unduly jacobin." Polevoi was one of the non-
aristocratic *raznočincy* (unclassed, plebeian—§ 22). In 1845
the tsar seriously thought of having obstacles imposed to
the entry of the *raznočincy* into the higher schools.

The events of 1848 caused intense anxiety to Nicholas,
and a regular witches' sabbath of reaction was inaugurated.
The members of the Petraševcy group (the two Dostoevskiis,
Pleščeev, Durov, etc.) were all prosecuted ; measures were
taken against Saltykov ; Ostrovskii, Turgenev, Kiřeevskii,
Homjakov, and Herzen, successively fell into disfavour—
Turgenev's offence being an obituary notice of Gogol ! It
was forbidden to mention the very name of Bělinskii, and
those who wished to refer to him had to employ circumlo-
cutions !

Censorship was developed to an almost incredible extent.
There were twenty-two distinct censorships. Criticism of
the government and of official proceedings was absolutely
prohibited. Even those who at a later date were considered
pillars of reaction, even such men as Bulgarin, were now suspect
as revolutionaries ; Pogodin suffered the same fate ; to the
ultra - reactionaries, Uvarov actually seemed insufficiently
reactionary, and he had to resign his position as minister for
education. Upon a ministerial report which concluded with
the word " progress," Nicholas wrote the comment, " Progress ?
What progress ? This word must be deleted from official
terminology."

Such intensity of reaction was only possible because society
(" society " still meaning the aristocracy alone) had completely
abandoned the enlightened and humanitarian ideas that culminated in the decabrist revolt. Nicholas I was possible
because such men as Prince Vjazamskii and Puškin had become

afraid of " jacobinism," and because Gogol had been able to torment and starve himself back into Orthodoxy.[1]

§ 19.

UNDER Alexander and Nicholas, Russian national consciousness continually expanded, increasing finally to a highly developed chauvinism, of which Uvarov's program was the expression.

The development of Russian national consciousness dates back to the eighteenth century. In opposition to the reforms of Peter, and in opposition to the favouring of foreigners characteristic of the court, Russian peculiarities were defended against foreign influences by historians and other writers, by Tredjakovskii, Lomonosov, Sumarokov, L'vov, Lukin, Ščerbatov, and Boltin. There was a natural reaction against the extravagances of Gallomania, and antifrench feeling was accentuated in the struggles against the French republic and the Napoleonic empire. The Frenchified Russian aristocracy became alienated from the regicides, and Russian authors lost the taste for French literature and philosophy. The strengthening of national feeling in Russia was analogous to what was taking place in Germany, the movement being intensified in both countries by linguistic changes, by the purification of the native tongue. In Russia, as in Germany, there was a reaction against French supremacy.

For the Russians the problem of the written language was one of peculiar importance. Only through the reforms

[1] Readers who desire to gain a more detailed picture of Russian civilization during the reign of Nicholas, must refer to the official journals of the period and to those that were officially permitted. I must content myself here with a reference to "Majak" (The Lighthouse), which championed Uvarov's ideas from 1840 to 1850. The editor, General Buraček, mathematician and designer of ships, wished to favour an education that should promote the spirit of Russian nationalism ; western ideas were to be resisted or corrected, for European notions conflicted with the gospels. In his view, the west was a prey to Roman heathenism, and from this antichristian spirit had sprung revolutions, freethought, the reformation, and the papacy. The kingdom of God, the realm of the easterns, would rise gloriously upon the ruins of the western world. In conformity with this spirit, the periodical published contributions from gardeners and other simple men of the people, who displayed their genuinely Russian " mind-intelligence " (um-razum) in stories of apparitions and the like. The newer Russian literature was practically united in its condemnation of this organ of pure Russian patriotism. Puškin as well as Lermontov, and, it need hardly be said, Bělinskii, were opposed to it. But a few authors, such as Zagoskin, were delighted with " Majak."

of Peter did the Russian vernacular come into its kingdom in the literary world, for hitherto the old ecclesiastical language had been the vehicle of literature. The new written tongue made its way against the authority of the church. Whilst conservative writers continued to cling to the ecclesiastical language, and to write in a stilted scholastic style, progressive authors, those affected by European influence, gave expression to their thoughts in the folk speech. Old Russia and New Russia were thus respectively manifested in a linguistic dualism, which was further displayed in the differences between the Slavonic alphabet used in ecclesiastical writings and the new alphabet introduced by Peter. In many authors we find a mingling of tongues and styles. It is often said that it was Karamzin's merit, in opposition to Šiškov, to have secured the literary dominance of the Russian tongue, but this assertion involves a chronological error. The modern literary language was already employed by such writers as Fonvizin. It is an important fact that literature and language should have undergone so notable a growth during the first half of the nineteenth century.

As the campaign against French influences developed, a preference for all that was German became established. Moreover, the Frenchified Russians had their attention strongly drawn to Germany by the writings of Madame de Staël (1810), and subsequently by those of Benjamin Constant and others. German literature and philosophy spontaneously aroused a feeling of respect, and a similar respect was inspired by English literature, above all by the works of Byron. The spirit of French classicism was replaced by the spirit of Teutonic romanticism. It was especially in philosophy that German influence was predominant. If Russia had been French under Catherine and had still been French under Alexander, it became German under Nicholas. German ideas were adopted, even though the German language made little headway.

In spite of this influence, and indeed with the assistance of German romanticism, Russian national sentiment continued to grow. Just as the European romanticists extolled the middle ages and the Old Teutonic epoch, so in Russia did a cult of Old Russia arise.

It was not by any chance coincidence that at the time when Fichte was writing his *Address to the German Nation*, Šiškov in Russia should have been railing against French influences, and against Frenchmen, whom he regarded as a combination of tiger and ape. From Alexander, Šiškov secured political preferment owing to the publication in 1811 of his work *Considerations upon Love of Country*, and he took the place of Speranskii. In 1824 he was appointed minister for education, being guided in this position by the principle that knowledge " in default of faith and simplemindedness " (Šiškov was a defender of serfdom) was injurious to the nation. Universal education would do more harm than good, and the immoderate diffusion of scientific culture was likewise deleterious. Even Filaret's catechism fell under the ban of Šiškov's censorship because the quotations from Holy Writ were in the Russian vernacular instead of church Slavonic.

Numerous writers vied with Šiškov in the idealisation of Old Russia. Karamzin, generally recognised as the chief of Russian historians, voiced the praises of oldtime tsarism and aristocracy. Deržavin, Zagoskin, Marlinskii, Polevoi in his later phase, together with the previously enumerated adversaries of Gallomania—all glorified Russia as contrasted with the west. The discovery in the year 1800 of the twelfth-century saga, *The Lay of Igor's Raid*, strengthened this tendency in poesy and imaginative literature. No long time elapsed before Russian national sentiment waxed so intense that Polevoi was able to Russify Turgot's phrase " patriotisme d'antichambre," and to speak of *kvaspatriotizm*.[1]

The west contributed in no small degree to this intensification of Russism. To Europe, Russia seemed interesting and new, and speedily secured admirers. Peter, the first tsar not merely to visit Europe but to make a cult of European ideas and institutions, became an object of wonder and admiration. Catherine, as already stated, was even more greatly admired, notably by Voltaire and Herder. Klopstock sang the praises of Alexander I, who was regarded by Madame de Staël as the " miracle of Providence," and many joined with these writers in acclaiming the saviour of France and Europe. Not merely was Russia interesting to Europeans, but, by a not unnatural illusion, she loomed with a false grandeur in the minds of the civilised and hypercivilised inhabitants of Europe, whose Rousseauism led them to imagine that in uncivilised Russia they had discovered the simple natural conditions for which they yearned.

[1] *Kvas* is a cheap effervescing beverage brewed from rye and malt (" champagne de cochon ").

We must never forget that in the west Rousseau as well as de Maistre had passed sentence of death upon western civilisation. Rousseau's hostility to civilisation had gained wide acceptance. It was not surprising that the Russians should adopt these ideas also from their teachers and masters. For this reason not reactionaries alone, but men of progressive inclinations as well, sermonised about the " corruption " of the west.

To a certain degree, Russian national sentiment was intensified by the awakening national feeling of the western and southern Slavs. Slavism or panslavism struck roots in Russia as elsewhere—not in official Russia, but to some extent among the intelligentsia and among the common people. As far as the last were concerned, this arose solely from religious sympathy with the Orthodox southern Slavs, struggling for liberation from Turkish dominion.

Alexander I aimed at the partition of Turkey. Constantinople, the cradle of Russian Christendom, was to become Russian. This design, however, was frustrated by Napoleon. But Napoleon, in his turn, was shattered against Russia, against the third Rome. In the political field, as well as in the domain of civilisation, Russian sentiment turned against France as the home of the revolution, and Alexander became leader of the holy alliance.

This strengthening of national sentiment must be taken into account by those who wish to understand, not merely the origin of the reaction under Alexander and Nicholas, but also the wide diffusion, the intensity, and the duration of the movement. We shall see, on the other hand, how love for the peasantry became associated with this Russism. The true Russian essence was discovered in the peasant, in the man of the common people, and a distinction came to be drawn between the folk and the nation. Democratic and socialistic influences were here at work, for the people were contrasted with the upper classes, with the aristocracy, the intelligentsia, the bourgeoisie, and even with the state.

§. 20.

DESPITE the reactionary increase of chauvinism and exclusivism in the economic field, Alexander and Nicholas were compelled to promote the Europeanisation of Russia. Agriculture, and still more industry, had to seek models in Europe. To some extent reaction positively favoured this Europeanisation, in so far as " Enrichissez-vous, messieurs " is the doctrine of every reaction.

Commerce had had its importance even in Old Russia, in the Russia of Kiev and of Novgorod. In the realm of Muscovy, and above all in the capital, trading considerations were dominant in the organisation and spread of home industry and of manufacture. On into the seventeenth and eighteenth centuries foreign trade consisted mainly in the export of natural products (honey, bees-wax, furs, and the like, but also linen and hempen textiles), the compensatory imports being European manufactures (arms, textiles, commodities of art and luxury, wines, etc.). In the year 1653, goods to the value of more than one million roubles were imported by way of Archangel, and it must be remembered that at that time the purchasing power of money was far greater than now. In the days of Muscovy the import of Europeans had already begun, and the inconsiderableness of the exports was in part dependent upon the fact that European merchants and handicraftsmen were settling in Moscow.

Peter energetically supported the development of manufacturing industry, which had been initiated by the mercantile classes, and this resulted in the growth of what are often termed "artificial" manufactures—meaning manufactures fostered by the state, and especially to supply the needs of the army.

In the reign of Peter the originators of manufacturing enterprise were mainly merchants, but a few of them were landowners. Labour was recruited from among the serfs, and here the noble landowners with private factories on their estates had an advantage, for their workmen belonged to them as serfs, whereas the owner of an ordinary factory had to procure labourers from a landowner. It is true that Peter made the adscription of serfs to the factories possible, but during the eighteenth century the number of the factories owned by nobles as hereditary property increased, more especially seeing that the state did so much to protect the nobles, in their manufacturing enterprises as well as in other ways.

The obrok relationship of many of the serfs was favourable to the growth of a class of factory workers. The peasant who paid obrok, a yearly sum due on account of the utilisation of land placed at his disposal by his lord, had more personal freedom than the peasant liable to the corvée.

A class of free operatives early came into existence side by side with those who remained serfs, so that at the opening of the nineteenth century about one half of all operatives were freemen. The employment of free workmen was more profitable to the entrepreneur, and for this reason the liberation of the peasantry became a demand of those who desired the strengthening of manufacturing industry.

In proportion as manufacture developed under Alexander, and in proportion as European technical skill found place in the factories, the opposition between agriculture and industry, and also the reciprocal dependence of agriculture and industry, forced themselves on the attention. Down to the present day, agrarianism and industrialism have continued to find exclusive champions. In Russia, as in the west, there were protectionists and free-traders, and members of both parties advocated the maintenance of serfdom. In conformity with his general foreign policy, Alexander adhered to the continental system, but Russian conditions and the increasing need for manufactured articles unobtainable in Russia gave the impulse towards a more liberal tariff policy. Simultaneously, Russian manufacturing industry underwent modifications in a similar direction, the operatives being more and more generally recruited from among the free and comparatively mobile elements in town and country. In 1825, fifty-four per cent. of the workmen were engaged by free contract.

Under Nicholas I, industry made rapid progress, Moscow and its environs becoming the centre of the growing industrialisation and capitalisation, especially as regards textiles. Nicholas declared that serfdom in Russia prevented commerce and industry from flourishing as they might otherwise have done. He had derived this opinion from Storch, his teacher in political economy, the most notable adherent in Russia of Adam Smith. It is significant of the political condition of the country that Storch's leading work, *Cours de l'économie politique*, could not be published in Russian, although the tsar shared the author's views. For a long period the official tendency in political economy had been to favour the agrarian outlook on industry, for it was still held that agriculture was a " natural," manufacture an " artificial " source of popular well-being, and manufacture therefore was no more than tolerated. None the less, manufacturing industry underwent notable expansion during Alexander's reign.

The development of home industries long proceeded side by side with that of industries pursued in factories. Some of the home industries were devoted to the satisfaction of everyday needs, but others were a domestic form of industrial enterprise. Not until the introduction of modern machinery and until the growth of railway communication, with its facilitation of exchange of commodities, was the parallelism of development between home industry and large-scale manufacture disturbed. The time when this change began coincided with that in which Nicholas was preparing for the liberation of the peasantry.[1]

§ 21.

THE reaction under Alexander and Nicholas was incompetent to arrest the development of modern Russian literature and journalism.

Romanticist sentimentalism and mysticism, replacing Voltairist classicism, accommodated themselves in the persons of their most notable exponents, Karamzin and Žukovskii,

[1] The following figures give a fairly accurate picture of the growth of large-scale industry in Russia :—

Year.	Number of Factories.	Number of Workmen.	Value of Manufactures in Millions of Roubles.
1765	262	38,000	5
1801	2,423	95,000	25
1825	5,261	202,000	46
1854	9,944	460,000	160
1881	31,173	770,000	998
1893	22,483	1,400,000	1,760
1896	38,401	1,742,000	2,745

According to another statistical table, compiled to 1861, the figures are :—

Year.	Number of Factories.	Number of Workmen.
1762	984	—
1796	3,161	—
1815	4,189	172,882
1843	6,813	466,579
1861	14,148	522,500

to the system of general reaction ; but willingly or unwillingly the more vigorous minds took another direction, negating the principles of the official and social reaction.

The lyricism of the epoch, finding expression in the works of Puškin and the so-called Pleiad, was a sign of the times. Forbidden political activities, men were turning their attention more and more inward, and this gave rise to reflective, analytic, and critical lyricism. It was characteristic that these moods should secure their most effective expression in verse, for modern prose—the novel—originated later. Besides Puškin, we have such notable poets as Batjuškov, Venevitinov, Barjatynskii, Jazykov, and Ryléev. Their poems are concentrated thought, philosophy in lyric form. Far-reaching analysis and criticism of life and its relationships had begun. Griboedov's *The Misfortune of being Clever* (1822–1823) is a penetrating critique of the Alexandrine age. Beside Griboedov the satirist may be placed the fabulist Krylov, who likewise after his manner probed the wounds of society. Puškin, more than all, in his *Onĕgin* (1823–1831) held up a mirror to his time.

The leading writers of the new school were more or less closely associated with the decabrist revolt. Ryléev atoned on the gallows for his endeavour to be a poet and citizen. Marlinskii, and in especial Griboedov, were privy to the plot. Puškin, directly questioned by Nicholas as to whether he had participated in the decabrist rising, returned a definite answer in the affirmative.

This peculiar analytical school of literature, known as "accusatory," continued under Nicholas. Puškin's analysis was carried forward by Gogol in *The Inspector-General* (1836) and *Dead Souls*. Lermontov belonged to the same school (*A Hero of our Time*, 1840). The tsar, who permitted *The Inspector-General* to be staged, laughed heartily at the play, although he might well have fitted on the cap.

Under Nicholas, in addition to Puškin and Gogol, the other great representatives of the newer Russian literature were growing to maturity, and began to become known towards the close of the reign : Dostoevskii, Tolstoi, Turgenev, Gončarov, Ostrovskii, Nekrasov, Grigorovič, and Pisemskii.

During the reaction whilst Alexander I and Nicholas were on the throne, the peculiarly Russian criticism typified by the writings of Bĕlinskii developed side by side with ordinary literature. In the reign of Nicholas, political and sociological journalism began. To sum up, that which is commonly spoken of as modern Russian literature, the Russian literature that is generally recognised as part of world literature, took its rise under Alexander and Nicholas. To-day, with inexact chronology, Russians continue to speak of " the forties," and of the " idealists of the forties." If Russian literature be esteemed for its characteristic realism, we have to admit that a factor in the development of this realism was the practical trend of the reaction under Alexander and still more under Nicholas.

Herzen describes the age of Nicholas as an extraordinary period of outward slavery and inward freedom. It cannot be denied that this inward freedom which, as we shall see, was extolled by the slavophils, and which even men of the west admire, was to a degree the outcome of that political abstinence which absolutism enforces. The " superfluous man," who plays so notable a part in the Russian literature of succeeding reigns, was born under Nicholas, if not before.

§ 22.

IT is characteristic of Nicolaitan Russia that under the theocratic oppression of Uvarov's system there germinated the philosophic and political ideals and tendencies which persist and are undergoing further evolution to-day. Through alienation from France, those Russians who longed for culture had their faces directed towards Germany, and French enlightenment was amplified by German science and philosophy. Politically, in fact, the Russians had exchanged bad for worse. But Nicholas and his henchmen of the Uvarov type were incompetent to understand that the Berlin lectures of a Schleiermacher or of a Hegel and his disciples (which the Russians might attend with exalted approval), that acquaintance with German literature and philosophy, would have a more persistent effect than acquaintance with the writings of Voltaire.

Attendance at German universities began in the eighteenth century, for it was natural that German professors and academicians summoned to Russia should induce some of their students to visit Germany. At the German universities the Russians studied various disciplines, devoting themselves above all to the officially demanded economic, legal, and technical culture, mining being the most important subject under the last head   Widespread was the influence of Haxthausen, who visited Russia in 1843 to examine the Russian mir and Russian economic conditions in general. Apart from their theoretical studies, it was inevitable that Russian students in Germany should be influenced by German philosophy and literature and by the political tendencies dominant in academic and cultured society. The philosophy of Kant and of Fichte had little direct influence in Russia, but the influence of Schelling and of Hegel was extensive. It was especially owing to the thoroughness of its theory of cognition, to its moral earnestness, and to its bearings upon ethics and practical conduct, that German philosophy owed its power in Russia. Schelling's aesthetics played a part in the development of Russian literary criticism ; and Schelling and Hegel, with their philosophy of history, did much to promote the foundation of Russian philosophy of history.

Especially notable was the success in Russia of the Hegelian left and, as we shall see, of Feuerbach.

German poets, too, had far-reaching influence. The writings of Lessing, Schiller, Goethe, and those also of E. T. A. Hoffmann and others, in conjunction with the writings of the German philosophers, positively revolutionised Young Russia. As Turgenev phrased it, the intelligentsia plunged out of its depth into the " German sea " of philosophy ; and he shrewdly characterised the practical needs of Young Russia with the words : " In philosophy at that time we sought everything in the world except lucid thought."

In the circle of the Moscow Schellingites, Odoevskii and his associates founded in the year 1824 " Mnemozyna," the first Russian philosophical periodical, which came to an untimely end owing to the decabrist rising.

The Hegelian left influenced progressive Russians in the direction of new France. Apart from this, intimate relationships with France had still continued, and widespread knowledge of the French tongue facilitated the influence of French philosophy and literature. The effect of French socialism was powerful. Saltykov gives the following account of French influence in Russia towards the close of the forties (1846–1847) : " From France, not of course from the France of Louis Philippe and Guizot, but from the France of Saint-Simon, Cabet, Fourier, Louis Blanc, and above all George Sand, we derived a faith in humanity ; France irradiated to us the conviction that the golden age lies not in the past but in the future."

Saltykov did not stand alone in his day as pupil of European socialists. Annenkov the critic wrote similarly concerning the powerful leaven of French socialism among the younger Russians. Identical, too, were the accounts given by J. J. Panaev, A. P. Miljukov, and other writers. From 1845 onwards there gathered round the publicist Butaševič-Petraševskii a circle of authors who became known as the Petraševscy. To this group belonged Dostoevskii, Bělinskii, Pleščeev, Apollon Maikov the poet and his brother Valerian the critic, Danilevskii, subsequently noted as a slavophil, and many others. The abolition of serfdom, the enfranchisement of literature and journalism, and the reform of judicial procedure, were standing topics of lively discussion. Petraševskii was an enthusiastic disciple of Fourier and Saint-Simon.[1]

The socialisation of literature was likewise indicated by the increasingly democratic tone of books and periodicals. In former days writers had belonged almost exclusively to the aristocracy, but now their ranks were recruited from the middle classes as well. Sons of impoverished nobles, sons of priests, officials, and merchants, became men of letters ; and there were even a few proletarian authors, as for instance Polevoi. This democratisation of literature and journalism was deliberate, as we learn from Marlinskii as well as from Polevoi, and above all from Bělinskii.[2]

The democratisation of literature and journalism had, further, peculiar social significance for Russia, inasmuch as it led to the constitution of the intelligentsia as a distinct caste. Down to our own day the definition of this concept remains an unsolved problem of Russian criticism and philosophy, but its first denotation was the oppositional intelligentsia.

In those days the influence in Russia of English philosophical thought was small. As has been shown, English con-

---

[1] Petraševskii, writing under the pseudonym of Kirillov, published a Dictionary of Foreign Terms. This non-committal title was to cover a species of progressive political encyclopædia, but the completion of the work was prevented by the arrest of Petraševskii and his friends. Petraševskii died in Siberia, but his comrades survived and returned to Russia.

[2] In this sense the Russians frequently speak of the entry of the *raznočincy* (plebeians) into literature. Glěb Uspenskii gives a casual definition of a *raznočinec* as " one who stands outside the professions and classes." In the dictionaries we are told that the *raznočinec* is " one without personal nobility belonging to no guild, and exempt from taxation."

stitutionalism helped to form the views of the decabrists and
their predecessors. Moreover, the Russians were interested
in the parliamentary reform of 1832, and still more in the
Chartist movement. But not until a later generation did
English philosophy come into its own in Russia. Carlyle
was the first philosophic writer whose works were widely known.
But long before this the influence of Byron had been considerable.

§ 23.

UNDER pressure of reaction a remarkable development
occurred in the literary movement of opposition and
revolution.

As a matter of course the schools and still more the universities were unsatisfactory to young men and were detested
by them, and but few of the professors were able to act as
leaders of youth or to form the mind of the rising generation.
Doubtless among the students, progressives were in the minority,
but at the outset the troops of opposition and revolution were
mainly recruited from academic youth. It has been characteristic of absolutism, and was above all characteristic of Russian
absolutism, that students should play so prominent a rôle in
all forms of opposition and revolution.

The insufficiency of the universities and of all other instruments of culture, in conjunction with the pressure of absolutism, resulted at an early date in making self-culture an
integral constituent of the progressive programme. During the
reign of Alexander, and still more during that of Nicholas,
there originated in loose association with the universities a
number of literary salons and small circles. Here persons with
like sentiments, or at least similar aims, forgathered. Here
theoretical problems were vigorously discussed, and before
long political and social topics were eagerly considered. These
circles were at the same time centres of propaganda. A natural
growth from the masonic lodges and secret societies, the circles
for self-culture subsequently developed into revolutionary
committees.[1]

---

[1] Renowned are the circles of Stankevič and Herzen, the former originating
ear y in the thirt es, the latter about 1842. The circle of Sungurov may likewise be mentioned. The members of this group were accused of forming " a
secret society associated with the decabrists." The legal proceed.ngs against
Sungurov and his comrades lasted nearly two years (1831–1833) and terminated

Down to the present day, Russian literature contrasts with that of the west by the way in which it abounds in self-tutored men. Nor was it by chance that such men were conspicuous during the epoch of the Alexandrine and Nicolaitan reaction —men like Polevoi and Bělinskii, the last-named being the writer to develop literary criticism into a weapon of opposition and revolution.

From the opening of the movement, the propaganda of progressive ideas was a leading aim of journalistic and critical literature, reviews coming to exercise great influence side by side with newspapers, and the leading aim of this literature being to popularise philosophy and new ideas.

Pari passu with the increase in reaction, the democratic literary opposition evolved into a revolutionary movement. Clandestine literature came into existence both at home and abroad. Works were circulated in manuscript, thousands of copies being made of Griboedov's comedies, for example, before Nicholas allowed them to be printed. Subsequently, secret presses were installed at home, and printing and publishing establishments came into existence abroad, the first of these being the Russian printing house founded in London by Herzen in the year 1853. Prohibited foreign works and Russian writings printed abroad were by an organised system clandestinely imported into Russia.

In this connection a word may be said concerning the suggestive method employed in the literature of opposition. In the earlier newspapers of Russia and in the novels and other books of that day we must read much between the lines. Veiled incitations are ofttimes more effective than plain language. Absolutism is not merely brutal, but stupid as well. Moreover, alike in St. Petersburg and Moscow reactionary journalism and literature were in every respect inferior to the literature and journalism of the progressives.

A movement of emigration was associated with the growth of clandestine literature. Emigration must be regarded as a permanent Russian institution. In Old Russia, during the days of the petty princes, we should speak rather of the persistence of a nomadic tendency ; but in the realm of Muscovy the political character of the movement had already become

quite à la Nicholas in the sentencing of the accused, some to quartering, some to hanging, and some to shooting, the punishments being then commuted to imprisonment.

apparent, as is evidenced by the case of Kurbskii. Reaction during the eighteenth century induced many Russians to emigrate, whilst in the nineteenth century the suppression of the decabrist rising was followed by a great increase in emigration. By its repressive measures (which failed to pay, even in the economic sense) the Russian government induced legions of Russians to take refuge in Europe, where they became Europeanised and were educated to be instruments of the revolution.

After the suppression of the decabrist revolt, constitutional government and the liberation of the peasantry remained the political ideals of the liberal opposition. N. J. Turgenev may be considered a representative of this political liberalism. Born in 1789, Turgenev was educated at Göttingen university and completed his political and administrative culture under Stein, to whom he had been recommended by the government. His *Attempt to Formulate a Theory of Taxation*, published in 1818, attracted wide attention. Judgment was passed on him by default for participation in the Welfare Society and in the decabrist movement, a death sentence subsequently commuted to one of imprisonment for life being passed upon him. Restored to civil rights by Alexander II, he paid two brief visits to Russia, but spent the rest of his life in Europe, dying in 1871. He advocated the constitutionalist ideas of the decabrists in countless French and Russian writings. Of his detailed memoirs the greater part remains unpublished. His relationship to the decabrists and his share in the movement requires further critical investigation.

His principal work, *La Russie et les russes*, was published in three volumes in 1847. Here Turgenev gives a history of his participation in the decabrist movement, writes a detailed criticism of the Russian administration, and formulates a scheme of essential reforms. He displays intimate knowledge of western literature and institutions, those of England, France, and Prussia. We note his familiar acquaintance with the plans of Speranskii, and we observe that he is in advance of that statesman in that he vigorously advocates the liberation of the peasantry. Turgenev pleads for the summoning of the zemskii sobor, which is to be granted legislative authority. The liberated peasants are to be given small plots of land. Living in Paris from 1833 onwards, he had become acquainted with the socialist or communist movement, and was unfavourable to it, though he recognised its importance, at least for Europe. He did not desire any organisation of labour in Russia ; constitutional government would suffice. The zemskii sobor was to have but one chamber, for the Russian aristocracy was not so important as the English ; suffrage was not to be universal. In addition, Turgenev demanded certain essential administrative reforms, especially as regards the administration of justice, the abolition of corporal punishment, local self-government, etc. As political writer, Turgenev was a man of many-sided culture, and was well versed in progressive and in reactionary literature. During the reign of Nicholas, he was the most efficient of the opposition publicists, was, it may be said, the only man of statesmanlike intelligence among the opposition before Herzen took the field.[1]

§ 24.

A MORE detailed account must be given of Nicholas' attitude towards serfdom. In political questions the emperor was a man of firm will, but as far as this social problem was concerned he displayed a vacillation strongly recalling the characteristics of his brother Alexander. As early as 1826 a privy committee was appointed to consider the matter, but nothing was done, although further privy committees were instituted in subsequent years. In 1841, and later, certain legal and administrative changes were made favouring the peasants, but the reforms remained almost without practical effect because they were so ill-conceived that the landowners were able to paralyse their working or even to turn them to advantage. Still, an attempt was made to reduce to written specifications the penal powers of the landlords, and it was forbidden to separate a serf from his family or to sell him apart from the land.

Nicholas recognised the seamy side of serfdom. Speaking

[1] At most this assertion must be modified by a reference to I. G. Golovin, who left Russia in 1844 and wrote against absolutism. His numerous historical works attracted some attention in their day, being rich in anecdotal details, and displaying the weaknesses of the court and the aristocracy ; but in political matters Golovin was conservative. To socialism and subsequently to nihilism he was far more strongly opposed than was Turgenev. Among his works may be enumerated : La Russie sous Nicholas I, 1845 (English translation, Russia under the Autocrat Nicholas the First (2 vols., London, 1846) ; Russia under Alexander II, 1870 ; Secrets of Russia, 1882; Russian Nihilism, My Relationships to Herzen and Bakunin, 1880.

of the large landowners, he remarked in the year 1847 that the aristocracy had rights in the soil but not in the men upon the soil. The alleged right to treat men as chattels had been secured solely through craft and deception on one side and ignorance on the other, and it was on account of serfdom that Russia was devoid of industry and commerce. It is recorded that upon his death-bed Nicholas commended the task of liberation to his son.

The reasons for the vacillation and indecision displayed by Nicholas are readily comprehensible. The tsar recognised that the foundation of his absolutism was serfdom. Count Uvarov, too, had made this exceedingly plain when he declared slavery to be the basis of aristocracy. According to Uvarov's conception of politics, autocracy, monarchy itself, had the same historic basis as the right to hold men in serfdom. Everything that had existed before the days of Peter had passed away, serfdom alone excepted, and to tamper with serfdom would be to shatter the entire edifice. Uvarov uttered warnings against any attempt to diminish the rights of the nobles over the serfs. Were this done, the aristocracy would become discontented and would seek compensation. The only source of compensation, said this tsarophil aristocrat, was to be found within the sphere of autocracy.

Other landowners, some of them friendly to the peasantry, recognised that there was an intimate connection between slavery, aristocracy, and tsarism. Such a landowner was Kiselev, who often discussed the matter with the tsar. Upon sentimental and rational grounds Kiselev favoured the liberation of the peasantry, but considered that it was essential to avoid allowing liberation to lead to democratisation. As regards the problem whether the enfranchised peasant should or should not be granted rights in the land, he recommended a middle course. The peasant should be given personal freedom, and in return for enfeoffment with a moderate area of land should have to perform definitely specified services. Kiselev recommended this plan because he considered that to liberate the peasants without giving them land would serve merely to create a class of proletarians, whereas to liberate them and at the same time to grant them absolute possession of the land they tilled would " destroy the independence of the nobility and would establish democracy."

Monarchy, and above all absolute monarchy, is no more

than a manifestation of aristocracy. However absolute his power, the tsar is merely par inter pares, and in ultimate analysis, as Uvarov clearly indicates, loyalty is nothing but loyalty upon conditions.

Nicholas was well aware of this, hence his Alexandrine vacillation in these ostensibly humanitarian designs, which were in truth the outcome of economic considerations. For his dread of democracy, Kiselev was rewarded with the title of count, and a prudent calculation led Nicholas to favour the interests of the nobles. During his reign a system of entail was established (1845), and it was characteristic of Nicholas that he was exceptionally free-handed in the distribution of the princely title.[1]

The peasants likewise understood the motives actuating their sovereign, and the consequence was that, side by side with the philosophic and political opposition of the progressive aristocracy, a social opposition came into existence, the opposition of " Orthodox " Russia, the opposition of the mužik.

Among the peasantry there arose a movement against the aristocratic great landlords, a movement that was not simply revolutionary, for it had definite social aims. During the reigns of Alexander I and of Nicholas there was persistent ferment among the peasantry, and it is unquestionable that many peasants sympathised with the liberal opposition and with the revolutionary movement. This is especially clear as far as the decabrist rising is concerned. The peasants were influenced by the opposition sentiments of the intelligentsia and the aristocracy, but their own economic and social distresses were yet more potent causes of discontent. Year after year, in the most widely separated districts, landowners were killed by the peasants, their mansions burned.[2]

[1] Paul created four princes; Alexander I, three; Nicholas, sixteen; Alexander II and III, none.

[2] In the archives of the ministry for home affairs during the reign of Nicholas we find reports of 547 jacqueries in the years 1828 to 1854. Another computation gives the following figures :—

Period.						Jacqueries.
1826–1830	..	..	..	..	..	41
1831–1834	..	..	..	..	..	46
1835–1839	..	..	..	..	..	59
1840–1844	..	..	..	..	..	101
1845–1849	..	..	..	..	..	172
1850–1859	..	..	..	..	..	137
Total	..	..	..	..	..	556

In addition, there were incessant mutinies. The military colonies on the frontier, reintroduced by Alexander I, could not be maintained. The troops and many of the officers were frequently in revolt, and it is further noteworthy that from time to time the soldiers rose against their officers as aristocrats.

In addition to these active symptoms of discontent, the serfs sometimes adopted methods of passive resistance, and a number of suicides occurred, officially recorded as instances of " sudden death." [1]

Finally, during the reign of Nicholas, serious labour troubles began. There had been disturbances in the labour world in earlier reigns, in those of Catherine II, Paul, and Alexander I ; but under Nicholas they became far more extensive.[2] In 1845 the first anti-strike law was promulgated. Nicholas' government watched with concern the increase of the proletariat, but the industrial interests of the capitalists and those of the state itself prevailed over the political fears of the police and the administration. In Russia, as in Europe, there were frequent attempts to prevent the establishment of new factories and thus to hinder an increase in the number of operatives, but the state was compelled to found factories of its own, and had often to support manufacturing industry in defiance of the aristocratic and agrarianising aims by which it was animated.

The intelligentsia, influenced by French socialist ideas, sympathised with the revolting mužiks. The eyes of Nicholas and his advisers might have been opened when, in 1848, the Petraševcy created the Fourierist league ; but Nicholas contented himself with sending Dostoevskii and the others to the scaffold, and surprising them at the last minute by commuting the death sentence to one of administrative exile.

Without exaggeration, 200 could certainly be added to this total   During the years 1855–1859, 152 landowners (among them 21 officials) were murdered, whilst there were 175 attempted murders.

[1] In the year 1841 for example, 1,622 such cases are enumerated, a very high figure for Russia and for that day. We are expressly told that after the liberation there was a notable decline in the frequency of suicide.

[2] In 1834, there occurred a great strike in Kazan, an acute manifestation of a struggle between the workmen and the factory owners which had been chronic since 1796. There were disturbances in 1817, 1818, 1819, 1820, 1823, and finally in 1834.

§ 25.

THE final outcome of theocratic policy and of the reaction under Alexander I and Nicholas I was the downfall of Sevastopol. Six years after the overthrow of the revolution in Hungary, Russia's sometime associates in the holy alliance made common cause with Turkey, which Alexander had desired to destroy.

It is not difficult to understand the effect which the Crimean defeat exercised upon theocratic power, an effect resembling that caused upon medieval minds by the failure of the crusades. Just as in earlier days Christians and Christianity had proved too weak to conquer their hereditary enemies, so now were Russian theocracy, Russian Orthodoxy, autocracy, and nationalism, compelled to capitulate to " degenerate Europe."

Orthodoxy, the essential basis of theocracy, was, indeed, in evil case if judged by its power over the Orthodox emperor-pope. Nicholas, like his brother Alexander, failed to find adequate consolation in the official creed. We learn from the testimony of his physicians that he harboured thoughts of suicide, and although he did not carry these into effect, during his last illness he hastened the end by thwarting medical assistance. His courtiers, who were playing cards when informed of his death, continued their game undisturbed.

No more in life than in death did Nicholas find moral help in his state church and its religion—unless we are to regard his cruelty and despotism as Christian manifestations. Was his private life Christian ? Was his relationship to his mistress Nelidov, Christian ? What are we to think of his confiscation of the estates and castles of the Polish aristocracy ? [1]

By the collapse of their traditional diplomacy and militarism, aristocratic officialdom and the court, hitherto content with veneer, were compelled to devote serious attention to internal affairs. What happened to absolutist Austria in 1859 and 1866, what happened to France in 1870 and 1871, happened now to Russia. The defeat at Sevastopol resulted from the bad equipment of the army, and from defects in leadership and military training. Russia's enemies were provided with modern artillery and small arms against the obsolete weapons of the Russians. The range of the Russian rifles was from 300 to 450 paces, that of the European rifles was 1,200 paces. The

[1] Cf. statistical data in § 68.

Russians had to fight steamboats with sailing vessels. In the days of the first Napoleon the Russians had been able to meet their enemies on comparatively equal terms, but now their schools were behind the age and their technical knowledge was consequently deficient. The army had been severely affected by deficiencies of administration. Bravery on the battlefield does not suffice to secure victory. For this end, highly trained officers and men, improved instruments of offence and defence, and an adequate supply of food, medicines, and stores of all kinds, are no less essential. There must be foresight. The history of the Crimean War teaches us how the inward corruption of theocratic obscurantism had affected army administration. When we study that history we realize the truth of Bělinskii's dictum concerning the whole regime of Nicholas I, that it was " a corporation of enthroned thieves and brigands."

A comprehensive survey of the entire period of reaction under Nicholas and his predecessors fills us with astonishment at the incapacity of the Russian reactionaries. We recognise how little they were competent even to promote their own interests, how unable they were to attain to so much as a partial grasp of Russia's historical evolution or to secure an organic picture of their country in its relationships with the world at large. Nicholas never ceased to regard revolution as the product of agitation, as the work of isolated demagogues and secret societies. His advisers took the same view. The crown and the government held that it was enough to enforce police methods of repression, mechanically imitating reactionary Europe. Nicholas followed the petty example of Metternich and his anti-revolutionary reaction, and followed it with identical results.

CHAPTER FOUR

LIBERATION OF THE PEASANTRY IN 1861.
ADMINISTRATIVE REFORMS

§ 26.

SEVASTOPOL ushered in the epoch of the " great reforms," for the reforms of 1861 and their consequences were thus named. Constitutional government was not introduced, but the peasants. were liberated and the administration had to be reformed. Similarly in Austria, the year 1848 heralded the liberation of the peasantry, but the constitution then inaugurated was ephemeral. Similarly after the battle of Jena, Prussia remodelled her administration, but a constitution was not granted until much later.

The majority of the population had in fact hitherto lived as slaves, for the tying of the peasant to the lord's soil, completed under Catherine, was practical slavery.

It is difficult to-day to realise even approximately the nature of Russian serfdom. Those familiar with the history of the institution are apt to confine their attention to its legal and economic aspects. It is necessary to grasp the moral and social implications of serfdom as it affected concrete life. We have to understand that the peasant was in actual fact another's property, soul and body ; that the lord could sell his serfs ; that down to the year 1833 he could at will break up the serf's family as irrevocably as death breaks it up, by selling an individual member apart from the family—for the serf, bound to the soil, could not follow the one who was sold, as the wives of aristocrats were able at their own charges to follow husbands exiled to Siberia. The serf was money, was part of the natural economy. The landowner could gamble away his " souls " at the card-table, or could make his mistresses a present of them. The slaves were at the absolute disposal of the lord, who was free to settle whether a gifted child should become cook, musician, or surgeon. The lord disposed likewise of his slaves' wives and daughters, deciding what couples might marry and what couples might not ; the lord's mansion was in many cases nothing but a harem. Terrible is the picture of serfdom given by the best authors in their reminiscences. An attentive reader of the older Russian literature will discern everywhere this peculiar moral and social background. Those who have observed and described Russian village and rural life make express references to the matter. "'Gryzlov,' said D.S., 'Marija Thedorova is making ready to go to Moscow. We need money. When I was driving through the villages I saw a number of children ; our chattels have been increasing in number ; take measures accordingly ! ' This signified that Gryzlov was commissioned to visit the villages of D.S., to seize some of the superfluous boys and girls, sell them, and hand the proceeds to the landowner." (Grigorovič, *Literary Memories*.) In the newspapers prior to 1861, such advertisements as the following were quite common : " For sale, a light carriage and two girls." Widely known was the girl market in the village of Ivanovka. Hither girls were brought from all parts of Russia and were sold even to Asiatic buyers.

Kropotkin, in his *Memoirs of a Revolutionist*, has recently given a detailed description of the moral effect of serfdom upon the Russian aristocracy. We have indeed to remember that slavery invariably exercises an influence upon slave-owner as well as upon slave. Every variety of slavery is always and universally twofold : as the master is, so is the slave ; as the slave is, so is the master. Both slaves and lords have servile souls. Herein lies the curse of slavery, that there exists a hierarchy of slaves, from the tsar at the top to the last village pasha at the bottom, a hierarchy of men who will not and cannot work because they are privileged to use their fellow men as instruments.

Herzen termed serfs " baptized property." Before Herzen's day, Gogol spoke of " dead souls." But Gogol was perfectly right when with all possible force he showed that Christian slavery was based upon the Bible. So Christian and so scriptural was the absolutist censorship that the publication of a Russian translation of *Uncle Tom's Cabin* was forbidden, lest Russian readers should be struck by the parallel between negro slaves and mužik serfs. Despite his close relationships with Nicholas, Žukovskii was forbidden to print the translation of Schiller's *Three Words of the Faith*—"Man is created free, and is free, even if born in chains." The tragic example of the poet Sibirjakov shows the limits imposed in Russia upon moral and spiritual freedom. Born in chains, what his lord valued in him was not his poetic gift, but his skill as pastrycook, the trade he had been taught. When Žukovskii and others became interested in the poet, and desired to purchase his freedom, compensation to the amount of ten thousand roubles was demanded.

A recognition of the social and moral bearing of serfdom made its abolition a primary demand of persons holding enlightened and humanitarian views. But these considerations were reinforced by economic calculation, which never ceased to demonstrate the comparative unproductiveness of servile labour. Finally, Russian aristocrats and landowners could not fail to understand the meaning of incessant jacqueries, château burnings, and assassinations.

Liberation of the peasantry was the pious aspiration of eighteenth-century humanists, of masonic and political secret societies, and above all of the decabrists. Not in vain was the death of Pestel; not fruitless were the sufferings of the exiles who languished in Siberia. Nor was it by chance that Prince Obolenskii, a decabrist, returning from exile in 1856, exercised in this matter a decisive influence upon Rostovcev, the counsellor of Alexander II and one of the leading promoters of this reform.

Uvarov's philosophy of serfdom fell with the fall of Sevastopol.

The history of the abolition of serfdom under Alexander II is brief but momentous. There was a fierce struggle between the progressives and the moderates, between the opponents and the supporters of the institution. The emperor's position was difficult, for with two exceptions (Constantine, Alexander's younger brother, and Helena Pavlovna, his aunt) all the members of the court were adverse to the reform.

After the conclusion of peace and the issue of the peace manifesto of 1856, the tsar seized the first opportunity to instruct the delegation of the Moscow aristocracy to consider the possibility of liberating the serfs. Following the path that had been trodden by his father, in 1857 he summoned a privy committee, but recognising the futility of this method, upon the first move made by the Lithuanian landowners on behalf of the liberation of the peasantry, Alexander issued a rescript recommending the formation of " preparatory committees " in the various administrative districts, publicity for the question being thus at length secured. The progressive press was not slow to seize its opportunity; in 1858 a central committee was appointed to settle the question; and on February 19, 1861, the manifesto of liberation was issued.[1]

The Russian aristocratic system, the work-shyness whose organisation was centuries old, had been broken down, and the struggle between light and darkness had ended in the triumph of light. The darkness had confused the intelligence of so great a man as Puškin, and had confused even that of Gogol; but speaking generally it redounds to the honour of Russian literature that the leading spirits of that literature were the most efficient adversaries of slavery. Modern literature combated slavery within the depths of the Russian soul. Towards the close of the forties, village life and the mužik became leading topics. The Village, 1846, Anton Goremyka (Anthony the Unlucky), 1848, both by Grigorovič, and A Sportsman's Diary, 1852, by Turgenev, belong to this period.

In his Literary Memories Turgenev tells us how he plunged out of his depth into the " German sea " to emerge purified and reborn, for he could no longer endure home life in Russia. " I had to move to a distance from my enemy, so that I might be able from a distance to hurl myself upon him with greater impetus. My enemy had a definite configuration, a known name : the enemy was serfdom. Under this name I subsumed everything which I should have to fight against to the day of my death, everything I had sworn never to make terms with. . . . Such was my Hannibal's oath, nor was I the only one to make it. I took my way to the west to enable myself to fulfil it better." Alexander II declared that the reading of 4 Sportsman's Diary had convinced him that serfdom must be abolished. In such matters Alexander was often a prey to self-created illusions, but the act was in itself of no less value even if he and his advisers were impelled

---

[1] Serfs acting as domestic servants had to be liberated within two years of the proclamation. The peasants were ordered to pay their lords the compensation due for emancipation in instalments spread over forty-nine years. The government, however, paid off the totals to the landlords in its own bonds, and collected the instalments from the peasants.

towards liberation by practical considerations. " It is better
to abolish serfdom from above than to wait until it is abolished
from below "—the words of the tsar liberator to the Moscow
nobles remind us of Catherine, and ring truer than the reference
to Turgenev.

§ 27.

THE favourable results of the liberation of the peasantry
were not immediately apparent either to the peasants or
to the landowners. The poet Nekrasov used the image of a
tightly stretched chain, which snapped under the tension,
one end striking the lord and the other the mužik. Both
for lord and for peasant, liberation was effected without intermediate stages, and a considerable time had to pass before the
peasant accustomed to service and the lord accustomed to
command could adapt themselves to new conditions. Moreover, the first economic and financial consequences were in
many cases unfortunate for both parties. All such libera-
tions have involved a certain period of disorder and confusion,
which has invariably been turned to account by speculators
of every kind. Not until a shorter or longer time has elapsed
do we find that the ideals and plans for which the reform was
brought about are to a certain extent realised.

Thus did it happen in Russia. If we are to appreciate the
essential nature of the Russian liberation we must remember
first of all that the position of the serfs was not everywhere
identical throughout the wide areas of Russian agricultural
land. The status of the serfs was very variously regulated,
and there were many degrees of serfdom. Speaking generally,
there existed the two main categories previously described,
but on closer analysis these may be subdivided into as many
as twenty varieties. The peasant owed the landowner either
personal service and labour (*barščina*) or else paid him yearly
dues (*obrok*). Work and dues varied according to the locality
and the circumstances of the time. The obrok was from
twenty to fifty crowns ; in some places there existed " half-
peasants," as they were termed, who paid their lords only half
the dues ; and there were other variations. Obrok was paid
either in kind or in money. In addition to the dues to his
lord, the peasant had to pay local and national taxes (poll tax).

Noteworthy was the difference between crown peasants
or state peasants and the peasants on private estates. In

1797, for the benefit of the imperial family, certain appanage estates were separated from the crown estates. The peasants upon the appanage estates were in approximately the same position as the crown peasants.

Before 1861 many of the serfs were extremely poor, but not a few were well-to-do, and some were even wealthy. Of the landowners, again, some were rich and some were poor. Not infrequently a serf would become a wealthy merchant or manufacturer, his relationship to the lord, who might be a much poorer man than himself, being thereby rendered unstable. One landowner would have thousands of " souls," in some cases as many as a hundred thousand ; others would have but a few hundred ; others again would have but two or three serfs, or perhaps no more than one. Two-thirds of all the landowners were in debt to the banks, for serfdom had been ruinous to landlord as well as to peasant.

Prior to 1861 the relationships had been further complicated by the differences in status between the crown and appanage peasants on the one hand and the peasants on private estates on the other. The crown peasants paid obrok, and were in most cases assessed at a lower figure than the private estate peasants. But there were different categories among the crown peasants ; and the peculiar position occupied by the odnodvorcy, or one-farm men, has already been described.

Nor must we forget that even before 1861 there existed a certain number of entirely free and independent peasants, men who had been liberated by the crown or by the landowner, men who had purchased their freedom, and so on.

In the year 1860, in the fifty administrative districts of European Russia, the number of male peasants was as follows :—

Crown peasants ..	..	..	..	10,340,000
Private estate peasants ..	..	..		11,910 000
Appanage peasants	..	..	..	870,000

Of the total population, 38·1 per cent were private estate peasants, 37·2 per cent were crown peasants and free peasants, and 3·4 per cent were appanage peasants.

The following table shows the percentage distribution of landed property before and after the liberation of 1861 :—

				Before liberation.	After liberation.
Crown estates ..	..	..	..	64·4	45·6
Private estates ..	..	..	..	30·6	22·6
Appanage	..	..	..	3·3	1·8
Free peasants and colonists	..		..	1·7	30·0

In the year of the liberation, only 140,000 landowners possessed serfs. But of these "landowners," from 3,000 to 4,000 owned no land, so that their serfs were merely personal servants.

It must further be remembered that even before 1861 the unfree peasant cultivated a small area of land for himself and his family, paying the landowner for the usufruct or discharging his dues in the form of labour. The land assigned to the peasants in 1861 was about one fifth less than that which they had previously occupied, the reduction being especially conspicuous in fertile regions where land had a high value. On the average each peasant received three to four desjatinas. In the north he was given seven desjatinas, in the steppes ten, in the region of the black earth no more that two desjatinas.[1]

There was one provision in the manifesto of liberation which led to the creation of a new social element of serious import, to the formation of a class of peasant proletarians numbering hundreds of thousands. This was the provision that peasants willing to content themselves with one fourth of the amount of land assignable to them (" gratuitous allotments " or " beggarly allotments ") would be immediately granted complete freedom by their lords. This scheme was a realisation of some of the older plans of enfranchisement, such as that of N. Turgenev.

When we remember that the peasant had to continue compensatory payments after the liberation, we shall not be surprised that he was discontented.

Finally, it is necessary to point out that the peasant was not granted full private ownership of the land, but could hold it only as communal property. In a sense the power of the mir over the individual peasant was thereby increased, for after 1861 the mir was responsible, not for the taxes alone, but likewise for the instalments of the redemption money.

By the obligation to pay redemption money the peasant was refettered to his lord, this condition of dependence persisting until the redemption money had been paid in full. Thus enfranchisement was in many instances retarded. The government had anticipated widespread disturbances among the peasantry in consequence of liberation, and took military measures accordingly. In actual fact, the peasant revolts which had been so frequent during the reign of Nicholas continued after the liberation. During the years 1861 to 1863

[1] The desjatina is 2·7 acres.

in twenty-nine administrative districts there were 1,100 jacqueries, many of which were suppressed by the military.

The consequence was that, soon after the issue of the liberation manifesto, numerous experts declared that the peasants had been given too little land and that the redemption money had been assessed at too high a figure. Nor was it radical publicists alone, such men as Čeryševskii and Dobroljubov, who spoke of the land hunger of the peasants. Even moderate writers, Kavelin for example, referred to the existence of an acute agrarian crisis, and demanded more land for the peasants. In 1881 (December 28th) the amount of redemption money was reduced. In 1882 the Peasants' Bank was founded, and further mitigations were introduced for the peasantry— although simultaneously the landowners' interests were not neglected, for the Nobles' Bank was founded in 1885, and the privileges of the peasants were restricted in various ways on behalf of the landed interest.

Declared opponents of liberation were not intimidated by the February manifesto. Organising their forces, they founded a periodical ("Věst"), placed all possible hindrances in the way of the realisation of the reform, and furthered an agitation on the part of the landlords to secure assistance from the state. Some of the social reactionaries who opposed liberation were advocates of constitutional government, but their thoughts went no further than an aristocratic representation by estates.

The liberation of the peasantry, as actually carried out, was the result of a compromise between the opponents and the supporters of serfdom and between the conflicting plans of the various parties. Whereas the peasants naturally desired their liberation to be accompanied by the assignment to them of the soil they tilled, no more than an infinitesimal minority of landowners favoured this idea. The best of the landowners proposed that liberation, if it was to be effected, should be accompanied by the granting of land to the peasants in return for compensation payable to the landowner by the peasant, by the state, or by both. In the Baltic provinces, liberation was effected without any grant of land, and the peasants had to rent whatever land they needed. Many landowners in other parts would doubtless have agreed to an arrangement of the kind, but even upon this matter there were conflicting currents. Some desired that the enfranchised peasant should have no land of his own at all; others were willing that he should be granted a small allotment ; others proposed a partial enfranchisement with a definite legal formulation of peasant right. The manifesto of 1861 aimed at meeting the landowners' wishes as far as possible.

Serfdom was abolished, and agrarian difficulties, which still persist, were the sequel of enfranchisement.

§ 28.

THE liberation of the peasantry rendered necessary a reform of the entire administration.

The landowner had lost his patriarchal and patrimonial status. He was no longer the privileged hereditary official of the tsar, the direct and indirect controller of the peasant, lord and economic exploiter. The demands of the decabrists, their constitutionalist designs put forward as supplementary to the liberation of the peasantry, the demands of N. Turgenev and Pestel, were partially realised under Alexander.

The first administrative effect of liberation was a mitigation of corporal punishment. In 1863, running the gauntlet, the use of the lash, and the branding of criminals, were simultaneously abolished. The use of the cane was continued ; not until 1904 did the volost courts cease to inflict sentences of caning, but the practice persisted in the penitentiaries. For women, corporal punishment was abolished, except in the case of administrative exiles.

In the year 1864 the new judicial procedure and the local government of the zemstvos were introduced.

Prior to 1864, state courts of law had indeed existed, but the nobility and the landowners had acted as judges, whilst the courts of first instance were in the hands of the police. It can readily be imagined how, in these conditions, justice was administered. The most important element in reform was the establishment of publicity in legal procedure. The judiciary was made independent of the executive, judges being declared irremovable. Justices of the peace were appointed and trial by jury came into use.[1]

The general effect of these reforms in the administration of justice may be gathered by the delight with which the opening of the new courts was everywhere hailed by the public,

[1] The appointment of justices of the peace to deal with minor offences was not universalised, being restricted in practice to the larger towns.

as in St. Petersburg on April 17, 1866. Some time, of course, elapsed before the new system was in full working order, and in certain regions its introduction was extremely slow. It was not installed in Kiev until 1881 !

The zemstvo constitution was likewise brought into force by gradations only, and in no more than thirty-four of the administrative districts in European Russia. The worst feature of the change was that absolutism and centralism endeavoured to maintain and to extend their wonted predominance. The lack of local efficiency furnished adequate cause for absolutist centralisation.

The towns were granted certain liberties somewhat later than the rural districts. The liberal aims of the townsmen had aroused considerable anxiety in the government, and the new towns' ordinance was not promulgated until 1870. A trifling humanisation of the military system in the spirit of the peasant enfranchisement was an even later reform. The serf had been sent into the army at the caprice of his lord. Once enrolled he had to serve for twenty-five years and to learn his duties under persons whose system of instruction was enforced by blows. The landowner selected for military service the sons of those peasants who were on his bad books. Further, his power in this matter had a money value, for the wealthier peasants and townsmen could naturally secure exemption by payment.

Arakčeev's military colonies were abolished in 1857. In 1874 universal obligation to military service was established, the term of service being reduced to fifteen years, of which seven had to be spent on active service. From among men who had attained military age, those actually required were selected by lot. Men of education were exempt.

In the finances, too, more order was secured. From 1862 onwards financial designs and the budget were made public, general attention being thereby directed to the problem of how health was to be restored to the chaotic national finances. After 1866, financial reports were published.

Certain reforms of taxation were made : the disastrous system of farming out the right to grant licences for the sale of alcoholic liquors was done away with in 1863, and in 1880 the salt tax was abolished ; but the burden of taxation was increased on the whole.

Nevertheless it proved impossible to do away with a deficit

during the reign of Alexander II. The Turkish war had been costly ; it was necessary to accelerate railway development ; money was needed for schools and for new institutions in general. In the year 1855 the regular revenue was 264,000,000 roubles ; in 1888 it had risen to 651,000,000 roubles. At the close of Catherine's reign, the national debt amounted approximately to 215,000,000 ; when Alexander I died the figure was 1,345,000,000 ; under Nicholas and his successor, although the finances were better administered, the increase in the debt was stupendous.

Educational reform likewise ensued. In 1863 a new studies' ordinance was issued for the universities, granting the academic senates fuller autonony and comparative freedom of teaching. The Nicolaitan regime was abandoned at the universities shortly after the accession of Alexander II. In the autumn of 1856, the faculty of law was once more allowed to resume the teaching of the constitutional law of European states, which had hitherto been banned ; more attention could be paid to philosophy ; were it only for practical reasons, educational policy was compelled to aim at the production of more efficient state servants and at the fuller elaboration of teaching energies. The students secured greater freedom, and in 1861 the obligation to wear uniform was abolished. The new statutes did not permit the formation of students' associations. Two additional universities were founded in the reign of Alexander II, that of Odessa in 1864 and that of Warsaw in 1869.

More was done than during the reign of Nicholas to promote the development of middle and other schools ; but owing to financial stringency public elementary schools, Russia's chief need, received less help than was universally demanded, and was desired even by the government. The newly founded zemstvos worked with especial energy on behalf of elementary schools, and the general interest in popular education brought notable educationists and authors into the field, such men as Pirogov, Ušinskii, Stojunin, Vodovozov, N. H. Korf, and also L. N. Tolstoi. The Russian public elementary school really came into existence solely as the outcome of the liberation of the peasantry. Before the liberation, the state was exclusively interested in the education of aristocrats and officials. A few writers, theologians in especial, boast that popular education was carried on in prepetrine Russia, but this assertion is erroneous.

The cadet schools were also improved.

An entirely new feature of this epoch was the inauguration of public education for women. After serfdom had been abolished it was necessary that the daughters of the growing class of cultured persons and the daughters of the nobility should have better tuition. There was an increasing demand for women teachers, women doctors—for skilled workers, without distinction of sex. Middle schools for girls (gimnazijas and progimnazijas) were established in 1869. Higher university training was rendered possible for women, at first by special courses, and subsequently (1878) by free admission of women to the universities. Before long, however, reaction became apparent in this field.

In general terms it must be said that all these " great reforms " were seriously defective because they were mere half-measures. The power of the centralised bureaucracy remained intact. The ancient caste system continued in operation, and thus the liberation of the peasantry failed to do all that progressive intelligences had anticipated. The segregation of classes which had characterised the Muscovite state persisted. The customs that had been established for centuries still dominated society.

CHAPTER FIVE

RENEWAL AND CONTINUATION OF THE NICOLAITAN
REGIME AFTER A BRIEF LIBERAL INTERLUDE.
GROWTH OF THE TERRORIST GUERILLA-REVO-
LUTION ; ALEXANDER II BECOMES ITS VICTIM.
ACCENTUATION OF THE THEOCRATIC REACTION ;
COUNTER-TERRORISM. ITS DEFEAT IN THE
WAR AGAINST JAPAN

§ 29.

RUSSIANS are still fond of speaking of " the sixties,"
and usually refer in this connection to " the forties " as
well. Unquestionably as a sequel of the liberation of the
peasantry and determined by that liberation, national energies
were unchained, and in all domains more vigorous activities
and endeavours became manifest. The changes resulting from
the reform of 1861 can be seen and measured in literature
and journalism. Censorship grew less severe, the bureaucracy had certain definite tasks to execute, by reform alone
could the army make head after its defeats. Ideas and programs, work and achievement, were generally expected,
demanded, and to some extent supplied.

The men whom Europe now counts as leading figures in the
Russian branch of world literature produced their most notable
writings during the reign of Alexander II and during the
opening years of that of Alexander III. The masterpieces
of Dostoevskii and of Turgenev were published under Alexander II ; and during this epoch Saltykov, Gončarov, Pisemskii,
Lěskov, Nekrasov, Ostrovskii, and L. N. Tolstoi, were also
active.

The rise of the so-called ethnographic literature, and in
especial of the imaginative analysis of folk life, is organically

connected with the liberation of the peasantry. In the late forties we have Turgenev and Grigorovič. Uspenskii, Zlatovratskii, and a number of novelists, must also be mentioned, men who studied the life of various regions in Russia, a country enormously variegated alike ethnographically and socially (Levitov, Jakuškin, Mel'nikov, Rěšetnikov, Pomjalovskii, and many others). All of those just named were " poets with a purpose," for the widespread distresses of the day forced upon thinking men an endeavour to overcome traditional evils and a desire to criticise proposals for reform. But besides the writers of this trend, there were a few men of note who inclined rather to cultivate art for art's sake, and among them I may name Aleksěi Tolstoi and Apollon Maikov.

After the death of Nicholas, the censorship, political and religious, became milder and more liberal. A. Nikitenko, author and censor, who had had personal experience of the bonds of serfdom (he had been liberated by his lord, Count Šeremetev, upon the recommendation of Žukovskii and others after he had already become known to the public), in his *Diary*, a well known work, indicated the accession of Alexander II on February 18, 1855, as the landmark of a new epoch. Now Nikitenko was well acquainted with the Russian censorship. It cannot be said that the government showed any undue haste to prove itself liberal. Preventive censorship upon large books was not abolished in the capital until 1855, nor until after the press had made special representations to the ministry for home affairs. But this much, at least, resulted from the preparatory work, during the first ten years of the new reign, for the liberation of the serfs and for the subsequent carrying out of that reform, that the ensuing reaction, whilst it could contest endeavours towards liberty, could no longer suppress these so effectively as had been possible under Nicholas.

Owing to the comparative freedom of the press and of literature, the various philosophical and historical trends, the various conceptions of Russia and of the tasks that lay before her, could develop more freely and could secure fuller expression under Alexander II. Ideas were now printed which during the reign of Nicholas had been discussed only in private.

During the reign of Alexander II and during that of his

successor, there existed comparative freedom for the literary expression of political and social ideas. The novel now became a forum for the sociological analysis of society and its evolution, verse yielding place to prose.

The position secured by criticism through the work of Bělinskii was maintained, and the opposition to official Russia was continued. In this connection must be mentioned the names of many authors unknown in Europe, those of Maikov and Miljutin, the Comtists, those of Družinin, Annenkov, etc. The realists of the sixties exercised great influence, above all Černyševskii, Dobroljubov, and Pisarev. Next to them comes Mihailovskii, whose work as critic continued for more than thirty years.

Conservative and reactionary literature was notably weaker than progressive literature, alike quantitatively and qualitatively.

Characteristic of the epoch and of its consolidating character are the historico-philosophical investigations which form the content and purport of Černyševskii's novel *What is to be Done?* whose title sums up the whole problem. The book in question is devoted to an account of these various philosophical doctrines, but in the present historical sketch no more than a brief reference can be made to the different trends.

The contrast between Russia and Europe, between Old Russia and New, between Moscow and St. Petersburg, is represented by two parties, the slavophils (Kirčevskii, Homjakov, etc.) and the westerners (Čaadaev, etc.). The počvenniki, those whose leading interest was the land (*počva*, soil), occupy an intermediate position ; so also do the narodniki, who take their stand upon the common people and upon the folk institutions of mir and artel.

Černyševskii marched forward to the adoption of western socialism ; so did Herzen, whose " Kolokol " was at this time exercising considerable influence abroad. Side by side with Herzen, and sometimes in conjunction with him, Bakunin became representative of revolutionary socialism and anarchism.

The conservative and reactionary tendency, led in the journalistic world by Katkov, found a spokesman in Pobědonoscev, and in Dostoevskii as well.

Alike practically and theoretically, the alternative between

Old and New Russia assumed a critical phase in the appearance of nihilism and in the discussion of these various revolutionary tendencies. Nihilism was peculiarly characteristic of the reform epoch of the sixties and of the next decade. The philosophical significance of Dostoevskii is to be found in his contest with nihilism. In a special section of the present studies independent treatment of this question will be undertaken.

It is further necessary to point out that theology, too, was influenced by the philosophic movement. Symptomatic of the time was the resignation of a professorship of theology in the year 1854 by Eliseev, subsequently a noted journalist. Buharev was one of the most distinguished liberal theologians of the day. In 1846 he had become monk and professor, but in the year 1863 he abandoned monasticism, relinquished his priesthood, and married, supporting himself precariously by journalistic work. To these external details of his personal history there corresponded a rich inner spiritual life, a struggle against faith in the letter, and a development of inclinations towards the world and worldly literature forbidden to the monk. Buharev's superiors and the synod opposed his teachings, with the assistance of reactionary writers, and above all with that of Askočenskii.

Western philosophy and literature, which had so powerfully affected the Russians during the days of Alexander I and Nicholas, continued its work, its influence being yet further increased by the vigorous impulsion of English philosophy. Positivism, in especial, secured in Russia numerous and congenial adepts. The positivism of Feuerbach, by which Herzen, Bělinskii, and Bakunin were decisively affected, was now deliberately carried a stage further under the influence of French and English positivism, and in particular under that of Auguste Comte and John Stuart Mill. The writings of Spencer and Darwin and of the evolutionists in general, likewise came before long to play their part.

From 1848 onwards German philosophy was continually at work through the writings of Hegel and Feuerbach, and through those of the anti-reactionary materialists, Vogt, Büchner, and Moleschott. During these years Schopenhauer had great influence in Russia.

The French socialist doctrine of the thirties and the forties was after 1848 rendered more precise (if I may use the term) by German socialism. Lassalle's thought was based upon that of Hegel; the thought of Marx and Engels was based upon that of Hegel and Feuerbach. As thinkers and socialist organisers, Lassalle, Marx, and Engels exercised decisive influence upon the more revolutionary Russians, and especially upon those who were in a position to study socialistic organisation abroad. Russian emigrants became acquainted with, and in part received their political education in, the international and the working-class organisations founded by Lassalle and the Marxists.

Like Marx and Engels, Stirner wielded some influence in Russia, but that of French socialism was more extensive.

The influence of Young Germany must here be given due weight, not forgetting its manifestations in the field of literature, and Heine's writings in especial. But all the similar movements had their effect upon Young Russia: Young Italy; Young Poland; the Mazzinist organisation known as Young Europe; and the analogous movements in France, Belgium, Spain, etc. Even before 1848, but still more after that year, during the epoch of reaction, Russian political refugees entered into association with German and other refugees in Switzerland, Paris, and London.

All these influences continued to affect the aristocracy, but the bourgeois intelligentsia was now increasing notably in numbers. The intelligentsia reacted upon the mužik, inclining the latter to the adoption of similar ideals. The mužik may be conservative or progressive, but is in any case oppositional and even revolutionary in outlook, as is shown by frequent revolts. The mužik is as a rule illiterate, but reading is not everything. He thinks and observes, doing these things often no less successfully than his cultured teachers. The mužik notes the technical changes and improvements rendered possible by scientific progress; he has a word with an official, an officer, a merchant, a commercial traveller; he hears what is going on in " Piter " (St. Petersburg); sometimes he reads, and passes on the result to his fellows. Ex-villagers return to see him from the town; as workman and as soldier he makes the acquaintance of a wider world; he has personal experience of the arbitrariness of officials and the indifference of popes; he experiences hunger and suffering, and again suffering and hunger—he becomes oppositional and revolutionary.

When, therefore, at the beginning of the seventies the members of the intelligentsia originated the movement " towards the people," among whom they lived as teachers, writers, workmen, etc., and when they began their practical propaganda of enlightenment, they found the soil prepared. It is an error to assert that the stimulating activities of these narodniki had no effect.

Thus the Russian mužik, no less than the intellectual, had his crisis to traverse ; and in the case of the peasant it was natural that this crisis should manifest itself chiefly in the domain of religion. The oppositional influence of the raskol has never ceased, but of late there has been superadded the influence of European Protestantism, which has begun to affect large masses of the peasantry. During the sixties stundism became diffused in the south ; during the seventies came stundobantism (now neo-stundism) ; other and analogous religious movements arose among the common people. In St. Petersburg, Lord Radstock and above all Paškov secured adherents. The religious aims of Tolstoi gathered all these tendencies to a single focus as it were, and for Tolstoi as for so many others the mužik was teacher.

Thus did the religious rationalism of the mužik take its place beside the positivism and nihilism of the intelligentsia. In his novel *Pavel Rudenko, the Stundist*, Stepniak (Kravčinskii) gives an accurate picture of this association, describing the way in which the believing stundist mužik makes common cause with the revolutionary student.

§ 30.

IN the political field, during the reign of Alexander II, progressively minded persons aimed at the inauguration of a constitution.

This idea was in conformity with decabrist tradition, which had been vigorously maintained by such refugee journalists as N. Turgenev and Herzen. As we have learned, in Russia as elsewhere, revolutionary political hopes were awakened by the year 1848, and were not destroyed by subsequent reaction. On the contrary, the desire for popular representation was stimulated by European example, for at the end of the fifties even reactionary Austria had to accept constitutionalism. The net result of 1848 was to teach the Russians that not the

French alone, but likewise the Prussians and Germans beloved of Nicholas and his successor, had effected a revolution. After the liberation of the peasantry, Russia and her official hereditary enemy Turkey remained the sole absolutist countries, if we except a few insignificant freaks like Mecklenburg.

In the beginning of the sixties discontent with the internal situation became apparent in all strata and classes of the population. The liberation of the peasantry aroused considerable excitement upon its own account, and its very incompleteness served to increase dissatisfaction. The mentality of those who regarded as inadequate the comparatively extensive liberties that had been secured, is not difficult to understand. The granting of these liberties in all spheres of administration stimulated the desire for larger freedom.

It was at the universities that dissatisfaction first broke out, the initial political demonstration of the students occurring in St. Petersburg in 1860, at the grave of the actor Martynov. Similar demonstrations followed in other universities, the result being that in the year of liberation the university of St. Petersburg was closed. Most of the dismissed students adopted revolutionary views. Mihailov, a man of letters, was arrested; an author named Avděev was expelled from St. Petersburg; excitement grew. The first constitutionalist secret society, "Velikorus'" (Great Russia) was founded in 1861. It had a secret printing press and issued a few leaflets. In 1862 came into existence a secret society known as "Zemlja i Volja" (Land and Freedom, the name adopted also by a later and better known society). *An Address to the younger Generation* had been issued as early as 1861. The proclamation *Young Russia* now appeared, preaching revolution and a socialist republic. Černyševskii and Pisarev were arrested.

Unquestionably this movement was associated with the preparations for the Polish rising.

In some of the administrative districts members of the nobility publicly advocated the establishment of constitutional government, and sent memorials to the tsar asking that the zemskii sobor should be summoned. The nobles of the Tver district adopted this course in 1862.

The suppression of the Polish revolt was the prelude to a declared reaction, of which Katkov was the chief leader amongst men of culture. The Poles were deprived of their constitutionalist rights; in 1864 Polish administration, pre-

viously distinct, was amalgamated with that of Russia ; simultaneously the peasants were openly supported against the
Polish aristocracy. Reaction was intensified because many
Russians participated in the rising ; and also because Herzen,
influenced by the suggestions of Bakunin, espoused the cause
of the Poles.

Russification speedily extended from Poland to other nonrussian areas, beginning in 1869 with the Baltic provinces.

It is true that administrative reforms were undertaken,
but the way in which they were carried out was soon influenced
by the spirit of reaction. The resolute character of the retrograde movement was displayed in 1864 by the condemnation
of Černyševskii, the most popular of progressive writers, who
was exiled to Siberia. Pisarev was sentenced to imprisonment in a fortress. The secret society of which Karakozov
was a leading spirit was now formed, and in 1866 took place
the first attempt on the life of Alexander II. Whilst reaction
became intense and more deliberate, opposition in its turn
became more energetic and increasingly revolutionary. It
grew ever plainer that the tsar was infirm of purpose, and his
autocratic inclinations could not long be veiled in liberal
phraseology. In 1869, Nečaev the Bakuninist was engaged in
anarchistic plots which ended in the assassination of one of
his own comrades, a student named Ivanov. Nečaev secured
few adherents among progressive and revolutionary youth
in general ; but in the early seventies began the propagandist
activity of the cultural societies, the first group under Čaikovskii
being exceptionally well organised. The political influence of
western Europe became yet more marked. The example of
the Paris commune, the growth of socialism and anarchism,
and the widespread agitation carried on with the aid of clandestinely imported literature, exercised a stimulating and encouraging effect. An additional factor in the movement was
the acquaintanceship young Russians had obtained with
Europe and European universities. During the reign of
Alexander II attendance at western universities was at first
permitted on a more liberal scale than had been the case under
Nicholas, and young people were not slow to avail themselves
of the privilege. Russian students of both sexes visited Zurich
by the hundred. In 1873 an order for their recall was suddenly
issued, and Russia was thereby peopled by large numbers
of persons belonging to the cultured opposition. From 1872

onwards propagandist activities were vigorous among the peasants (" towards the people ") ; propaganda among the operatives dates from a year earlier.

It can by no means be said that these efforts were guided by a uniform spirit. Individual groups (Societies for Self-Culture and Practical Activity) consisted of adherents of Bakunin, Herzen, Lavrov, and Tkačev. The teachings of the narodniki, socialism and communism, liberalism and anarchism, were frequently disseminated by members of one and the same circle.

From 1874 the government openly attempted to suppress the entire movement. Hundreds of young men and women were imprisoned. After a lengthy term of preliminary arrest, which would sometimes last for years, the accused were tried in batches (" the trial of the fifty," " the trial of the hundred and ninety-three," etc.).

A new revolutionary party known as " Zemlja i Volja " was organised in 1876. The war with Turkey in 1877 increased revolutionary sentiment, for the incapacity and corruption that prevailed under the absolutist regime were continually coming to light. The bold deed of Věra Zasulič took place early in 1878 at the very time when the Russian army was close to Constantinople, and this gave the signal for open war. The shooting of General Trepov, prefect of St. Petersburg, had an exceptionally powerful effect because Věra Zasulič was tried by jury and acquitted. The shooting of Trepov in January was followed in August by Stepniak's assassination of Mezencev, chief of police.

In the following year (1879) the Zemlja i Volja was sub-divided into the " Narodnaja Volja " (people's will) consisting of declared terrorists, and into the party which aimed at socialistic propaganda among peasants and operatives, this latter being known as " Černyi Peredĕl " (black redistribution —of the soil, to wit). The terrorists were led by the much talked of executive committee (Ispolnitel'nyi Komitet)

Once again the military and diplomatic failures of the Turkish war urged a change of front upon the absolutist government. The increase in public demonstrations, and still more the frequency of desperate and self-sacrificing attacks upon high dignitaries and upon the tsar himself, induced the reaction to reverse its policy. In 1878 there began a series of arbitrary and repressive measures. Administrative exile was increasingly frequent; courts martial were established in various districts; the entire population of the towns was subjected to supervision, concierges being made tools of the police; the governors were given extraordinary powers, and at length special governors-general were appointed with dictatorial authority. On November 2, 1879, the tsar issued an appeal to all classes to co-operate in the struggle against the terrorists, but in vain. With the appointment of Loris-Melikov as minister for home affairs (1880) there ensued a mitigation of the anti-revolutionary repressive measures, the Nicolaitan third section being abolished, the censorship rendered less severe, and so on. In addition Loris-Melikov designed the introduction of positive reforms in favour of the peasantry, and hoped to reform the administration, but it was too late.

On March 9, 1881, in a ukase to the minister for home affairs, the tsar approved what was known as the constitution of Count Loris-Melikov. The promulgation was postponed until the twelfth. When tidings of a new conspiracy reached him he ordered that on the following day (March 13th), the ukase should be published in the official gazette. On the 13th the "tsar liberator" was blown up by the bomb thrown by the peasant's son Rysakov at the very time when Loris-Melikov's proposal was handed in to the state printing office.

It is beyond dispute that Loris-Melikov had no idea of granting a constitution. His "dictatorship of the heart" amounted merely to the legal regulation of repressive measures, with an attempt to strengthen absolutism by reforming and cleansing the bureaucracy. "Preparatory committees" were to investigate the respective departments of the administration, and to draft proposals which would be submitted to a "general committee." Various members of the preparatory committee would be nominated by the tsar to the general committee, which would contain also delegates from the zemstvos and the larger towns (St. Petersburg and Moscow were to have two members each), and a few persons nominated from the administrative districts where there were no zemstvos. The general committee was to sit for no more than a specified period, and was to have deliberative powers only. After being passed by the general committee, the proposals were finally to be submitted to the council of state.

This can in no sense be regarded as a constitution. It was a conservative concession to the moderate supporters of the existing system. A similar scheme had been drafted by Count Valuev as far back as 1863, elaborated in 1866 by Grand Duke Constantine Nikolaievič, rediscussed in the beginning of 1880 by the tsar and some of his advisers, and then rejected. It was the doom of Alexander that he should fail to make the concessions whose necessity he had recognised on ascending the throne.

§ 31.

AT the opening of his reign, Alexander III ordered that his father's intentions should be carried out unchanged, and that Loris-Melikov's constitution should be adopted. Speedily, however, he rescinded this resolution, and reactionary oppression became dominant in all departments. This reaction took the form of exacting revenge for the murder of Alexander II, and it became known as the white terror.

Even the most rigid of legitimists must admit that immediately after the death of Alexander II the revolutionary executive committee issued a formal despatch to the tsar, admirably written, indicating that the granting of a constitution was the only means by which Russia could be tranquillised. As if in answer, on March 18th a " council of deputies " was created to collaborate with the prefect of St. Petersburg. This body, which had but a short life, was popularly known as the " rams' parliament," for the prefect of St. Petersburg was named Baranov, and *baran* is the Russian for ram. " Restrict education " was the tsar's formal command to the minister for education.

The manifesto in which Alexander promised to maintain and to strengthen the autocracy entrusted him by God, was described by Katkov as " the heavenly manna . . . which restores to Russia the Russian autocratic tsar, empowered by God and responsible to God alone."[1] In this spirit the adminis-

[1] The Christian and legitimist zeal of the new tsar's immediate advisers is sufficiently indicated by the fact that Pobědonoscev and his friends founded a secret anti-revolutionary " Holy Retinue " (known also as the " Voluntary Protectors "), aiming at the destruction of the enemies to the throne by all possible means, including murder. Towards the end of 1882, these Jesuits of absolutism entered into relationships with the executive committee of the Narodnaja Volja (the negotiations were conducted by Lavrov, Mihailovskii,

tration was now centralised in such a way as to increase the strength of autocracy.

The election of justices of the peace was abolished ; the competence of the jurors' courts was reduced ; the zemstvos were placed under the supervision of the *zemskie načal'niki* (provincial authorities) and were aristocratised. Urban administration underwent similar modifications.

In August 1881 the police absolutism which had been introduced under Alexander II was strengthened and systematised by the regulation " concerning measures to protect civil order and to secure social tranquillity." This protection (*ohrana*) was of two kinds, an " augmented " and an " extraordinary," the former being introduced for a year and the latter for six months. The minister for home affairs could, however, get the ministerial committee to prolong both varieties, and in actual fact Russia has remained under this " exceptional " regime since 1881.

Administrative repression was deliberately supported by the restriction of education which was desired by the tsar. Pobědonoscev came to reinforce the endeavours of Katkov ; and Pobědoncscev, whose influence at court lasted until the close of the year 1905, did his utmost to enforce cæsaropapism against the revolution. He had been tutor to Alexander III (who himself acted as tutor to Nicholas II), and it was the spirit of Pobědonoscev, chief procurator of the holy synod, that characterised the mental tendencies of the reaction.

He was the spiritual father of the church schools established in 1884. In the same year, owing to the continuous denunciations of Katkov, the universities were furnished with new statutes, reducing scientific studies to a minimum and practically suppressing the teaching of philosophy and sociology. The only permissible lectures on philosophy must relate to the doctrines of Plato, Aristotle, and their predecessors ! Progressive professors were dismissed, to be replaced by persons whose views were agreeable to the government, and the wearing of uniform was reintroduced for the

and others), desiring to learn its strength and the names of its leaders. But in December 1882, Count Tolstoi, being appointed minister for home affairs, put an end to these activities, for in his view the Holy Retinue was itself revolutionary, and was a nuisance to the police. It seems that these reactionaries were the founders of the periodical " Volnoe Slovo " (Free Word) which was published abroad to play the part of agent provocateur. For a time Dragomanov acted as editor of this paper, not realising its true character.

students. Nevertheless, in 1888 a university was founded at Tomsk in Siberia.

The middle schools were closely supervised. During the reign of Alexander II the reaction had already begun to work its will in this domain. Count Tolstoi, in 1865 chief procurator of the holy synod, and minister for education from 1866 to 1880, carried out his celebrated classicist reform, which was enforced from 1871 to 1893. He declared war on the modern schools, and the old endeavour to play off classicism against the spirit of revolt was renewed. Schools for girls likewise suffered, for Count Pahlen a reactionary, had discovered as early as 1874 that revolutionary propaganda was carried on mainly by women. A forcible argument had been furnished to the reactionaries by Sophie Perovskaja's participation in the assassination of the tsar. A few commercial and industrial schools were founded for practical instruction.

Struggle furnished the philosophical foundations for progressive and liberal efforts, and for conservatives and reactionaries nihilism ever remained the enfant terrible. To give the government a freer hand in this contest, a few concessions were made in other fields. It was characteristic that during the era of Pobědonoscev the raskolniki were treated with more toleration, and from 1884 onwards their cult was officially sanctioned. On the other hand, extreme intolerance was displayed towards Jews and Catholics.

Russification continued in the frontier territories, whilst army and civil administration were energetically nationalised.[1]

---

[1] At the close of the reign of Alexander II, the percentage of Germans in the various departments was as follows:—

	Per cent.
Civil Service	32
High Military Command	41
Imperial Council	36
Senate	33
Ministry for Foreign Affairs	57
Ministry for Home Affairs	27
Ministry for Public Instruction	28
Ministry for Finance	27
Ministry for the Domains	34
Ministry for Ways and Communications	34
Imperial Audit Office	18
Ministry for Marine	39
Ministry for War	46
Ministry for the Imperial Court } Imperial Aides-de-Camp	39
Post and Telegraphs	62

At this time the percentage of Germans among the general population was 1·1.

During the years 1881 to 1883 numerous antijewish pogroms occurred in the south.

In the reign of Alexander III, revolutionaries were treated with ruthless cruelty. Executions, it is true, were comparatively infrequent, numbering no more that twenty-six during the thirteen years Alexander was on the throne, but the treatment of prisoners and exiles was positively inhuman. In 1884, the fortress of Schlüsselburg was devoted to the punishment of the gravest political offences, and what went on within its walls has become known through numerous reports. The reinstated rod became a favourite instrument of justice. Political prisoners and Siberian exiles were abominably treated, all their natural human feelings being unsparingly outraged. In 1888 whole sections were simultaneously ill-used; in Yakutsk, in 1889, the martyred exiles offered active resistance and appealed to the veto of Europe, whereby the horrors were somewhat mitigated.

The revolutionaries carried a few plots to a successful conclusion and made two attempts on the life of the tsar. On the whole during the reign of Alexander III political depression and stagnation were conspicuous, not only in Russia, but also among the revolutionary parties working on Russia from abroad. The same statement applies to the Narodnaja Volja. The revolutionaries had become disheartened; many of them were abandoning the principles of terrorism and nihilism, and were experiencing an extensive reaction on their own account. The influence of Dostoevskii was increasingly felt in this direction, whilst Tolstoi's preaching against the use of violence was beginning to exercise considerable effect. The intelligentsia was devoting itself to the consideration of religious questions, and was to a large extent inclining towards the adoption of an extremely nebulous ethical anarchism.

Still weaker during this epoch were the liberal secret organisations.[1]

[1] From 1861 there existed in Russia and abroad secret liberal associations which maintained the decabrist tradition in their demand for a constitution, but these secret organisations were of an entirely different character from the revolutionary secret societies. They had no propaganda worth considering, and displayed little power of attraction. Not until 1878 and 1879 did the liberals attempt to get into touch with the revolutionaries, but negotiations proved fruitless. A few secret societies were organised during the Loris-Melikov era, but remained without influence. Better known are the societies Liga, and the Union of Zemstvos and for Self-Government. The periodical " Volnoe Slovo," edited during and after 1883 by Dragomanov, has been generally

During this epoch of reaction, which was likewise an epoch of internal transformation, the revolutionaries seemed paralysed. For years after 1884 they did practically nothing. Typical of this crisis was the conduct of the revolutionary leader Tihomirov, who went over into Katkov's camp. The spread of Marxist ideas contributed to the paralysis of the terrorist movement. As early as 1878 Stepniak, the man who had stabbed Mezencev, wrote : " We are not fighting the state but the bourgeoisie." In 1883 the first party of declared Marxists was founded, under the name Liberation of Labour. Provisionally established in Geneva, it remained in close touch with the intelligentsia and the working classes of Russia.

The whole of cultured Russia was occupied during the eighties and has been occupied to the present day in considering the problems forced upon the attention by Marxism. Above all were people interested in the dispute between the narodniki and the Marxists concerning the economic and capitalistic development of Russia. It is incontestable that Russian revisionism (Struve) developed under the influence of the narodniki. A return from materialism to philosophic idealism was associated with the growth of revisionism. " Idealism," was the cry heard on all sides, " idealism versus materialism ! "

This appeal came not only from the revisionists, but from the jurists as well (Novgorodcev), and above all from the advocates of that literary idealism, of that mystical religious movement which during recent years has been associated with the teachings of Dostoevskii and of the philosopher Solov'ev. A peculiar position in this connection is occupied by Leont'ev, the theocrat, a man of original mind.

The development of the poet Čehov was characteristic of the political and social fatigue that prevailed during the reign of Alexander III. He ushered in the literary decadence, the movement known as neoidealism or neoromanticism. Merežkovskii and Volynskii may be mentioned as representatives of this school, the former as poet and essayist, and the latter as critic.

regarded as the organ of these associations, but it is more probable that it served the aims of the before-mentioned reactionary group Holy Retinue. The leading point in the Union of Zemstvos and for Self-Government was the demand for a national duma (elected from the whole empire by universal suffrage) and a zemstvo duma. The latter was to be the organ of local self-government, the former the organ of centralisation.

Similar was the theological trend towards a "new learned monasticism," initiated by Dostoevskii and Ivan Aksakov. The writers of this school desired that the church should be liberated from the state in the interest of religion.

§ 32.

THE champions of reaction did not fail to recognise that the economic and financial regeneration of Russia was essential. Economic reform was to sustain and justify reaction. Tsar Alexander III led a far simpler life than his predecessors. Himself thrifty, he did not hesitate to check the extravagance of his relatives.

To restore order to the national finances, the ministers Bunge, Vyšnegradskii, and Witte increased the revenue by enhanced taxation and higher protective duties, and were able to overcome the deficit, although large sums were needed for the nationalisation of the railways. After the accession of Nicholas II, during the years 1895 to 1897, a large gold reserve having been accumulated, the gold standard was introduced.

Theocratic Russia, though spiritually exclusive, had to attract foreign and unchristian capital to the country, The reactionary tsar, nolens volens and despite the protective tariff system, had to pursue a Europeanising foreign policy. Owing to the ill success of the Turkish war conducted by Alexander II, his son was estranged from England and Germany. As we now know, after the Berlin congress Bismarck was quite erroneously regarded as the hereditary enemy (" the way to Constantinople is through the Brandenburg Gate "). The tariff war with Germany initiated in 1891 came to a speedy close in the autumn of 1893 with the suspension of the autonomous Russian tariff, and in January 1894 a most-favoured-nation treaty was concluded in Berlin. But with France Russia entered into an alliance, tsarist absolutism becoming leagued with the French republic, for in 1892 the Parisian bourse had extended its ægis over Russian paper.

Economic policy is apt to lead Russian diplomacy into difficulties. Since Germany is Russia's immediate neighbour, it is Germany that can supply Russia most freely and can buy from her most extensively. In actual fact Russia's trade with Germany is the largest ; next comes England ; China and the United States do more business with Russia than does France. The political factor is of great importance in international relationships.

Russia is still a predominantly agricultural country, with a mainly rural population, although of late the growth of the towns and of manufacturing industry has been comparatively rapid.[1]

Under Alexander III and his successor the peasants were granted certain concessions. From 1883 onwards the poll tax was abolished by progressive stages (in Siberia not until 1899). But during the reign of Alexander III there was a great increase in indirect taxation. The Peasants' Bank founded in 1882 helped the peasants to acquire land, but the Nobles' Bank was of still greater assistance to the nobility. After the liberation a severe crisis affected the noble landowners, but the trouble had in truth begun before 1861, for about two-thirds of the owners of serfs were heavily indebted.

During the reign of Alexander III financial support and strengthening of the nobility became a deliberate policy. In 1883, in opposition to previous law and custom, a new law was promulgated concerning estates where the succession had failed. In future these estates were to accrue to the corporation of the nobility instead of to the state. The Nobles' Bank was founded in 1885, its aim being, as explained in its charter, to secure for the nobility the leading position in army, local administration, and judiciary, so that the example of the nobles might diffuse rules of faith and loyalty and establish sound principles of national culture.

In this spirit and with this aim financial privileges were continually being granted to the nobility, and it was in this spirit that the reforms of the period were conceived; but the

	Year.					Percentage of Towndwellers.	Round Total of urban Population.
1	1724	..	..	..	..	3·0	300,000
	1784	..	..	..	..	3·1	800,000
	1796	..	..	..	..	4·1	1,300,000
	1812	..	..	..	..	4·4	1,600,000
	1835	..	..	..	..	5·8	3,000,000
	1851	..	..	..	..	7·8	3,500,000
	1878	..	..	..	..	9·2	6,000,000
	1890	..	..	..	..	12·8	13,900,000
	1897	..	..	..	..	13·25	17,100,000

Between 1724 and 1897 the urban population increased fifty-onefold and the rural population eightfold. In France the urban population comprises nearly 41 per cent. and in England more than 75 per cent. of the total.

government and the tsars, despite the best will in the world, could do little to help the nobles.[1]

Little, too, could be done to help the peasant, whose land hunger remains intense, and whose land is no less gravely burdened with debt than that of the great landowners.

The size of the peasant farm has been reduced through increase in population. The mean landholding per head of the male peasant population was in 1860, 4·8 desjatinas; in 1880, 3.5 desjatinas; and in 1900, 2·6 desjatinas.

Whilst land hunger has thus continually increased, since the liberation the price of land has more than doubled. The average price per desjatina of land was:

1868–1877 ..	..	..	..	..	19·1 roubles
1878–1887 ..	..	..	· ..	..	26·5 ,,
1888–1897 ..	..	..	..	..	42·5 ,,

It is by no means easy to appraise the actual position of the peasantry in respect of landownership in various regions to-day. But if we remember that on the average a peasant family requires 12·24 desjatinas for a satisfactory livelihood, it is evident that about three-fourths of the peasant families have insufficient land.

The land hunger of the Russian peasantry gives rise to a need for food which is chronic, with acute exacerbations. This is illustrated by the following data: 70·7 per cent of the peasants secure less from the land than would suffice for a decent existence; 20·4 per cent can feed themselves but cannot feed their stock; only 8·9 per cent can buy anything more that the bare necessaries of daily consumption. According to trustworthy reports, in the south, upon the fruitful black earth, after all taxes have been paid by a Russian family consisting of five persons, no more than eighty-two roubles remain for the entire year's subsistence.

The agrarian committee appointed by Witte in 1903 reported as follows: " When the harvest is normal, the amount of nutriment obtainable by the peasant is, on the average, 30 per cent below the minimum physiologically requisite to maintain the strength of an adult worker on the land."

[1] Between 1863 and 1892 the landowners, chiefly noble landowners, lost about twenty-five million desjatinas of land. To-day the total loss considerably exceeds forty millions. Since the liberation, land has been bought freely by well-to-do peasants, by merchants, and by the towns.

The annual yield per head is—

Cereals—in Russia, 246 kilos, in Germany, 316 kilos.
Potatoes   ,,   131   ,,   ,,   620   ,,

In Russia, when the need for food becomes acute, conditions prevail which were familiar enough in Europe during the middle ages and in the days of classical antiquity, but which are now known only in such countries as India. In western Europe, acute famine has long been a thing of the past. And yet hungry Russia has to export grain !

The great famines of 1891 and 1892 are of recent memory ; in the latter year cholera was epidemic.

During the sixties the state disbursed 797,000 roubles per annum for the support of the poverty-stricken population. Between 1870 and 1880 the average annual payments on this account were 1,780,000 roubles. Between 1881 and 1890 the figure was lower, for the harvests were good, and the area under cultivation was comparatively large ; during this period the disbursements averaged about 1,000,000 roubles per annum. But from 1891 to 1900 the annual cost increased to 19,100,000 roubles. During the years 1901 to 1905, owing to the failure of the crops the total disbursements were 118,057,000 roubles ; whilst in the single year 1906 the expenditure under this head amounted to 150,000,000 roubles.

During the sixties, governmental help was requisite in eight administrative districts ; during the seventies in fifteen ; during the eighties in twenty-five ; during the nineties in twenty-nine ; and during the years following 1900 in thirty-one.

These data are all the more alarming seeing that the yield of the soil has permanently increased since 1861, although Russian agriculture lags far behind that of European countries.[1]

During the years of famine, Alexander III's government was able to display all the strength of its compassion. The autocrat's uneasy conscience actually led him to look askance at and to interfere with the philanthropic projects of the cultured and well-to-do classes. The movement "towards the people" was never regarded with favour !

---

[1] Cattle breeding, too, is relatively on the down grade. The head of cattle per hundred inhabitants numbered 37·2 in 1880, 33 in 1906, 30 in 1909. Statistics further show that the weight of the stock has declined, and more particularly that there is a reduced yield of milk. (It should be noted that the decline in cattle breeding leads to the soil being less efficiently manured !)

A further evidence of land hunger is afforded by the increasing migration of peasants to Siberia.[1]

It need hardly be said that land hunger is not the sole explanation of chronic and acute famine. In certain regions there is a positive superfluity of land. I am not thinking here of the districts inhabited by nomads and semi-nomads, but refer to such areas as those in northern Caucasia, where the average farm often exceeds 20 desjatinas in extent. Yet here also, just as in Siberia and in all parts of Russia with the exception of the northern regions, the peasant complains of land hunger. There are numerous contributory causes of chronic famine, and among these it is necessary to refer to the backward state of Russian agriculture.

According to comparative statistics published in 1907 by the Russian ministry for finance, the yield of wheat per desjatina is in Russia 42 poods, in Italy 50, in North America 60, in Austria 75, in Hungary 77, in France 78, in Germany 120, and in England 137.

It must not be supposed that the peasant is solely responsible for the defective returns from Russian soil ; general conditions, remoteness of the cultivated areas from the peasants' dwellings, and similar causes, are contributory. But it remains true that the peasant's lack of culture and capacity for work, together with the backward state of civilisation in general, are, in conjunction with the unjust distribution of land, the principal causes of the agrarian crisis.

Since the liberation, the development of manufacturing industry has been comparatively vigorous. The growth of manufacture was, indeed, a contributory cause of the liberation ; but, conversely, the enfranchisement of the peasants promoted the growth of industry and commerce.

Enfranchised peasants flocked to the towns and crowded into the factories, which before long assumed a European and even an American character. Wages are decided by free contract ; modern machinery is employed ; with the aid of foreign capital, great industry and capitalistic enterprise

---

[1] Between 1885 and 1896, the emigrants to Siberia numbered 912,000 ; they numbered 1,387,532 between 1897 and 1906 ; from that year down to 1913 they numbered about two and a half millions. There have also been extensive migrations to Caucasia and to Central Asia. Emigration to the west (America) remains inconsiderable, but began about 1891. Jewish emigration has been extensive, more than one million Jews having left Russia between 1899 and 1906.

develop. Old Russia is being economically and socially transformed, the former class divisions being replaced by the new segregation into a class of capitalists and a class of operatives. Contemporaneously there has occurred a transformation of commerce, and since the beginning of the sixties the locomotive and the steamboat have facilitated the export of grain to Europe.

So rapid was the evolution of Russian industry, so prompt the adoption of capitalistic methods of production, that no long time elapsed before the labour problem was superadded to the peasant problem. Philosophical historians and other writers could not fail to discern the mighty changes which the growth of large-scale manufacture was effecting. Hence arose the socialistic and semi-socialistic theories of the narodniki and the early Russian socialists, who hoped to save agricultural Russia and the Russia of home industries from the onslaughts of hungry foreign capital.

The position of Russian operatives is far worse than that of the same class in Europe. Labour protection laws are comparatively inadequate, and social legislation is less efficient. Flerovskii's book, *The Condition of the Working Class in Russia*, published in 1869, though based upon imperfect statistical evidence, gave an accurate picture of the unhappy condition of the peasants and workers. Since then, more trustworthy data have become available. We know that in Russian factories accidents are far commoner than in the west, the percentage in some establishments being as high as 22. The popular poetry of the working classes has long been concerned with these lamentable conditions.[1]

[1] No accurate statistics regarding the numbers of Russian operatives are at present available, but the following figures may be considered approximately correct.

Year.	Factory Hands in Establishments subject to Inspection.	Miners.	Totals.
1900	1,618,000	716,000	2,334,000
1901	1,617,000	683,000	2,300,000
1902	1,624,000	627,000	2,251,000
1903	1,684,000	610,000	2,294,000
1904	1,660,000	599,000	2,259,000
1905	1,685,000	582,000	2,267,000
1906	1,718,000	643,000	2,361,000
1907	1,762,000	657,000	2,419,000
1908	1,765,000	—	—
1909	1,789,000	—	—

§ 33.

ALEXANDER III died in the belief that Russia was the greatest and strongest monarchy in the world. He spoke of Russia as the sixth continent, and the following anecdote is related of him. He was fishing in Finland, when Giers, the minister for foreign affairs, came to ask his decision upon some urgent matter, saying that Europe was waiting for an answer. Alexander rejoined, "When the Russian tsar is fishing, Europe can wait."

Before the outbreak of war with Japan the Russian army was ten times as numerous as that of her opponent, and the Russian fleet was nearly three times larger than the Japanese. The Siberian railway, begun under Alexander III for the protection of the far east, had been completed.

The Japanese war was entered upon with a light heart. Even before Kuropatkin's revelations, it was known that the motives of the clique which had done most to promote the war had been petty and sordid. Although Nicholas II had, when heir to the throne, visited Japan and Siberia, and although the official writer who described the tsarevitch's travels announced Russia's panasiatic program governmental Russia at the time of the war knew nothing of the great question which was subsequently voiced in the catchword of "the yellow peril."

The reader may be referred to Prince Uhtomskii's account of Nicholas' journey in eastern Asia during the years 1890 and 1891. He will find it recorded in black and white that panasiatism had become the national program of official and Orthodox Russia.

From Byzantine orthodoxy to panasiatism! According to the fantasies of Prince Uhtomskii, all the peoples of Asia would gladly accept the rule of the white tsar, for in Russian civilization, in the Russian national character, they would rediscover elements in inward correspondence with their own outlook on the universe. In the Asiatic races Uhtomskii discerned the mystical faith, the religious introspectiveness, which the slavophils regarded as essentially Russian and Orthodox qualities.

On the average the English workman earns twice as much, the American workman nearly four times as much, as the Russian. The standard of life of the Russian workman is extremely low. Fourteen roubles a month is considered a good wage for a male operative. Russian workmen are as hungry as Russian peasants.

Ever since Muscovy had become great through its victory over the Tatars, dominion over Asiatic peoples, extension of Asiatic empire, had consciously or unconsciously been the Russian goal. The south and the east of the existing empire were Asiatic, and the same might be said of the north. Rule over Asia had been extended step by step. In 1701, during the reign of Peter, Siberia had been entirely incorporated ; there had been wars with Turkey and Persia, the two greatest Mohammedan realms, and these wars had been the opening of a struggle still undecided ; Crimea and Caucasia had become Russian ; Central Asia and the Amur region had been occupied ; in Asia, now, Russia was coming into contact with her European rivals, was awakening the slumbering empire of China, and was unchaining the energies of the watchful island realm.[1]

It is indisputable, therefore, that Asia is of profound importance to Russia. So far as this is true, there is nothing particularly striking about Uhtomskii's program. Even the utopian romanticism of panasiatism would have been by no means censurable if the advisers of the future tsar had conscientiously weighed the pros and cons of the Asiatic problem. But the most characteristic feature of Uhtomskii's work was the incredible superficiality with which he estimated the Asiatic powers, and above all Japan. While the coming tsar was indulging his panasiatic dreams, the Japanese were learning all that was to be learned from Europe ; and with the aid of European civilisation they were able to force upon Russia the peace of Portsmouth (U.S.A.).

Defeat was sustained in Manchuria, not by the Russian soldier, but by Russian army administration, the Russian general staff, the St. Petersburg court and its diplomacy, the Russian bureaucracy — in a word, the whole regime of Pobědonoscev. Nonchristian, unbelieving Japan overthrew Orthodox, Holy Russia.

I do not consider that the Japanese performed any deeds of extraordinary strategic significance, and their financial resources for the conduct of the war do not seem to have been very considerable (cf. Helferich, *Das Geld im Russisch-Japan-*

---

[1] Russian territory in Asia comprises 16,550,000 square kilometres ; European territory in Asia comprises 9,906,000 square kilometres. Siberia alone is larger than Europe (including European Russia). But it must be remembered that the Asiatic possessions of Russia are uncultivated, and for the most part unfitted for economic exploitation.

ischen Kriege, 1906). But in the light of these considerations Russia's defeat appears all the more disastrous. From the Russian side we are frequently and perhaps truthfully assured that notwithstanding her reverses Russia would have been able to pursue the war to a successful conclusion had it not been for the outbreak of revolution at home. Can we level a graver accusation against Russian policy and administration ? It is not to be denied that upon the battlefields in the far east Russia was conquered, not by the Japanese, but by the enemy within her gates, that the author of her defeats was cæsaro-papist absolutism.

Numerous Russian works have been published of late dealing with the Russo-Japanese war. Andreev's *The Red Laugh* is well known in Europe. Bĕlorĕckii, who had personal experience at the front, analyses the war successfully. In a number of tales he depicts for us the mood of the Russian army. The general title of his stories is *Without Idea.* The various characters endeavour to discover " the idea," the meaning, of the war. In the end, however, one of the officers sums it up by saying : " What is the meaning of the war ? Its principal meaning is that it has no meaning at all. . . ."

CHAPTER SIX

THE FIRST GENERAL REVOLUTIONARY MOVEMENT AMONG THE MASSES; THE BEGINNINGS OF THE CONSTITUTION. THE COUNTER-REVOLUTION

§ 34.

TOWARDS the end of the reign of Alexander III, constitutionalist aspirations grew stronger. During the last days of the tsar's life the draft of a constitution was circulated in manuscript, and after his death the demand for a constitution was openly voiced in some of the zemstvos. Nicholas II, the new tsar, seized the opportunity to declare categorically to the representatives of the nobles who came to congratulate him on his wedding that he would uphold the foundations of autocracy no less firmly than his father.

Two days later there was circulated in St. Petersburg a plain answer to this program of Nicholas II. In reply to his declaration of war against liberal aims it was asserted: "You have begun the struggle, and the battle will not be long delayed."

In fact, there was little delay.

The repressive policy of Alexander III was continued, and was in many respects made more drastic than ever. In the new tsar, however, there was lacking the harsh but widely recognised authority of Alexander III, whose father's assassination had been regarded as a partial justification for the use of repressive measures. Under Nicholas, no serious attempt was made to solve the great social problems that were crying for solution, the agrarian question and the need for reform of the corrupt administration being ignored. Despite the continuous increase in the number of operatives, nothing was done to promote labour legislation. The activities of the schools, of scientific corporations, and of the press, were officially restricted. Before long it was generally recognised that the tsar, unlike his father, had no will of his own, and that Nicholas was in effect a prisoner in the hands of Pobědonoscev and the sordid clique of Bezobrazov, Saharov, Alekséev, etc., whose mouthpiece was Katkov's newspaper.

A more irritable and revolutionary mood began to prevail, not among the intelligentsia alone, but likewise among the operatives and the peasantry. During and after 1895 there were serious labour troubles; in 1896, the great strike of 30,000 textile workers took place in St. Petersburg; the Jewish workman became organised in the social democratic "Bund." In Minsk, during the year 1898, was constituted the Russian Social Democratic Labour Party.

Remarkable and characteristically Russian was the opposition movement in the universities, for by 1899 these had become positively impregnated with revolutionary feeling. The government retaliated by repressive measures, students who participated in the movement were forcibly enrolled as soldiers, and this increased the ferment.

Professors and writers of advanced views now took their places boldly in the front ranks of the opposition. I may recall the protest of the literati against the inhuman treatment of the people by the police and the Cossacks on March 17, 1901.

The socialists were opposed to individual revolutionary acts, their aim being to promote the economic organisation and strengthening of their party ("the economists"); but as the number of organised workers increased, ideas of a mass movement for political revolution began to prevail. The various opposition parties drew closer together, so that a peculiar political alliance resulted, and constitutionalist liberals co-operated more harmoniously with the working class and with the resurgent terrorists than had seemed possible in previous campaigns. The terrorist groups of the Narodnaja Volja had undergone disintegration, but in the year 1901 this body became renascent as the Social Revolutionary Party. In contradistinction to the Social Democratic Labour Party, the Social Revolutionary Party advocated the weapon of terrorism, reviving in its "fighting organisation" (*boevaja organizacija*) the traditions of the "executive committee." Under pressure of this party, whose propagandist activities were pursued mainly among the peasantry, the social democrats, too, for the nonce recognised terrorist attacks as permissible in exceptional circumstances. Throughout the various revolutionary parties there was manifest a tendency to unite for common measures, and seeing that all revolutionary parties are socialistically inclined there was general agreement that in Russia political revolution was to pave the way for social revolution. The Russian Marxists, and above all the revisionists, were busily at work. Orthodox Marxism and economic materialism were tempered by revisionism, so that the state was recognised as possessing equal rights side by side with the conditions of economic production. Marxist aloofness from " mere " politics came to an end ; the economic campaign against the bourgeoisie was abandoned ; operatives, capitalists, and great landlords were unanimous in their demand for political reform.

The bourgeoisie and the liberal aristocracy took the lead, pushed forward by the working class and by the peasantry. Struve, the revisionist social democrat, founded at Stuttgart in the year 1902 the periodical " Osvoboždenie " (Deliverance), whose publication was continued until October 1905. In January 1904 the constitutionalists established the " Sojuz Osvoboždenija " (League of Deliverance), which was to organise for joint action all the radical and revolutionary parties of Russia. The task was far from easy, for in Russia each nationality has its special program ; but for a time at least community of need enforced community of effort.[1]

In September 1905 the League of Deliverance was transformed into the Constitutional Democratic Party.[2]

War against the tsar opened in 1901 with the assassination of Bogolěpov, minister for education. In 1902 followed the

[1] The names of the parties affiliated to the League of Deliverance aptly characterise the political situation. They are as follows : 1. Russian Social Democratic Labour Party ; 2. Social Revolutionary Party ; 3. Polish Socialist Party ; 4. General Jewish Labour Union ; 5. Social Democracy of Poland and Lithuania ; 6. Proletariat (a Polish socialistic party) ; 7. Lithuanian Social Democratic Party ; 8. Lettish Social Democratic Labour Party ; 9. Union of the Lettish Social Democracy ; 10. Little Russian (Ukrainian) Social Democratic Party ; 11. Little Russian Revolutionary Party ; 12. Georgian Social-Federalist-Revolutionary Party ; 13. Armenian Social Democratic Workers' Organisation ; 14. White Russian Socialist Union ; 15. Armenian Revolutionary Federation ; 16. League of Deliverance ; 17. Polish National League ; 18. Finnish Party of Active Resistance.

[2] As early as 1891 there had come into existence a party of " popular rights " which aimed at uniting the liberals and the revolutionaries, but this organisation had little political influence.

murder of Sypjagin, minister for home affairs, who during his thirty months of office had ordered the arrest on political grounds of 60,000 persons.   The turn of Pleve came next (1904) : the assassination of Grand Duke Sergius followed ; the attempt on Pobědonoscev miscarried.

Apart from these isolated terrorist deeds the organised workers made ready for a mass struggle.   From the day of Nicholas II's advent to the throne, continuous increase in the strength of the political opposition was noticeable, culminating in the widespread revolutionary movement of the year 1905.[1]

Doubtless the tsar's government and advisers marked the threatening storm, but they continued to hope that petty concessions would suffice to save absolutism.   In a manifesto promulgated in March 1903 the tsar made a few obscurely formulated promises ; in June 1903 the Poles were granted the privilege of giving religious instruction in the Polish tongue. But there was no change in administrative methods ; discontent continued to increase in Russia proper, in Finland (where Bobrikov, the governor-general, was assassinated on June 16, 1904), in Caucasia, and universally. Svjatopolk-Mirskii, appointed Pleve's successor on September 8, 1904, wooed " the confidence of society," but his attitude towards the zemstvo congress in Moscow showed how weak was his liberalism.

[1] The following data of proceedings against political offenders give a picture of the growth of the revolutionary movement after Nicholas' ascent to the throne.

Year.	Legal Proceedings.	Number of Persons.	Administrative Proceedings.	Number of Persons.
1894	158	919	56	559
1895	259	944	90	623
1896	309	1,668	67	561
1897	289	1,427	122	1,474
1898	257	1,144	149	1,004
1899	338	1,884	166	1,325
1900	384	1,580	144	1,363
1901	520	1,784	250	1,238
1902	1,053	3,744	347	1,678
1903	1,988	5,590	1,522	6,405

The information is derived from the secret reports of the ministry for justice, which were published by the social revolutionaries. The arrests made by the police during the year 1903 under Pleve's regime numbered 64,000.

A great impression was made throughout the country by this congress. At first authorised by Svjatopolk-Mirskii, it was subsequently prohibited at the instigation of Pobědonoscev and some of the grand dukes. Held none the less on November 19, 20, 21, 1904, it demanded a constitution, extensive administrative reforms, and general measures of social utility.

The mass revolutionary movement may be considered to date from the procession of St. Petersburg operatives led by the pope, Gapon. The workmen organised by Gapon in St. Petersburg, like those organised by Zubatov in Moscow, were loyal subjects of the tsar. Reinforced by some of the social democrats, they made their ingenuous demonstration in front of the winter palace.

It is true that the assembly was dispersed by the imperial troops, but bloody Sunday, January 22, 1905, was nevertheless the defeat of absolutism. It is proved that the workers went in peace to the winter palace, the only disorders occurring on the Vasilii-Ostrov, where some barricades were erected and some stores of arms plundered. Excitement was greatly increased by the slaughtering of the defenceless people. Strikes were general in towns and country districts. Bulygin's ministry endeavoured to pacify the country, and in the beginning of March was promulgated a manifesto containing a rescript to the minister (instructing him to summon deputies to consider legislative proposals) and a ukase to the senate (granting the right of petition to the ministerial council) ; but these concessions failed to restore tranquillity. The sanctioning of religious freedom in April produced a better impression. The preparations for the organisation of a panrussian peasant league, and the congress held by this body in Moscow from August 14th to 16th, could not fail to convince the government that Bulygin's plans were an anachronism.

During the summer of 1905 the whole country was in an uproar—not alone Russia proper and the Russian capitals, but in addition Poland and the Baltic provinces. The disorders in Livonia, in Finland, and in Caucasia, were especially grave ; and the ferment extended even into Siberia. For these reasons, immediately after the close of the Japanese war in the peace signed at Portsmouth on August 16, 1905, a constitution was granted on August 19th, based upon the decrees of March, and the law concerning the establishment of the national duma and the electoral law were promulgated. Bulygin's constitution, however, which granted the people and the popular representatives no powers beyond those attaching to a consultative parliament, never came into existence, for the zemstvo congress refused to accept it, whilst the great strike in October showed what the working classes and society at large thought of the matter. It may indeed be said that this was not simply a strike of the working class, but a strike of society at large. Employers and merchants made common cause with their employees. In the railway strike which determined the issue, middle-class officials were on strike just as much as workmen. The October strike was a magnificent protest of united Russia against tsarism.[1]

[1] The figures in the following table will give a sufficient idea of the importance of the movement. Political and economic strikes are taken together.

Year.	Number of Strikes.		Number of Workers on Strike.	
	Absolute.	Percentage of Factories affected.	Absolute.	Percentage of Workers affected.
1895	68	0·36	31,195	2·01
1896	118	0·62	29,527	1.94
1897	145	0·75	59,870	3·99
1898	215	1·13	43,150	2·87
1899	189	0·90	57,498	3·83
1900	125	0·73	29,389	1·73
1901	164	0·96	32,218	1·89
1902	123	0·72	36,671	2·15
1903	550	3·21	26,832	5·10
1904	68	0·40	24,904	1·46
1905	13,995	93·20	2,863,173	163·80
1906	6,114	42·20	1,108,406	65·80
1907	3,573	23·80	740,074	41·99
1908	892	5·90	176,101	9·70
1909	340	2·30	64,166	3·50

According to "Proletarii," the organ of the Social Democratic Labour Party, in September 1906 the number of Russian socialists (paying members of organisations) was as follows:—

Russians	..	..	..	..	..	31,000
Poles	..	..	..	..	..	26,000
Letts	..	..	..	..	..	11,000
Bund	..	..	..	..	..	30,000

In Germany it may be pointed out there are about 400,000 subscribing members of the socialist party; in Saxony alone there are about 39,000. In Italy the party numbers about 45,000 members.

The seriousness of the revolutionary aims was proved by the organisation of the council of workers' deputies which from the thirteenth of October for fifty days conducted the movement in St. Petersburg. The council did not consist solely of workmen and socialists, but was an attempt at the deliberate fusion of all oppositional and revolutionary energies.

The October strike was followed on October 17th and 30th by the promulgation of the October constitution. The tsar renounced his absolutist authority ; he granted to the national duma legislative and constitutionalist rights ; he conceded inviolability of the person, freedom of thought and utterance, the right of public meeting, and the right of combination.

On November 21st Pobědonoscev retired on pension. The chief procurator of the holy synod had understood the signs of the time. After the promulgation of the constitution the metropolitan of Moscow instructed the popes of his diocese to preach sermons favouring reaction, but on October 29th the Moscow clergy issued a public proclamation against their spiritual chief.

All classes, all schools of political thought, were united in the struggle against absolutism.

The town operatives and those of the rural industrial centres constituted the main strength of this first mass revolution in Russia, the various sections of Marxists working hand in hand with the social revolutionaries.

After the October strike and after the promulgation of the constitution the peasants rallied to the side of the workmen, and their lead was followed by the radical intelligentsia in the zemstvos. At the close of the year the movement among the peasantry assumed a threatening character, and in the course of 1906 it took the form of innumerable local riots and acts of violence directed against landowners Hence the landowners and the nobility soon cooled towards the revolution, and joined forces with the government, which had in the meanwhile gathered strength.

The middle and higher bourgeoisie participated in the struggle for freedom ; manufacturers and other employers continued to pay wages to men on strike ; the salariat joined with workmen and peasants in carrying out the decrees of the revolutionary committee. Even by the moderate parties the revolution was recognised for a time as the power that had gained the victory over absolutism.

All the universities participated in the uprising, students and professors, authors and journalists, following the best traditions of Russian literature and publicism.

The new spirit prevailed likewise among the clergy, for the altar could no longer sustain the burden of the tottering throne. A liberal group of clergy formed the Brotherhood of Defenders of the Renovation of the Church, and as the outcome of their impulsion the synod called upon the government to summon a council. In conformity with this demand a committee was appointed to supervise the necessary preliminaries.

The tsarist system was torn by internal dissensions. The commander-in-chief against Japan had, under the eyes of the victorious enemy, to offer resistance to the camarilla. Thousands of officers and soldiers, wounded, crippled, shattered in health, had had bitter experience of the effects of tsarist absolutism. They suffered in mind no less than in body, these soldiers and officers who, for all their self-sacrificing spirit, for all their courage, were compelled to withdraw shame-stricken from the Asiatic theatre of war. To the wide plains of Russia there now returned thousands upon thousands of cripples, and soldier peasants to the number of hundreds of thousands, who would relate to coming generations the sins of tsarist absolutism.

In the navy, dissatisfaction was even more rife than in the army, as was shown by the mutiny of entire ships' complements.

All classes and schools of thought, the peoples of all nationalities, differing in language, tradition, civilisation, and religion, united against the common enemy, displaying a splendid natural unity in face of the unnaturalness of theocratic despotism.

Nineteen hundred and five was the logical sequel of eighteen hundred and sixty-one. The liberation of the peasantry had removed the broad foundation of absolutism. The peasants, from among whom the operatives were recruited, had imbibed the teachings of the intelligentsia, and with horny hands they now realised the hopes of Radiščev and the best of his successors. The revolution of 1905 was not evoked by the defeat upon the great battlefields of the far east : it was the continuation of the decabrist rising ; it was the fusion of the countless isolated struggles of the terror ; it was the fruit of philosophic and political enlightenment.

Gor'kii, proletarian and barefooted vagabond, was literary spokesman of the victorious revolution.

§ 35.

THE Romanovs had been in no hurry to grant a constitution, although it was to the zemskii sobor that they owed their own election to the Russian throne.

But one who recalls how in my own land of Austria the political omnipotence of absolutism was relinquished hesitatingly and as it were drop by drop, one who knows the history of reaction under Napoleon, of the Bourbon restoration, and of similar restorations in other countries, would hardly expect anything better of tsarism.

The October manifesto was merely the promise of a constitution. Fulfilment ought to have been effected in accordance with the best European models and through the instrumentality of the legislative assembly; but the worst European models were those chosen for imitation by the tsar and his advisers.

Under Witte a ministerial council was formed to act as cabinet (November 1, 1905), the suffrage was somewhat extended (December 24, 1905), and Bulygin's duma statute was improved. The council of state was transformed to constitute a kind of senate (March 5, 1906), being enlarged by the addition of elected members, the tsar reserving the right of appointing the president and of nominating members in equal number to those elected.

The duma assembled on May 10, 1906. On May 6th a new revision of the fundamental laws was published, to specify in particular the legal position of the tsar, for whom was reserved the exclusive right of initiative in the alteration of the fundamental laws. The promulgation of these fundamental rights took place quite autocratically, by way of ordinance.

The first duma was elected by indirect suffrage. The rural constituencies were comparatively numerous, and while it is true that the preference thus given to the country over the towns was in conformity with Russian conditions, it is obvious that the government speculated upon the political apathy of large rural areas and upon the lack of political training in these. Moreover, special powers were assigned to the landowners.

Nearly half the members of the first duma were peasants. To be precise, on June 13th, of 478 deputies, 204 were peasants, this being 45·5 per cent. The other members were adherents of the intelligentsia. Speaking generally, from Russia proper and from the electorates of the other national sections, the best elements were sent to the duma. No more than two illiterates were elected.

On May 10th in the winter palace, the duma was opened by the tsar with a speech from the throne. Muromcev, a cadet (vide infra), the man who during the reign of Alexander III had been dismissed from the chair of Roman law at Moscow university, was elected president.

Before and still more during the elections occurred the formation of the first publicly and legally recognised political parties. As a matter of course they were at this time inchoate, for program and organisation could only be developed and tested in actual working. One hundred and five of the deputies were independents.

It need hardly be said that all three sections, the right, the left, and the centre, were represented in the duma, and that each of them consisted of several subsections. In the first duma the party of the right was the weakest. At the outset there were a few independents really belonging to the right, who subsequently constituted themselves as a group of progressists, twelve in number ; these progressists led the opposition, which was friendly to the government. The left and the centre formed a very large anti-governmental majority.

The left, too, at first consisted of independents. About one hundred of these combined to form the Labour Party (*trudoviki*). To this belonged the few social democrats and social revolutionaries in the house, for some had been elected although both these parties had boycotted the duma. Not until later were some social democrats elected in Caucasia in conformity with the tactics of the minority of the party. They formed an independent group in the duma, comprising seventeen deputies. The social revolutionaries did not constitute a distinct party.

The centre consisted of four sections. The main body contained the constitutional democrats, 160 in number. There was a small body of democratic reformers ; there was a party of " peaceful renovation " ; and there were the members of the union of October seventeenth. The centre groups became known as "cadets" from the initial letters of the name of the largest section among them ("constitutional" in Russian being spelled with a k—the "K.D.'s" were termed the "kadets").

The five national parties, the Poles, Esthonians, Letts, Lithuanians, and Little Russians, acted in common as the League of Autonomists. There were about seventy of this group, but its numbers fluctuated greatly, as its members adhered to other parties from time to time.[1]

From the very first the government and the bureaucracy were hostile to the duma. Doubtless the demands of that body were of a radical character, but the ultra-revolutionary parties, and in especial the social revolutionaries, had expressly renounced terrorist methods ; and moreover, all the revolutionary parties, Social Democratic Party, Social Revolutionary Party, and the League of Deliverance, had undergone notable changes amid the new conditions.

In the Social Democratic Party two groups had been constituted, a "majority," consisting of advocates of revolutionary methods, and a "minority". (led by Plehanov and others), desiring to use social democratic methods, and to have recourse to revolution in exceptional cases only.[2]

The majority desired to boycott the duma, but the minority wished to participate in the elections.

[1] Outside the duma there were yet other parties. At the beginning of 1906 eleven parties had been constituted with a definite program. I. *Right and Reactionary* : 1. Moderate Progressists ; 2. National Economists ; 3. Panrussian Commercial and Industrial Union ; 4. Union of October Seventeenth ; 5. Party of Law and Order ; 6. Constitutional Monarchists (Tsarists). II. *Centre* : 7. Constitutionalist Democrats ; 8. Liberals ; 9. Radicals. III. *Extreme Left* : 10. Social Democrats ; 11. Social Revolutionaries.

At the end of 1906 twenty-three parties and combinations were enumerated. I. *Conservative and Reactionary* : 1. Russian Monarchist Party ; 2. League of the Russian People ; 3. Russian Association. II. *Centre* : 4. Commercial and Industrial Union ; 5. Union of October Seventeenth. III. *Liberal Democrats* : 6. Party of National Liberty (Constitutionalist Democrats) ; 7. Party of Democratic Reform ; 8. Liberals ; 9. Radicals. IV. *Revolutionaries (Extreme Left)* : 10. Russian Social Democratic Labour Party ; 11. Social Revolutionaries ; 12. Populist Socialists (Young Narodniki) ; 13. Bund (Jewish) ; 14. Social Democracy of Poland and Lithuania ; 15. Lithuanian Social Democracy ; 16. Ukrainian Revolutionary Party ; 17. Lettish Social Democracy ; 18. Polish Socialists ; 19. Armenian Revolutionary Party ; 20. Georgian Social Federalists ; 21. Old Russian Peasants Union ; 22. Railway Union ; 23. Teachers Union. This is not an exhaustive list of parties and combinations, for only the most important and the strongest have been specifically enumerated.

[2] Further details regarding the social democrats will be found in § 152, and regarding the social revolutionaries in § 167.

The social revolutionaries were subdivided into the moderate folk-socialists (also termed young narodniki or neo-narodniki) and the terrorist "maximalists"; there was also a centre group in this party with indeterminate trends.[1]

The first duma had two leading tasks to perform. It was necessary to solve the agrarian problem. Not merely must political liberties be legislatively secured, but the control and the reform of the administration must be placed upon a sound basis. In the address submitted in response to the speech from the throne, both these demands were voiced. An agrarian program was sketched, aiming in principle at the abolition of private property in land; legal and administrative guarantees were demanded for the fundamental rights; there was to be an amnesty for political offenders.

After the elections Witte was replaced by Goremykin. The address was answered by a declaration of war, and the duma was dissolved on July 10th. The agrarian program was the immediate cause of the dissolution. The government having reiterated in decisive terms its dissent from the duma's proposals, the duma issued a manifesto to the people, and was dissolved on that account.

Goremykin's cabinet came to an end with the disappearance of the duma, and Stolypin, who had been minister for home affairs under Goremykin, now became premier.

At this juncture one hundred and eighty members of the duma met in Viborg, and resolved to issue a manifesto to the people, urging them to refuse the payment of taxes and to resist enrolment in the army. This manifesto was not signed by the duma as such, but by the individual members who issued it. Proceedings were instituted by the government against the signatories, and these were consequently excluded from the second duma.

[1] In a circular issued by the police department in the beginning of January 1907, the following groups and parties are specified as revolutionary groups and organizations: 1. Social Revolutionaries; 2. Anarchist Communists, Irreconcilables, Mahaevcy; 3. Russian Social Democratic Labour Party, both "majority" and "minority"; 4. General Jewish Workers Union in Poland, Lithuania, and Russia (including the Bund, chiefly influential in the west); 5. Polish Socialist Party, Social Democrats of the Kingdom of Poland and Lithuania, Proletariat; 6. Armenian Party of Federalist Revolutionaries (Drošak or Dašnakcujutn); 7. Georgian Party of Federalist Revolutionaries (Sakartvelo); 8. Finnish Party of Active Resistance; 9. The independent organisations of the Military Revolutionists, the Zionist Socialists (Poalei Zion), and the League of Deliverance.

The life of the first duma lasted barely three months, and from July 10, 1906, to February 20, 1907, Russia was without a duma.

The reactionary measures of the government had disastrous results. Whilst political revolutionary sentiment increased and spread throughout the country, there spread in addition an unpolitical anarchy, manifesting itself in murders and in the theft of public and private moneys. Thereby political agitation was rendered extremely difficult, above all for the revolutionary parties.

Courts martial were instituted by the government as a protective measure. These courts acted promptly, but with great injustice. It is known that in quite a number of cases innocent persons were executed.

Military justice was, of course, blind on suitable occasions. It proved impossible to discover the assassins of Herzenstein, a member of the duma, although it speedily became known that the deed had some criminal association with the League of the Russian People.

The disorders among the peasantry continued. The harvest of 1906 was a very bad one, and in consequence of hunger, the mužiks' ancient enemy, the countryfolk became profoundly discontented. Owing to the extremity of need, political demands were forgotten. The political agitation carried on by the radical and revolutionary parties secured but little attention, more especially seeing that the government, desiring to forestall the next duma, undertook on its own initiative to deal with the agrarian problem. Consequently, after the harvest of 1906, the ukase was promulgated which exercised decisive influence upon the organisation of the communes and upon the position of the peasant as landowner. By the ukase of October 5, 1906, the peasants were placed upon the same footing as other classes in respect of the subdivision of family property and in respect of freedom of residence, the power of the mir over the individual peasant being thereby broken. By the ukase of November 9, 1906, every head of family was empowered to claim from the mir his share of land, to be held as private property. To carry out these decisions " committees for supplying the peasants with land " were established, and upon them officials and landowners held a decisive majority (ten votes as against three peasant representatives). By the labours of the committees, with the assistance of the Agrarian Bank, the government was able to appease the peasantry before the assembly of the second duma. A contributory cause of the pacification was doubtless the influence of the cavalry patrols dispatched to various districts. But it is unquestionable that the government's agrarian legislation diverted the attention of the peasant towards the notable changes which the law of November 9th and the associated reforms in the judiciary, the educational system, etc., effected in his life.[1]

In the towns and industrial districts, excitement among operatives was comparatively intense, an accessory cause of disturbance being the industrial crisis which began in the autumn of 1906.

By concessions to the old believers and the sectaries the government endeavoured to assume a liberal aspect, but despite this the general mood remained antagonistic. Although by the new suffrage system introduced by Witte on December 11, 1906, and by certain decrees issued by the senate, the passive suffrage (eligibility for election) was falsified in order to secure the defeat of undesired candidates, an opposition majority was returned to the second duma. The government was indeed able to ensure that what had been lacking to the first duma, a properly organised right, should now come into existence. On the other hand, many more social democrats and social revolutionaries were elected to the second duma. The right consisted of twelve members of the League of the Russian People, forty-three moderates (among whom was the Party of October Seventeenth), and fifty independents.

To the centre belonged ninety-six constitutionalist democrats, the president (this time Golovin) being again chosen from among this group, forty-six Poles, and one member of the Party of Democratic Reform.

The Cossack group, numbering seventeen members, occupied an intermediate position between the centre and the left.

The left comprised sixty-nine social democrats, thirty-seven social revolutionaries, a hundred and three members of the Labour Party, and fifteen young narodniki.

[1] Notable was the law of June 19, 1910, by which the peasant whose property had not been partitioned since the liberation was declared a property owner. Notable, too, were the subsequent laws of 1910 and 1911, whereby heads of families were made sole proprietors. Other members of the family, who had hitherto been entitled to a share, were now deprived of their co-proprietary rights without compensation.

The Mohammedans, twenty-eight in number, inclined towards the left.

The second duma lasted but a few days longer than the first, from March 5th to June 16, 1907. It was natural that superstitious persons should regard it as a sign of ill omen when on March 15th the ceiling of the chamber fell in. Apart from this, thoughtful politicians and good observers had reason to expect that in the case of the second duma also the vital threads would soon be cut. From the outset it was the aim of the right to provoke the majority by reactionary and partisan proposals and to demonstrate that the duma was unworkable.

On June 1st the government demanded suspension of parliamentary immunity in the case of sixteen deputies who were declared to be criminal conspirators, and demanded further that thirty-nine members of the Social Democratic Party should be excluded from the house. The committee appointed to discuss the question was unable to come to a decision, and on June 16th the second duma was dissolved by a manifesto from the tsar, who adduced various grounds of censure, among which the chief were that the duma refused to express condemnation of murders and acts of violence and refused to surrender conspirators against the state and the throne.

On the day of the dissolution the government arbitrarily issued a new electoral law. The number of deputies was reduced to 437; the suffrage of the towns, the operatives, and the peasants (nearly half the electors), was enormously reduced, whilst the power of the landed gentry and the zemstvo bureaucracy was greatly increased. The third duma, therefore, was predominantly aristocratic, a duma of conservative great landowners. The party of the right, and the centre comprising the Octobrists (107), together controlled nearly three-fourths of the votes; the cadets (56) and the greatly reduced radicals and revolutionaries had become a small minority; in addition the cadets had lost a number of their best men. The social democrats held no more than seventeen seats, the Labour Party and the young narodniki no more than sixteen, whilst the social revolutionaries had boycotted the third duma.

The economic crisis of 1906 found its logical continuation in 1907. Once more the crops failed in many administrative districts; the effects of the industrial crisis were manifested in several strikes; and, in the south, to all these evils was superadded an epidemic of cholera. The extent to which

Russia suffered economically is indicated by the decline in the population of Odessa, a decline amounting to 100,000.

The elections were concluded on October 1st, and the third duma met on October 2nd. The nature of the new situation was promptly shown by the election of the president and his aides. Homjakov, Octobrist and governmental henchman, a descendant of the celebrated slavophil, was chosen president, and the vice-presidents were likewise members of the right.

During the debate upon the address, Bishop Mitrofan demanded recognition of the tsar's autocracy, a proposal rejected by the house; but Stolypin in his declaration expressed the same idea in a somewhat masked form, whilst in the preamble to the declaration the autocracy was recognised clearly enough. Stolypin uttered grave threats against the revolution and the parties of the extreme left.

The character of the third duma was shown most clearly in the election as deputies of nearly sixty clerics of various grades; but Petrov, a liberal priest, who with a few other clerics had adhered to the opposition in the second duma, failed to secure re-election.

Aided by the majority in the duma, Stolypin's government did all that was possible to restore the old regime. The nobility and in particular the conservative and reactionary landed gentry, now reaped a renewed harvest. The government and the church (the synod) rescinded all the liberties that had been granted. The press, the schools, the unorthodox, priests and officials of liberal views, were harassed and their convictions were outraged. The third duma, like its predecessors, debated the political rights of citizens and the fundamental right of the individual, for these important factors of the constitution had been dealt with by the tsar alone and in a partial manner. Arrests continued in large numbers, so that the prisons were crowded with political " criminals."

Collective trials of a positively ludicrous character were deliberately undertaken. On December 12, 1907, the social democratic " conspirators " of the second duma were sentenced; and on the same day the trial of the 169 deputies of the first duma was begun—of course these, too, were condemned.

The fourth duma, elected in 1912, was similar in composition. The left, however, had gained in strength. The united efforts of the government and of the synod, intervening openly and directly on three occasions through the instrumentality of an electoral board, did not secure the expected majority.

§ 36.

IF we desire to understand absolutism and the revolution we must examine the methods of the counter-revolution somewhat more closely.

The October strike alarmed and confused the government of the tsar. In 1848, in a similar manner, the Viennese government lost its head, and at the outset yielded ground before the revolution. The disordered state of the Russian government was most conspicuously displayed in its dealings with the press laws.

On the strength of the October manifesto, Russian journalists assumed without further parley that freedom of the press had been established. Faced by this pressure, in December 1905 the government abolished preventive censorship as far as the towns were concerned, and made a few other liberal concessions, whilst leaving intact certain old oppressive regulations and supplementing these by new. In actual fact, after October 1905, St. Petersburg journalists wrote with a freedom which is still unknown in Austria. Not merely were the predecessors of the reigning tsar criticised without reserve, but for a time even Nicholas II was subjected to more cautious criticism. Large freedoms were likewise assumed as far as books were concerned. As if between night and morning the book market was transformed. Works previously prohibited, both native and translated, were now freely published, and often simultaneously by several firms. Thus were promptly circulated in large numbers the writings of Radiščev, the decabrists, Herzen, Kropotkin, Černyševskii, etc. ; the confiscated works and the censored portions of the works of Dostoevskii, Turgenev, Tolstoi, etc. ; the writings of Marx, Lassalle, Plehanov, etc. ; the works of Spencer, Strauss, Feuerbach, Spinoza, Diderot, and Voltaire ; the pamphlets and larger books issued by the socialist publishing house in Stuttgart ; and so on. Russia was furnished with a supply of revolutionary literature for the coming epoch of reaction, and not until later could there be leisure for the quiet perusal and digestion of the vast quantities of matter rapidly issued from the press.

But after certain vacillations in the revolutionary direction, the government collected its forces, and towards the end of December 1905 tsarism initiated a deliberate counter-revolution. Above all, the government endeavoured to save absolutism by obscure and ambiguous utterances. This relates more especially to the concept of autocracy (*samoderžavie*), which may be interpreted in the sense either of European monarchy or in that of Byzantine despotism. The government seized every opportunity of stressing the latter aspect, whereas the constitutionalists naturally interpreted the term as signifying nothing more than constitutional monarchy.[1]

It is for this reason that certain journalists and statesmen have asked whether Russia possesses a constitution at all. Certainly Russia has a constitution—but it is one based upon the Prussian model.

The police and the administration endeavoured to save their customary absolutism by the most ludicrous expedients, nor was it long before the government proceeded to a formal restriction of fundamental rights. For example the right of public meeting was left intact, but preventive censorship over advertisements was retained and it thus remained possible to restrict the effectiveness of electoral meetings.

Laws and ordinances concerning freedom of the press, freedom of conscience (the right to change one's religion), freedom of combination, freedom of study and teaching, were unceasing topics of parliamentary and journalistic discussion. In the beginning of November 1909, Stolypin withdrew the proposals for toleration which had been laid before the duma in the previous summer. Many similar instances might be given.

Freedom of speech and writing was repressed after the ancient manner. The list of books and newspapers confiscated between October 30, 1905, and January 1/13, 1909, fills 160 large octavo pages. Books and pamphlets which could be published in 1905 and 1906 were again prohibited (works of Tolstoi, Kropotkin, etc.).

---

[1] The fundamental law of May 6, 1906 runs as follows (§ 4) : " To the tsar of all the Russias appertains supreme autocratic authority. God himself commends us to obey the tsar's authority, not from fear alone, but also as a duty imposed by conscience." (For the text of 1832 vide supra, pp. 109–110.) We see that in 1906 the term " absolute " has been dropped, but that there is express insistence upon " autocracy." Members of the duma discontinued the oath of fealty to " his tsarist majesty and autocrat of all the Russias." In drafting the constitutional charter, the government did everything it could to avoid the use of European constitutionalist or parliamentary terminology ; the expressions, constitution, parliament, and chamber (palata), are not employed.

The history of the duma suffrage shows what the absolutist administration was capable of. It suffices in this connection to compare the first and second dumas with the third, or to read a report of the doings of the government in individual elections.

The electoral law of June 16, 1907, was issued by arbitrary decree, although in the state fundamental law it is expressly stated in several paragraphs that the tsar is competent to promulgate laws only in conjunction with the duma (and the council of state). In the relevant section (87), which is modelled upon § 14 in the Austrian constitution, the regulation of the suffrage is expressly removed from the tsar's competence, but the coup d'état was carried out in defiance of this specification.

The electoral law, with its electoral geometry, may in the political field be compared in the artistic and the æsthetic field with the Moscow Vasilii Blažennyi (the cathedral of St. Basil, built in the reign of John the Terrible).

A pamphlet exists recording all prosecutions instituted against deputies to the first duma. The members of almost all the parties were prosecuted for one reason or another. Similar prosecutions were initiated against the liberal deputies of the second and third dumas. Even the octobrists were too " red " for the police !

Reports concerning the " white terror " constitute a permanent rubric of the daily press from 1906 onwards. The white terror began with the suppression of the December revolt (1905), which in Moscow was characterised by fierce barricade fighting. The " days of freedom " of October and November had passed away. Not merely was the revolution suppressed, but in most of the larger towns (eighty-five are enumerated) with the connivance of the police there occurred the well-known pogroms directed against the Jews, but in some cases also (as in Tver and Tomsk) against the intelligentsia.

My pen is reluctant to describe the infamies of this reign of terror. In actual fact, every one in Russia is still [1913] an outlaw. It may be said without exaggeration that during the white terror the fear of death ceased to exist. It had been driven away by pogroms ; by the death sentences of courts martial and field courts martial ; by arrest and martyrisations in the prisons and on the road to Siberia ; by the extremities of cruelty and torture ; by the frequency of suicide in the prisons ; by illness, epidemic disease, and famine. During the first year of the constitution, from October 1905 to October 1906, 22,721 persons suffered physical injury in pogroms and other civil disorders.

In August 1908 Stolypin the premier informed Stead the English journalist that the number of executions averaged fifteen per month. Kropotkin promptly contested this statement in the *Times*, and subsequently in *The Terror in Russia* (1909) he published a critical compilation of the facts concerning the methods recently employed by the government and the police. I extract the following data:

	Death Sentences.	Executions.
Courts Martial 1905	96	32
,, 1906	773	280
,, 1907	1,432	508
,, 1908	1,835	802 [1]
Field Courts Martial August 19, 1906, to April 20, 1907	—	676
Field Courts Martial January to March 1909	396	235

These data refer only to civilians.

The government alleged in excuse that in consequence of the revolution there had been a great increase in murders and in crimes against property. On June 3, 1909, the following data referring to murder and attempted murder were laid before the duma by the government.

	Persons murdered.	Persons wounded.
1905 (Middle of October to end of December)	222	217
1906	1,126	1,506
1907	3,001	1,076
1908	1,820	2,083

---

[1] The figures for November and December are not included. These data may be compared with those relating to executions under Alexander III, which numbered 26 in thirteen years. In 1909 the minister for home affairs issued a circular to the governors of the administrative districts recommending that in order to tranquillise the country the death penalty should be inflicted as seldom as possible. The following figures relating to the period from August 1, 1910, to September 1, 1912 (old style), show the result of this circular.

	1910.	1911.	1912.	Totals.
Trials followed by death sentences ..	81	136	81	298
Number of persons sentenced to death	185	293	214	692
Sentence modified	88	101	77	266
Executed..	29	73	83	185

During the years 1905 to 1910 there were in all 7,101 death sentences and 4,449 executions. In Germany during the year 1882 there were 95 death sentences, and during the year 1907, 31. In England, since the year 1811 there have been in all 893 executions. In Finland there has been no execution since 1826.

These figures merely show that in the year 1907 there was a great increase in murders. If we examine the data relating to murders and murderous assaults in previous years we find that the increase in murders cannot be explained as the outcome of the revolution. In the year 1904 there were sentenced to death for murder 2,800 persons, whilst 3,778 were sentenced for murderous assaults. During the period 1884 to 1893, the average annual number of trials on account of murder and murderous assaults was about 5,000. Thus the only exception that remains to be explained is the year 1907 with its greater number of murders (during this year there actually occurred a smaller number of murderous assaults). The probable explanation is that while during 1905 and 1906 the workers' organisations and revolutionary committees were still functioning, there was no notable increase in the number of murders, but that the suppression of these organisations and committees had as its consequence the murder of many manufacturers, captains of industry, landowners, and their managers or stewards. This was the upshot of the anarchy inaugurated by the government, which day in and day out provided the spectacle of murders and murderous assaults—for the government hoped to increase the effect of its death sentences by carrying out executions in public.

The reader can study all these cruelties in Kropotkin's record. I will content myself here with referring to the letter from Lomtatidze, the duma deputy imprisoned in Sevastopol, a translation of which was published in the " Daily News " of April 13, 1909. This simple report of what was personally seen and experienced, influences our imaginations more powerfully than such a work as Andreev's widely circulated *The Seven that were Hanged*. In his pamphlet entitled *The Hanging Tsar* Tolstoi stigmatises the cruelties of tsarist repression.

What explanation can be given of the massacre in April 1912 at the Siberian gold mines of the Lena company, when the soldiers killed 270 workmen on strike and wounded 250 others ?

In earlier days, it is true, even more persons were executed. Under the father of Peter the Great, Alexis Mihailovič, the executions of coiners alone numbered 7,000. If we turn to England we find that during the reign of Elizabeth there were more than 89,000 executions. The executions under Nicholas have not yet attained so high a figure, but (even if we leave the victims of the Japanese war out of consideration) more human lives than 89,000 have already been sacrificed by the fault of the government. Consider all the victims, beginning with the thousands who perished on the Hodynskoe Field at the coronation of Nicholas II ; consider the premature deaths in Siberia and in the prisons ; and consider all those who have been slaughtered in pogroms. . . . Does the tsar know all that is done in his name ? Does he countersign thousands of death sentences without reflecting what these terrible figures mean ? Whether he knows or not, whether he reflects or does not reflect, in any case the official defenders and legalist supporters of tsarism will find it hard to continue their justification of absolute monarchy. Yet this was the tsar who summoned the peace congress at The Hague.

I am aware that the blame for all that happened does not attach to the tsar and his government alone. A large section of society, cultured as well as uncultured (for the officials instrumental in carrying out the white terror belonged to the intelligentsia), demanded and co-operated in these brutal methods of repression. The white terror was supported by a vigorous agitation in the press. The reactionary journals, which during the years 1904 and 1905 had joined with the others in clamouring for reforms and legality (" Novoe Vremja," " Svět," " Graždanin," etc), had now become the journalistic and literary defenders of blood-stained reaction.

In 1906 was constituted the terrorist League of the Russian People, with its branch organisation, the Party of Active Struggle against the Revolution, whose reactionary agents and organisations, composed of the dregs of society, became notorious throughout the world after the Kishinev pogrom, under the name of " black hundred." Those only who have read at least one issue of one of the party organs, such as the " Russkoe Znamja " or the " Věče," can fully grasp the limitless barbarism of these groups ; but some idea can be gleaned from the antisemitic journals of Vienna and Prague, which borrowed freely from the columns of the " Russkoe Znamja." In the Reichsrat, Brežnovský, through his interpellation of December 17, 1906, rendered accessible the contents of a Russian pamphlet entitled *The Secret of Jewish Policy, its Methods and its Results, ascertained with the Aid of Science and of Pseudo-liberalism.* It need hardly be said that Russia, like other countries, possesses also a silk-hatted mob. There were to be found university professors willing to write lying pamphlets and lying books, to furnish historical and social arguments justifying the doings of the black hundred. In these compilations all who display any tincture of liberal sentiment, and in especial all freemasons, Jews, Englishmen, and revolutionaries, are not merely denounced, but are represented as the spawn of an antirussian inferno.

There exists documentary proof that the police and various other instruments of the government, including some of the high officials, did not merely neglect to suppress the pogroms, but positively furthered and organised these atrocities. It has been demonstrated that the League of the Russian People was privy to the murder of Herzenstein, to that of Jollos, etc. We read, for example, in the " Věče " : " O Russians, save Russia while salvation is yet possible. The death of Herzenstein cannot atone for all the murders of our Russian men, whose blood still calls for vengeance " ! ! !

The League of the Russian People had various branches and brother organisations, among which may be mentioned the League of the Archangel Michael, led by the notorious deputy Puriškivič. This league sent the monarchical sections a description of students who had disturbed lectures at the mining institute, and did everything in its power to promote denunciations.

It was the deliberate aim of the League of the Russian People to bring about the salvation of the fatherland by the use of such means as have been indicated. With this end in view absolute monarchy, Orthodoxy, and the Russian national spirit were to be strengthened, thus reviving Uvarov's trinitarian doctrine. At the congress of all the affiliated organisations held in October 1909, among the demands voiced were the re-establishment of the patriarchate, the annexation to Russia of Finland and of the Chelm administrative district, the expulsion of the Jews (who were not even to be allowed to write Russian), and so on. In a word, the demand was a panrussian, " For God, Tsar, and Fatherland."

Shortly after the issue of the October manifesto, Nicholas II received a deputation from the League of the Russian People. The spokesman, the notorious President Dubrovin, begged the tsar not to relinquish his autocracy. In response Nicholas pledged himself in words borrowed from Katkov, saying : " I shall continue to reign as autocrat, and to no one but God shall I render account of my doings." [1]   Accepting the offered badge of the union, he said : " Tell your friends that with God's help and the assistance of the League of the Russian People I hope to destroy my enemies."

It was reported in the newspapers that after this audience Stolypin begged leave to resign. It must be remembered that in the legal proceedings initiated on account of the murder of Herzenstein, Dubrovin was cited by the Finnish court as an accessory. He preferred not to put in an appearance, and it was stated in the press that Theophil, the tsar's new spiritual adviser, had interceded on his behalf.

Contemporary tsarism and the counter-revolution cannot be properly understood without taking into account police participation in crime through the instrumentality of provocative agents. The history of the agent Azev is known in its main lines. This man served both the police and the social revolutionaries, organising not only the attack on Pleve but also that upon Grand Duke Sergius. Let the reader reflect upon the significance of this, that tsarism, in its desire to quell the revolution, should be willing to sacrifice its own adherents, persons of such distinction. Nor was Azev the first, for he was but one instrument in a system. In the reign of Alexander III, Sudeikin, chief of the ohrana, endeavoured to persuade the terrorist Degaev to join with his associates in the assassination of Tolstoi (then minister for home affairs) and of Grand Duke Vladimir. This would enable Degaev to betray the secret society with real efficiency, Sudeikin would be promoted to the ministry, and could then protect the person of the tsar. Degaev, under the influence of liquor, betrayed himself to a comrade, who declared that Degaev must kill Sudeikin if he wished to avoid being put out of the way. Degaev assassinated Sudeikin and escaped to America.

The government of the tsar-pope, the man whose rule was of God and for God, the man who was not responsible to the duma but to God alone, this government continued for a lengthy period, for the safety of the tsar to employ Azev the assassin, and continued to do so after Azev's murderous handiwork had been plainly proved and publicly stigmatized.

The work of the counter-revolution and the promotion of

---

[1] Metternich had also held the view that to sovereigns alone belonged the guidance of the destinies of nations, and that to God alone were princes responsible for their actions.

police absolutism were in the hands of a widely ramified " black cabinet," which supervised all domestic and foreign correspondence. The most highly placed dignitaries were not exempt from the attentions of this cabinet.[1]

The facts that have been adduced suffice for the condemnation of tsarism in the past as well as in the present, for the condemnation of the entire system. Theocratic cæsaropapism cannot be justified if it can be upheld only by such means —it cannot be true that the absolute tsar governs by God's grace, it cannot be true that God commends obedience towards the tsar, it cannot be true that such obedience is enjoined by conscience. The existence of the white terror under Nicholas proves that section four arbitrarily incorporated by him in the state fundamental laws, the section referring to the theocratic essence of the tsar's supreme authority, is false. Absolutism has no foundation either in religion or morals.

The deduction we have to draw from this reaction which has now lasted for many years applies also to the state church, the theoretical and practical basis of tsarism. From the first the church has defended tsarism against the opposition and against the revolution, and now the church has approved the reaction, has approved the black hundred, has availed itself of the services of that body in the interest of reaction. Finally, in the elections for the fourth duma, the church openly intervened on the side of reaction. The synod, Sabler the chief procurator, and the hierarchy, organised the election of numerous members of the clergy, in order to secure the presence in the fourth duma of a clerical party far larger than the one which had existed in the third, and it was designed that these clerical deputies should be led by some of the hierarchs, who were likewise to secure election. But the result of the elections was a disagreeable surprise to the reactionary ecclesiastics, for whereas there had been forty-four priests in the third duma, there were but forty-three in the fourth.

The aim of the synod and the hierarchy was to transform the clergy into thoroughly pliable police tools of the anticonstitutionalist reaction. With this end in view a program was drafted whose two main points were as follows. In the first

[1] After the death of Pleve, Lopuhin, chief of police, whose name became so widely known in connection with the Azev affair, when examining Pleve's papers discovered a copy of one of his own letters. At an earlier date, Loris-Melikov had had occasion for urgent complaint because his correspondence was not safe from the secret police.

place, the clergy were to be paid by the state, to make them economically independent of the ecclesiastical authority; thus priests, like other officials, would become entirely subject to the good will of the government. Secondly, there was to be a modification in the educational system. The spiritual academies were already fitted to the purposes of reaction. By the curriculum of these seminaries, persons being trained for the priesthood were for practical purposes completely cut off from secular literature and thought, and were trained entirely in the spirit of theology.

But further changes were in contemplation.

Hitherto at the seminaries priests and teachers had been educated side by side, but seminaries were to become purely theological schools, for the training of priests alone, in order that the pupils at these institutions could no longer have the chance of adopting a secular career, for the more efficient and energetic young men were now refusing to take orders, and the church was suffering greatly from a dearth of candidates for the priesthood.

From the clerical side the same aim was followed in the proposed reorganisation of the church schools which had been founded during the reign of Alexander III. The curriculum in these schools had at first lasted two years, and had subsequently been extended to three. They were now to be transformed into institutions containing six classes, and were to give a purely theological general education, so that it would be impossible for pupils to pass from them into other schools.

These suggested reforms were a return to the plans of Archbishop Antonii. They imitated the training given in Catholic theological schools. The state church was to return to the middle ages, to the prepetrine Moscow of the patriarch-tsar Filaret. It was the hope of the reactionaries that the reintroduction of the patriarchate would subserve the same end, although the majority of the clergy expected it to strengthen the church and to emancipate the church from the tutelage of the state. At court, medieval superstition was dominant, as was shown by the Rasputin affair and by other indications.

If the white terror forces on us the conviction that tsarist absolutism is not a divinely ordained institution, we learn also from the sanction which the church is so ready to give to absolutism that the latter has no justification in appealing to God and to God's will for its policy and for its existence.

§ 37.

THE moral and legal justification of the revolution manifests the legal and moral danger of absolutism to society
and to the state, and shows how impossible it is to transform
absolutism by peaceable measures—for aristocracy and absolute
monarchy have learned nothing and forgotten nothing.

A sanguinary revolution as the ultimate means of escape
from an existing system of coercion can never be faultless,
quite apart from the consideration that in every revolution
those co-operate who are not chiefly aiming at the overthrow
of absolutism. The Russian revolution committed faults,
thereby giving absolutism specious grounds for reaction.
We shall have to consider this matter in fuller detail, but it
may be said here that even though it be necessary to admit
that the revolutionary tactics of expropriation were erroneous,
there is no ground for considering that the political revolution which aimed at the overthrow of absolutism was responsible
for the occurrence of the innumerable acts of theft and robbery.
The anarchical conditions which ensued upon the revolution
were the fault of the government and of its police. The official
education of the masses had produced general instability ;
the repressive measures practised by the organs of state, to
which mendacity and crime had for many decades been welcome
weapons, had trained up the present generation of expropriators
and pogromists, and had made the most barbarous hooliganism
a scourge throughout the country.[1]

Discussion concerning the nature and significance of the
revolution was carried on by all parties ; the tactics of the
struggle were criticised ; the question as to the chief justification for the revolution was mooted ; and the results of the
revolution were appraised.

After the revolution a serious crisis affected Russian society.
The more conservative elements on the liberal side were
content with what had been gained, and complained of the
utopianism of the radicals. To the reactionaries it seemed

[1] It was reported in the newspapers of December 12, 1912, that according
to reports issued by the ministry for home affairs between January 14, 1907,
and November 14, 1912, there had occurred 38,094 attacks by armed persons,
and that in the course of these 1,719 officials and 5,997 private individuals
had been killed, while 2,499 officials and 5,747 private individuals had been
wounded. During the first ten months of 1913 there were 2,148 attacks by
armed persons.

that the prevalence of marauding and of expropriation by robbery warranted, not merely repressive measures, but a return to absolutism.

The radical parties considered the constitution inadequate, but even within these parties there existed notable differences of opinion. Some hailed the frustration of the revolution almost with satisfaction, as sustaining their theory that political methods of reform were of no avail; others contended that the continuance of the revolution demanded by the more radical was needless.

The reaction, however, supplied more water to drive the radical mills. It was monstrous that the political organisation of the social democrats should be prohibited. Owing to this prohibition, the social democrats, who as deputies were legally immune, were forced to engage in clandestine activities. In like manner the agitation of the social revolutionaries was driven underground. Even lawful working-class organisations, trade unions, co-operatives, and institutes for working-class education, were persecuted.

Most of the revolutionary leaders were put out of action by the repression, but their places were taken by others. For about a year [1] a revolutionary mood has been conspicuous, not in journalistic utterances alone, but likewise in renewed strikes and demonstrations.[2] Even the reaction seems to have wearied of its executioner's work; fatigue became apparent by 1910, even if there was no purposive change for the better. Nor were the peasants fully satisfied with the government's agrarian program and with the way in which that program was carried out.

After the numerous political and economic strikes, manufacturing industry required peace and security, and the capitalists were consequently inclined to seek security and peace

[1] This work was written in 1913.

[2] The number of persons engaged in political strikes during the last eight years has been as follows:—

1905	1,083,000
1906	515,000
1907	522,000
1908	91,000
1909	8,000
1910	4,000
1911	40,000
1912	950,000

at the hands of reaction, though reaction endangered their own existence. The home market for manufactures was improving, business was taking a favourable turn, the national revenue was increasing rapidly from 1908 onwards, and the reaction secured ready help from capitalist entrepreneurs. Even in this quarter, however, were heard isolated protests against reaction.

In literature and philosophy, after the revolution, those tendencies were strengthened which, as we have already seen, were characteristic of the prerevolutionary epoch, namely mysticism and a return to religion. With this religious revival was associated a turning away from revolution. The loudest preachers of these movements were deserters from the Marxist camp; but among the narodniki and the social revolutionaries Dostoevskii and Solov'ev now enjoyed enhanced prestige.

In literature, decadence became conspicuous in the form of irritable and stimulating sexuality; the boundary between art and pornography was often blurred; even among young people at school, clubs and societies for the promotion of " free love " came into existence (" Saninism," after Arcybašev's *Sanine*). The disciples of decadence delighted in religious mysticism.

Whilst by one section of the intelligentsia, during this period of disillusionment with the revolution, crude hedonism came to be accepted as a logical consequence, and to be regarded almost as a means of salvation, another section succumbed to declared pessimism, which frequently culminated in suicide. Among the young, in fact, there was a positive epidemic of suicide.

It may well be considered that all these phenomena subserved political and ecclesiastical reaction. Hence, in the progressive camp, they were felt to be reactionary and were resisted on that ground.

Despite these morbid manifestations, there have on the progressive side been encouraging symptoms of resanation. The experiences of the revolution have diffused so much light that thoughtful persons have subjected the programs of their respective parties and movements to critical revision, and have endeavoured to bring about an organic expansion of such liberties as have been won. A sense of renovation has spread and strengthened, the newer tasks have been recognised, and work on behalf of the realisation of general progress is being joyfully continued.

CHAPTER SEVEN

PROBLEMS OF THE PHILOSOPHY OF HISTORY AND
OF RELIGION IN RUSSIA—A SUMMARY STATEMENT

I

§ 38.

AFTER this glance at the leading facts of Russian history,
we have to attain to clear views concerning the chief
problems of the philosophy of history and of religion in Russia.

As an initial step, it will be well to say something about
Russian philosophy in general. The task is far from easy.
There is no history of Russian philosophy to which we can
refer, for as yet the Russians have made no more than preliminary essays in this field. E. Radlov has recently published
A Sketch of the History of Russian Philosophy. The author
knows his subject well, and I shall therefore avail myself of
his characterisation of Russian philosophy.

Radlov admits that Russia has not yet produced a thoroughly
original and independent system of philosophy. He refuses,
however, to accept the sceptical view that, while philosophy
is known in Russia, there is no Russian philosophy. Radlov
distinguishes three spheres of mental life wherein Russian
philosophical thought has made itself manifest. Individual
spiritual needs find expression in the philosophical trend
which is characterised by the writings of Skovoroda, the
slavophils, Vladimir Solov'ev, and Tolstoi, and which may
be regarded as a reaction against the unceasing transference
to Russian soil of the data of foreign thought. The thinkers
of a second group are concerned with educational philosophy
at the universities and ecclesiastical academies. Finally,
Radlov distinguishes the political and social trend, manifesting
itself chiefly in journalism and sociology ; literary criticism is

represented as belonging to the same sphere ; Radlov refers in this connection to Radiščev, Bĕlinskii, Černyševskii, Mihailovskii, Grigor'ev, and Strahov.

This classification manifestly lacks precision, for Radlov fails to distinguish accurately between " sphere " and " trend." He goes on to say, in amplification, that Russian philosophers have no interest in the more abstract problems of philosophy, such as the theory of cognition, but that they delight in practical questions. Ethics, in particular, is the favourite field of Russian philosophy. It is from this practical predilection of Russian thought that Radlov deduces the second leading quality he ascribes to it, namely the mysticism which permeates all manifestations of the Russian mind.

Radlov confirms my own views upon Russian philosophy, but it seems to me that a more precise definition of certain concepts is essential.

It is perfectly true that Russians are now mainly busied with ethical questions. To use Tolstoi's phrase, they desire to grasp the meaning of life in order to apply their theory to practical living. We need not now discuss whether this is a specific characteristic of the Russian spirit. At any rate, western philosophy was for a long period, and still is, largely busied about these same ethical problems.

Ethics leads on logically to politics. The political and social trend of Russian philosophy is ethical ; ethical theory is to be practically applied to extant society. In concreto, therefore, we have to do with socialism and its justification. To carry matters a stage further, we have to ask how the goal of socialism is to be attained, whether by reform of the existing political organisation or by revolution. The problem of revolution, an ethical problem, is the crux of contemporary politics.

But socialism does not involve politics merely, the principles of social practice, it involves sociology in addition, the theory of social organisation and evolution ; and it is here that history and the philosophy of history have their parts to play. Russian thinkers are not satisfied with enquiring as to the meaning of life in abstracto ; they wish also to learn the meaning of Russian life, Russian social order, and Russian history.

But this implies a comparison of Russia with the west. It implies, in a word, the problem, Russia and Europe, if we conceive the contrast between these two areas as expressed in existing evolutional differences.   Thus is the contrast conceived by the Russians.

Analysis of ethical fundamentals leads likewise to the religious problem, for morality is an extremely important element of religion, of the Christian religion, of the Christian church.   Naturally and by logical development, Russian moral philosophy becomes a philosophy of religion.

Thus we arrive at mysticism, which Radlov associates with ethics.   From the logical outlook, the problem with which we are concerned is that of the relationship between morality and religion.   In actual fact, when we analyse Russian ecclesiastical religion we find mysticism in the foreground of the picture, for Russian religious sentiment is impregnated with mysticism to a far greater extent than the same sentiment in Europe.   We have, of course, to grasp the quality of this mysticism.   To formulate the problem in other words, we must examine Russian mysticism psychologically, must define it more precisely in the light of the theory of cognition.

Radlov is right in holding that Russian literary criticism is philosophic criticism, for literary criticism has a quite peculiar significance in Russia.   Let me hasten to add that Russian literature is itself peculiar in that it pays peculiar attention to ethical, socio-political, and religious problems.

Finally, Radlov aptly points out a comparative defect of Russian philosophy, and it is that Russian philosophers evade the discussion of the theory of cognition.   Provisionally, and in unduly summarised phraseology, I may say that whilst literary criticism is known to the Russians, they lack epistemological criticism.

I have at least shown, I believe, that the association in these studies of the philosophy of history with the philosophy of religion is in conformity with the character of Russian philosophy.   This will be rendered clearer by a brief excursus on the evolution of Russian philosophy.

II

§ 39.

FOR purposes of comparison a suitable summary of European philosophy would be useful.   It would be possible to refer to a number of authorities on this subject, but I will myself give a brief outline of European philosophy, for such comprehensive statements are not numerous. Moreover, for the benefit of competent students of philosophy, I desire to define my outlook. A preliminary survey of this character will prove helpful when we come to the description of individual Russian thinkers.

I shall confine myself to the later history of philosophy, beginning, like Radlov, with the eighteenth century.

First let us consider the problem of the philosophy of history.

The century of the enlightenment was characterised by the rise of the historic sense. Scientific historiography, the new method in history, begins with the latter half of the eighteenth century. Prior to this date the historic sense was lacking; there was no comprehension of the significance of comparing historical epochs, and there was no historical enlightenment. Chronology existed, but scientific history was unknown. This is not to say that there were no initial attempts at the new outlook, but the eighteenth century is the first we can speak of as thinking historically, the first century to secure a clear grasp of the concept of historical progress.

In the development and organisation of historical science, the profounder historic sense of the age was displayed in the scientific investigation of history, in the study of social life and its development. More especially was it manifest in the establishment of the new historical and sociological disciplines.

It was no chance matter that in every country numerous men of note became busied in this field. In his *New Science*, Vico produced the first philosophically planned treatise on sociology, a work in which the philosophy of history found a logical place as an integral constituent. French writers, in particular, devoted themselves to the philosophy of history. Voltaire was the first to use the term. Among other Frenchmen who were fruitful workers in this field may be mentioned Condorcet, Montesquieu, Turgot, and Rousseau. In Germany, we have Lessing, Herder, Schiller, and many other writers; and here, too, concrete historical investigation was methodically pursued (Schlözer, Schlosser, etc.). In England, Ferguson and other writers were at work, whilst Hume undertook historical research and wrote many sociological essays. The economic doctrines of Adam Smith have an important bearing upon sociology, and so have those of Malthus and the statisticians

(Süssmilch, Schlözer, Achenwall), who all endeavoured to grasp the nature of social organisation and evolution.

With reference to Kant a doubt may be expressed whether his century, the century of the enlightenment and of rationalism, may also be regarded as characterised by an increase in the historic sense. At any rate Kant paid but little attention to historical and social problems, and it has therefore frequently been suggested that a contrast exists between rationalism and the historic outlook. But. in conflict with this contention reference may be made to notable rationalists and distinguished adherents of the enlightenment who were likewise characterised by a well marked historic sense, to such men as Hume, Voltaire, Lessing, and at a later date Comte. Rationalism and the historic outlook are not mutually exclusive. Kant was a mathematician and a physicist, and in so far as he was these he belonged to the group of philosophers who from the days of Descartes onwards thought along the lines of mathematics and natural science.[1]

In view of the powerful effect exercised in Russia by German philosophy, this matter was one of considerable significance to Russian philosophy. Kant had comparatively little influence upon Russian thought, whereas since the eighteenth century the philosophico-historical and sociological outlook has been dominant in Russia.

Kant's successors, and above all Hegel, simultaneously represented rationalist and historical views. Indeed, the idealism of Kant and of the postkantians was no less predominantly historical than contemporary French and English philosophy

Not by chance were Hegel and Comte contemporaries. Both represented the historical trend of thought, just as the socialists, culminating in Marx, likewise endeavoured to base their systems on a historical foundation.

The philosophers of the restoration and of the reaction, the opponents of the revolution and of the new philosophical trends, such writers as de Maistre, de Bonald, Savigny, Stahl, etc., were also predominantly historical ("historical school of law").

The sense of historical evolution became yet stronger during

[1] Although Kant devoted little time to history, it is possible to maintain that he possessed a historic sense. I cannot discuss the question here, but may refer to the able study by Fritz Medicus.

the nineteenth century with the growth of natural science and the formulation of the theory of evolution. Darwin is but the representative of the intensive historical thought which characterises the labours of the entire century. History of men and of the human race underwent expansion into history of the world and of the universe. On the other hand, history fructified natural science. Darwin's thought was based upon that of Malthus.

§ 40.

THE increasing vigour of the historic sense, the fact that during the eighteenth century people became aware of the existence of historical evolution, is largely explicable on the ground that at this epoch the development of society, social changes, the historical process, were perceived and felt more plainly than before. The social changes which had accumulated as the outcome of the reformation and the renaissance, those innovations which were realised and appraised as progress in the sense of perfectionment, were now being recognised. A new idea of progress and a new faith in progress had arisen, and concurrently there developed the new historic outlook. History came to be conceived as a history of the future. Such is the meaning of the enthusiastic philosophical disquisitions on progress penned by numerous eighteenth-century writers, as for example by Condorcet.

The theoretical historic outlook and historic enlightenment are intimately associated with practical endeavours towards reform, and in the new era history becomes *vitae magistra*, history guides practical life, guides politics. Strengthening of the historic sense and a belief in progress manifest themselves as an impulse towards reform, as an effort to bring about the essential reconstruction of social organisation. This impulse, this endeavour, leads to revolution, to the great revolution. The great revolution is defeated by the restoration, that is to say, by a reactionary revolution, and it therefore becomes necessary to think out anew and to rediscuss the problems of social organisation and reorganisation. The restoration is followed by the July revolution; a further reaction is followed by the general revolution of 1848; Europe fails to attain to repose, and has to make a choice between the old regime or the acquirements of the revolution. The problem of revolution as a whole must be grasped in its true significance, which is not political merely, but philosophical as well. In the study of philosophy, of literature, and of the sciences which deal with man and society, thinkers become aware that the revolution signifies a new age, a new life. We speak of renascence in all domains, a renascence which must be deliberately conceived in theory and must be efficiently carried out in practice.

§ 41.

THE eighteenth century is generally and rightly termed the century of the enlightenment and of rationalism. The titles of two works of this epoch, Paine's *Age of Reason* and Kant's *Critique of Pure Reason*, are distinctive of the rationalising enlightenment.

The *Critique of Pure Reason* provides the epistemological foundation of philosophical criticism. In opposition to the blind faith that had hitherto prevailed (which Kant speaks of as " dogmatism "), but in opposition also to the scepticism of David Hume, Kant demonstrates that a critical awareness of the powers of the human intelligence is the only possible and the only correct attitude for the philosopher to assume. This is the historical, the world-historical significance of criticism.

In concreto, Kant's criticism, like Hume's scepticism, was directed against theology, for theology makes belief in authority the basis of our entire outlook on the universe. It was in this sense that Hegel defined the philosopher's task as follows : " to disturb to the utmost of his power the theologians who with the zeal of ants are endeavouring to assemble critical building materials for the firm establishment of their Gothic temple, to make everything difficult for them, to whip them out of every corner of refuge, until, no longer finding shelter, they are compelled to expose their nakedness to the light of day."

This opposition between philosophy and theology is at the same time opposition towards the church as a religious organisation upon a theological basis. In ultimate analysis the new philosophy is philosophy of religion. If the new philosophy is so frequently conceived as hostile to religion, all that this really signifies is that between philosophy and historically extant religion, the so-called positive religion, an opposition exists, that there is hostility towards the doctrine and the practice of the church.

In one form or another, the church is a state church. Since the middle ages, even, church and state have constituted a unity, this unity being based upon identity of general outlook. Theology furnishes the official outlook of the state, and, in conformity with this unity, society is theocratically organised.

Philosophy, therefore, as philosophy of religion, is a criticism, not merely of theology, but in addition of theocracy, of church doctrine, church morality, church politics—of official doctrine, morality, and politics in general.

§ 41 A.

IT must be carefully noted that the opposition is between philosophy and theology, not between philosophy and religion. It is true that philosophy is opposed to the religion of the churches.

Hume's scepticism was directed against metaphysics and theology, but in addition he rejected religion on the ground that it was an inherited system of tranquillisation. Since he considered that the essence of religion was anthropomorphism, religion was in his view equivalent to superstition.

The Kantian criticism endeavoured to show that transcendental concepts and ideas lack critical justification. In the last resort, however, Kant was willing to tolerate a " more subtle " anthropomorphism when it was necessary to discuss the concept of God, the most important of all concepts. The tendency to anthropomorphise transcendental concepts of the reason was in Kant's view the outcome of natural and inevitable illusions and sophistications of the pure reason itself, illusion and sophistications from which the wisest of mortals cannot hope to be free.

After Kant, Auguste Comte developed yet further the contrast formulated by Hume between anthropomorphism and sceptical critical thought. Three stages, said Comte, can be recognised in the historical development of the human race : the theological, the metaphysical, and the positive (or scientific). The theological stage may be subdivided into three : fetichistic, polytheistic, and monotheistic. The metaphysical stage is no more than transitional.

Here Comte was merely developing Vico's ideas systematically. According to Vico the first of the three stages of human development was the era of gods, demigods (heroes), and men.

Elsewhere Vico terms the first epoch the poetic epoch, saying that poets were the first philosophers. In this age we have expression given to the outlook of the senses and the imagination in default of rationalised activity, and the outlook is chiefly conditioned by fear. This is the age in which nature is animated and deified by the poetic imagination; self-surrender and piety prevail, whilst manners remain rude and barbarous. There follows an epoch of partial awakening. Still later comes the era of complete awakening, of enlightened reason, and of humanitarianism.

In German philosophy, Feuerbach referred religion to anthropomorphism, becoming thereby the real founder of the Hegelian radical left. In this teaching Feuerbach was followed by Strauss, and above all by Stirner and Marx. In England, Spencer, and Tylor the ethnologist, studying primitive man, perfected Comte's doctrine in certain details.

This problem, or rather these problems, cannot be fully considered here, but for our purposes the following points must be emphasised. First of all I should like to render my terminology precise. Following Plato's example, I wish to take my stand with those who replace the term anthropomorphism by the term myth, and to speak therefore of mythopoiesis, which is contrasted with critical, scientifically precise thought and behaviour of human beings vis-à-vis the world. Behaviour of human beings, let me repeat, for we are concerned, not with religion alone, but also with morality, with the whole conduct of man in relation to the world and to society. At a certain stage of development man is not only characterised by having a mythical religion, but in addition his philosophy is mythical; mythical too are his poetry and his art, his ethics and his economics, his language. To express the matter briefly, the essence of myth is found in man's purely objective attitude, in man's complete self-surrender to the object, in his explanation of the world and of himself by analogies, and by hasty analogies. Contrasted with this are scientific and critical thought and conduct. By the critical mind, things are deduced from other things as a result of careful observation and comparison; the critical thinker generalises and makes abstractions; he thinks, in fact, thinks scientifically and critically.

Thus the historical significance of Kantian criticism arises out of the way in which it conceives the attitude of the critical thinker towards the world and towards himself, as opposed to myth, but also as opposed to scepticism. Comte, with his positivism, endeavoured to rest content with critical and scientific thought as developed in the special sciences, and to justify such thought historically as the latest stage of evolution. But such a naïve historical outlook is inadequate ; it is necessary, with Kant, to establish epistemologically the opposition between mythopoiesis and scientific thought. It is a case of criticism versus positivism.

From the history of European thought we learn how among the Greeks there occurred a gradual severance between mythical and critical thought. Philosophers became more fully aware of the contrast as soon as individualism and subjectivism gathered strength during the age of Socrates, the sophists, Plato, and Aristotle.[1] Thenceforward the opposition between mythology and philosophy had become established.

After Aristotle, philosophical thought grew weaker, mythology stronger. The mythical thought of the east was superadded to that of Greece, and from this syncretism theology developed as Christian mythology. Christian mythology was the child of Greek philosophy. Theology, the name given to the most important section of the Aristotelian metaphysic, is the correct denotation for Christian dogma.

Just as classical mythology was contrasted with philosophy, so was Christian dogmatics, Christian mythology, contrasted with scholasticism. Primarily scholasticism was the handmaid of theology, but from it the new scientific philosophy developed and promptly displayed its opposition to theology. This opposition was epistemologically expounded by Hume and Kant. Theology is to-day recognised to be the instrument of myth, philosophy to be the instrument of science.

It is at length possible for us to come to an understanding concerning the relationship of philosophy to religion.

The reader need not be alarmed. I do not propose to say much to him about the essential nature of religion. He will know enough if he will turn the subject over in his own mind. It is a subject to which every one is compelled to attend in view of the existing situation.

Religion, piety, has hitherto been mythical in character. Religious knowledge was at first mythology, subsequently

---

[1] In his History of Greece, Grote, basing his demonstration upon the ideas of Comte, gives a clear account of this development.

theology and theosophy. God was the summum of theology
and religion. Man's attitude towards myth was entirely
objective and uncritical ; God's revelation (in teaching and
miracle) was the mainspring of knowledge and of conduct ;
thinking mythically, man blindly accepted the objective revelation as the absolute guide of thought and action ; belief,
faith, was the foundation of the mythical, theological, system
of knowledge. Revelation was absolute, was valid for all
times and for all men, was catholic. Quod ubique, quod semper,
quod ab omnibus creditum est—thus was the principle of
catholicity formulated as early as the fifth century.

Belief in divine revelation, belief in God, has ever been,
and is of necessity, belief in mediators between God and man,
belief in priests. This belief, this faith, created the church,
created theocracy.

Philosophy, in contrast to theology, is the instrument of
science, is scientific. God is no longer the sole object of contemplation. Philosophy aims at knowledge of the All in all
its parts ; science is specialised knowledge, and philosophá is
the instrument of the specialised sciences. Science and philosophy issue from man, and man has become his own object
of contemplation ; theism has yielded place to anthropism.

One who thinks and acts scientifically is subjectivist and
individualist. Individualism and subjectivism have become
for him the great epistemological problem.

The scientific thinker has ceased to belief in revelation,
has indeed ceased to " believe " at all. He doubts, he criti-
cises ; he endeavours to attain certainty. To belief, to credulity,
to blind faith, he opposes convictions based upon reasoned
knowledge. Critical thought has replaced authority and
tradition as the decisive test of truth. Herein, once more,
lies the historical importance of Kantian criticism. Criticism
is the attainment of complete self-consciousness by modern
man vis-à-vis the world and society.

The scientific, the critical thinker, recognises no mediator
between God and man. He trusts no longer in priests and their
church but in science and philosophy. To theocracy he opposes
anthropocracy or democracy. The man of science, indeed,
recognises catholicity, not the catholicity of external authority,
but that of deliberate and critical agreement.

Hume erred when he rejected religion as anthropomorphism
Anthropomorphism is in truth nothing more than the method

of mythical thought. Kant reduced religion to morality. Comte began, like Hume, with the rejection of religion, but subsequently relapsed into fetishism.

To-day the religious problem may be formulated as follows. Can there be an unrevealed religion? Can the scientific or critical thinker, can the philosopher, have a religion; and if so, what religion?

§ 42.

THE eighteenth century is, in addition, the age of humanitarianism. This concept is conceived extensively and intensively. The brotherhood of the entire human race is to be realised through the inborn love of man for his fellows. To human love, Kant superadds the sense of human dignity.

In this respect, too, Kant and Hume are of historical importance. Hume called a halt to his scepticism when he came to consider ethics, whilst the critical philosophy of Kant culminated in a moral outlook on the world. For the very reason that they had uprooted theology, both these philosophers endeavoured to safeguard ethics, to establish morality upon a natural foundation.

This is why, in modern philosophy since Descartes, so much stress is laid upon the idea of naturalness. Men seek natural religion, natural law, natural morals, a state of nature, natural reason. Art, above all, strives to be natural. The enlightenment had led to the abandonment of the theological basis of thought and conduct. Enlightenment, humaneness and humanity, naturalness—these became synonyms.

During the nineteenth century, owing to the practical trend given to philosophy by Hume and Kant, rationalism, in so far as it was one-sidedly intellectual, was supplemented by emotionalism and voluntarism. These, in their turn, have been apt to receive a one-sided cultivation, commonly in opposition to intellectualism, as in the philosophy of Schopenhauer.

In my own formulation of the problem I contest the existence of a natural opposition between reason and emotion on the one hand and will on the other. My conception of the relationship between the three fundamental energies of the psyche differs both from that of the rationalists (or intellectualists) and from that of the voluntarists (and emotionalists). It is worth noting that in this psychological scheme Kant, the arch-rationalist, accepted feeling or emotion as a distinct basic category, following here the example of Mendelssohn and Tetens, both of whom had been pioneers in placing the emotions beside the intellect and the will as fundamental elements of the human mind (1776 and 1777). Kant's tripartite critique of the *Pure Reason*, the *Judgment*, and the *Practical Reason*, was in conformity with this distinction.

In a word, democracy is opposed to theocracy in the fields alike of practice and of theory.

§ 43.

THE effort to secure a natural and human system of morals logically culminates in political reforms, and may in the last resort lead to revolutionary reforms. Implicit in the enlightenment was the proclamation of the rights of man by the French revolution. Paine, who played a part in the great revolution, gave in his *Rights of Man* a vivid demonstration of these tendencies.

The wider endeavour to secure social reforms awakened pari passu with the growth of the movement for political rights and reforms. It is true that the French revolutionists had the socialists executed as communists, but during the postrevolutionary restoration and the period of reaction, socialism ceased to be the political program of isolated individuals and became that of the working classes at large.

Socialism and sociology frequently appear in association as practice and theory. The enlightenment and the humanitarian philosophy had to throw light above all upon the social and historical domains, upon the most complicated of all facts and phenomena. It has already been pointed out that there is no opposition between Kantian rationalism and the historical outlook. Just like the French and the English enlightenment, German idealism, founded by Kant as a moral outlook upon the world order, led to socialism.

Finally, too, the idea of nationality is deducible from the humanitarian ideal. Herder was one of the first thinkers to contrast the nation as a natural organisation with the state as an artificial organisation, and he attempted to show that the essence of nationality is to be found in literary monuments and above all in folk poetry. After Herder, philosophy tended more and more to devote itself to the problem of nationality, as we see in the writings of Fichte, Schopenhauer, etc. During the nineteenth century the principle of nationality ripened to become a great political force.

§ 44.

THE development and strengthening of the historic sense, enhanced understanding of the evolutionary process in human society and in the universe, made reflective persons fully aware of the antithesis between the individual and the whole of which he forms a part. It is to-day regarded as an obvious fact that the modern age is individualistic in comparison with earlier days. For us this signifies that the modern human being, through his critique of cognition and of his own mental processes in general, has become critically aware of the antithesis between the individual and the collectivity, that collectivity wherein the individual is himself comprehended.

Kant conceived individualism also as subjectivism, for in opposition to epistemological objectivism (realism) he made the assumption that the object adapts itself to our faculty of cognition instead of conversely. From this assumption, which Kant compared with the bold speculation of Copernicus, Fichte and Stirner advanced to solipsism.

Kant's critical rationalism, inasmuch as it was subjectivist, was thoroughly activistic. Cognition seemed to him to be an active process of the understanding. He extolled the auto-procreation of our reason, valued reason for its spontaneity as contrasted with receptivity. Voluntarism, in fact, began with Kant.

Epistemologically and metaphysically, however, even Kant failed to carry his subjectivism to its logical conclusion, and for this reason Fichte spoke of him as a " three-quarters-head." Holding that consistent subjectivism, solipsism, was an absurdity, Kant assumed the existence of an objective thing-by-itself. But even Fichte, despite his verdict upon Kant's half measures, evaded solipsism. If we examine the Fichtean ego closely, its " logical fanaticism " (Jacobi) vanishes. Fichte helped himself out with the expedient of diversified egos (the absolute ego, the ego of intellectual contemplation, the ego as idea, the individual ego), and took refuge in history and the philosophy of history, discovering there nationality. as the objective to which he subordinated the ego. Fichte, too, and Fichte above all, applied subjectivism to the cultivation of morality.

After Fichte, Schelling turned away from Fichte and Kant, and turned back to nature and history. Hegel escaped solipsism by pantheism ; Stirner, Hegel's pupil, was the first to conceive solipsism as egoism ; whilst Schopenhauer transformed subjectivism into his voluntarist nihilism.

We shall see how the question of subjectivism and objectivism, and in particular the problem of solipsism, caused a great commotion in Russian thought. Nor is this surprising, for consistent subjectivism, the solipsistic autoapotheosis to which Fichte and Schelling were prone, is brutal and positively absurd. From the critical outlook, Stirner's egoism is nothing more than a bogey to terrify the philistines—and a not particularly terrifying bogey after all. From Hegel, Feuerbach advanced objectivistically towards socialism, desiring to reconcile the ego with the tu. Marx, on the other hand, conceiving historical objectivism in an absolute sense, went so far as positive elimination of the ego and his individual consciousness, extreme subjectivism thus evoking extreme objectivism.

§ 45.

IN conclusion, then, what has been said about modern philosophy may be summarised in three antitheses. Philosophy is absolutely opposed to theology, anthropism to theism ; but this must not be taken to imply that theism is utterly false, or that anthropism is atheistic, for all that is meant is that the anthropistic outlook and point of departure has come into its own in modern philosophy. At the same time, in the political sphere, democracy is counterposed to theocracy, to theocratic aristocracy, this signifying that democracy, likewise, possesses theoretic and philosophical importance. In ultimate analysis, modern philosophy has ceased to be the queen of the sciences. It does not occupy a higher plane than the special sciences, but ranks beside them. It is *scientia generalis.*

III

§ 46.

RUSSIAN philosophy of history, sociological analysis of the motive forces of evolution, and the attempt to grasp the laws that regulate the temporal succession of social phenomena, date from the time of Peter the Great, for they arose in connection with the reforms effected in his reign and in that of his successors. It is true that Russians have been without clear ideas concerning the existence of Russian philosophy of history and of philosophy of history in general. Nevertheless, closer contact with Europe compelled thinking Russians to compare their home with the foreign world, and judgments of the present necessitated judgments of the past.

The Russian chronicler who passes by the name of Nestor propounded tasks for Russian historiographers substantially identical with those undertaken by writers of the seventeenth and eighteenth centuries. The Kievic twelfth-century historian drew attention to the conglomeration of ethnic types prevailing in Old Russia, and referred also to the peculiar relationship of the Russians as Slavs to their numerous nonslavic neighbours. More especially did Nestor lay stress upon the polyglot character of the Russian state.[1]

Conditions were still much the same in the state of Peter. The prevalence of foreign (chiefly Teutonic) influence, and the fact that in the parts of Russia adjacent to Europe the rôle of the Germans was so decisive for Russia, gave Nestor's utterances a living contemporary meaning. Remarkable for his day was Nestor's knowledge of the various Slav stocks, In the eighteenth century the relationship of the Russians to the Poles entered a critical stage ; the incorporation of the greater part of the Polish state gave occasion for the discussion of the Slavic tongues, all the more because at this epoch the Slavs in Austria and in the Balkans were experiencing a cultural and political awakening. The historical and Slavic researches of these nonrussian Slavs, and the similar researches of the Germans, found attentive and sympathetic readers in Russia.

All these conditions were extremely favourable to the development of Russian historiography. In addition to the polyhistor Lomonosov, whose *History of Russia* was completed in the year 1763, there came a whole series of historians, Tatiščev, Tredjakovskii, Ščerbatov, and Boltin. The name of Karamzin may be added to complete the list.

[1] I refer to the oft quoted passage which describes how during the years 860 to 862 the Variag Norsemen were invited to become rulers. I draw especial attention to the fact that according to Nestor the invitation was jointly issued by the Slavs and the Finns.

German writers exercised notable influence upon the development of Russian historical research. Bayer (who came to Russia in 1725), G. F. Müller, above all Schlözer, whose attention was turned to Russia towards 1770, and in addition Ewers and Reutz, form a stately series.

In accordance with the spirit of the age, the interest of these historians was concentrated upon the chronicle of the reigning dynasty and its origin. Now began the controversy whether the Russian state had been founded by Norsemen, whether it was of foreign origin. The patriotism of Tredjákovskii led him to defend the Slavic theory ; other writers followed in his footsteps, contending further that the Russians and the Slavs in general were autochthons. German writers, led by Bayer, denied the indigenicity of the Slavic Russians, and assumed the Norse origin of the Varangians. It must be conceded that these German historians of Russia were here following Russian chroniclers, and that apart from this they excelled their Russian colleagues in respect of critical perspicacity and method.

But if Russian historians idealised the primal age of Russia, in doing so they followed the general view. It must be admitted, too, that similar idealisation was voiced from the German side, notably by Herder ; whilst, on the other hand, Ščerbatov and Boltin displayed a more critical spirit than Tatiščev and Lomonosov.

It was natural that extremely hazy ideas should prevail concerning happenings in primitive Russia, for even to-day accurate knowledge is scanty.

In general, Russia was identified with the dynasty, and it seemed to these writers that tsarist absolutism constituted the true essence of Russia and of its civilisation. For the development of this absolutism Tatiščev propounded a formula which was subsequently adopted in the main by Karamzin, and was still held at a later date. From the first, he said, the Russian state was a hereditary monarchy. Through subdivision of the inheritance among the heirs, decay set in, this rendering subjugation by the Tatars possible. But from the days of Ivan III onwards Muscovy abolished the " democratic " polyarchy of the petty princes, Russia was reunited, and became strong once more. Opinions varied in points of detail, but this general view as to the nature and value of absolutism continued to prevail. German historiographers accepted the same estimate of absolutism and endorsed Tatiščev's formula.

In the spirit of Peter and of the age, Tatiščev conceived absolutism as enlightened absolutism. He was himself permeated by the German philosophy of enlightenment. In the reign of Anne he advocated the constitution of a deliberative senate.

Karamzin defended absolutism in the spirit of the post-revolutionary reaction. His panegyric upon Alexander I was extended to cover all the rulers of Russia. Before him, indeed, Lomonosov advanced the theory that no notable progress had taken place among the Slavic peoples because there was no reason for them to alter. In Karamzin's opinion, as far back as the ninth century Russia had been the greatest and most civilised state in the world.

During the period of reaction in the reigns of Alexander I and Nicholas I, this opening epoch of Russian historical research was superseded by new historical trends. Fresh and important material was discovered in the state archives and in the monasteries, the value of this material to the historian receiving due recognition. To an increasing extent, history, which had hitherto been purely political and dynastic, became enriched by historical studies dealing with administration, law, and economics.

Schlözer, following the example of Achenwall, had already made extensive use of statistics, which he termed " quiescent history " (whilst, conversely, for him history was " statistics in motion "). Storch, the political economist, had compiled detailed statistics of the Russian realm. In his historical retrospects he was the first to draw attention to the socio-political significance of trade for Kievic Old Russia.

The content of history was further enlarged by the history of literature, language (Slav linguistic studies), and the other activities of civilization (art, etc.) More and more, history expanded from the field of pure politics to cover the whole story of civilisation.

Comparative historiography played its part in this development. Granovskii, of whom a more detailed account will shortly be given, was perhaps the first Russian to write a universal history.

It need hardly be said that after the days of Schlözer, Russian historiography was continually assisted by the progress of German historical research. It can, for example, be shown that Niebuhr exercised considerable influence in Russia.

The greatest changes in the conception of history were those resulting from the experiences Russians acquired in contact with Europe and actually in Europe. Moreover, as has been previously pointed out, historical thought in Russia was stimulated and matured by German philosophy.

Russia participated in the European revolution. Russia fought against republican and Napoleonic France. Russia had joint experience with Europe of the postrevolutionary restoration and reaction, so that the European problem became a Russian problem as well. The causes which led in Europe to the rise of the philosophy of history and to the foundation of sociology were likewise responsible in Russia for the origination of Russian philosophy of history and Russian sociology. With the aid of German idealistic philosophy (in especial that of Schelling and Hegel), and simultaneously with the aid of French socialist thought, after the decabrist rising, the July revolution, the Polish revolt, and the year 1848, Russian philosophy became predominantly historical.

It was during the reaction under Nicholas and under Uvarov his minister for education that Russian philosophy of history became organised as an independent discipline (Čaadaev and the slavophils).

Following Hegel came Comte, Buckle, and the English evolutionists to exercise a notable influence on Russian sociology. Of late, and above all, the teaching of Marx and the Marxists has been predominant. The subsequent studies will attempt a detailed account of this epoch of Russian historical and social philosophy.[1]

[1] Section 47 of the German edition, containing a list of authorities for the study of Russia, is printed as an appendix to Vol. II of the English edition.

PART TWO

SKETCHES OF RUSSIAN PHILOSOPHY OF HISTORY AND PHILOSOPHY OF RELIGION

CHAPTER EIGHT

P. J. ČAADAEV. CATHOLIC VERSUS ORTHODOX THEOCRACY

§ 48.

THE decabrist rising was suppressed in blood, Poland was pacified, and under the supervision of the third section Count Uvarov, in the name of the official trinity of Orthodoxy, autocracy, and nationality, had just proclaimed the infallibility of Tsar Nicholas' policy, when there suddenly appeared Čaadaev's *Philosophic Writing* wherein in the name of religion Uvarov's formula and the entire history of Russia were declared null.[1]

[1] Petr Jakovlevič Čaadaev was born in Moscow on May 17, 1794. His mother was the daughter of Prince Ščerbatov the historian, and, after the early death of his parents, Petr and his brother Mihail, his elder by eighteen months, were brought up by his aunt Princess Ščerbatova. Čaadaev was well read at an early age. Entering the army in 1812, he was under fire at Borodino, Leipzig, and elsewhere, and sent in his papers in 1821. He associated freely with the decabrists, and was for a time an active freemason, but left his lodge in 1818. The years 1823 to 1826 were spent in a visit to Europe. Upon his return to Russian soil he was arrested for complicity in the decabrist rising, but was set at liberty after a brief examination. He lived in Moscow, solitary at first, just as in Europe he had lived a lonely life, for in 1820 he had experienced a spiritual conversion, immersing himself in the study of certain mystics, and it seems that the state of his nervous system was not perfectly normal. His brother was likewise an eccentric, living an isolated village life, haunted by fears inspired by the decabrist rising. But in the year 1831, Petr Čaadaev, acting upon medical advice, joined the English club, and spent the rest of his days moving in the best circles of Moscow society, delighting in the impression he produced, not only by his philosophic views, but also by his faultless attire and by his studied courtliness of manner. Count Pozzo di Borgo, the celebrated Corsican in the Russian service, described Čaadaev as " un russe parfaitement comme il faut." Čaadaev never left Moscow, not even during the summer months, and died there on April 14, 1856. His literary reputation was secured by the publication of his Philosophic Writing, which appeared in Nadeždin's " Telescop." It was first composed in French in 1829, and was addressed to a lady. Three other essays of Čaadaev's are extant. The

Russia, we are told in the writing, has neither history nor tradition, for she has no guiding ideal, and nations cannot live and thrive unless they have an ideal and realise it in practice. Russia has not given a single thought to the world, the world has been able to learn nothing from the Russians, for all individual Russians and the Russian people as a whole are poor-spirited, empty and dead in soul—Čaadaev's essays are dated from " Necropolis." He considered that the universal spiritual inactivity was actually stamped upon the Russians, that Russians had no physiognomy.

The *Philosophic Writing* contains the outline of a philosophy of history. With full awareness of the import of his demand, Čaadaev insists that Russians need an entirely new philosophic outlook upon history, so that they may attain to clear views regarding their position in historical evolution and the tasks they have to fulfil. He follows here the path indicated by western philosophy, in especial by Schelling and in part also by Hegel, but it was inevitable that the suggestion should seem monstrous to the champions of official patriotism, seeing that Uvarov's philosophy of history had formulated perfectly clear prescriptions as to Russia's place in the world and the duties incumbent upon Russians.

To Čaadaev human history is the history of Christianity and of the church, the history of the realisation of God's kingdom upon earth, the history of religious education. To him the Christian religion is no mere system of morality   Above all it is the eternal, divine energy, not acting upon the individual alone, but infused into society at large. The dogma of the one true church implies such a social influence   Christianity has organised society ; Christianity has actually realised God's kingdom upon earth ; Christianity is not merely an ideal, for it is a living energy, the divine energy incarnate.

second and the third continue the correspondence, and refer to several previous writings; the fourth treats of Gothic and Egyptian architecture, and conveys Čaadaev's views upon Christianity and upon the antique. These four essays are spoken of as Čaadaev's philosophic writings, in contradistinction to a number of his letters which have been preserved. There is likewise extant a fragment written in 1836, entitled A Madman's Apology. The four essays are included in Oeuvres choisies de P. Tschadaieff, publiées pour la première fois par le Prince Gagarin de la Compagnie de Jésus, 1862. A work by V. Frank, Russisches Christentum, 1898, contains epitomes of the first and second essays, together with the Apology, two letters to Schelling, and certain other extracts from Čaadaev and opinions about his writings. Frank's publication, like Gagarin's was to subserve the aims of Catholic propaganda.

The principle of unity, indivisibility, and uniformity, by which religion has displayed itself as the central and leading force of history, is found by Čaadaev in Catholicism alone, for only in the Catholic church has the world-embracing Christian ideal been embodied. Despite the individuality of separate nations, he considers that in the spiritual sphere the medieval church realised cultural unity. In his enthusiasm for this unity, he is not content with rejecting the reformation as presented in the Lutheran and Evangelical churches, but in addition he refuses to recognise the Orthodox church of Russia. The Byzantine church originated in the ambition of Photius ; by adhesion to that church Russia shut herself out from the Christian community, and owing to her consequent isolation remained without a living civilisation, for genuine, living, and inspiring civilisation is attainable only in the great community of nations. According to Čaadaev, Moscow imposed upon the Russians a yoke far heavier than that of the Tatars. Russia, in her isolation, was devoid of religion as well as of civilisation. The Russians were Christians, indeed, but only in name. The Abyssinians were also Christians. Russia has a culture of her own ; but, asks Čaadaev contemptuously, have not the Japanese likewise a culture ? Where are the great men of Russia, her sages, the leaders of the Russian nation and of a wider humanity ? The writer does not share the views of those who look hopefully towards the great masses of the population. The masses are blind ; none but heaven-sent great men can be accepted as representatives of the people, and there are no such men in Russia. Moreover, Russian life is not inspired with a genuinely Christian spirit. Čaadaev points to the English as exemplars of a truly religious people, for to him England, not Russia, is the promised land.

The ideals of duty, of justice, of law and order, are at home only in the west, not in Russia.

Čaadaev expressly condemns the chauvinistic glorification of Russia and the east vis-à-vis the west, a supervaluation common in the Russia of his day. The Christian consciousness must be based upon truth, not upon blind national prejudices which serve only to keep men apart. Russia, continues Čaadaev, does not belong to the east either geographically or historically. It has remained isolated between east and west, and for this reason has failed to share in the advantages of the east or to co-operate and participate in those of the west. Precisely on account of its peculiar geographical position, Russia, leaning in the east on China and in the west on Germany, should have endeavoured to co-ordinate the two great principles of mental life, the imagination and the reason, and to unify in her own civilisation the history of the entire globe. But Russia failed to do anything of the kind, merely imitating the intellectual life of the west, and taking over western ideas ready made. This imitation, this acceptance of the ready made, is disastrous. Ideas must be developed by spontaneous activity if they are to work as living thoughts. It is through such an elaboration of idea that individuals and nations acquire a specific spiritual tendency. Russia's misfortune lies in this, that Russians have accepted ideas in the finished state, and therefore lack the definite trend, the peculiar methodology, the logical and syllogistic thought of the west, which in the west is realised through ideas. " We grow, but we do not ripen."

This spiritual isolation and inactivity are paid for by every individual Russian. The Russians have no common life, no common tradition ; each one of them endeavours as best he can to enter upon his own account into relationships with historical evolution.

Čaadaev compares the position of the Russian nation in respect of European civilisation with the social position of illegitimate children. Without inheritance, without any union with the men who have gone before, the Russians have no part in the tasks which devolved upon humanity before they themselves appeared upon the stage of history. . . .

The effect of the *Philosophic Writing* was stupendous. Herzen compared this effect with that produced by Griboedov's comedy. He exaggerated, but its influence was in truth powerful and impressive, like that of the cry of " fire " in the quiet of night.

When Nicholas read the essay, he made a marginal note to the effect that the work was an impudent absurdity which could only have been written by a madman. It is impossible to say whether this judgment was based solely upon the perusal of the writing or whether the tsar had been informed regarding Čaadaev's eccentricities and nervous peculiarities. However this may be, orders were now issued that Čaadaev should be examined daily by the police physician and should be declared insane. Naturally the author was watched also by the police, but the physician soon discontinued his visits, whilst the police ceased to concern themselves about the author after he had been forbidden to write. In fact, Čaadaev never published anything in book form.

The Philosophic Writing of Čaadaev was given to the world without the writer's authorisation ; by 1836 his views had undergone modification, and the essay had never been intended for the general public. But in this very point lies the significance of the work, and it is for this reason that it has become a literary document of the Nicolaitan epoch. It was addressed to a lady quite unknown in the literary world, and it was through its artless character, through its intimate tone of conviction, and through its frankness, that the *Writing* exercised so inflammatory an effect. The appearance of this heretical and revolutionary essay in Nadeždin's journal " Telescop " was, moreover, characteristic of tsarist absolutism and the censorship of that day. Nadeždin, it is related, adroitly extorted an authorisation to print from the censor when the latter was, as usual of an evening, engrossed at the card table. A passionate devotion to cards was a characteristic fruit of the Russian prohibition of thought. The censor's carelessness, the energy of an editor speculating in a sensation, in a word, the publication of the *Philosophic Writing* with its attendant details, reproduce for us the essence of Nicolaitan civilisation. Another characteristic touch is that the signal for the philosophic revolution should have been given by a soldier, for at that time the officers constituted in a sense the most cultured and independent class in Russia. Čaadaev took his place as successor of the decabrists. Further, his essay was written in French. At the close of the twenties, the cultured Russian, though he studied German philosophers and accepted many of their ideas, was still predominantly under French influence. Beyond question Čaadaev's essay is a literary document of surpassing interest.

§ 49.

ČAADAEV grew up among the decabrists, and was subjected to the same influences as his friends N. Turgenev, Jakuškin, Griboedov, Puškin, etc. He shared the views of the decabrists, but in addition he watched the restoration of the old regime in France and elsewhere in Europe, attuning his mind to the philosophy of that restoration. Frenchified by his education, he had become acquainted with the change of philosophic front in France; had familiarised himself with the thoughts of Chateaubriand, of Madame de Staël, de Maistre, de Bonald, and Ballanche; had learned something of German philosophy —from Schlegel a little, from Schelling a great deal, and somewhat from Hegel. Among classical thinkers he had paid great attention to Plato. Writers of his own day had exhibited the counter-revolution to him as a great historical problem with which humanity was faced; in his own land and in his personal experience he had acquired first-hand knowledge of this counter-revolution and of the part played in it by the Russia of Alexander and of Nicholas. He had participated in the war against Napoleon. At a later date (1820), a mutiny occurred in his regiment, and he was ordered to report on it by Tsar Alexander, who was then in Troppau. After a prolonged sojourn in Europe, in his *Philosophic Writing* Čaadaev proclaimed his dissent from the Nicolaitan system.

Čaadaev's literary remains are fragmentary; they have not hitherto been subjected to adequate criticism; reports as to his views are indefinite. For these reasons I cannot attempt a decisive judgment.

Beyond question Čaadaev passed through a religious crisis, like so many of his contemporaries. He moved away from the rationalist outlook of Voltaire to romanticist mysticism. From available evidence it is impossible to determine whether and to what extent he returned to Voltairism. Even though as late as 1837 he described the philosophy of the decabrists as mere frigid deism culminating in doubt, this must not be taken as implying that by that date he had himself ceased to doubt. It seems probable that towards the year 1820 he inclined towards mysticism, a mysticism intense to a degree that was almost morbid. This much, at least, is certain, that he was greatly interested in the writings of Jung-Stilling and Eckartshausen, and was pondering about the spirit world. I think, however, that he got the better of this mysticism. There is no mystical element in his *Philosophic Writing* or in his other known works. It is true that thoughts are occasionally expressed by him which may be the outcome of a mystical contemplativeness, but side by side with these we find disquisitions with no trace of mysticism, and his conception of the philosophy of history is entirely unmystical. His demand for spiritual passivity, and above all his demand for the annihilation of the ego, may be mystically interpreted. Čaadaev speaks of his contempt for the world, rejecting on this ground all participation in the political improvement of the world ; he even contends that the world is our work and can therefore be annihilated by us at our own will : these and similar sayings may be mystically interpreted. There is a mystical ring about his presentation of eternity as the life of the righteous, and about his claim to have eliminated the concept of time (" thou opinest that the shovel of the gravedigger stands between thee and heaven "—1837) ; and a similarly mystical interpretation may be attached to his conception of immortality in the sense of the Platonic pre-existence ; but these utterances may also be interpreted unmystically. His *Philosophic Writing* is not mystical. At the outset of the essay Čaadaev commends to his correspondent the practice of all the ceremonies of the church. This is the very reverse of mysticism ; it is perhaps a romanticist prescription à la Chateaubriand, but does not remind us of Tauler Similarly, Čaadaev's religious philosophy is devoid of mysticism. He lays great stress upon the church and upon its political power. For him religion and the church are identical concepts. He lays especial stress upon the objective aspect of religion as contrasted with the subjective, explicitly rejecting the Protestant doctrine of the invisible church. In so far, too, as he analyses the nature of religion, his outlook is unmystical. He stresses the truth of religion, valuing before everything the struggle of religion towards truth and towards the ideal. Love of one's neighbour has for him a logical basis ; in the search for truth a man is defeated by his own ego, because this ego hides the truth from him ; he must therefore overcome his ego if he is to find truth.

Finally, Čaadaev's leanings towards Catholicism and his fondness for the papacy are evidence against the view that he was a mystic. In these respects he was conquered by de Maistre the politician, and not by mysticism.

I devote considerable space to this question, because of late much emphasis has been laid upon the mystical aspects of Čaadaev's work, and because it seems to me expedient to elucidate the religious foundations of this writer's philosophy of history.[1]

[1] I have at my disposal Čaadaev's writings in the Russian translation by Geršenzon (P. J. Čaadaev, Life and Thought, 1908). Here the word social'nyi

Even though at a later date Čaadaev gave a psychological explanation of the characteristics of his *Writing*, attributing it to a condition of morbid mental irritability which had even led him to entertain thoughts of suicide, I hesitate to accept the characterisation. In any case, the occurrence of this mood of despair would suggest that his earlier attitude of doubt had not been definitively replaced by religious conviction.

For all his gifts, Čaadaev was not a profound thinker, for he lacked scientific steadfastness and power of elaboration. He said of himself that he had but one idea. It is true that in his eyes history was the realisation of only one idea, but even this he fails to formulate with sufficient clearness and to trace without ambiguity. The defect in his work is associated with and exemplified by his attitude towards Catholicism. He never went over to Rome, and when questioned on the matter he would take refuge in indefinite phraseology, or would explain that he regarded Catholicism as a kind of regulative principle for faith. He was not a strong, firm man, being much more the dandy of the English club than the man of faith. In my view, he was greatly impressed by French civilisation, and in accordance with the Catholic philosophy of his day he regarded this civilisation as the fruit of Catholicism, which, once more in the French spirit, was identified by him with Christianity. He was fortified in such a position by his romanticist predilection for Catholicism. We are justified in assuming that he noted the progress made by Catholicism in the west, especially among the Protestant peoples, for this progress was notorious. Moreover, he himself tells us that from 1833 onwards he had observed the spread of the Puseyite movement in England. Catholicisation was a widespread phenomenon of the day. In Russia, Čaadaev was not the only Catholiciser. I may remind the reader of Alexander I and of his hopes of the pope. Since the days of Tsar Paul, among the Russian aristocracy there had been much sympathy with Catholicism and above all with Jesuitism. Several highly placed nobles were Catholics, and some were actually Jesuits, like Prince Gagarin, the editor of Čaadaev's *Writing*. An interesting career in this connection was that of Pečerin, at one time professor of philology at Moscow, who sought refuge from atheism

is frequently employed with reference to the political significance of the church. Čaadaev even speaks of " the social problem," but he means no more than the problem of the influence of the church upon society, its political influence.

with the Redemptorists. The conversion of Gagarin and of
Pečerin took place after the appearance of Čaadaev's *Writing*,
which was perhaps contributory. Čaadaev himself did not
become a Catholic, and his views upon the Russian church
underwent a change. But we lack sufficient information as
to Čaadaev's thoughts concerning the leading problems of
theology and religion, and above all we are ill informed as
to his views upon the relationships between the two leading
Catholic churches, as to his estimate of their differences in point
of dogma and as to his detailed hopes for their reunion. The
abstract character of his fondness for the papacy is plainly
shown by his selection of England, rather than France, or
Austria under Metternich, as the ideal of a religious land.

Čaadaev's sympathy with Catholicism and the papacy
prejudiced him with the liberals as well as with Uvarov, as is
manifested by the protests of Odoevskii and Puškin. Puškin
unfortunately took part against his friend in the Vjazemskii
denunciation of Čaadaev to the minister for education. Dostoevskii, when composing the greatest of his novels, desired
to make Čaadaev, with his fondness for Catholicism, the leading
figure in the story. Thus persistent was the influence of
Čaadaev, and thus extensive was the significance attached to
him by his successors.

§ 50.

ČAADAEV was astonished at the vogue of his *Writing*, and
he endeavoured in his *Apology* to justify and expound the
earlier work. It is undeniable that the exposition weakened
his criticism of Russia, but it must also be admitted that in
the *Apology* many of the utterances of the *Writing* are clarified.
In the last-named work, some of the concepts are presented
with inadequate precision, and this makes it difficult to decide
whether Čaadaev's later views represent a natural development or the withdrawals of a weakling. It is necessary to
emphasise the crudity of the *Writing*. Almost childish is the
way in which Čaadaev fails to recognise that his commendation
of England and of the English religious spirit conflicts with the
fundamental thesis of his work. The more closely we examine
that work, the more strongly are we impressed with the indefiniteness of its leading ideas. Čaadaev is no more than a
philosophic improviser, an aphorist whose views had not been
logically thought out and systematised.

In the *Apology* he admits that the criticism voiced in the *Writing* had been acrid and excessive. But he accounts for this by his extreme distaste for the "fanatical Slavs," that is to say for the slavophils who, chauvinist in method and in aim, have uncritically panegyrised Russian history. Čaadaev has a perfect horror of nationalism, and above all of the national prejudices which hold men apart. To him the patriotism of the slavophils seems a mere national instinct, and he demands that national instinct shall be enlightened by reflective ideals. For Russian patriotism "the day of blind amours" is past. "I have never learned to love my fatherland with lowered eyelids, bowed head, and closed lips. In my view those only who see their country with clear vision can be helpful to their country. . . . I love my fatherland as Peter the Great taught me to love it. I admit that I have no sympathy with ecstatic patriotism, that indolent patriotism which sees everything rose-tinted, and succumbs to the slumber of illusion. . . . Love of country is a great thing, but there is a greater love still, the love of truth. . . . The path to heaven leads upward, not through the fatherland, but through the field of truth. . . . Love of country engenders heroes, but love of truth creates sages."

Čaadaev reiterates the thesis of the uncivilised character of prepetrine development. The calm recognition of this fact does not seem to him unpatriotic, but it proves that Russians excel men of other nations in taking unbiased views of themselves. In their lack of culture the Russians, less overloaded with ideas, have fresher minds, are more receptive, are comparatively unprejudiced. The Russian spirit is receptive precisely because it is empty, and all that Russians have to do is to choose from Europe what is best. But they must choose ; they must not blindly imitate ! Such, contends Čaadaev, was the aim of Peter the Great. Peter found his country a blank scroll. With his strong hand he inscribed on this blank the words "Europe" and "the West." Since then the Russians have belonged to Europe and the west. Peter showed that Russia's mission was to effect a deliberate synthesis of the best elements in European civilisation.

Čaadaev's meaning is plain. Russia is to take over the conduct of human history. He does not say this in so many words, but it is the corollary of his estimate of Russia and of Europe. As early as 1831 he writes apocalyptically in a letter, " An obscure feeling convinces me that a man is destined shortly to appear who will reveal to the age the truth of which it is in need." Was it to be some Saint-Simon to found a political religion, or some Lamennais to establish a new Catholicism ? However this may be, Čaadaev looks for the completion of human destiny and for a new evangel from heaven. In the *Apology* (1837) he gives expression to his profound conviction that the Russians have been appointed to solve many social problems, to perfect a considerable part of the ideas formulated among the older societies, and to supply the answers to the most difficult questions that confront humanity.

In the *Writing* he demands that Russia shall effect a synthesis of east and west, but in the *Apology* he modifies this view. At the outset he completes his characterisation of east and west. The east is religiously contemplative, the west is active ; hence the east has left the conduct of affairs entirely in the hands of government, whereas the west bases government upon law. Both east and west have done great things ; the east was the pioneer ; but the west, more energetic, subsequently absorbed the east. Ultimately the east fell asleep in its indolent " synthesis." In this characterisation of the east Čaadaev takes sides definitely against the slavophils, who conceived Russia as of the east and played her off against the west. Čaadaev recognises the importance of the east, but its importance is subordinate to that of the west, and he will not admit that Russia is essentially eastern. This is inconsistent, for in the *Writing* he represents Russia as of the east, and at a later date (as, for example, in a letter to Schelling in 1842), we find that Čaadaev refers to modesty, bashfulness, and ascetic contemplativeness as characteristic of the Russian spirit—and at that time these traits were regarded, and by many are still regarded, as typically oriental.

In the *Apology* Čaadaev is inclined to refer Russia's defects to her geographical situation, to her position on the uttermost limit of civilisation. He frequently refers to this position in the world, emphasising the assertion that the Russians are northlanders, and he insists that the Russians have to a predominant extent allowed themselves to be guided by government. When he makes this an occasion for a compliment to Nicholas and his dynasty, we are reminded of the negotiations which in 1833 Čaadaev conducted with Benckendorff with a view to securing an official post. Čaadaev then wrote that for Russians there was no other way of progress than by remaining faithful subjects, by subordinating their own feelings to the feelings of the tsar, and by an attitude of absolute humility towards the autocrat. It must be remembered that Čaadaev had strongly condemned the revolution of July 1830, and indeed the French of that date.

It will be seen that Čaadaev was not notably courageous. In his *Apology* he calumniated Herzen in a most distasteful manner. When taxed with this by a friend, his excuse was: " Mon cher, on tient à sa peau."

In the *Apology* Čaadaev speaks of Peter, Lomonosov, and Puškin as Russian sages and as the teachers of mankind. Their existence is a proof that Russia, at any rate the Russia of Peter the Great, progresses. But in prepetrine Russia, too, he discovers a valuable and significant civilising factor, the Russian church, and the Christian humility which it has stamped upon the Russian people. Čaadaev was an opponent of serfdom, as we learn from his letters and from the reports of his friends. N. Turgenev, whom we know to have been a strong opponent of serfdom, endorsed Čaadaev's views. Further, Čaadaev deplored the subjugation of church to state, this implying censure of cæsaropapism But should he not have asked himself whether these phenomena had any connection with the way in which the Russian church had inculcated prayer and humility upon Russians ?

In these matters Čaadaev's position was embarrassing. His condemnation of Gogol's *Correspondence with Friends* in the year 1847 suffices to show that even after 1836 he had no great love for the Russian church and its humility. Still later, he spoke of the Crimean war in a way which was ill calculated to promote a spirit of humility towards the autocrat of all the Russias.

§ 51.

IN his philosophy of history Čaadaev vacillates above all in respect of the fundamental idea of progress. On the one hand he is inclined, with Pascal, to assume that progress is continuous. On the other hand he regards the Christianisation of the world as a miracle, as the outcome of supernatural intervention ; on a single day there perished, to be reborn, not alone the Roman empire, but the entire world of classical antiquity.

In like manner Čaadaev arrives at peculiar estimates of classical civilisation in general. In Greek civilisation he esteems its material beauty alone, condemning Socrates, Marcus Aurelius, the stoics, the Platonists, and Homer " the corrupter of mankind." The old world was not destroyed by the barbarians, but fell to pieces at a touch, for it was already a corpse. None the less he has praise for Epicurus and his ethical system, for therein he discerns the factor that binds human beings together. It is equally uncongenial to find that while he esteems Mohammed and Islam, and also the religions of Hindustan, he has no word of commendation for Aristotle and his undeniable services. Apropos of the settlement with Islam he is bold enough to admit that Christianity can adopt divers religious forms, and that in case of need it may even enter into alliance with error in order to attain its aims to the full ! Two of his philosophical essays are devoted to these questions.

Čaadaev simultaneously touches on the problem of freedom. On the one hand he admits the determinism of many historical events and facts, as when he refers to the influence of geographical situation. He insists, too, upon the internal logicality, upon the " syllogism," of historical development, thus reminding us of the Hegelian dialectic. On the other hand he maintains that the individual is free, for " the absolute freedom of the human spirit " has been preserved by Christianity ; and he desires also to rescue the " universal reason." In the letter written to Schelling in 1842 he condemns the Hegelian dialectic as a fatalistic logic which practically abolishes free will. It cannot be said that he even approaches to a clear formulation of the problem. He tells us that history is the product of the divine energy ; but how can we conceive the freedom of the individual and of the universal reason as reconcilable with this theism ? What is the general significance of the immanence of God ; what is the individual reason ; and what is the " universal reason " ? What is the relationship of immanent teleology to freedom and to necessity ?

It would seem that these problems flitted through Čaadaev's mind, though he failed to formulate them adequately. He was familiar with the difficulties which Tolstoi (among others) was subsequently to encounter in the elaboration of a philosophy of history.

Frequently he contemplates the kingdom of God on earth sub specie æternitatis, so remote from time that men, the world, and history become mere symbols. Thus for him Rome is a symbol of the entire history of the world ; the eternal city is a real point, where concretely and physiologically man can conceptually grasp all the memories of the human race, whilst the pope is a mere idea, a pure abstraction, not a man, but an all-powerful symbol of time.

In association with these problems Čaadaev had to consider how the individual is related to social development. He contrasts society with the individual, and subordinates the individual to society. Not merely does he demand humility and the religious subjugation of the ego, but for him the " universal reason," as he terms it, is the social whole, which is subject to the will of God, but which, as a whole, has an independent and spontaneous existence vis-à-vis the individual. As people this whole is conceived to be something distinct from the mere government, but (at least when he is dealing with the middle ages) he postulates the federative system of nations as a whole, and it is this whole which he terms " the Christian nation," wherein individual and national differences disappear or are subsumed. What view are we to take of divinely sent great men as leaders of the people ? " To genius all things are possible." Schelling seemed to him the one man great enough to lead all the leaders of the crowd. What are the blind masses when compared with their leaders ? In 1837, without relinquishing his respect for " universal reason," Čaadaev had energetically combated Lamennais' doctrine of the universal spirit, although Lamennais terms it " la raison universelle du genre humain," which is identified with the tradition and consciousness of the Catholic church, with Catholicism.

If I am to aim at a decisive judgment, I must express my regret that no complete critical edition as yet exists of all Čaadaev's fragmentary writings. In the works of this author we have a concrete example of the difficulty to which I referred in the preface, the difficulty while in Europe of writing about Russia. For an adequate study of Čaadaev it would be necessary to consider manuscript memorials, to collect all the available fragments, and to arrange them in chronological order. Thus only would it be possible to present Čaadaev's mental development.

I have treated Čaadaev as the first Russian philosopher

of history. He was, in fact, the first Russian who endeavoured, following the lines laid down by German philosophers of history, to attain to clear conceptions concerning the nature of the philosophy of history and of history in general. He was especially interested in the philosophical demonstration and valuation of the ideas of which historical facts are the expression. To Čaadaev the history of every nation is no mere succession of facts, for it is in addition a concatenation of ideas. In this and in similar respects Čaadaev reiterates the Hegelian dialectic and reproduces the Hegelian outlook. As we have seen, he employs Hegelian terminology, speaking of the logic and syllogistic of the " universal reason " as it evolves in history. To the Russians, in their adaptation to a commencing Europeanisation, a philosophy of history was especially necessary.

In this matter Čaadaev occupied a peculiar position between two parties that were then in process of formation, that of the slavophils and that of the westernisers.

He accepts the fundamental thesis of the slavophils, that society and historical development are to be conceived, above all, in a religious sense. But he is distinguished from the slavophils in that when he thinks of religion and the church he thinks of the militant and conquering church of the west, whereas the slavophils had in mind rather the contemplative religion of the east with its mystical renunciation of the world. Thus it was that Čaadaev, instead of shutting himself up in a Russian monastery, sought out the world, becoming as it were a monk in a frock coat.

To Čaadaev the slavophils seemed to be retrospective utopists, learned apostles of a national reaction, whereas his aim was towards a world church, a universal church, modelled on the papacy. Čaadaev's papistical leanings constituted a stumbling-block for his slavophil friends and opponents, but in Moscow he had personal associations with Ivan Kiréevskii, Homjakov, and the other founders and advocates of slavophilism from whom he derived his later esteem for the Russian and eastern church.

In this way Čaadaev drew nearer to the program of official theocracy, though he continued to think rather of a " theocracy of consciousness " in Schlegel's sense than of theocracy as it was understood by Count Uvarov, and for this reason he was an object of suspicion to the government no less than to the first slavophils. In 1852, when the police compiled a register of slavophil suspects, Čaadaev was included. Fun has been made of this police catalogue of men of letters, but as far as Čaadaev was concerned it did not err.

He was, however, distinguished from the slavophils by his unreserved admiration for Peter, and for the same reason he was esteemed by the westernisers, above all by Herzen. In the sphere of abstract politics he never abandoned the ideals of the decabrists, although he detested their method, the method of revolution. At bottom, indeed, Čaadaev too desired a revolution, but it was to be on the European model. In the west, writes Čaadaev in his first essay, all political revolutions were in reality spiritual revolutions ; interests followed ideas instead of leading them.

Čaadaev shared with the westernisers an unsparing criticism of Russian conditions. He shared their aversion to national chauvinism, which since the Napoleonic campaigns had grown to constitute the official nationalism of Uvarov, and which Čaadaev regarded as national nihilism. We learn this from Jazykov, the slavophil poet, who fiercely censured Čaadaev for his antipatriotism.

Although Čaadaev's conceptions had a theocratic basis, the westernisers discovered in this writer an essential scepticism upon religious questions, and therefore felt at unison with him.

Čaadaev exercised powerful influence over his contemporaries and successors. We see this not only in Herzen, but also in Puškin, N. Turgenev, and even Dostoevskii. The influence is in part explicable through Čaadaev's remarkable duplex position, a position recognised by Puškin in his criticism of this man whom he termed a " curer of souls." In Rome, said Puškin, he would have been a Brutus, but in Athens a Pericles.

CHAPTER NINE

SLAVOPHILISM. THE MESSIANISM OF ORTHODOX THEOCRACY. SLAVOPHILISM AND PANSLAVISM

I

§ 52.

WITH the aid of German philosophy the "fanatic Slavs," as Čaadaev termed them, transformed Uvarov's theocratic program into a philosophical system. In his religious westernism Čaadaev remained isolated, but continued to exercise an influence upon friend and foe, for the slavophil movement culminated in the establishment of a school.

Slavophil philosophy was first formulated in the literary circles of Moscow, being directly connected with the system of Schelling, whereas to the westernisers, the opponents of slavophilism, Hegel's system served as foundation. At the outset the two tendencies were not precisely differentiated, but by about 1845 a clear division of principle was recognised, and therewith the adherents of the respective views entered opposite camps. Owing, however, to the severity of censorship under Nicholas, the literary and journalistic formulation of the conceptions in question did not ensue until some years later, at the beginning of the fifties and in the opening years of the reign of Alexander II.

Certain historians of literature refer to nationalist predecessors of the slavophils, telling us that Šiškov, Karamzin, or Küchelbecker was the first slavophil. The only sense in which this is true is that the slavophils developed yet further the strong nationalist tendency which had become manifest during the reign of Alexander I and that they defended and treasured Russian civilisation. In this sense, predecessors of slavophilism are likewise to be found among the first advocates of Russianism during the eighteenth century and even earlier. But I consider it necessary to insist that in its primary form and as advocated by its founders slavophilism was not a nationalistic but an essentially religious movement, and that equally with westernism its philosophic sources were to be found in the west.

The original meaning of the term slavophil was a love for Slav literature, not for Slavism. The word was first used to denote the nationalism of Šiškov. This writer declared that church Slavonic was the root and foundation of the Russian vernacular ; with the church tongue came the church Slavonic alphabet, and of course the church spirit as well. The word " slavophil " was ironically employed by Šiškov's opponents, and was subsequently transferred to the new trend. Kirěevskii spoke of his own views as Orthodox Slavonic, others referred to " the Slavs " ; Gogol used the expression " Slovenists and Europeists."[1]

Čaadaev's friend Ivan Kirěevskii was the founder of slavophilism. Homjakov is frequently spoken of as the founder, and it is contended that Homjakov influenced Kirěevskii, and practically effected the latter's conversion to slavophilism. The statement is inaccurate. Kirěevskii, as we are about to learn, was at the outset of his development a supporter of western culture, but he was likewise an opponent of contemporary liberalism in so far as this was indifferent or hostile to religion. Subsequently he became more conservative and his ecclesiastical and religious feelings strengthened. Only for this intensification of his ecclesiastical leanings can Homjakov, P. Kirěevskii (the brother of Ivan) and others be regarded as responsible. Even in this direction the influence of Kirěevskii's wife and of her clerically minded acquaintances may perhaps have been more important than that of Homjakov. To Kirěevskii we owe the most profound and the most general formulation of slavophilism as a philosophic doctrine, and Homjakov was more influenced by Kirěevskii than Kirěevskii by Homjakov. As a matter of mere chronology, Kirěevskii was the philosophic founder of slavophilism.[2]

---

[1] Slavophils spoke at first of themselves as "slavenofils," and subsequently the forms "slavjanofil" and "slavofil" came into use.

[2] Ivan Vasilievič Kirěevskii was born in Moscow on March 22, 1806, and belonged to an old and well-to-do family. His education was influenced by Žukovskii the romanticist, a great uncle on the maternal side. Žukovskii had

Kireevskii, like Čaadaev and his other friends and acquaintances, was brought up on German philosophy and literature, Schelling having above all influenced him. At an early age Kireevskii was introduced to the ideas of Schelling by his stepfather and tutor Elagin, who translated into Russian Schelling's *Philosophical Letters Concerning Dogmatism and Criticism*. In this work are to be found the leading epistemological positions that were subsequently expounded in Kireevskii's own writings. The influence of Schelling may likewise be traced in the essay entitled *The Nineteenth Century*, and in the program of Kireevskii's review " The European." In a word, the Europeanisation of Russia was Kireevski's program immediately after his return from Europe.

exercised considerable influence upon his niece, Kireevskii's mother, interesting her and her son in the study of German romanticist literature. Kireevskii's father died in 1812. In 1817 his mother married Elagin, and from 1821 onwards she played a leading part in Moscow society, at first in the literary circle which gathered round Polevoi (Vjazemskii, Küchelbecker, Ševyrev, Pogodin, and others, including Puškin) ; and subsequently in the circle of the lyric poet Venevitinov (Puškin, Vjazemskii, Barjatynskii, etc.). In 1824 Kireevskii became an employee in the Moscow record office, the largest Russian collection of historical documents ; among his fellow employees were Petr Kireevskii, Prince Odoevskii, the poet Venevitinov and his brother, and Ševyrev. In 1830 Kireevskii went to Berlin, attending lectures on philosophy, theology, and history (Carl Ritter, Stuhr, Raumer, and Schleiermacher). Already well acquainted with Hegel's works, in Berlin Kireevskii made the philosopher's personal acquaintance. He also met Gans and Michelet. After two months in Berlin he went to Munich, associating there with Schelling and Oken. He remained less than a year in Germany, and returned home without having attained the desired philosophical satisfaction. In 1832 he founded the review " Evropeec " (The European) to which Puškin, Žukovskii, Barjatynskii, and Jasykov were to contribute, but Kireenskii's essay The Nineteenth Century and a critical sketch of Griboedov proved the ruin of the review, and S. T. Aksakov, the censor who had passed the contributions, fell into disfavour. " The European " was suppressed after.the second number, Kireevskii married in 1834. During the forties, literary and philosophic Moscow assembled in Mme. Elagin's salon. Hither came Gogol and Jasykov, K. Aksakov, Samarin, Homjakov, D. A. Valuev, Granovskii, Herzen, Čaadaev, and many others. Kireevskii had hoped to be appointed professor of philosophy, but failed to obtain this post. In 1845 he was entrusted by Pogodin with the editorship of " Moskvitjanin " (The Muscovite), but abandoned the position after the issue of three numbers. In 1852, in conjunction with others of the like way of thinking, he launched the " Moskovskii Sbornik " (Moscow Magazine), but his essay On the Character of European Civilisation and its Relationship to Russian Civilisation proved fatal to this literary undertaking. In the year 1856, after the author's death, in " Russkaja Beseda " (a slavophil periodical published from 1856 to 1860) appeared a sketch entitled The Need for and the Possibility of new Foundations for Philosophy. This posthumous work was a fragment, for it was uncompleted when Kireevskii died of cholera on June 11, 1856. Petr Kireevskii (born February 11, 1808, and died October 25, 1856) was known as a collector of folk songs.

Čaadaev might well take delight in Kirěevskii's writings of the year 1832 ! Kirěevskii unreservedly accepted European culture as it had developed from the middle of the eighteenth century onwards. With Schelling, he considered this culture to be the highest stage of intellectual development, regarding it as the phåse of artistic creative energy which completed the practical and theoretical phases. At the same time, this culture was the harmonious solution of the oppositions which had found transitory expression as revolution and counter-revolution, as Voltairism and romanticist mysticism. Kirěevskii considered that the French revolution had exercised a wholesome influence upon Europe. He hailed the return to religion and the religious spirit, for like Čaadaev he looked upon this as a social energy tending to unify mankind. In his view, religion was not merely ceremonial and inward conviction, but was also a spiritual unanimity of the entire nation. As such it must be displayed in all manifestations of social life. Religion must permeate the entire historical development of the nation.

To Kirěevskii the culture of the new Europe was the natural sequel and perfectionment of classical culture as fructified by Christianity. Russian civilisation before the days of Peter was in his eyes defective because Russian Christianity, the Russian church, though purer and holier than Catholicism and the Roman church, had been incompetent to diffuse their energy throughout Russian life as a whole, to permeate state, civilisation, art, the economic organism, society at large. For the Russians the classical factor was lacking, and there was consequently also lacking the renaissance influence which in the west was so peculiarly associated with Christianity. The Russians remained uncultured. In Novgorod and Pskov alone did there exist offshoots from the general culture of Europe.

Kirěevski praised Peter and Catherine for having articulated Russia to Europe, and he condemned the national chauvinists who desired for Russia a purely national and independent culture. He inveighed against those who wished to separate Russia from Europe by building a Chinese wall. True civilisation was to be found, not in national peculiarities, but in participation in the general life of the civilised world. The Russians should not direct their gaze backward towards Old Russia ; they must and could undertake the direct adoption of the newer European civilisation. They must become Europeanised, for to strive after a separate nationalism was tantamount to aiming at uncivilisation.

There are numerous lacunæ in Kiréevskii's philosophy of history, and in especial we have to note the lack of analysis of that Russian Christianity which was " purer and holier." Moreover, if religion was to permeate the entirety of social life, how was the new western culture, modern Europeanism, to be directly associated with the Russian church and religion ? In this association, what was to be Russia's rôle ?

The work is too sketchy. The individual phases of historical development are not adequately described. For example, the reformation receives no more than passing mention ; we are not told why the new culture has outstripped the older, Christian, culture ; and so on. Further, the leading concepts, state, nation, humanity, civilisation, religion, etc., are not defined with sufficient precision. Nor did Kiréevskii attain to clear views regarding the true significance of his Europeanism. The Nicolaitan government, however, had no doubts about the matter, and gave Kiréevskii's " European " short shrift. Culture implies freedom ; the activity of the reason signifies revolution ; the " adroitly chosen middle course " leads to a constitution. Such was the minister for education's interpretation of the essay, and no one can say that he was wholly wrong.

§ 53.

AFTER this literary mishap Kiréevskii remained in the background, publishing no more than a few literary studies, anonymously. When he married he became acquainted with Father Filaret an ascetic monk of the Novospassian monastery in Moscow, Mme. Kiréevskii's confessor. This acquaintanceship contributed much to the clarification of Kiréevskii's religious views, and strengthened the influence exercised by his brother Petr and his friend Homjakov. Kiréevskii had hoped to bring his wife, a woman of education, over to his side ; but within two years of marriage, as his friend Košelev reports, he shared the opinions of his wife. From his estate at Dolbino in the administrative district of Tula he paid frequent visits to the hermitage of Optina, entering into close relationships with some of its older occupants. After the death of Filaret in 1842, Kiréevskii's confessor, Father Makarii, influenced him greatly. His Orthodox bias was further strengthened by the study of the Greek fathers of the church, and it was in the frame of mind thus induced that he wrote the two essays of 1852 and 1856.

The leading ideas of these works and of other fragmentary articles and thoughts may be briefly expounded as follows.

In its intimate nature Russia differs from Europe. The contrast between the two civilisations is determined by religious and ecclesiastical differences. It is the contrast between faith, and knowledge inimical to faith ; between tradition and criticism ; between eastern Orthodoxy, on the one hand, and Roman Catholicism and predominantly German Protestantism, on the other. Orthodoxy is for Russia the buckler of revealed religion ; the Orthodox creed is the mystical expression of absolute and divinely revealed religious truth. European Catholicism, and above all Protestantism, made an unfortunate attempt to show that divine revelation was in conformity with reason, the net result of this rationalism being to destroy the faith of the western church and to divide the human spirit against itself. Culture, too, as based upon the faith and upon the church, differs in Russia and in Europe. The dominant philosophy of Russia is that of the Greek fathers of the church, but in Europe scholasticism and the essentially Protestant philosophy which sprung from scholasticism have been the mainsprings of culture. For this reason Russian art has its peculiar characteristics, for to it beauty and truth are one, whereas in Europe the conception of abstract beauty leads to visionary untruths.

The Russian state has grown organically out of the commune, the mir ; the European state originated through armed occupations and the subjugation of foreign peoples. Moreover, modern parliamentarism with its majority rule is merely the continuation of the materialist principle of government. Kirěevskii took the same view of Louis Philippe as did Nicholas I.

Russian law, too, has developed organically out of the convictions of the people, whereas European law, imposed by the Roman conquerors, finds its climax in outward legalism and in the formalism of the letter.

Above all, therefore, the relationship of state to church differs in Russia and in Europe. The Russian state is entirely distinct from the church, the former having none but secular tasks to fulfil. The European state is merged into the church ; the church usurps power over temporal affairs and neglects spiritual affairs. "Holy Russia" does not signify what the politically Holy Roman Empire had signified; Holy Russia is a treasure house for relics.

In Russia property is communal (the mir), for the individual has a value as such; in Europe the individual is valueless, for the meaning of European private property is that the human being is adscript to the soil—it is the soil which has value, not the individual.

In Russia, consequently, the family has an entirely different constitution from that which obtains in Europe. The Russian family is patriarchal; by the ties of blood its members are associated to form a moral unity from which have originated by organic growth the commune and ultimately the state with its patriarchal ruler. The European family is individualistic and therefore egoistic; it leads to the emancipation of women and children.

Russian life is simple, but Europe seeks luxury and comfort. Political economy is the science of the life of material enjoyments.

The Russian finds genuine civilisation, Old Russian, Slavic, prepetrine civilisation, upon the land; its sustainer is the peasant, the mužik, the community at large. The European has his modern civilisation, whose focus is in the town, and whose sustainer is the bourgeois. Bourgeois industrialism dominates social life; bourgeois philanthropy is essentially the outcome of egoistic calculation.

The fruits of these differing outlooks and activities are likewise fundamentally diverse. The Russian is spiritually unified; though he never fails to be aware of his imperfections, his conscience gives him repose and satisfaction. The European has a conviction that he is perfect, and yet has no feeling of happiness or satisfaction, for his spiritual nature is utterly disunited, and he is plunged into scepticism and unbelief; but without faith it is impossible to live.

Kirěevskii, having been led to formulate this dualism by an analysis of contemporary Russia and Europe, next endeavours to explain it on philosophic and historical grounds. In his view the contrast between two civilisations and two worlds existed already in antiquity in the contrast between Rome and Athens (later replaced by Constantinople). Christianity mitigated national peculiarities. Within the unified worldwide church, local and national qualities were pushed outward to the frontier. In course of time, however, Latin peculiarities gained the upper hand, and this resulted in schism, in the great historical dualism of east and west.

The Latin half of the world was unable to withstand its ancient juristic and formal fondness for the syllogism, for logic ; it modified its dogma (" filioque "), and it evolved scholasticism, which was to make Christian teaching comprehensible to the reason. Yet precisely by this logical route did scholasticism and the Roman church become hostile to reason, and despite their rationalism they submitted blindly to the authority of the hierarchy and of the pope.

Not merely the church but culture as a whole came to the west in an exclusively Latin form. In all its elements, therefore, this culture has a juristic and formal, outwardly logical character. In the moral sphere, the western character is manifested in the Roman pride which constitutes the essence of patriotism, the greatest of the Roman virtues. The Greek loved his home, but the patriotism of the Roman was the pride of one who, in loving his fatherland, loved in truth his party and his own egoistic interest. In a word, the acceptance of the Roman system gave its peculiar stamp to the whole of western culture—and that culture was confined to externals.

To a degree the reformation saved religion for the west. In the main, however, Roman rationalistic scholasticism continued in force, Protestantism engendering modern Teutonic philosophy. Through the work of Hume, Kant, Fichte, Schelling, and Hegel, western thought, essentially Roman, western syllogistic rationalism, was brought to its term. The old unity of Catholicism was disintegrated through the triumph of individualism and subjectivism, whereby too, the west was socially atomised. Just as in the middle ages every knight in his castle was a state within the state, so now in the modern age we have the cult of unrestricted individual authority, the proclamation of personal conviction ; revolution, as typified in the French revolution, has become the precondition of progress.

Very different was the development of eastern Christianity. Kirěevskii fails to give us as precise a demonstration of the essence of Greek and Byzantine civilisation and culture as he has given us of the development of the west. He contents himself with explaining the Greek conception of religion, which, in contrast with the outwardly logical rationalism of the west, is characterised by an intensity of mystical contemplation.

The great schism weakened Byzantium from the cultural outlook, but did not lead to any decay of religion. From Byzantium Russia received true Christianity and therewith the foundations of true civilisation. Unlike the nations which accepted Roman Christianity, the Russians had no civilisation prior to their conversion, and were therefore able to adopt Christianity more readily and to maintain it in greater purity. They cherished, not only Christian doctrine, but also Christian morals and the genuinely Christian character. The Russian is typically contrasted with the Latin ; the Russian's Christian humility is the very opposite of the Latin's ostentatious pride. Kirěevskii is, indeed, forced to admit that in latter days the man of the people, the mužik, has alone preserved true Christianity ; and he further concedes that Russia also took a false step in her development, mistaking the form for the substance. The substance of Christianity, the meaning of Christian doctrine, finds expression in outward form, in ritual. Deceived by the intimate association between substance and form, the Russian has mistaken the form for the substance, and thus Old Russian culture and Russian social life became encumbered with formalism. In this domain of form there actually resulted a kind of schism, the sixteenth-century raskol.

Kirěevskii was even inclined to explain the reforms of Peter as an offshoot of Russian formalism. Russia, in her devotion to form, adopted the formalistic system of the Romanised west. Yet Kirěevskii, rejecting Peter's reforms and rejecting the civilisation of the west, himself reproduces Peter's error ; he even commits the original sin of Rome, and endeavours to provide a philosophical foundation for the true religion of the Orthodox east. " What sort of a religion would the religion be which was incompatible with reason ? " This is the question he addresses to those men of the west who jettison philosophy in order to save religion.

Thus in the end Kirěevskii comes to the view that German philosophy may constitute a transitional stage on the way to an independent Russian philosophy. Western philosophy, he considers, has attained its climax, has found its definitive form, in German idealism, and is incapable of further development. The understanding must recognize this, and must resolve upon a change of outlook ; the cold analysis of the critical understanding, which since Roman days has been the leading power in the west, must be replaced by a return to reason; from logic, syllogistics, dialectics, we must return to mystical contemplation. The critical understanding has isolated the individual psychical faculties, has attempted to make them independent one of another, has led to an inner division in the human spirit. Rescue from this state can be secured in one way only, by a return to faith, to contemplation, to intuition, in a word to that reason wherein all the spiritual energies, acting as a perfect unity, constitute a living whole. This unity of the spirit was, he says, most perfectly attained among the Greek fathers of the church; but Kiréevskii recognises that it has become impossible for mankind to regain their standpoint. Philosophy is at once the outcome and the foundation of the sciences, and the leader in the path we have to take between the sciences and faith. The new knowledge demands a new philosophy. Hence Kiréevskii based himself upon Schelling, who after his return to mysticism could lead the new knowledge and the new civilisation back to the true faith. At any rate, the saving Russian philosophy could be established upon the foundation of Schelling's teachings; the Greek fathers would serve this philosophy as signposts, would offer it the principles requisite for the guidance of life.

It is manifest that Kiréevskii is endeavouring with the aid of Schelling, and especially with the aid of Schelling in his later developments, Schelling entangled in theosophy and mythology, to confute Kant and Hegel. To put the matter in psychological and epistemological terms, Kiréevskii accepts the datum of Kantian criticism that the highest religious truths are not cognisable by the understanding. With the establishment of this proposition Kant deprived European rationalist civilisation of its roots, but he failed to take the further step that was necessary. Schelling was the first to turn away from rationalism to intuition, to intellectual contemplation. And yet Kant desired by means of his criticism to find a way back to faith. " Consequently the leading characteristic of believing thought is found in the endeavour to fuse all the individual parts of the soul into a single energy, to discover that inner concentration of being wherein the reason, the will, and the emotions, but also the conscience, the beautiful, the true, the wonderful, the object of desire, justice, compassion, the totality of reason, flow together to form a living whole, so that the essence of personality becomes re-established in its primitive indivisibility." To Kiréevskii the chief peculiarity of " Orthodox thinking " lies in this, that " it does not endeavour to transform individual concepts in order to bring them into harmony with the demands of faith, but aims at elevating the understanding to a level higher than that which this faculty commonly occupies ; it endeavours to secure that the very source of apprehension, the very mode of thought, shall be sympathetically attuned to faith " [1]

§ 54.

HAVING endeavoured to make a brief sketch of Kirĕevskii's slavophil philosophy of history and of religion. I will now venture a short critical discussion of that philosophy.

It is easy to grasp the distinction between Kirĕevskii's earlier views and those which he subsequently formulated. We see that there had occurred a real change of tendency, and not a mere change of outlook upon certain points (as, for example, in his attitude towards the French revolution). It is true that in his first work Kirĕevskii recognised religion to be the most important among social forces. As early as 1827 he condemned the " stupid liberalism " which had no respect for religion. In his second phase, however, religion, which was first conceived by him in the sense of Schelling, was considered in the historical form given to it by the Byzantine Russian church. Whereas Schelling desired to see the opposition between catholicism (Petrus) and Protestantism (Paulus) done away with in the Johannine church of the future, Kirĕevskii found his ideal in the Russian church—though it must be admitted that Kirĕevskii constructed an ideal Russian church for himself.

We can learn Kirĕevskii's mentality and outlook from an enumeration of the philosophers by whom, in addition to the Greek teachers of the church, he was chiefly attracted. Besides Schelling and such men as the Schellingian Steffens,[2]

---

[1] Kirĕevskii's terminology is based upon Kant and Schelling. He employs the Kantian distinction between " understanding " (razsudok) and " reason " (razum, or um). The mystical contemplation of the reason (zrĕnie uma) is what Schelling terms contemplation (Anschauung or intellectuelle Anschauung). In Russian the common interpretation of this term " zrenie uma " (literally " mind sight ") is what we understand by " intuition," not necessarily employed with any mystical meaning but rather with the sense of " a priori." Homjakov attempts a fuller analysis of this theory of the spiritual energies.

[2] Characteristic of Kirĕevskii is the epitome he gives of the autobiography of Steffens, who was converted from Protestantism to Catholicism, but ultimately

we have Vinet, Pascal, and similar writers. He considered Schleiermacher, to whom he had listened in Berlin, too rationalistic. Of Hegel's work he would accept only the introduction to the philosophico-historical dialectic. As has already been explained, he rejected the Kantian criticism in toto.

Rejecting modern philosophy, he is likewise opposed to scholasticism, which he regards as the mother of modern philosophy. Consistently enough he condemns Byzantine scholasticism as well as the scholasticism of the west, and in general has much that is critical to say of Byzantinism.

Kiréevskii wishes religion and revelation to be kept perfectly pure, and therefore, in common with Schelling, he advocates a peculiar mystical receptivity, a mood of immediate contemplation. Catholicism and Protestantism are for him no religion at all because they aim to make faith comprehensible by the understanding, to give it a rationalistic basis. Even dogma is in Kiréevskii's eyes revealed truth, and he therefore considers that theism, in its revealed form of the trinitarian doctrine, is the essential Christian doctrine. (The essay of 1856 was designed as the introduction to a treatise on the doctrine of the trinity.)

Of course mystical contemplation does not suffice Kiréevskii. Nolens volens he requires a theory of religion, and he therefore decides in favour of Joannes Damascenus (Chrysorrhoas) and Schelling. Kiréevskii conceives mysticism as a species of gnosis ; he is akin to those medieval scholastics who were simultaneously mystics ; it was by this trend that he was led towards Schelling, a Protestant thinker, under whose influence he remained to the end.

Kiréevskii did not experience any such mystical crisis as had been passed through by Čaadaev. He had a great affection for the Greek fathers of the church and helped his monastic friends in the publication of their works, but he knew that the contents of these works could not suffice for modern times. Himself no mystic, he endeavoured to immerse his mind in Old Byzantine mysticism and to explain that mysticism psychologically, but as far as his personal attitude was concerned he got no further than a revival of the spirit of antique faith and the acceptance of ecclesiastical forms of piety.

became an Old Lutheran. 'Steffens was opposed to the (Prussian) ecclesiastical union. Kiréevskii considered that much was to be learned from Steffens' religious experiences.

Though he sought strength and aid in intercourse with monks and believers, he was never able to rid himself completely of the sting of doubt.

Doubtless Kirěevskii experienced a change of views, becoming more conservative, but he exhibited no intolerance towards those who held opinions he had discarded, and he maintained freedom of judgment vis-à-vis his slavophil associates.[1]

Above all Kirěevskii demanded that there should be unity, not only in philosophical views, but likewise in personal and social life. Upon the foundation of a defective philosophy of cognition borrowed from German idealism he established a psychological, epistemological, and historical, dualism which was to give expression to the contrast between Russia and Europe. His consistent application of this dualism to historical evolution is a quite creditable performance, but his history and philosophy of history constitute rather a deductive artifact than an empirical demonstration of actual occurrences.

In his analysis of European dualism Kirěevskii laid bare the errors and the defects that had characterised the dichotomisation of Russian development since the days of Peter ; but the errors and defects which he perceived in Europe had in fact forced themselves on his attention in regard to Russia and in regard to himself. It cannot be denied that this dichotomisation exists in Russia and in Europe, but Kirěevskii erred when he objectivised his own life ideals, when he transferred them to the philosophico-historical plane and to Old Russia. His mistake was the one made by all European romanticists since the days of Rousseau, when they sought the ideal for the future in the past, some among the ancient Teutons and Gauls, others among the ancient Slavs, and yet others in the age of the apostles. Kirěevskii transferred Schelling's church of the future to the third Rome or discovered it in the Russian mužik. He strongly idealised the third Rome, and this idealisation of Old Russia and of Orthodoxy was in reality a severe criticism of extant Russia. The literary henchmen of Tsar Nicholas were. well aware of this, condemning as " quite peculiarly

---

[1] A characteristic utterance was one to Granovskii : " I am closely akin to you in feeling, but I am far from sharing all your intellectual convictions ; in faith I am with our friends, but differ from them greatly in other respects." To Homjakov he wrote in 1844 : " You perhaps regard me as an arch-slavophil. Let me tell you that only in part do I share the slavophil's outlook, and that from the remainder of their opinions I am as remote as from the most eccentric of the views of Granovskii."

mischievous " the panegyric of Old Russia published by Kirěevskii in the year 1852. To Kirěevskii, faith was no mere belief
in a conviction imposed from without, but was a genuine
devotion of the inner life bringing the individual into direct
communion with a higher world. The official state church,
with its authoritarian creed, could not tolerate such a view.
Obviously, moreover, it was mere self-deception for Kirěevskii
to restrict to Catholicism and Protestantism his demonstration
of the religious inadequacy of the churches.

In the gross and in detail Kirěevskii's philosophy of history
is imperfect. His concepts are unduly abstract, and he does
not analyse historical facts with sufficient precision. But the
same criticism applies to Kirěevskii's German teachers, and
Kirěevskii's work was important notwithstanding all its
defects. For Russian ecclesiastical historians, the imposing
institution of theocracy constitutes the true content of history.
By Kirěevskii, in the spirit of these historians, the disastrous
dichotomisation of the church and of mankind is regarded
as a new Fall (schism), reproduced, with trifling alterations,
in Russia (the Russia of Peter).

In his exposition, such concepts as church, state, nation,
and people are unduly abstract, whilst historical facts are
distorted, often in the most ingenuous manner. To Kirěevskii,
Plato and Aristotle seem typical representatives of two distinct
outlooks on the universe, Plato being a mystic, Aristotle a
syllogist and rationalist. Kirěevskii utterly fails to remember
that these two thinkers were Greeks and contemporaries, and
that between Hellenism and Romanism there was no such
simple contrast as that which he assumes to have existed; the
difficulty is not overcome by assigning Aristotle to the west.
Kirěevskii fails to recognise that his Greeks systematised
theology and scholasticism. He does not endeavour to ascertain how and when classical Hellenism developed into Byzantinism. We are not told how in respect of national character
the Russians and the Slavs are more closely akin to the Greeks
than are the Teutons and the Romans. It need hardly be said
that the concepts west and east are very loosely formulated.
But there are even graver difficulties in Kirěevskii's philosophy
of history. Above all, we have to ask ourselves how the true
and unitary church universal could have been defeated so
disastrously by Roman pride, the divine overthrown by the
human. Kirěevskii himself moots the question why Russian

civilisation, in view of its advantages, failed to develop more fully than European civilisation. Why, he enquires, did not Russia outstrip Europe? Why did not Russia become the leader of civilisation? Why has Russia had to borrow her civilisation from Europe? We have further to ask how the uncultured Russians could possibly preserve the treasure of divine truth intact and pure for humanity? Kirĕenskii, the believer, solved this historical enigma in a spirit quite opposed to that of the parable of the buried talent.

In contrast with Schelling and with the devotees of romanticist hero-worship, Kirĕevskii turned for help to the mužik, to the man of the common people. For him the mužik was the ideally religious man. He insisted that the thoughts which were to save Russia must be elaborated by the totality of the faithful, and he declared genius to be superfluous if not positively harmful. Here Kirĕevskii's views were in striking contrast with those of Čaadaev.

Kirĕevskii's religious agrarianism had likewise a social basis. He greatly admired the mir, and extolled it as the fundamental social unit of the Russian political system.

Quite consistently, Kirĕevskii believed in Russia's messianic mission. Russia's true faith would bring salvation also to the west. But Kirĕevskii remained modest and tolerant, conceiving that this salvation would take the form of a synthesis of Russian and of western civilisation, and that the saviour would receive many cultural acquirements from the saved. His slavophilism was less exclusively nationalistic than that of his successors, and for him the true motive force of Russian messianism was ever to be found in the advantages and the absolutism of the orthodox creed. Since, however, a faith cannot exist without believers, Kirĕevskii was obliged to consider the national peculiarities of the Russians and of the other peoples of the world, was obliged to ponder the problem why the Russians were to undertake the salvation of mankind at one specific epoch. As early as 1829, in a report on Russian literature, Kirĕevskii had advocated the articulation of Russia to Europe. The European nations, he wrote, had all completed their tasks; in respect of civilisation Europe was now a unity which had swallowed up the independence of the individual nations out of which it had been composed. Hence, for the continuance of its organic life as a unity, Europe required a centre. This centre must be found in a single nation, able to dominate the others both politically and intellectually, and Russia was predestined to fulfil the function. Russia would become the capital, as it were, the heart of the others, would in her turn occupy the position that had been successively filled by Italy, by Spain, by the Germany of the reformation, by England, and by France. In addition to Russia, Kirĕevskii did indeed envisage the United States of America, a country no less young and vigorons than Russia, but it was too remote from Europe, and its preponderantly English civilisation was unduly one-sided. The foundations of Russian culture had been laid by all the nations. Russia was European in character, whilst her geographical situation would also lead her to exercise a notable influence upon Europe. In Kirĕevskii's opinion, the flexibility and impressionability of the national character would tend, in conjunction with the political interests of the Russian state, to promote the same end. " The fate of every European state depends upon a union of all European states ; the fate of Russia depends on Russia alone. But the fate of Russia rests upon Russia's civilisation, which is the determinant and the source of all her advantages. As soon as we have turned these advantages to full account, we shall share them with Europe, thus paying back our debt a hundredfold."

As previously said, this messianism was still modest. Moreover, it was realistically based upon the youth and vigour of the Russian people, upon the political power and geographical situation of the country, and upon the national character.

Subsequently Kirĕevskii's views underwent modification. In the essay of 1852 we read that racial peculiarities do not suffice for the foundation of future hopes. These peculiarities, like the soil upon which the seed falls, may accelerate or retard the growth of the seed, may supply satisfactory or unsatisfactory nutriment, may furnish free scope for development or may choke the desired growth with tares—but the character of the fruit depends on the character of the seed.

Even if we accept the simile of soil and seed, we ask for an adequate study of the soil. It is here that Kirĕevskii's exposition is so imperfect. To the Russians (he speaks sometimes of " Russians," sometimes of " Slavs ") he ascribes a peculiarly pacific tendency which is manifestly considered the offspring of the Christian's love for his neighbour. Having discovered a Russian state that had grown solely through the arts of peace,

Kirěevskii asked himself whether the love of peace peculiar to the Russian was a congenital or an acquired characteristic. This critical problem and a number of similar ones are propounded, and some of them will require further consideration when we pass to the study of Kirěevskii's successors. It is evident that Kirěevskii had accepted the humanitarian ideal of the German enlightenment and had translated it into Russian.

Another observation may be permitted upon Kirěevskii's character as manifested in his literary fragments. For the very reason that we have no more than fragmentary works from his pen, we get a good picture of the man's literary isolation. The censorship and the repressive measures of the reign of Nicholas robbed him of the joys of creation and made him a literary hermit. Retiring into himself, Kirěevskii, in conformity with his own theory, devoted himself to contemplation, for he lacked inclination and courage for the struggle against oppression. In 1848, for example, when even Pogodin was urging that an address should be sent to the tsar wherein literary men should make a joint complaint against the censorship, Kirěevskii advised against this course, lest suspicion be aroused that he and his friends were not loyal supporters of the government. To preserve Russia from internal disorders and to obviate a war in which Russia might help the Germans against the Slavs, well-disposed persons should be willing to sacrifice literature for two or three years. In the social question, too, and above all in the great Russian problem concerning the liberation of the serfs, Kirěevskii's views were extremely conservative.

Kirěevskii's outlook tended towards quietism. He was here more strongly influenced by Russian conditions than by German philosophy. By Kant and Fichte, but also by Schelling, his attention had been directed to the consideration that the will has an importance side by side with the intelligence. In the treatise translated by Kirěevskii's stepfather Elagin, Schelling pointed to the will as the source of self-consciousness, whilst in the later and entirely mystical writings of the German philosopher, the will was spoken of as the real being (*das Ursein*). Kirěevskii, too, pondered the problem of the will, and it was characteristic of his mentality that this should lead him to quietism. In a letter to Homjakov he complained that the present differed from antiquity in its failure to understand

how to strengthen the will.   Strong individualities were doubtless to be found, like that of Napoleon, but these remained
exceptional.   The will was born in seclusion and was trained
by silence.   To Kiréevskii, Russian monks and the ancients
were the true heroes, heroes of the will, and with them he
decided in favour of seeking an asylum from the world.
Despite all differences, we see here a certain conformity of
teaching between Kiréevskii and Čaadaev.

§ 55.

IN close association with Kiréevskii, and yet independently,
Homjakov and Konstantin Aksakov elaborately perfected the development of slavophil doctrine, Homjakov being
mainly concerned with its theological and Aksakov with its
political aspects.[1]

Homjakov was the polemist, the missionary, the agitator
of the slavophils.   His opponent Herzen speaks of him as
having polemised throughout life.   In writing and by word
of mouth Homjakov presented counter-arguments to the
westernisers and also to his own allies (Samarin and Kiréevskii).
His dialectic method, above all in historical questions, consisted in an attempt to present the facts in another light.
Speaking generally, Homjakov followed the method of theologians who endeavour to make their fixed theses palatable.
I am thinking especially of those theologians and men of
learning whose good faith is beyond dispute.   To Homjakov
slavophilism had the cogency of a creed.   Let me give a single

---

[1] Aleksěi Stepanovič Homjakov was born in Moscow on May 1, 1804.   His
mother, née Kiréevskaja, provided for him from early childhood a strictly
religious education.   Homjakov's father had a taste for literature, but a passion
for cards, and gambled away more than a million roubles.   Homjakov promised
his mother to remain chaste until marriage, and kept his word.   His chief
interests were mathematics, literature, history, theology, and philosophy ; he
also painted, and wrote poems and dramas, but neither Puškin nor Bělinskii
admired him as a poet.   In 1822 he entered the army.   While in St. Petersburg he associated with the decabrists, and especially with Rylčev, but dissented
from their views.   He spent 1825 and 1826 in Europe.   In 1828 he rejoined
the army to fight against the Turks, and distinguished himself in various skir-
mishes.   During the thirties and the forties he developed his views in intercourse with friends and opponents (among the former being the brothers Kiréevskii, K. Aksakov, Samarin, Košelev, Valuev, and among the latter Herzen and
Granovskii).   In 1836 he married a sister of the poet Jasykov.   He numbered
Gogol among his acquaintances.   In 1847 he again visited Europe (Prague,
England, Germany).   On September 23, 1860, he died of cholera.

example. The westernisers drew the slavophils' attention to the fact that extremely harsh and inhuman corporal punishments were inflicted in Byzantium, the cradle of the pure faith. Homjakov replied that Byzantium was Roman before it became Christian, and might well therefore have acquired its severities from Rome. He failed to observe that if we accept this derivation of Byzantine cruelties we have to admit that in an important respect Christianity proved too weak ; but he agrees that Byzantium was far from setting a good or beautiful example in social matters, and here he differs from his friend Kiřeevskii ; at the same time he endeavours to save the slavophil position by the contention that pure Christianity withdrew into the monasteries and hermitages.

Samarin spoke of Homjakov as " a teacher of the church," declaring that it had been his transcendent service to initiate a new era for Orthodoxy. Homjakov did in fact desire, with the help of philosophy, to secure for Russian theology an equal rank with Catholic and Protestant theology. With this end in view he carried on a species of philosophic polemic against Catholicism and Protestantism.

In philosophy and history Homjakov's opinions were derived from those of Kiřeevskii. It was his endeavour to carry Kiřeevskii's teaching a stage further in the fields alike of psychology and epistemology, but I cannot think that he was successful. There are many points of detail wherein Homjakov differs from Kiřeevskii, but these differences are of no essential significance.

With Kiřeevskii, Homjakov starts from the thesis that human life as a whole finds its true fulcrum in religion. He regards history as the history of religious development ; and to him religion, or to speak more precisely faith, is the motive force of history. History is itself a continuous struggle between freedom and necessity. If religion be the true historic energy, it follows that there must be a struggle between two divergent religious outlooks, the religion of material necessity and the religion of spiritual freedom. This struggle ends with the establishment of the religion of the spirit and of freedom.

Homjakov did not systematically elaborate this fundamentally Hegelian doctrine, but expounded it in numerous annotations for a universal history.

In the most primitive forms of fetichism, down to the philosophy of Buddhism with its apotheosis of non-existence,

Homjakov discerns the cult of matter and of material necessity. The spirit striving for freedom must recognise matter as evil, must fight against matter, must liberate itself from matter —for the slave of matter yields to necessity. Homjakov considers that Buddhism effected a certain development of spirituality, but this spirituality is servile and not free, for the Buddhist finds his freedom solely in self-annihilation. Homjakov further declares that all forms of anthropomorphism are a cult of matter, for the materialist is one who can comprehend divinity in no other form than his own. Judaism was more spiritual than were the various polytheistic religions, but the perfectly spiritual and free religion made its appearance with the coming of Christianity. Christianity, however, suffered a schism, for under the influence of materialist Rome and its juristic logic (likewise purely materialist) spirituality was confused with mere reasonableness.[1] Rome detached herself from the church universal, but the eastern church remained faithful to the true doctrine. The orthodox creed is notably distinguished from that of the west, and this is sufficiently shown by terminology. The west has " religio," obligation, that is to say unfreedom ; but the Russian, the member of the orthodox church " believes " voluntarily, from free inward conviction, and without any outward obligation, for his faith is a primary matter of the heart.

By an inner necessity Roman Catholic rationalism gives birth to the yet more rationalistic Protestantism. Within its limits, Catholicism aimed at unity, and secured unity, but at the cost of freedom, whereas Protestantism sacrificed unity to freedom. Catholicism begat Protestantism, and Protestantism begat German philosophy. Kant was the continuation of Luther, and Feuerbach the continuation of Zwingli and Carlstadt. In Feuerbach and Stirner, postkantian German philosophy reached its nadir, individualism and subjectivism manifesting their true essence—egoism. Protestantism is rationalism in an idealist form, whilst Catholicism is rationalism in a materialist form. To Catholic rationalist materialism, Homjakov gives the name of " talismanism," holding that the Catholic prayer is a mere conjuration, whereas the Orthodox Christian maintains a genuine spiritualism in ritual and in prayer.

---

[1] Homjakov speaks of the contrast between material and spiritual religion as the contrast between Kushitism and Iranism. He divides Kushitism into Sivaism and Buddhism, whilst Iranism comprises Judaism and Christianity.

Just as there is only one God and only one truth, the truth of God, so is there but one church. This is not the visible society, the community of the faithful; it is the spirit and the grace of God living in this community. The church is holy and universal (catholic), its unity is absolute. The living, the dead, the heavenly spirits (the angels), and the generations yet to come, are all united in the one church. The church has therefore existed since the creation of the world and will endure till the end of all things.

In the forties Homjakov wrote a catechetic exposition of church doctrine, and it was characteristic that he should stress the all-embracing unity of the church. This signified that Homjakov, like Kirĕevskii and Čaadaev, rejected religious individualism and subjectivism. The individual as a religious being was by him subordinated to the religious whole, for he considered such subordination to be the necessary consequence of the existence of the one God who has revealed truth to man. Homjakov thus attained to a civitas Dei wherein was abolished the distinction between this world and the next, the individual becoming already in this world a dweller in the city of God.

Subsequently, during the fifties, Homjakov wrote certain polemics against Catholics and Protestants. In these works he insisted upon the absolute character of revelation, and in one place he positively identified dogma with the church. He attained to Rousseau's formula of the universal will. For Homjakov, as for Rousseau, universality (catholicity) did not consist in the totality or in the majority of the members of society (the church). " The church," he wrote, " does not comprise more or fewer of the faithful; it is not composed of the majority of the faithful; it is not even constituted by the visible union of the faithful. The church is the spiritual bond which unites them." God, Christ, is the head of the church.

In view of these and similar formulations it has been contended that despite Homjakov's hostility to Protestantism his own idea of the church is Protestant, and above all it has been maintained that he reproduces the Protestant doctrine of the church invisible. There is considerable force in the objection, but we must remember that the doctrine of the church invisible has been very variously conceived, and that it exists in both the Catholic churches, the Roman and the

Orthodox, side by side with the doctrine of the church visible.

Homjakov found it difficult to establish a precise distinction between the material and the spiritual, between the realm of necessity and the realm of freedom. He conceived the unity of the church as the spiritual unity of divine truth, losing sight in this conception of the individual members of the church. But since he was unable to ignore these individual members completely, he helped himself out with the concept of a living body or organism. The church, since it had to be spiritual, was not in Homjakov's view authoritative in character, seeing that every authority is something imposed from without. To him the church was truth itself, the grace of God, living in all. By this route Homjakov attained to a species of pantheism. The individual understanding could grasp divine truth in no other way than through " a moral harmony with the all-existing understanding." Christ is head of the church ; but the bodily, the visible Christ, says Homjakov, would be an imposed truth, whereas truth must be free, must be voluntarily accepted.

Thus the problem of individualism involved Homjakov in great difficulties. He vacillated between the Catholic and the Protestant outlook, and was unable on the epistemological plane to formulate clearly the relationship between the individual and the church as a whole.

The concept of faith, so important a part of Homjakov's doctrine, is involved in like obscurity. In this case he was unable to master the epistemological relationship between subject and object. If truth be objectively given as divine revelation, how does the individual become aware of this truth ? In the letter to Bunsen, Homjakov terms the Bible the written church and speaks of the church as the living Bible.

In the letter to Samarin, written in 1859 and 1860, Homjakov attempted an epistemological exposition of the idea of faith in the form of a critique of philosophy from Kant to Hegel. It is important for our understanding of Homjakov that we should recognise how incapable he was of dealing with the real problems of the theory of cognition and how he attempted to formulate his own outlook quite illogically by derivation from certain positions of the German philosophers. Homjakov set out from Kiŕeevskii's assumption that faith is the central and unitary cognitive energy of the mind, and he assumed, like Kirěevskii, that there is an opposition between faith and analytical understanding. Kirěevskii made no attempt at a more precise psychological study of this outlook, but Homjakov endeavoured to provide it with psychological foundations in the Kantian criticism and in the philosophy of the post-kantians. His starting-point was that reason (*razum*) and will were identical. He spoke of a " willing understanding," thus insisting upon the spontaneity, the creative energy, of reason. Thus Homjakov, in defiance of his fundamental view, accepted that which he had contested elsewhere, the individualism and subjectivism which secured epistemological and even metaphysical expression in the work of Kant and his successors. Homjakov, like Kirěevskii, was directly influenced by Schelling, referring to Schelling's view concerning the nature and significance of the will. Doubtless, too, Homjakov had learned from Hegel that the essence of self-determining freedom is to be found in the unity of will and thought.

I do not know whether Homjakov had any intimate knowledge of Schopenhauer's doctrine of the will.[1] However this may be, upon a foundation of German idealism, reason and will are conceived as one, but Homjakov subdivides will into belief and understanding (*razsudok*). Belief is defined as thát capacity of the reason which becomes aware of realities and transmits them to the understanding for analysis and cognition. Belief, we are told further, is the inner and living awareness of things; it is the immediate grasp of things as a whole ; belief renders immediate and evident what is objective and what is subjective, requiring neither proof nor reasons for this. Belief is " pure thought," is rational contemplation, is intuition, of which in its completeness man is not capable on earth, but whose power he will enjoy to the full in the other world.

It is obvious that Homjakov has not advanced beyond Schelling, or beyond German idealism and subjectivism ; but

---

[1] Zavitnevič, the Russian expounder of Homjakov's theological system, compares Homjakov's view of the will with the doctrine of Maine de Biran. I am not aware whether Homjakov was acquainted with the works of the French philosopher, but the Russian's theory of cognition was exclusively derived from German philosophy. Besides, Maine de Biran passed through several phases of development, and in the last of these phases his earlier doctrine of the will was modified. In any case, the French philosopher's theory of the will is likewise individualistic and subjectivistic.

we see that he has been influenced by his friend Kirěevskii, and has thus been led to formulate a pedagogy of the will. In contrast with Kirěevskii, Homjakov was energetic, enterprising, and active, and in this respect his doctrine of the will is expressive of his personality. We must not fail to note that in certain passages Homjakov conceives the process of cognition in a thoroughly voluntaristic sense. He speaks in plain terms of " the will to understand," conceiving the process of understanding as an energy, and thus emphasising the activity of the understanding in the sense of Kant and his successors. But in Homjakov's case this voluntarism is altogether futile. The essence of Kant's active understanding lies in this, that the individual understanding begets or creates knowledge independently and subjectively ; whereas Homjakov accepts the theological doctrine that the most important truths are revealed, and for him therefore knowledge is mainly a passive belief—the acceptance of the given truths with the belief which is posited as the central energy of cognition, and which (in accordance with the teaching of Schelling and Kirěevskii), is conceived as an inward cognition or contemplation. Homjakov rejects the idea of spontaneous cognition, of the active creation of knowledge ; in his view the sole purpose of belief is to accept the objectively given and complete revelation. Consequently Homjakov is opposed, not merely to sensualism and materialism, but also to empiricism and above all to rationalism, for he rejects individualism and subjectivism. Revelation furnishes objective knowledge, cognition, which the human being has simply to accept. This acceptance is effected by way of belief, regarded as a special faculty or part-faculty.

Thus Homjakov is in agreement, not with Kant or Fichte, but with Schlegel and the latter's " theocracy of consciousness " and " theocracy of science " ; but Schlegel endeavoured to explain this theocracy psychologically, separating the believing soul from the cognising and rebellious spirit. Homjakov's analysis of reason into belief and (critical) understanding has much similarity with this doctrine. The stress that Homjakov lays on the will has as its ultimate significance that man knowingly and voluntarily subordinates his understanding to revelation. Homjakov could just as well have spoken of the " will to believe " as of the " will to understand."

It is thus plain that Homjakov, though perhaps somewhat

more orthodox than Kirěevskii, was no mystic. In his theological polemic we perceive the scholastic rather than the mystic.

Homjakov entirely rejects German philosophy, though he endeavours to turn this philosophy to his own account. Kirěevskii recognises German philosophy, and in especial the philosophy of Schelling, as an instrument and even as a guide. Homjakov, in contradistinction to Kirěevskii, rejects even the last phase of Schelling. He concedes with Kirěevskii that Hegel in his *Phenomenology* rendered imperishable services ; but in this very book " the last titan of the understanding " condemned rationalism. Rationalism must be absolutely abandoned ; Hegel, rationalism incarnate, is himself forced to recognise and to admit this. In Stirner, Homjakov discovers a terrible but instructive proof of the aberrant tendencies of German Protestant rationalism. Rationalist individualism and subjectivism terminate in the evangel of the crassest egoism. The history of the age, writes Homjakov (*Concerning Humboldt*, 1849), is a living commentary upon Max Stirner.

§ 56.

HOMJAKOV speaks of his system as " true conservatism," espousing the cause of the tories against the whigs, but what he preaches and extols is in reality theocratic absolutism.

He recognises that the state must necessarily exist side by side with the church, but does so with one great reservation. Christ is a citizen of the two distinct social orders, the perfect and heavenly order, the church, and the imperfect earthly order, the state. Life in the state, and in concreto the state law and administration, must conform wholly to the prescriptions of divine law, of religious doctrine.

In especial, Homjakov gives his approval to the Old Russian state, as he supposes it to have existed, assuming it to have originated by organic growth as a joint organisation of the communes and without the use of coercion. Wholly established upon an ethical and religious basis, this state is nothing other than the body of the church. The Russian state, contends Homjakov, organised the church and received its power from the hands of the people. In the west, on the other hand, the state is coercive in character, having originated by conquest.

Of this character was the Roman state, and also the Roman-Teutonic state which the Teutonic princes and their foreign retainers introduced into Russia, and which was subsequently strengthened by Peter. Thus Homjakov repudiates the western state just as he repudiates the western church, and repudiates therewith the state of Peter, insisting that Peter borrowed inorganic elements from the west and above all from Protestantism.

Homjakov censures Byzantium on the ground that the Byzantine state, corrupted by Rome, imposed restrictions upon the church. His grievance against the state of Peter is of like character, seeing that since the days of Peter the church has passed under the dominion of the state. Homjakov complains of Catholicism for having made the state completely subordinate to itself, whereby the church was secularised; and the church thus became a mere "believing state." Protestantism, conversely, in that the state subjugated the church, secularised the church yet more, and may almost be said to have abolished it. The true relationship between state and church can, he considers, be found only in the east, and he thinks here of a parallelism wherein state and church fulfil their respective duties without any mutual interference. Of course this parallelism must not be conceived in the sense of the modern theory of a free church within a free state. We must think rather of an organic, free, spiritual, reciprocal working of body and soul, and our general outlook must be that of spiritualist and anti-materialist theory.

Homjakov's conception of the Russian and western churches was unduly abstract and lacked adequate historical foundation, and for this reason he failed to write clearly concerning the relationship between church and state. If we are to avoid discussing this relationship in a purely schematic manner, we must comprehend the actuality of religious and political organisation, must comprehend it in its historic entirety. In the analysis of the church, the nature and the power of the clergy are decisive. The celibate Catholic priest exercises a different power over the faithful from that exercised by the married Russian priest, and the social position of the two is entirely different; quite different again from either is the position of the Protestant pastor, who is no longer a priest. The political and social power of clergy and hierarchy varies accordingly. In this connection we must think above all of the power of the monasteries, and it is important to remember that the hierarchy of the Orthodox church is drawn from the world of monks.

When Homjakov finds fault with Protestant cæsaropapism, he forgets that the reformation did away with priesthood and the hierarchy, and that for this reason in the Protestant church and in Protestant society there no longer exist priests to form with their hierarchy a state within the state in that they constitute a peculiar religious and political aristocratic element.

Homjakov fails to understand that the reformation, by abolishing priestly intermediaries between the believer and God, transforming religion into religious individualism and subjectivism, made it more a true matter of the heart and of inward conviction. The church lost its significance as an objectively given external authority as soon as it ceased to be possible for this authority to derive spontaneously and by tacit consent from the living faith of persons holding like beliefs. The development of hundreds and hundreds of larger and smaller Protestant churches is a natural process of evolution in the modern religious world, for it was essential that religion should be de-ecclesiasticised. The church undergoes transformation into a comparatively free religious community, and a small free church suffices for religion and the genuinely religious life.

In contrast therefore with medieval theocracy, Protestantism tends towards emancipation from the church. Rothe, a theologian of the Hegelian school, has formulated the tendency by saying that the growth of the modern state as a comprehensive organisation of moral and religious life has rendered the church superfluous.

Homjakov was forced to admit this, or at least to recognise it, for such is the sense of his own formulas concerning the invisible church ; but his belief in revelation, and the objective formulation of that belief, leading him to rank the Bible and the church side by side, impel Homjakov towards Catholic ecclesiastical imperialism, more especially since he wholeheartedly accepts the institution of the priesthood (" talismanism ") and its hierarchy. Neither Christ nor the Bible, but the church, is for Homjakov the decisive religious authority, and in the concrete world of political life the hierarchy and its most notable leaders constitute the church

It need hardly be said that I have been referring only to the principle of Protestantism and to its general evolutionary tendency. It is not to be denied that here and there intolerable forms of cæsaropapism have prevailed under Protestantism, as in England in earlier days, in Prussia, etc.

For Homjakov, who laid so much stress upon the unity of the church, it should have been a matter of importance to demonstrate these concrete historic differences between the churches. Had he done so, he would have grasped the difference between the monarchical centralised papacy, the federation of the orthodox and so-called autocephalic churches, and the temporarily unorganised free alliance of the Protestant churches ; he would have understood the nature of the various theocracies. Such a comparison would have enabled him to understand why popery with its centralisation was impossible in the east, and why the Greek emperor acquired more influence over the church than the Roman emperor. Under similar conditions to those which prevailed in Byzantium, the Russian tsar as protector of the church became its master, until Peter, by abolishing the patriarchate, completed the transformation of the church into a state institution. Homjakov might have detected the similarities and differences between the three leading churches, and it would have interested him greatly to note the marked resemblances between the Russian church as a priestly church and the Roman ; he would have understood, for instance, why Gallicanism was possible, and why the French king gained so much power over the church. Moreover, after the reformation, despite the papacy those sovereigns who opposed the reformation became masters everywhere of their respective state churches. The counter-reformation was analogous in the political field to the defence of Orthodoxy against unorthodoxy at home and abroad by the Byzantine and Russian state. In like manner there are numerous resemblances between Protestant and Russian theocracy.

The most important point, however, is that Homjakov, like the Catholic theorists, conceives the relationship between state and church as a relationship between body and soul, and that, like these theorists, he refers to the body as a negligible quantity. From this in practice it is but a step towards the toleration and recognition of the existing state.

This step was taken by Homjakov. Although he could not bring himself wholly to recognise the Petrine state, in practice he recognised the state and the government of Nicholas. In the end he acted like Photius, who, as we have learned, made Christ a minister of state and church. Homjakov accepted the autocracy, and he condemned the decabrist revolt. He regarded a military revolt as an absurdity, seeing that the army is intended for the defence of the nation. Homjakov was but twenty years of age when he first naïvely put these views before Ryléev, but he continued to hold them in later life, as we learn from his polemic against the Jesuit Gagarin in the year 1858. In a pamphlet entitled *La Russie sera-t-elle catholique?* published in the year 1858, the editor of Čaadaev's writings attacked Uvarov's formula, and could see therein nothing beyond the revolutionary idea of the nineteenth century. In his view those who advocated this formula were light-heartedly sacrificing Orthodoxy and autocracy to nationalism and to radical, republican, and communistic doctrines. Homjakov contemptuously rejects the " religious Machiavellianism " of the Russian Jesuit, stigmatising it as quite unfounded. He might have reminded the Jesuit of the Jesuit advocates of tyrannicide. His withers would have been unwrung had Father Gagarin rejoined by speaking of Protestant apostles of tryannicide, for the Jesuit could not have mentioned any Orthodox Russian defenders of regicide. But under Nicholas it was inexpedient even to talk about regicide, and Homjakov therefore let the argument alone.

Like many theocrats, logically and upon the abstract plane Homjakov regarded the state when compared with the church as an imperfect and earthly institution, but none the less the concrete, historic state was to him " holy and sublime," for it protected against enemies from without and within. One who idolised the Orthodox church as did Homjakov, one who demanded faith and humility before tradition and authority as insistently as did he, was able to reconcile himself even with the Nicolaitan state, although he might at times express his dissatisfaction with certain state institutions and functions. Occasionally Homjakov expressed energetic condemnation of the censorship. There were times when " holy " Russia seemed to him no longer holy. For example, he thanked God for the reverses in Crimea, taking them as a sign that Russia must be converted. In the end, however, he invariably returned with satisfaction to his ideal of Orthodox Christianity, discoverable in pristine purity in some monastery or elsewhere.

So cautious, however, was the Nicolaitan government that it considered the ideal of slavophil theocracy anything but flattering to the historically extant theocracy, and the slavophils were therefore placed upon the same index with the revolutionary westernisers.

Homjakov, with his " true conservatism " and his religious zeal for the faith of the church and the city of God, was unable to grasp this interconnection, although it had already become manifest to some of his opponents in the camp of the westernisers.

His personal energy notwithstanding, Homjakov was in fine nothing more than a political and religious quietist, and a justificatory argument may be found for his quietism. He accepts autocracy, he tells us, because he feels and thinks unpolitically. The west accepts spiritual autocracy because the west detests political authority ; but the Russian, the slavophil, favours civil autocracy because he will have nothing to do with autocracy in spiritual affairs.

When we read such arguments, we are seized with a doubt whether this sophistry must not have been plain to Homjakov himself. Manifestly in his polemic writings in the French tongue (translated into Russian at a later date by Samarin and others) the Orthodox church is presented to Protestants and Catholics in a better light than in the Russian essays. Homjakov, being anglophil, would gladly have induced the Anglican church to amalgamate with the Russian (it must be an amalgamation, not an alliance, for the church is one), and on this ground he was sparing in criticism.

As theologian Homjakov is a scholastic. Just as he accepts autocracy in the name of the church, so in truth does he favour the democratic principle of popular sovereignty, for he refers to the election of the Romanovs, and speaks of the sovereignty of the people in set terms. But he does not forget to insist with equal emphasis that his thought is antirepublican and anticonstitutionalist ; he tells us that the obedience of the people is the outcome of its sovereignty !

§ 57.

KONSTANTIN AKSAKOV, son of the respected author Sergěi T. Aksakov, expounded the theocratic political doctrine of the slavophils in a number of historical sketches.

In especial he defended on peculiar lines the theocratic view that the state is of comparatively little value, and even a practical impossibility.[1]

According to Konstantin Aksakov, in the political sphere Russia has a twofold organisation, as country and as state. By "country" he understands the organic fusion of all the individual communes into a single community—the country. The country is the complex of tilled land, the complex of the individual mirs, but the mir is a purely ethical community grounded upon the unanimity of all its members. Aksakov rejects the principle of majority rule as a coercive institution ; in their deliberative assemblies the Slavs have ever been willing to take action solely upon unanimous decisions. The Slavic organisation, pacific in character, based upon free conviction and upon the consciences of all the associated individuals, is termed by Aksakov the way of " inner truth " ; contrasted therewith is the " outer truth " manifested in the organisation of the European state by coercive and conquering authority. Where " outer truth " is established there must be law, legal formulation, and written guarantees.

How can we explain the origin of the extant Russian state side by side with the " country " ? To this question Aksakov replies that the state is a necessary concession to human frailty. If all men were holy, the state would be superfluous. Aksakov consoles himself with the reflection that while the Russian state did not originate from the people, but was imported and organised from without, this took place because the state was

[1] Konstantin Aksakov grew up in the Moscow circles in which the views of Homjakov and Kirĕevskii were formed. His opinions ripened during years spent amid the same circumstances and influences, and his agreement with his friends is explained by intimate spiritual association and by devotion to like ideals. Aksakov was born in 1817. In the year 1832 he was entered at the university of Moscow, and received his leading impressions in the circle of Stankevič and subsequently in that of the slavophils. He visited Europe in 1838, but this journey had no notable influence on his mind. At first Aksakov was an enthusiastic disciple of Hegel. He subsequently became an ardent champion of slavophil ideals, wearing the national costume as an outward index of his devotion to this propaganda. In the year 1848, however, the police interfered to this extent, that he was forbidden to wear a beard, which was regarded as a revolutionary symbol. Aksakov wrote a number of historical essays, and was much occupied in grammatical and etymological studies. He was likewise a literary critic, and made attempts in the poetic field (dramas and philosophical poems). He died in 1860. It may be mentioned that the Aksakovs derive their descent from a Variag chieftain and that Konstantin's grandmother was a Turkish woman.

needed as a protection against external enemies and also as a means for allaying internal disorders. Aksakov thus explains the genesis of the foreign Variag state as a necessary evil. Per se the Slavs, and above all the Russians, are "people without a state."

Thus in the course of history Russia was organised by two great social forces, that of the country and that of the state, and the history of Russia is the history of the relationship between these two forces. In the Kievic epoch the state element was still weak. The princes stood at the head of the free communes ; the communes had their deliberative assemblies (věče) ; the relations between commune and prince were peaceful, and peaceful also were the relations between the separate communes ; the deliberations of the princes constituted the foundation of the subsequent zemskii sobor.

The state element was strengthened by the Tatar inroads and by the internal dissensions of the princes. Moreover, it was to the interest of the communes to liberate themselves from the princes, since these were adopting feudal methods of organisation. There thus came into existence the unified state of Muscovy, whereby the country, too, was fused into a single whole through the amalgamations of the communes. Aksakov does not fail to admit that the example of the khan of Tatary suggested absolutism to the grand prince of Moscow ; but in this absolutism he contemplates the single state and the single country of Russia as a whole, the individual věčes being replaced by the zemskii sobor, the territorial assembly.

Aksakov was reconciled to the state of Muscovy, and he gives full recognition to the election of the Romanovs. In 1612 Russia was in a condition similar to that which obtained in 862. Once again there was no state, and once again the country elected a ruler, not from without this time, but from within.

The state of Peter and his successors was repudiated by Aksakov as an imitation of the European state.[1] He consoled himself with the hope that the existence of this state would prove no more than a transient episode in the history of Russia. He considered that the year 1812 and the liberating deed of Moscow proved that Russia (country and people) was still

---

[1] In his dissertation of the year 1846 for the degree of master of arts Aksakov gave due recognition to the Petrine state.

the true Russia and that Moscow was its capital ; he held that the state of Muscovy still existed.

Most energetically did Aksakov contest the westernisers' view as to the tribal origin of the state. In the first beginnings the Russian community was a tribe, but the next and subsequent stages did not take the form of tribal patriarchalism but of the democratic family and of the mir with its assembly (věče) developing therefrom. Aksakov opposes his own theory of the primitive mir and the věče to the patriarchal tribal theory.

Aksakov repudiates Europe and the European state in the strongest terms, going so far as to see nothing in Europe but slavery, whereas he discerns true freedom in Russia. He considers that the United States is wanting in freedom ; and the constitutionalist European state with its constitutional guarantees is for him merely a proof that in Europe peoples and rulers lack mutual trust. Europe, devoid of internal freedom, lapsed from absolutism into revolution ; Russia, being endowed with internal freedom, need not bow the knee before the new European idol of revolution—it is plain that Aksakov has forgotten the decabrists. But perhaps the oversight was intentional, for he too was harassed by the Nicolaitan censorship. When Alexander II ascended the throne Aksakov composed one of the customary memorials, those memorials which, besides advocating well-meaning constitutionalist utopias, demanded freedom of speech and the summoning of a deliberative zemskii sobor.

The official title " Holy Russia " was taken literally and in all earnestness by Aksakov. He regarded prepetrine Russia and the Russia of the mužik as sacred. There were doubtless sins in this Russia, but no vices, and he was inclined to make a distinction in this respect between Moscow and St. Petersburg. Whilst Homjakov spoke of Moscow as the laboratory of Russian thought, Aksakov saw in Moscow the ideal ethical capital of the holy land of Russia, whereas to him St. Petersburg was merely the residence of Peter and his European bureaucracy.

It is needless for me to expose the utopianism of this teaching. It must be obvious to every reader that Aksakov imaginatively creates for himself in and behind the Russian state a " country " that has never existed. In actual fact Aksakov had to satisfy his appetite with his own words. We have to postulate Aksakov's " country " side by side with the state, his " ethical

capital " side by side with the actual political capital where
the ruler dwells, and so on.

His utopianism contains a large tincture of anarchism.
We have seen that Aksakov declared the Slavic nations and
above all the Russians to be pre-eminently a people " without
a state."

This anarchism is derived by Aksakov from his false view
concerning the nature of the church and of religion ; religious
mysticism leads him to flee from the state and from the world.
He turns history to the service of his orthodox mysticism.
In good earnest he ascribed a mystical element to science, in
so far as he assigned to science a part in the foundation of
life, itself a mystery. In sum, to him life was and remained
mysterious. Restricted within the narrow limits of his slavophil
circle, he projected his own moral relationship to his friends
into the history of Russia.

§ 58.

TO the state Homjakov opposed not only the church but
also the nation. In his system the nation occupied an
intermediate sphere of activity between that of private persons
and that of the state. Nation and society were here identical
concepts ; all qualities of soil and people had their place in
social activity, and this social activity filled the " chasm "
between the activities of private persons and those of the state.
To Homjakov the state was no more than the outward expression
of the living national activity, and indeed he regarded the
state as nothing more than an instrument of coercion, which
must be called upon in case of need to protect the community
at large against the evil passions of individuals—for society,
that is to say the community at large, is founded exclusively
upon points-of-view, peace, and voluntary agreement

Spiritual energies, he wrote on one occasion (1839), originate
in the people and in the church ; " the function of government
(a narrower concept than the concept of the state) is solely
to awaken or to modify the play of these energies by a more
or less harsh use of its authoritative powers." To Homjakov,
K. Aksakov, and the slavophils in general, the state is nothing
more than a variant of the well-known liberal nightwatchman.
Homjakov is opposed to the westernisers and to their leader
Hegel, decisively repudiating the idolisation of the state and
the rationalist doctrine of the folk-spirit.

In this opposition to Hegel, Homjakov takes the side of most of the romanticists and above all that of Schelling and of the advocates of the historical doctrine of law. Since the days of Herder, German philosophy had discovered in the nation and in the folk-spirit the source of all social manifestations and organisations. Poetry, art and literature, language, morals, in the last resort law (and therefore also the state) and religion, were regarded as such manifestations of the " folk-spirit." They were, it is true, unconscious manifestations. It is impossible here to enter into details and to analyse this view. In different thinkers differences in formulation and in groundwork will naturally be discoverable. It must suffice to refer to the basic conception of romanticism and to its preference for the so-called folk-spirit as the creator of all social activity. We may add that the nation or the folk (the terminology and the concept were then and still are vague) were imagined to be an organic portion or an organ of mankind ; the idea of nationality and the humanitarian doctrine were brought into intimate association, nationality being based upon the humanitarian ideal extensively and intensively, politically and morally, socially and historically.

The humanitarian ideal of the eighteenth century led up to the ideal of nationality. Herder (vide supra, § 43) was unquestionably one of the first to regard the nation as a natural organ of mankind, and it was in this sense that he wrote his history of philosophy. Herder likewise opposed the state, as an artificial product, to the natural products of folk-life.

Hegel protested against this romanticist view, and the Hegelian left and Young Germany joined energetically in the protest. It is true that Hegel recognised the significance of the folk-spirit, and even emphasised its importance, but he considered that the folk, the nation, became a unity through the instrumentality of the state. Hegel regarded the government as " the simple soul or the self of the folk-spirit," and he looked upon the state as a self-conscious and willing divinity, as the divine will. In a further logical development Hegel came to consider that only the monarchical state and the monarch were genuine manifestations of the divine will ; he looked forward to a general organisation of mankind, which was not to result from a fusion of the nations, but from a fusion of the states to form a world state. For a time he regarded Napoleon as the world soul and as the future rightful lord of the world, saying, " The lord of the world is the colossal self-consciousness, knowing itself to be the true God." Thus Hegel's pantheism and panlogism manifested itself as a monarchical universal absolutism. " The state is the divine will as a contemporary spirit evolving itself in a real form and as the organisation of a world."

Homjakov, as an adversary of the religious enlightenment, was an opponent of the political enlightenment and of rationalism. He opposed Hegel's theory of the state, and accepted the views of Schlegel, those of Savigny's romanticist successors, and their historical theory of law. Upon the same outlook was based his opposition to Roman law and its logic, and his preference for customary law in accordance with the doctrines of the historical school of law.[1] The historical school of law conceived the folk-spirit mythically and mystically, quite in the sense of the romanticists and without any precise analysis of the concept. It was all the more natural that this should please the romanticist slavophils, since Puchta, the leader of the Germanist jurists, found in God the ultimate source of law. Homjakov regarded the state, to use an expression of his own, as a living and organic protective mantle for society (that is to say for the folk). Such was the normal state, but there exist also abnormal and morbid states, those whose activities develop inorganically, without the aid of the folk and in opposition to the folk. The living protection then becomes a dry crust, a fistula in history, filled with the dust of corrupted nations. . . . It is obvious that here Homjakov is thinking of the state of Peter and his successors, and of the Russian bureaucracy.

Just as little as he analysed the concepts church and state did Homjakov analyse the concepts of nation and folk-spirit. In opposition to the German historical school of law and in opposition to those romanticists who were radical in politics, he assigned to the nation but two spheres of activity, art and science. These two activities alone, he said, are national in the strict sense of the term, these alone are expressions of the folk-spirit. The German romanticists did not thus emphasise the national aspect of science. They regarded art, and above all literature, language, morals, law, and in some cases also

---

[1] In 1850 Kiręevskii, too, attended Savigny's lectures in Berlin, and thus became acquainted with the German jurist's system.

philosophy, as national. Herder likewise considered religion a product of the national character.

In this matter Homjakov follows the logical development of the Orthodox theocrat. If religion and dogma, and if in conjunction with religion the principles of law, morals, and politics are revealed, little sphere is left for folk-activity. It is true that Homjakov did not think the matter out sufficiently. From the religious standpoint Čaadaev dispensed with nationality, leaving place only for the " Christian folk," for the church. Homjakov left scope for nationality, but within narrow limits, and he failed to define the precise significance of nationality in the spheres of morals and of law. He considered that the Russian state originated through church and nation, and from this outlook it could be conceded that folk-character somehow found expression in the state and in its laws.

Strictly speaking, Homjakov leaves nothing but art for the domain of the folk-spirit, and here he involves himself in difficulties as far as church art is concerned, especially in the matter of Byzantine and Russian iconography. The relationship of the individual artist to the community at large is specified by Homjakov by saying that the artist does not create out of his own energy, but that the spiritual energy of the folk is the motive force which drives the artist.

Science, says Homjakov, inasmuch as it is truth, is universally the same ; but in the positive sciences and in history, the way in which a truth finds expression, the way in which we attain to truth, is subject to conditions of time and space. Twice two is four, universally, so that there can be no " Russian arithmetic " or " Russian astronomy." The sciences which formulate simple external laws are not national. Those sciences alone are national which are concerned with the moral and spiritual endeavours of human beings.

Such problems of art and science need far more thorough investigation. Homjakov frequently devoted his attention to such matters.

Kiréevskii here diverges from Homjakov, whilst K. Aksakov diverges yet more conspicuously. Both Kiréevskii and Aksakov discover in the Russian or Slavic national character a notable source of anti-european views of life ; whilst Kiréevskii contends that the Romans, the Latin nations, and the Teutons have led western civilisation into devious paths. A more detailed critical investigation would have involved the asking

of numerous questions concerning the relationship between
national character and religion ; above all it would have been
desirable to examine to what extent the adoption and maintenance of true religion was due to national character, or what
had caused the peculiar Russian competence in these respects.
The founders of slavophilism would have done well, too, to
formulate the problem of nationality in far more precise terms.

§ 59.

SINCE from the philosophers and publicists with whom
we have now to deal we shall hear a great deal more
about the problem of "nation" and "nationality," it seems
wise at this stage to discuss the most important problems of a
critical philosophy of nationality, so that I may expound the
grounds for my judgment of the various views.

Even in scientific works, the definitions given of the vaguely
used terms "nation" and "nationality" have hitherto been far
from precise.   When further, the concept of nation and nationality is used in conjunction with the equally vague concepts
of state, church, and humanity, an absolute chaos of discon-
nected thoughts is apt to be presented.

Great care is needed in the use of these terms.   If when
we speak of "nation" we refer to the great collectivity itself,
by "nationality" we shall understand the essence of the
qualities of the nation, although the word "nationality" is
sometimes used as a synonym for "nation."   The terms "idea
of nationality," "sentiment of nationality," and "principle
of nationality," are sufficiently comprehensible.   The use of the
words "nation" and "folk" involves difficulties.   "Nation"
signifies rather the political whole organised as a state.   "Folk"
is used in a more democratic sense, denoting the nation intensively considered as a mass engaged in collective action.   We
speak of folk-songs, folk-art, and the folk-spirit ; less often
of national songs and the national spirit, and when we use the
latter terms it is in a somewhat different sense.[1]

[1] In relation to the development of these ideas in Russian, etymology has
some significance. "Narod" is used in the sense both of nation and folk. Since
properly speaking the term denotes the so-called common people only, the
foreign word "nacija" is used to help out the meaning.   "Narod" is connected
with "rodit'," to beget (just as the Latin "natio" is connected with "nasci ");
from the same root come "rod" (race, kind), and "rodina" (birth-place, and
in some of the Slav tongue,s family).

Nationality, the national character or " spirit," is displayed not only in language, but also in manifold manners and customs (clothing, etc.), in the methods of settlement and habitation (arrangement of houses, villages and towns), work and domestic economy, law and the state, morals, religion, science and philosophy, culture and art—any and all of these may be regarded as expressions of national character. Thus the idea of nationality is extremely intricate.

If we enquire what is the character of a nation, what is the essence of nationality, we may be told that it is to be discovered in one or in several of the before-mentioned departments, or in the complex of them all. Of late, people have become aware of racial differences, and therewith arises the problem, wherein " race " consists; whether we are to conceive it in a physiological sense only or psychically as well.

Moreover, when we are determining a national character, we must not confine our attention to single elements, but must consider the synthesis of all these elements into an organic whole. For this synthesis to be possible it must be presupposed that the various elements have been fully grasped and appropriately valued in their mutual dependence. We must then select the most important, most characteristic central element, and appraise its relationship to the others.

Obviously, too, each individual element must be subjected to further, detailed analysis. Think, for example, how rich in content is the idea of language, and how in practice language is apt to be chosen as the favourite index and characteristic of nationality.[1]

Attention must be drawn to another extremely important problem of the philosophy of nationality. We accept the idea of development and progress in all departments of social life. National character too, therefore, must develop, and what are the causes of this evolution ? How extensive is the change ? Is the modern Russian the same in essence and character with the Russian who lived under John the Terrible and the Russian who lived under Vladimir of Kiev ? Manifestly we are not

---

[1] We have to think of the concepts of mother tongue, dialect, and written language; of speech as a means of communication (the language of daily intercourse); of the parallelism between speech and thought, between feeling and willing; of language as an object of art. Writing, too, as a means for giving a fixed and permanent form to what is spoken, is of significance here, and we think of the different methods of writing.

concerned here solely with changes in opinion, for we have to think whether nations and races change anthropologically and ·ethnically. Does the structure of the skeleton become modified ; do the shape and size of the skull vary ; if so, what causes the changes ? Are they brought about by modifications of diet, by changed methods of work, by modifications in climate or place of residence, etc ? Are nations subject in addition to psychical changes ? Does the mode of feeling vary ? Is the outward, the physiognomical aspect of peoples subject to change ?

These are extremely complicated problems, which must be approached methodically and with great caution. Above all, in this connection, we must give due weight to the special problem of racial and national minglings. Using the popular catchword, we have to ask ourselves whether such a thing as a " pure race " really exists, or whether all races and nationalities are not in truth of mixed blood. As far as Russia is concerned, the doubt is of extreme significance, for during the Kievic period we know that as a historic fact a continuous mingling of races and peoples was in progress. In my biographical note on K. Aksakov, the reference to his Turkish grandmother was deliberate. We often hear of the African ancestors of Pužkin, of the Tatar ancestors of Ivan Turgenev. Does the essence of the Russian character persist despite such racial minglings ; to what extent does it persist ; above all if it persists, how is its persistence secured ?

What are we to say about denationalisation ? When a nation abandons its language to adopt another, or when an individual or a number of individuals belonging to any nation experience such a change, what modification occurs in the national essence ? Ševyrev, to whom we shall have to refer again shortly, said of the Russians of his day that they thought as Germans, and expressed themselves as Frenchmen. Were these still genuine Russians ?

Such critical enquiries involve numerous and thorny problems, and they are problems to which as yet scant scientific attention has been paid.

Subjectively we have to think of the sentiment of nationality, of the fact that men love their nation, their nationality, their folk, more than they love foreigners.

We love also our country (love of fatherland, patriotism), and in the concrete we love the particular place where we were born or grew up. This love, this sentiment, may be intensified to the point of disease, manifesting itself as the malady of home-sickness.

The object of the sentiment of nationality (country, nation, folk) is one extremely rich in content, and every man who contemplates the idea of nationality and concerns himself about the sentiment of nationality will tend after his own kind to concentrate his attention upon one or more special elements of that content. The idea and the sentiment are determined by men's social, economic, and cultural level. The aristocrat, the bureaucrat, the soldier, the man of culture, the peasant, the townsman, the manual worker, the proletarian —each of these will have his own idea of nation or folk, and the sentiments of each will be peculiarly tinged.

The sentiment of nationality may be blind, instinctive, and elemental. As with love in general, so with love of folk and home, the question arises in each case how far the sentiment is conscious, deliberately motived, based upon clear ideas and judgments.

Nor must we forget that variations in the sentiment are qualitative as well as quantitative. Besides being more or less intense, it may be different ; it may be noble and elevated, or it may be comparatively crude.

It is equally obvious that the idea of the nation, and therewith the national sentiment, undergoes modification and development. At different times, in divers epochs, the love of home and the love of folk vary. Without going too far back in history, it will suffice to point out that the love for one's folk among the eighteenth-century rationalists must have been different in character from that which prevailed among the nineteenth-century romanticists, or from that which prevailed at a later date among the naturalists and realists.

Of great importance to the determination of the sentiment and of the idea of nationality is the state of thought and feeling towards other nations, towards foreigners in general, and more particularly towards neighbour nations. We have to ask to what extent strangers are known, for in the foreign nation the same wealth of qualities has to be considered as in our own ; the knowledge of foreigners and the quality of feeling towards foreigners are just as variable and manifold as the knowledge of one's own folk and the feelings associated with that knowledge. A great many people really care very little for their own compatriots, but they hate anything foreign. Yet it is possible to learn to love a foreign language, foreign ways, ideas, and modes of feeling ; it is even possible to come to prefer the foreign to the native, and this happens often enough in every department of life.

To a certain extent it may be said that our own national essence is first made clear to us by comparison with the foreign essence. For this reason the sentiment of nationality in a multilingual state is more self-conscious and more critical than in a state where " state " coincides with " nation." This is especially true of Russia, of Austria-Hungary, and of the Balkan lands. The force of contrast is yet more powerful when multiformity of language is associated with the dominance, partial or complete, of a single language and a single folk. Once more we think of Russia, of Austria and Hungary, of the Balkans, and to some extent also of Germany. The dominance may be political, economic, linguistic, cultural, or ecclesiastico-religious. It may be such a predominance as was exercised by the French in eighteenth-century Russia and also in eighteenth-century Germany ; it may be the predominance of Russian as an official language ; and so on.

The course of historical evolution displays to us a continuous severance and differentiation of individual nations, whilst simultaneously interactions occur in the political, economic, and cultural fields. There have been multilingual states, and at times these have been organised to form world-wide realms (Alexander, the Roman empire, the Frankish realm, the medieval emperordom, the Napoleonic empire, modern imperialism) ; there exist also world-wide churches, world-wide economic unions, etc. The organisation of great areas of the world, of entire continents, and ultimately of humanity as a whole, makes continuous progress.

Between the incessant struggles and suitable combinations of the petty stocks and tribes in a primitive stage, on the one hand, and the struggles and alliances of the great states and nations of modern times on the other, we can discern numerous transitional forms of this simultaneous differentiation and assimilation. Nearly every one of us to-day is member and instrument of some superstate, superchurch, or other world-wide organisation.

The modern sentiment of nationality and the modern idea of nationality originated in the west with the reformation and the renaissance. At this epoch men became more conscious of their nationality, more aware of peculiarities of language and other specifically national characteristics; they came to realise nationality as an entity side by side with the organisation of state and of church. The medieval theocracy was based upon religion and determined by religion. The reformation as a folk-movement led to the replacement of Latin by the folk-speech for religious uses; the vernacular likewise became the tongue of literature and the tongue of culture; the whole development was one leading towards the individualisation of the separate nations. To Herder, therefore, nationality seemed "natural" in contrast with the "artificial" state; similarly the church could be regarded as "artificial."

In the eighteenth century, literature, language, religion, all the vital activities, came to be considered manifestations of national character. People spoke of the national spirit or folk-spirit, thinking of it as analogous to the individual spirit. The folk or nation was conceived as an individual, as a person, as an organism. Such was Herder's view, and such at a later date were the views held by the advocates of the historical school of law and by the romanticists.

Yet during this same century, cosmopolitanism appeared as a characteristic trend in almost every nation, whether large or small. It was especially easy for the French to become cosmopolitans since their language and literature were universally known. The Germans, the English, and the Italians, were inspired by cosmopolitan sentiments and used cosmopolitan phraseology. Above all was this true of the Russians, who adopted the French language and French civilisation. The humanitarian ideal became universally diffused, being intensively and extensively conceived as the organisation of humanity and as a general process of humanisation, above all in the sphere of sentiment.

The period of reaction against the revolution and against Napoleon, the restoration period, was characterised · everywhere by a strengthening of nationalism. Simultaneously, however, humanitarian ideals became more powerful. This may be discerned in the foundation of the socialist international, and in the continuous growth of international organisations and the increasing frequency of international congresses. These developments were nowise inferior in significance to the councils held by the theocracy.

The increase in bilinguality and multilinguality, attempts at the construction of an artificial language, the organisation of the literature of translation, interest in the affairs of the entire world (an interest gratified by the daily press)—all these things afford proof of the increasing unification of the differentiated and still differentiating nations.

The discovery and utilisation of the steam engine and its application to facilitate communication, served during the nineteenth century, not merely to promote freedom of movement within individual countries (after the peasantry previously chained to the soil had everywhere been freed), but they rendered it possible to effect national migrations which in respect of their extent and the importance of their consequences were nowise inferior to the so-called national migrations which marked the closing days of the Roman empire. This matter is of importance, not in relation to America alone, but equally so in relation to Russia and to the colonisation of her home territories and of Siberia.

The eighteenth century, as the century of the enlightenment and of humanitarianism, solemnly proclaimed the rights of man, and in the ensuing epoch an advance was made towards the codification of the language and nationality. Beyond question this development was associated with increasing democratisation. In multilingual states the idea of nationality took a democratic form in contrast with the unifying and denationalising centralist tendencies of aristocratic and theocratic absolutism.

State and nation have never as yet been coterminous ideas. No national state has hitherto existed in Europe. I mean that if we except such political curios as Liechtenstein there is no instance in which all the members of a state belong to a single nation. Even little Montenegro is multilingual. Italy and Serbia respectively contain people who are not Italians and Serbs. Still, the idea of nationality becomes more and more vigorously state-constructive.

As a rule the extant multilingual states of Europe consist to a preponderant extent of a single stock. In Russia, however, the percentage of nonrussians is very large, and some of the nonrussian peoples of Russia are highly civilised, standing in respect of culture upon a loftier plane than the Russians proper. In Hungary the Magyars, though in a minority, are politically dominant. Switzerland has its own peculiar characteristics as a multilingual state. It is obvious that the relationship between state and nationality and the bearing of extant political methods upon the principle of nationality require closer examination. Special problems are constituted by the nationality of the dynasties and of the aristocracies. In Poland and in Russia, for instance, we find social and economic differences between peoples of one and the same state.

Knowledge of nationality becomes more and more definitely organised in specific disciplines, and above all in anthropology and ethnography. The domain of what is termed folk-psychology is somewhat vague but this department belongs to the sphere of sociological research. History and linguistic science have, of course, important bearings upon the philosophy of race and nationality.

After Herder's preliminary essays in this field, the further development of the philosophy of nationality was first undertaken by Fichte. It was quite in accordance with the spirit of his age that he should incline to ignore the political state whilst attaching much importance to the nation, and that he should advocate a national system of education for the Germans. Contemporary with Fichte and subsequent to him came the romanticist philosophers of nationality, and above all certain representatives of the historical school of law ; but in this connection we must think also of Hegel, of Schopenhauer and his pupil Hartmann, of Lagarde, Richard Wagner, and Gobineau, and in quite recent times of Houston Chamberlain, and others.

When the philosophy of nationality has been more precisely formulated it will doubtless become possible to speak of a science of nationality analogous to the science of religion or to the science of language.

When we thus endeavour to attain to clear ideas concerning the functions of a scientific philosophy of nationality, it becomes plain that the slavophils were unequal to the task. By this I do not mean to imply that the German philosophers, the teachers of the slavophils, did not effect a good deal in the new field of research. But the earlier German writers were comparatively sterile, and especially striking to the critical observer is the naïve way in which Hegel makes use of the " national spirit " as a historical and social category without troubling to subject the concept to precise analysis. In general terms we may say that it is the great fault of Hegel that he fails to subject to critical analysis the most important of his historical and social ideas. Hence the defects in all that he has to say concerning the relationships between state and nation, between nation and church, and so on. In Hegel's writings (and it is equally true of the writings of Schelling and of those of their predecessors), the philosophy of history is still uncritical.

The same defect is characteristic of the slavophil philosophy of history. All the slavophil writers employ the words state, nation, folk, society, church, and humanity, as if they were dealing with terms to which clearly defined notions were attached, whereas in truth, though the concepts in question are in general use, their interpretation is anything but clear and unambiguous.

§ 59A.

HOMJAKOV was more nationalist than Kirěevskii. In the year 1847 he accepted the interpretation of the name slavophil in a nationalist sense, admitting that he loved the Slavs. To the Russians the other Slavs were the "most immediate neighbours," and this was especially true of the Orthodox southern Slavs. The domestic life and the simple habits of the Slavs gave him a homelike feeling, and he often boasted of the Slavs that their manners and customs had come down unchanged out of the primeval age. Homjakov classified nations as agriculturists and conquerors respectively; thinking here rather of natural qualities than of economic institutions. The Slavs, he said, had ever been and still were agriculturists by taste and were consequently peaceful, whereas the Teutons and the Romans were conquerors. It was their inborn love of peace which had enabled the Slavs to make true Christianity so speedily their own, and to preserve for themselves this Christianity of love and humility, whereas western Christianity, after the schism at any rate, became a religion of conquest and subjugation.

Homjakov visited the Slav countries; in Prague he made the acquaintance of Hanka; and at first hand he studied the Poles, the Bulgars, and the Serbs. But his views contained numerous hazy and uncritical elements. In his nationalist enthusiasm he adopted the national dress without troubling himself about the question whether this costume was not more or less Tatar in origin. In general terms it may be said that Homjakov and his colleagues were little concerned about the critical question whether Slav manners and customs were, after all, as primitive as the slavophils were in the habit of assuming. In any case, what does the acceptance of this aristocratic genealogical tree prove as to the excellency of Slav customs ? The national character may evolve, may change, may improve or deteriorate ; but the slavophils were impervious to such considerations,

A further question arises how far the individual Slavic peoples are essentially identical in character and in other respects, for it must not be taken as a matter of course that the Slavs are as homogeneous as Homjakov assumes. The assumption requires critical examination. In point of civilisation the existence of marked differences is indisputable. Homjakov himself separates the Poles from the other Slavs. The Poles, having adopted Catholicism and other institutions from the conquering nations of the west, took the side of the Germans against the Slavs.

Homjakov does not discuss the question of Czech and Croat Catholicism. Kirěevskii approved the Czechs and Hussitism in that he considered them to have preserved reminiscences of Orthodoxy. To the Moravian brethren he even ascribed the Orthodox doctrine of the trinity.

More precise acquaintanceship with ecclesiastical history could not fail to destroy this illusion, although the later slavophils endeavoured to associate the Czech reformation far more directly with the eastern church. They had little success here, although the Slav apostles Cyril and Methodius had diffused Byzantine doctrines throughout Moravia.

Homjakov when he speaks of Slavs thinks chiefly of Orthodox Slavs, holding that the Slavs (including the Russians) possessed the qualities rendering possible their conversion to Christianity and the maintenance of true Christianity. It is difficult to understand how Kirěevskii, Homjakov, and their successors could fail to take into account that in addition to the Slavs, the Byzantines and other eastern peoples adopted Orthodox Christianity. Are the Greeks (Byzantines) more akin in essence to the Slavs than the Romans, the Latin peoples, or the Germans ? Do the Armenians resemble the Russians (Slavs) more closely in character than the Germans or, say, the Abyssinians, a people concerning whose Christianity Čaadaev had more accurate ideas than have the latest founders of the Abyssinio-Russian religious community ?

Doubtless in ecclesiastical and religious matters the various Orthodox nations are closely associated. Community of custom has in many respects been diffused owing to ecclesiastical community, just as we find that among the peoples of the west their ecclesiastical community is responsible for many similarities. But the slavophils would have done well to analyse these differences and resemblances with more precision, for they would thus have secured clearer and more definite ideas concerning both east and west.

It may be briefly pointed out that there is no historical or sociological warrant for Homjakov's contrast between agriculturists and conquerors. The history of all the Slavs, and above all the history of the Russians, affords striking proof that the idyll of the " dovelike nature " of the ancient and of the modern Slavs must be completely discredited. It was time in Homjakov's day for this idyll to be decently buried.

I cannot but call to mind Hegel's characterisation of the Germans and their national talent for the reformation, which to Hegel seemed to embody true Christianity just as to the slavophils Orthodoxy seemed to embody it. Hegel declared that the other nations were aiming at secular dominion, at conquests, and at discoveries. Luther, the simple German monk, sought and found perfection in the realm of the spirit. In Hegel's view pure Christianity as a folk-religion made its first appearance among the Teutons. The Greeks and the Romans could neither adopt nor realise the pure teaching of Christ ; the Teutons were the first to be capable of true Christian piety, and in them (in Hegel's view) was first manifest the most beautiful and the most heartfelt devotion. Medieval Catholicism was of value only in so far as it was established by the mingled Romance and Teutonic people, but solely through the reformation did the German essence and pure Christianity first attain full development.

In medieval Catholicism and among the Latins its founders, Hegel discovered a cleavage such as the slavophils discovered between Catholics and Protestants, but in Hegel's view this was due to the mingling of Romance and Teutonic national elements.

Hegel, I may add, likewise considers that the Slavs were primarily agriculturists, but his deduction is that among the Slavs, therefore, the institution of slavery was retained by the landowning aristocracy. Hegel, just like Čaadaev, attributes to the forces of nature a great influence upon the destiny of the Slavs, considering that they have but little spontaneity and subjective activity.

Hegel was germanophil precisely as Homjakov and Kiréevskii were slavophil, and the German's views require to be criticised just as severely as those of the Russians. It is really amusing to read the slavophil condemnation of German philosophy and German rationalism, and then to note how these Moscow writers utilise Berlinese rationalism and at times turn it topsy turvy. I could give additional instances, but will content myself with a significant parallel. Hegel finds in the Catholic middle ages, as a peculiar contradiction, that the Germans (Germans or Teutons, for he uses the terms interchangeably, just as the slavophils wrote promiscuously of Slavs and Russians), despite their beautiful and heartfelt piety, were uncultured and superstitious barbarians. In the same way, to Homjakov, the Old Russians were barbarians, but they preserved true Christianity and exhibited the most beautiful and heartfelt piety. Hegel refers barbarism to the spheres of intelligence and will, whilst piety springs from the heart. The thought of Homjakov and Kiréevskii was essentially similar, except that in their view imitativeness, the state, and the geographical situation, were to a certain extent responsible for the barbarism of the Old Russians.

§ 60.

WE have dealt with the two founders of slavophilism, but it is necessary to refer in addition to a few other writers if we are to become thoroughly acquainted with slavophilism as a school.

The place of next importance is occupied by Jurii F. Samarin (1819–1876). In philosophy he was a follower of Homjakov. In his essay (1844) concerning Stefan Javorskii and Theophan Prokopovič he endeavoured to show apropos of these two contemporaries of Peter (vide supra, § 9) the one-sidedness and the defects of Catholic unity and of the Protestant principle of individual freedom. It is important to note that Samarin was more strongly opposed to Catholicism than to Protestantism. He held with Homjakov that Protestantism was merely the negation of Catholicism, and that Catholicism therefore, being the positive enemy, must be more positively resisted. Samarin made an exhaustive study of Catholic dogmatics, being especially concerned with the work of Möhler, and he borrowed likewise from Baader. Baader interested him as defender of Catholicism against the papacy, and, as a Catholic, one who (to quote his own expression) preferred the aristocratic organisation of the Orthodox church to the despotism of the Catholic and to the democracy of the Protestant church. In the epistemological field also, Baader exercised an influence on Samarin, and perhaps on Homjakov and Kirěevskii as well.[1]

After the writing of his essay Samarin traversed a crisis. He desired with the aid of Hegel to prove the correctness of the Orthodox position, thus doing the very thing which he had previously condemned. Samarin's earlier view had been that belief neither can nor should be rationally demonstrated, and to this view he returned after the crisis in question. At this period Gagarin, who subsequently became a Jesuit, influenced him as well as Hegel. His hostility to Catholicism was shown later in his polemic against the Jesuits, and above all against the Russian Jesuit Martynov. Samarin energetically attacked the ethical system of Jesuitism (Busenbaum's moral teaching).

[1] The dependence of the slavophils upon German philosophy thus becomes plainer than ever. Baader had intimate relationships with Russia for a lengthy period. In a memorial composed in the year 1814 he elaborated for Tsar Alexander I, for the emperor of Austria, and for the king of Prussia, the fundamental lines of the holy alliance, and probably contributed to the establishment of that alliance. This memorial, entitled, Concerning the Need Resulting from the French Revolution to Establish a New and more Intimate Connection between Religion and Politics, was dedicated to Prince Golicyn, friend of Alexander I, and at that time minister for spiritual affairs. From 1818 onwards Baader sent the prince regular reports, receiving for a long period a considerable salary on this account (140 roubles a month). In 1815 Alexander I commissioned Baader to write a religious work for the Russian clergy. Baader wished to found in St. Petersburg an archæological academy which was to favour an intimate association between religion, science, and art, and was in addition to promote the reconciliation of the three churches. In 1822 he set out for Russia, but had to turn back just before he reached Riga, for Baron Yxkull, his enthusiastic patron and travelling companion, had visited Benjamin Constant and had consequently fallen into disfavour. This incautious proceeding cost Baader his Russian salary. Another of Baader's works was, Eastern and Western Catholicism considered Rather in Respect of its chief Internal Relationships than in Respect of its Outward Relationships, 1818. One chapter of this work consists of a letter written in French by Ševyrev to Baader under date February 22, 1810. The essay, Concerning the Practicability or Impracticability of Emancipating Catholicism from the Roman Dictatorship in the Matter of the Science of Religion, 1839, is dedicated to the author Elim Meščerskii. The essays, Sur l'Eucharistie and Sur la Notion du Temps may be parts of the work intended for the Russian clergy. (I have been able to find nothing noteworthy about Baader in Russian literature.)

Samarin's anticatholicism acquired a political trend through the Polish rising of 1863, Catholicism taking a concrete form for the Russians in Polish nationalist propaganda and in Jesuitism. Samarin considered that the Poles presented a living verification of the slavophil philosophy of religion and philosophy of history. Upon the basis of Catholicism, the Poles had become untrue to their country and to themselves, and had therefore entered the path of destruction. The Polish question was insoluble without a rebirth of the Poles. Samarin referred to the Czechs, saying that a nation with such memories as those of the Hussite movement could never die out. During the revolt of 1863 Samarin was willing to concede linguistic and administrative autonomy to the Poles, and he declared that the complete surrender of the kingdom of Poland was not " per se " impossible, and would not absolutely conflict with Russian interests.

Samarin was likewise alive to the political importance of the Baltic provinces. Warmly, too warmly, did he commend to the Russians the Esthonian and Lettish rural population as natural allies against the dominant German aristocracy.

Despite his ardent slavophil convictions, Samarin remained an advocate of western culture, and he was on terms of intimate friendship with Kavelin the westerniser. He worked conscientiously in favour of the liberation of the peasantry, and after the liberation he continued to labour in the same spirit. Like K. Aksakov he esteemed the mir constitution of the communes very highly, regarding it as a primitive Russian institution.

§ 61.

THE younger Aksakov (1823–1886) likewise belonged to the earlier generation of slavophils.

At first Ivan Aksakov was extremely critical towards historically extant Russia. We have undeniable proof of this in his letters to his friend Herzen (down to the year 1861). Subsequently he took more conservative views, but continued to make a difference between official Russia and the Russia which, as he contended, developed out of healthy popular energies. Not until 1881 did he draw closer to the reaction, but even then this reactionary trend was not persistent. His was a thoroughly virile character, as we see from his frank answers to the third section. He was examined before this department for the letters he had written to his father during the arrest of his friend Samarin.

To Aksakov, as to so many in Europe as well as in Russia, the year 1848 brought proof that European civilisation was decadent, and he considered that the day of nonrevolutionary Russia had now arrived. All that he desired was that Russia should maintain her spiritual independence and should not become involved in western affairs. But Russia, Orthodox Russia, once more moved her armies westward to stamp out the revolution in Hungary and to support Austria, a land for which the nationalist slavophils had no liking. In the year 1850 we read: " Russia will soon separate into two halves ; Orthodoxy will take the side of the state, the government, the infidel nobility, and those of the clergy whose faith is luke-warm, whilst all others will turn towards the raskol." In 1856 he wrote : " For God's sake be careful in the use of the words nationality and Orthodoxy " ; and he declared that it was impossible to have any sympathy " with prepetrine Russia, with official Orthodoxy, or with the monks." Aksakov delighted in frequent visits to Europe.

Ivan Aksakov was the journalist of slavophilism. More especially after the death of Kirěevskii and Homjakov did he maintain the slavophil tradition in his periodicals, formulating the doctrine in relation to the questions of the day.

He held firmly to the teaching of Homjakov, regarding ideal Orthodoxy as the guardian of nationality, but in practice he did not invariably succeed in distinguishing this Orthodoxy from the state church.

Homjakov's religious outlook, logically adopted, could not fail to induce a repulsion from the errors of the state church and from ecclesiastical religion, but the quietism of the slavophils was apt to induce them to tolerate the official church. Aksakov displayed his own religious sentiments as an official in his any-thing but conciliatory attitude towards the raskolniki, and subsequently in his approval of Gogol's religious conversion.

Aksakov thought that the church could be strengthened against the state by the revival of the patriarchate, which had been abolished by Peter. The priesthood was to be invigor-ated by the introduction of district councils and provincial councils. He referred to the paragraphs of the legal code, more than a thousand in number, by which the relations between state and church were regulated, saying that these proved that the church lacked freedom. He also demanded freedom of conscience in the church's own interest, but this demand remained purely academic. Moreover Aksakov associated Orthodoxy so inseparably with Russianism, saying that while Orthodoxy might exist outside of Russia, Russia could not exist without Orthodoxy, that he was compelled willy nilly to make concessions to the official police church.

Russia contains a notable percentage of nonrussian inhabitants, whose Russification had long been part of the official program, but this Russification was carried on quite mechanically by the administration and the army. In the eastern frontier lands there were differences of religion as well as differences of nationality, and here the slavophil theory supported Orthodoxy as the national religion against Catholicism and Protestantism.

Aksakov did not withstand the temptation, and he approved the official Russification of the Eastern frontier lands.

But he did not desire the Russification of the Poles. " It is impossible," he wrote, " to sympathise with the movement of the Ruthenians against the Austrians in Galicia, a region whose possession is legally (or rather illegally) profitable to the Austrians as the possession of the kingdom of Poland is profitable to us, whilst simultaneously regarding as without justification the endeavours of the Poles to free themselves from their dependence towards us." These words were penned a year after the revolt. In 1863 he had proposed that the purely Polish areas, those which had not belonged to Russia prior to the partition, be granted entire liberty should the Polish people decide by referendum in favour of internal autonomy under Russian suzerainty. In 1848 Homjakov had recommended a similar solution of the Polish problem.

At the time of the rising in Bosnia-Herzegovina, and during the Russo-Turkish war, Aksakov once more subordinated slavophil ideals to official policy. In the interim, after the death of Pogodin, he had become chairman of the Slav Welfare Committee. But the issue of the war and the upshot of the congress of Berlin having been described by him as a " colossal absurdity," he was banished from Moscow. In Bulgaria, however, some of the electors nominated him as candidate for the Bulgarian throne.

The increasing activity of the opposition after the Russo-

Turkish war and the growth of revolutionary sentiment at this epoch impelled Aksakov more and more towards the right, and after the assassination of Alexander II he became fiercely embittered against Europe. To Aksakov the deed of March 13th was a bloody confirmation of slavophil doctrine, for the terrorist atrocity was in his view an inevitable outcome of the idea of the Roman coercive state which Peter had transplanted from Europe into Russia.

It would be inaccurate to regard this declaration of Aksakov as nothing more than a complaint against the Petrine state and the bureaucracy. The complete argument here involved contains the fundamental conception of slavophilism and must therefore be briefly capitulated.

It is found in the speech which Aksakov delivered on April 10, 1881, before the St. Petersburg Slavic Society after a solemn requiem for Alexander II. He accused the intelligentsia of treason to their own nationality, describing the assassination of the tsar as a crime against the primitive Russian idea and primitive Russian institutions. By these, he said, the tsar was intimately associated with the people, being their father, leader, and sole representative. He condemned nihilism, which had now taken the form of terrorism, censuring it not merely as anarchism, for he included in a general condemnation all the liberal political endeavours of the west. Aksakov's formula ran as follows : " Nihilism=anarchism=revolution=socialism =constitutionalism=liberalism=westernism."

The Roman state founded upon force (the " outer " truth of Konstantin Aksakov) is the very opposite of Christianity, being not simply unchristian but positively atheistic, devoid of spiritual leadership and without belief. The western nations adopted and continued the Roman state, and Peter likewise adopted it. But Christ cannot simply cease to be Christ ; he will carry on the struggle against the god who has been enthroned in his place ; he will do this both inwardly and in social life ; he will rebel against the Christian principle which permeates all historically extant societies ; hence the lot of every Christian society which severs itself from Christ must inevitably be rebellion and revolution. A society which has thus made revolution a principle of development stumbles from revolution to revolution, arrives at anarchy, and ultimately achieves complete self-negation and self-slaughter. The man of the present denies God and erects his own reason as an idol. Not content with half measures, with inexorable logic his negation proceeds to the destruction of this idol as well ; he casts away his soul and idolises the flesh to become slave of the flesh ; the man without God becomes Nebuchadnezzar, becomes a beast.

Whilst Samarin endeavoured to verify the slavophil philosophy of history by applying it to the Catholic Poles, Aksakov extended the thesis to the entire west and to the Petrine state, declaring the revolution to be a falling away from God, from Christ, and therefore from Russian Orthodoxy, from true Christianity. Unquestionably in making this declaration Aksakov had before his eyes the analysis in which Dostoevskii deduced the reign of terror from atheism. The germs of this idea are indeed to be found in the works of the early slavophils, for Kirĕevskii represented the cleavage in the souls of European and Russian men as despairing pessimism, whilst Homjakov deduced negation from materialism.

During the first days of the reaction under Alexander III, Aksakov moved towards the position of Katkov and Pobĕdonoscev, but he soon moved away from the reactionaries when he perceived that the reforms of 1861 were to be sacrificed.

§ 62.

IVAN AKSAKOV'S explanation of the revolution finds its practical culmination in the glorification of Uvarov's absolutism, and N. Danilevskii moved forward to the stage of extolling Uvarov's nationalism. Danilevskii, like Dostoevskii, was implicated in the so-called Petraševscy conspiracy, but was punished merely by banishment from St. Petersburg. Devoting himself to the study of natural science, he had the advantage of working under von Baer for some years. As student of natural science Danilevskii acquired reputation by the books he published in opposition to Darwinism. In 1871 appeared his work on *Russia and Europe*, which became the handbook of slavophilism in its later phase.[1]

In this work Danilevskii aims at demonstrating that historical development exhibits to us ten types of civilisation embodied in as many national or racial types : (1) Egyptian ; (2) Chinese ; (3) Assyrio-Babylonic-Phœnician, Chaldean, or

---

[1] *Russia and Europe* first appeared in serial form in 1869. Danilevskii was born in 1822 and died in 1885.

Old Semitic ; (4) Indian ; (5) Iranian ; (6) Hebrew ; (7) Greek ; (8) Roman ; (9) New Semitic or Arabian ; (10) Teutono-Romance or European. (No more than passing allusion is made to the Mexican and Peruvian civilisations.)

In the natural course of development, the Slavic type is destined to separate from the Teutono-Romance or European type, and it will elaborate in a comprehensive synthesis the cultural elements that have undergone partial development at the hands of the other types. The extant types have secured a ripe development for religion alone (the Jews), for culture alone (the Greeks), or for the art of government alone (the Romans). The Teutono-Romance stocks were successful both in the political and in the cultural fields, but their civilisation has a one-sidedly scientific and industrial character, and among them the state is based on coercion. It is for this reason that Europe has lapsed into anarchy. In religion this anarchy takes the form of Protestantism ; in philosophy it takes the form of materialism ; and in the socio-political field it takes the form of the struggle between political democracy and economic feudalism. The Russians will be the first to effect an organic union of the four chief elements of civilisation (religion, culture in the narrower sense, political development, and socio-political organisation), and they will display their originality by furnishing the correct solution of the socio-economic problem.

Politically the task of Russia will be to organise a Slav federation, led by Russia herself. She must win Constantinople as capital of this federation, and in the struggle with Europe she will work out a solution of the Slav problem and therewith of the European problem and the problem of humanity at large. It is true that the Slavs are pacific by nature (Danilevskii is an opponent of Darwinism !), but the struggle with Europe is nevertheless essential and will be none the less salutary.

The concept of the types of civilisation is sufficiently clarified by Danilevskii. His ideas contain a somewhat mechanical association between the zoological notion of race and the historical notion of nationality. This enables him to identify race with church and religion, and in the process he annexes for the Slavic type, not only the Orthodox Rumanians and Greeks, but also the Protestant and Catholic Magyars.[1]

[1] The philosopher Solov'ev considers that Danilevskii's types are taken from H. Rückert's Universal History (1857) ; the Russian writer of a history

Hostility towards Europe and fondness for Old Russia led Danilevskii to the view which was not uncommon among the later slavophils, that Turkish rule was better for the Slavs than the rule of European states. The Turks, he considered, had preserved the Slavs from contact with European civilisation and had not denationalised them. It is true that in his synthesis Danilevskii proposes to accept European civilisation, thus in a sense continuing the work of Peter—for clearness and definiteness are not conspicuous qualities in this writer, nor in the slavophils in general. But in any case Danilevskii instilled a few valuable drops of zoology and of biologically based nationalism into the slavophil philosophy of religion and philosophy of history. From biological nationalism it is but a step to biological patriotism, to which many of the later slavophils succumbed. On the theoretical plane Danilevskii's explanation of historical development was extremely hasty ; his judgments concerning the spread and transmission of civilisation, concerning the decay of civilisations and nations, and the like, were prematurely formulated ; and it is obvious that his valuation of individual historical forces was altogether one-sided. The anthropological content of his view (definition of race, racial classification, racial mingling, the relationship between race and nationality) was inadequate ; and he had very little that was noteworthy to adduce concerning the relationship between physiological and mental characters. But I must not be unjust, and it is necessary to concede that in Danilevskii's day European science had little that was more valuable to offer upon these topics.

II

§ 63.

THE complete understanding of slavophilism will be facilitated by a brief comparison with the contemporary development of the national idea among the other Slav peoples, for these and Russia influenced one another mutually.

of literature deduces them from Pogodin. I may point out that Homjakov in his sketches of universal history classified the human species according to races, states, and religions, basing his conception of historical development upon these three principles. I have not myself followed up the precise affiliation of the idea, thinking it sufficient to point out its lack of clearness.

In the first place, slavophilism was related to the peculiar historical manifestation known as the Slav renaissance.

The eighteenth century, the century of the humanitarian movement, of the enlightenment, and of the great revolution, induced a political and national awakening, not in the west alone, but likewise in the east and south-east of Europe. Ideas of liberty could not fail to exercise a potent influence among the oppressed and dependent peoples under the absolutist rule of Austria, Turkey, and Russia; and it was inevitable that the national contrasts within these multilingual states should strengthen nationalist sentiment. At the opening of the nineteenth century the universal effect of the Napoleonic wars was to favour the growth of national consciousness. In the ensuing epoch of absolutist restoration and reaction, the liberal and democratic efforts of the revolutions of 1830 and 1848 favoured an extension of equal rights to nations and languages hitherto oppressed, while subsequently the socialist movement, its internationalism notwithstanding, promoted the growth of independent nationalist sentiments. Not in multilingual Austria alone, but likewise in Germany, nationally unified though politically disintegrated, the growth of national consciousness was resisted by absolutist governments, for nationalist sentiment was everywhere directed against the absolute state, and adopted everywhere a comparatively democratic and liberal program.

In Austria it was the Czechs and the Magyars above all who underwent a national awakening during the reigns of Maria Theresa and Joseph II, and in the year 1848 the awakening took a political form. The other peoples under Austrian and Turkish rule likewise experienced national and political awakening. In the Balkans one people after another secured freedom—Serbs, Greeks, Rumans, and finally Bulgars. The evolutionary process is not yet completed.

From the outset the national renaissance of the Slav peoples was guided by a more or less openly declared panslavist program. The similarity of the Slav tongues and of Slav manners and customs, ties of proximity and of political community (in Austria and in Turkey), and the example of the analogous movements known as pangermanism, panromanism, and pan-scandinavianism, furthered the progress of the idea of Slav union. In the lesser Slav states a consciousness of political and cultural weakness and pettiness made union with the greater Slav states, nations, and civilisations seem desirable. In the program for unification it was natural that a peculiarly important rôle should be assigned to Russia, in view of the increasing political and cultural prestige of Russia in the European world. Apart from Montenegro, Russia was the only independent Slav state ; five Slav nations (or six if the Serbs of Lusatia be included) were under German or Turkish rule, and the territories they inhabited were subdivided into almost five times as many administrative areas.

The formulation of the Slav program of unification was extremely vague, at least in the early days of the Slav renaissance.

The general idea was of a nonpolitical mutuality which was to facilitate the reciprocal study of the Slav tongues by a sort of cultural exchange. The union was conceived as ideal merely, as confined to the realm of the spirit. Many ingenuous persons went so far as to contemplate the artificial construction of a universal Slav tongue.

The political program of Slav union was geographically defined by extant political frontiers. Its advocates referred especially to Austro-Slavism or to Illyrism. There was little thought of the political union of all the Slavs ; but even under absolutism a few persons were bold enough to think of a republican or monarchical federation, and whether republican or monarchical the Russians or else the Poles or the Czechs were to play the leading rôle.

At first, therefore, and in its subsequent developments, panslavism was purely academic, the creation mainly of learned Slavists and historians. Owing to the lack of cultural and economic associations there was but little practical mutuality between the various Slav nations. The unifying antagonism towards the dominant foreign languages and civilisations was enormously outweighed by the positive fact that the individual Slav peoples were in truth independent nations and not mere tribes, as were the Germans, whose disintegration was purely political, not linguistic or cultural. The Slav peoples had distinct political and cultural histories, and a strengthening of any one of these peoples could be effected solely by the deliberate cultivation of its own language and its own civilisation. Among the various Slav nations and sections it was necessary that leading minds should consider ways and means of realising this more practical program.

Panslavism notwithstanding, the number of Slav nations and tongues was increased by the universal nationalist movements which followed the eighteenth century, and which resulted in a separation between the written tongues of the Hungarian Slovaks and of the Czechs, and which led also to a nationalist movement among the Ruthenians, who detached themselves from the Great Russians. A like process of national and linguistic differentiation was manifested also among the Slovenes who, had political conditions been different, might without much difficulty have undergone linguistic assimilation with the Croats. A similar differentiation is manifest in the evolution of the Croats and the Serbs, but here one and the same nation has undergone differentiation owing to religious and political dissimilarities, and owing to the varying influences of diverse cultural and geographical conditions.

The nature and evolution of the national renaissance of the Slav peoples was theoretically formulated in a number of programs wherein the matter was considered from the outlook of the philosophy of history and from that of the philosophy of nationality. It was natural that in drafting these programs people should be influenced by the historico-philosophical movement that originated in the eighteenth century and was stimulated by the great revolution. Just as in Russia at this date a philosophy of history and a philosophy of nationality came into existence, so do we find that at the same epoch there were attempts to found such philosophies among the other Slav peoples.

Side by side with the growth of the philosophies of history and of nationality there originated a Slavistic movement for the historical study of the Russian and other Slav tongues and civilisations ; this movement was analogous with the Romance and Teutonist movements, and was partly influenced by the last-named (by the works of Grimm and similar writers).

§ 64.

AFTER these general observations, passing now to the individual programs of the Slav nations in the matter of the philosophy of history and of the philosophy of nationality, we must begin with the Czechs.

The Czechs were the first theorists of the national renaissance of their own and of other Slav peoples. In their peculiar position as a threatened nationality, from the outset dependence upon the other Slavs was an important element in the idea of the national renaissance. Dobrovský (ob. 1829), the great founder of the Slavistic movement, had doubts about the vital efficiency of his own nationality, but he was the first russophil to bring forward reasoned grounds on behalf of his ideas and sympathies. He paid a visit to Russia in the year 1792. In Bohemia he had several predecessors, most of whom wrote in German. Dobrovský himself, the most vigorous reawakener of his nation, like Dobner, Voigt, Pelzel, etc., wrote only in German and in Latin. There were likewise German Slavists (Alter of Vienna, etc.), and there were German historians (Anton, etc.) who occupied themselves with the history of the Slav nations. In Russia at this epoch historical interest was limited to the Russian past.

To Dobrovský the most notable element common to the Slavs was the linguistic, but he considered they displayed likewise a community of manners and customs, and he believed that it was possible to detect a Slav national psychology.

Upon the foundation established by Dobrovský, Kollár developed Herder's historico-philosophical and slavophil ideas into the notion of the literary mutuality of the Slavs. Kollár's studies at the university of Jena and his experiences of the German nationalist movement (at the Wartburg festival etc.) exercised no small influence on his mind. The aggressive nationalism of the Magyars also affected him very powerfully —he was born in Hungary, and in Pesth he became Protestant preacher to the Slovako-German congregation. The Slavs, he contended, must create for themselves a Slav universal culture, for it was their mission to take over the historic leadership of the world from the decayed Teutons and Latins. In point of program Kollár's Slav ideal was quite unpolitical; he wholly accepted Herder's humanitarian ideal, and he dreamed of a nonpolitical fraternity of the nations under the leadership of Slav civilisation. The study of Slav tongues was to subserve this end, and the extent to which they were to be mastered was graded in accordance with the learner's degree of culture. An ordinary well-educated man was to be able to speak the four main living languages, Russian, " Illyrian," Polish, and Czecho-Slovak; the more learned Slav should know also the dialects, Little Russian, Croatian, Wendic, and Bulgarian; finally the man of learning, the Slavist and historian, must be familiar with the living and dead languages and dialects.[1] In the spirit of Kollár worked Šafařík with his study of Slav archæology, and Jungmann. Especially active in this field was Hanka, the most diligent forger of Old Czech literary works and documents (the Königinhof manuscript and the Grünberg manuscript).

The Slavist labours of the Czechs had a certain practical result in the Slav congress held in Prague in the year 1848, as imitation and rival of the Frankfort parliament.

Kollár's successors, and notably Palacký and Havliček, the political leaders of 1848, effected considerable modifications in Kollár's abstract ideal. Panslavism as a vague cosmopolitanism was replaced by a fully conscious Czechism ; instead of " great " panslavism there came into existence " lesser " panslavism, or Austroslavism. Palacký and Havliček entered protests against the Russian universal monarchy. Palacký wrote for the Czechs the first philosophically conceived history wherein the reformation effected by Huss and above all by the Moravian brethren was presented as the climax of Czech and European development. Palacký, too, elaborated the first political program. Upon the foundation of Herder's humanitarian ideal and by a process of natural law, a democratic federation of all the peoples of Austria in their several ethnographical boundaries was to come into existence. This program was journalistically defended and democratically equipped by Havliček with unrivalled mastery.

Havliček was one of the first if not the first of the Czechs to acquire an intimate knowledge of Russia. In the years 1843 and 1844 he was tutor in the house of Ševyrev. He would have nothing to do with official Nicolaitan Russia, but he was equally averse to the doctrines of the slavophils, adhering consistently to the philosophy of the enlightenment and to the democratic system of universal suffrage. His was the proposition " Secular absolutism is pillowed upon religious absolutism." He considered, however, that a closer union of the Austrian Slavs was a practical aim.

[1] Consult the writing, Concerning Literary Mutuality Between the Various Stocks and Linguistic Families of the Slav Nations, published in German in 1837 (2nd edition, 1844). The fundamental idea had previously been given to the world in Czech in an essay and in several other works, and among these in the annotations to the epic poem, Slávy Dcera (The Daughter of the Sláva) which appeared in 1821. Russian translations were published in 1838 and 1842, and a Serb translation in 1845.

Not until after the political experiences of the reaction that followed 1848 and not until after the creation of Austro-Hungarian dualism did Palacky tend towards panslavism and Russism. He took part in the panslavist congress held at Moscow in 1867.

Towards 1848 certain Slovak philosophico-historical writers modified Kollár's ideal. Overestimating the importance of the sometime Great Moravian realm and of its reputed Orthodox church founded by the Slav apostles, they proposed with the help of Russia and the Orthodox church to incorporate the Slovaks in a kind of panslavist federation.[1]

§ 65.

A MONG the southern Slavs also, the program of national renaissance goes back to Herder and the German philosophy of enlightenment. One of the earliest humanitarian philosophers was the Serb Obradovič (1739-1811), a monk who worked indefatigably at self-culture, one to whom a book was dearer than the sound of monastery or church bells. He was succeeded by the Slavist Vuk Karadšič ; and subsequently, in the thirties and forties, by Gai, who under Kollár's influence was the founder of Illyrism. In the year 1848 Illyrism acquired a strong political trend through its antagonism to the Magyars, which was fostered by Vienna, and through the fate of the Serbs under Turkish rule.

The national unification of the Serbo-Croats was long hindered by the religious differences between the Catholic Croats and the Orthodox Serbs. Križanič, indeed, the Croat priest to whom we have previously referred, preached panslavism ; but not until quite recently did Croats and Serbs make the first attempt to subordinate their religious differences to the joint national interest, encountering thereupon vigorous nationalist and ecclesiastical opponents in Buda-Pesth and in Vienna (the Serbo-Austrian conflict).

Peculiarly difficult is the position of the smallest Slav nation, the Slovene. Oppressed by two great civilised peoples the Italians and the Germans, and administratively divided

---

[1] Štúr was one of the most notable of this group. His writing, Slavdom and the World of the Future, a Message to the Slavs from the Banks of the Danube, existed in manuscript only till 1867, when Lamanskii translated it into Russian and published it in that tongue.

into a number of crown lands, it has been extremely difficult
for the Slovenes to preserve their consciousness of national
independence ; or at least, traditions of the past have failed to
keep memories of this independence alive as in the case of
the other Slav peoples.   The Bohemians, Poles, Serbs, Croats,
and Bulgars, have been politically independent and have
effected noteworthy performances in the fields of statecraft
and civilisation.   It is owing to the small-scale character of
Slovene development that the intelligentsia of this people
tends in cultural matters to lean upon the Croats and the
Czechs.

In this connection reference may also be made to the seg-
ments of nongerman nationalities in Germany, the Wends
and the Kassubs, some of whom deliberately endeavour to
foster a separatist national sentiment, seeking cultural associations with the Slav peoples respectively nearest to them
linguistically and geographically, the Wends turning to the
Czechs and the Kassubs to the Poles.

Whereas the Russians are an extremely numerous people,
the other Slav nations are comparatively small ; a similar
numerical disproportion is displayed between the lesser Slav
peoples on the one hand and the Germans and other great
nationalities on the other ; hence arise difficult problems for
sociologists and statesmen, both as regards the little nations
and the great ones.

In an epoch of association and of political alliances and
ententes, the notable national similarities between the Slav
peoples, their geographical proximity, and the political dependence of many of them, have close associations with the
panslavist question.

In the Turkey of earlier days there long existed religious
relationships between the Serbs and the Bulgars on the one
hand and the Russians on the other, and these tended indirectly
and directly to assume a political complexion.   At an early
date official Russia formulated her antagonism to Turkey in
a program of liberating the Christian nations of the Balkans.

The relationships between Russia and Austria-Hungary
were determined by like considerations.

The Bulgars partly owed their political enfranchisement
to their relationship to Russia, but their idea of national
renaissance dates from the eighteenth century, and may be
considered to have originated with the appearance in the year

1762 of a *History of the Bulgarian People* written by a monk named Paisii. Among Paisii's successors may be mentioned Venelin (1762–1839), a Ruthenian medical man, educated in Russia, who collected folk-songs and manuscripts in the south, his historical, archæological, and ethnographical studies stimulating the growth of national consciousness. Religious relationships with the Greeks were important to the Bulgars. During the fifties the religious question powerfully promoted nationalist sentiment, the Bulgars demanding Bulgarian bishops, and this demand securing sympathetic understanding in Russia. In 1870 the Bulgarian exarchate was founded, Ilarion, the first exarch, being a warm advocate of national liberation.

The example of Serbia, too, exercised a certain influence upon Bulgaria. It was under Serbian influence that Paisii was led to write his history, and Serb struggles for political freedom invigorated the similar Bulgarian endeavours. Before long, however, there ensued violent struggles between these two neighbour nations, especially over Macedonia. But this very antagonism served on both sides to promote the progress of nationalisation, and ultimately, for the purposes of the war of liberation against Turkey, there originated that Serbo-Bulgarian understanding which was the real foundation of the Balkan federation.

Bulgaria, having acquired independence, found it necessary like the other Balkan nations to devote herself to making up for lost time in the way of cultural development, which had been hindered under Turkish rule. The Bulgars, too, have to solve the ethnographical and religious problems of their multilingual state. The southern Slav problem is peculiarly complicated owing to the religious disintegration of these Slavs into Catholics, members of the Orthodox church, and Mohammedans.

§ 66.

OF a quite peculiar character is the Little Russian problem. Some of its difficulty is already indicated by the lack of any generally accepted name for this people. They are sometimes termed Little Russians ; in Austria they are commonly spoken of as Ruthenians ; and they are also denominated Ukrainians. Independent Poland oppressed the Little Russians alike nationally, economically, and in the religious field. It was hostility to Poland which induced the Little Russians to become part of the Muscovite realm, but after their incorporation into Russia antagonism began to make itself manifest between the Great Russians and the Little Russians ; and this antagonism was not solely nationalist and linguistic, but extended likewise into the administrative and economic spheres. Through the partition of Poland and the acquisition of Bukowina a considerable proportion of Little Russian territory accrued to Austria. In Galicia, Austria inclines to protect the Little Russians in so far as this suits the aims of her policy towards Russia and the Poles. In Hungary the Little Russian tongue is proscribed.[1]

The linguistic and economic differences between north and south induced a nationalist movement among the Little Russians, a movement known as Ukrainism. At the outset the demand was for the cultivation of the folk-speech in the schools and in literature and for its use for official purposes, without political separation. Even Russian pedagogues, Ušinskii, Vodovozov, and others, laid due weight upon the linguistic differences, insisting on educational grounds that Little Russian should be used in elementary schools ; for the same reason the St. Petersburg academy recently recommended that Little Russian should be employed as the medium of instruction. The use of repressive measures has led in course of time to the growth of a political separatist movement, social differences contributing also to this development.

The first ukrainophil program went so far as to demand that Ruthenians should be guaranteed autonomy and linguistic independence in a panslavist federation (republic) after the American model. The Great Russian language was to be no more than a general means of communication. This plan was based upon the theories of those historians who considered that the essence of the Russian state was not to be found in Muscovite tsarism but in the republic of Novgorod and in the South Russian Cossack state. In addition to Kostomarov, the historians P. V. Pavlov and Ščapov advocated this theory. In the year 1845, upon the basis of these historical ideals, Kostomarov founded in Kiev the Cyrillo-Methodian secret society which may be regarded as a continuation of the society

[1] The numbers of the Little Russians are given as follows : in Russia, twenty-two to twenty-six millions; in Austria (Galicia and Bukowina), more than four millions ; in Hungary, half a million.

of the United Slavs. The poet Ševčenko expanded Kostomarov's ideas to constitute a more profoundly conceived cultural
panslavism. Kostomarov's society was suppressed in 1847.
Kostomarov, Ševčenko, and several other members, were
banished from Little Russia and punished in other ways,
Ševčenko being forced into the army and treated by Nicholas
as previously described. Henceforward the use of Little
Russian was regarded with increasing disfavour. On the
other hand, under Austrian rule, Lemberg tended more and
more to become the literary centre of the Little Russians.

Both in Russia and in Galicia the Little Russian problem
was increasingly complicated by the growth of socialism and
the development of political propaganda. The Little Russians
became involved in relationships, not merely with the Russian
administrative machine and with Russian tendencies towards
economic centralisation, but also with the Poles and the Jews.
There are now in Ukraine more than five million Jews
whose civilisation is divergent from that of the Russians, so that
they constitute an ethnographical and cultural whole. Whilst
Kostomarov regarded the problem from the nationalist outlook
and was influenced by the national panslavist movement,
Dragomanov, who had been dismissed from the university
in 1876, in his political writings of the eighties interpreted the
essential ideas of Kostomarov's federation in the sense of
autonomy and self-government, endeavouring to effect an
organic union between these ideas and the demands of moderate
socialism and democratic constitutionalism. This was done
without prejudice to the scientific question whether the Little
Russians really constitute a peculiar nationality. Dragomanov did not favour the idea of political separatism, and
in a literary feud with Lamanskii he actually opposed the
separatist movement.

I am here concerned solely with the facts of historical
development, and shall not enter into a detailed discussion
of the question whether extant linguistic and other differences
suffice to constitute a distinct literature and a distinct nationality. History teaches that languages and peoples differentiate
owing to the co-operation of numerous factors, and that, among
these, political factors play a notable part. When the inhabitants of a particular area feel themselves to be a distinct
nation and organise a national literature for themselves, it
is their will to this end that is decisive, and the sentiment

of unity is not the issue of questions of grammar or linguistic research.[1]

The revolution (1905) brought the Little Russians certain freedoms in the matter of the public use of their tongue, the publication of Little Russian newspapers being permitted, and so on. The program formulated in 1863 by Minister Valuev on the ground that a Little Russian nationality " never has existed, does not exist, and cannot exist," has at least been modified by the government.

The religious question plays a certain part in the matter. The Little Russians of Austria are Uniats whilst those of Russia are Orthodox. Some of the Little Russians in Poland are Uniats.

Among the White Russians the idea of differentiation has originated only in very recent days.[2]

§ 67.

THE Poles lost their political independence much later than the other northern and southern Slavs, and for this reason the national sentiment of the Poles is peculiarly political and is directed towards the re-establishment of the Polish state. This is manifested by the two revolutions against Russia, the country under whose sway the majority of the Poles are now living.[3]

Polish philosophy developed under the influence of the German postkantian philosophy of history, being based in

---

[1] Beyond question the Slovaks have no language that is peculiarly their own, and nevertheless political conditions had led to the segregation of the Slovak dialect as a literary tongue. In Germany certain dialects are quite as distinct from the literary speech as Little Russian is from Great Russian. In Germany no obstacles are imposed upon the literary cultivation of the dialects, whilst the teachers in the schools and the officials in the discharge of their duties help themselves out with dialect in case of need. It is doubtless difficult to create a literary speech and a literature in rivalry with a literary tongue already extant and accessible, but it is questionable whether the linguistic development of the Russians will follow the laws of linguistic centralisation in Germany, France, England, etc. As has been said, the question is not a literary one merely, for its solution depends primarily upon political considerations. A Great Russian monthly review has recently been founded in the Little Russian interest.

[2] The White Russians number about six millions.

[3] The Austrian Poles number three and a half millions, the German Poles three and a quarter millions, and the Russian Poles eleven millions ; of these last there are eight millions in the kingdom of Poland and about three millions in Lithuania, West Russia, and South Russia.

especial upon the doctrines of Schelling and Hegel, but it exercised little influence upon Russian philosophy of history. The Polish problem was formulated in a number of notable historico-philosophical and literary works, and it would be of great interest to undertake a comparative study of these in relation to the other historico-philosophical systems of the Slavs. After the revolution of 1830 the messianism founded previously by Wronski (1778–1853) acquired a definitely political trend in the hands of Mickiewicz, who at a later date contended that upon a Catholic basis and with the help of Napoleon III, Poland would bring salvation to humanity and to herself. His program was at first political, and deliberately militarist, but subsequently assumed a more distinctively social form. Krasinskii recommended inward and spiritual reforms to his fellow-countrymen who had been dispersed by emigration. Whilst Mickiewicz had summarised his revolutionary program in the words, "The slave's only weapon is treason," Krasinskii endeavoured to supersede revolutionism by religious development. In contrast with Russian Orthodoxy and German Protestantism, Catholicism was idealised by the Polish messianists, who conceived it just as mystically as the Russian messianists conceived the idealised Orthodoxy of their own land. This mysticism was reduced to a system by Towianski (1799–1878), a writer who exercised much influence upon Mickiewicz and others.

Among the Poles, too, at the opening of the nineteenth century, the Slavistic movement called a learned panslavism into life. In 1816, in the kingdom of Poland, the Polish government ordered that lectures upon the kindred Slav tongues should be delivered at the Polish universities of Warsaw and Vilna, the aim being to promote the progress of the Polish cause.

Among the Poles panslavism has always taken a more abstract form than among the Czechs, the southern Slavs, and the Ruthenians. Only among the Poles and the Russians did the messianist idea gain ground—only among the two greatest Slav nations, the latter of which had always been independent whilst in the case of the former memories of independence were still fresh. There was, however, a notable distinction between Russian and Polish messianism. The Poles desired to secure the salvation of mankind with the aid and practically under the leadership of the French, who

21

were not Slavs, whereas the Russians felt strong enough to undertake the task for themselves. The Czechs (and the Slovaks), aware of the smallness of their own powers, whilst conceiving the idea of a universal and mighty Slavdom, were inclined always to rely upon the help of humanity at large and of civilisation in general. Themselves restricted to Austro-Hungarian territory, their tendency was to concentrate upon the Slavs distributed among other states. Though Kollár was a theologian, he had abandoned the theocratic ideal. As a nation the Czechs had experienced the reformation, but they had afterwards been forcibly reconverted to Catholicism by Rome and Austria, and they had therefore remained inwardly estranged from the victorious church. The Russians, the Poles, and the southern Slavs relied upon the church but the Czechs relied upon culture. Mickiewicz condemned the humanitarian cultural ideal of the Czechs in the name of sentiment and inspiration. The generation following that of Mickiewicz, enlightened by the issue of the revolution of 1863 and by the decline in European sympathy for the Polish cause, entered the path of culture and social reforms. Many Poles believed that the most effective support could be secured from Austria and from the antirussian policy of that country but Mickiewicz, in his *Improvisation*, recommended a different policy :—

> The Austrian gives him vinegar to drink,
> The Prussian gives him gall to drink,
> And at the foot of the cross stands
> Mother Freedom, weeping.
> But look ! The Muscovite warrior
> Springs forward with the lance,
> Thrusts it into the innocent side—
> Blood gushes forth ! What hast thou done,
> Most stupid and most fierce of all the executioner's servants ?
> He alone repents, he alone,
> And him God will pardon !

The revolution of 1905 and the granting of a constitution have made it possible for Poles and Russians to come into closer and more direct contact in the duma. In this way there may arise an understanding of their joint national interests, and each side may come to realise the other's needs.

§ 68.

A S we have seen, Russian national sentiment was an independent development of the peculiar historical and geographical problems which Russia had to solve in internal and external relationships ; consideration for the Slavs played a very small part. Certain relationships of religious intimacy existed only in the case of the Orthodox Bulgars and Serbs. Križanič, it is true, preached panslavism to the Russians, but had to dream out his political dreams in Siberia. Only with the development of political activities among the Serbs and the Greeks did there arise a certain political interest, inconsiderable at best, on behalf of the Slavs, for the attitude of the Russian government and of the tsar towards the revolting Slavs and Greeks remained legitimist.

The panslavist movement took root to some extent among the freemasons. There existed a lodge of United Slavs, secret of course ; after 1825 there was also a political secret society aiming at a federation of Slav republics, and this society was broken up during the trial of the decabrists. Several of the decabrists cherished panslavist ideals, as for example M. A. Fonvizin, but Fonvizin conceived his panslavist program at a later date than the decabrist rising, in the forties, during exile in Siberia.

In the reign of Nicholas, literary panslavism was encouraged by the Slavistic movement, whose beginnings in Russia can be traced back into the eighteenth century. In this matter Schlözer, the German historian, directed Russian attention towards the Slavs by the chapter on the Slav apostles in his translation of Nestor.

The influence of the Czech Slavists played a part, above all that of Dobrovský, one of whose Russian acquaintances was Šiškov (1813). Dobrovský's successors in Prague were likewise concerned in the movement, and in special Kollár, who did not sufficiently separate the provinces of poetry, archæology, and philology. Czecho-Russian mutuality was to a certain extent favoured by the Russian campaigns in Europe, when the Russian armies marched across Bohemian territories. Youthful Russian historians and philologists visited Prague, but during the fifties these literary efforts cooled. The labours of Dobrovský and Šafařík left little scope in Prague for Russian

Slavists.[1] Hanka entered into close relationship with various Russians, and among them Count Uvarov, whose Orthodox clericalism he flattered with the suggestion that Bohemia received Christianity from Constantinople and in Orthodox form. But these panslavist whimsies could not maintain their ground in face of the political movement which now, under western influence, was beginning in Austria and Bohemia. Kollár and Hanka were replaced by Palacký and Havliček, and panslavism was driven out by democracy and liberalism.

Official Russia was too conservative and too Orthodox to think of panslavism. Šiškov, for example, was infuriated by the very idea of writing Russian in the Latin script, and said that any Russian who did such a thing ought to be beheaded. Magnickii denounced Köppen for his article upon Cyril and Methodius. Köppen's plan to invite the three Czech Slavists, Šafařík, Čelakovský, and Hanka, to Russia was frustrated by the fears and the indifference of the government and the academy of sciences. Nicholas. as legitimist, was the declared enemy of panslavism.

In 1849 Ivan Aksakov was examined by the police, and was compelled to give written answers to various questions, especially as concerned the nature of slavophilism. Tsar Nicholas wrote interesting marginal notes upon these answers, expressing his emphatic disapproval of the panslavist movement, and saying that the union of all the Slavs " would lead to the destruction of Russia." To the tsar, panslavism seemed a revolutionary program, seeing that a union of the Slavs could only be effected by revolts against God-given monarchs. In 1847 Kostomarov's Cyrillo-Methodian Union was prosecuted. A writing issued at this date by the ministry for education and expounding the true Russian program opposes this program to " the purely imaginary Slavdom " imported into Russia from Bohemia.

Most of the Russian Slavists gave expression to these or to similar tendencies. As political representatives of the move-

[1] The first Russian Slavist who made his way to visit the Slav countries was Köppen, son of a Prussian immigrant from Brandenburg to Russia. Köppen came to Prague in 1823. In 1837 and subsequent years other noted Slavists to visit Prague were Bodjanskii, Srezněvskii, and Preis. The plan to transfer Šafařík and Čelakovský to Russia came to nothing. The first chair of Slavistics was established at Moscow in 1811, being held by the historian Kačenovskii. In 1826 Šiškov, who had become minister for education, inaugurated at the universities and at the newly founded pedagogic institute, chairs in Slavistics to which the before-mentioned Russian Slavists were subsequently appointed.

ment I may mention the historian Pogodin (1800–1875) and the historian of literature Ševyrev (1806–1864).

In youth Pogodin had at times been dominated by romanticist notions of liberty, but in due time he became conservative and reactionary in accordance with the program of Uvarov's official nationalism. In 1835 Uvarov appointed him professor of history at Moscow, to defend " historical Orthodoxy."

Ševyrev was professor of the history of literature at Moscow university. He was a hard worker, but a pedant and a poor thinker, one well fitted to bring Schelling's philosophy and the teaching of the German romanticists into harmony with Uvarov's program. He advised Gogol to devote his literary talents to descriptions of the upper classes ; whilst Pogodin as an editor treated his collaborators as the Russian great landowner treated his peasants. To Ševyrev we owe the oft-quoted formula, " The west is putrescent ! " To him western civilisation was poisonous, and the west was a pre-destined corpse whose deathlike odour already tainted the air.

If such men as these had panslavist inclinations, their panslavism was properly speaking panrussism. As a rule they thought only of a union of the Orthodox Slavs, whilst the Catholic Slavs were left to the west. Pogodin visited Prague in 1835, and made the acquaintance of Palacký, Šafařík, and Hanka, but these relationships were restricted to the scientific field.

Even if Pogodin and Ševyrev termed themselves slavophils, and if after their manner they rough-hewed the doctrine of Kirěevskii and Homjakov, these reactionary chauvinists must be distinguished all the more sharply from the first slavophils precisely because the two doctrines are so often labelled with the same name. This name, as I have shown, properly attaches to the early slavophils, the founders of the doctrine, for its subsequent exponents strayed into the paths of Pogodin.

The slavophils were far too much inclined to base Russia's civilisation upon religion for it to be possible for them to be nationalist and political panslavists. " Without Orthodoxy our nationality becomes fudge," said Košelev, and this expression, rough though it be, sums up exceedingly well the fundamental outlook of the slavophils. The difference between slavophilism and political panslavism is well shown in Samarin's polemic (1875) against the reactionary political views of General Fadĕev,

writer on military topics, friend of Černaev of disastrous
memory.

The attitude of the slavophils towards the Slavs was determined by their theocratic outlook. During his European
journey Homjakov visited Prague and became acquainted with
Hanka. The Slavs were dear to him, but dear above all were
the Orthodox southern Slavs. Similar were the feelings of the
later Slavophils. Ivan Aksakov, for example, took an extremely
critical view of the pilgrimage of the Czechs to Moscow, and
laid stress upon religious differences.[1]

Lamanskii subsequently suggested the possibility of parti-
tioning the Bohemian territories. Bohemia with the liberal
Czechs was to go to Germany, whilst southern Moravia and the
Slovaks were to become Russian. But just as Bismarck from
his Protestant standpoint rejected the idea of a union with
Catholic German-Austria, so were the Russian slavophils and
panslavists horrified at the thought of annexing the Liberal
and Catholic Slavs.

Certain Russian slavophils and panslavists attempted,
however, to show that the Czech Slavs have a right to stand
on the same footing as the Russian Slavs, attributing to them
adhesion to Orthodoxy, on the ground that the Czech reformation had been due to the influence and existence of Orthodoxy
in Bohemia since the days of the Slav apostles. Kirěevskii
was the first to formulate this historical doctrine, which is
manifestly false ; subsequently it was expounded in fuller
detail by Hilferding (*Huss, his Relationship to the Orthodox
Church*, 1871) ; and it is held even to-day, notwithstanding
the overwhelming proof to the contrary (Palmov, *The Moravian
Brethren*, 1904).

Vis-à-vis the Orthodox southern Slavs, both slavophils and
panslavists adopted a different standpoint, for here the tie of
a common faith existed, and there were old associations. Moreover, official Russia was the antagonist of Turkey and appeared
as liberator of the southern Slavs—the conquest of Constantinople
and the erection of the three-barred cross on the dome of St.
Sophia becoming a national ideal. Catherine II had regarded
Constantinople as capital of the Russo-Greek realm.

Towards the Poles the attitude both of slavophils and of
panslavists was always peculiar. Russism as Orthodoxy
contrasted with Sarmatianism as Catholicism, and further,

[1] Aksakov condemned Rieger's political aims as ultramontane half-measures.

the political factor was decisive rather than the national. Poland was the old political enemy, the country which, after having been an adversary for centuries, had been incorporated into the Russian realm as a semi-independent land. Owing, too, to the tripartition of the Polish nation the Polish question was predominantly political, and this matter of the partition dictated the political relationship to Austria and to Germany. As early as the end of the eighteenth century the political agitation against Russia was conducted in Poland by secret societies, and abroad by Polish refugees ; the first secret society in Warsaw appears to date from the year 1796. After 1815, when by the congress of Vienna the major part of Poland was reallotted to Russia, the agitation of these societies became accentuated, and at this time Poland had her own constitution and was freer than Russia. The Polish secret societies consequently acquired influence over liberal elements in Russia ; the Russian secret societies, and above all the decabrists, being in communication with the Polish societies. We have previously made acquaintance with Pestel's sarmatiophil program, but we have also learned that not all Russians, nor even all decabrists, shared Pestel's views upon the Polish question.

Liberals continued to display sympathy for Poland. Advanced Russian authors like Polevoi drew attention to the writings of Mickiewicz, and advocated a reciprocal drawing together of the two countries, whilst Mickiewicz received a cordial welcome in Moscow. On the other hand a few Poles were unfortunately found to take service as Russian writers on behalf of the official reaction of the twenties and thirties. I may mention Bulgarin and Senkovskii (Baron Brambeus). Not merely was the latter opposed to liberalism and western philosophy, but he used extremely opprobrious language about his fellow-countrymen.

Poles and Russians were mutually estranged by the revolution of 1830, and the widespread confiscations nourished the feeling of bitterness.[1] The economic differences between Russia and Poland had and still have great importance in relation to the Polish problem. Poland was economically

---

[1] During the years 1832 to 1835 persons to the number of 2,338 had their property confiscated, and during the years 1835 to 1856 persons to the additional number of 551 were affected ; the value of the confiscated lands was reckoned at 141,000,000 francs.

more advanced, and Russian manufacturing industry, that of Moscow above all, attempted to defend itself against Polish competition by various repressive measures, dealing with communications, tariffs, etc.[1]

In the fifties and sixties, when the slavophils and the westernisers were formulating their respective views, the Polish question was vigorously discussed by both parties. The opinions of the slavophils (Samarin and Ivan Aksakov) have already been expounded. Among the westernisers reference may be made to Čičerin, who in 1859 advocated the old Polish policy of Alexander I, and declared that the Polish fatherland ought to be restored to the Poles. At a later date, long subsequent to the rising of 1863, Čičerin returned to the matter (this was in 1901 in an answer to Rennenkampf's writing of 1898, *Letters Concerning the Jewish and Polish Question*). It was Čičerin's hope that a satisfactory solution of the Polish problem would increase Russia's influence in the Slav world.

The rising of 1863 induced an unfavourable mood among Russian liberals, who dreaded the consequences of the anti-revolutionary reaction upon Russia herself. Herzen had to suffer at this time for his sarmatiophil tendencies. Conservatives and reactionaries pointed to the Polish rising as justification for general reaction. At this time Katkov was the chief spokesman of Russian nationalism. But in 1863 all that Katkov demanded was the Russification of the eastern parts of Poland, those which had of old belonged to Russia. As far as the kingdom of Poland was concerned he asked only for joint administration of army and finance, considering that this area might well remain independent nationally and linguistically. In Katkov's view the difficulty of the Polish question was solely conditioned by the utopian demand of the ultras that Poland should be restored, with the frontier of 1772. He was even willing to allow Polish priests to engage in propaganda, provided this was undertaken from sincere conviction.

The official Russification of the Poles in educational and administrative affairs was not effected immediately after the revolt, but took place step by step from 1865 onwards. The steps, it is true, followed in rapid succession, and by 1870 the

---

[1] Haxthausen informs us that he learned in Moscow in the year 1843 that a Moscow deputation made representations to the government against the complete incorporation of Poland, protesting against this measure upon industrial grounds.

system may be said to have been in complete working order. This system, for whose defects the Russians too had to pay, developed in such evil fashion that the best officials and administrators refused to serve in Poland.[1]

In the complex of questions which make up the Russian problem, the Polish question is one of the most important, and it has therefore always been a matter of profound concern, not merely to politicians and partisans, but also to the philosophers of history. The Polish question is itself a complex of difficult problems. Should historical Poland or ethnographical Poland be granted independence within the Russian empire, and if so in what form and to what extent? The interests and aims of Russians and Poles, of Little Russians, Lithuanians, White Russians, and Jews, conflict in this matter. Socially and economically the relationship of Polish manufacturing industry to Russian manufacturing industry and to aristocratic landlordism is a burning question, especially in nonpolish areas. Culturally Catholicism is opposed to Orthodoxy, whilst the Uniats constitute a peculiar problem. Alike in Russia and in Poland the Jewish question is extremely thorny. Last of all there has to be considered the relationship of Russian Poland to Austrian and Prussian Poland, the panpolish problem in general.

It is upon the Polish question that Russian panslavism has been shipwrecked.

The reaction under Alexander II and still more under Alexander III endeavoured with increasing energy to realise the official nationalist program of Uvarov in accordance with which all the nonrussian peoples of Russia, Germans, Finns, Lithuanians, Letts, etc., as well as the rebellious Poles, were to be Russified. Administrative centralism, hitherto easygoing and intellectually sluggish, was transformed into a state-privileged linguistic aristocracy of the dominant nation, the language question becoming continually more acute, above all in the civilised frontier lands adjacent to Europe.

In Europe, the importance of Russian panslavism is greatly overestimated, especially by the German-Austrian, Polish, and Magyar press. It is necessary to remember that the

[1] In 1867 the following special privileges were granted to the bureaucracy in Poland. One year of service was to count as four, a bonus of 15% was added to all salaries, and the right to a pension was acquired after five years' service.

inhabitants of Russia (European and Asiatic) comprise at least forty-eight distinct nationalities. Many of the inhabitants are not even of Indo-European origin, but have sprung from Finnish, Turkish, Mongolian, and other nonaryan stocks. Some of these peoples are very numerous, the Finns, for instance, the Tatars, the Kirghiz, and above all the Jews. If we leave out of account fragmentary Bulgarian colonies, the only non-russian Slav people under Russian rule are the Poles, and the relationship of the Russians to the Poles is sui generis. The Little Russians are not yet recognised as a separate folk, and consequently as far as Russia herself is concerned there is no ground for panslavism. The Russians have religious ties of old standing with some of the southern Slavs, but the Russian boundary does not march with that of the southern Slavs. Speaking generally we may say that the frontier between Russia proper and the Slav dependency of Russia, the frontier between Poland and Little Russia, does not possess the political significance of the other Russian lines of demarcation, those which separate European Russia from the Germans, the Swedes, and the Rumanians, and those which separate Russia in Asia from the Chinese, the Japanese, the Turks, and the Persians. If under Nicholas II panasiatism has been officially proclaimed as the program of Russia, we cannot but recognise that this program is more in conformity with actual relationships than is the panslavist program.

A panslavist program does indeed exist, but is taken seriously by no more than a few Russians. This is proved by the fiasco of the so-called neoslavism, the name coined within the last few years for a réchauffé of panslavist slavophilism—a dish that has speedily cooled.[1]

---

[1] In the west people continue to talk of the Slav Welfare Association, although less is now heard of it than during and after the Russo-Turkish war. Founded in Moscow by Pogodin in 1858, called at first the Slav Welfare Committee, in 1877 its name was changed to Slav Welfare Association. Branches were formed in St. Petersburg, Kiev, and Odessa, in 1868, 1869, and 1870, respectively. Pogodin's chief object in launching the committee was to use it as a weapon against Roman Catholic propaganda in the Balkans. According to the published accounts for the years 1868 to 1893 the receipts of the association during this period amounted to 2,629,247 roubles. Of this sum, 2,403,379 roubles were spent in the Slav lands of the Balkans for the maintenance of the churches ; 25,395 roubles went to the schools ; the remainder was devoted to literary and other purposes. Historically the association was analogous to the Gustavus Adolphus Association, and this also was stigmatised by the Catholic clericalists as a body constituted solely for purposes of political agitation. (Between 1832,

The danger to Europe or to Germany and Austria-Hungary does not arise from the panslavist movement, but from the fact that European and Asiatic Russia contain 170,000,000 inhabitants, who may, should circumstances favour this development, become a gigantic military and economic force. During the last half century the population of Russia, which in 1859 was 74,000,000, has more than doubled. What will the numerical relationships be in 1950, and what will they be at the close of the twentieth century?

According to one estimate, the populations of A.D. 2000 will number as follows, in millions : Hungary, 30 ; Austria, 54 ; Italy, 58 ; France, 64 ; British Isles, 145 ; Germany, 165 ; European Russia, 400 ; Russia including Russia in Asia, 500 ; the United States, 1,195.

Will the triple alliance still exist at that date? However this may be, the relationships of population between the countries of the triple alliance on the one hand and the countries of the triple entente on the other will be far less favourable to the former group than those which now obtain. Persons who regard physical force as decisive in national life may, as their standpoint varies, console themselves or alarm themselves with the contemplation of these calculations ; they will do well not to forget the growth of Japan, China, India, etc. ;

the year of its foundation, and 1884, the Gustavus Adolphus Association disbursed 19,686,532 marks.) During recent years the Slav Welfare Association has ceased to have any practical importance. Suggestions in the European press that the spoutings of its orators possess political significance are utterly erroneous. Apart from the fact that the membership of the association is numerically insignificant, pensioned generals like Kiréev are without influence in Russia. There is no lack in Russia of pensioned generals and officers of lesser rank, and these sometimes beguile the weary hours with excursions into what they dignify by the name of Slav politics. The aforesaid Kiréev, in a speech delivered in 1893, declared that slavophilism would prove the salvation of the world, would deliver Europe from anarchism, parliamentarism, unbelief, and dynamite. But it is necessary to distinguish between slavophilism of this type and the slavophilism of Kiréevskii. The first slavophils associated their doctrine with the country and the folk, whereas Kiréev and other slavophils of late date look towards the autocracy. After Pogodin's death Ivan Aksakov became chairman of the Moscow branch of the association, and Aksakov was doubtless a publicist of note. The choice fell upon him in preference to the prince of Bulgaria, but he was not strictly speaking a panslavist. At the present date General Čerep-Spiridovič is chairman of the Moscow branch, and as far as I can learn no one but the Paris Cri d'Alarme takes his political views seriously. A few years ago certain so-called neoslavist associations were founded as a counterblast to the reactionary associations. Their aims were distinctively nonpolitical, their interest being in Slav culture. Little, however, is heard of them to-day.

and they should bear in mind the awakening of an Asiatic consciousness.

In truth the question of numbers must be taken into serious account. In 1789 the population of France exceeded that of any other European state, and in part at least the power of the France of that day is explicable upon this ground. In millions the actual populations were : France, 26 ; Turkey, 23 ; Austria, 19 ; British Isles, 15 ; Prussia, 6; Poland, 9; European Russia, 20 ; Russia in Asia, 5.

The growth of population in Russia has been exceedingly rapid. At the time of Peter's death the populations under Russian rule numbered barely 15,000,000 ; at the opening of the nineteenth century they were 38,000,000 ; in 1900 they were 135,000,000 ; to-day they are 170,000,000.

Through the natural growth of population changes occur in the relative greatness of states and nations. France, formerly a great power, threatens to drop into the second rank, whilst other powers, whose inhabitants multiply, grow stronger. The philosophical statistician must turn his attention to the problem of the greater and the lesser nations and to their political and national destiny.[1]

§ 69.

SLAVOPHIL messianism is not identical with national chauvinism and national panslavism.

If we are to understand the messianist movement thoroughly and to explain its literary origins, we must look back into the time when in their Moscow circle the slavophils were developing their views in conflict with the westernisers. This was during the second half of the reign of Alexander I and during the reign of Nicholas I. In Europe and in Russia it was the epoch of restoration and of reaction after the revolution, the epoch of

---

[1] It will be interesting in this connection, in view of Haxthausen's relationships with the slavophils, to recall that writer's contributions to Slav philosophy of history. The Czechs, he said, were too petty a folk to play a notable political rôle. Their place and task among the Slavs was that of intermediators. The Poles, he considered, could not form an independent state, but they might preserve their national peculiarities. (It was all to the good that the Germans, too, did not compose a homogeneous state. As for the Russians, their mission in the world, said Haxthausen, was to intermediate between Asia and Europe. He considered panslavism of value as an expression of reciprocal Slav sympathies.)

deliberate reversion to prerevolutionary social institutions and whenever possible to those of the middle ages. The most momentous and thorough expression of the tendency is found in romanticist Catholisation, as witnessed by the fact that not governments alone, but poets, philosophers, and statesmen, above all that many Protestants in Germany and England, adopted Catholicism. It was not only de Maistre and the other French conservative philosophers who sang the praises of Catholicism, but the same sentiments were voiced by Protestants and converts, by such men as Stolberg, Schlegel, Novalis (who was never actually received into the church though he accepted its tenets), Gentz, Haller, Müller, and Overbeck the painter. In England the number of converts was very large. From the Roman side there were already being made energetic efforts in favour of union, directed mainly towards the Orthodox churches.

Rousseau had attempted to prove that civilisation was decadent. Even in Rousseau's own day, the Rousseauist movement, the longing for more primitive, elemental, nay, barbaric energies had already secured wide support, whilst after the revolution its spread was yet more extensive. The horrors of the French revolution were regarded as confirmation of the theory, many persons considering the revolution to be the outcome of philosophy and of its secondary effects. The reader may recall in this connection the Indian children of nature depicted by Chateaubriand, and the numerous successors of these in the different national literatures ; he may recall Faust and the renunciation of the wisdom of the schools ; he may recall Byron's revolt against society ; and he may recall Musset's analysis of the malady of the century.

The historians and the philosophers of history confirmed Rousseau's thesis. Evolution appeared to them as a succession of leading nations and states. One folk thrust another from the pre-eminent position ; one nation after another attained to the leadership, only in its turn to decay. Antiquity presented a succession of declining peoples and perishing civilisations, conquered and swept away by fresh and uncorrupted barbarians. Passing to the later middle ages, the fall of Byzantium was an example of the same process. Such were the ideas of Herder and of many of his successors ; such, in especial, were the ideas of the romanticists.

The socialist movement, which was soon to undertake the

organisation of the great masses of the workers, was guided by the same notion of the decay of all hitherto extant civilisations ; the working class was to take the leadership in society and in the development of philosophy.

Characteristic of the period was a historical preference for the study of the very earliest times (archæology in all its departments). The middle ages were rehabilitated.

Associated with this flight into the grey past were the idea and the conviction that new foundations must be discovered for society and for philosophy ; widespread was the belief that in these respects a thorough change was essential. Associated therewith was the conflicting conviction that an entirely new era was beginning, and that progress would issue from the endeavours of this reactionary historical movement, which fled from the present into the primal age.

Philosophy, led by Hume and Kant, proved that a new philosophy and a new outlook on the world were indispensable. Widespread was the assurance that change, that thoroughgoing reform, was needful, though some desired reforms in the direction of progress whilst others thought that reforms would best be secured by a return to the past.

The new philosophy of history endeavoured to take stock of the needs of the postrevolutionary epoch and to influence future developments.

In Russia the intelligentsia participated in all these European endeavours, the slavophils, and the westernisers no less, taking the side of those who demanded a return to the past. From Rousseau, Herder, and many of the philosophers of history, above all from those of socialistic views, they learned that civilisation, that Europe, that the west, was falling into decay. Russia was without civilisation, and Kiréevskii's deduction was that this was advantageous to Russia, for the Russians were the chosen people, fresh and uncorrupted, competent with undiminished energies to carry on the task of civilisation. Sčerbatov and Boltin had already adduced proofs that in the moral sphere the Russians were more efficient than the French. The trifle of civilisation with which Peter had inoculated the Russians would do no harm. Even Čaadaev, Europe's great admirer, ultimately came over to this view.

Puškin's analysis of European Russia must be interpreted as a confirmation of the essential rightness of Rousseau's and Byron's views ; the simple country girl, the Cossack's daughter, are the pillars of society; the good old times must be rehabilitated. Gogol, too, points to the futility of his contemporaries, and teaches a return to the past. Still more modern writers, led by Turgenev, extolled the mužik and village life.

Philosophers and historians had shown that a nation with unimpaired energies must assume the leadership. We, said the Russians, are such a nation. It was true that Hegel and others did not believe that the Teutons were decadent, and it was to the Teutons that they looked for the desired salvation, while the Latin races, and the French in particular, were jettisoned by Hegel. Had not Herder, the great German philosopher of history, prophesied the most splendid future for the Russians? Had not Voltaire, the oracle of cultured Europe, done the same?

It was, indeed, difficult to believe that the Russians were entitled to drive the coach of history merely because they were barbarians. Doubt might arise, moreover, whether the Russians were really as young and fresh as was suggested; it was long since the days of St. Vladimir, and the analogy with the German barbarians and the decadent Romans was not altogether easy to apply. Still, Hegel had suggested a way out of this difficulty. If the reformation was to furnish the Germans with enduring capacity for the leadership of civilisation, surely the Russians were still more competent, for they had a purer form of Christianity, whilst philosophers, poets, artists, and politicians were abandoning Protestantism. Such men, indeed, were turning towards Catholicism; even Alexander I was inclined to look to the pope for help; and Čaadaev sang the pope's praises. Puškin and Gogol defended Orthodox Old Russia, and Uvarov was a tower of strength.

Had not Russia conquered Napoleon and the decadent Frenchmen, thus affording proof of her energy? Was not Russia respected and admired throughout Europe? Why, Napoleon himself had prophesied that Europe would be Cossack in fifty years. The Russian mužik was the Messiah longed for by Rousseau. During the eighteenth century European men of letters had discovered Teutonic folk-poesy and folk-art, but at the same epoch the Old Russian folk-songs had been collected, whilst new epics, admired by all Europe, were coming to light (*The Lay of Igor's Raid*).

French and German socialists had shown that the masses must effect social reform, but Haxthausen, a German, expressly declared that in the mir the Russians had long possessed the basis for the essentials of social reform, and even Marx had recognised the truth of this statement.

For the Russians, therefore, the only practical question remaining to be solved was whether they should trouble themselves with degenerate Europe. Should they trample Europe under foot, or should they save it? "We will save it," they said, " for we are the true Christians, and love our enemies; besides, a tincture of Europe can do us no harm, and we will even make the externals of European civilisation and European culture our own. Among other elements in declining Europe, the humanitarian philosophy is something really worth having. . . ."

Kirěevskii preached the humanitarian ideal, and so did Homjakov, though far more of a nationalist. One inspired by nationalist sentiment, said Homjakov, is opposed to what is individually alien, but has no objection to what is universally human; the Russian is peculiarly fitted by his inborn characteristics to make what is universally human his own; because he is Russian, he is a man; it is his gift to understand the peculiarities of other nations. Homjakov admitted that the Germans had discovered Shakespeare, but they were rendered capable of doing so because they had first learned from other nations. The Russians, under Peter's leadership, had likewise learned from others; they had adopted foreign elements, to make these entirely their own; as soon as they were ready to return to themselves, even more then than the Germans would they be able to understand both themselves and others. Slavophilism would furnish the possibility of making this return most speedily. Should any one take exception to the slavophil campaign against all that was foreign, it would suffice, said Homjakov, to remind the objector how Klopstock, Fichte, and Schiller had railed against all that was foreign. (He made no mention of Lessing.) The Russians were thoroughly competent to become leaders and saviours of mankind; the nations of Europe could follow Russia willingly; their needs would be fully understood by the Russians. In Dostoevskii's interpretation of Slavophil messianism, Russian comprehensive humanity is to be something very different from a Babylonian welter of the nations. The one and only Russian people would be representative, leader, and saviour of mankind—and would naturally be master as well, for Europe must not forget that Russia is the sixth continent;

and (as the calculations recently quoted show) before so very long she will dispose of 500,000,000 men, destined in due course to become 1,000,000,000.

III

§ 70.

WE are now sufficiently prepared to form a definitive judgment concerning the nature and development of slavophilism, and in doing so it will be possible to adduce certain details in amplification of our view.

Slavophilism is a school, and something more than a school, namely a tendency, represented by a group of thinkers, who differ, however, upon numerous points of considerable importance.

The strongest of the slavophil thinkers is Kirěevskii ; his is the most philosophical mind, although it must be admitted that in respect of the philosophy of religion and the philosophy of history the characteristic teaching of the slavophils was somewhat fragmentary.

As expounded by Kirěevskii, slavophilism is a system of the philosophy of religion and philosophy of history deriving wholly from the postrevolutionary mood of the restoration, and its leading thought is that theocracy must overcome and replace the threatening revolution. In this matter Kirěevskii agrees with Čaadaev, the slavophil with the westerniser, both being here intimately associated with the thought of the European world, and Kirěevskii being in this respect just as much a westerniser as Čaadaev.

I. Aksakov considered that the central idea of the tendency was to be found in nationality, and this view was reiterated by V. Solov'ev, who said that the " national element " was the most important item of slavophil thought, an element to which everything else, including religion, was subordinate. But it is necessary to point out that true Russism, the principal element of the Russian national idea, was constituted according to the slavophils by the one and only genuine Orthodoxy.

It is further of importance (and this is what Aksakov really wished to say), that the slavophils have not only to explain Russian civilisation, but to justify and defend it ; the slavophils are russophils, Russian patriots. It may be conceded that this

22

patriotism was justified in face of the negation of Čaadaev and the radical westernisers. In this sense even Herzen recognised that slavophilism was the reaction of "outraged national sentiment" against exclusively foreign influences —though slavophilism was not so wholly instinctive as Herzen opined. Moreover, what has been said is valid only as regards the philosophic founders of slavophilism, and strictly speaking it is valid only for Kiréevskii. The other slavophils proclaimed as historical reality what to Kiréevskii was no more than ideal, and in their hands philosophic and religious messianism became political imperialism and nationalist chauvinism. To him applies the denotation *moskvobĕsie* (Moscow frenzy) which became current after the Polish rising.

The first slavophils recognised and admitted Russia's errors. In a poem circulated in manuscript throughout Russia (for the censor had refused his imprimatur) Homjakov apostrophised Russia, the chosen of God :

> Persist in thy endeavour. To be God's instrument
> Is hard for earthly beings ;
> Sharp are His judgments with His servants,
> And, alas, how many fearsome
> Sins hast thou harboured.
> Black is thy fate through black falseness,
> And heavy upon thee presses the yoke of slavery ;
> Filled art thou with godless and devastating lies,
> With dead and infamous sloth,
> And every kind of baseness !

Kiréevskii's criticisms, and still more those of Homjakov, were directed against prepetrine Russia as well as against contemporary Russia, the fruit of Peter's reforms. To Samarin the two crowning errors, the two most disastrous maladies of Russia, were usury and formalism.

Peter's reforms were not rejected in their entirety by all the slavophils. Kiréevskii's judgment of Peter's work was comparatively mild. K. Aksakov, on the other hand, was utterly opposed to Peter's work, whilst his brother Ivan considered that the assassination of Alexander II was a direct issue of Peter's reforms. Whilst Homjakov was inclined simply to value Moscow from the literator's outlook and to prize it as a laboratory of western thought, I. Aksakov's sentiments towards the capital that had been founded by Peter were already quite nationalistic. Well-known is his letter to Strahov

(1863), in which he declares that no truly popular journal can be published in St. Petersburg, for the first prerequisite of a free national sentiment is to hate St. Petersburg whole-heartedly and in every thought.   To Ivan Aksakov the northern capital and the west in its entirety were incorporations of Satan.   But some of the slavophils continued to approve Petrine reforms, and some, like Lamanskii, regarded them as an organic continuation of Muscovite evolution.   If we find it necessary to demur strongly to Ivan Aksakov's nationalism, the nationalism of the later slavophils must be still more decisively condemned.   In these subsequent developments the philosophy of history becomes more and more conspicuously replaced by a superficial interest in current politics ;   the philosophy of religion is overshadowed by official clericalism ; and endeavours towards religious development are overcast by the Russifying ecclesiastical policy of the holy synod.   Inas-much as the slavophils considered that the foundations of civilisation were established upon religion and the church, the nationalist basis was not with them a matter of principle. Danilevskii diverges here from the first slavophils, for in his outlook the idea of nationality assumes far greater importance and independence.   Kirěevskii and Homjakov conceive the church in a universal sense, but both of them, and especially the latter, incline to identify the Orthodox universal church with the Russian national and state church.   When they speak of the importance of ritual to the Russians, some, Šiškov for example, put a mystically high value upon church Slavonic, whilst others, and above all K. Aksakov, lapse into a mystical adoration of the Russian language, speaking of it as the most beautiful and most independent of all tongues.   In like manner, in the theoretical and philosophical field, Kirěevskii's broad religious and historical program narrows into the program of Uvarov ; and after 1863, subsequent to the Polish rising, the victory of Uvarov over Kirěevskii is decisive.

In their struggle for religion the founders of slavophilism turn away from the new philosophy, but even here we cannot speak of the absolute negation of western thought.   The rejection of the western religions, of Catholicism and Protestant-ism and of the philosophy that has issued from these creeds, is made with certain reserves.   It is only in so far as they are considered one-sided that Catholicism and Protestantism are condemned, and some of the systems of German philosophy (notably that of Schelling) find acceptance. Orthodoxy in idealised form is presented as the measure of thought and action. Within Orthodoxy, orientalist and Russian mysticism are made supreme, and rationalism is rejected. Kiréevskii distrusts reason, and Homjakov and Samarin feel this mistrust still more strongly. Samarin considers rationalism analogous to absolutism. For the rationalist, he says, everything is subject to rules and regulations ; tradition and personal inspiration go by the board ; a general lassitude results from the autocracy of the understanding. From time to time, however, doubts arise as to the accuracy of this logic. Homjakov once wrote to Samarin saying that while Granovskii did not walk hand in hand with the slavophils, Zagoskin was perfectly willing to do so, and that this was proof that acceptance of slavophilism was a matter not of understanding but of instinct.

By a logical sequence, the passive Christian virtues were esteemed ; even suffering was a good thing ; conciliatory, patient, pious humility and lowliness (*smirenie*) was posited as the chief Christian virtue of Orthodox Russians.

Quite in the sense and after the model of the restoration in the west, a secure foundation for antirevolutionary absolutism was sought in the doctrine of revelation and tradition. Religious irrationalism was deliberately opposed to philosophic rationalism. It was for this reason that the slavophils turned away from the philosophy of Hegel, the philosophy cultivated by the westernisers, and based their position upon Schelling, Baader, and the French philosophers of the restoration. Homjakov armed himself against historical relativism, and attacked Hegel's dictum of the reality of the rational and the rationality of the real.

Slavophil conceptions of history were inspired by the romanticist flight from the present into the past.

In the sphere of practice the slavophils aimed at theocracy. The state was subordinate to the church precisely as the natural and the human were subordinate to the divine.

Primitive slavophilism was non-political. The slavophils themselves (Homjakov) expressly declared it, whilst the westernisers (Kavelin) pointed it out as a slavophilist principle.

It was natural that from their theocratic outlook the slavophils should despise the state, or should at least tend to thrust it into the background. They endeavoured to justify their nonpolitical program with reference to the inborn qualities of the Russian people. It was the natural gift of the Russian people to be nonpolitical; Russians had no desire to rule, and preferred to leave the exercise of the powers of state to a foreign European government. Konstantin Aksakov elaborated an entire political system of this character.

The opponents of the slavophils are apt to say that there was a tincture of anarchism in the views of these writers, but the assertion amounts to very little.

The Russian absolutism of the time misled many people to this unpolitical standpoint; the theocratic ideal of the slavophils was a refuge from the theocratic reality. To be unpolitical often signifies the possession of strong political views, conservative views, and this was true in high degree of most of the slavophils who, as respected aristocrats and members of the wealthy landowning class, were ultraconservative in politics. Accepting tsarism as the given form of autocracy, they were content to idealise it, and it was from above not from below that they hoped for the coming of the reforms they desiderated. For themselves, for their own class, they wished a number of radical reforms, and in especial freedom of the press and the establishment of a territorial assembly (in which they would of course play the leading rôle). The territorial assembly, modelled upon the design of the zemskii sobor of old days, was not to be a legislative parliament, for K. Aksakov and Samarin, in full agreement here with Kirěevskii's teaching, protested against constitutionalism. In this respect the slavophils were more logical and more conservative than the Catholic liberals of that day, Tocqueville and Montalembert. Samarin, at any rate, disapproved their policy, and in his attitude towards constitutionalism agreed rather with Nicholas I, who, as is well known, "could understand" republicanism and absolute monarchy, but "could not understand" constitutional monarchy. He looked upon this form of government as infamous. In the sphere of politics the slavophils did not advance beyond the standpoint of absolutist patriarchalism, and from this standpoint of agrarian patriarchalism and patrimonialism the slavophils, like the aristocrats in general, were opponents of the bureaucracy.

The church and ecclesiastical tradition being recognised as the supreme authority, and much emphasis being laid upon catholicity, it was logical that in every department individualism should be bluntly rejected. European liberalism fell with individualism, and European constitutionalism fell with liberalism. It is true that the slavophils recognised the need for reforms, but these were to be "inner" reforms only. Hence they were declared opponents of political revolution. To them, as to so many monarchists and legitimists, it seemed that Russia was on principle opponent of the revolution, and not opponent merely, but, as a historic datum, the positive contradiction of every possible revolution. Tjutčev, the most notable of the slavophil poets, in some verses published in the year 1848 entitled *Russia and the Revolution*, contrasted Russia, as a truly Christian land and indeed the only Christian land, with the revolution, with antichrist. I. Aksakov loathed the revolution, not merely in its nihilist manifestations, but when it presented itself as liberalism and constitutionalism.

Tsar Nicholas and his government had no love for the slavophils, despite their hostility to the revolution and their unpolitical program. Kiréevskii's journal was suppressed. Homjakov, in 1854, on account of his poem *To Russia*, was forbidden to have his works printed, and in recent years his writings and studies concerning the Russian church have been posthumously prohibited. Both the Aksakovs had trouble with the censorship and with other authorities. To the official mind it seemed that the early slavophils belonged to the same political school with the westernisers. Not until the reign of Alexander II was comparative freedom granted to the slavophils. In 1855 K. Aksakov demanded from the tsar the freedom of the press and the summoning of the zemskii sobor.

Against the disastrous individualism and subjectivism which Stirner had introduced into Europe, Homjakov was not content merely to appeal to religious catholicity. In an extremely characteristic manner he supported his religio-philosophical reasoning with an argument drawn from the agrarian field. Agriculture, he said, offered a protection against individualism. It was the guardian of " true conservatism " and democracy, and the Teutonic warrior and the conquering state were contrasted by him with the Russian state of peasants and great landowners. The Russian landowner was likewise an aristocrat, but of a very different species from the aristocrat of the west ; the Russian aristocracy was democratic, and was associated with the peasantry upon terms of Christian love. Samarin went yet further, pointing to Europe, where conservatism found its main foundations in the aristocracy, whereas in Russia conservatism was at home in "the darksome room of the peasant."

Their theocratic standpoint made it impossible for the slavophils to appraise the various social forces in a sufficiently concrete manner. Preferring to deal with the abstract concept of folk or nation, they failed to secure clear understanding of Russia's economic and social position.

It is true that the slavophils were keenly interested in the peasant and his liberation. Interest in the question was so acute and so widespread that the slavophil messianists could not fail to give it their attention. Most of the slavophils favoured the liberation of the peasantry, but very few of them conceived this liberation in a genuinely liberal sense. Kirěevskii did not discuss liberation in any of his public utterances, but referred to the matter in his letters. Homjakov wrote about it on one occasion. Shortly after the Crimean war, Samarin, advocating the abolition of serfdom, wrote, " We succumbed through our own feebleness, and not owing to the objective force of the league of western powers." When public discussion of the question became possible after the accession of Alexander II, the slavophil organ " Russkaja Besěda," a periodical issued during the years 1856 to 1860, published in 1885 and 1859 a supplement edited by Košilev and entitled " Selskojo Blagoustroistvo " (rural wellbeing).

Slavophilism and its religious quietism, the idea of the political social order and fraternity of Old Russian social institutions, prevented the philosophical founders of the doctrine from realising the social significance of the liberation of the peasantry. Homjakov and Ivan Aksakov, no less than Kirěevskii, would not hear a word of English political economy. Aksakov, desiring to keep alive the genuinely Russian sense of benevolence, desired also and for this end to maintain the existence of the poor. In his view, the western system of poor relief was a politico-economical device and was not moral at all ; if you asked for an example of a practical man and a good political economist, he would mention Judas.[1]

---

[1] Semevskii, the historian of the liberation of the peasantry, reports that upon Homjakov's estates the condition of the peasantry, in conflict with their lord's theories, was worse than that which prevailed in the domains of neighbouring landowners. In 1851 Košelev reported that Homjakov had defended the purchase of serfs for purposes of colonisation (Košelev was personally opposed to purchase and sale). In 1861 Dostoevskii reproached I. Aksakov for having

The reactionary party among the nobility, agitating against the liberation of the peasantry, took occasion in their periodical "Věst'" to denounce the slavophils as Russian Saint-Simonians. This was gross exaggeration, for the slavophils vigorously opposed socialism as unrussian. Homjakov and his friends counterposed socialism with the Russian mir and the Russian artel, but these institutions were conceived ethically and religiously, not economically and socially. In the mir they saw a means for averting the proletarianisation of the masses, and thus based upon the mir as against French socialism their agrarian hopes for the undisturbed development of Russia. For the slavophils the Russian mir was a foundation established by Christian love, was the foundation of the social organisation of the entire Russian people, which thus became a great family under the patriarchal leadership of the tsar. But we must not on this account speak of the slavophils as "Christian socialists."

In this idealisation of the mir, the slavophils were supported by Haxthausen, who was then studying Russian agrarian conditions on the spot.[1]

Speaking generally, the slavophils continued to cherish Rousseauist agrarianism. Kiręevskii contemned towns and urban civilisation, sharply contrasting with European civilisation the Old Russian Orthodox and religious civilisation, speaking of the latter as characteristically rural. Kiręevskii, too, was hostile to the growth of manufacturing industry, which was fostered by the state, and his followers remained faithful to

uncritically favoured the relationship of serf and lord in the interest of the lord. Košelev wrote as follows to Ivan Kiręevskii in 1852: "I cannot understand, my dear friend Kiręevskii, how you, a Christian, can fail to be horrified at keeping men in servitude to yourself." But Kiręevskii's quietist passivism made it quite easy for him to tolerate the institution of serfdom. In 1847, when his sister wished to liberate her peasants, he dissuaded her from the step. In a discussion with Košelev, he said that if the peasants must be given land, they ought not to have five desjatinas, but one only: "This will help the peasant along, but he will still have to seek other work; in default of such necessity all the landowner's fields would remain untilled."

[1] In his third volume Haxthausen refers to his relationships with the slavophils ("Young Russia"), expressing his agreement with their views. He is especially enthusiastic about Konstantin Aksakov, referring to him as "one of the most talented men with whom I became acquainted in Russia." He met also Kiręevskii, Homjakov, and Samarin, and in addition Čaadaev and representatives of the westernisers (Granovskii, for instance). According to Herzen it was from Konstantin Aksakov that Haxthausen derived his view as to the importance of the mir and the artel.

this view. The industrialisation of Moscow, the slavophil centre, was advancing with vigorous strides during the epoch under consideration. Haxthausen, the German slavophil, recognised that the nobles' town had already become a manufacturing town, and he did not fail to perceive and to point out that the process of industrialisation had been furthered by the nobles themselves.[1]

With considerable justice, Pisemskii and others reproached the slavophils on the ground that the latter had no real knowledge of the folk, of the peasantry, and that their disquisitions did not rise above the level of "religio-linguistic sentimentalism."

The slavophils had already drawn attention to the class organisation of society, and might have learned much concerning the class struggle from French historians and socialists. They were, however, unable to realise the existence of classes and class contrasts in Russia, contenting themselves with a vaguely homogeneous conception of "country." Their failure here was in part a failure in the scientific field, for they were affected by the tendency to undue simplification that has always characterised the beginnings of sociological research.

Slavophilism, as a general trend based on the philosophy of history, had close relationships with the general literary movement. Kirěevskii was a historian of literature, whilst his brother acquired a deserved reputation as collector of folk-songs. Others among the slavophils did much to encourage the profounder study of folk-poesy, but Turgenev considers that as artists and thinkers the slavophils never created anything truly vital, for they did not face reality with a sufficiently untrammelled spirit. The criticism is just.

During the Napoleonic wars a patriotic tendency found expression in verse, and the writers of this school immersed themselves in the Russian past, the work of Sergěi Aksakov being a notable example. These trends fortified the slavophil movement (Sergěi's sons being among the founders of slavophilism), but they cannot be regarded as distinctively slavophil.

In youth Sergěi Aksakov had read much anent the ideals

[1] Schulze-Gävernitz carries Haxthausen's idea a stage further when he shows how the slavophils actually promoted the industrialisation of Moscow and Russia by their romanticist glorification of agrarianism and by their campaign against economic individualism—by their insistence upon the independence of Russia vis-à-vis Europe, and so on.

of Novikov, and he endeavoured to combine them in harmonious unison with those of Šiškov. The appearance in "The European" of Kirěevskii's essay *The Nineteenth Century* cost Aksakov his office as censor. He was not blinded by his friendship with Gogol, and would not accept without qualification the fallacies of Gogol's religious mysticism. His sons were less unprejudiced in their relationship to Gogol. Konstantin compared Gogol with Homer, and ascribed to him a position above all the writers of Europe. Bělinskii, champion of Gogol as literary artist, found it necessary to dissent from this view, and at length in 1880, at the Puškin festival, Ivan Aksakov hailed Puškin the greatest of the truly Russian poets. Prior to this the slavophils had given that place to Gogol.

But Gogol was no slavophil, nor was Ostrovskii. The relationships of both to the Moscow slavophils were those of personal friendship rather than of doctrine. Tjutčev, on the other hand, may be counted among the slavophils, and so may Jasykov. Homjakov and the two younger Aksakovs expounded their views in philosophic poems and dramas rather than directly. Apollon Maikov had strong classical leanings ; the Greek and Latin elements in his work are too numerous for us to classify him as a slavophil poet. Nevertheless, he was seduced by the slavophil Byzantine-Russian outlook, with its essential contradictions (see his lyrical tragedy, *Two Worlds ; or the Two Romes*), into the strange aberration of writing an apotheosis of John the Terrible. Kohanovskaja (1825–1884) had likewise close literary relationships with the slavophils (Konstantin Aksakov), and exemplified slavophil ideas in her novels.

Dostoevskii, last of all, had imbibed the ideas of Kirěevskii and the other slavophils, and may himself be termed slavophil if religious messianism and the philosophico-historical outlook be admitted as principles of slavophilism. But Dostoevskii developed his views towards religion and the church independently, following a different route from that taken by the slavophils. To put the matter paradoxically, Dostoevskii is too slavophil to be reckoned among the slavophils—there is nothing in him of the Old Slavic sentiment which Homjakov and Ivan Aksakov combined with the religious philosophy of Kirěevskii.

Early slavophilism was a modification of the Russist or Old Russist tendency that had been previously displayed by Boltin, Ščerbatov, and Šiskov. Philosophically the slavophils had advanced a stage, had arrived at a profounder conception of the problem of Russia in relation to Europe, being helped here by German philosophy, and indeed by European thought in its entirety, influenced as that thought was by the sanguinary experiences of the revolution and the counter-revolution and faced as it was with the need for choosing between the old regime and the new. Russia was so far Europeanised and since the days of Peter had been so closely involved in the European system of states, that after the end of the eighteenth century European influence became extremely potent in Russia, and all the more potent because Russia, through her internal development, had to encounter the same difficulties and to solve the same problems as Europe.

From the outlook of the history of literature, slavophilism is a parallel phenomenon with the romanticist restoration in Europe, as manifested in art and above all poesy, in philosophy and theology, in history, in jurisprudence, and in politics. Though slavophilism was an outgrowth of Russian conditions, the movement was none the less in high degree European, and it developed under European influences just as much as did the opposed movement of westernism. Western philosophy furnished the slavophils with arms against westernism. If Hegel, Feuerbach, Stirner, Fourier, and Saint-Simon were Europeans, so also were Schelling, Baader, de Maistre, de Bonald, and Görres.

Slavophilism was the philosophic attempt to renovate theocracy. Philosophically considered, slavophilism was the first deliberately conceived philosophy of religion and philosophy of history.

The scientific weakness of slavophilism depends upon the inadequacy of its foundations, upon the inadequacy of its epistemological criticism. It was impossible to attain to the philosophic goal with the aid of the protean philosophy of Schelling. Hegel, the Hegelian left, and materialism, could not be effectively resisted, and certainly could not be put to rout, by the forces of Schelling and Baader. Still less could this end be secured with the aid of Joannes Damascenus.

The historical and economic foundations and aims of slavophilism are likewise inadequate, though this may in part be condoned by the insufficiencies of Russian historical research in that epoch. It was owing to these insufficiencies that past and present appeared under false illumination, and like considerations explain why in the philosophy of history the constructions of the slavophils were so arbitrary.

The inadequacy of slavophil philosophy of history is well shown by the inferences the slavophils made from the reputedly peaceful invitation issued to the Varangians. Though the alleged invitation lacks adequate historical confirmation, inferences were drawn as to the nature of the Old Russian state, and it was supposed to furnish a demonstration as to the characteristics of the Old Russians in general.[1]

The poverty of historical research at that date is partly accountable, too, for the political errors of the slavophils, and explains their fondness for tsarist absolutism. Karamzin had decorated Muscovite tsarism with a halo, and had taught the first slavophils what they knew of Russian history.

Slavophil ideas developed in association with theological doctrine and theological church history. It would be interesting to compare slavophil philosophy of history with that of Janssen, the Catholic historian. Here, from a theological doctrine closely resembling that of the slavophils, the development of Christian society is deduced in a strikingly similar manner. Lagarde's religious nationalism may likewise be compared with the views of the early slavophils. Tönnies, a German writer, in his book *Community Life and Society* (1887), a treatise on communism and socialism as empirical forms of civilisation, has arrived at views resembling those of the slavophils.

These historico-philosophical theories give the slavophil system a scholastic stamp, for the slavophils should at least have endeavoured to prove their main propositions. The scholastic trend is unpleasing even in Homjakov, and in the case of the later slavophils it becomes positively repulsive, owing to the way in which it is carried out altogether regardless of the truths that have been established since the doctrine was first formulated. Gor'kii was not wholly wrong in his contention that the slavophils (the narodniki and Dostoevskii) displayed a union of talent with truly oriental unscrupulousness and Tatar cunning.

Theoretically considered, this philosophy of religion and its epistemological basis are quite untenable.

The weaknesses of the system facilitated the subsequent

---

[1] Attention has recently been directed to a parallel circumstance recorded by the chronicler Widukind, who informs us that the Teutonic Anglo-Saxons were invited to England by the British (likewise presumed to be Teutons).

transformation of slavophilism to become a nationalist political system which was not conservative merely but positively reactionary. The slavophil philosophy of history was replaced by political Slavism, the slavophil philosophy of religion by the ecclesiastical policy of the synod. For the inadequate but noteworthy philosophical essays of a Kirěevskii and a Homjakov were substituted political tracts and unmethodical disquisitions voicing an academic Slavisticism pursued for political ends, a doctrine which continues to drag out a pitiful existence even to-day.

Some of the slavophil professors have doubtless written important historical and Slavistic works, but no philosophical successor to Kirěevskii has ever appeared.[1]

The influence of slavophil teaching was great and persistent, affecting not merely the prevalent philosophic view of Russian civilisation and history and the intellectual valuation of these, but inducing likewise a mood of enthusiasm, which is attributable to the personal influence exercised by the founders of slavophilism—for Kirěevskii, Konstantin Aksakov, and Homjakov were estimable and amiable men. In multifold transformations, the general thesis and certain individual slavophil doctrines are held by many to-day, whilst slavophilism continues to work also by contraries, through the opposition it arouses. In Miljukov's view the development of slavophilism has been a decadence rather than a simple transformation, for he considers that the philosophical and nationalist elements of the doctrine, those which were united into an integral whole by the founders of the system, have become segregated to undergo independent development. This independent and one-sided development is seen according to Miljukov in Leont'ev the ultra-nationalist and Solov'ev the philosopher, but it was, he says,

[1] There is no occasion to name all the later slavophils, and it will suffice to allude to men of European reputation. Košelev, a vigorous and cultured publicist, has been mentioned. Běljaev is a meritorious historian whose writings deal with Russian law, the mir, and the peasantry. Hilferding was as Slavist and historian greatly influenced by Homjakov. Lamanskii, a Slavist, was regarded with much enmity in Austria, but this was unjust, for Lamanskii was not a supporter of the government as were so many of his slavophil contemporaries and pupils, and his character enforced the respect of liberal opponents. Budilovič, Slavist, defended panrussism (consult his The Literary Unity of the Slavs, 1879). K. Bestužev-Rjumin, historian, was from 1878 to 1882 president of the St. Petersburg Slav Union. Kojalovič, historian of the Uniat churches of Russia, has written a work upon the spirit of Russia as displayed in historiography.

already manifest in Danilevskii and Grigor'ev. This formulation is tenable. But the important point is that the slavophil trend and slavophil attempts towards a philosophical view and valuation of Russia and Europe continue to influence thought to-day, and that the vitality of the doctrine is due to the persistence of the conditions under which slavophilism took its rise.

During the forties and the two following decades the westernisers were under slavophil influence. We have seen how Čaadaev in later years drew nearer to the slavophils. Bělinskii and Herzen, Bakunin and the earlier Russian socialists such as Černyševskii, derived their faith in Russia and her social mission from and in conjunction with the slavophils. The radical westernisers, like the slavophils, extolled the mir and the artel as Russian and Slav institutions. Bakunin derived from the slavophil criticism of the state more than one suggestion for his anarchist theories. The narodničestvo is also partly deducible from slavophilism, though more indirectly (by way of Herzen) ; whilst Russian Marxism was in its inception influenced by the narodničestvo.

But when we are considering the relationships between the westernisers and the slavophils, we must not think only of agreement in certain doctrinal details, however important. Yet more noteworthy, perhaps, is the mutual stimulus which each doctrine exercised on the other during the polemic about their respective philosophical fundamentals. In Bělinskii and still more in Herzon and Ivan Turgenev, we see how slavophilism spurred on the westernisers to opposition.

From the outlook of metaphysical materialism it is comprehensible that Cernyševskii should have regarded Kirěevskii as a dreamer merely and not a philosopher, and should have looked upon Pisarev as a Don Quixote, but the judgments are one-sided. Plehanov, in like manner, from his Marxist standpoint, declares that sympathy with the slavophil theory is necessarily treason to the cause of progress, even if the treason be unintentional and unconscious, and he attempts to class the early slavophils with Pogodin. But this is unfair; the opinions and the general mode of thought of Kirěevskii and Homjakov have foundations utterly different from those upon which are established the views of Pogodin.

Though Leont'ev, again, builds upon the slavophils, we must not hold them entirely accountable for Leont'ev's views.

Dostoevskii took much from the slavophils, and especially from Kirěevskii. After his manner, Dostoevskii may be said to have positively provided a new foundation for slavophilism, through the intermediation of the počveniki (Grigor'ev).

Philosophically Solov'ev, despite his subsequent opposition to the doctrine, may be considered to have carried a stage further the religious philosophy of slavophilism.

Among the most recent philosophers of religion, the influence of Dostoevskii and Solov'ev can be plainly traced side by side with that of Homjakov and Kirěevskii. These two founders of the doctrine are again and again referred to (Geršenzon, Berdjaev, etc.), and we are told that the slavophils did good service in that they duly esteemed the importance of religion, even though their position inclined too much towards the right.

Exponents of official theology were but little inclined to think well of Kirěevskii or Homjakov, their disapproval having other and obvious causes besides Homjakov's strong censures upon official theology (for example, upon Makarii's book). None the less a few theologians were early found to regard slavophil teaching with respect. Of late a more progressive tendency has been noteworthy in theology, led by Antonii in Volhynia and by his pupil Sergii in Finland. In this development the influence of slavophilism, together with that of Dostoevskii, is well marked.

CHAPTER TEN

WESTERNISM. V. G. BĚLINSKII

I

§ 71.

THE harmless geographical designations "westernism" and "westerniser" connote a definite program, the Europeanisation of Russia, the continuation of Peter's reforms.

What do we mean by Europeanisation ? Europe contains various cultural elements, specifically distinct civilisations. It is undeniable that the differences between French and Germans, between Germans and Englishmen, etc., are considerable. To the Russian, however, these differences appear trifling in comparison with the remove between Russia and the countries of European civilisation. To Russia, in its hunger for civilisation, the west seemed " the land of miracles " (Homjakov).

Westernism, like slavophilism, originated in the days of Nicholas I. Since European influence was then restricted in every possible way, thinking persons became for the first time fully aware of the contrast between Russia and Europe.

As we have learned, the influence of Germany was at that time preponderant, but France continued to play a stimulating part in Russian development ; the influence of England was comparatively small, whilst that of Italy and the other European countries was insignificant.

Westernism in the wider sense of the term dates from the epoch when European influences began to exercise considerable effect upon Russia, and in this wider sense all the later progressive tendencies, including the Marxist tendency, are westernist. But more commonly the concept is interpreted in a narrower signification, the term being used to denote the theories and tendencies that were formulated in the literary dispute with the slavophils.

The contrast between westernism and slavophilism was not definite at the outset, nor was it equally marked in all questions. The slavophils were of one mind with the westernisers in recognising that a great cultural difference exists between Russia and the west, and the members of both schools were in truth agreed that Russians would do well to learn from the west. Divergence between the two tendencies became marked in the answer they respectively gave to the question whether Peter, as Čaadaev expressed it, "had really had before him nothing but a blank sheet of paper"—whether Russia did or did not contain cultural elements peculiarly her own, valuable elements which it was desirable to retain and foster side by side with those introduced from Europe. The westernisers differed from the slavophils in their answer to the great historico-philosophical question concerning the significance, the value, and the trend of Russian development. This main question and the subsidiary questions it involved were not answered by all the westernisers in the same manner. On many points the westernisers agreed with the slavophils and pursued the same aims. The members of both schools constituted at first a single circle and drew nourishment from the same European source. It is true that the friendship did not long endure, and that the two camps speedily became hostile, the animosity often taking a personal form. As early as 1841 Bělinskii was censured by Ševirev for lack of patriotism. Jasykov, Homjakov's brother-in-law, wrote some verses in which he levelled accusations of heresy, and this made bad blood. He spoke of Čaadaev as an apostate, of Granovskii as a corrupter of youth, of Herzen as a lackey in western livery. In 1845 Granovskii became permanently estranged from Aksakov and Samarin, though Aksakov by no means approved of those who, à la Jasykov, regarded themselves as "Slav gendarmes in the name of Jesus Christ." A year later a breach occurred between Herzen and Granovskii.

As I have previously pointed out, Europe contained de Maistre and Stahl as well as Hegel and Proudhon. From Europe the Russians could derive reactionary as well as progressive ideas, could learn reaction as well as revolution. The great revolution was followed by a strong reaction. Europe was and still is split into progressive, democratic Europe and conservative, aristocratic Europe. We must bear this main distinction in mind when we are appraising slavophilism and westernism as tendencies, and no less when we are forming our estimates of the individual representatives of these tendencies, and we must distinguish between the separate doctrines of the systems. It is often far from easy to classify a particular thinker, to decide whether he is to be designated westerniser or slavophil. Of Kirěevskii, for instance, it is certainly right to maintain that he always remained a westerniser; whereas Čaadaev, though a typical westerniser, was extremely conservative.

Marked differences exist between individual westernisers, and between individual slavophils.

As regards the general distinction between the westernisers and the slavophils, the most important divergence of outlook concerned ecclesiastico-religious and metaphysical questions. Even here, however, manifold transitional phases and numerous points of agreement can be discerned. To the westernisers, too, it seemed that the most profound cause for severance in minds and in tendencies was discoverable in variations of outlook upon ecclesiastico-religious and metaphysical questions.

The westernism of the eighteenth century and of the opening part of the nineteenth was "enlightened." It contained elements derived from the rationalism of the German philosophy of enlightenment; many of its advocates were inclined towards Voltairism. They were sceptically minded. Alleging themselves superior to the superstition of the mužik, in actual fact they were indifferent in religious matters, though, following Voltaire, official religion seemed to them necessary on political grounds. Some, however, in religious matters held the views of Rousseau rather than those of Voltaire. Of these was Radiščev, who during his banishment to Siberia defended theism (using Robespierre's terminology and speaking of the " grand être suprême "), and championed the doctrine of immortality with especial warmth. Most Russian freemasons held similar views.

In Russia too, after the French revolution and the Napoleonic wars, there ensued a movement equivalent to a restoration. German idealist philosophy, the philosophy of Kant, Fichte, Schelling, and Hegel, practically thrust Voltairist liberalism into the background. This was as obvious in the case of

Čaadaev the westerniser as in that of the early slavophils.
But even before Čaadaev and Kirěevskii, such liberal westernisers as Odoevskii and Galič expressed themselves as decisively
opposed to scepticism, demanding that there should be " firm
convictions for the conduct of life." Galič, a Schellingian,
declared, " One cannot live without conviction." " To be
happy," wrote Odoevskii, "man must have a luminous axiom,
an axiom of wide implications, one that is all-embracing, one
that brings deliverance from the torment of doubt." In
harmony with this aim, Odoevskii considered that it was the
fundamental characteristic of his time " to flee from scepticism,
always to believe in something," and his beliefs were grounded
on the sciences.

For these reasons enthusiasm was demanded and stimulated
in all fields. Such was the dominant spirit in the circle of
Stankevič, who then exercised great influence. Stankevič
declared that a frigid man was necessarily a rascal, and was
himself an enthusiast for music (Schubert) and literature.
His most intimate friends were of like mood. It is noteworthy
that the primary ideas of the westernisers and the slavophils
were struck out in personal intercourse, and that the literary
formulation of these views came later. Neither Čaadaev nor
Stankevič nor Granovskii was a prolific writer. They were
all concerned quite as much with new ideals of life, with new
trends, as simply with ideas and views. Both parties to the
conflict we are considering were believers, enthusiastic believers,
the westernisers in European ideals and the slavophils in Russia.

But as regards the content of their respective beliefs there
is this great divergence between the westernisers and the
slavophils, that the westernisers turned away from the Orthodox creed, whereas the slavophils clung to it, though in
idealised form.

Philosophically the difference between the westernisers
and the slavophils is tantamount to the difference between
Hegel and Schelling. Cherishing Hegel, the westernisers
cherished the rationalism condemned by the slavophils, and
Schelling's belief in the absolute was replaced by Hegel's
relativism. Whereas, with de Bonald, the European philosophy
of restoration and reaction declared reason to be an emanation
of the devil, the westernisers, though they frequently admitted
the one-sidedness of rationalism, were of the school which
does not underestimate the importance of reason.

But this differentiation in Russia between the schools of Hegel and of Schelling was not manifest at the outset, for the first westernisers were, like the slavophils, Schellingians.

Within the westernist movement, the religious and metaphysical question was the cause of a segregation into right and left camps. This segregation occurred on exactly the same lines as in German Hegelianism.

We can follow the matter in Herzen's reminiscences.

From childhood upwards Herzen had been a Voltairian and a freethinker. At the university of Moscow, where he studied natural science and medicine, he was a materialist and an atheist. He tells us that his renewed and profounder study of Hegel led him to this metaphysical and religious outlook. A light broke in on him when he recognised that Hegel was "the algebra of revolution." Whilst his friends were intoxicated with Hegelian scholasticism and were satisfied therewith, Herzen, with Hegel's aid, liberated his mind from all traditional political and religious views. Feuerbach's anthropologism likewise played a notable part in this development. To Herzen, therefore, science in the positivist sense became absolute mistress, whereas many of the liberal westernisers, no less than the slavophils, were moving in the direction of religious romanticism. Herzen detested the expedient of liberal symbolism and allegory, deciding clearly and unambiguously in favour of materialism and atheism, which in his belief were imperiously dictated by science. It was for this reason that in 1846 he definitely broke with many of his friends, and especially with Granovskii. Granovskii desired to leave the religious question open, and himself cherished a belief in personal immortality. Botkin's metaphysical outlook was identical, and Čičerin held similar religious views.

French socialism likewise exercised a decisive influence upon Herzen. Hegel, Feuerbach, and Proudhon were his spiritual leaders. A man, said Herzen, who has not vitally experienced Hegel's *Phenomenology* and Proudhon's *Contradictions* cannot be considered a complete, a thoroughly modern (" contemporary ") human being. Feuerbach brought enfranchisement from mysticism and mythology. Materialist, positivist, scientific sobriety was to free Young Russia from inherited religious mysticism ; the sobriety of science was to disintegrate, dispossess, and replace the ardency of mysticism.

Herzen was followed by Bělinskii ; by Ogarev, who inde-

pendently arrived at the same results as Herzen and introduced
Feuerbach's work to Herzen; by Bakunin; and by the youth
of Russia, despite their love and veneration for Granovskii.
Herzen's philosophy was the education of the more radical
generations, and is still to a large extent their education to-day.

Young Russia thus became differentiated into three camps,
that of the slavophils (I refer here to the founders of the school),
the liberals, and the socialists or radicals. These designations
lack precision, it is true. They fail, above all, to give an
adequate indication of the religious and metaphysical outlook
of those found in the respective camps, though it is this outlook which constitutes the classificatory mark. Herzen spoke
of his own tendencies as materialist and positivist, and the
term atheist might just as well be applied.

To conclude, we may say that, while the contrast between
the slavophils and the westernisers is striking, in concreto, in
the phenomenal world of history, manifold and numerous
transitional phases exist, and the representatives of the two
trends mutually influence, correct, and supplement one another.
The contrast between Russia and Europe is no more absolute
than the contrast between present and past.

The advantage, or perhaps it would be better to say the
charm, of the slavophils as defenders of Russia and her past
is that they have a circumscribed general outlook, which is,
however, rather an artificial, imaginative construction than the
product of active research. The strength of the westernisers, as
defenders of Europe and modernity, consists in their scientific
elaboration of certain debatable theories. Whilst the slavophils were chiefly philosophers of history, the westernisers
were rather historians, jurists, specialists. The westernisers
were representative of scientific Russia and progressive philosophy; the slavophils were conservatives in philosophy. The
slavophils believed in Russia ("Russia cannot be grasped
with the understanding; one can only believe in Russia," said
Tjutčev); the westernisers believed in Europe, but were critical
alike of their fatherland and of Europe, and desired to attain
the utmost possible scientific clarity concerning both.

In the political field the slavophils were conservatives and
reactionaries, whilst the westernisers, as liberals and socialists,
distinctively constituted progressive and democratic Young
Russia.

The Hegelian left in Russia, like the Hegelian left in

Germany, was radically opposed to absolutism. The positivist materialism of Herzen and his radical associates found its fiercest opponent in official Orthodoxy, in the theocratic program of Nicholas and Uvarov. Since in Russia (and indeed in Europe as well) the state is so intimately associated with the church, metaphysical opposition to the church and church doctrine simultaneously became political opposition to the state. As time passed, this opposition developed, and displayed varying degrees of intensity. If the earlier liberals, such men as N. Turgenev, had been compelled to emigrate owing to their political demand for a constitution, it was all the more natural that Herzen and his fellow radicals should be forced to take refuge in Europe.

Westernism is sharply distinguished from slavophilism by the political trend of the former. The slavophils were unpolitical ; they desired merely " inner," moral and religious reform, whereas the westernisers' aim was for " outer," political reform. Thus westernism became radical, oppositional, and directly revolutionary.

§ 72.

THE westernisers were distinguished from the slavophils by their estimate of the value of the state and of politics. To the westernisers the state was a political rather than a moral entity, and they attached to it a greater value than did the slavophils. But this is true only of the liberal westernisers, those of the right or comparatively conservative wing, for the radical westernisers, Herzen for instance, agreed rather with the slavophils in their valuation of the state and of politics. A difference further exists between the theories of the westernisers and those of the slavophils as regards the origin of the state in general and of the Russian state in particular.

Whilst the slavophils considered that the Russian state originated in the family community and the village community, the westernisers taught that the Old Russian state, like all European states, had developed out of the patriarchal tribal organisation. To the westernisers (and indeed to the slavophils as well), patriarchalism was the explanation and perhaps the justification of absolutism. Konstantin Aksakov, however, was strongly opposed to the patriarchal theory, and expressed the view that Russia least of all had been a patriarchal state.

Aksakov thus defended the moral nature of the Russian state, and to this extent was perfectly right in that he considered that patriarchalism was not eo ipso ethical. It has already been pointed out in sketching the development of the Kievic state that the tribal theory does not adequately account for the facts.

The westernisers, and especially the historians and jurists among them, attempted to show that political and legal institutions had developed along analogous lines in Russia and in Europe, and in both cases out of the same or very similar conditions. They considered, for example, that feudalism prevailed in Russia during the middle ages. They were little inclined to stress the independence and peculiarity of Russian law ; they discovered traces of the influence of Roman law ; the differences between Russian and western law to which the slavophils pointed with much emphasis were by the westernisers reduced to differences in point of customary law, and so on. Both westernisers and slavophils were able to turn to account the conflict in Europe between the Latinists and the Teutonists. In the political field the demands of the westernisers differed from those of the slavophils. The latter asked for the reintroduction of the Muscovite zemskii sobor, whereas the westernisers desired a constitution. In certain respects, however, they voiced identical demands, both favouring freedom of the press, and both espousing the cause of the raskolniki (though for different motives).

The westernisers looked upon Peter the Great as the most vital and splendid representative of the state and its cultural tasks.

The westernisers' valuation of the state differed from the slavophils' valuation because the former were in opposition to the church even if they considered religion of importance. Whilst the slavophils looked upon the church as the leading historical and social force; the westernisers considered that the state was this force. The westernisers, consequently, conceived the relationship between state and church in a way peculiar to themselves, their outlook being for practical purposes legalist. Čičerin, for example, was opposed to the thought of an intimate union between state and church ; in religion's own interest he accepted Cavour's formula of a free church in a free state.

A word must be said here about the Russian bureaucracy,

against which the slavophils were animated by aristocratic prejudices. It was doubtless far from being an ideal institution. Nevertheless the bureaucracy never failed to number among its members intelligent, legally cultured, and liberal officials. To a certain extent the bureaucracy was westernist, in so far as since the days of Peter the administration had sought its models in Europe, and in so far as a university education was essential to the maintenance of the state machine and of the army. If the slavophils opposed bureaucracy, so also did Pobědonoscěv. It need hardly be said that the bureaucracy was instrumental in carrying out the reaction dictated by the court and by the decisive powers in the Russian state.

Gradovskii reproaches westernism for its apotheosis of the state machine. The accusation applies mainly to the conservative westernisers, and in especial to the jurists.

The two parties differed in their valuation and explanation of the mir. The westernisers, led by Čičerin, inclined to regard the mir as an institution of comparatively late development, predominantly administrative in function, fiscal in its aims. But some of the westernisers, the more radical among them, while accepting the slavophil theory of origins, gave the mir and the artel a socialistic significance. The mir, they held, preserved Russia from the growth of a proletariat, and represented the communism desiderated by the socialists.[1]

As regards the liberation of the peasantry, the outlook of the westernisers was more energetic because more distinctively political. Stankevič, indeed, held that serfdom ought first to be abolished, and a constitution subsequently

---

[1] In the grey primeval age, says Čičerin, the mir may indeed have been patriarchal, but during historic times it was produced by political organisation from above. The commune was a fiscal organ of the state, each commune, as a whole, guaranteeing the payment of a definite sum in taxes. The state of Kiev originated in the conquests of the Variag Norsemen, the soil becoming, as in the west, the conqueror's private property. Čičerin's article, Survey of the Historical Development of the Peasant Community in Russia, was published in 1856. As early as 1851, Běljaev, writing in opposition to Čičerin, had endeavoured to adduce historical justification for the slavophil view. Solov'ev the historian, writing in 1856, endeavoured to mediate, and so did Kavelin the jurist, and many others. Čičerin, like the slavophils, agreed with Haxthausen, who held that the mir was a patriarchal expansion of the family. The institution had disappeared before the Muscovite epoch, but had been revived in the eighteenth century under the impulsion of the Petrine poll tax. Haxthausen extolled the mir as a means for preserving Russia from proletarianisation.

introduced, but the majority of the westernisers, following N. Turgenev's example, favoured the simultaneous introduction of the two reforms.

In contrast with the slavophils, the westernisers took a lively interest in economic problems.

As regards the nature and significance of nationality, the westernisers were cosmopolitans and humanitarians in the eighteenth-century sense, whilst the slavophils, being nationalists, considered nationality more important than the state. Whereas Karamzin had insisted : " The national is nothing as compared with the human. The main thing is to be men, not to be Slavs," the slavophils declared that man was man only as a Russian, a Frenchman, etc. Samarin therefore finds that expression is given to nationality even in individual sciences, but Čičerin opposes him in the name of science. It cannot be said that all the westernisers rejected nationalism in toto, for the liberals advocated a moderate nationalism, but the radicals as a rule were antinationalists.

All differences notwithstanding, it is necessary to point to an agreement where questions of nationality were concerned. Both parties subordinated nationality to a higher principle, the slavophils to religion and the church, the liberals to the state. On individual points, therefore, peculiar and astonishing agreement was manifest. The more conservative among the westernisers, placing a high value upon nationality and the state, approximated to the bureaucratic conception of " official " nationality. The later slavophils went so far as to demand Russification, doing so in the name of religion and of the church, but many of the westernisers voiced similar demands in the name of the state—Pestel among the first ! On the other hand, the stressing of nationality led to liberal and democratic views, in so far as nationality was opposed to political centralism, and considered to be of superior importance.

The westernisers were opponents of panslavism, both in its slavophil and in its political forms.[1]

The rejection of panslavism was not, however, universal, nor when it occurred was it always equally vigorous, and we

[1] In the liberal periodical " Otečestvennyja Zapiski " (1845) the Turks were considered to be more interesting than the Slavs they had subjugated. The " Atheneum " (1859) ascribed an important civilising rôle to the Austrian police in Slav countries. The slavophils and panslavists protested against such views.

have previously referred to the panslavism of the freemasons and the decabrists. In any case it cannot be asserted that the westernisers had no political interest in the Slavs, and we might even speak of westernist panslavism as more realist than that of the slavophils. Pypin, the westerniser, did much more to promote knowledge and due appreciation of the eastern and southern Slavs and their respective civilisations than did the panslavist and slavophil utopians. In the political field, Čičerin considered the importance of the Slavs to Russia (thinking of a free Russia) as a European power.

The difference of outlook of the two parties upon the national and Slav question is especially notable in their attitude towards the Poles. The westernisers sympathised with Polish efforts to secure liberty, and even with the Polish revolution. The decabrists had had direct associations with Polish secret societies, and these relationships were renewed by the more radical among the westernisers (Herzen, Bakunin). Conservative westernisers were adverse to the Poles.

It is necessary to emphasise the fact that the westernisers had just as strong an affection for Russia as the slavophils. Herzen says of the two parties : " By them and by us from youth upwards a powerful, unpremeditated, instinctive, and passionate sentiment was operative, a sentiment of unbounded and all-embracing love for the Russian folk, for the Russian way of life, and for the Russian mode of thought. : . . We were their opponents, but opponents of a quite peculiar kind. We and they were animated by a love that was single though not identical ; like Janus or the two-headed eagle, we looked in different directions while a single heart was beating within our breast."

The westernisers criticised Russia and hated the errors and defects of their country, but their knowledge of Europe taught them to love Russia with all her errors and defects. This combination of love and hatred was extremely characteristic of the westernisers. More than one among them came to the conclusion that Europe had the same defects as Russia, and had them perhaps in even greater degree. Odoevskii, who intellectually and emotionally was westernist through and through, declared that Europe was perishing. Among the later westernisers no less a man than Herzen had for Europe a feeling tantamount to hatred. We see the same thing to-day in Gor'kii.

The westernisers differed from the slavophils mainly in this, that the westernisers, not admitting the existence of absolute differences between Russia and Europe, recognised in Europe the same faults as in Russia. Hence the westernist messianism of a Herzen or a Bakunin was less passivist than slavophil messianism ; to the westernisers it seemed that the salvation of Russia and of Europe lay in revolutionary reconstruction. Some of them, whilst recognising that Russia had her peculiar mission, did not believe that the European nations were decadent. In this matter the westernisers were in agreement with Schelling, the slavophils' chosen philosopher, for Schelling held that every nation had its mission. Hegel, the philosopher of the westernisers, spoke of the mission of the Teutons and the mission of the Latins, but left the Slavs out of the reckoning.

§ 72 A.

A BRIEF account will now be given of some of the leading westernisers.

Čaadaev is commonly referred to as one of the first westernisers. The possibility of doing this is an illustration of what has previously been said, that opposition to slavophilism was the leading characteristic of westernism. At the same time, it is manifest that Čaadaev, the advocate of romanticist Catholicisation, preached a restoration and reaction which were not westernist in nature. Čaadaev's passivism brings him nearer to the slavophils than to the progressive westernisers.

In Moscow, Stankevič, pupil of Pavlov the Schellingian, exercised great influence over his friends and associates. Pavlov was supposed to deliver lectures upon political economy and physics, but he really lectured upon Schelling's natural philosophy. His pupil Stankevič became centre of a circle of men of like aims, who eagerly discussed Schelling, Hegel, German literature (Hoffmann, Schiller, Goethe), and Shakespeare. Bělinskii, I. Kirěevskii, K. Aksakov, Bakunin, Botkin, Katkov, Granovskii, Ketčer (the translator of Shakespeare), etc., belonged to this circle. Stankevič went to Berlin to study philosophy, and here Turgenev was influenced by him.

Stankevič, at first a Schellingian, subsequently became a Hegelian. His was one of those beautiful personalities which in the German literature of that day are displayed before the reader's eyes like figures compounded of morning mist—gifted, aspiring, but without the strength of body and of mind requisite for the fulfilment of his aspirations. We owe to Stankevič the discovery of the folk-poet Kolcov.[1]

Similar was the lot of Granovskii, from whom we learn that Stankevič's influence upon himself and his friends was boundless and all for the good. As professor of history his lectures on universal history had considerable effect, though only of a preparatory and stimulating kind. He, likewise, was too weak a man to do much in the time of Nicholas I to promote the development of character in others.[2]

On the other hand the influence of Bělinskii, the critic, was extensive and indeed decisive for Russian readers. In addition to Bělinskii there were a number of literary critics and historians who made Russia acquainted with the world of European thought: Naděždin (1804–1856); Annenkov (1812–1887); Družinin (1824–1864); Botkin (1810–1869); V. Maikov (1823–1847). Among more recent writers Pypin, the learned historian of literature, may be mentioned. In his larger works and in numerous essays he was an antagonist of slavophilism.[3]

Among publicists and journalists Polevoi (1796–1846) deserves mention, and has been previously referred to. A critic of Karamzin and author of a history of Russia, Polevoi recognised that Russia had her own task to fulfil in history, but as regards the other nations of Europe he considered that these were far from being decadent, and that their task was only now beginning. Bělinskii reacted vigorously against Polevoi and his literary criticism.

Čičerin may once more be named as representative of moderate liberalism in politics and the social movement,

---

[1] Stankevič (1813–1840) studied from 1831 to 1835 at the philosophical faculty in Moscow, where he was influenced by Kačenovskii, leader of the sceptical historical school. In 1837 he went to Berlin, where he was on terms of intimate friendship with Werder, the Hegelian.

[2] Granovskii (1813–1855), who studied law at the university, was in Berlin during 1837 and 1838, where he worked under Werder, Ranke, Ritter, and Savigny. From 1839 onwards he lectured at the Moscow philosophical faculty. His lectures to the wider cultivated public were especially popular.

[3] His history of Slav literature was published in German translation during the years 1880 to 1884, the section on Polish literature being contributed by Spasowicz.

whilst N. Turgenev, the decabrist, living abroad, was likewise an advocate of constitutionalist liberalism.[1]

Kavelin the jurist (1848–1908), personally acquainted with the slavophils and the westernisers, endeavoured to adopt an intermediate position between spiritualism and materialism. He had discussions with the slavophils and also with Herzen.[2]

Gradovskii (1841–1889) was another member of the younger group. A meritorious historian and systematic writer on Russian public law, he worked also as journalist. He agreed with the slavophils in his esteem for folk-organisation, and considered that Russian development was a manifestation of the universally human.

Among historians, S. M. Solov'ev (1820–1879) may be mentioned. As regards Old Russia he attached especial importance to the tribal theory, and he considered that Russian development and European development ran on parallel lines. Whereas Karamzin had written a history of the Russian state and above all of Russian absolutism, Solov'ev's *History of Russia* was a history of the Russian people. From the time of John IV onwards, he said, Russia had been striving for organic union with Europe, and this union was effected during the seventeenth and eighteenth centuries.

Herzen and Bakunin, the exiles, were leading founders of the more radical tendency in politics. Herzen's friend, the poet Ogarev, another émigré, was full of ideas but weak in the field of action. In Russia, Černyševskii and Dobroljubov represented similar tendencies.

The younger literary generation of this epoch was liberal and westernist, the most typical representative of the trend being Ivan Turgenev.

[1] Čičerin (1828–1901) was professor of constitutional law in Moscow. His works deal with the philosophy of law, the history of political ideas, constitutional law, ethics, and philosophy. Though a Hegelian, his ethical principles were borrowed also from Kant. He took the field as an opponent of the philosopher Solov'ev and was likewise an antagonist of Herzen. Čičerin was burgomaster of Moscow, and while holder of this office delivered a liberal speech on the occasion of the coronation of Alexander III, this costing him the imperial favour.

[2] In the year 1861, when the disorders among the students (vide supra) began, he was compelled to leave the university, and the like fate befell a number of others : Pypin ; Stasjulevič, for many years editor of the liberal newspaper "Věstnik Evropy"; Spasowicz, Polish liberal, historian of literature, and eloquent lawyer ; Utin.

II

§ 73.

VISSARION GRIGOR'EVIČ BĚLINSKII was leader of
the progressive westernist intelligentsia owing to his
indefatigable and many-sided literary labours. He was a
really hard worker, whereas Stankevič, Botkin, and Granovskii,
and even Čaadaev and Kirěevskii, must be spoken of rather
as improvisers than as workers in the literary field.[1]

Bělinskii's works were published a long time back in twelve
large volumes which ran through several editions. Of late

---

[1] Vissarion Grigor'evič Bělinskii was born on May 30, 1811, in Sveaborg,
where his father was stationed as army surgeon. In 1816 his family removed
to the town of Chembar in the administrative district of Penza. Home-life
was a martyrdom for this vivacious and gifted boy, for neither father nor
mother could or would give their son an education. Bělinskii had to leave
the third class of the gymnazija prematurely, for he preferred working at
home to being bored at school. In 1829 he began to attend the philological
faculty of the university of Moscow. Here he was introduced to German
philosophy and literature by the professors Naděždin and Pavlov. In the year
1832, having in the previous year written a drama, Dmitri Kalinin, submitted
in manuscript to the university censorship, he was compelled to leave the
university. The drama, a fierce protest against serfdom, was declared immoral
and a scandal to the university, but his rustication was ostensibly attributed
to incapacity and weak health. Thenceforward Bělinskii spent his days in
the circle of literary and philosophic friends to which we have previously alluded
(Stankevič, Herzen), remaining always the omnivorous reader he had been
since childhood. He secured a scanty livelihood by private tuition, translations
(translating, for example, works of Paul de Kock), and minor literary labours.
His first important literary work, and the first to attract attention, appeared
in Naděždin's review (1839) and was entitled Literary Fantasies, A Prose Elegy.
German philosophy in its chronological and logical development, and notably
Schelling (1832–1836), Fichte (1837), and Hegel (1837), exercised decisive influence upon Bělinskii. Among German poets to affect his mental development should be mentioned Goethe, Schiller, and Hoffmann. The celebrated
essay on the battle of Borodino was written in St. Petersburg, whither Bělinskii
had removed in October 1839 to make a living as collaborator on the liberal
newspaper "Otečestvennyja Zapiski." In St. Petersburg Bělinskii moved onward from the Hegelian position to that of the Hegelian left (Feuerbach), and
in 1842 to that of French socialism. His most comprehensive work was his
analysis of Puškin (1844). He kept up close literary and philosophical associations with Bakunin, Herzen, Nekrasov, Turgenev, Kavelin, Annenkov, etc.
He was on intimate terms with Gončarov, Grigorovič, and Dostoevskii. Botkin
was his friend and helper from the time when they first met in Moscow. Bělinskii married in 1843, and, characteristically, took a very serious view of marriage.
In 1845 illness compelled him to begin a long stay in the south, and in 1847
he visited Salzbrunn spa, whence he fulminated his fierce protest against Gogol.
He died on May 18, 1848.

more accurate and completer editions have appeared, furnished with introductions and notes. His extensive correspondence is unfortunately known in part only, through the efforts of Pypin and recently through those of Ivanov-Razumnik, the historian of literature. In the days of Alexander I, and still more in those of Nicholas I, literary criticism became the philosophical forum for the discussion of questions of the day, and therefore became also a political forum. The autocracy was able to harass literature and literary criticism, but could not completely suppress these activities.

Bělinskii's personal development was characteristic of the progressive endeavours of the thirties and the forties. While still no more than a schoolboy, he was devoted to literature, the theatre being an education to him ; when he was a student at the university, German philosophy and literature played their part ; when he became an author, he was influenced by French socialism. At the outset Bělinskii trod in the footsteps of Schelling, then Fichte attracted him greatly, but he soon turned to Hegel. It was in Stankevič's circle that he first became acquainted with the ideas of Schelling. To Bakunin he owed his knowledge of those of Fichte. In the same circle Bakunin was the promulgator of Hegelianism ; by Bakunin, too, Bělinskii was initiated, like Proudhon in Paris at a later date, into the philosophy of the Prussian philosophers of court and state.

Ripening experience and the philosophy of Feuerbach, to which he was introduced by Herzen, turned him during his fourth decade towards democracy and socialism in the form these had taken in France after the July revolution. In the metaphysical field, Bělinskii, like many other Russian progressives, passed on from German idealism and romanticism to positivism, materialism, and atheism.

It is by no means easy to give a more precise account of this development. It was Bělinskii's way to take up new foreign ideas with great enthusiasm, but this enthusiasm was soon succeeded by a phase of sober criticism. During the stage of transition he was apt in his literary compositions to continue to expound his older views, whilst in letters and conversations the new faith was already fermenting. Letters and criticisms must therefore be weighed one against the other, for whereas in the letters things are cooked over a hot fire, in the criticisms they are served comparatively cold. Hence the interpretation of Bělinskii is difficult, and divergent opinions are possible. Moreover, about persons his views were liable to frequent and rapid changes.[1]

Some biographers and literary historians distinguish three periods in Bělinskii's development. The first, extending to the year 1840, was that in which he was engaged in the recognition of reality, with Hegel's assistance. From 1840 to 1847 he was devoted to the struggle for western culture and social institutions. In 1847 occurred a sort of slavophil conversion, leading to a campaign on behalf of nationality.

This classification is extremely superficial. As regards the third period, it is obvious that a recognition of the importance of nationality is not peculiar to slavophilism. We need only recall that in 1847 appeared the writing directed against Gogol, a convert to Orthodoxy, for this will suffice to convince us that Bělinskii was no slavophil. Besides, in this very year 1847 Bělinskii expressed himself very energetically and in extremely definite terms as opposed to the slavophil doctrine of the mir and the artel. If in 1847 (it was really in 1846) Bělinskii experienced a new crisis, it was of a different kind, for at this epoch he became somewhat unsympathetic towards socialism.

Agreement with the slavophils in certain respects is characteristic rather of the first of the alleged phases. At the university Bělinskii, having been made acquainted by Pavlov with the work of Schelling, passed under romanticist influences, but simultaneously Nadeždin drew his attention to the pitfalls of romanticism, and his youthful drama is permeated by this cleavage of views. Through renewed acquaintanceship with Schelling and German philosophy in Stankevič's circle he came in certain important respects to share the opinions of the slavophils, and employed some of the expressions which the slavophils had made current. He spoke of the importance of the "inner" life as contrasted with the "outer"; he condemned the French for the way in which their understanding tended to lapse into criticism (making use of the word *razsudok*); he considered that will was the essence of the mind—and we have seen that all these views were characteristic of the slavophils. At this period for Bělinskii eternity was, as he puts it,

---

[1] For example, in 1839, Bělinskii produced an appreciative judgment of his teacher and literary patron Nadeždin, both in respect of authorship and of personal character. But a year later he condemned Nadeždin's character in strong terms.

no fantasy, and he would not allow his reason to instil critical doubts during the intoxicating minutes of faith. These are moods and opinions which manifest his agreement with the slavophils in leading points. Bĕlinskii himself speaks of this first phase of the thirties as his epoch of " abstract heroism," and he analyses it psychologically by saying that he then lived in the sphere of feeling alone, giving feeling precedence over understanding, whereas at a later date, he tells us, he came to recognise that feeling and understanding are identical. Thus, did Bĕlinskii write at the end of 1837.

In this state of inward disintegration he endeavoured (1836) to find relief in " sensuality," seeking " to tranquillise desperation by dissipation," fruitlessly, it need hardly be said. About this he wrote to his friends quite openly and with a certain repressed wrath. In the same year appeared Čaadaev's protest against Russia, but for the time being Bĕlinskii would pay no heed to him. In philosophical and political matters he had for a short time been taken captive by Fichte, but now shook himself free with Hegel's aid. At this period he wrote an extremely weak play entitled *The Fifty Year Old Uncle,* and hoping to earn money he compiled a grammar for which no purchaser could be found.

Despite these internal and external troubles, Bĕlinskii for a brief period now became reconciled with reality. Pogodin would have had more reason than the slavophils to rejoice over the Bĕlinskii of the years 1837 to 1839. He was opposed to politics, which might alter the real ; he was opposed to the French, to politicians, to philosophers (Voltaire !), and to poets ; poets were too political for him, and therefore he clung to Goethe. " To the devil with politics. Long live science ! . . . . German philosophy is a development and exposition clear and distinct as mathematics, a development and exposition of the Christian doctrine founded on love and on the idea of raising man towards the divine." Hegel notwithstanding, his view of civic freedom resembles that of the slavophils, for he says that it can derive only from the inner freedom of the individual. He rejects European constitutions and French politics, with their insistence on experience and history. But he praises Germany, and even Prussia, appealing to the pure understanding and to idealist and apriorist philosophy. Germany is to him " the Jerusalem of the new humanity." In this phase Bĕlinskii goes so far as to forget the youthful drama which had closed for him the portals of the university, coming to terms even with the reality of serfdom. He gives utterance to the proposition, "Might is right, and right is might." But Bĕlinskii did not shut his eyes to the fact that Russia was culturally weak. "We suffer from the weight of Chinesedom," he said in 1839, and four years later he again expressed his horror of Russian Chinesedom. To the same period belong Bĕlinskii's essays upon the battle of Borodino and upon Wolfgang Menzel which are regarded by critics as the climax of this phase of development.

Liberal historians of literature, affected by a kind of shame and unwilling to put weapons into the hands of their opponents, are apt to refrain from a close analysis of these essays. As a rule *Sketches of the Battle of Borodino* is dismissed with a casual mention, the reader being told that in this article, with the aid of Hegel's proposition " The rational is real and the real is. rational," Bĕlinskii had reconciled himself to Russia and to the state of Nicholas, and that Herzen quarrelled with Bĕlinskii on account of the article—Herzen refused to shake hands with Bĕlinskii, and even the gentle Granovskii considered Bĕlinskii's article " vulgar." [1]

Tolstoi considered the battle of Borodino unmeaning ; Napoleon declared it a struggle of titans ; to Bĕlinskii it seemed "the manifestation of the eternal spirit of life," for thus was he influenced by Glinka's book, worthless from the literary and scientific outlook, but penned in an access of mystical ecstasy. To Bĕlinskii this revelation is simultaneously the revelation of the folk-spirit, and he seizes the opportunity to deliver himself concerning the folk-spirit—a subject about which at that time much was being written in Germany.

To Bĕlinskii the Russian folk, the nation, is identical with the state, folk and state being a historically given and full-grown organism. The state, continues Bĕlinskii, is the work

[1] The article appeared in December 1839 as a review of Sketches of the Battle of Borodino by Theodor Glinka. It was the literary continuation of discussions Bĕlinskii had had with his friends in Moscow, discussions in which Bĕlinskii had been advocate for the defence of autocracy. Theodor Glinka was a writer on military topics, and had for a time been member of a political secret society ; in 1826, therefore, after the suppression of the decabrist rising, he was cashiered from the army and banished from the capital. His brother, Sergĕi Glinka, was editor of the " Russkii Vĕstnik " which from 1808 to 1824 was chauvinistic champion of the patriotism of the day, antifrench and anti-napoleonic in its manifestations.

of heroes, and in the case under consideration it is the work
of the tsar whom Bělinskii places upon the same footing with
God, hero, and nation—for the concepts merge into a single
mythical and mystical complex. Bělinskii is so obsessed by
this political anthropomorphism, or rather sociomorphism,
that in the name " tsar " he discovers, like every Russian,
poetic depths and a mysterious significance. " Our tsar "
is of course Tsar Nicholas. Bělinskii reiterates the patriarchal
theory of the origin of Russian absolutism, and he opposes
the Russian state and the Russian folk to Europe, just like
the slavophils, and also just like Count Uvarov.

From this standpoint, cosmopolitanism was to Bělinskii a
phantom, something hazy and impalpable, and in no sense
a living reality ; liberalism as a whole was nothing but French
chatter. Power, says Bělinskii, with Paul, is from God ;
the tsar is the real " vicegerent " of God ; a president, like
the president of the American republic, is doubtless respectworthy, but he is not sacred, for he owes his existence to the
revolution.

If we were to judge Bělinskii's article on Borodino solely
by political canons, we could appeal on his behalf to the great
authority of Hegel. In his acceptance of reality Bělinskii
was certainly no worse than Hegel. Whilst Hegel came in the
end to discover his mystical and mythical " absolute reason "
in the Teutonic world, in the Prussian state and the Prussian
monarchy, in Frederick William III of Prussia, Bělinskii, for
the same reason and with much the same justification, could
be an enthusiast for the Russia of Uvarov and Nicholas. But
Bělinskii could appeal to other authority besides that of Hegel.
Bakunin approved the article, and at this time the views of
Bělinskii's friends in Moscow were, speaking generally, far
from being clarified and differentiated. Of Bělinskii, too,
it must be said that he lacked philosophical clarity. Besides,
in his essay on Borodino he is by no means the orthodox
Hegelian that he might be supposed in view of his adopting
the proposition concerning the rationality of the real. This
is plain from his insistence upon the organic growth of the
Russian state, and from his whole conception of the world as
an organism, for here Bělinskii inclines more towards Schelling,
the romanticists, and the historical school of law, than towards
Hegel. Again, he identifies the Russian state with the nation
in a manner which is not wholly Hegelian. He stresses the

distinction between the state and the nation, and in the case of Russia alone are state and nation identical. In a more detailed exposition of Bělinskii's views due weight would have to be given to these and to many other considerations. The essay upon Wolfgang Menzel, which is in the form of a review of a translation of Menzel's *German Literature*, likewise betrays the composite factors of Bělinskii's views. He condemns Menzel, clings to Goethe and Hegel, but energetically opposes the ethics of George Sand, and so on. It is impossible here to undertake a precise analysis of all these works, nor is such an analysis within the scope of the present sketch, which aims merely at a reference to the philosophical and metaphysical problem which busied and disquieted Bělinskii in his essay on Borodino, namely (to use the phraseology of the schools) the fundamental problem of the relationship between subject and object, between I and not-I. Fichte continued to disturb Bělinskii's mind; but Hegel's rational reality of history was in the end to overthrow Fichte's extreme individualism and subjectivism.

§ 74.

BĕLINSKII, too, plunged into Turgenev's "German sea," but he did not wish to drown in it, nor was there any reason why he should, seeing that in Germany itself Fichte and his successors refused to perish there (§ 44).

Bělinskii accepted objectively given history, and above all the objectively given state, just as Hegel and also Schelling and Fichte accepted them—the two last-named in so far as they sought objective standing-ground upon historic data.

Bělinskii was fully aware that his historism was directed against subjectivism. In Hegel's sense he endeavoured to avoid a cleavage between the subject, as individual and as chance product, and the object, the world-all, as universal and necessary, in this way, that the subject was to give itself up to the object so that the individual and chance-given might raise itself to the level of the universal and necessary, and become justified thereby. The universal and necessary is discerned in history, and properly speaking in historically developing society; society is identified with the state; but never for a moment does Bělinskii forget himself, the subject, continually enquiring, What must this ego, the subject, do to render possible the giving of itself up to the whole, and how is the sacrifice morally justified ?

Bělinskii concedes to the subject the right and even the necessity of negating the object, for the individual human being must struggle with the object ; but this negation of the object, of society, and of history, can be nothing more than a transient stage of development, and must not long endure. The contest with society is necessary, but this contest must not degenerate into revolt, into revolution ; it must be a striving towards perfectionment, and must end in the recognition of society. " Woe to those who are disunited from society, never to be reconciled with it. Society is the higher reality, and reality insists that man shall live completely at peace with her, shall completely recognise her ; failing this, reality crushes man beneath the leaden weight of her giant hand."

Ultimately the conflict between extreme subjectivism and objectivism is reduced to the following formula. The subjective side of man is likewise real, but extreme subjectivism, like any one-sided truth pushed to an extreme, leads to an absurdity ; through extreme subjectivism the understanding is narrowed, concepts are rendered arbitrary, feeling is degraded to arid and immoral egoism, and the will in action manifests itself as evil-doing and crime.[1]

Bělinskii thus combats extreme, absolute subjectivism, solipsism, which for him degrades the world into illusion and in effect annihilates it ; he clings to Hegel's reality, which in

[1] A more extended account of Bělinskii's reasoning concerning this important matter may be given in his own words. " Quâ personality man is individual and a chance product, but quâ spirit (that spirit of which his personality is the expression) he is universal and necessary. Hence the cleavage between his situation and his endeavour ; hence the struggle between his ego and all that lies without the ego, all that comprises the non-ego. In relation to his personality, the non-ego, the objective world, is hostile ; in relation to his spirit, the expression of the infinite and the universal, this objective world is to him essentially akin. That he may become more real, that he may cease to be the mere semblance of a man, his personality must become the individual expression of the universal, the restricted manifestation of the infinite. Man must therefore free himself from his subjective personality, recognising it to be an illusion and a falsehood ; he must reconcile himself with the universal, with the world-all, by coming to understand that here alone are truth and reality to be found. And since this world-all or universal exists, not in the subject but in the object, he must become akin in essence thereto, must coalesce into a unity therewith. Thereafter he will again become a subjective personality, but this subjective personality will now be real, for it will no longer give expression to the chance-given individual, but to the universal, to the world-all— in a word there will be spirit in the flesh."

his view is identical with God. But he combats also extreme, absolute objectivism. Of peculiar philosophic importance in this connection is an account given by Bělinskii in 1839 of two prophetical books published at that time. In this criticism he rejected absolute objectivism on the ground that it led to superstition and was itself superstition. The essay is one of the most original of Bělinskii's philosophic writings and bears witness to the penetrating powers of his understanding. Superstition, we are told, is a developmental phase of the individual ego, a phase in which the ego seeks truth exclusively in the object. In this extreme and absolute objectivism, the ego denominates as truth the very thing which is diametrically opposed to the understanding, and that precisely is selected for esteem which is most alien and most void of thought. Bělinskii therefore distinguishes between the mysterious that is beloved of superstition and the mysterious of mysticism. The mysterious in which superstition lives is cold and dead, and its mystery originates in despotism and caprice.

As far as I have been able to discover, the importance of these aperçus is nowhere recognised in the literature dealing with Bělinskii, and they have been simply ignored by his critics. Yet here Bělinskii touches upon the deepest problems of German idealism and of philosophy in general.

In the ancient dispute over the relationship between subject and object, a dispute so profoundly treated by German philosophy, Bělinskii rejects both extreme subjectivism in the form of solipsistic, egoistic individualism and extreme objectivism. For him the dilemma is one of crime versus superstition. He refuses to be intimidated by this dilemma, categorically insisting that we need have neither crime (revolution) nor superstition. He gets rid of the dilemma by refusing to admit that either subjectivism or objectivism is valid beyond a certain point, and by endeavouring to establish a harmony between them.

He turns away from Fichte, and still more from Stirner. He knew nothing of Marx and Engels as extreme objectivists, but interesting and brilliant is his discovery that in extreme objectivism lies the essence of superstition. In precisely the same manner did Vico and Hume characterise as extreme objectivism the first stage of mental development, and, following the lead of these philosophers, Feuerbach represented that the essence of religion was anthropomorphism, was extreme

objectivism. Not until later did Bělinskii become acquainted
with the ideas of Feuerbach after he had been introduced to
them by his friends Herzen and Bakunin, and all the more
interesting, therefore, was the insight he displayed into extreme
objectivism.

I do not contend that Bělinskii grasped the problem accurately and in its entirety. Systematism in philosophy and
epistemology was not his gift. He was content with an ethical
solution of the problem, with demonstrating its limits, and
with pointing out how to harmonise subjectivism and objectivism. His subsequent development enables us to learn what
were the ethical ideas which did him this important service.

§ 75.

IN St. Petersburg, Bělinskii was able to watch the realities
of Russian officialdom close at hand. Three or four
months, he tells us, sufficed to inform him regarding these
matters, and henceforward to the day of his death he was
at one with Herzen on the subject, whilst diverging in outlook
from Polevoi, who had now grown reactionary. Hardly had
the article been published when to his friend Botkin, Bělinskii
reported the intellectual crisis through which he had been
passing, and anathematised the detestable whimsey which had
led him to make peace with the detestable reality. Removing
Goethe from the place of honour in his critical sanctuary, he
now extolled Schiller, the noble advocate of humanity. "I am
told; Develop all the treasures of thy spirit that thou mayest
achieve free self-satisfaction for that spirit ; weep to console
thyself ; mourn to bring thyself joy ; strive towards perfection ;
mount towards the highest steps upon the staircase of development ; and shouldst thou stumble—well, thou wilt fall ! The
devil take thee then, for thou wert fit for nothing better. . . .
Most humble thanks, Egor Feodorovič Gegel [Hegel], I bow
before your philosophic nightcap, but notwithstanding my
respect for your philosophic philistinism I must dutifully assure
you that if I should succeed in creeping up the developmental
stairs to attain the topmost step I would endeavour, even
there, to take into the reckoning all the victims of vital conditions and of history, all the victims of misfortune, of superstition, of the inquisition of Philip II, and so on—and in default
would hurl myself headlong from the summit. I do not desire

happiness in any other terms, and I must be tranquillised concerning the fate of every one of my blood brothers." Such were the sentiments animating Bĕlinskii in 1841, and more and more he tended towards the conviction that "every man is an end for himself," and that universal harmony is too dearly bought at the cost of individual disharmonies, disharmonies in individual lives.

Bĕlinskii readily came to understand that the idealisation of the all, the idealisation of history (this to include Russian history, and Russian history to include Nicholas), was too gross an imposition. He could not fail to say to himself that just as little as Napoleon and the "respectworthy" president of the United States, was Nicholas a truly real reality. In a word, the basing of the political theory of legitimacy upon Hegelian pantheism had to Bĕlinskii become suspect through and through. It is true that Bĕlinskii might have transferred to Bakunin's shoulders some of the responsibility for the Borodino essay, but Bĕlinskii was not the man to attempt to shuffle off responsibilities in this way. Besides, Bakunin too had perceived his error, and had come to the same way of thinking as Bĕlinskii.

A light had broken in on the latter with the recognition that the Hegelian metaphysic, that Hegelian pantheism, could be used to demonstrate that the illegitimist rulers as well as the legitimist, that Robespierre and Napoleon as well as Louis XVI and Nicholas, were "an expression of the universal and the infinite." Both are historically given, and if we hold fast to history we pass from Hegel to revolution. Herzen, as we know, found in Hegel "the algebra of revolution," nor was it difficult to Herzen and Ogarev to induce Bĕlinskii to share the new outlook. "The executioner exists, and his existence is rational, but he is none the less repulsive," wrote Bĕlinskii at the close of the year 1840.

Herzen and Ogarev brought about Bĕlinskii's movement from Hegel to the Hegelian left and to Feuerbach. From Feuerbach it was but a step to Young Germany and to Heine. It would be inaccurate to say that Bĕlinskii abandoned Hegel and went over to Feuerbach and the socialists. Nor did Bĕlinskii himself throw his Borodino essay altogether overboard, for all that he would admit was that he had drawn false conclusions from correct principles. The man harassed by Fichte's subjectivism had accepted the Hegelian reality as a God, and by degrees only did he come to recognise the nature of this god. He came to recognise that we are not concerned with every reality (his friend Stankevič had warned him, quite needlessly, that these doctrines are not meant to apply to the realities of commonplace life), but with the objective reign of law manifest in and revealed by the succession of phenomena, that reign of law which in social life he recognised as the realisation of humanity.

Feuerbach showed the Russians, who were wholly objectivist, how to harmonise objectivism with subjectivism. Whilst Bělinskii, as he admits, had hitherto considered subjectivism and objectivism only in their more extreme and radical aspects, he now learned from Feuerbach that a logical and methodical peace could be made between moderate subjectivism and moderate objectivism, learned, indeed, that such a peace offered the only possibility of understanding the essential nature of philosophical development and above all of German philosophy, and that it offered the sole means of bringing that development to its proper conclusion. Feuerbach made of man the only goal and issue of human experience, and to Bělinskii, stimulated by Fichte, he displayed the boundary line between ultra-subjectivist illusion and objectivistically true and rational reality.

Whereas Bělinskii had conceived the ideas of God, tsar, hero, and nation, as a complex unity, Feuerbach had shown him the fallacious character of this fusion, and with Herzen and Ogarev he had become an opponent of theocratic theism and tsarism. The anthropomorphic God having been deposed from his heavenly throne as unreal, it naturally followed that the divinely appointed earthly throne of the tsar fell with it, whilst the president, previously no more than " respectworthy," was now raised to the rank of " sanctity."

For the Hegelian left of Russia, Feuerbach's anthropologism and his explanation of religion as anthropomorphism were now reinforced by Strauss. Bělinskii had learned from Strauss to take an adverse view of Christianity and Christ. Vogt and the whole materialistic current fortified him and his intellectual colleagues in their materialist views.

Bělinskii now preached humanity quite in the sense of Feuerbach. But " man," he said, was identical with " liberal," and by liberalism he understood freedom from the oppression of Nicholas. Bělinskii modified the Hegelian program. France became the new Jerusalem ; her policy and her revolution were the determinative example of the self-sacrificing idea of humanity ; monarchy was anti-human. The French always exercised much influence over Bělinskii even though German ideas constituted his program. He tells us that he could not speak German well. We know that he studied Hegel in Russian translation, and it is improbable that he had much knowledge of the original writings of any of the German philosophers.

After this estrangement from reality and especially from Russian reality he came again to a more friendly view of the French, recognising that in their revolution French blood had been poured out for the sacred rights of humanity. He knew well enough that there were many phrasemakers and chatterers in France ; but Germany, too, had her Hofrats, philistines, and other rabble. He came to admire Robespierre. The millennium would be constructed on earth, not by the sugary and stilted phrases of the idealist and fastidious Gironde, but by the terrorists and by the two-edged sword of word and deed wielded by Robespierre and Saint-Just. Bělinskii thus passed from the " inner " to the " outer " truth.[1]

In 1841 Bělinskii went over to the French socialists. George Sand was rehabilitated, for the woman's question had always seemed of great importance to him. He desired for women equality of position with men and an identical education ; marriage was to be free from conventional contracts, and was to secure its moral value as a true union of love. Saint-Simon and Fourier, Pierre Leroux, Cabet, Proudhon, and Ledru-Rollin, instilled into him the conviction that socialism was " the idea of ideas, the being of beings, the question of questions, the alpha and omega of belief and knowledge " ; for him socialism now embraced history and religion and philosophy. Louis Blanc, in his *Histoire de dix ans*, had made clear for him the nature of the bourgeoise, and had enabled him to understand the proletarianisation of the masses which the bourgeoisie had brought about. But we must not suppose that Bělinskii owed his interest in social problems solely to these theorists

---

[1] In 1837 he had written : "Civic freedom must be the fruit of the inner freedom of all the individuals composing the nation, but inner freedom is attained through self-consciousness. Such is the splendid way in which we shall gain freedom for our Russia. All will be secured without conspiracies or revolts, and will therefore be better organised and more enduring."

of socialism. From the first he had been socialistically and democratically inclined, for he was numbered among the earliest of the writers who then really constituted the third estate. Doubtless, like almost all Russian authors of his day, he sprang from the nobility, but he belonged to the petty and impoverished nobility. The liberation of the peasantry, liberation in general, had always been his ideal, as we may learn from his youthful drama which, modelled upon Schiller's *Robbers*, freely condemned serfdom. " Sociality is my watchword," he tells us after his philosophic discussion with Herzen. We must be careful, however, to avoid the mistake of confusing Bělinskii's socialism with the socialism of to-day, with Marxist socialism. Bělinskii remained throughout a strong individualist, resembling in this Lassalle rather than Marx, considering that the individual must not be sacrificed to the whole. As we have seen, he will not accept happiness on any account if one fellow-man, if a single brother, continues to suffer ; and we often read assertions which imply that wellbeing cannot exist in a community if individual members suffer.

Bělinskii modified Louis Blanc's exposition of the rôle of classes, at any rate as far as Russia was concerned, for he considered that in Russia literature had enriched the bourgeoisie with " a kind of class," the intelligentsia. This class was composed of members of all classes, and was brought together by the love of culture. Such a view was expressed by Bělinskii in 1846. In the following year he explained more precisely that the development of all nations had proceeded by way of class differentiation, and he stated in set terms that the bourgeoisie, as a middle class, was essential to the welfare of the state. He did not fail to see the evil of modern class society as manifested in the dominion of capitalism, but he did not consider that the bourgeoisie and manufacturing industry were responsible for this dominion. It was his opinion, further, that the Russian aristocracy must undergo transformation into a bourgeoisie, for not until then in Russia could the internal process of civic development begin.

Civilisation and culture are regarded by Bělinskii as the most important motive power of progressive peoples, and he often adds the humanitarian idea as an additional energising factor, whilst he regards the intelligentsia, the supplementary bourgeois class, as the instrument of civilisation and culture. He accepts the given gradation of classes, and accepts more especially the intellectual leadership of the intelligentsia, this leadership being exercised by select individualities. He thus rejects (1848) the " mystical faith in the people " characteristic of the slavophils and the socialists.

It is indisputable that from the German and French socialism of his day he took over the principles of the philosophic and political revolution without accepting the economic doctrines, the economic materialism, of the movement. It must, however, not be forgotten that in those days, when the revolution of 1848 was brewing, Marx had not yet clearly formulated his economic materialism, and it must be remembered that he was then revolutionary in sentiment, revolutionary in the political sense of the term.

Bělinskii's closing years (from 1846 onwards) were, therefore, characterised by a more vigorous insistence upon individualism, which found expression in sharp sayings about the French socialists. It never became clear to him that his struggle for the rights of the individual personality must not conflict with socialism. But Bělinskii did not cease to participate actively in the campaign against superstition and mysticism.

He was a born fighter, and in describing his own polemic attitude he says, " I am by nature a Jew." His mission as combatant was to organise progressive Russia against absolutism. A cell was already prepared for him in the fortress of St. Peter and St. Paul, and it was only his premature death which saved him from occupying it.

Bělinskii's philosophical credo secured its climax of expression in his *Letter to Gogol*. For years Bělinskii had championed Gogol, and in the end was forced to turn against him. In 1847 Gogol published his *Selected Passages from Correspondence with Friends*, drawn for the most part from letters written in 1845 and 1846, when Gogol's religious emotionalism was tragically in the ascendant. In the *Correspondence*, Gogol unreservedly favours the old order and the established Orthodox religion, having good words even for the abomination of serfdom, his passivist Christianity now leading him to approve the institution. Bělinskii, who was then in Europe and could write without troubling himself about the censorship, incorporated a flaming protest in a *Letter to Gogol*. This was circulated far and wide throughout Russia in manuscript copies ; men of the cultured classes learned it by heart ; Dostoevskii and the Petraševcy had to atone in Siberia for reading it in public ; and it became the living program of progressive Russia. "Russia does not need Orthodox mysticism," exclaims Bělinskii ; "she needs rights and laws in harmony with the healthy understanding and in conformity with justice. At an epoch when and in a country where men sell men like cattle, Gogol wishes to soothe our minds with empty sermons."

The *Letter to Gogol* throws light upon Bělinskii's general outlook as well as upon his personal character.

Feuerbachian atheism and materialism take the form of a socialistic struggle against the old order of the Russian theocracy. Feuerbach's socialistic sentiments are elucidated and fortified by those of the French. Bělinskii now feels towards the French the sympathy which Saltykov declared characteristic of himself and the younger generation. This is not to say that Bělinskii turned from Feuerbach to Stirner, and indeed Annenkov tells us that Bělinskii rejected Stirner's teaching most emphatically. He did not, however, entirely reject egoism ; he clung to Feuerbach's ego and alter ego. But egoism was valid solely upon a moral basis, and this moral basis was social and socialistic altruism. Not even Homjakov was more vigorous in his refutation of Stirner. Bělinskii's fighting spirit enabled him to sense the passive bourgeois in the ostensibly radical anarchist.

Nor, on the other hand, did Bělinskii fall into the error of Marx. Marx and Engels, passing beyond Feuerbach in their opposition to the idealist subjectivism of German philosophy, arrived at a no less extreme objectivism, not merely throwing Stirner overboard, but sacrificing the individual to the mass. From Feuerbach, Bělinskii learned a moderate objectivism, and contended that the individual, as a strong personality, should carry on the struggle against society. In this matter Bělinskii thought and felt as a Russian. In the Russia of that day the masses were composed of the peasantry, they were illiterate serfs, and it was impossible therefore for Bělinskii to subordinate (as did Engels) the " paltry " individual to such a mass. Nor could Bělinskii see in the Russian masses those who would carry on the tradition of German idealistic philosophy, as for Lassalle and Engels the German working classes seemed predestined to carry it on. Bělinskii read Marx's essays in the " Deutsch-Französische Jahrbücher," and recognised their radicalism, but Bělinskii remained unsympathetic towards the philosophy of Marx, despite the latter's atheism and materialism.

Bělinskii's study of Hegel had not led him to the objectivist historism adopted by Marx and Engels. He expressly declared that the freedom of the idea must not be sacrificed to the fetters of the time and to deadening fact, and he refused to offer up ethics to history, as the Marxists and positivists had done.

There was doubtless a positivist element in Bělinskii. Like Marx and Engels, he first became acquainted with positivism in a German form, in the teaching of Feuerbach and Hegel— for the historism of Hegel and Feuerbach is to a large extent positivist. Moreover, from 1846 onward Bělinskii was acquainted with the work of Comte and Littré, and was thus familiar with the more precise formulations of French positivism. To the Russians in general as well as to Bělinskii this French and German positivism was a welcome elucidation and reinforcement of their native realism.

But it is important to note that Bělinskii did not regard the realism and positivism of time and fact as the real and true reality. He was, as he said, unwilling to abandon the capacity for freedom of movement in the moral sphere.

Continually, and at every opportunity, Bělinskii fought scepticism and especially the " hectic " scepticism of Russia. From 1840 onwards Bělinskii condemned scepticism just as had Stankevič or Odoevskii, and had indeed expressed his opposition at an earlier date. Scepticism seemed to him an abnormal mental state, one apt to be widely diffused during periods of transition, when the old has been abandoned whilst the new has not yet come into being. In scepticism, too, there existed degrees and differences. In a sense scepticism seemed to Bělinskii a necessary condition of progress, but this form of scepticism was not a cold negation. None but the petty and the base fall prey to such negation ; men of great and vigorous nature, suffering under their scepticism, react against it by creating new and higher things. This dissertation conveys an excellent psychological analysis of Bělinskii's own *Letter to Gogol*, and indeed explains his literary activities in general, his literary work of opposition and revolution.

This revolution had, properly speaking, but one opponent, theocracy and its ecclesiastical religion. The enthusiasm of Bělinskii's campaign was directed against the superstition and mysticism of the Russian church, Hegel, Feuerbach,

Comte, and their positivist rationalism, were to scare away superstition and mysticism. Bělinskii knew Russia and knew himself.

For from the first, Bělinskii was by no means inaccessible to mysticism, of which throughout life he had a lively appreciation. As a good Russian he could only understand religion as a form of mysticism. Similarly the slavophils were zealous advocates of mysticism, whilst their most conspicuous opponents, Kirěevskii, Homjakov, and Samarin, had strong mystical leanings.

We learn from Turgenev, Dostoevskii, and others how much the religious problem interested Bělinskii, and we can see this for ourselves in his *Letter to Gogol* and in his whole struggle for light and knowledge. Dostoevskii is unjust to Bělinskii in that he fails to understand the latter's blasphemous antichristian utterances. Not the historic, the real Christ, but ecclesiastical Christianity, the falsified Christ, was a stumbling block to Bělinskii. " We have not yet solved the problem of the existence of God—and you say you want your dinner ! " he once reproachfully exclaimed to Turgenev who had become weary of a philosophical discussion. This reproach conveys the whole Bělinskii. Neither in social nor in metaphysical questions did he show any trace of the indifferentism not uncommon in liberals.

As we learn from his correspondence, Bělinskii was troubled by the question of personal immortality as well as by that of theism. He was not satisfied with faith, as were Botkin and Stankevič. Being no longer able to believe, he wanted to know. In these questions, too, he desired light. Hence romanticist renunciation and resignation did not suffice him, and outspoken atheism and materialism seemed preferable. In the *Letter to Gogol* he passionately defends the thesis that by nature the Russians are profoundly irreligious. They are superstitious, but civilisation will drive out superstition ; in his inward soul the Russian is indifferent to an exemplary degree. It is true that much religious zeal was shown by the raskolniki, but these sectaries were so few in number as to be negligible.

The very passion with which these views are expressed, the passion that animates the whole *Letter to Gogol*, confutes Bělinskii's own contention. Gogol roused the religious sentiments of his contemporaries, but in their spiritual need these were as little able as Gogol himself to find a way out of the difficulty.

Bělinskii carries on his campaign against mysticism with the aid of the philosophy of history as well as with that of the philosophy of religion. The contrast between mysticism and rational knowledge is the standard by which he judges Russia and Europe, the standard he applies to the old Russia and the new. The disciple of Feuerbach and Strauss recognised in the old Russia a well-developed national and independent life, but this life was one of unconscious contemplation, essentially mystical, such as is characteristic of the east, of Asia. The Russian consciousness awakened with the coming of Peter; Russia began to live the European life of willing and knowing; the Russian struggled towards the light and endeavoured to strengthen his individuality. But since the days of Peter, Russia had been cleft in twain, for the people continued to live as of old, whilst the world of society had abandoned and forgotten the ancient tradition, and continued to stride forward along the path of Europeanisation.

The agreement with Čaadaev and also with the slavophils is plain, but the agreement with the slavophils extends only to the recognition of the difference between Europe and Russia and the difference between prepetrine and postpetrine Russia. When the difference comes to be appraised, there exists between Bělinskii and the slavophils the difference between Europe and Old Russia, the difference between rationalism and mysticism—if we may use these concepts summarily in Belinskii's sense. The word mysticism is applied by Bělinskii to religious mysticism, but he uses it also to denote the theological outlook in general, the entire outlook of Old Russia on the universe.

Dostoevskii tells us that Bělinskii, when he went for a walk, was fond of going to watch the building of the first railway station at St. Petersburg. " It cheers me to stand there for a while and watch the work going on. At last, I say to myself, we are going to have one railway at least. You can't imagine how this raises my spirits ! " Dostoevskii here gives us the real Bělinskii. His delight in the building of the railway is his faith in Europe and in Young Russia, his faith in the saving power of knowledge, his faith in the deliverance of Russia from the slackening bonds of theocratic absolutism.

Bělinskii fights superstition, and, as he uses the term, superstition embraces religion and theology in general. Feuerbach and Comte lead him astray, lead him to the old fallacy to which Hume had succumbed, the identification of religion with anthropomorphism and superstition. The struggle against official church doctrine and official religion perpetuates this fallacy even to-day, and it is therefore easy to understand why Bělinskii and his contemporaries were prone to it.

Bělinskii failed to undertake a thorough and systematic discussion of the basic problems of philosophy, and failed especially to discuss the epistemological problem, for in the reign of Nicholas he was more concerned with practice than with theory. He was content to make the most of the practical and ethical tendency of German philosophy, deriving from that philosophy his general epistemological outlook. He was mainly busied with questions of the day as shown forth in literature. He was not a philosopher in the German sense, not a professor of philosophy ; the Germans with their thoroughness and their elaborate systematisations seemed to him unduly philistine. He reproached Gončarov with being a German and a philistine. He esteemed the Germans as " the seminarists of mankind " ; but he frankly declared that a successful coup against Bulgarin and Greč gave him more pleasure than an article weighty with detail. He was, in fact, a literary revolutionist, and Gončarov spoke of him as a " tribune."

Bělinskii had an almost morbid thirst for knowledge. " Learn, learn, learn ! " was his earliest watchword, and one to which he remained true throughout life. Most of his critiques were in fact written for self-instruction, and this is why they exercised so lively an influence. His opponents were not slow to reproach him as a callow student, to censure him for defective culture, and the reproach was again and again reiterated. It is true that in literature Bělinskii was a self-made man, but so were many of the most talented authors of his day.

Bělinskii was aware of his own defects, but he had a fine intelligence. With the aid of German philosophy he grasped clearly enough the nature of Russia's essential defects, and ardently throughout life did he strive to mend them (" the vehement Vissarion "). He was but thirty-seven when he died. Had his life been prolonged he might have written one or more books for which he cherished plans, but his work as it was was more important to his contemporaries than that of many who have lived an orderly literary career. Nor must we forget that Bělinskii's friends and Bělinskii's opponents, the slavophils and many of the westernisers, likewise failed to produce systematic works.

§ 76.

A S critic and æstheticist Bělinskii was able to appraise rightly the individual poets and other writers whose works comprise Russian literature, and was at the same time competent to give an accurate characterisation of the development of that literature. He had a notable influence upon contemporary poets. In his very first writings he gave due recognition to Puškin's talent, whilst Gončarov, Turgenev, Grigorovič, Nekrasov, Dostoevskii, Kolcov, and Poležaev, learned much from Bělinskii.

Bělinskii showed his contemporaries that the thoughts of great poets, such men as Griboedov (whom Bělinskii did not understand before 1840), Puškin, Gogol, Lermontov, Dostoevskii, and Gončarov constitute a positive national treasure, one of supreme, nay of vital importance. Benediktov, who was then much overvalued, was appraised at his proper worth. Homjakov's didactic partisan verse was estimated at its just value. Bělinskii may be reproached for having failed to understand the character of Tatjana in Puškin's *Onegin*, and for other failures of insight, but it is important to note that he thoroughly recognised the positive Russism of Puškin's and Gogol's work, and that as far as Gogol, in particular, was concerned he recognised that this writer's realism (which he spoke of as belonging to the " natural " school, as contrasted with the " rhetorical ") was a Russian way of regarding life.

Great was Bělinskii's influence upon the literary circles of Moscow and St. Petersburg. This was shown by his relationships with the slavophils and the westernisers, and in particular by his relationships with the literary critics Naděždin and Annenkov, and with many other connoisseurs of literature, who already abounded in Russia.

Despite the derivation of much of his thought from German philosophy, in æsthetics Bělinskii was an empiricist. Art, he declared, existed before æsthetics, and æsthetics therefore must be guided by art, and not conversely. Bělinskii had no theory of æsthetics worked out in all its details ; he was concerned almost exclusively with poesy and the written word, his realism leading him to advocate the characteristic view that the poet thinks in pictures. But he did not fail to emphasise also the work done by the poet in the field of thought. In 1842 he wrote that living contemporary science had become the foster-mother of art, for without science talent was weak and enthusiasm lacked energy.[1] At an earlier date Venevitinov had said that Russian literature " must think rather than create "—a one-sided rule, but one whose formulation was readily comprehensible in the Russia of Nicholas.

These views remind us of Schelling, but also of Hegel, for in æsthetics as in philosophy Bělinskii was influenced by both the German thinkers. The giving of art precedence over practice and theory is Schellingian, and when the author is in this vein we are told that the good is based upon æsthetic sentiments ; but after Bělinskii has made acquaintance with Hegel his tendency is rather to range the beautiful beside religion and philosophy, and to insist that the beautiful too is moral.

We find echoes of Schelling and Hegel, in addition, in the conflict between romanticism and classicism which continues unceasingly in Bělinskii's mind, and which Russian realism hoped to bring to an end. But Bělinskii himself is as little successful here as in his attempts at a more precise demarcation between subjectivism and objectivism in general. On the one hand we are told that art, as the product of genius (genius being appraised à la Schelling) is subjective ; yet at the same time he assures us that art is objective and must be nothing else. During the years when Bělinskii was idolising reality it was natural that in the sphere of æsthetics he should insist that art must represent reality alone.

The question whether art may have a purpose, exercised Bělinskii's mind greatly. At one time he would insist that art must never be tendentious, and yet shortly afterwards he would say that art pure and simple must be supplemented by tendentious belletristics, for this was extremely useful.

Bělinskii never failed to esteem the beautiful, the artistic, most highly ; but as his mind matured he came more and more to look for ideas, for thought-content, in works of art. This

---

[1] In 1843 Bělinskii said that art was one of the absolute spheres of " cognition." In similar fashion he had ere this spoken of poetry as philosophy and thought, in so far as it was the task of poetry to present the idea as viewed concretely.

thought-content, he insisted, must derive from society viewed as a whole.

Literature, in particular, is to Bělinskii the consciousness, or the growth into consciousness, of the people. He adopts the theory which is referable to Schelling that the poet is the orator, the instrument, of his nation. But it was not Schelling's authority alone which led him to form this estimate of poetic art. It is generally held that at that epoch in poetry alone had the Russians produced original work, whilst further, and before all, it is necessary to remember that before the revolution of 1848 (for here I am not thinking of Russia alone) poetry and literature in general had to function as a parliamentary forum. Bělinskii never failed to advocate the view that the poet's gifts must be such as to enable him to sympathise directly with the ideas and the spirit of his age, for Bělinskii regarded the poet as the instrument, not of party or sect, but of the hidden ideas of society as a whole. In accordance with Hegel's teaching, he declares it to be the poet's mission to give expression, not to the individual and fortuitous, but to the universal and necessary.

It was beyond Bělinskii's powers to analyse more precisely the nature of nationality, but here the slavophils and other Russian writers of the day failed no less. He was content with casual references to certain physiological peculiarities which might have been brought about by the influence of climate and soil, and some of which might manifest themselves in the mental sphere. He advanced beyond Hegel in his distinction between nationality and state, but as far as the Russians were concerned it sufficed him to note that they possessed well-marked national lineaments. He demanded, therefore, that the ideas created by the foreign world should be independently elaborated by the Russians in the spirit of their own nationality. Russia, he said, possessed the energy to complete this task and to say " her word " to the world.

In contradistinction to the slavophils and the romanticists Bělinskii's conception of nationality was not mystical, and in individualistic fashion he attached more importance to individual poets, this determining his critical outlook towards folk-poetry. All he could see in Russian folk-poetry was childish lispings, sound without sense; and for the like reason he considered prepetrine literature practically valueless because it had not yet awakened to consciousness. I may mention in this connection that Bělinskii formed an unfavourable estimate of the literary attempts of the Little Russians. (He condemned Ševčenko's political endeavours without further ado.)

Bělinskii paid homage to the slavophils for their fidelity to conviction. As regards the substance of their doctrine he said that humanity in the concrete consists of definite nationalities, that as a historic fact the universally human finds its expression in distinct nationalities. To him, as later to Turgenev, humanity in the abstract, humanitarian cosmopolitanism, was a phantom. The excellence of his disposition is shown by the continuance of his cordial friendship with the slavophil Konstantin Aksakov, notwithstanding their dissent upon theoretical matters.

Bělinskii's enthusiasm for Europe has led the historians of literature to regard as a lapse into slavophilism his disquisitions upon nationality, formulated in 1847. It was alleged, moreover, that his critical attitude towards Maikov the positivist was due to personal dislike. This is erroneous, We have already referred to his attitude towards the slavophils. In the opening period of his literary activities he declared himself opposed to cosmopolitanism, and continued to hold this view throughout life.

Whilst in his first critical writing (1834) he said that Russia did not yet possess a literature, he subsequently came to recognise Russian literature as an independent and notable entity. At an early date he considered that the work of the four poets, Deržavin, Krylov, Griboedov, and Puškin was of the first importance ; in 1841 he added to his list of noteworthy Russian writers Žukovskii, Batjuškov, Gogol, and Lermontov ; finally, in 1844, he took it as a matter of course that Russia had a genuine literature of her own.

Æsthetic feeling, artistic understanding and sympathy, have been denied to Bělinskii because he considered that the Sixtine Madonna manifested indifference to earthly needs, deficient love, a proud consciousness of a high mission and of personal. perfection, whilst in the Christ child, he thought, was foreshadowed the development of the Old Testament God of revenge. But surely Bělinskii was within his rights in thus interpreting Catholic mysticism ? Kireevskii, too, declared that he found this Raphael Madonna incomprehensible, though Žukovskii, with romanticist enthusiasm, was eager to bring the divine repose of the picture home to the understanding of his contemporaries.

As historian (and before all he was historian of literature) Bělinskii was unable to arrive at a unified result concerning the tasks of history and in especial those of the history of literature. Hegel's influence did not make itself felt in any consistent application of the dialectic method. Nor can we discover in Bělinskii's work unified and distinctly formulated theories regarding the motive forces of historical development. Bělinskii was neither sociological expert nor philosophical historian, although he took frequent occasion to express his views concerning the evolution of Russia. We have learned what he thought about the struggle towards culture and humanitarianism, and I may reiterate here that Peter's personality and Peter's reforms seemed to him a confirmation of his opinion regarding the historical importance of leading individualities. All his efforts were directed towards the intensification of Peter's great work, which Bělinskii regarded as the necessary civilising impulse coming from without.

Bělinskii's influence upon his contemporaries and upon the younger generations was enormous. Down to 1856, during the reaction that followed upon 1848, he could not be mentioned by name, and writers alluded to him only as " the critic of the forties " or " the critic of the Gogol epoch." Bělinskii directed the rising generation into the political and social path, and contrasted the freedom of democracy with the absolutism of theocracy. In this matter, of course, he was not alone; nor was he the first, for he was himself influenced by Bakunin and Herzen; but he had a remarkable understanding of the way in which men's minds could best be stirred despite the pressure of the Nicolaitan censorship. He felt democratically. Even though often enough he uttered complaints against the masses, he had ever before his eyes the reading public and the difficult and responsible mission of the Russian author. His humanitarian teaching was necessarily directed towards readers and not towards illiterates, but he was well aware that in point of character the cultured man may be no higher than the uncultured. I may recall as typical the utterance : " The masses live without thinking, and live meanly ; but to think without living—is that any better ? "

From the very first, alike from friends and from opponents,

Bělinskii's personality received due appreciation. Not infrequently, indeed, such praises were lavished upon the goodness of his heart that the prestige of his head might well suffer in comparison !

Bělinskii became political, social, and philosophic leader of the younger generation. His work, it is true, was that of literary critic, but for him criticism applied, not to books, but to the life which, as he said, was mirrored in literature. Ivan Aksakov relates that during an inspection tour made in 1856 he encountered large numbers of persons intimately acquainted with Bělinskii's *Letter to Gogol*, which many of them knew by heart. Bělinskii touched upon the most important and profoundest problems of his time. Half unconsciously, with the aid of his philosophy of religion, he preached the political and social revolution under the very eyes of Nicholas' censors. Bělinskii's youthful drama is his own life program.

This work could not have direct effects in Bělinskii's own day, for it was not published until eighty years after it had been written, but the thoughts which Bělinskii here conceived for the first time, recurred continuously in his later works, being reproduced with greater precision and in more intimate association with the interests of the day.

Kalinin the hero, son of a serf, loves his lord's daughter. They enter into a free union of hearts, hoping that the approval of the family may subsequently be secured. But the family desires to bestow the girl in marriage upon a prince. Kalinin thereupon arms for defence, has a quarrel with Sof'ja's brother, who apostrophises him contemptuously as " slave." Having killed the brother in this quarrel, Kalinin then kills Sof'ja at her own request, and subsequently makes away with himself, for he has learned that he is Sof'ja's half-brother, and that his suicide will merely put the crown upon the crimes of incest and murder.

Kalinin is thus at war with society and the social order, but his censures are chiefly directed against the all-powerful God who has arranged the world so ill and who has fore-ordained that man should be powerless. In the character of Surskii, Kalinin's friend, Bělinskii delineates the optimist, the believer in divine providence who accepts life and all that it brings, seeing in the world and in life a harmony that is perfect even if it be not fully understood.

This antithesis of the two characters reminds us of Schelling and his three epochs, that of blind destiny and that of mechanical determination by natural law being succeeded and superseded by the stage of providential workings. Kalinin represents the first two stages, Surskii the third stage, wherein the history of the world assumes the aspect of a pre-established harmony. But the newer German philosophy and literature may have acted jointly with the work of Schelling to lead Bělinskii to deal with the problem of freedom and necessity.

However this may be, Bělinskii at nineteen years of age formulated the problem of freedom and responsibility. This is not to say that he solved it, for the problem is one which continued to vex the maturer man until the close of his career.

Dmitri Kalinin is poor as a work of art. It is the program of an immature mind in revolt against the Nicolaitan social order. Bělinskii's Kalinin preaches the right and duty of revolution. If laws conflict with the rights of nature and humanity, with the rights of the understanding, man must disregard the laws. Kalinin rails against the " snakes, crocodiles, and tigers which live on the bones and flesh of their nearest, drinking blood like water ; he introduces us to several types of slave-holders ; he struggles against the bonds of marriage, sanctioned by the church but fundamentally immoral, setting up against marriage the ideal of free love. Nor is Bělinskii content with levelling complaints against society and its official props. In blasphemous pride he calls God to account, for this lying and miserable world is God's work— or is it after all the work of Satan ?

We can understand why this play led the professors to threaten Bělinskii with Siberia, and we can understand, too, how his literary misadventure, in conjunction with these threats, threw the youthful revolutionary into a fever.

Now that we are acquainted with the vicissitudes of Bělinskii's philosophical development we shall be able to understand his continued vacillation between the philosophy of Kalinin and that of Surskii. He first endeavoured to find peace in Schelling, next in Fichte, and subsequently in Hegel, Feuerbach, and the socialists in turn, ever searching, moving ever to and fro between faith and doubt.

Again and again we read in his letters of metaphysical struggles concerning God.

At the time when he clung to reality as to a god he declared (1838) : " I am God's soldier, and I march at His word of command." But in 1840, when he learned of the death of Stankevič, he pondered much over life and death. "To what end," he asks, "are we in the world? We die and rot, men and nations perish, the world itself will perish, Shakespeare and Hegel will be as if they had never been." A year later Bělinskii declares that negation is his god. A year later still he writes to Bakunin : "What is man without God? A cold corpse. Man's life is in God ; he dies and he prospers, he suffers and he rejoices, in God."

We have seen that Bělinskii desires faith, seeks faith. "Without faith," he writes in 1842, "I cannot live." When he found faith in socialism he said : "I can live more easily . . . In my soul there is now that without which I cannot live, the faith that furnishes answers to all questions. But this is not faith merely, nor is it knowledge, but it is religious knowledge and conscious religion."

By the analysis of these and many other of Bělinskii's sayings it might be possible to secure a more precise definition of the concepts faith and religion, but it is enough for our purpose to know that the problem occupied his mind. His demand for " a conscious religion " and for " religious knowledge " is significant, and we learn from his letter to Gogol that in his opinion official religion offers nothing of the kind. In 1846 he had declared that for him the terms God and religion signified darkness, ignorance, chains, and the knout.

In the analysis of Lermontov (1840) he discerns in *The Hero of our own Time* " the lapse of the spirit into tormenting reflection, the disintegration of feeling and self-consciousness." Bělinskii exposed here the secret of his own searching and struggling soul.

For in Bělinskii, also, there dwelt two souls. From the æsthetic outlook he embodied the contrast between romanticism and realism, even though for Bělinskii himself this was a contrast between two utterly divergent outlooks on the universe. Romanticism was for him the inner mystical world of mankind, and by mysticism he practically meant the same thing as religion. The struggle with and concerning romanticism was therefore the struggle with and concerning religion. On one side was the yearning for faith, the faith that can move mountains ; on the other side were reason and negation. " Long live reason and negation ! To the devil with tradition, forms, and ceremonies!" wrote Bělinskii in 1840 to his friend Botkin.

Like significance must be attached to his campaign against the religious slavophils, whom he numbered among the romanticists. There was much that was congenial to him in these opponents. In fighting them he was fighting himself, his own religious past. But, said Bělinskii once, "the man of noble mind does not perish in the light, as bourgeois philosophers hold." We know, too, Bělinskii's utterance concerning strong and creative scepticism.

CHAPTER ELEVEN

THE SYNTHESIS OF WESTERNISM AND SLAVO-PHILISM. APOLLON GRIGOR'EV.

§ 77.

PECULIAR interest attaches to Apollon Aleksandrovič Grigor'ev the critic. His first literary works were produced in the middle of the forties. By the close of the fifties his leading views had already been elaborated. Shortly after 1860 he gave a comprehensive exposition of these, writing now chiefly in the two reviews edited by the brothers Dostoevskii.[1]

Grigor'ev is frequently classed among the "younger" slavophils, but some prefer to consider him a conservative. His outlook was really a modification of slavophilism, and at the same time he attempted a synthesis of slavophil and westernist views.

Dostoevskii spoke of Grigor'ev and his supporters as *počvenniki*. The root of this world is *počva*, signifying soil, ground, foundation. The počvenniki were considered to be established upon the solid basis of the Russian folk, but the double significance of the term počva is reflected in the philosophical foundations of the počvenniks' programme.

By 1861 the contrast between the slavophils and the westernisers had in Grigor'ev's view been transcended. The distinct trends no longer existed, or at any rate lacked justification for existence, now that Puškin had succeeded in effecting the organic synthesis of the two cultural elements. Art, said Grigor'ev, is the instrument of nationality, of the national spirit, whilst the nation is the instrument of mankind,

---

[1] Grigor'ev was born in Moscow in the year 1822, and left Moscow university in 1842. In the southern capital he was exposed to the same influences as his westernist and slavophil friends and contemporaries. He died in 1864.

for mankind exists only in distinct nations. Men of genius are the spokesmen of the nations. The author is a prophet ; he creates out of his thoughts and feelings ; in sorrow doth he bring forth his children. The truly great author invariably speaks a " new word." Puškin was such a genius and prophet of the Russian people. Puškin had had personal experience of the contrasts between Russian and Europeanism, but had transcended these contrasts, and, being a great genius, had created a new and perfectly independent type, a genuinely Russian type which must be counterposed to the European.[1] Grigor'ev considers that full and accurate expression of the Russian folk-spirit is given in the figure of Bělkin and similar characters in Puškin's works—Dubrovskii, for instance, and the captain's daughter. The Russian soul first secured complete expression through Puškin. Pečorin, on the other hand, the central figure of Lermontov's book *The Hero of our own Time*, was an unrussian, an antirussian type, such as Europe,. or rather European romanticism, had forced upon the Russians. The Russian type was the peaceful, good-natured, unassuming man, with his simple healthy mind and sound sentiments. Pečorin, the brilliant, passionate hero, seemed to Grigor'ev an embodiment of the predatory type. But among Lermontov's figures Grigor'ev finds that of Maksim Maksimyč congenial. Puškin's Tatjana, he considered, incorporated at once the positive feminine type and the positive Russian ideal.

It will thus be seen that Grigor'ev does not look upon art as the mirror of life, but as an instrument for the guidance of life, presenting positive ideals in the types it creates. In conformity with this view Grigor'ev assigns a constructive and positive task to literary criticism. Criticism must be " organic," the word being used in much the same sense as that in which Homjakov spoke of the church as an organism, being used as it was employed by Saint-Simon and above all by Carlyle. We trace here, too, an idea of Carlyle, a writer who exercised much influence on Grigor'ev, and even on the Russian's literary style. Grigor'ev elaborates Carlyle's distinction

---

[1] Grigor'ev describes the creative process more or less in the following way. The great writer becomes acquainted with the figures depicted by foreign poets, but he does not take these over to make them his own, for they serve merely to arouse kindred images in his mind. The Byronic types became part of Puškin's mental experience, but these were not the types he gave to the world as his own ; he fought with them, and his own Russian types were the issue of the struggle.

between two historical epochs, the healthy, positive epoch based on faith and imagination, and the retrograde, negative epoch of decadence based on thought and reason. It is true that Grigor'ev opposed romanticism, but his own philosophy was romanticist through and through. He gave emotion the preference over reason ; in the name of mysticism he condemned rationalism ; in common with the romanticists he conceived the ideal of humanity in a nationalist sense. To him, as to the romanticists, art was the leading instrument in the movement of nationality, for unawares he identified art with religion and religious ardour. Grigor'ev's political outlook and his Carlylean hero-worship were likewise romanticist. Since great geniuses are the leaders of mankind, there is no justification for parliamentary democracy or for the revolutionary struggle to secure progress. It was logical that Grigor'ev, holding these views, should oppose the westernisers, and especially that he should oppose the commencing political propaganda.

This organic criticism is, properly speaking, conceived by Grigor'ev as a philosophy of history, or as philosophy in general. He employs it to counteract the " historical " criticism of Bělinskii, whilst he is still more strongly opposed to " theoretical " criticism, using this term to denote the political and utilitarian trend of Černyševskii's school. Grigor'ev ranks Pisarev above Černyševskii and Dobroljubov, but he censures Pisarev for one-sidedness and undue devotion to abstract logic, whereby, says Grigor'ev, Pisarev was led into the error of describing art, nationality, history, science, thought itself, as nonentities.

Despite these differences there are points of contact and agreement. His subsequent analysis of Ostrovskii reminds us in many respects of Dobroljubov, whilst Grigor'ev is at one with Pisarev in his anti-historical outlook. Grigor'ev rejects Hegelianism, historism, and relativism. The human spirit has eternal energies attaching to it as an organism. These energies manifest themselves in thought, science, art, nationality, and history (the omission of religion from the enumeration is characteristic) ; they are not ephemeral results and stages of development ; once more, they are everlasting.

It need hardly be said that Grigor'ev will have nothing to do with the æstheticists and their cult of art for art's sake.

Grigor'ev was obviously right in his insistence upon the point that the thoughtful Russian's great task must be, not merely to take over novelties from Europe, but to elaborate these acquisitions and to build upon the new foundation. Grigor'ev's "organic" criticism was a formulation of this task. The demand had been made before; Bělinskii in his ultimate phase had entered the same path, and had largely anticipated Grigor'ev'; almost all Grigor'ev's ideas may, separately considered, be deduced from Bělinskii; but Grigor'ev's peculiar service was the unified formulation of his fundamental idea, that of the organic.

Grigor'ev attempted with notable discernment to indicate the positively new in Russian literature. The false judgment which made him rank Ostrovskii beside Puškin, and the injustice he displayed towards Gogol, must not induce us to underestimate his own excellence and originality. He gave his approval to some of Turgenev's work (*A Nobleman's Retreat*), and greatly esteemed that of Tolstoi. It was necessary that an attempt should be made to delimit the idea of nationality more precisely. Grigor'ev made such an attempt, and was guided in it by modern ideas, differing here from the slavophils, who built upon the foundations laid by the Greek fathers of the church.

Grigor'ev displayed moderation, too, in his attempts at synthesis. He had more approval for the westernisers than for the slavophils. He was extremely sympathetic towards Čaadaev, and he recognised Bělinskii's merits; but he condemned the extravagances of the westernisers and their negation of all that was Russian. He had full confidence, likewise, in Homjakov and Kiréevskii, though he considered their views extravagant. To the later slavophils, with their petty ideals, he was definitely opposed.

Since he himself had a strong mystical trend, Homjakov's and Kiréevskii's insistence upon the mystical factor was agreeable to him. His philosophy was largely based upon that of Schelling, whose influence was reinforced by Carlyle's. But in the case of his European teachers he effected a synthesis similar to that which he demanded for Russia; Schelling and Carlyle were rationalised by Hegel. He was especially adverse to the realists, and to the nihilists, with their positivist aridity. In this respect Dostoevskii appealed to him, and in co-operation with the latter he made the two reviews edited by the brothers Dostoevskii into an organ of antinihilism.

Grigor'ev's personal life, ill-regulated, romantic, and

brilliant, gave expression to his antipositivist mood and outlook. Considering himself animated by peculiarly genuine Russian sentiments, Russian life seemed to him a synthesis of very remarkable elements. In the drunkard, for instance, he would discover the manifestation of the pure soul, and his judgments were characterised by numerous similar aberrations. He once delineated himself aptly as a " turbulent " humanist—the Russian word *naglyi* has the connotation of impetuosity or brutality. There was a morbid element in Grigor'ev, an element we shall find more fully developed in Dostoevskii. Grigor'ev spoke of " irrational happiness," of the " pride of sorrow," of the " repellent sweetness " of certain spiritual troubles, and so on.

Grigor'ev did not found a school, for he lacked energy and endurance. His thought was aphoristic in character ; his ideas were not sharply or clearly formulated. Grigor'ev had no love for logic-choppers who reason simply for reasoning's sake. In fact his own mysticism was often on extremely bad terms with logic. Nevertheless Grigor'ev moved amid kindred spirits, and through their intermediation exercised enhanced influence. The most notable among his associates was Dostoevskii, who learned much and borrowed much from Grigor'ev. In his whole nature Dostoevskii had much in common with Grigor'ev. In addition to Dostoevskii I may mention Strahov, the editor of Grigor'ev's works.[1]

---

[1] Strahov (1828–1896) was one of the chief contributors to the Dostoevskiis' reviews. He wrote a number of philosophical and literary works (The World as a Whole ; the Fundamental Concepts of Psychology and Physiology ; The Struggle with the West ; Critical Essays on Turgenev and Tolstoi ; etc.), and he translated portions of Kuno Fischer's History of Philosophy and of Lange's History of Materialism. Strahov was a diligent worker, and so amiable was his disposition that only in the form of mechanical compromises could he effect the synthesis demanded by Grigor'ev. Thus it was that Tolstoi became his mentor as well as Danilevskii and Dostoevskii. Of Dostoevskii, Strahov has given us reminiscences.

CHAPTER TWELVE

ALEKSANDR HERZEN. PHILOSOPHICAL AND POLITICAL RADICALISM

§ 78.

EVEN before Bělinskii's weary eyes had closed, Herzen was preparing to carry on the work of literary opposition and revolution. A political thinker, and animated by a strong impulse towards political activity, Herzen could not possibly remain unmolested in the Russia of Nicholas. He was already attracting the attention of the authorities when Uvarov was formulating the official program, and after he had been prosecuted several times he determined to take refuge in Europe. Quitting Russia in 1847, he spent the rest of his life in Europe. Even during the era of comparative freedom under Alexander II, he was unable to return home.

The significance of the emigration and of Herzen's journalistic activities during the reign of Nicholas has already been discussed in connection with our account of the reaction of 1848. Among his collaborators, Herzen had men of the finest intelligence—Ivan Turgenev, Ivan Aksakov for a time, Kavelin. Samarin, etc. He had many sources of trustworthy information regarding the defects of the administration and the government. It may be imagined how the uncensored articles written by and for Herzen would exercise a striking influence in Russia. The circulation of Herzen's publications in Russia was well organised. They were read by young and old, and the Tsar perused every issue of " Kolokol." The effect of the detailed criticism and of the revelations was enhanced by a brilliant style. At first his literary efforts were somewhat weak, but he soon became one of the best if not the best Russian author of the day. His work was characterised by Gallicisms and anomalies which shocked Turgenev, but Turgenev himself recognised how living, ardent, nay scorching, were Herzen's writings. Herzen cultivated a literary form peculiar to himself, producing a species of memoirs wherein the history of his own time was philosophically expounded and criticised. His literary works might have been published under the general title, " The Development of Russia and Europe as I see it." This intimately personal outlook gives a peculiar charm to his narrative of the events of the day. He coined words to suit his ideas, speaking as a materialist of " pure brain " and " brain equality " ; he ventured on audacious neologistic phrases and incisive figures of speech, such as " Petrograndism," the " puritans of demagogy," the " theology of the scourge," " baptised property " (serfs); he was resolute to call a spade a spade, then a bold thing to do in other places besides Russia ; all these characteristics, in conjunction with the emotional strength of his conviction, his use of irony and paradox, the poetry of his language, and the unaffected art with which his sentences were combined to produce an impressive whole, could not fail to attract public attention. On suitable occasions Herzen availed himself of imaginative writings for the conveyance of his ideas, composing a novel entitled *Who is to Blame?* and a number of short stories. These are novels with a purpose ; pros and cons are actively debated ; but the description of the circumstances amid which the characters move and act are admirable, and form notable contributions to the psychological depiction of the time.

Herzen was the most brilliant representative of the progressive generation that flourished under Nicholas. After the collapse at Sevastopol he became the boldest spokesman of the liberal era of Alexander II, and was teacher of the young reformers of the so-called sixties.[1]

---

[1] Aleksandr Ivanovič Herzen was born in Moscow on March 25, 1812. His father, Jakovlev, was a wealthy member of the old aristocracy. Herzen was an illegitimate child, the mother being a German girl who had accompanied Jakovlev on his return from Stuttgart in 1811. Jakovlev and his brothers, men of high standing, lived in a way characteristic of the half-cultured Russians who were survivals from the days of Catherine. Herzen's father is said to have had as tutor a relative of Voltaire, but despite his French culture his domestic ways were thoroughly Asiatic. It is true that he gave his love child the name of " Herzen," but frequently enough he would make the boy's illegitimacy the occasion for displaying inhuman contempt towards mother and child. In early youth Herzen learned the open secret of his origin, and this was a source of coolness and even bitterness in his relations with his father. His experience of the way in which the serfs were treated, served further to alienate him, and

An incomplete edition of Herzen's works has been published in Geneva in the Russian tongue. They cannot even yet [1913] be freely published in Russia. The first Russian edition appeared in St. Petersburg in 1905, but there had been many excisions.

In philosophical matters Herzen, like his friends in Moscow, was nourished on Hegel and Feuerbach. Bělinskii played the part of John the Baptist to Herzen, and Herzen provided the organic continuation of Bělinskii's work. Just as Hegel and the Hegelian left attacked romanticism from the positivist

induced a hostile mood towards the aristocracy. He had a number of French teachers whose work of tuition was very ill performed, and in his father's library he made early acquaintance with the writings of Voltaire and other French authors (Beaumarchais, le Mariage de Figaro !). The French revolution and the republic became the boy's ideals. At the age of thirteen he entered into a life-and-death alliance with Ogarev, whilst the decabrists and above all Pestel were canonized by the boys. It is true that the decabrist program as they conceived it smacked rather of Schiller's Don Carlos than of historical reality. Throughout life Schiller was one of Herzen's favourite authors. His religious education exercised a notable influence on Herzen. His mother brought him up in the spirit of her own Lutheran faith, but simultaneously the lad practised the ritual of the Orthodox church ; to the grown man the gospels remained a holy book. French and German influences were reinforced by those of Russian literature, by the reading of Puškin, Rylčev, etc. A cousin somewhat older than himself, the legitimate son of one of his uncles, led him to conceive profound and enduring respect for chemistry and the natural sciences. At the university Herzen studied physics and mathematics, and on graduating in 1833 presented a thesis on Copernicus. Pavlov initiated the university student into the mysteries of Schelling and Oken ; but more important to Herzen than the university was the circle of friends among whom his philosophical and political development proceeded during the thirties and forties. In 1834 he was imprisoned in connection with the doings of this circle, and in 1835 was sent to Viatka. While in prison and at Viatka, Herzen became affected with an intense religious and artistic mysticism, reading Eckartshausen, Swedenborg, and the work of occultist writers like Eschenmayer ; a few years earlier he had studied the writings of Čaadaev, with whom he was personally acquainted. In 1838 he was transferred from Viatka to Vladimir on the river Klyazma, where he was in military service, contracting here a romantic marriage with Natalia Aleksandrovna Zahar'ina, whom he had loved for several years. In 1839 he returned to Moscow, and in 1840 removed to St. Petersburg. At this time for a brief period he was estranged from Bělinskii. The years 1841 and 1842 were spent in Novgorod, and from thence till 1847 he lived in Moscow. To this epoch belong his study of Hegel and Feuerbach, his friendship with the slavophils, his subsequent detachment from them (1845), and his breach with the liberals (with Granovskii in 1846). He turned to German materialism (Vogt), and to French and English positivism (Comte, Littré and Mill). Herzen was now much occupied with the ideas of the French socialists, Saint-Simon, Fourier, Louis Blanc, Considérant, and Proudhon ; he was interested, too, in the philosophers of history, Vico, Herder, Michelet, etc. ; and it need hardly be said that he studied such political writers as Montesquieu and Bentham. Leopardi and Byron became his favourite poets. His father died in 1846, leaving him a considerable fortune, amounting to half a million roubles. He quitted Russia standpoint, so was Herzen's whole outlook an attack on romanticism, and he had to wage war against the romanticism rooted in his own nature. Here, again, he resembled Bĕlinskii. Basing himself upon Feuerbach, he endeavoured to eradicate the inborn tendency to myth and mysticism, calling positivism and materialism to his aid, appealing to Comte as well as to Feuerbach, and to Vogt as well as to Comte.

Herzen came to Europe and to Paris at the very time when the February revolution was in its inception. In boyhood he

in January 1847. After spending some time in Paris, Italy, and elsewhere, he settled in London in 1852, remaining there till 1867. His last years were spent in Paris, Geneva, Nice, and elsewhere. He died in Paris on January 21, 1870. In Europe he made the personal acquaintance of a large number of influential persons, and while in London was an associate of such refugees as Mazzini and Garibaldi. His first notable literary work, which succeeded a few casual essays, was the novel, Who is to Blame? which appeared in 1847. From 1850 onwards there issued his characteristic essays (From the Other Shore, 1850, etc.). By this time his pseudonym Iskander was well known in Russia. The review "Poljarnaja Zvĕzda" (1855–1862) and the periodical "Kolokol" (1857–1867, and in French from 1868) gained world-wide renown. In addition to his contributions to periodical literature, Herzen issued a number of vigorous and widely read works (Memoirs of Catherine II, The Writings of the Raskolniki, etc.). In 1853 he founded The Free Russian Press in London. A few additional details regarding his life may be given. His need for friendship was characteristic. His boy friendship with Ogarev was a refuge from the cold and gloomy life of his home, and in manhood he gained many friends in Russia and in Europe. The calf love of the thirteen-year-old lad for the woman who afterwards married Herzen's friend Vadim Passek can in part be accounted for by this general need for friendship ; and his love for Natalia is to some extent assignable to the same cause. This love notwithstanding, while in Viatka he had with the wife of an official a liaison of which he speedily wearied ; in Novgorod his relations with his wife were disturbed by a passion he conceived for a servant girl. Later (1850) his wife's intimacy with Herwegh was a terrible blow to him. Natalia left husband and children, but returned to Herzen a year later. A few months after this, his mother and two of his children perished in a shipwreck. Natalia died on May 2, 1852. The following are Herzen's principal writings : From the Other Shore, 1850 ; Letters from Italy and France, 1850 ; Social Conditions in Russia, 1854 ; A Russian's Memoirs, 4 vols., 1855–6 ; Who is to Blame? 1851 ; Duty above All, 1857. In French : De l'autre rive, 1851 ; Du développement des idées révolutionnaires, en Russie, 1851 ; La conspiration russe de 1825, suivie d'une lettre sur l'émancipation des paysans en Russie, 1858 ; La France ou l'Angleterre ? Variations russe sur le thème de l'attentat du 14 janvier 1858, 1858 ; Le peuple russe et le socialisme. Lettre à M. Michelet, 1858 ; Les mémoires, three volumes, 1860–62 ; Camicia rossa, Garibaldi à Londres, 1865 ; Lettre addressée à l'empereur de Russie, 1866 ; La Mazourka, un article du Kolokol, dédié avec profonde sympathie et respect à Edgar Quinet, 1869 ; Lettres sur la France et l'Italie, 1871 ; Nouvelle phase de la littérature russe, 1868. German : K. Kavelins und I. Turgenev's sozialpolitsche Briefwechsel mit Herzen. Mit Beilagen und Erläuterungen von Professor M. Dragomanov, 1894 (Schiemann's Bibliothek russischer Denkwürdigkeiten, iv.).

had been an enthusiast for the revolution and the republic, and his study of the French socialists had strengthened in the man the imaginative longings of the child. Animated by a positively mystical faith in the revolution and in human progress, he hastened to the promised land of revolutions. In France during 1848 he was in intimate spiritual sympathy with the forward movement, but his experience of this revolution and of the rapidly ensuing reaction and restoration taught him that the revolution is destroyed, not by the reaction, but by itself. As a result he lost faith in revolution.

The first of his works to be issued in Europe (*From the Other Shore*, 1850) is an analysis of this sobering from the mysticism of revolution. For the Russian edition of this work he wrote the *Epilogue to 1849*, which opens with the words : " A curse upon thee, year of blood and madness, year of victorious stupidity, brutality, and dullness. A curse upon thee ! "

The old social order was based upon religious illusion. Since religion and the church are one with politics and the state, it seemed to Herzen that the first awakening of mankind from the religious dream of the Catholic and feudal (aristocratic) middle ages was effected in the revolution which introduced Protestantism and philosophy and which terminated for the time being in the great revolution of the eighteenth century. This revolution was led by a minority ; the masses were unmoved by it. The minority repudiated its principles as soon as it attained to power ; even Robespierre had Anacharsis Cloots guillotined for professing a religion different from his own. The revolution had fallen, and its fate was inevitable because its ideals were the ideals of a minority. All these ideals, all these enthusiasms and convictions, were unavailing, for faith in the justice of one's ideals did not suffice ; brain equality was no less essential, and this did not exist. Hence the heroes of freedom and the leading revolutionaries were not the heirs of the revolution, and its fruits were harvested by the bourgeoisie. But the bourgeoisie contented itself with half-measures in religion and politics, with Protestantism and liberalism. Liberalism is the religion of the bourgeois, of the trader, of the man without individuality, of the intermediator between the possessor and the non-possessor. An instrument, a means to an end—such is the bourgeois.

The bourgeois fondness for half-measures is well suited by

English parliamentarism, this gigantic treadmill which seems specially created to demonstrate the internal arrest and marasmus of bourgeois liberalism, whilst French republican formalism is of identical character. A bourgeois republic is worth just as much or just as little as a monarchy. The very men, the very bourgeois, who brought about the great revolution, hastened thereafter to set Napoleon and then the kings upon the throne. After the July revolution came Louis Philippe. After the February revolution, as early as June, and under the republican regime, the workers were shot down by Cavaignac (Herzen and Turgenev were confined to their dwellings by the police, and listened to the rattle of the musketry ; these writers gave brilliant descriptions of the June days). The masquerade terminated with the accession of Napoleon III.

What is the significance of these chronic revolutions and restorations ? Hitherto the revolutions have been mere Don Quixotisms, the republics nothing but forms of the old regime, which must be destroyed from its foundations if the revolution is to have any real meaning. The sentiments of the European masses remain monarchical and Christian, and, pending the destruction of authoritarianism and religion, political scene-shifting is devoid of significance. A true revolution to-day must be socialist, atheist, and materialist. While the masses, while the revolutionaries themselves, are still Christian believers, bourgeois revolts terminate in cæsarism. The struggle of the non-possessors with the possessors, communism, will destroy cæsarism, but therewith will destroy civilisation, to which the masses owe nothing but tears, misery, ignorance, and debasement. Socialism will conquer, but will do so in utterly foolish forms. In the struggle between the revolution and " order," Europe will be transformed until it comes to resemble Bohemia after the Hussite wars ; civilisation will take flight to England, or more probably to America, where the new social order is already flourishing. But the new order will be driven out by a yet newer order, the minority will once again revolt —the flux and reflux of history. " Thus will revolutions break forth anew, thus again will blood flow in streams. And the upshot ? Who can tell ! But come what may it is enough that in this flaming up of folly, hatred, revenge, and strife, there will perish the world which oppresses the men of the new time, which restricts their lives, which forbids the realisation of the future. Long live chaos, therefore, long live destruction! Vive la mort! Make way for the future. We are the executioners of the past!"

Again: "Our historic mission, our peculiar task, is that through our disillusionment and our sufferings we attain to repose and humility in face of the truth, and are enabled to preserve future generations from like sorrows. Through our work mankind will be sobered; we are the crapulence, we are the birth pangs of humanity. Should the end of the birthpangs be fortunate, all will be well; but we must not forget that in the process child or mother may succumb; perhaps both may perish—and history with its Mormonism will begin a new pregnancy. . . . E sempre bene!" In a word, the meaning of life and history is that life and history have no meaning.

The French revolution and German science are the Pillars of Hercules of Europe. The French revolution proclaimed freedom of thought and life, but failed to recognise that this freedom was irreconcilable with the Catholic organisation of Europe (Herzen frequently employs the word Catholic as a synonym of Christian, regarding Protestantism and liberalism as mere phases of Catholicism). German science is a speculative religion, is nothing more than the latest phase of Catholicism—Rousseau and Hegel were Christians; Robespierre and Saint-Just were monarchists.

The republic of the National Convention was a pentarchical absolutism and at the same time a church with civil dogmas; the people remained "laymen," subject to guidance.

But the world of custom, ceremonial, and authority, trembles at the dread name of liberty, and the old body cannot survive with this poison in its veins. Hence, after the irrational epoch of emperordom, people awakened to a sense of the national danger, and all profound thinkers awaited a cataclysm—Chateaubriand, Lamennais (in his first phase), de Maistre, Hegel, and Niebuhr. At last came two giants to bring this historic epoch to a splendid close: Goethe and Byron. Byron was "the poet of doubt and indignation, at once confessor, executioner, and victim."

Byronic pride, the mood of Lucifer in *Cain*, this is the only way to salvation. Even Goethe's *Faust* remains a play for children; his Mephistopheles is still content with vacillation; the tragedy, the temporary despair, end in salvation, after the German manner sub specie æternitatis. The French help themselves through their troubles with political chatter. Byron, the " terrible titan," had the courage to express his contempt without circumlocution, to say without circumlocution that there was no issue. He gives us no brilliant phrases about negation; he does not sport with unbelief; he does not delude himself with sensuality; he does not attempt to job us off with simple girls, wine, and brilliants; unemotionally he depicts for us murder and crime. This disillusioned certainty can alone bring peace. Herzen refers to his own example, tells us how he has learned to endure the death of the being who meant everything to him. " The mists seemed to close in around me, I passed through a period of savage and dull despair but I did not attempt to console myself with false hopes. Not for a moment did I endeavour to stifle my sorrow with the stultifying idea of reunion beyond the grave." To Kavelin, in like manner, when Kavelin's son died, Herzen recommended work and duty as sole consolations.

The task of the few, of the righteous men in Sodom and Gomorrah, those who are strong of spirit though weak of hand, remains the preaching of the tidings of death as joyful tidings of approaching deliverance. To the objection that this gospel of the death and destruction of civilisation may deprive us of all delight in action, Herzen makes answer that to understand is itself to act, to realise.

The work on which Herzen thus buries and destroys his revolutionary illusions is dedicated to his son, then fifteen years of age. " I do not wish to delude you; I desire that you should know the truth as I know it; this truth shall be yours as a birthright, so that you need not discover it through painful errors, through murderous disillusionments. . . . Seek no unriddlings in this book; you will not find them; they are not for the men of our time. What is unriddled is done with, but the coming transformation is only in its inception. Not our task to build, but to destroy; we promise no new revelation, but we destroy the ancient lies. The man of to-day, an unhappy pontifex maximus, does no more than build the bridge, which will be crossed by an unknown in the unknown future. You, perhaps, will catch a glimpse of that unknown. . . . Do not stay on the old shore. . . . It is better to perish than to remain safe in the madhouse of reaction. The religion of the coming social reconstruction is the only religion I bequeath you. In that religion there is no paradise, no recompense, outside the individual consciousness, the personal conscience. When the right hour comes make your way homeward to our own people to preach to them this gospel ; there men once liked to hear me and perchance will recall my name. . . .

" My blessings upon you in the name of human reason, personal liberty, and brotherly love."

§ 79.

I DO not know if I shall have succeeded in giving the reader an impression of Herzen's literary art. As far as possible I have employed his own words and have followed his expositions uninterruptedly.

In his analysis of religious illusion we have a charming synthesis of the views of those two philosophers with whom Herzen was best acquainted, Comte and Feuerbach, but there is intermingled here some of Stirner's pitilessly logical desecration. Comte is responsible for Herzen's identification of Christianity with Catholicism, for his depreciation of Protestantism as the negation of Catholicism, for his estimate of metaphysics, and for his insistence on the political character of Catholicism. Herzen's setting of the problem, however, is derivable rather from Proudhon, and in part from Saint-Simon. Moreover it was by Čaadaev that Herzen was awakened to the significance of Catholicism. Herzen's first literary efforts, *A Young Man's Memoirs* and *Further Memoirs of a Young Man*, written in 1840 and 1841, dealt with Čaadaev's work, and the two writers were on terms of friendship. Herzen's historico-philosophical estimate of civilisation betrays the influence of Rousseau and the French socialists. His description of history as moving in a circle recalls the terminology of Vico, whose views were modified, however, for Herzen by the influence of Carlyle. Herzen owed his inexorable materialism to Vogt, with whom he was personally acquainted, and we recall in this connection the breach with Granovskii owing to Herzen's disbelief in personal immortality. His mood was at times influenced by Schopenhauer and Voltaire, and we have reminiscences of Goethe's Mephistopheles. His views on practical conduct were suggested by Byron's Lucifer.

Herzen has been accused of ecclecticism, but the reproach

is not entirely deserved. He was acquainted with European thinkers ; he lived in Europe and derived his culture from Europe ; but he adopted only what was congenial to him, and from the diverse elements that have been enumerated he constructed a whole that was expressive of his own individuality. He displayed the energy of organic synthesis.

Some of the European cultural elements by which he was influenced were operative in Russian elaborations. We trace in his mind the influence of Bělinskii, Homjakov, Kirěevskii, Čaadaev, Bakunin, and above all Černyševskii ; he read Puškin and Gogol as well as Goethe and Byron.

There is no occasion to undertake a detailed exposition of the points in which Herzen agrees with his predecessors, teachers, and friends, or to trace the derivation of his views from theirs. Nor need I consider further how far Herzen modified his opinions in the year 1848. A close study will convince us that he carried Feuerbach's thought to its logical conclusion, moving in the direction of Stirner ; but nevertheless Herzen's mood differed greatly from Stirner's. For Herzen, positivist disillusionment destroyed, not the religious illusion alone, but also the political illusion, the illusion of revolution.[1]

Herzen's philosophy of religion and philosophy of history are of interest to us. First of all it must be pointed out that Herzen, like Bělinskii (and like Feuerbach, Comte, and Hume), confused religion with mythology. Moreover, Herzen failed to distinguish clearly between religion and the church, between religion and ecclesiastical religion.[2]

---

[1] A closer comparison between Herzen and Feuerbach is desirable, at least as concerns the attitude of the two thinkers towards the revolution of 1848. Feuerbach analysed the personalities of the leading actors of this year, and considered that they failed to rise to the level of his philosophical demands. " In thought he deferred the revolution to later times, abandoning it as far as his own was concerned." (Grün, Feuerbach, vol i. p. 331). Feuerbach himself says (Grün, vol. ii. p. 329), that whereas emotionally he is an unconditional republican, intellectually his republican views are subject to limitations ; he is for the republic only when time and place are favourable, when men in general have attained a standpoint suitable to this form of political constitution. Herzen's estimate of America is to be found in Feuerbach and so is his valuation of monarchy. Herzen's rejection of atheism as negation, shortly to be discussed in the text, is pure Feuerbach.

[2] I append examples of his confusion of religion with myth. Herzen employs the most diversified words to express this view. Frequently he speaks of " religious mania." In his Aphorismata, compiled in 1867 for the circle of his philosophic friends (Schiff, Vogt, etc.), we are told that history is " historical irrationalism " ; religion is variously jumbled together with the ideas of fantasy,

Christianity to him, like all religion and all mythology, is from the ethical standpoint a system of passivity, and he speaks of it as " the apotheosis of death." He writes : " Sub specie æternitatis death has no meaning, but from this outlook there is no meaning in anything else." Thus does Herzen characterise the Christian renunciation of the world. We may assume that when Herzen adduced this argument against Christianity (1853), he was thinking chiefly of the Orthodoxy of his native land. This is manifest in his judgment of Catholicism, which he contrasts with Orthodoxy as capable of further development. His judgment of Orthodoxy and Byzantinism is most unfavourable ; they represent for him a lower form of Christianity ; the characteristics of Byzantine art are to him a proof of this thesis. In 1843 he spoke of Orthodoxy as in a condition of absolute arrest. Nevertheless in the weakness of Orthodoxy, as in the weakness of Russia in general, Herzen discovers a great negative advantage, and this is that the Russian church has acquired no influence on life, whereas the life of Europe has been permeated by Catholicism. For Herzen, therefore, Catholicism is Christianity par excellence, whilst Orthodoxy is no more than " an evil possibility." Orthodoxy and its lack of influence have so far been good for Russia in that Russia as yet has done nothing, and therefore must and can do all the more in the coming time.

As regards Orthodoxy, Herzen makes an honourable exception in the case of the old believers. He regards them as constituting the most energetic and healthiest element of the nation. We owe to them the preservation of the national ideal, of the folk-spirit, of national tradition, national manners and customs.

When Herzen refers to Čaadaev and his Catholicising tendency, he tells us that Catholicism, when contrasted with Russian Orthodoxy, possesses many excellent qualities which impress the Russian mind favourably, and which therefore have led many others besides Čaadaev towards Catholicism. In Herzen's view, the positive definiteness of Catholicism gives it the advantage over the comparatively negative Orthodoxy.

It is obvious that Herzen must himself be numbered among

mythical fables, faith, falsehood, the Bible, the Apocalypse, mysticism, and illusion ; history, as " consecrated irrationalism," is presented as a pathological or phantasmagorial religious condition. Logic and mathematics are contrasted, as anti-social, with this socially unifying condition—and so on.

those who are impressed by Catholicism, and that this is why
he adopted the Catholic view concerning the negativity of
Protestantism, a view expressed by Comte and also by de
Maistre. Herzen is too ready to identify Protestantism with
German science and philosophy and with liberalism. Like
Comte, he makes no distinction between theology and religion.

§ 80.

IN boyhood Herzen was already a Voltairian, but Voltaire
did not preserve him from romanticism and mysticism.
Nevertheless Herzen moved on speedily and with comparative
ease from mysticism to Hegelianism and the Hegelian left.
After he had become intimately acquainted with French and
English positivism it was his persistent endeavour to follow
the positivist trail, but he found more difficulty in doing so
than he was himself perhaps aware.

Herzen's own characterisation of his transition from
romanticism and mysticism to positive science is that from
the first, as mystic, he was a mystic of science, meaning to
imply that, whilst the object of his belief had been transformed,
there had been no change in the belief itself—no such change
as that with which he reproaches the revolutionaries and the
bourgeoisie. He assigns to this phase the entire period of
his " mystical " belief in the revolution. Herzen then believed
in mankind, in socialist utopias, and so on. But, he asked
himself, Is not such a belief ridiculous and stupid, if it be
ridiculous and stupid to believe in God and in the kingdom
of heaven ?

To Herzen, positivism, scientific sobriety, seem always to
have come as the " bitter " fruits of philosophical struggle,
to have been felt as " a heavy cross." In the first years of
his Feuerbachian period (1843), he writes of the " dreadful
vampire," of the " coldness " of positive science, and uses
many similar expressions which are employed also by German
and French romanticists, and indeed by the founder of positivism himself. Herzen knew that positivism must be gained
through struggle ; he knew that the vigorous thinker must,
as Jesus phrased it, lose his soul in order to find it ; he must
fight through the stages of scepticism (" moral suicide ") and
of dull, purely negative atheism. Amid all his strivings for
positivism the wish frequently recurs, If I could only pray !

And he had actual experience of yielding to this desire. In the year 1839 he, his wife, and his friend Ogarev prayed together from joy and thankfulness on account of the friendship between the two families. Ogarev, in his religious ecstasy, then craved for martyrdom.

The reaction following 1848 brought disillusionment to Herzen. He desired at length to be a consistent positivist, but the unpositivist moods recurred none the less, they were a " curse" with which he was frequently afflicted. I have quoted the strongly-worded passage concerning the stultifying idea of immortality, this dating from the year 1852 ; but in no long time thereafter milder utterances were to be found in Herzen's writings. In 1855, for example, he refers to the death of a friend, Worzel, the Polish refugee. To the last Worzel remained the " old idealist " ; he continued to believe in the realisation of his utopias. Herzen never found courage to expound to Worzel his own convictions in all their nakedness. Mazzini closed Worzel's eyes : " Worzel needed prayers for the dying, not truth."

It is true that Herzen formulates rules at times to effect the pitiless awakening from mysticism, but in 1855 he confesses that in his despair he has been saved by his children, by some of his friends, and by his work (the writing a description of his personal development). Herzen declares that, speaking generally, despite all disillusionment, he has continued to cling to " the religion of individuality, to the belief in two or three human beings, to confidence in himself and in the human will."

Above all, however, he soon finds a faith in Russia. " Belief in Russia saved me on the brink of moral destruction," he writes in 1854 ; " for this faith, for this recovery of health, I have to thank my country. I do not know if I shall ever see Russia again, but my love for Russia will endure until I die." In 1857 he formulates his programme of future work as follows : " Work, active work, on behalf of the Russian people, which has laboured enough on our behalf ! "

Is that the mental atmosphere of positivism ; is that the critical intelligence of positivism ?

If Herzen thus fails to attain to Vogt's scientific positivism, he recognises the failure, he realises that this sobriety of disillusionment is beyond his powers ; he is too fond, he tells us, of " the poesy of tragical thrills, and of morbid emotions, which we love as we love all that quickens and stings us." Herzen frequently declares that the Russian is melancholy, sceptical, and ironical; he leaves the question undecided whether these qualities are congenital or acquired. In his view the antithesis of faith is not knowledge but doubt, and he admits that he recurs ever to the mood of doubt, Byronic doubt, for Byron was "the poet of doubt and discontent." He is aware that he is here treading in the footsteps of Hume instead of in those of Comte, for the definite aim of the latter's positivism was to effect the overthrow of Hume's scepticism.[1] For Herzen the pain of disillusionment is keen, the pain of the disenchantment that follows the cure of his "religious mania"; it is therefore impossible for him to be a consistent and tranquil positivist.[2]

Herzen, like Bělinskii, is constrained to believe; his scepticism is not chronic, and the mood of the Byronic Lucifer is not persistent. Herzen has an intense craving for love and friendship, and his experiences in this domain temper with gentle melancholy his moods of contemptuous pride and biting irony. More than once during the tragic happenings of a life rich in personal experience, Herzen found relief in tears. At such times positive science seemed inadequate. Yet he had faith in science, and found consolation in the acquirements of science. He sent his friends a newspaper cutting containing a report of the despatch of the first cablegram from New York to London as proof that science alone has absolute values in life; but this, after all, was but a passing mood, and other sentiments were usually predominant.

From the outlook thus sketched it was inevitable that Herzen should come to terms with the nihilist movement now maturing in Russia. Like Herzen, and taught by Herzen, the nihilists consistently opposed materialism to romanticism and mysticism. This coming to terms was promoted, not merely by the literary activities of Černyševskii and his followers, but also by the direct polemic against Herzen,

[1] For Herzen there was, speaking generally, no scepticism in the eighteenth century, but conversely intense faith; the proclamation of scepticism came with the proclamation of the republic. Diderot and England constitute exceptions. England had long been the home of scepticism. Byron walked consistently along the path trodden by Shakespeare, Hobbes, and Hume.

[2] The Russian term for disillusionment, razočarovanie, signifies literally disenchantment, for čarovat' is to charm, to bewitch.

and by the discussion which followed Turgenev's analysis of nihilism in *Fathers and Children*, a novel published in 1861.

In 1867 A. A. Serno-Solov'evič, belonging to that younger generation which had already turned away from Herzen, brother of N. A. Serno-Solov'evič who was banished to Siberia and killed on the way to the place of exile, published a caustic pamphlet against Herzen.[1] The pamphlet was sent by Herzen to his friend Bakunin as corpus delicti for an attack upon nihilism. Bakunin rejoined with a defence. Thereupon, in 1869, Herzen finally accommodated himself to the Bazarov type.

Herzen sees in nihilism " a sublime manifestation of Russian development "; he interprets nihilism in the sense of his positivist " disillusionment "; but he attains in the end to very different conclusions, for he modifies the idea of disillusionment.

" Nihilism," he writes, " is logic without restriction, science without dogmas, the unconditional acceptance of experience, the unresisting acceptance of consequences, whatever their kind, if these are the fruit of observation and are dictated by the reason. Nihilism does not reduce *something* to *nothing*, but discerns that *nothing* was taken for *something* under the influence of an optical illusion, and that every certainty, however much it be opposed by fantastic imaginings, is healthier than these imaginings, and must be accepted in their place." Nihilism, protests Herzen, does not transform facts and ideas into nothing; it is not barren scepticism, nor yet arrogant and despairing passivity (for in this sense Turgenev and his favourite Schopenhauer might be regarded as " the greatest of nihilists "); it is the realistic criticism of Old Russia, such as we find in Gogol's *Dead Souls* and in the works of Bělinskii. " But nihilism has not brought new foundations or new principles."

Herzen refuses to accept Pisarev's interpretation of Bazarov. He complains that Bazarov leaves nothing in repose, and contemplates everything in Russia from above, complaining in especial that Bazarov failed to understand the decabrists and their significance.

" Science would bring salvation to Bazarov; he would

---

[1] *Russian Affairs*, a Reply to Herzen's article, Order Reigns, in No. 233 of "Kolokol." A German translation of this pamphlet was issued by L. Borkheim in 1871.

cease to look down upon people from above in profound and unconcealed contempt. Science, even more than the New Testament, teaches us humility. Science cannot look down on anything from above, for to science this expression " from above " has no meaning. Science knows nothing of contempt, does not lie to secure an end, nor conceal anything through caprice. Science faces facts, as investigator and often as physician, but never as executioner, never with hostility and irony. Science (there is no reason why I should hide words in the depths of my soul), science is love, as Spinoza says of thought and knowledge.

Byron's Lucifer and irony are definitively dethroned ; their place is taken by love, by that humanity which Herzen adduces as characteristic of Bělinskii and his Russian friends and opponents. Despite all the " fanaticism of conviction," this Russian humanity is on occasions gentle and yielding. At any rate Herzen finds peculiar " hesitations " in himself. In 1863, for example, he made concessions to Bakunin, in defiance of his own convictions.[1]

In the same year in which he makes a confession of faith in the nihilism of love, he comes to terms with Bakunin, and declares : " To say, Do not believe ! is no less dictatorial and in truth no less foolish than to say, Believe ! "

Herzen attains to the idea of duty as well as to the idea of love.

In his first philosophical essays Herzen expresses his hostility to Buddhism and to dilettantism in science. Pure philosophical theory without bearings on life has for him neither value nor meaning. " Man," he says, " does not live by logic alone ; man has his work to do in the social-historical morally free and positively active world. Man does not merely possess capacity to formulate ideas of renunciation, but he possesses also will, which may be termed the positive, the creative understanding." This formulation, derived from German idealism, and published in 1843, frequently recurs in Herzen's writings. (Homjakov's identification of will and understanding dates from 1859, and is derived from the same source.)

The problem of duty, the question why the individual ought to act in one way rather than in another, why he decides

---

[1] In the essay of 1866, Superfluous Persons and Spiteful Persons, the superfluous persons (Oněgin, Pečorin) are defended against the realists. The essay is by some regarded as a polemic against Černyševskii.

in this way or in that and feels himself morally bound so to decide, Herzen attempts to solve by saying that " the development of science, its present state, compels us to accept certain truths, regardless of our desires." This solution was furnished by Herzen in 1845 in the discussion with Granovskii to which reference has previously been made. To the objection that this duty is relative merely, and appears in the end to be not a duty at all but a historical problem, Herzen makes answer that such truths cease to be a historical problem, and become " simple and irrefutable facts of consciousness." When Herzen goes on to compare these " facts " with the theorems of Euclid we must admit that from the epistemological outlook the comparison is unfortunate, but the important point to note is his insistence upon the obligatory character of certain truths. He continually recurs to this view. We have seen that in his essay on Turgenev's Bazarov he maintains the universally obligatory character of those truths which come as an absolute demand of the rigidly scientific understanding. " Barren scepticism," irony, the mood of the Byronic Lucifer, are thus decisively rejected.

§ 81.

IN the Byronic mood following the experiences of 1848 Herzen abandoned himself to contempt for his fellows, to the pride of Lucifer in *Cain*. His mood, indeed, was not one of contempt merely, but positively criminal, nay murderous. Herzen, like Bělinskii and Bakunin before him, was led to the problem of crime by way of idealism.

Faced like Bakunin and Bělinskii with the problem of subjectivism versus objectivism, he decided in favour of a harmonious combination of the two. The evolution of German philosophy, of whose principles he gave an account, strengthened his inclination towards this solution. The work in which it was presented, entitled *Letters Concerning the Study of Nature*, was the most detailed of Herzen's philosophical writings, and exercised a formative influence upon the development of Russian philosophy. It was completed in 1865. With Feuerbach, Herzen decided on metaphysical grounds in favour of positivism and materialism, and advocated the bridging over of the crude contrast between subjectivism and objectivism. In Hegel (not in Schelling, not even in Fichte, not in Kant)

Herzen discovered the last word in German philosophy, and for him this was the last word of philosophy in general, for Herzen prized German philosophy as the non plus ultra of the new thought. Herzen could not conceive of any progress to be made by philosophy beyond Hegel, and he declared that the Hegelian left, including Feuerbach, had produced nothing really new, but had merely brought to light what existed already in Hegel in an undeveloped state.

The history of German philosophy from Kant by way of Fichte to Schelling was compared by Herzen (who in this followed Edgar Quinet) with the political development which is typified in the corresponding names of Mirabeau, Robespierre, and Napoleon. Hegel, he said, was the first to discover the true standpoint, with his abolition of the dualism of objectivism and subjectivism. Herzen passed the same judgment as Bĕlinskii and Bakunin upon extremist, one-sidedly epistemological and metaphysical subjectivism (Robespierre). It contained an element of intolerable impudence ; it was arrogant and ruthless in its criticism ; owing to its one-sidedness it could just as little attain to truth as the opposed doctrine, one-sided objectivism (Napoleon)—or as Herzen, following the terminology of the German schools, preferred to call it, one-sided empiricism. Herzen's formula was that empiricism must combine with rationalism.

From the ethical outlook, too, Herzen rejected extreme subjectivism and individualism as egoism. When he first passed under the influence of Feuerbach, he employed the latter's terminology, contrasting mankind with the tu, contrasting the heart as individual with the general, contrasting the individual with the species, and allotting equal rights to both. In *Who is to Blame ?* the individual was contrasted with the family. After Herzen became acquainted with the work of Stirner, individualism was more definitely conceived by him as egoism. Man, he said, is endowed both with natural egoism or individualism and with sociability or the social instinct— this is the best translation of the term employed somewhat vaguely by Herzen, *obščestvennost'*. Not infrequently he uses the word altruism, which he takes from the French. Often enough these two natural qualities of mankind are referred to ; it is recognised that both have their place ; and sometimes egoism is expressly defended. " The Slav," he says " is less egoist than any others." Why, asks Herzen, should egoism, self-will (*svoevolie*) be subordinated to " others-will " (*čyževolie*) ? The individual, the personality, is " the climax of the historic world," is " the living and conscious instrument of his age "—at least this is true of the man of genius. Herzen agrees with Bělinskii that such persons are the instruments of the nation and of mankind. Revolutions, in so far as Herzen approves them, have not been begun and carried through by a class, and least of all by the bourgeoisie ; they have been the work of free men : of such men as Ulrich von Hutten, the knight ; Voltaire, the aristocrat ; Rousseau, the watchmaker's son ; Schiller, the regimental surgeon ; Goethe, the descendant of craftsmen—these were free men belonging to no class in particular, and the bourgeoisie as a class merely reaped the harvest of their labours.

But side by side with this extreme individualism we continually encounter Feuerbachian formulas. In *From the Other Shore*, for example, we read that there is no antagonism between ego and tu ; and Herzen warns us that despite the sacrosanctity of individuality we must not shiver society into atoms. From this standpoint there is no logical place for Byronic crime, either metaphysically or ethically.

What did he understand by Byronic crime and murder at the time when he was invoking curses on revolution ? Bělinskii makes his Kalinin commit murder, but the murderer kills himself too ; it is certain that Herzen had no desire for such a solution, while Bělinskii got the better of his own hero. The Byronic mood and a deliberate decision to murder are something different from the murder done by Kalinin, who was driven by circumstances to unpremeditated deeds.

Herzen was faced by the problem of revolution and was forced into a decision. Europe set Russia an example in revolutions ; the thought of the decabrists was sacred to Herzen, and this is why, in his revolutionary enthusiasm, he hastened so hopefully to Paris. As a Russian, as a foreigner, it was obvious that he could take no part in the revolution. As a Frenchman he would have been under no obligation to participate actively. But was he right in his condemnation of the revolution ?

Moreover, what has become of his decision in favour of murder after the example of Byron's *Cain* ? Why does he despise mankind on account of 1848, despise men who like Herzen himself had decided in favour of murder—and had carried out their decision ? To one who thinks clearly and pursues his thoughts to their logical conclusion, revolution, the revolution of 1848, signifies crime and murder among other things. Must we then choose between crime and crime, between murder and murder ?

In 1848, as an actual fact, Herzen expressed his opposition to the revolution ; and his Byronic mood of that epoch, his decision in favour of murder, was but moral window-dressing. This is obvious from Herzen's reconsideration of his views on the revolution.

As early as 1840 Herzen was a Feuerbachian, and in 1845 he reconciled objectivism with subjectivism. He was by this time a positivist, and yet in 1848 he was still capable of revolutionary fervour. Not until after 1848, when he had witnessed the reaction in Austria, Hungary, Germany, France, and elsewhere, did he turn against revolution. Most of Feuerbach's disciples in Germany were enthusiasts for the revolution, and many of them were makers of revolution, but Feuerbach himself, like Herzen, was an opponent, and on the same grounds. Decision for or against revolution in general, and in particular for or against personal participation in revolutionary struggles, were questions which could be variously solved from the Feuerbachian outlook.

It is hardly necessary to show in detail that Herzen was somewhat premature in his execrations of 1848. How could he fail to see that the revolution, despite its failures, produced much of political and cultural value ? Why could he not grasp that evolution moves step by step, that it is a gradual process ? Even if we agree that his censure of the errors of the revolution of 1848 was justified, is the real problem solved by this censure ?

Moreover, Herzen's estimate of the republic or of the various attempts at establishing the republic, was too hastily formed. He was right in holding that the republic of 1848 was not in essentials very different from the monarchy, but was there in fact no difference at all ? He himself demands a socialist republic ; but is not the political republic, the bourgeois republic, a step towards his ideal ? Many political thinkers were concerned about these questions after 1848. Herzen's friend Bakunin, and Carl Marx who opposed both Herzen and Bakunin, attained to sounder views on this matter.

It is obvious that the unqualified rejection of constitutionalism and parliamentarism is wrong-headed. Had Herzen recalled how Tsar Nicholas condemned constitutional monarchy as a lie while expressing an "understanding" of the republic, his thoughts concerning this matter might have been more statesmanlike. Herzen appeals to Paine and to the American example generally, but did not America gain her liberties and her republic by revolution?

The appeal is to Paine? But in Paine, whose healthy understanding Herzen prizes so greatly, the Russian thinker might have discovered an important signpost. Paine expressly points out that for political freedom, religious and philosophical freedom are indispensable; he tells us that in case of need it is our duty to work politically in order to pave the way for religious freedom, and conversely. Paine, though an Englishman, participated personally in the French revolution.

Herzen could not avoid returning again and again to the problem of revolution. His friends in Europe among the political refugees believed in the possibility of a speedy renewal of the revolution. Russian believers in the revolution, those alike who remained in Russia and those who had fled to Europe, Ogarev and above all Bakunin, forced the problem on his attention. When compelled to give a direct answer, Herzen declared himself opposed to revolution, and specifically opposed to personal participation in revolution.

From the age of thirteen (he wrote thus to Mazzini in 1851) he had been devoted to a single idea, to waging war against every oppressive power in the name of the absolute independence of the individuality. He would therefore carry on his own little partisan struggle. He would be a genuine Cossack, acting "on his own initiative." He was indeed attached to the great revolutionary army, but he would not enroll himself in its regular cadres until the character of these had been completely transformed. These words clearly demonstrate that in Herzen's view the definitive revolution would not be necessary for a long time to come. For the time being he puts his trust in men rather than in institutions, and he therefore considers the spreading of enlightenment by philosophic, literary, and journalistic labours more important, and in truth more revolutionary.

Despite his intimate associations with notable political leaders in France, Italy, and Germany, Herzen took no personal part in political agitation. He was opposed on principle to secret societies, and never became a member of any of the Russian revolutionary parties which were now coming into existence. As Bělinskii had done in 1837, Herzen condemned secret propaganda as an obsolete method, however radical its aim. In 1853 he expressed his contempt for the propaganda. So decisively did he condemn Karakozov's attempt upon the tsar (1866), so adverse was he to political assassination in general, that the leaders of the revolutionary groups were moved to protest.

At length, in 1869, Herzen comes to grips with the revolution in his *Letters to an Old Comrade* (Bakunin).

Herzen agrees with Bakunin as to the goal, which is the transformation of the bourgeois state into a folk-state, but he considers that the revolutionaries are mistaken in their tactics. The folk, the entire people, the masses, cannot be educated for the folk-state by a coup d'état or by a coup de tête. Property, the family, the church, and the state have been and still are means for the education of mankind towards freedom—freedom in rationality.

Society evolves, moves gradually forward. The state is doubtless a transitional form, but its function is not yet superseded.

Herzen does not now believe that history advances by leaps ; he desires to move step by step ; he has no faith in the old, the obsolete, revolutionary method ; above all, he expects nothing from force or from terrorism. Nor does he believe in the vigorous agitation advocated by Bakunin. He holds that men can be outwardly enfranchised only in so far as they are inwardly free.

Herzen does not dread the objection that he is a mere progressive, that he is an advocate of compromise. He who is unwilling that civilisation should be founded on the knout must not endeavour to secure liberty through the instrumentality of the guillotine. No honourable man can desire to play the rôle of Attila. " Let every conscientious person ask himself whether he is ready. Let him ask himself whether the new organisation towards which we are advancing presents itself as clearly to his mind as do the generalised ideals of collective property and of solidarity. Has he conceived the process (apart from simple destruction) by which the transformation of the old forms into the new is to be effected ? If he be personally content with himself, let him tell us whether the environment is ready, that environment upon which, circumstances being what they are, depends the possibility for action."

We must therefore wait and work. The strength of the old order lies not so much in political power as in the fact that it is generally approved. We must influence men so that this approval may cease, and we must therefore preach to them and go on preaching. Impatient opponents will say that the time for words is passed, that the time for action has come. " As if words were not actions ! As if the time for words could ever pass ! Our enemies have never made this distinction between word and deed ; for words they have exacted punishment as severe as for deeds, and more severe in many cases." Herzen refuses to be a blind instrument of destiny ; he will not be the scourge of God, God's executioner. Not for him the simple faith, the uncomplicated ignorance, the wild fanaticism, the immaculate childishness, of revolutionary thought. He does not believe that history, that the course of events, can make men involuntary instruments for the destruction of the old regime. The knower and thinker decides freely for himself, and his decision must be : " Preaching is necessary for mankind, incessant preaching, provided it be rational, preaching directed alike to worker and employer, to burgher and to tiller of the soil. We have more need of apostles than of officers of the advance guard or sappers of destruction. We need apostles who will preach to opponents as well as to sympathisers. Preaching to the enemy is a great deed of love. Our enemies are not to blame because they are enabled, with the aid of a kind of persistent variant of the morality of earlier days, to maintain an existence outside the current of the time. They arouse my pity like the victims of illness or accident, these persons who stand on the edge of the abyss burdened with a load of riches which will drag them down into the depths. We must open their eyes for them ; we must not simply sweep them out of our way ; we must give them a chance of saving themselves if they will." For himself and his fellows Herzen recognises only one power, " the power of reason and understanding. If we reject this power we become outlaws from science and renegades from civilisation."

After 1848 Herzen had invoked curses on the revolution, abandoning the bourgeoisie to the contempt of Byron's Cain and threatening it with the weapon of crime. But towards the close of his career, a few months before his death, we find him expressing sympathy for the bourgeois. " I am sorry not only for men but for things, and I am oftener sorrier for things than for men." At this time, writing to his friend Ogarev, who shared the ideas of Bakunin, Herzen urges him to renounce the thought of an abortive liberation in accordance with the plans of Nečaev. " It is possible in history to make a rapid move, but if you want anything of the kind you must steel yourself against sympathy with those who will perish on the occasion, sympathy with individuals. In truth such sympathy was known neither to Pugačev nor to Marat."

Once before, Herzen had proclaimed the victory of the Galilean, when Tsar Alexander II had decided in favour of the liberation of the serfs. After twenty years' experience as a refugee among refugees he once again and definitively expressed his confidence in the Galilean, saying that sympathy and love of our enemies, not contempt or crime, would bring about equality, brain equality. We must follow Christ not Byron. " Go ye, therefore, and teach all nations."

The younger generation could not follow Herzen here. They followed the Herzen who had preached Byron's Cain, who had despised the bourgeoisie, who had taught that the religion of Christ must be overcome as the religion of death.

Thus Herzen ended his days as a Christian, a Christian in the sphere of practice, for he frankly accepted the gospel of humility—an. unbelieving Christian ! He had represented the revolutionaries of 1848 as believing Christians, and this position is very different from that of the unbelieving Christian. But may we say that for practical purposes Herzen moved on to the acceptance of bourgeois tactics and policy ?

Not entirely, for had he done this he must have ended by giving his approval to the bourgeois revolution.

We need no longer be alarmed because we were threatened with Byron's Cain. Cain has been transformed into Faust, the Faust whom Herzen had so strongly condemned. Nay more, Cain has been degraded, and placed among the " superfluous persons."

§ 82.

IN 1850, when Herzen first achieved a comparatively connected formulation of his philosophy of religion and of history, he had already long passed beyond the stage of philosophical studentship and philosophical errantry. He was then eight-and-thirty years of age, and his work at this period may serve as the starting-point for an analysis of his sociological ideas. All the more is this the case seeing that when he was a student of Hegel he had made a methodical attempt to secure a precise outlook upon history and the natural sciences and upon knowledge in its widest sense.

His diary dealing with the years 1842 to 1845 tells us how he busied himself with the problem of the nature of knowledge and of science, building mainly upon Hegelian and Feuerbachian foundations. To the same period belong certain essays, *Dilettantism in Science* and *Letters Concerning the Study of Nature*, wherein he attempted to formulate his views. He did not in these essays arrive at satisfactory results, and we note in them that no reconciliation is achieved between Hegel and positivist materialism. According to Hegel, in history as in the world at large reason is supreme. Herzen does not yet deny this, but he contrasts logic with history, pointing to the logical characteristics of the former and to the essentially human characteristics of the latter. Herzen distinguishes historical thought as an activity of the species from the logical thought of the individual, which is, he says, thought properly speaking. In the positivist sense, Herzen lays especial stress upon the exact thought of natural science, and we already find him voicing complaints concerning "the heavy cross of disillusioned knowledge." From the outlook of this disillusioned knowledge, which he opposes to all forms and degrees of religious illusion, Herzen fights against dilettantism. Man is at variance with nature and himself, and his only resource therefore is exact knowledge ; in his disintegration it is essential that he should attain a clear outlook. Herzen proceeds to attempt a history of philosophy which shall convey a more detailed formulation of this view, but he does not give us a clearer statement of principles, and the contrast between Feuerbach and Hegel is not transcended.

In this stage Hegel has still so much influence that Herzen recognizes a progressive movement in history, and admits the possibility of a foreknowledge of the future, writing : " We are the premisses out of which the syllogism of the future is constructed, and we can therefore cognise the future in advance."

Such is the language of Herzen in 1843 ; but by 1850 all this has been forgotten, and Hegel with it.

Positivist disillusionment has now destroyed for Herzen, not religion alone, but likewise faith in the meaning of history. Abandoning theology, Herzen abandons also teleology, and in especial the teleology of historical development. He does not believe that progress occurs, even though he admits that man can grow better, accepting this as a simple fact of observation. The reasons why man grows better may doubtless be analysed, but no ultimate aim towards which human improvement tends is discernible. History is a record of the brute understanding of the masses, sanctified irrationality, religious mania. The power and the glory of history are not found in reason, nor yet in happiness (as the old song says), but in irrationality. As late as 1867 Herzen reiterates in this fashion his views of 1850, putting them into the mouth of an anatomist named Leviathanskii. The name, of course, derives from *Leviathan*, for Herzen finds in Hobbes the climax of materialism. The name is likewise intended to suggest that history, the social organism in general, must be looked upon as a monster. In 1864 he refers to history as a disorderly improvisation, and this is his enduring conviction. For Herzen there exist only individual moments weighty with meaning, but no history. He does not admit historical evolution as a whole. His style, his characteristic dazzling aphoristic style, is itself an expression of this conviction.

We trace in Herzen two distinct thought sequences. Sometimes individuality and its " sacredness " (1847) are so vigorously stressed, that society and its development recede into the background, or even disappear from our ken. Individuality must not be made into a means for a remote end ; it is an end in itself ; it does not subserve any " Moloch," any historico-philosophical artifact. Like Bělinskii he discerns in the misery and in the death of a single human being, no less irrationality and disharmony than in the misery and destruction of the entire human race by some cosmic catastrophe. He admits that the future holds out numerous possibilities, but he declines to accept the theory that there is a predestined path, discoverable in advance, for this would infringe the freedom of individuality. Again and again he expresses his dissent from fatalism.

Herzen adduces an additional argument, rejecting the distant goal in the name of the present. " The present is the true sphere of existence," he wrote as early as 1842, and he

presented life in general, or life in the present, as man's one
and only true goal   He seemed to overlook the fact that the
present, too, is history, even though it be history in its most
recent manifestation.

Herzen, like Bělinskii, is an adversary of historism ; he
refuses, like Bělinskii, to be the slave of time and events.

Subsequently, as we have seen, Herzen admits that there
is progress, but even then his materialist outlook distinguishes
him from Hegel.   In materialism Herzen finds support for his
vigorous individualism.   Definite and thoroughly individual
brains will, he says, have nothing to do with pantheism or with
any organisation of these brains which makes them no more
than parts of a whole.   Brain monads, but no pre-established
harmony—thus we may summarise Herzen's metaphysics.

When I thus emphasise Herzen's materialism, I must not
be taken as implying that he failed to recognise thought as the
motive force for individual men and the motive force of history.
But Herzen explains thought materialistically as brain activity.
From this outlook he sometimes hopes that progress will be
secured by an improvement in brains.   Reforms, social and
historical reforms, are the outcome of changes in " cerebrin."
He is doubtless speaking ironically here, as also when he
compares human progress with the progress of the cattle which
man himself has tamed; and yet this very irony is the sequel
of the positivist and materialist process of disillusionment, of
the struggle of knowledge against religious mania and sanctified
irrationality.

§ 83.

THE developments subsequent to 1850 led Herzen away
from his historical nihilism.

The Crimean war gave a powerful stimulus to political
interest in Russia. Sevastopol and its consequences, the
new regime and its preparations for reform (in especial for the
liberation of the peasantry), attracted much attention from
Herzen ; the consideration of practical political possibilities
compelled him to take up a position in relation to precisely
defined aims and to co-operate for their attainment. Hence,
although a refugee, Herzen came to live with and in Russia,
and he discovered that for this Russia which he had been so
glad to leave he felt a strong and saving love. The importance

of history and of the people as a whole was recognised by
him, his unruly individualism was moderated, subjectivism
was subordinated to objectivism.

An observation will be here in place concerning Herzen's
despair of the revolution. It must not be supposed that this
despair was solely the outcome of political experience. The
curse uttered in 1850 has so personal a ring that we cannot but
regard Herzen's change of front in that year as to a large extent
the objectivisation of intimate spiritual experiences. Through
becoming a refugee he was cut off from old associations and
his family life was disturbed ; these circumstances dictated
the curse. Many of Herzen's letters and reminiscences relating
to his more intimate experiences remain unpublished. I
believe that these documents would give us a better understanding of his mental struggles and a clearer view of his
positivist and materialist development.

His analysis of Europe and of the revolution convinced
Herzen that the socialistic folk-state he desired to see brought
into being would be likely to remain long unrealised were it
not for the existence of a people competent to undertake the
great task of bringing about the true social revolution in
contradistinction to the bourgeois revolution. Such, he said,
was the mission of the Russian people.

Herzen tells us how he became aware of the distinction
between the St. Petersburg government and the Russian
people, and how his faith in his fatherland was thereby restored.
Acquaintanceship with Europe taught him that the Russian
westernisers had an utterly false conception of Europe. He
censured his friends for being able to see nothing but cultured
Europe, and for knowing only the Europe of the past. Experience of contemporary Europe and of Europe as a whole afforded
a pitiless demonstration that the Europe of their ideals was
non-existent.

It may be noted that Herzen's very first impressions in
1847 led him to take an unfavourable view of Europe.

The Russian people, on the other hand, seemed to him
capable of realising aspirations for genuine political and social
freedom. It was true that the Russian government and
tsarism were little if at all better than the European governments. Even the Russian people was full of faults, and it
appeared to Herzen that Gogol's *Dead Souls* furnished a true
and universally valid indictment of contemporary Russia.

Nevertheless there was no reason to despair. Regarding Peter the Great as a strange combination of the genius and the tiger, Herzen could only accept Peter's reforms with reservations; like the slavophils, he contrasted Moscow with St. Petersburg, the people with the bureaucracy.

Herzen reiterated what Čaadaev and the Rousseauist slavophils had said about the lack of civilisation in Russia. It was an enormous advantage for the Russian people to be free from the restricting traditions of Europe. Russia had not suffered from the three great scourges, Catholicism, Roman law, and the bourgeoisie. Feudalism, Protestantism, and liberalism were merely developments of these three principles; feudalism derived from Catholicism and Roman law; Protestantism and liberalism were the ultimate phases of Catholicism; hence Russia knew nothing of feudalism, Protestantism, and liberalism. In the letter to Michelet (1851), in which Herzen, with ardent affection, defended the Russian people and the Russian character against westernist misunderstandings, he summarised his comparison between Russia and Europe in the following propositions: Russia will never be Protestant; Russia will never be juste-milieu; Russia will not make a revolution simply in order to get rid of Tsar Nicholas and to replace him by tsar-deputies, tsar-judges, and tsar-policemen.

Herzen now found himself able to explain certain undesirable historical facts quite in the slavophil manner.

Take tsarism, for example. Tsarism is not monarchy. European monarchy developed out of feudalism and Catholicism, and is animated by a peculiar social and religious ideal. The tsar is tsar for tsardom's sake. He is nothing more than an unlimited dictator. When the time comes and when the people is ready, the tsar will make way for the socialist republic and will become its president. In contrast with old and moribund Europe, young and vigorous Russia can offer two notable guarantees, the younger generation of the landowning aristocracy and the peasantry.

The aristocracy showed and tested its vigour in the decabrist revolt. Philosophically these Russian aristocrats have gone much further than Europeans in the negation of the old world. Above all, the successors of the decabrists no longer believe in their right to own land.

The Russian peasant on the other hand, believes in his right to do so; he has a religious faith in his right to the soil, and a religious faith in the mir ; for Herzen the foundation of new Russia is to be the mir.

There are, says Herzen, three elements of exceptional value in the Russian mir : the right of every individual to land ; the common ownership of land ; the self-government of the village community. These elements, considers Herzen, are worth more than the political and social development of Europe. It is true that in the middle forties, before he left Russia, Herzen had recognised that the mir is not an exclusively Russian or Slav institution, and he knew that it exists in India and various other countries. At that time, too, Herzen believed that the Russian village community was the outcome of defective development, the issue of primitive patriarchalism and uncivilisation. If, at a later date, he came to esteem the mir so highly it was because in 1848 Europe had displayed her utter incapacity for socialism.

Herzen recognised that the mir had one great defect, the absorption of individuality into the mir. But the artel, he said, and the Cossacks, would suffice to save for Russia a not inconsiderable measure of individualism. Moreover, the defect could be cured, the freedom of the individual and that of the mir could be harmonised, and the liberation of the peasantry would bring this about. " The freeing of Russia will begin either with a revolt of the serfs or else with their liberation," said Herzen in 1854. When in 1857 Alexander II had declared his intention to liberate the peasants, Herzen and Ogarev enthusiastically exclaimed, " Thou hast conquered, O Galilean !"

Herzen could not fail to consider the counter-argument, could not fail to ask himself whether Russia would not have to pass through the same stages of development as Europe. Could Russia realise the folk-state and socialism by one step from her present primitive condition ; could she dispense with traversing the phase of European civilisation and with passing through the economic evolution of capitalism ? Herzen set his mind at rest with the consideration that if Russia, because in fact essentially akin to the European peoples, had to follow the same course of development, this development might none the less take a special form, since for liberty many historical possibilities are open. Herzen does not recognise the validity of any historical law in accordance with which Russia must follow exactly the same path as the European nations. Without a bourgeoisie and without Catholicism, but upon the foundation

of the mir, Russia can advance straightway to a higher level
of development.

Herzen could invoke the authority of European socialists
in support of this assumption that Russia might overleap the
capitalist epoch. The matter will be discussed later in detail
when we come to consider the identical view of the narodniki.
Of late much emphasis has been laid upon Herzen's
" westernist socialism," and Herzen has been praised as founder
of the narodničestvo. It is true that Herzen's socialism paved
the way for the narodničestvo movement ; that he uttered the
watchword, Land and Liberty ; and that he directed the intelligentsia towards the mužik. Herzen, however, was distinguished from the narodniki by the way in which he stressed
the philosophic aspects of socialism, and tended to leave the
economic side of the question out of account. The narodniki
developed their views in opposition to Marxism, and their
economic and social outlook approximates far more closely
than did Herzen's to that of Marx.

Herzen frequently endeavoured to ascertain which among
the Russian characteristics would prove especially advantageous to the progress of Russian evolution. He considered
that the Russian character exhibited remarkable plasticity,
that it was endowed with great capacity for the acceptance and
elaboration of the acquirements made by the foreign world.
To him this seemed the most human side of the Russian disposition. The Russians, too, precisely because they were so
accessible to the universally human, were better able than the
French, the Germans, and the English to harmonise theory
and practice. Herzen also extolled Russian realism. Finally
he regarded the work of Puškin as a titanic manifestation full
of glorious promise, the fruit of the vigorous Russian understanding and its capacity for culture.

Nor did Herzen forget to attach due importance to the
size of the Russian state. Sixty million people ; in less than
half a century the number of Russian soldiers would be imposing, of soldiers who had already shown Europe their mettle.
The Russians, too, had quite remarkable powers of resistance,
for they had been able to maintain their peculiarities under
the Tatar yoke and under the regime of German bureaucrats.

When he analysed the defects of the mir, Herzen was also
aware of the defects in the Russian and Slav character.
Passivity, humility, effeminacy, lack of individuality, char-

acterised the Slav, and therefore, despite the mir, he remained a slave. Contrasted with the Russian, the Teuton was a vigorous individualist, and in European political history the Teuton realised the individualistic ideal.

Russian critics have disputed whether Herzen became a slavophil. Herzen himself threw light on this accusation and rejected it, saying that his metaphysical and religious outlook on fundamentals differed from that of the slavophils, and that the distinction was essential. The assertion would have been perfectly correct had not Herzen modified or at least toned down his fundamental outlook under the influence of slavophil political views. Turgenev reminded his friend on one occasion (November 8, 1862) of the earlier phase : " A foe to mysticism and absolutism, you kneel mystically before the Russian sheepskin, discerning therein all the blessings, all the novelty and originality, of coming social forms—discerning, in a word, the absolute, that absolute over which you make merry in the philosophical field. All your idols have been shattered, and yet, since man cannot live without an idol, you suggest that we should erect an altar to this sheepskin, to this unknown god. Happily we know nothing about him, and we can therefore once again pray, believe, and hope."

Turgenev is right. Herzen appraised the Russian people and the mužik from the standpoint to which Homjakov gave the name of talismanism. In Moscow, Herzen had frequent talks with the slavophils concerning such matters, and Homjakov would have nothing to do with Herzen's antiteleological philosophy of history. In Europe, however, in 1859, Herzen came to recognise that he had a much closer kinship with the slavophils than with the " westernist old believers " (the liberals)

After 1848, in fact, the Herzenian solus ipse felt distinctly out of sorts, and the disorder was not metaphysical merely, but political and social as well ; the Byronic intoxication was succeeded by the customary fit of headache and depression. " We are at once the corpses and the assassins, the diseases and the pathological anatomists of the old world. I have long considered that it is at least possible to begin a new personal life, to retire into oneself, to get away from the old-clothes market. It remains impossible, however, as long as there is any one about you with whom you have not broken off all ties, for the old world will return to you through him." But now Herzen does not fear contact with the Old Russian world.

With true Russian fatalism he consoles himself with the example of Karazin, who, after the death of Tsar Paul, communicated political advice to Alexander I in epistolary form. When we recall Karazin's subsequent antisocial activities, the chosen instance seems unfortunate !

Now that Herzen was far away from St. Petersburg and Moscow, now that he led the solitary life of a refugee, he came to look upon Russia as an enchanted land and upon the mužik as a saviour. At first, indeed, he imagined that America was the land of promise, and at times his thoughts turned towards Australia, but in the end his faith became centred in Russia. He forgot the tragical and debasing experiences of his paternal home and became reconciled with the Russian aristocrat. At one time he had looked upon aristocracy as a more or less cultured form of anthropophagy ; the landowner, the man who would strike his serfs, was simply one variety of cannibal ; and he hoped that this cannibal system would be brought to a close by the labourer's refusal to work for another's ends. But now the aristocrat has taken Herzen's sermon to heart, is about to renounce his rights in the soil, and is going to recognise the mužik as a brother !

In matters of foreign policy (with which, were he consistent, he would have nothing to do) Herzen is likewise in accord with the slavophils. During the Crimean war (1854) he wishes to give Constantinople to the Russians. After the war he opposes France and Napoleon and advocates an alliance with England (1858).

Thus Herzen, once more like the later slavophils, takes a leap towards panslavism.

The historical rôle Herzen assigns to the Russians is now generalised by him, and assigned to the Slavs at large. The socialist republic is not indeed to be replaced by the Slav federation, but the federation will modify the republic or will pave the way to it. The national movement has become more important than the social. Herzen has forgotten that the Poles and the Czechs have no mir, and he has forgotten the southern Slavs (though as far as these last are concerned the zadruga may be accepted in place of or as a supplement to the mir). At one time he had been extremely reserved in his attitude towards panslavism, especially in the Czech form. But under the influence of Proudhon's federative doctrines he first thought of the federative solution of the Polish question, and then went on to advocate a federation of all the Slavs. Beyond question, too, in this matter the ideas of Bakunin modified those of Herzen.

Thus did Herzen draw near to the slavophils, even though great differences continued to exist upon matters of principle, and in the social and political fields as well as in the sphere of metaphysics. For example, his explanation of tsarism as a dictatorship was anything but legitimist, but neither his foes nor his friends took these differences adequately into account, their estimate of Herzen's conversion being determined by its political consequences. Formerly he had declared that Europe was essential to Russia, as ideal, as example, and as reproach ; and he had maintained that if Europe had not existed, it would have been necessary for Russia's sake to create it imaginatively. But now Russia had become the ideal for Europe.

It is hardly necessary for me to defend myself against the accusation that I disapprove of Herzen's love for his homeland. I have done no more than reproduce his utterances regarding natural affection for the native soil, and for the life which despite all its defects custom has made congenial to a man's mind. Well do I know how experience of the foreign and the unaccustomed is apt to awaken home-sickness. I am aware that after his arrival in Europe Herzen found it necessary to defend progressive Russia against the false views and erroneous judgments that were prevalent in Europe. It was inevitable that such opinions on Russia as were uttered by Michelet should produce a feeling of irritation. But for Herzen to preach Russian messianism was a very different matter.

§ 84.

HERZEN, though he passed through a mystical period, grew up amid the liberal traditions of the eighteenth-century philosophy of enlightenment and humanitarianism ; he soon became a radical, an admirer of the decabrists, and above all of Pestel ; in the middle of the forties, as we have learned, he separated from the liberals and adopted socialist views.

Herzen became acquainted with the writings of the French socialists and with those of Weitling and Owen before he had studied the works of Hegel, but it was the influence of Hegel and Feuerbach which revolutionised his outlook and made him a socialist. He wrote a brief sketch of socialism in Russia, representing the Petraševcy and Cernyševskii as precursors of socialism. After 1848 he discarded French and European socialism as futile, but he continued to term himself a socialist and to look forward to the true social revolution. In " Kolokol," especially in the later issues, the socialist note is extremely prominent, being stressed in polemic against the younger revolutionists who were dissatisfied with Herzen.

Herzen speaks of his socialism as " Russian." It is agrarian socialism, the socialism of the mužik and of the artel. But he advocated in addition municipal socialism, political socialism, and district socialism. Thus was Herzenism distinguished from Marxism, which looks chiefly to workers and proletarians for its fulfilment. Herzen's " Russian " socialism often spoken of as " Russian " communism, is further distinguished from Marxism by this, that Herzen, though a materialist, did not teach economic materialism. His own account of Marx in London shows, moreover, that Marx and the Marxists were to him personally uncongenial. He sided with Bakunin against Marx, and when the first edition of Marx's magnum opus was published in 1867, Herzen paid scant attention to it.

His primary demand, as has been recorded above, was for brain equality. He knew that civilisation is impossible to the hungry, and he knew that the civilisation of the minority depends on the physical toil of the majority. From Louis Blanc and others he learned of the class struggle in Europe, and he himself levelled accusations against the " Manicheism of society," but he was definitely opposed to the class struggle. He insisted that the function of socialism was not merely to put an end " to anthropophagy " and especially to capitalism, but above all to annihilate everything monarchical and religious. Herzen looked to socialism for a new philosophy, and it seemed to him that Saint-Simon and Fourier had uttered no more than the first lispings of the future philosophy.

His socialism was based upon a positivist and materialist outlook. Shortly before his death, in *The Physician, the Dying, and the Dead*, he censured the socialism of his contemporaries as being still a religion, that is to say illusion, and from socialism of this texture he expected nothing but a new blood-letting, and not the true act of liberation.

In his demand for brain equality Herzen is no communist

extremist. He does not suggest the complete abolition of private property, and would content himself with its investment by society in a manner analogous with that of the Russian mir. But it is plain that Herzen detests the capitalists more than the great landlords, and his views concerning the Russian aristocracy are recorded above. Throughout, Herzen's socialism remained essentially philosophic. He was little concerned about economic questions, and in this domain Proudhon was his leading authority. Proudhon likewise influenced Herzen greatly in his political views, and confirmed his individualism and individualistic federalism. I have previously referred to Herzen's great esteem for Proudhon, and I may mention that Herzen supplied Proudhon with funds for the latter's journal " Voix du Peuple " (1849–1850).

If Christianity as monotheism be regarded as embodying the essence of monarchism, Herzen's socialism, as materialistic atheism, may be regarded as predominantly antimonarchism.

This antimonarchism has the folk-state as its ideal. Herzen has an especial loathing for political centralisation, returning to this again and again, and declaring from time to time that the Slav is by nature opposed to centralisation, to the state. The language resembles that of Konstantin Aksakov. Herzen was afraid of the cultured and hypercultured absolutist state ; he dreaded " Genghis Khan with telegraphs, steamships, and railways, with Carnot and Monge on the staff, his soldiers armed with Minié rifles and Congreve rockets, and led by Batu Khan."

In the *Letters to an Old Comrade* the abolition of the state is presented as an ideal, and we are told that the majority must attain to its full mental stature, since this is an essential preliminary to the abolition of the state. Proudhon's federalism and anarchism likewise find reiterated expression.

After his spiritual return to the Russia of the slavophils Herzen contented himself with the liberation of the peasantry in 1861, in place of the great and definitive social revolution which in 1848 he had contrasted with all previous revolutions. Either despotism or social revolution, had been Herzen's cry in the forties. The events of 1848 were to him a proof that Europe was incompetent for the social revolution. But in 1861 Russia taught him that she was capable of carrying through this revolution successfully, and of doing so without bloodshed. We must not forget that Herzen himself worked energetically on behalf of the liberation of the peasantry, and that he endeavoured to win over the aristocratic landowners to the idea of liberation. Truthfully and in moving terms he showed them how the free lords were themselves degraded by the institution of serfdom, writing : " We are slaves because we are masters. We are servants because we are landowners. We are ourselves serfs because we keep our brothers in servitude, those brothers whose origin, whose blood, and whose language we share."

The Russian mir has become for him the " lightning conductor " of revolution ; and the supreme value of the mir consists for him in this, that the mir is not an abstract theory of cultured socialists, but a practical institution prevailing among a huge population—a population of illiterates.

The contrast between Herzen's views after 1861 and the socialism of his earlier phase will now be plain. The goal for Russia is no longer a social revolution but a political revolution, and the social revolution has become merely means to an end. Herzen now demands for Russia all that Europe possesses, the things which to Europe (according to his previous view) had been valueless. He demands civilisation, culture, and a parliament. In 1864 he insists upon the need for a zemskii sobor or a duma, elected by universal suffrage. In Europe, he has told us, the suffrage is a contemptible " arithmetical pantheism " which has given the vote to undeveloped orang-utans (of French men four-fifths are orang-utans, of Europeans nineteen-twentieths). But in Russia the suffrage, above all thanks to the existence of the old believers, will secure the genuine representation of the Russian people.[1] The intelligentsia will introduce " the idea of modern science." Do we discern here the brain equality of his earlier days ?

As we have already learned, Herzen further tells Bakunin that he accepts the Russian state. " If the sunrise takes place without blood-tinged clouds " it really does not matter whether the sunrise wears Monomach's crown or the Phrygian cap.

It is by no means easy to say what Herzen really meant by his " sunrise." In the letter to Bakunin he says the time has come to ascertain whether we are all ready for the definitive deed of liberation. Herzen often speaks of this readiness.

---

[1] In the " Poljarnaja Zvĕzda," from 1862 onwards, Herzen published the before-mentioned collection of documents relating to the raskolniki

In 1862 he tells us that the Russian revolution must be a return to the folk and to the mir, and writes : " Preach to the people, not Feuerbach or Babeuf, but a religion the people will understand, the people of the soil. . . . Make ready, for the day of destiny is at hand." Then follows his tirade about the rising sun, accompanied or not with " blood-tinged clouds."

We must now see whether Herzen furnishes clear suggestions as to what is to be the relationship between Europe and Russia when Russia comes to fulfil her messianic mission vis-à-vis Europe. In his answer to Michelet's scepticism about Russia (1855), Herzen tells us that revolutionary Europe will as a matter of course join forces organically with Russia. " In Russia the man of the future is the mužik, just as in France the operative. Tsarism will disappear, and so will the Russian intelligentsia, for the latter's sole function is to mediate between the Russian people and revolutionary Europe.

Nevertheless Herzen was ever somewhat inclined to regard the masses from the outlook of a superior person. In 1850, when he demanded a socialist folk-state, the realisation of this ideal was deferred to a remote future. After 1861, however, he talks of immediate realisation, speaks favourably of the masses, not of the mužiks alone, but also of European operatives ; and he even gives the intelligentsia its congé. How and why is the intelligentsia to disappear ? Is it because Rousseau passed sentence upon civilisation— or does Herzen foresee the immediate organisation of brain equality ?

According to the plan of 1862 the tsar in his Monomach crown is not to vanish, provided only that the sun rises unaccompanied by blood-tinged clouds, and it is plain that Herzen could readily contemplate the retention of the tsar, seeing that he did not consider the tsar to be a monarch in the strict sense of the term.

But what is the drift of this criticism ? It is that Herzen did not whole-heartedly believe in the Russian saviour, and was never able completely to overcome his own scepticism. The task he assigned to Russia was far too great for him to hope that the Russian mir would ever be able to achieve it in its entirety.

The kernel of his philosophy of history is as follows. The old world was perishing beyond hope of rescue. Christianity, which had renovated the Roman world, was in process of decomposition. . . . The reformation and the great revolution had been no more than temporary expedients. Just as the aging Rome had rejected Christianity, so now did the aging Christian world reject socialism.

No doubt Herzen was quite in earnest when to the decrepit and dying Europe he represented Russia as the saving new world. He endeavoured to show that Russia and socialism were one and the same, and he desired to communicate the belief to Europe. Such was the chief aim of the letters he wrote in 1854, *The Old World and Russia*. But Herzen would not have been Herzen had he failed to recognise that the historico-philosophical analogy between socialism and Christianity was not convincing, and was the less convincing since, generally speaking, socialism was for him above all a new outlook. Were the Russian mir and the Orthodox mužik to constitute the new world, to embody the new doctrine ? As early as the beginning of the thirties Herzen had made acquaintance with the works of Saint-Simon and with the attempts of the Saint-Simonian school to secure a new socialistic outlook ; somewhat later Owen and the " new Christianity " came under his notice, and he now looked to this source for the doctrine of salvation. The study of Hegel and still more the study of Feuerbach strengthened these yearnings, and Feuerbach showed Herzen how the human being must develop out of the Christian. Is it possible to think that Herzen could without scepticism regard the mužik as the desired saviour ? This is why he placed the operative beside the mužik, and this is why he became reconciled with the bourgeois. The approximation effected by Herzen was of Russia to Europe, not of Europe to Russia.

§ 85.

HERZEN'S career recalls the fate of Goethe's Euphorion. Radiating light he rises, on high he shines, but he is dashed to pieces on the earth. In the fifties and in the early sixties Herzen was the spokesman of progressive Russia ; after the liberation of the peasantry and after the Polish rising he became more and more isolated, increasingly lonely.

His criticism of Russia contributed much towards the realisation of the reforms before and after 1861 ; his influence upon all circles and strata of cultured Russia, not excepting the bureaucracy and the court, was powerful. The stimulating and directing effect of Herzen's personality and writings upon his friends in Moscow and in St. Petersburg has often been pointed out, and I have referred to the continued influence he exercised from Europe. " Vivos voco ! " was the motto of " Kolokol," a motto taken from the favourite poet of his boyhood. And Herzen's " Bell " was heard throughout Russia. Ševčenko devoutly kissed the first numbers of the periodical to reach him.

Herzen was an awakener, his was the voice of one crying in the wilderness. Recognition is due to his character as well as to his literary activities. He said of himself that hypocrisy and duplicity were the two errors most alien to his disposition. Herzen could not be better portrayed.

Herzen helped the leaders of liberalism, such men as Čičerin, Kavelin, etc., to clarify their principles ; the slavophils had to come to terms with Herzen ; and even the reactionaries had to try conclusions with him.

His influence declined after the Polish rising of 1863. The decline has been ascribed to Herzen's sarmatiophil policy, and also to Bakunin's undesirable influence in " Kolokol." The number of subscribers to the periodical fell from three thousand to five hundred.

When we consider Herzen's Polish policy it is necessary to discriminate. He did good service by his protests against the brutal subjugation of the Poles, but in his approval of the revolution of that day he went too far, further than his own principles justified. Herzen himself admitted this. Katkov, who had at one time recognised " Kolokol " to be a power, came in 1863, as leader of official nationalism, into an attitude of opposition to Herzen.

I do not believe that the waning of Herzen's influence was solely due to his views upon the Polish rising. After 1861 his opinions and his policy forced him into a difficult position. Herzen's philosophy remained practically unchanged throughout life. Having become a Feuerbachian, a Feuerbachian he remained, as we learn from all his utterances down to the very last. Doubtless he mitigated his positivist disillusionment, and abandoned the Byronic Cain, but he held fast to his positivist materialism. It was natural that this philosophy should seem odious to conservatives and reactionaries, but some even of the liberals were repelled by it (Granovskii, Čičerin, etc.). Moreover, some of the liberals were antagonised by Herzen's socialism.

On the other hand, young men of socialistic and radical

views considered Herzen too vague, and found his policy unduly conservative. The first proclamation issued by Young Russia reproaches Herzen for misunderstanding the situation and for conservatism. At this epoch, too, political endeavours were in the ascendant in Russia, where the leaders of the movement resided; publicist and political interests were concentrated in Russia; the powerful influence exercised by Černyševskii during the early sixties, if not the direct cause of the coolness felt towards Herzen, at least paved the way for its onset.

The reaction and repression which began in 1863, led to an increase in radicalism, and sent a new stream of refugees to Europe, refugees already unfriendly to Herzen. His removal from London to Geneva, the new refugee centre, availed nothing; an understanding was impossible. Not merely did Herzen remain estranged from the younger revolutionaries, but he was never able to harmonise his outlook with that of Černyševskii, though the two writers built on the same philosophical foundations.

Herzen knew and admitted that he had changed, but he had changed, he said, because the entire situation had altered. Modification of views is natural to a vigorously aspiring man, but the important question is, in what direction the modification occurs and by what it is determined. Much as I admire Herzen as author and as man, my liking for him has its reserves. His change of views disturbs me, though not for quite the same reasons that made his friends uneasy.

It was not in early youth, but in the maturity of manhood that Herzen declared himself a disciple of the Byronic Cain, and it therefore seems to me that his subsequent change was hardly natural—unless we explain the anathema uttered in 1850 as the expletive of a young man in a hurry. But the remove from Byron to N. Turgenev is a very great one, and between the two writers there is a chasm hardly to be spanned ! It was natural that N. Turgenev should exercise an attraction on Herzen, for Turgenev had thought out his constitutionalist plans with some care, and the decabrist tradition was likewise on his side.

For the very reason that Herzen appeals to us because of his many brilliant qualities we must endeavour to come to an understanding about his defects.

In philosophical matters Herzen's inadequacy was due to this, that he failed to criticise and recriticise the foundations of his philosophy, and that he uncritically continued to cling to Feuerbach and positivism. Marx and Engels advanced beyond Feuerbach, and even Stirner attempted to do so. At the outset Herzen passes on from Feuerbach upon the line of Marx towards revolution; he advances to crime, in Byronic fashion; but after remaining long content with breathing threatenings and slaughter, after prolonged "hesitation," he turns away to liberalism.

Now I, too, believe that Feuerbach's philosophy is defective. The identification of religion with myth is fallacious, and Feuerbach's materialism is of as little avail as materialism in general. Marx prudently transmuted it into economic materialism. Herzen deduced the political consequences of the Feuerbachian doctrine "homo homini deus"; but he remained too much on the abstract plane; he failed to undertake a precise analysis of the real relationships between religion and politics, between church and state; and he failed to secure any profounder insight into the nature of theocracy and into its development and forms.

To the last, Herzen remained an opponent of Orthodoxy, and yet he concluded a peace with the believing mužik and the old believers, to find the positively Russian in his folk-duma.

It was a grave defect, too, that Herzen failed to secure a better understanding of socialism, its true significance and its internal and external development. I am aware that it is by no means easy to arrive at clear views from a study of the writings of the French socialists. I admit, moreover, that the practical demands of these socialists were not such as most of us would consider practical (the Saint-Simonians, for example, wished to have all their clothing to button behind, so that it would be impossible for the individual to dress himself unaided, and his neighbour would be compelled to exercise the faculty of altruism!). But it was a weakness in Herzen that he failed to study Marx, that he did not observe the labour movement and the economic and social developments of his day, and that he did not grasp the influence that these changes were exercising in the political field.

Nor were Herzen's views of the mužik and the mir based upon close investigation of economic and social relationships. He says with justice of the slavophils that their holy-picture ideals and the fumes of incense made it impossible for them to understand the true condition of the people. But may we not say almost the same of Herzen's adoration of the mužik ?

His knowledge of history was defective. Though he had a keen and profitable interest in the living present, he erred gravely through failing to undertake a thorough historical analysis of contemporary events. Unduly one-sided is the manner in which history is reduced to the biography of Herzen. In fact all Herzen's writings are extraordinarily subjective, far too subjective for a philosopher who desired to transcend German idealism and to escape its subjectivist pitfalls.

In the political field Herzen's subjectivism takes the form of anarchism, socialistic anarchism or anarchistic socialism— it does not matter which name we use. Herzen's anarchism derives from the defects of his subjectivism, and this is itself dependent upon Herzen's social position.

He was a refugee, stranger among strangers, economically and socially independent, living upon income drawn from Russia, an opponent of capitalism, but not necessarily an opponent of Rothschild, of whom he could make an adroit literary use in opposition to the fiscalism of the Russian government and the tsar (*James Rothschild the Emperor, and Romanov the Banker*). In a word, this economic and social isolation made Herzen unpractical. Helplessness in practical matters, becoming objective in the philosophic and literary fields, took the form of anarchism.

In course of time, lack of practical experience is apt to lead to contempt for practical experience. Herzen was inclined to share Plato's aristocratic disdain of politics and politicians, and the reason was the same in his case as in Plato's. To the philosopher, one who studies the ultimate principles of all being and life, and writes about these abysmal matters, the details of everyday politics seem petty ; to him, officials, ministers, even the tsar, are no more than unimportant wage-earners appointed by the people. They can therefore be tolerated readily enough ; it matters little whether we have to do with tsar or president, with one who wears Monomach's crown or a Phrygian cap. Thus abstract and theoretical anarchism becomes in practice legitimism, but it is natural that the real practitioners should look askance at this practical legitimism.

Herzen, moreover, has in his composition a considerable element of the anarchism peculiar to authors, and a brilliant and well-informed article seems to him more valuable and more important than all the tsars !

Herzen's futility in practical matters was the evil heritage of Russian absolutism. Tsarism, especially under Nicholas I, condemned to inactivity the best and the most energetic of the Russians, and for the refugee this inactivity was perpetuated and accentuated.

If, finally, we take into account the aristocratic factor in Herzen's mentality and his associations from childhood upwards, we have a sufficient explanation of his anarchism. Though at first he despised the bourgeois, he became reconciled later with " collective mediocrity " (he quotes Mill's phrase) and its " Chinesedom." He is sorry for the unfortunate bourgeois, and becomes reconciled with him after the manner of an aristocratic superior. In 1848 no less a man than Bělinskii thought it necessary to protect the bourgeoisie against Herzen's onslaughts. After a time, however, Herzen came to admit (1863) that Russia would perhaps traverse the bourgeois stage. Later still, he practically accepted this as inevitable. It was natural that Herzen should look upon the " autocratic masses " rather from the outlook of the aristocrat than from that of the historian or politician. He makes fun of the bourgeois because he buys his clothes ready-made, and because he replaces parks with orchards and palaces with hotels. As a romanticist Herzen detested the bourgeois ; " accuracy and moderation " irritated him ; he could see nothing in the bourgeois but indifferentism and stagnation ; he despised " chameleopardism " devoid of strong racial and individual qualities, for all that was individual was typified for him in " the restless and the eccentric."

He achieved little with his conception of Byron's Cain as nothing more than the antibourgeois. Herzen did not adequately appraise the revolutionary defiance of Byron's Cain and Lucifer, and this is why his Cain capitulated to the bourgeoisie. Physical-force-anarchism was transmuted by Herzen into sermonising. In addition he adopted a positivistic categorical imperative, tincturing this with Schopenhauer's compassion.

Herzen was never able to transcend a paralysing scepticism ; hence arose the " hesitation " which he so justly diagnosed in himself ; and this is why Herzen did not become a permanent leader either in the theoretical or in the practical field. Louis

Blanc was once branded by Herzen as a bourgeois in the following terms : " His intellectualist religiousness and his lack of scepticism surrounded him as with a Chinese wall, so that it was impossible to throw within the enclosure a single new idea or a single doubt."

Herzen himself was one who threw thoughts broadcast. It is undeniable that he made many apt observations concerning both Russia and Europe. He is often commended for having in 1867 foreseen the fall of Napoleonic France and the victory of Bismarck and Prussia.

At the outset of his literary career Herzen devoted much consideration to the relationship between scientific specialists and philosophers. He dreaded specialisation as unindividual ; he was afraid of becoming such a man as Wagner in Goethe's *Faust* ; and he therefore turned towards generalities, towards philosophy, although conversely he sufficiently recognised the dangers of dilettantism. He never attained to the goal of his desire, the perfect synthesis of these two extremes. Rather was it his privilege " to live a many-sided life," to embody both philosophically and politically the proverbial breadth of the Russian nature.

We involuntarily recall Beltov in *Who is to Blame ?* where this " superfluous man " is ably and unsparingly analysed by Herzen. The Russian, who has received a thoroughly European education at the hands of Genevese Frenchmen, astonishes the German specialists by his versatility and astonishes the French by his profundity ; but whereas the Germans and the Frenchmen achieve much, he achieves nothing. He has a positively morbid love of work, but he is unable to secure a practical position in relation to life, incompetent to make contact with an environment wholly foreign to him. He lives only in thoughts and passions, a frigid dreamer, eternally a child. Half his life is spent upon the choice of a profession, and again and again he begins a new career, for he has inherited neither culture nor traditions from his father, nothing but property which he does not know how to manage. Thus Beltov's life is the Russian active inactivity, and Beltov is only a generalised human being, a moral Caspar Hauser as it were.

Herzen here gives a masterly portrait of his friend Ogarev. Beltov desired to reveal the secret of the world, of its development and history, which was to be disclosed to astonished humanity in one of the most thorough and most profound philosophical works ever written ; but he never got beyond the preface, and even this was not completed. Others of Herzen's friends besides Ogarev are figured in Beltov. Herzen considered that Stankevič, for example, was one of those who had achieved nothing. In a sense and to a degree Herzen limns himself, too, in Beltov. It is true that Beltov is only a caricature of Herzen, but the best portraits are really caricatures.

These considerations must not discredit the true and living interest which Herzen took in all the questions that stirred his time, the interest he took in all that was human. Herzen's many-sided interests converged in a single direction, upon a single object—Russia.

CHAPTER THIRTEEN

M. A. BAKUNIN. REVOLUTIONARY ANARCHISM

§ 86.

WE have already made the acquaintance of Bakunin in Stankevič's circle, and have learned how Bakunin, a self-made man in matters philosophical, introduced his Moscow friends to the thought of Hegel. Bakunin is solely comprehensible as product and victim of Russian conditions under Nicholas I. Brought up from the very outset amid decabrist memories, he betook himself to Europe, plunged into Hegelian philosophy, and was urged on towards the revolution by the Hegelian left and by Proudhon. The years before 1848 and the year of revolution were spent by him in revolutionary movements of all kinds, for he hoped to realise his ideal of a free humanity through personal participation in the revolution, no matter where. His experiences in European and Russian prisons, and in Siberia, accentuated his hatred of the existing order, and made of him a professional revolutionary. The world as it was, Russia pre-eminently but Europe as well, extant civilisation and extant institutions, infuriated him, and his head was ever filled with revolutionary thoughts and plans, which, however, never attained to maturity. Neither in the field of practice nor in that of theory did Bakunin know anything of method or order. A genius and yet half-cultured (not wholly by his own fault), an egoist to the pitch of childishness, he was never troubled by the question whether, in the last resort, and amid the universal wretchedness, he might not to some extent share responsibility for his own individuality. The roots of all evil were elsewhere than in himself. The old order and its supporters, nature and the universe, including the Almighty, had personally injured him, were to him a continuous provocation; and he spent his life in frantic attempts to transform the world by force and to remould it in accordance with his own ideas. Without the beginnings of a clear conception as to the nature of the new constructions, and equally devoid of real knowledge of the world, Bakunin devoted himself to the career of a cosmopolitan agitator. At work now in England and now in France, then again in Belgium and Germany, and subsequently pursuing secret intrigues in Italy and Switzerland, he was never able to discover the fulcrum from which he might lever the world out of its bed. Thus revolutionary unrest and revolutionary fever mastered him. Mistaking his agitations for actions, he lost the sense of reality, and became unable to appraise at its true value the work done by his fellows. Not only did he reproach Herzen for thinking literature more important than practical activity, for preferring a man of letters to a " man of action," but he even declared Černyševskii to be no more than an arm-chair philosopher. Yet every revolutionary dreamer could lead him by the nose, and could fire him with enthusiasm for subversive designs, however preposterous.

Immediately after the failure of the Swedish enterprise on behalf of the Poles (1863), Herzen wrote to Bakunin: " Divorced from practical life, from earliest youth immersed over head and ears in that German idealism out of which the epoch constructed a realistic outlook ' as per schedule,' knowing nothing of Russia either before your imprisonment or after your Siberian exile, but animated by a grand and passionate desire for noble deeds, you have lived to the age of fifty in a world of illusions, student-like unrestraint, lofty plans, and petty defects. When, after ten years, you regained liberty, you showed yourself to be as of old a mere theorist, a man utterly without clear conceptions, a talker, unscrupulous in money matters, with an element of tacit but stubborn epicureanism, and with an itch for revolutionary activity— lacking only revolution itself."

The characterisation is just.[1] I would draw special attention to what Herzen says about Bakunin's unscrupulous-

[1] At a much earlier date Bělinskii described his friend Bakunin in the following terms : " Savage energy ; restless, stimulating, and profound mobility of mind ; incessant striving for remote ends without any gratification in the present ; even hatred for the present and for himself in the present ; ever leaping from the special to the general."

ness in money matters, for the accusation is confirmed in the reminiscences of Gué, the painter, the well-known friend of Tolstoi. Gué gives a specific instance. This trait, and indeed Bakunin's whole character, must be taken into account if we wish to form a sound estimate of his socialism. One who desires to provide the world with an entirely " new morality," one who wishes to reconstruct it in all essentials, must put up with the moral standards of everyday life. It is true that Bakunin's political opponents, especially Marx, Engels, and their adherents (some of whom were Russians), vilified Bakunin, to a large extent unjustly, but Bakunin's intimates were hardly more favourable in their judgments of Bakunin the man. Herzen and Ogarev were guarded in their language, but their impression was obviously unfavourable. Herzen, in his diary of 1848, makes an allusion to Bakunin which shows that those well acquainted with the latter were already saying, " He is a man of talent, but a bad lot." It is recorded that on more than one occasion the arch-conspirator displayed the most petty inclination towards gossip and other unmanly propensities. Kropotkin gives an extremely favourable account of Bakunin's personal character. I should value this testimony highly had it been based on personal observation, but Kropotkin never met Bakunin.

Bělinskii says of Bakunin that he loved ideas, not human beings. To this man of half-thoughts and half-deeds, his fellows were never more than means to an end. Half-thoughts, I say, and half-deeds. Hardly any of Bakunin's literary works were completed, nor did he display endurance and constancy in his practical undertakings. If history, as Herzen declares, be an improvisation, there must be individual improvisers, and such was Bakunin.

Bakunin's philosophical development resembled that of Bělinskii and Herzen. His relationship with Herzen, with whom he made acquaintance in 1839, was important to Bakunin and to Herzen as well, and was of a very peculiar nature.

Like Herzen, from Kant, Fichte, and Schelling, Bakunin passed on to Hegel, and from Hegel to Feuerbach. On coming to Europe, Bakunin met various members of the Hegelian left, and his relationships with these continued down to the rising of 1848. He knew Ruge, and subsequently met Stirner. In Paris he was on friendly terms with Proudhon. Influenced by Comte and by Vogt, he became definitively positivist and materialist. During his second period of European life he was confirmed in his materialism by the influence of Marx (for Bakunin contrasts here with Herzen), and by that of Darwinism, which by Bakunin as by so many others was taken as proof of materialism. He was fond of referring to the descent of men from monkeys, of speaking of the gorilla as man's ancestor. At this time, too, Bakunin was influenced by the ideas of Schopenhauer.

We see, then, that Bakunin's philosophical development and training closely resembled Herzen's. This is all the more comprehensible seeing that Bakunin remained in correspondence, and in part upon terms of personal intercourse, with his radical friends, and above all with Herzen. For a long time Herzen continued to agree even with the later radical ideas of Bakunin. It may be said that the thoughts to which Herzen gave expression in *From the Other Shore* remained those of Bakunin throughout life. The two friends sought the same goal, but differed as regards tactics.

We have already heard of Herzen's *Letters to an Old Comrade,* written in 1869. During this year Nečaev began his agitation among the Moscow students, and Herzen therefore felt it necessary to settle accounts in the theoretical field with Bakunin and the younger revolutionaries. In point of tactics the difference between the two friends arose out of the Herzenian " hesitation." Bakunin never hesitated for a moment ; as if by reflex action, we may say, he responded with a blow of his revolutionary fist to all the stimuli of the objective world, of the real world of society. He took delight in the thought of shattering the world to bits. He sought this delight in all directions, and when it was unobtainable in the form of concrete revolutionary activities, he would find it in passionate criticism and negation of the existing social order.[1]

---

[1] Mihail Bakunin was born in 1814. His father, who belonged to a wealthy family of good position, was a highly cultured man ; educated in Italy, he took his degree as doctor of philosophy at the university of Turin, and after his return to Russia was in touch with the decabrists. Bakunin's mother was related to Murav'ev-Apostol, one of the executed decabrists. In 1828 Mihail Bakunin was entered at the artillery school to be trained for a military career. Becoming an officer in 1833, he served for a brief period, but sent in his papers in 1834. For the next few years he lived in Moscow, in continuous association with the members of Stankevič's circle, and through Stankevič his thoughts were directed towards philosophy. He acquired a knowledge of German by the study of Kant and Fichte, and in 1835 translated Fichte's Lectures on the

§ 87.

BAKUNIN'S translation of Hegel's *Gymnasial Lectures* appeared in 1838, being published in "Nabljudatel" (The Observer), a periodical edited by Bělinskii.

In his introduction to this work Bakunin anticipated Bělinskii's explanation of the Hegelian proposition, "All that is real is rational."

Vocation of the Scholar. Having become a Hegelian in 1838, he translated Hegel's Gymnasial Lectures, and wrote an Introduction to the work. His ardent Hegelian propaganda led Bělinskii at a later date to give him the title of "spiritual father." Herzen, returning from exile in 1839, endeavoured to make clear to him the intrinsic meaning of the Hegelian philosophy, but for the moment with small success. Bakunin's sisters likewise had close relationships with their brother's Moscow friends. Ljubov was betrothed to Stankevič, but died before Stankevič, in 1838. Tatjana was an intimate friend of Bělinskii, whilst the latter was for a considerable period in love with Aleksandra. Aleksandra was attached to Botkin, but the parents forbade the marriage. In 1840 Bakunin went to Europe. At Berlin university he attended lectures given by members of the Hegelian school, and came into contact with Young Germany (Ruge and others), deriving from this last source an intimate knowledge of the philosophy of Feuerbach. In 1842 Bakunin published in the "Deutsche Jahrbücher" his Essay Concerning the Reaction in Germany, and wrote an impassioned pamphlet against Schelling in defence of Hegel. Before this he had attended Schelling's lectures, and had written, Schelling and Revelation, a Critique of the Latest-Reaction against Philosophy. In Switzerland he made the acquaintance of Vogt. Owing to his relationships with communist societies, the Russian government ordered him to return to Russia. Disregarding the summons, Bakunin went to Paris, where he became a friend of Proudhon and initiated the Frenchman into the mysteries of Hegel. In Paris he also made the acquaintance of George Sand and of Marx. Paris was at this time the rendezvous of the refugees. Especially intimate were Bakunin's relations with the exiled Polish revolutionaries, and he was henceforward an ardent advocate of Polish independence. During 1847 Bakunin encountered in Paris his old friends Herzen and Ogarev, and also met Bělinskii there. Expelled from Paris for his speech at the commemorative festival of the Polish insurrection of 1830, he went to Brussels, where Marx, too, was staying, but in 1848 hastened back to Paris to take an energetic part in the organisation of the workers. After the February revolution he left Paris for Prague to attend the Slav congress and was leader of the Prague rising. In 1849, having played an active part in the Dresden rising (in which Richard Wagner was also concerned), he was arrested and sentenced to death, the sentence being subsequently commuted to one of perpetual imprisonment in a fortress. In 1850 he was extradited to Austria, to experience there the same fate of death sentence, reprieve, and subsequent extradition to Russia, considerations of economy being doubtless the determining cause of the extradition. From 1851 to 1854 he was imprisoned in the fortress of St. Peter and St. Paul. He was then sent to the Schlüsselburg, and there, suffering severely from scurvy, he lost all his teeth, and his digestion was permanently impaired. In 1857 he was exiled to Siberia, where he came into close relationship with his cousin Murav'ev Amurskii, governor-general of Eastern Siberia, and in 1858 married a Polish woman. Escaping from Siberia, he returned to Europe by way of Japan and

Bakunin here settles his account with extreme subjectivism, and in particular with Fichtean solipsism. Building on a Hegelian foundation, he arrives at a position opposed to that of Kant, his former leader in philosophy, and opposed above all to that of Fichte, speaking of extreme subjectivism as egoistic self-contemplation and " the annihilation of any possible love." He condemns Schiller, the Kantian revolté ; he condemns Voltaire and the French philosophers of the

America, visiting Herzen in London in 1861. He now renewed his ties with the Polish refugees, and in 1863 endeavoured to come to the help of the Polish rebels by naval operations initiated in Sweden. We have already recounted how Bakunin's sarmatiophil influence proved injurious to Herzen's " Kolokol." The failure of the Polish rising and the triumph of reaction in Russia led Bakunin for the future to devote his attention to the west. From 1864 to 1868 he lived in Italy, where he founded the secret society International Brotherhood (known also as Alliance of Revolutionary Socialists), which lasted until 1869. Bakunin had relations with the Russians of the younger generation and with the Russian revolutionary secret societies then in process of formation. The International Working-Men's Association having been founded in 1864, Bakunin joined it in 1868, and there ensued a fierce struggle between him and Marx. In 1868 Bakunin also founded the Alliance internationale de la démocratie socialiste, with a secret brotherhood of whose central committee he was dictator. The same year, in conjunction with N. Žukovskii, he edited at Zurich the Russian journal " Narodnoe Dĕlo," but from the issue of the second number it was already in the hands of his opponent N. Utin. In 1869 he became intimate with Nečaev. In 1871 he took part in the disturbances at Lyons, where it was hoped to establish the commune. The struggle with Marx ended at the Hague congress in 1872, when Bakunin was excluded from the International ; at Marx's suggestion the grounds for the exclusion were recorded by Utin in a report describing Bakunin's share in Nečaev's machinations. As early as 1871 Bakunin had withdrawn to the Fédération jurassienne ; in 1872 he founded a Slav section in this body, which had but a short life, breaking up in 1873 owing to internal dissensions and the conflict with Lavrov ; in 1873 Bakunin quitted the Fédération. After participating in 1874 in the abortive rising at Bologna, much disheartened, he desisted from his activities. Attempts were frequently made to bring about a reunion between Bakunin's followers and the Marxists, and this was effected at Ghent in 1877, the year after Bakunin's death, which took place on July 6, 1876, in a hospital at Berne. The following are the principal works dealing with Bakunin. Mihail Bakunin's Correspondence with Aleksandr Herzen and Ogarev, with a biographical introduction, appendixes and elucidations by Mihail Dragomanov. A German translation (by Boris Minzes) of this Russian work is to be found in Theodor Schiemann's Bibliotek rüssischer Denkwürdigkeiten, 1895, vol. vi. No more than twenty-five lithographed copies were circulated of Nettlau's biography of Bakunin in three vols. (1896–1900). There is a précis by the author, M. Bakunin, eine biographische Skizze von Dr. M. Nettlau mit Auszügen aus seinen Schriften, und Nachwort von G. Landauer, 1901. Bakunin's friend James Guillaume has written a biographical sketch in the second volume of his collected edition of Bakunin's French writings, M. Bakounine, Oeuvres, Paris, 1907 et seq., seven vols. The edition is incomplete, but can be supplemented by Dragomanov, and by Guillaume's L'Internationale, documents et souvenirs, 1864 to 1878, 2 vols., Paris 1905-7.

eighteenth century ; and he condemns Saint-Simon. All are repudiated owing to their hostility to Christianity. Like Granovskii, Bakunin expressly defends the doctrine of immortality.

According to Bakunin, subjectivism leads to despair and self-destruction. " Reality is ever victorious ; man has no choice but to come to terms with reality, to immerse himself deliberately in reality, and to love reality, for in default of this he must destroy himself." This anti-subjectivist formula of Bakunin is very different from the formula of Bělinskii and Herzen, for whereas the two latter discern in subjectivism the premises for crime, murder, and revolution, Bakunin discovers the premises for suicide. Many years afterwards, in 1874, when the rising in Bologna miscarried, Bakunin wished to take his own life, but was dissuaded by a friend. Yet Bakunin had then abandoned subjectivism, and upon objectivist grounds had preached murder—the right to kill.

§ 88.

FOUR years later Bakunin rejected, not Russian reality alone, but European reality as well, his rejection being no less emphatic than had formerly been his defence.

I refer to the essay in Ruge's " Jahrbücher " for the year 1842. From this writing it is customary to quote as characteristic of Bakunin's anarchism the saying, " The desire for destruction is at the same time a creative desire." But the essay should be read in its entirety, for it is the best that Bakunin ever wrote, and furnishes a genuinely philosophical program of democracy.

Bakunin declares war on Schelling and his positive philosophy, which Schelling had counterposed to Hegel's negative rationalism. In 1841 Frederick William IV, " the romanticist on the throne," had summoned Schelling to Berlin, and Bakunin had heard Schelling lecture. Turning away from Schelling's romanticist mythology and revelation, Bakunin contrasts with the German's theosophy the theory of rationalistic democracy. The things which in Schelling's dreams were to appear in his Johannine church of the future were for Bakunin to be realised here and now by democracy.[1]

---

[1] Reaction in Germany, a Fragment, by a Frenchman. The essay is signed Jules Elysard and has a prefatory note by Ruge. " Deutsche Jahrbücher für Wissenschaft und Kunst," October 17–21, 1842.

Bakunin attempts to discover the true essence of democracy by throwing light upon its opposition to the reaction of the post-revolutionary epoch of the restoration. The theoretical basis of this reaction is found in Schelling's positive philosophy and in the historical school of law ; the reaction has but one practical aim, to maintain the old social order.

Conversely the task of democracy is to create a new world. The essence, the principle, of democracy is the most general, the most all-embracing, the most intimate of factors ; it is what Hegel speaks of as the spirit which reveals itself and develops itself in history. Such is the principle of democracy, but somewhat different is the democratic party, which has not attained to clear views concerning its own principle, and hence its weakness. The party must learn that the task of democracy does not consist merely in opposition to rulers, it must not aim solely at some particular constitutional or politico-economic change, but must bring about a total transformation of the state of the world. Democracy is a religion ; it must be religious, must be, that is to say, permeated by its principle, not in the sphere of thought alone, but also in real life, down to its minutest manifestations. Not until this is effected will the democratic party conquer the world.

As a party, the democratic party is not the general, but merely a particular ; it is the negative contrasted with the other particular, the positive. The whole significance and the irresistible energy of the negative are found in the destruction of the positive ; but in destroying the positive, the negative, too, perishes. Since democracy does not yet exist in its affirmative wealth, but only as an incomplete negative, it must first perish with its opponent, before it can rise renewed in all the fulness of life. This transformation of the democratic party will be qualitative as well as quantitative. The democratic party must become conscious of the priestly office of democracy, must become aware that democracy is a new living and vitalising revelation, a new heaven and a new earth, a young and glorious world, wherein all existing discords will be resolved into a harmonious corcord.

Hence the weakness of the democratic party cannot be cured by any superficial union with the positive, for negative and positive are incompatible. Now the negative, considered in its contrast with the positive, appears void of content, and positive thinkers reproach the democrats on this ground. But they err ; the negative is nothing by itself, and in isolation would in actual fact be absolutely nothing. Its whole being, its content, are, however, found in its opposition to the positive, and its vital energy consists in the destruction of the positive.

The reactionary party is considered by Bakunin to exhibit two trends, for there are, he says, the pure or logical reactionaries, and the compromising or illogical reactionaries. The logical reactionaries are well aware that their positive can only be secured through the suppression of the negative, but they do not see that their positive is positive only in so far as it is opposed by the negative, and that if it were to secure complete victory over the negative, it would, in the absence of its opponent, no longer be the positive, but rather the completion of the negative. Blindness, however, is the leading characteristic of all positivists, and insight is vouchsafed to negativists alone. These pure positivists desire to be honest and complete human beings ; they detest half-measures just as much as do the democrats, for they know that only a complete human being can be good, and that half-measures are the tainted source of all that is evil.

Bakunin proceeds to show how the reactionaries hate the democrats, and how they would like to use any means, to use the inquisition were it still possible, in order to annihilate the democrats. The democrats, on the other hand, even though they may often be guilty of unjust and partisan actions, derive from the sublime principle of democracy energy enabling them to carry on their struggle religiously as well as politically, making a religion of freedom, whose only true expression is justice and love. Even in the heat of the struggle the democrat continues to obey the greatest of Christ's commandments, and to realise the essence of Christianity, which is love.

Bakunin next explains how and why the reactionaries take refuge in the past as it existed before the appearance of the opposition between negative and positive. They are to this extent right inasmuch as this past was a living totality and was consequently richer than the disintegrated present ; but they fail to understand that to-day this totality can manifest itself to them in no other form than as a self-created, dissolving, and disintegrating contrast ; they fail to understand that the totality, as a positive, involves also the negative, and is nothing but the soulless corpse of its old self given up to the mechanical and chemical process of reflection. Not understanding these things, but sensing the absence of life, they throw the whole blame upon the negative. Being unable to satisfy their desire for love and truth, their incapacity becomes transformed into hatred of the negative.

The compromising positivists are more strongly affected than the uncompromising positivists by the reflective malady of the age. They do not reject the negative unconditionally, but concede to it a relative and temporary justification. They lack, however, the energy of simplicity, and they know nothing of the endeavour to attain to completeness and honesty of disposition. Theoretical dishonesty is the standpoint of the compromisers. Bakunin speaks of this dishonesty as theoretical because he cannot believe that an individual evil will can really exercise an inhibitive influence upon the development of the human spirit, but he admits that of necessity theoretical dishonesty almost always manifests itself as practical dishonesty.

The compromising positivists are wiser than the logical positivists ; the former are the wise men, the theorists par excellence, and are therefore the leading representatives of the present. Bakunin characterises them by quoting a well-known dictum concerning the juste-milieu : " Le côté gauche dit, ' deux fois deux font quatre ' ; le côté droit dit, ' deux fois deux font six ' ; le juste-milieu dit, ' deux fois deux font cinq.' " The compromisers speak less clearly and definitely than the logical positivists ; they evade the simple practical urge for truth ; they are too astute to follow the simple practical dictates of consciousness. The democrats say that only the simple is true, real, and creative ; the compromisers, with immense trouble, construct an artificial patchwork, so that they may distinguish themselves from the stupid and uncultured mob. They know everything, and being men of world-wide experience they allow nothing to astonish them. They have sampled the entire material and spiritual universe, and after this long and tedious reflective journey have come to the conviction that the real world is not worth the trouble involved in securing a genuinely living contact with it. It is difficult to know what to make of these people. They never say " yes " or " no." They say, " You are right to some extent, but still . . ." When they have nothing more to say, they tell us, " Yes, it is rather odd."

Nevertheless the democrats cannot venture to ignore the party of the compromisers. Despite their instability, despite their incapacity to effect anything, theirs is numerically the most powerful party ; they have no substance, but they are in the majority, and are one of the most important signs of the times.

The whole wisdom of the compromisers is found in their contention that those who represent the two opposed tendencies, the positivists and the negativists, are necessarily one-sided, therefore err ; truth lies in the middle, and a compromise must be secured between the opposites. But this is erroneous. Compromise is de facto impossible, for the only aim of the negative is to destroy the positive. The compromisers set forth the two terms of the proposition, and from their own standpoint they ought to allow the opposition due weight ; but this opposition leads us to a dissolution, to a negation, not to a compromise. Bakunin appeals here to Hegel's logic, to Hegel's exposition of the category of contrast and its immanent development. This doctrine is of the utmost importance, and, since the category of contrast is the main category, is the very essence, of the present, Hegel is the greatest philosopher of the present, stands at the summit of modern theoretical culture. In so far as Hegel grasped and resolved this category, he was the starting-point of the necessary self-resolution of modern culture. Thus he is at once above theory and within theory. He postulates a new practical world, which will not be attained through the formal application and diffusion of ready-made theories, but only through the primordial activity of the practical and autonomous spirit.

The contrast between the positive and the negative is of such a character that the two elements are mutually exclusive, so that we are forced to ask how these two conflicting elements can be conceived in a totality. Those who wish to do this may arbitrarily turn their backs upon the cleavage, and endeavour to escape from the contrast by returning to the simple totality which existed before the cleavage occurred—but such a return is impossible. The. alternative is the endeavour to compromise, but this is likewise impossible, and the would-be compromisers are in reality quite unable to succeed.

Bakunin attempts to show that the positive has a twofold significance in relation to the negative. The positive may be the quiescent, immobile, apathetic, and pure positive, excluding all that is negative. But this exclusion is itself activity, movement ; and thus the positive, because of its very positiveness, is no longer the positive but the negative. By excluding the negative from itself, it excludes itself from itself, and destroys itself. It follows from this that the positive and the negative do not weigh equally in the scales; the contrast is not an equilibrium, for the negative scale is far more heavily loaded. The negative determines the life of the positive, includes within itself the totality of the contrast, and alone therefore possesses an absolute justification for existence.

This deduction seems to conflict with what was previously conceded by Bakunin, namely that the negative, taken by itself and considered in the abstract, is just as one-sided as the positive. This is indeed so, in so far as the negative excluded from the positive is itself positive. When the positivists negate the negative in its quiescent relationship to itself, they are discharging a logical and even sacred function, though they know not what they do. They believe themselves to be negating the negative, but they are negating it only in so far as they themselves convert it into a positive. They awaken the negative from the philistine repose for which it is ill-suited, and lead it back to its great mission—to the unresting and relentless destruction of all that positively exists.

Bakunin admits that the positive and the negative are equally justified when the latter, quiescently and egoistically withdrawing into itself, is untrue to itself. But the negative must not be egoistic; it must lovingly give itself up to the positive in order to absorb the positive. With growing enthusiasm Bakunin sociomorphises the logical contrast between the positive and the negative. In his relentless negation the negative appears simultaneously as that which is common to the two terms of the contrast, and as the superposed, the superior, the solely justified term; it is the manifestation of the contemporary practical spirit (which until the contrast has thus been resolved remains indiscernible)—the spirit which by its vigorous mission of destruction exhorts to repentance the sinful souls of the compromisers, the spirit which announces its imminent coming, its imminent revelation in a genuinely democratic and universally human church of liberty.

One who understands the spirit of the time and is permeated by that spirit, can wish no other compromise than the self-resolution of the positive by the negative. The effort to secure compromise is nothing but stupidity or lack of principle. The able and moral man is one who gives himself up whole-heartedly to the spirit of the time and is permeated by that spirit.

The compromisers, like the democrats, recognise the totality of the contrast between positive and negative, but they desire to rob this contrast of its mobility, its life, its soul, for the vitality of the contrast is something essentially practical in its nature, and is therefore unendurable by their impotent demi-souls. To the positivists, too, they wish to forbid the negation of the negative. They would like to preserve the decayed and withered remnants of tradition, and to live with the positivists in these traditional ruins, in this irrational rococo world. They would like to make themselves permanently at home in the positivists' world; in a world where not reason but long continuance and immobility are the measure of the true and the sacred; in a world where China with its mandarins and floggings with the bamboo are the incorporation of absolute truth. But since the negativists gather strength daily, the compromisers desire to weaken the negativist movement by urging the positivists to make a little room for the negativists in their society, by casting out of the positivist historical museum a small number of " ruins which are indeed quite venerable, but have after all fallen utterly into decay." They endeavour to persuade the positivists that the negativists are merely young people who have been embittered by poverty, whose behaviour will be quiet and modest as soon as they are permitted to enter the respectable society of the positivists. In like manner do the compromisers attempt to appease the negativists. They recognise the nobility of the negativists' aims and admire their youthful enthusiasm for purity of principle. But pure principles, they say, cannot be applied in practical life, where an element of eclecticism is in place. We must give way to the world if we are to influence the world. . . .

The upshot of this impossible superficial compromise is that the compromisers are despised by both parties.

Bakunin refuses to accept the suggestion that the compromisers serve the cause of progress, whereas the negativists desire to shatter the world to bits. The attempts of the compromisers to effect progress by gradations do not secure progress, but result in the maintenance of the mean and pitiful conditions that now exist. They wish the positive and the negative to continue to exist separate, one-sided, and unrelated ; to preserve for themselves in addition the enjoyment of the totality—a totality lacking life. For this reason the compromisers, since they are not truly permeated by the spirit of the present, are immoral, seeing that morality is impossible beyond the limits of the only saving church, the church of free men. Bakunin cites against them the words of the writer of the Apocalypse : " I know thy works, that thou art neither cold nor hot : I would thou wert cold or hot. So then because thou art lukewarm, and neither cold nor hot, I will spue thee out of my mouth. Thou sayest, I am rich, and increased with goods, and have need of nothing ; and knowest not that thou art wretched, and miserable, and poor, and blind, and naked."

To history also, Bakunin applies this Hegelian doctrine of contrast. The principle of freedom was active from the first in the old Catholic world, manifesting itself in the numerous heresies which kept Catholicism alive and vigorous, but did so only whilst they existed within Catholicism, only whilst the oppositions were combined into a totality. In Protestantism, whose spirit had at first developed within Catholicism, the principle of freedom became independent, and the contrast became manifest in its purity.

The compromisers maintain that the contrasts of the present day are less acute and less dangerous. Tranquillity, they contend, is universal ; everywhere movement has subsided ; no one thinks of war, for material interests, which have now become the leading concerns of politics and universal civilisation, cannot be furthered without peace. Bakunin, however, points out to the compromisers the great signs of the time. He shows them the mysterious and terrible words, liberty, equality and fraternity, graven upon the temple of liberty upbuilded by the revolution. He points to Napoleon, who did not tame democracy, but, as son of the revolution, disseminated the democratic levelling principle throughout Europe. He refers to Kant, Fichte, Schelling, and Hegel, showing that philosophy established in the intellectual world the identical levelling and revolutionary principle, and the principle of the autonomy of the spirit, which conflicts absolutely with all positive religions and churches. The revolution has not been overcome. It is merely gathering strength for a fresh onslaught. Strauss,

Feuerbach, and Bruno Bauer are preaching negation anew; they find listeners and followers everywhere, even among the positivists.

Mankind can secure satisfaction and repose in no other way than by the adoption of a universally practical principle, one which comprehends within itself the thousandfold phenomena of the mental life. But where is this life-creating principle to be discovered? Is it in Protestantism? Protestantism is given up to the most deplorable anarchy, and is split into innumerable sects; the Protestant world has no enthusiasm, and is the most disillusioned world imaginable. Is it in Catholicism? Catholicism, once a world-controlling power, has become the obedient tool of an immoral policy foreign to itself. Is it in the state? The state is affected by a profound internal conflict, for the state is impossible without religion, without a vigorous and universal sentiment. Neither Protestantism, nor Catholicism, nor yet the state, is the comprehensive, tranquillising, satisfying principle.

In conclusion, Bakunin once more apostrophises the compromisers in the following terms: " Look within, gentlemen, and tell me honestly whether you are content with yourselves, and whether you possibly can be content with yourselves. Are you not without exception gloomy and paltry manifestations of a gloomy and paltry age? Are you not full of contradictions? Are you complete men? Do you believe in anything real? Do you know what you want, and indeed are you capable of wanting anything? Has modern reflection (introspection), this epidemic malady of our day, left any part of you truly alive; are you not utterly permeated by this malady, paralysed by it, and broken? In fact, gentlemen, you must admit that our epoch is a gloomy epoch, and that we, its children, are yet more gloomy."

Bakunin's hope is therefore fixed upon the spirit of revolution, which will speedily manifest itself and will soon hold its assize. On all hands, and especially in France and England, socialistic-religious unions are coming into being. The people, whose rights are recognised in theory, but who by birth and circumstance are condemned to poverty and ignorance, and therewith also to practical slavery, the people, comprising the great majority of mankind, begin to number the thin ranks of their enemies and to demand the realisation of the rights which have already been theoretically conceded. All nations and all men are inspired with a premonition, and every one who is not affected with paralysis looks with tense expectation towards the near future, about to utter the word of deliverance. Even in Russia, which we know so little and for which perchance a great destiny is in store, lowering clouds are gathering, the heralds of storm ! The atmosphere is sultry, pregnant with tempests ! " To the positivists we say : ' Open the eyes of your mind ; let the dead bury their dead ; realise at last that the spirit, the ever-young, the ever-reborn, is not to be discovered in mouldering ruins ! ' To the compromisers we say : ' Throw open your hearts to the truth ; clear your minds from pitiful and blind wisdom, free yourselves from the theorist's arrogance and the slave's dread, which have withered your souls and paralysed your movements ! ' Let us put our trust in the eternal spirit which only destroys and annihilates because it is the unsearchable and eternally creative source of all life. The desire for destruction is also a creative desire ! "

Immediately after its appearance, Bakunin's essay attracted considerable and favourable attention from the liberal press of Europe and of Russia. Herzen, without knowing who was the author, thought highly of it, for Bakunin had roughed in the outline for Herzen's analysis of the revolution of 1848. Herzen's *From the Other Shore* was no more than the filling in of this outline with historic content. The abstractness of the exposition is characteristic of Bakunin and his anarchism. Not merely did Bakunin conceive Hegel's dialectical process in a purely schematic manner, but he conceived it unhistorically. According to Hegel the higher historic form develops out of the contrast between thesis and antithesis. Bakunin presents Hegel's formula in a way which indicates that the two contrasts are to be entirely superseded, and to give place to a completely new form. I suspect that Bakunin had already conceived, though not perhaps very clearly, the thought of Russia's messianism. Russia was for Europe the something wholly new, and Europe was perishing from its internal oppositions. Unquestionably when Bakunin spoke of the positive he was thinking of the medieval third and second Rome ; and in the struggle between the positive and the negative he presented an accurate schematic representation of the development of the modern age.

Bakunin's article gave clear expression to the revolutionary mood of the circle in which he moved, and to a degree therefore to the revolutionary mood of his time. It must further be admitted that he provided a successful interpretation of democracy in its philosophic aspects when he conceived democracy as a general outlook on the universe. In this matter, too, Herzen followed in Bakunin's footsteps. In Bakunin's conception of democracy as religious in character we trace the influence of French socialism. Noteworthy are the energetic protests against scepticism and the longing for a saving faith.

We must consider Bakunin's analysis of bourgeois liberalism in this light, and in this light we cannot fail to give it our general approval.

§ 89.

THE programme of religious democracy was transformed by Bakunin into the program of anarchistic pandestruction. He was led along this course, not merely by his multiform personal experiences, which increased his hostility to existing society, but in addition by the development of his philosophical thought. Bakunin accepted Feuerbach's anthropologism in the form of a sharply defined materialism, adhering to Herzen's exposition of its principles in *From the Other Shore*. Bakunin's tendencies in this direction were reinforced by the influence of Proudhon (owing to his attack upon the church and the state in 1858, in his book *De la justice dans la revolution et dans l'église*, Proudhon had to flee from Paris), and by that of postrevolutionary and antireactionary materialism. Thus religious democracy became antireligious democracy.

With Herzen, Bakunin now came to conceive the present as a definitive transition from theological illusion to the positivist disillusionment of realistic materialism. In the program for the peace congress at Geneva (1867), antitheology was placed beside federalism and socialism as the third essential demand. After the Lyons disturbances he had one of his recurrent paroxysms of theorising, and wrote the most detailed of his philosophical fragments, *Dieu et l'état*, which was first published in 1882 by the press of the Jura federation. Ecrasons l'infâme—thus may be summarised his philosophy of religion and philosophy of history as formulated in 1875. (" L'église et l'état sont mes deux bêtes noires.")

Atheism is alone competent to bring true freedom to mankind, and it is therefore the first prerequisite of the social revolution. " If God exists, man is a slave ; but man can and must be free, therefore God does not exist "—this onto-logical demonstration of atheism is vigorously presented by Bakunin. If the authority of God and the church be overthrown, there falls therewith the authority of the state, of which the church is a main prop. " As slaves of God, men must likewise become slaves of church and state, in so far as state is sanctified by church." All authority, therefore, is overthrown, all authority save only the authority of Bakunin. Just as Comte promoted himself to the rank of positivist pope, so did Bakunin look upon himself as anarchist pope.

Bakunin, like his teachers, conceives ecclesiastical religion as a superstition which originated in poverty and enslave-ment. The church is for him a kind of heavenly tavern (Bakunin naturally has in mind the Russian *kabak*) ; and con-versely the tavern is the heavenly church on earth. In the church and in the tavern the mužik can for a moment forget his sorrows and his poverty, drowning them in the former in irrational faith, and in the latter in vodka—the same drunkenness in both cases.

Bakunin does not conceive religion merely as theism, but lays great stress in addition upon the doctrine of immortality. To him as to his predecessors atheism is at the same time materialism in the sense of antispiritualism. Bakunin appeals in especial to Comte for the reduction of psychology to a branch of biology, one of the natural sciences.

The assumption that there exists an undying and therefore infinite soul seems to him to conflict with the theological doc-trine of God's absoluteness, but theology has found it possible to subordinate the infinite to a higher infinite. To mitigate the absurdity theologians have conceived the doctrine of the devil ; the infinite is in revolt against the absolutism of the infinite ; revolution is dominant even in the spirit world. Nay, the anchorites, revered as holy, were animated by this principle of revolt, which in their case took the form of a revolt against the infinite as typified in human society.

Religion, or superstition, will be overthrown and replaced by positive science and the disillusionment science brings. Bakunin, therefore, esteems logic highly. " You, my friends, may say what you will. Great is logic ; perhaps it is the only great thing " (1868).

History, like psychology, becomes materialistic. Bakunin draws this conclusion, and is therefore forced to recognise the universality of natural determinism ; but he takes all possible pains to preserve freedom for the individual. We feel that here Kant, and more especially Fichte, are at war in his mind against Hegel, Comte, and Vogt.

§ 90.

THE goal of history and of individual effort is the equality of all men, absolute equality, such as will render impossible the domination of one human being by another, and will therefore put an end to exploitation. Bakunin refuses to recognise any authority whatever. When God's authority is overthrown, authority of every other kind is likewise overthrown, and above all that of the state. Even science, which is to play so great a part in freeing mankind from the yoke of authority, must not issue commands. Science, or its representatives, must not dominate life, but must merely illuminate. The intelligentsia must bring culture to the masses, but this does not give the teacher any rights over the pupil ; and besides, inequality in point of culture is but transient, and the teacher may well come to learn from the pupil.

Absolute equality will not lead to the atomisation of society, will not break up mankind into fragments. It offers, on the contrary, to mankind the possibility of a true social union. Bakunin accepts Proudhon's program of federation, federation " from below upwards," conceiving the future society as a federative organisation of communes.

Bakunin continues to cling to the Hegelian dialectical formulation, and writes : " Statehood (centralisation) is the thesis, anarchy or amorphism is the antithesis, and federation will be the synthesis."

Bakunin looks for an entire reconstruction of society, and as a preliminary, therefore, existing society and its order must be destroyed root and branch. Pandestruction (when he uses this word " pan " means " wholly " as well as " all ") is essential because every element of the old social order would be capable, were life left in it, of proliferating anew, and of leading to the recurrence of the old.

From his antitheological outlook, the "alternative" of the year 1842 seems to Bakunin essential. Since theism, since religion in general, is the foundation of the existing social order, nothing short of the complete destruction of religion can effect the overthrow of the political order that has hitherto prevailed. Alike in the religious, in the political, and in the social field, atheism must be opposed to theism.

For Bakunin there exists no middle term between theism and atheism, and for him therefore pandestruction is above all the annihilation of theism, of religious faith. Bakunin sees (influenced, perhaps, by the theories of Strauss and Renan) that religions are historic growths, have been formed by society as a whole. Bakunin expresses his meaning by saying that "public opinion," which he ranks above state and church, has brought religion into being, and that "public opinion," men themselves and not their institutions merely, must therefore be fundamentally altered. Nevertheless, so runs his naïve argument, it will perhaps be easier to overthrow state and church, and we must consequently make a beginning with these.

Absolute pandestruction being thus reduced to partial destruction, we find that in certain other respects Bakunin is not disinclined to make a few concessions.

It is true that he continually returns to his demand for absolute amorphism, but in proportion as he works for the practical realisation of this aim he makes concessions and is content with partial modifications. Despite his "écrasons," he is actually inclined, as far as Russia is concerned, to tolerate "superstition." When his views began to gain attention in Russia and it became necessary for him to draft a program of political activity, Bakunin made concessions in matters of tactics, agreeing in especial that the religious question need not occupy the first place. Judged by his own program of 1842, Bakunin became a compromiser, a liberal reactionary.

Nor did he find it possible to reject the evolutionary idea. As previously stated, he accepted Darwinism, and had therefore to admit that the desired goal must be attained by numerous transitional stages. His historical knowledge was, however, inadequate, and the idea of gradual progress, rejected by him in 1842, was not clearly conceived or definitely elaborated.

In point of theory Bakunin makes further concessions

to Marxism and to historical materialism. Like Herzen, he conceives individual mental energy as a primary historic force, but in his postsiberian period his thought tended to become more economic, and was at times almost Marxist. His contest with Marx in the International compelled Bakunin to gain a clearer understanding of his opponent's theories, and despite all differences of opinion between himself and Marx he began a translation of the first volume of *Capital*.[1]

§ 91.

BAKUNIN attempted on more than one occasion to formulate the philosophic principles of revolution. In his leading work, the motive force of individual action and of history is discerned in three principles, animality, thought, and revolt ; man has an inborn need for revolt, a revolutionary instinct. This ranking of revolt beside thought and animality is manifestly a transference of the Bakuninist revolutionary nervous impulse into the domain of psychology ; but it is plain that revolt as a primary psychical element is atrophied in many human beings, or at least that it is " inborn " only in certain periods.

In his program for the Alliance Internationale de la Démocratie Socialiste, which was published in 1873, Bakunin formulated an ethical theory of revolution which was no less typical of his thought than the instinct theory.

---

[1] In Dieu et l'État, we are told that religion or theism is the groundwork of social slavery, that science and culture are the proper means to secure enfranchisement from religious illusion, from church and state, and consequently from slavery and exploitation. In the speech at the Berne conference (September 1868), he tells us, on the other hand, that the populace must be economically secure before it can become cultured, and that a social revolution is therefore necessary before we can hope for the destruction of religion. " Intellectual propaganda " will not suffice. Atheism will be attained through the social revolution, not conversely. Again, we read : " Economic revolution has an immeasurable advantage over religious and political revolution in the sobriety of its foundations." Thus positivism is represented as the consequence or accompaniment of economic revolution. In an undated letter published by Dragomanov, an arithmetical computation is even given of the relationship between the economic and the ideal endeavours of mankind. Half the human race, we are told, looks for the satisfaction of material needs, whereas the other half desires the satisfaction of spiritual or ideal needs, and history affords proof of this duplex trend of endeavour. But Bakunin inclines to give the primacy to spiritual needs. Even during the "phase of social-economic development" men will not devote themselves exclusively to promoting their material interests.

Starting from his materialistic determinism, Bakunin denied freedom of the will that he might be enabled to repudiate law, and above all criminal law. The individual, he said, was the " involuntary " product of the natural environment and the social milieu, by which criminals and kings are alike produced. Neither the criminal nor the king is responsible or blameworthy, since both are the natural products of one and the same society. To enable itself to punish criminals, society insists that it is necessary to hold the individual responsible for his actions, but this theory of responsibility derives from theology, which is compounded of absurdity and hypocrisy. The individual is neither punishable nor responsible.

Bakunin failed to note the objection that by this theory the judge and the executioner, just as much as the criminal, are " natural " products of society, so that it is plain that he had forgotten Bělinskii. Nor did he trouble himself to explain why the kings, as the topmost points, were to be overthrown, if they were no more than the blameless victims of the society to which they belonged.

Bakunin deduced all immorality (had he been consistent he would have said " so-called " immorality !) from political, social, and economic inequality. But this inequality, he said, is dominant only in the period of transition, and will disappear after the universal revolution, after a revolution which is simultaneously social, philosophical, economic, and political. During this period of transition, the sole right of society vis-à-vis the criminal is, in self-protection, to kill the criminal whom it has itself produced ; but society has no right to judge or to condemn. In connection with this right to kill, Bakunin is of course thinking of the individual assassinations and the mass killings of the revolution ; and the right to kill, to assassinate, is not by him properly conceived as a right but as a " natural fact," tragical but inevitable.

Bakunin, indeed, tells us in express terms that this " natural " fact is not ethical at all, but simply natural. The idea of justice is valid only during the period of transition ; it is a negative idea, in whose terms the social problem and social ideal may indeed be formulated, but the positive solution of that problem, the positive attainment of that ideal, can be effected solely by fraternity, by the actual realisation of equality. Bakunin further concedes that " natural " murders will even be useless if the oppressors thus removed are merely to be replaced by new oppressors. He condemns the jacobins and the Blanquists for dreaming of bloody revolutions directed against individual human beings, whereas the ultimate and universal revolution must be directed against the "organisation of things" and against "social positions." This radical revolution must destroy private property and the state, and may endeavour to protect individuals in so far as this will not injure the revolutionary cause. Bakunin does not shrink from speaking of this radical revolution as anarchy (anarchy, he says, is the "complete manifestation of the folk-life"), out of which equality will develop ; but for this very reason every authority must be annihilated, whether it be known by the name of church, monarchy, constitutionalist state, bourgeois republic, or revolutionary dictatorship. This entirely new revolutionary state [so we cannot get on without the state after all !] "will be the new fatherland, the alliance of the universal revolution against the alliance of all the reactions."

Such in broad outline is Bakunin's justly renowned philosophy of "deed," built up upon the old confusion between determinism and fatalism, which repudiates moral responsibility. For some reasons Bakunin would like to save individual freedom, but for other reasons this would be inconvenient. Bakunin shelters behind the positivist screen of "natural" facts. In his address to the Russian youth he defends on similar lines Karakozov's attempt on Alexander II, representing it as "natural" and "epidemic" passion of youth ; but, being aware of the precarious character of this exculpatory suggestion, he demands that "individual deeds" shall become more and more frequent, until they take the form of "deeds of the collective masses." The work will grow continually easier in proportion as panic gains ground in the stratum of society devoted to destruction. The uncorrupted minds of youth, argues Bakunin, cannot fail to grasp that it is far more humane to poniard or to strangle the objects of hatred by dozens or even by hundreds than in alliance with these same hated ones to participate in systematised legal murders. Bakunin therefore preaches the holy war of destruction ; evil is to be fought by all possible means, "with poison, the knife, or the noose— for the revolution sanctifies all equally." The true revolutionist knows nothing of scruples or doubts, and has nothing to rue. "Repentance is excellent if it can alter things or lead to improvement. Otherwise, it is not merely useless but injurious."

Bakunin inveighs energetically against those who demand from the " man of to-day " a precise plan of reconstruction and of the future. It suffices if we can achieve no more than a hazy idea of the opposite to all that is loathsome in contemporary civilisation. Our aim is to raze things to the ground ; our goal, pandestruction. " It seems to us criminal that those who are already busied about the practical work of revolution should trouble their minds with thoughts of this nebulous future, for such thoughts will merely prove a hindrance to the supreme cause of destruction." Bakunin rails against the literature of the day, composed by informers and flatterers, by those in the pay of despotism, who write belletristic and scientific works in defence of the old order, and who have thought out this lie concerning the positive plan for the future. It is true, adds Bakunin, that there are honest dreamers, and socialists among them, who spin cobweb plans of a better life, but this is once more the same detestable business, for they construct their pictures of the future out of the repulsive material of existing conditions. " Let the deed alone now speak."

The absurd, scholastic, sophistical, and positively Jesuitical character of Bakunin's anarchistic humanism must be plain to every thinker. I have already said that this " new morality " (Bakunin considers the old morality, based upon religion, patriarchalism, and class tradition lost beyond hope of rescue) is essentially founded upon materialistic and naturalistic determinism ; but in addition it may be pointed out that it is Schopenhauerian voluntarism which is here presented to us as the gospel of the deed. Bakunin, like so many other politicians, insists upon the merits of practice as contrasted with theory. Schopenhauer's misanthropic tendencies notwithstanding, his philosophical nihilism is transformed by Bakunin into pandestruction.[1]

We have already learned what Bělinskii and Herzen thought of the deed as contrasted with the word.

Bakunin, despite his positive preference for science, combined with voluntarism a vigorous hostility towards intel-

---

[1] Insistence upon the deed was characteristic of the revolutionary mood of the forties. Proudhon continually demands deeds ; and Hess, the Proudhonist, wrote a Philosophy of the Deed (1843) ; revolutionary practice was placed above theory. It must not be forgotten that postkantian philosophy in Germany had demanded on principle that theory should recede into the background as compared with practice. Fichte categorically demanded the deed.

lectualism. He refused to recognise science as the sole guide
in life. Science cannot alone control society, for control by
science would mean that mankind would be stupefied, that men
would become dumb driven cattle. Bakunin frequently used
strong expressions directed against the intelligentsia, which
he regarded as just as bad as the aristocracy, and as no less
callous than the bourgeoisie. Yet notwithstanding this verdict
he demanded of the members of the intelligentsia, not that
they should instruct the populace, but that they should revo-
lutionise it. At any rate Bakunin had far less admiration
for preaching than had Herzen.

In conformity with this philosophy of the deed, Bakunin
approved, not mass revolution alone, but individual assassination and individual expropriation as means for the production
of general panic, and he looked upon terrorism as an educative
instrument on behalf of the revolution.[1]

He unhesitatingly accepts Jesuitism and Machiavellianism.
The secret societies of the Poles and the Italians would naturally
encourage this tendency.[2]

We cannot ascertain how far Bakunin was guided by Nečaev
in issuing his secret instructions. Bakunin had cut adrift
from Nečaev, but his relations with the conspirator had been
of a somewhat questionable character. (Consult Dragomanov's
Biography in Minzes' German translation of Bakunin's letters,
p. xcii).

Notwithstanding the most thorough devotion to anarchy,
the revolution of pandestruction must in the end be regulated
and led, and Bakunin provided for this with the aid of the

[1] Debagorii-Mokrievič, the revolutionist, declares that Bakunin worked ever
in favour of an organised rising, and did not desire individual acts of political
assassination, carried out at individual discretion. Not merely does this
assertion conflict with what has been referred to above, but from Bakunin's
standpoint the philosophically grounded rejection of such individual outrages
is hardly possible.

[2] The details of Bakunin's and Nečaev's secret instructions to revolutionists may be read in the secret rules of the Carbonari League ; they coincide
in part with the rules of the Mazzinist secret society Young Italy. Bakunin
opposed Mazzini's religious views, but borrowed from Mazzini the plan for a
secret universalised league of Young Europe and the idea of the absolute
obedience of the members. At that time, moreover, the design had spread
throughout the continent. Even before 1848 Bakunin had been a member of
secret societies, and I believe that in Siberia his intercourse with the Polish
political exiles served to confirm him in his predilection for this type of activity.
As early as the twenties the Polish secret societies had similar programs and rules,
as we see in the Union of National Carbonari (1821), etc.

central committee, a secret body quite outside the ken of most of the members of the revolutionary association. Bakunin expressly appealed to the example of the Jesuits, saying that the individual revolutionary " must renounce his own will."

As tsar of the secret society Bakunin was, after the Russian model, absolutely irresponsible, and this is why he detested plans for the future. Now it is true that plans for the future are easily formulated when they are no more than a collection of wishes. But from one who arrogates on behalf of his reforms even the right to kill we may demand as a preliminary a precise and conscientious analysis of social institutions and their defects. We may also demand a precise and conscientious analysis of historical evolution, that it may be possible to forecast with reasonable probability the course of future evolution.

Marx was not always just to Bakunin in individual points, but his condemnation of Bakunin's fondness for blind ventures was thoroughly justified.

Moreover, Bakuninian great deeds shrunk lamentably when attempts were made to realise pandestruction. Bakunin was incessantly advocating petty disturbances and conspiracies, the promotion of unrest among peasants and operatives, ferments and revolts of all kinds. These were to keep the revolutionary spirit alive, and to pave the way for the ultimate catastrophe. Bakunin and his adherents spoke of the method as " parlefaitisme " (propaganda by deed).

Bakunin remained the confirmed Russian aristocrat. Everything that he casts up against the Russian aristocracy was preeminently applicable to himself and his anarchism. It is the blinded spirit of aristocracy which conjures up before his vain imagination the spectre of great deeds. It is this same spirit of aristocracy which inspires his willingness to subject the common revolutionists to Jesuitical drill, as a preliminary to making corpses of them. His revolutionism notwithstanding, Bakunin ever remains the defender of serfdom, the lord separated from his revolutionary slaves by the impenetrable wall of the secret society. This secret society business is a mere copy of absolutist aristocracy with its secret police and its secret diplomacy. Bakunin has no inkling that the essential and universal precondition to democracy must be publicity and mutual criticism. Secret societies are an incorporation of the aristocratic spirit with its illusion of great deeds and its contempt for the petty details of work—its shyness of work in general.

Bakunin with his social democracy reaches, in fact, the same result as was reached by Renan, the declared aristocrat, with his ingenious machine. The machine can break the world into fragments, but the élite of the intellectuals, those who alone understand the working of the secret mechanism, are enabled to impose fear and order upon the masses. Bakunin has not discovered an all-destroying machine, but he has discovered the all-destroying revolution, to be directed by the élite of his secret society under his personal leadership.

Bakunin's individualism culminates in the negation of individuality, culminates in absolutism. Crime and murder were dreaded by Bělinskii and Herzen as inevitable consequences of German philosophical subjectivism and individualism. With dauntless inconsistency Bakunin elevated them into a system and proclaimed the right to kill. In early days he had objected to German subjectivism and individualism on the ground that the doctrine led to suicide, but discarding this train of thought Bakunin himself came to advocate assassination.

Bakunin desires an-archy (he expressly revives the etymological significance of the term as the destruction of all authority). He preaches a war of annihilation after the manner of the robber chieftains of popular saga. In 1869 he declares that brigandage is one of the most honourable forms of Russian political life.

" We need something very different from a constitution ; we need storm and life, a world that is lawless and consequently free," he had exclaimed in 1848. Similarly in the secret rules of 1869 we read that the international brethren must combine " revolutionary fervour " with intelligence, energy, faithfulness, and discretion—must have a spice of the devil in them.

In Bakunin's own composition there was this spice of devilry, and he nourished his devil with the feelings of revenge that he cherished throughout life. We can understand that the regime of Nicholas I could not fail to inspire sentiments of hatred and a desire for revenge, but hatred and revenge make people blind, and those animated by such passions cannot hope to strike victorious blows.

In Gué's reminiscences (see p. 432) we are told that the painter's wife once asked Bakunin what were his aims and what were his beliefs. The answer was : " I believe in nothing.

I read nothing. I think of but one thing : twist the neck, twist it yet further, screw off the head, let not a trace of it remain ! "

§ 92.

AT the close of his life Bakunin recanted from Bakuninian anarchism and Jesuitism. At any rate, on October 21, 1874, he wrote as follows to Ogarev : " Realise at length that nothing living and firm can be upbuilded upon Jesuitical trickery, that revolutionary activity aiming to succeed must not seek its supports in base and petty passions, and that no revolution can achieve victory without lofty and conspicuously clear ideals." Dragomanov considers that these words embody a complete renunciamento on Bakunin's part, but I can see in them no more than a momentary doubt, such as often affected him in his loneliness, especially after the death of Herzen. He was always accessible to the words of a friend.

In 1870 he had broken with his adept Nečaev, and had branded him a traitor. In 1872 Bakunin accused Nečaev of Machiavellianism and Jesuitism.

In confirmation of his own interpretation Dragomanov refers to an incident recorded by Malon, who tells us that in February 1876 Bakunin rejoiced over the republican victory in the elections, saying : " La liberté mondiale est sauvée ! est sauvée encore une fois par la grande France ! " Other writers refer to this utterance as a proof that Bakunin's anarchistic and antipolitical views had undergone modification. To me, however, it seems that we have here no more than one of the numerous improvisations characteristic of Bakunin's impulsive temperament. Moreover, these retractations do not concern the revolution itself but the method of revolution. We must not forget that from time to time Bakunin considered the possibility of revolution without bloodshed, and would then give it the preference over a bloody revolution. Read, for example, what he wrote in the year 1862, in the essay *The People's Cause.* Having declared that he would rather follow Alexander II as the people's tsar than he would follow Pugačev and Pestel, he continued : " Owing to human stupidity, bloody revolutions are frequently necessary, but they are invariably an evil, a terrible evil and a great misfortune." Even in his secret instructions he refers similarly to revolutions as the outcome of human stupidity, but the trouble is that he collaborates in this stupidity, and demands that others should collaborate. Nevertheless when he writes thus he can no longer be conceiving revolt as a primordial mental energy.

§ 93.

MARX and the Marxists, and some of the liberals as well (Ruge, and others), accused Bakunin of nationalist panslavism, and reproached him therefore with being illogical. Even to-day many of the historians of socialism continue to puzzle their brains over the question whether (as was frequently maintained in Marxist circles) Bakunin did not become a Russian agent towards the close of his career.

It is true that in 1862 Bakunin continued to wonder whether the tsar would not carry out his plans for him, and we have just read that Alexander II seemed to him preferable as a leader to Pugačev and Pestel. Proudhon entertained similar illusions regarding Napoleon III. Mickiewicz, again, and many others based their hopes at times upon the thought of their most powerful enemies' conversion. Herzen cherished like aspirations, and Bakunin shared such a plan with Herzen, a plan which is certainly opposed to the idea of effecting change "from below upwards."

The views common to Bakunin and Herzen were not the expression of political and nationalistic panslavism, but were derived from slavophil messianism. In contradistinction with Herzen, Bakunin laid stress rather upon Slav than upon Russian messianism. The difference is explicable from the consideration that Bakunin had come into personal contact with other Slav revolutionaries—Poles, Czechs, and southern Slavs.

Marx and the Marxists, and also Ruge and other of the German opponents of Bakunin, are right in considering that Bakunin overestimated the revolutionary capacity of the Slavs. In other respects, however, Bakunin's Slavist program was no more nationalist than that of Marx and the liberals. Marx proposed an antislav combination on the part of Germans, Poles, and Magyars, preaching russophobia, czechophobia, and croatophobia. Bakunin, on the other hand, in the *Appeal to the Slavs* (1848) which was so strongly criticised by Marx, invited the Slavs to espouse the cause of the Magyars against Windischgrätz. In like manner Bakunin was for the Poles and also for the Germans (the people of Germany, not the despots). The essential difference is merely that Bakunin was a Russian, whereas Marx, Engels, and Ruge, being Germans, were animated with German sentiments.[1] In an earlier work of my own,[2] I have furnished proof of the assertion that at a considerably later date, Marx and the Marxists were still inspired with German nationalist sentiments, and cherished antipathies towards the Slavs. It is necessary to refer to the fact once more to-day, in view of the nationalist struggles now in progress within the ranks of the social democracy.[3]

To this view, which certainly cannot be termed chauvinist, Bakunin continued to adhere. He was a Russian, and as such desired that the Russians and the Slavs should become members of the revolutionary family of the nations. In the year 1848 he participated in the Prague rising ; in 1863 he wished to help the Poles ; at this time, too, he assisted in the commencing revolutionary organisation of the Russians. He had faith in the revolutionary energy of the Slavs.

If we wish to account for Bakunin's fondness for the Poles, we have only to recall that enthusiastic sarmatiophilism was almost universal at this epoch, and to remember Bakunin's personal acquaintanceship with Poles in Europe and in Siberia. We know, too, that his wife was a Pole.[4] Political relationships had existed between the radical Russians and the Poles ever since the partition of Poland.

When in 1848 the Czechs and the Ruthenians drew up their program of federation, Bakunin was won over to this cause. Bakunin belonged to a multilingual state, wherein distinct nationalities were struggling for national and linguistic rights. To him, consequently, the distinction between the centralising state and nationality was clearer than it was to Marx, by whom

---

[1] Marx's criticism of Bakunin's appeal (Appeal to the Slavs, by a Russian Patriot, M. Bakunin, Member of the Slav Congress in Prague, 1848) was published in the "Neue Rheinische Zeitung." It will be found in Die gesammelte Schriften von Karl Marx und Friedrich Engels, 1902, vol. iii. p. 246).

[2] Grundlagen des Marxismus, § 119.

[3] While still in Siberia Bakunin wrote as follows (1860) : "Nationality, just like the individual, just like the processes of life, digestion, and breathing, has no right to concern itself about itself until that right is denied. This is why the Poles, the Italians, the Hungarians, and all the oppressed Slav peoples, naturally and rightly stress the principle of nationality ; and this is perhaps why we Russians concern ourselves so little about our nationality, and ignore it in favour of higher questions."

[4] Writing from Siberia in 1861, Bakunin declared that the Polish question had been an "idée fixe" with him since 1846.

this differentiation between state and nation was far less vividly perceived. At the congress of the League of Peace and Freedom held at Berne in 1868, Bakunin drew express attention to the distinction between state and folk. We have seen that Herzen wanted a folk-state, and in like manner Bakunin differentiated folk from state, and had a democratic conception of the folk. For the rest, enough has been said in earlier chapters regarding the principle of nationality and kindred problems.

Proof that Bakunin's panslavism was not nationalist in character is further afforded by the fact that he did not accept the Czech program altogether uncritically. He approved neither Palacky nor Rieger, for in opposition to these two leaders he desired to make common cause with the Magyars against Austria. He wished, too, to take the Rumanians into his Slav federation, for he desired the break up of Turkey as well as that of Austria. As regards all these designs, there were doubtless differences of outlook and differences in the estimate of the political situation, as between Bakunin on the one hand and Marx and the German radicals on the other, but we must not for this reason refer Bakunin's views to Slavist chauvinism. We may admit that Bakunin, like Herzen and Russians in general, was less sympathetic towards Germans than towards Frenchmen, Italians, and other members of the Latin races. Here, however, traditional influences were at work, and more especially family traditions, for Bakunin's father had had a predilection for the Latins, and above all for the Italians. When Bakunin's plans on behalf of the Poles and the Slavs were shipwrecked in 1863, he turned to the Latins. It must not be supposed that Bakunin had any national aversion for the Germans, but he disliked German conditions in general and the German bourgeoisie in particular.

To conclude, Bakunin, like Herzen, regarded the Russian people as predestined to establish the social revolution. In support of this view he referred in 1868 to the existence and significance of the mir. In the opinion of the Russian folk, he said, the soil belongs to the folk alone, to the genuinely working masses, to those who till the ground. Now this outlook, says Bakunin, enfolds all the social revolutions of the past and of the future. The Slavs, he contends, and above all the Great Russians, are the most unwarlike of the nations, and they therefore have no desire for conquests, but are inspired by an unalloyed and passionate eagerness for the free and collective utilisation of the soil. By instinct, continues Bakunin, giving free rein to his imagination, the Russians are socialistic ; by nature they are revolutionary ; the Russians, therefore, will initiate the federation of the world.

These fancies do not belong to the domain of realist thought, and they are all the more open to censure seeing that two years earlier Bakunin had given utterance to extremely critical opinions regarding the Russian mir. In his letter to Herzen and Ogarev (1866) he strongly condemned the patriarchalism of the mir, saying that it repressed individuality, permitted no internal revolution, and (before all) sacrificed woman. The mir as an institution was the incorporation of Chinese immobility.

In this connection it may be well to point out that Bakunin's opponent Marx, and Engels no less, held at first regarding the Russian mir, and therefore regarding the Russian people, views no less uncritical than those of Bakunin.

After 1863 Bakunin modified his Slavist designs and practically abandoned them. Henceforward he placed more confidence in the French and in the Latins generally, whilst, as we know, he discovered the revolutionary instinct in all men and all nations. Once only, in the year 1872, in response to a German appeal, he elaborated the program for a Slav section of the International in Zurich. The Slavs, including more particularly the Czechs, were to be won over to the cause of revolution and to be weaned from reactionary panrussism. In this program Bakunin expressly declared that the Slavs were not to be organised for their own sake ; their organisation was merely to serve as means for their incorporation in the general organisation of the International.

§ 94.

IN order to clarify our outlook concerning Bakunin's philosophical and political views, we will now undertake a comparison between Bakunin and Marx. This will throw much light upon the relationship between anarchism and socialism, in so far as Bakunin may be regarded as one of the principal founders of anarchism, whilst Marx may be looked upon as the founder of contemporary socialism, and thus the contrast between the two men may be envisaged as the contrast between anarchism and socialism.

First of all it is essential to bear in mind that Marx and Bakunin both went through a developmental process, that both men modified their opinions as time passed. Further, in making the comparison, we must differentiate between Marx and Marxism, and must not overlook the distinction between socialism and social democracy.

Turning from these methodological preliminaries to consider the immediate question under review, we cannot fail to find it significant that the opposition between Marx and Bakunin endured for many years.[1] This suffices by itself to justify the conclusion that the difference of outlook was based (even though not invariably) upon essential differences in point of principle.

In philosophy, both Bakunin and Marx started from the same point, from Hegel–Feuerbach and the Hegelian left; both learned from Proudhon and the French socialists; both were positivists and materialists; the two men lived for a considerable time in similar circumstances and in the same localities; both participated in the revolution; both had to suffer from the same reaction and from its effects upon personal safety and freedom.

But under the influence of German philosophy Bakunin remained subjectivist and individualist, whereas Marx (and all that is said here applies equally to Engels) was much more influenced than Bakunin by French and English positivism, passed on to extreme objectivism, and came to regard history and the social totality as the determining influences in social life. Bakunin, too, abandoned the extremer forms of subjectivism and individualism (Introduction to Hegel's *Gymnasial*

---

[1] In the year 1848 Marx was annoyed at the ill-considered rising in Baden of which Herwegh was the leader. At the time Bakunin defended Herwegh, but subsequently agreed that Marx had been right. In the same year, in the "Neue Rheinische Zeitung," Bakunin was accused of being a Russian agent, the accusation being based upon the alleged testimony of George Sand. Marx published the contradiction of this piece of gossip. In 1849 Marx animadverted against Bakunin's panslavist policy, but here, too, there was no serious difference upon matters of principle. Such a difference was first displayed during the struggle in the International. Marx was doubtless right in considering that the foundation of the Bakuninian second International was a tactical error. Bakunin appealed in justification to the difference between the Latin and the Teutonic lands. Marx was right, too, in respect of Nečaev, but the behaviour of Bakunin's opponents was not altogether above criticism.

Lectures, 1838). A few days before his death, talking about Schopenhauer, he condemned individualism, writing : " Our whole philosophy is established upon a false foundation when it conceives human beings as individuals, instead of looking upon them, as it should, as members of a collectivity. Hence arise most philosophical errors, the upshot of which is that happiness is looked for in the clouds, or else that pessimism ensues, like that of Schopenhauer and Hartmann." In 1838 he considered suicide the necessary consequence of extreme subjectivism and individualism, in 1876 pessimism was the consequence—the distinction is not very great. It is not clear how Bakunin represented to himself the relationship between the individual and the collectivity. His formula of 1876 smacks of Comte, not of Marx–Engels. This corresponds with Bakunin's demand for collectivism, not communism. The question how much individualism and how much collectivism was not precisely formulated by Bakunin.

As compared with Bakunin, Marx is more scientific, more critical. The German is the theorist, whilst the Russian's attention is directed rather towards political practice. At first, and even later, Marx's outlook did not in essentials differ from that of Bakunin. Marx, too, was a revolutionary, and took personal part in the revolution of 1848, although much more cautiously than Bakunin ; Marx, again, wished to destroy the state, and believed in the speedy attainment of an ideal condition of society. But Marx abandoned the revolutionism of his youth, devoted himself to scientific study, spent his days in the British Museum library, and endeavoured to provide positivist and materialist foundations for political economy and the philosophy of history. Bakunin, on the other hand, was an organiser of revolts in which he took an active share, and only on occasions did he endeavour to collect his thoughts theoretically.

This is why Marx so greatly excels Bakunin as sociologist and still more as philosopher of history.

Vis-à-vis revolutionism the main difference is to be found in Marx's historical materialism and in his conception of the determinism of historical development. But Marx and his disciples did not at the outset deduce the logical consequences of historical materialism ; and, moreover, the doctrine was not at first (if ever) clearly and unambiguously formulated. Historical materialism led Marx and the Marxists to views differing from those of Bakunin concerning the state, law, and ideology in general—for it must be remembered that to Marx the state and state policy were likewise "ideology." State, law, church, etc., were not primary elements in social life, were not motive forces; and therefore political revolution was not decisive in its effects. Above all, in the Marxist view, the continual fomenting of revolution, Blanquism and Bakuninism, is inefficacious; decisive issues result from the orderly ripening of great historical epochs and from the definitive overthrow of the entire social edifice. It is true that Marx looked to the near future for the fulfilment of this expectation, and was therefore willing to lend a hand to the ever-recurring revolts, all the more since he did not profess to know what were the unmistakable indications of the coming of the decisive moment. Scientific history cannot pretend to offer apocalyptic signs of the time, and the prediction of the definitive cataclysm has not been fulfilled.

The force of Blanquism has moreover been weakened by the acceptance of Darwinism and the evolutionary idea. If social evolution proceed according to natural law, if it be the outcome of the class struggle, waged unceasingly as part of the natural order of things, then acute revolution is no more than a special case of chronic revolution, and our estimate of acute revolution must be revised. We conceive revolution as an evolutionary manifestation.

From Hegel, and yet more from Comte, Bakunin adopted the idea of an orderly development in great epochs. Bakunin, too, became a Darwinist; and yet he remained faithful to Blanquism.

Bakunin always recognised Marx's superior strength in philosophical and scientific matters. He translated the *Communist Manifesto* for Herzen's "Kolokol," and began a translation of the first volume of *Capital*. Bakunin accepted historical materialism and the theory of the class struggle, often expounding these doctrines and recommending them, after his own fashion. Even during the contest with Marx, Bakunin unhesitatingly admitted his opponent's merits as theorist and organiser.

At an early date Marx was distinguished from Bakunin and also from Herzen by his contemptuous neglect of the church and its political significance. In this respect Bakunin remained a Feuerbachian, or, better expressed, continued to adhere to views formed in his age of faith. In the Introduction to Hegel's *Gymnasial Lectures*, Bakunin formulated the essence of theocracy by saying, "where there is no religion there can be no state," and "religion is the substance, the quintessence, of the life of every state." Such was his opinion throughout life, the only change being that in maturer years he wished to replace religion by philosophy. The two men had at first similar ideas regarding the state, but the views and conduct of Marx underwent modification in proportion as he elaborated his historical materialism and his philosophy of history. From the first and subsequently (after 1863) Bakunin was more hostile to the state, which to him seemed more important than it did to Marx. Bakunin discovered the leading political and social evil in the principle of the state, in authority itself, not in political forms, which seemed to him matters of comparative indifference ; this is why he was continually engaged in the organisation of conspiracies for the final destruction of the state. Marx was likewise opposed to the state, but desired to use it for his own ends ; Marx, too, looked forward to a condition in which the state will no longer exist ; but this is to be brought about with the help of the state, the state is to abolish itself.

From the very outset, Marx and Bakunin differed in their respective conceptions of political and social administration. Marx was a centralist, Bakunin a federalist.[1]

Bakunin remained a revolutionary. Marx and the Marxists did not abandon the revolutionary idea, but they tended increasingly to postpone revolutionary practice to a distant future ; political effort, participation in parliamentarism, was to prepare the way for the realisation of the revolution. When Bismarck granted universal suffrage, Marx and Engels forged their weapons out of it in such a fashion that shortly before his death (1895) Engels declared revolution to be needless, and was eloquently silent concerning the definitive revolution. Bakunin would not hear a word of universal suffrage or of any other political institution ; he looked upon Marxism as nothing more than state socialism. Even the worker, when he becomes a ruler or a popular representative, is taking part in the state, and the state is the secret or overt source of slavery. All political activity is essentially bourgeois. Bakunin

[1] In the beginning Bakunin fought only against state absolutism; as late as 1868, like the Marxists, he would hear of nothing but a republic.

had an immoderate hatred of Bismarck, regarding Bismarckism as nothing but "militarism, police economics, and financial monopoly, united into a system." In agreement with Bismarck, Bakunin considered the Germans to be a state-loving race. In 1874 he declared that his hope was in the Slavs and the Latins, who were to react against pangermanism, not by the establishment of a great Slav state, but by the social revolution, which would bring into being a new, lawless, and therefore free world. Bakunin has no approval of petty reforms, desiring "revolution from the prime foundation." He aims at total disorganisation, entorganisation, political amorphism, and chaos, in the hope that the future society will spontaneously upbuild itself from below.

The Marx-Engels view of the state is therefore more dispassionate, for Marx and Engels, as historical materialists, recognise the socio-political primacy of economic organisation. Bakunin also admits the importance of economic foundations, entertains plans of a general strike, but invariably returns in the end to the expedient of political revolution. Nevertheless, as has been shown, attentive criticism of the utterances made by Bakunin at different epochs discloses a marked vacillation between the idea of economic primacy and that of political and religious primacy. It was impossible that Bakunin should remain uninfluenced by his contact with Marx, a contact which became closer for the very reason that he was engaged in a struggle with Marx.

Like Bakunin, Marx gave the name of "anarchy" to a condition in which there would be no state ; in the confidential circular directed against Bakunin, he defined anarchy as the disappearance of state and government. It is true that he here had in view, as he himself formulates it, the transformation of the government into a mere administration. But in Bakunin's writings, also, we can find passages wherein he interprets the annihilation of the state as nothing more than a radical transformation and reorganisation.[1]

It is possible, moreover, to quote from Bakunin passages in which he utters warnings against ill-considered fights and revolts. Apropos of the discussion concerning Karakozov's attempt on the life of Alexander II, he expressed doubts as to the utility of assassinating the tsar, but this scepticism is

---

[1] See, for example, Œuvres, i. p. 155, in Fédéralisme, Socialisme et Antithéologisme (1867).

quite casual, and therein lies its weakness. Again, he shook off Nečaev owing to the accusations made against the latter. The fact remains that Bakunin looked for a rising in every village in Russia—an incredible piece of revolutionary extravagance.

We must not overlook that Bakunin, as he boasted to Marx, possessed some talent for organisation. He collaborated in the organisation of the International, and proved his mettle as organiser of other societies.

Bakunin was the originator of the term " social democracy." Like Marx, Bakunin is in favour of communism, but he wishes this communism to be federally organised, not to be centralised.[1] When Bakunin thus emphatically speaks of himself as a collectivist and refuses to accept the designation of communist, the administrative outlook is determinative, not the social outlook. He desires economic equality and free association " from below upwards." But we find in his writings occasional utterances which may be interpreted as supporting private ownership. For example, in 1868, in the address to the congress of the League of Peace and Freedom, he advocates the abolition of the right to inheritance in a manner which would seem to imply that this is as far as he desired to go. Plehanov adduces this as proof that Bakunin was not vigorous enough in his opposition to private property. Plehanov further points out that Bakunin proposed that the French peasants should retain their property after the social revolution. But it must be remembered that this was simply because Bakunin regarded peasant proprietorship as a matter of trifling importance, and was prepared, just like some of the communists of to-day, to concede small-scale private property in land. Marx wished to establish his society with the aid of the industrial workers, the proletarians ; Bakunin looked rather for help to the peasants, especially in the case of Russia.[2]

Nor is there any real difference between Bakunin and Marx in their outlook on nationality. The former is Russian and Slav, just as the latter is German. Bakunin's wish to inspire the

[1] He distinguishes " revolutionary socialists or collectivists " from " authoritarian communists."

[2] In his first Slav program Bakunin demanded that in the Slav federation every burgher should have a right to land. He was thinking here of the agrarian communism of the mir. Speaking generally, Bakunin as a Russian (it must be remembered this was many decades ago) had his eyes on the peasant masses, whilst Marx looked towards the operatives.

Slavs with revolutionary ardour is quite comprehensible, far more comprehensible than Marx's antipathy to the Russians, the Czechs, and the Croats. Bakunin's hostility to the Germans was no greater, not even when he was directly attacking them (as in 1862, when he wrote apropos of federation, "that which is endurable to the Slavs is death to the Germans ").

Taking everything into consideration, we cannot find that between Bakunin and Marx there existed such an absolute contrast as the Marxists and anarchists of to-day, opposing one another on principle, are apt to contend. Bakunin is more individualist than Marx, more revolutionary, if we think of the longing for revolution as instinctive, or temperamental ; Bakunin's mind works more along political lines, and does so because he is not a consistent historical (economic) materialist. Bakunin is notably distinguished from Marx by his approval of terrorism in the form of individual outrages and by his approval of individual acts of expropriation. Marx appeals only to the decisions of the mass, and thereby his policy of course becomes more considered, more mature, and more effective.

It cannot be denied that Bakunin was, to a degree, anarchist in the sense of aimless and turbulent disorder. But Laveleye does him an injustice when he insists that this was the leading factor in Bakunin's views.

Primitive revolutionary feeling, purely negative revolutionism, which were so strongly characteristic of Bakunin, were known also to Marx. In the first volume of *Capital* the revolutionary mood finds vigorous expression, but we see how Marx is endeavouring to bridle it, and to transform it into positivist dispassionateness. Bakunin could never look on things so impersonally as did Marx, for in the Russian the sentiments of the hunted refugee, the injured outlaw, continually found expression. Marx could be impassioned on occasions, as in his defence of the Paris commune, but when he was impassioned he was strong. Bakunin's excitement betrays weakness.

Bakunin is a revolutionary, Marx a statesman and tactician. Marx was more nice in his methods. Bakunin did not see through Nečaev until his friends remonstrated and the scandal had become notorious. At Prague, again, in 1848, Bakunin was only playing at revolution. Herzen is quite right in his judgment here, and Kropotkin really agrees with Herzen, so does Lavrov, whose adherents could not get on with the Bakuninists. Those anarchists err who extol Bakunin as a man of action ; he was a dilettante, and his practical life no less than his theoretical was a collection of fragments. I do not deny that Bakunin was a man of genius ; I am not over-persuaded by the arguments of Marx, Engels, and others ; but I consider that on the whole Marx was right and Bakunin wrong. Marx understood the nature of democracy better than Bakunin, understood better how democracy might be realised. Bakunin's revolutionism and anarchism are the freedom of the Russian Cossack, the pseudo-hero whose characteristics have been so ably depicted by the painter Vereščagin, the pseudo-hero who made such a poor showing in the Russo-Japanese war. For Russia, Bakunin believes in brigands à la Pugačev and Razin ; for Europe, he believes in the dregs of the proletariat.

Bakunin, who desired to transform the world from its foundations, remained throughout life nothing better than a dreamer. When living in a villa near Locarno, an heirloom of his friend and disciple Cafiero which had been placed by the latter at the master's disposal, he wished to organise a rising in Italy, and had thoughts of boring a tunnel through which his anarchists could make their way into that country unnoticed. A manifestation of this same foolish simplemindedness was his antisemitism, which was displayed from time to time in his attacks on Lassalle and Marx.

We must not forget that Bakunin, during his second period of residence in Europe, lived in the Latin countries, whereas Marx was in England. Both men involuntarily constructed their ideas of the future and their thoughts regarding the organisation of society mainly out of the enduring impressions of their respective environments. Bakunin, who wherever he went remained the unresting foreigner, moved by preference in the comparatively unorganised strata of the working class, whereas Marx was influenced by English and German experiences.

This was why the Paris commune impressed the two men so differently.

Bakunin's anarchism is largely explicable by his restless, positively nomadic life in Europe.

Bakunin exercised a powerful influence upon the development of the opposition in Russia, the development by which it became revolutionary and terrorist. The younger generation of the sixties and seventies gave ear to Bakunin, not to Herzen. During 1872 and 1873 there were in Switzerland, and notably at Zurich, hundreds of Russian students, many of whom became Bakuninists, and transplanted Bakuninism to Russia.

Peculiar is the combination that has been effected between Russian realism and Bakunin's unrealism. Pisarev's " destructive criticism " has become pandestruction ; the nihilistic word has become the revolutionary deed ; to an increasing extent " word and deed " is the revolutionary slogan.

In contradistinction to Herzen, Bakunin conceived nihilism, not as Byronic revolt but as Blanquist revolt. He defended the nihilists against Herzen's attacks ; defended their practical activities, while admitting that they were guilty of vacillations, contradictions, and even scandalous and foul abominations. For Bakunin these aberrations were no more than the inevitable accompaniments of inchoate conditions. He regarded them as proofs that the younger generation was striving to construct the new morality. Though he belonged to the older generation, Bakunin numbered himself among those who were seeking the new morality, and indeed he believed himself to have definitively formulated it.

Nevertheless Bakuninist tactics did not find application in Russia, if we except Nečaev's attempt and the peasant revolt in the Chigirin district (§ III, iii.).

In the theoretical field Bakunin did little to further the formulation either of socialism or of anarchism, but his example was suggestive to theorists as well as to practical men. It is not difficult to understand why such writers as Kropotkin, Čerkezov, etc., honour Bakunin as their teacher ; Turgenev, too, was much preoccupied by Bakunin's ideas. As a man Bakunin was good-natured, but simple, frivolous, and undisciplined.[1] Consistently desiring to realise his ideals, he did not shrink from the risks of action, and was ever willing to set his life upon a cast ; this deserves recognition when we contrast him with his two opponents, the hesitating Herzen and the

---

[1] Bakunin's heedlessness was often crudely displayed. I may recall the instance given by Herzen, that the new government in Paris, desiring to be rid of Bakunin, sent him 3,000 francs and told him to go to Germany, to carry on his revolutionary activities there. This is not denied by Bakunin's biographers.

calculating Marx. In this sense Annenkov has aptly termed him " the father of Russian idealism."

A final judgment upon anarchism will not be attempted here, for we have first to make acquaintance with Bakunin's successors.

INDEX OF NAMES

Achenwall, 203, 216
Adam Smith, *see* Smith
Adrian (Patriarch, died 1700), 61, 63
Aksakov, Ivan, 161, 287-291, 308, 310, 312, 315, 321–323, 326, 327, 330, 375, 384
Aksakov, Konstantin, 239, 254, 266-274, 276, 287, 290, 322, 325, 326, 328, 330, 333, 337, 342, 343, 347, 373, 419
Aksakov, Sergei Timoféevič, 239, 266, 329, 330
Aleksandrovič, Daniel, 20
Alekséev, 171
Alexander I, Tsar of Russia, 67, 77, 83, 84, 85, 87, 88, 89, 91–95, 97, 102, 105, 110, 111, 114, 115, 116, 117, 119–122, 125, 128, 130–132, 144, 149, 216, 226, 228, 286, 290, 316, 319, 326, 351
Alexander II, Tsar of Russia, 66, 67, 75, 104, 107, 110, 112, 127, 130, 136, 137, 142, 144, 146, 147, 153, 156, 157, 158, 161, 237, 269, 313, 322, 327, 384, 385, 407, 413, 452, 457, 458, 466
Alexander III, Tsar of Russia, 67, 130, 146, 156, 159, 160, 161, 162, 167, 170, 179, 189, 193, 195, 291, 313, 349
Alexis Mihailovič, Tsar of Russia, 29, 48, 52, 67, 190
Alexis Petrovič (son of Peter the Great), 57, 67
Alter, 297
Amurskii, Murav'ev, 434
Anacharsis Cloots, 388
Anastasia, Tsarina of Russia, 67
Andreev, 169, 190
Anne, Tsarevna of Russia, Duchess of Brunswick, 67
Anne, Tsarevna of Russia, Duchess of Holstein-Gottorp, 67
Anne, Tsarina of Russia, 66, 67, 71, 79, 216

Annenkov, 148, 348, 350, 365, 370, 470
Anton, 297
Antonii, Archbishop of St. Petersburg, 195
Antonii, Archbishop of Volhynia, 335
Antoninus, *see* Aurelius
Antony, Duke of Brunswick, 67
Apostol, *see* Murav'ev-Apostol
Arakčeev, 93, 94, 110, 143
Arcybašev, 198
Aristotle, 157, 208, 233, 250
Askočenskii, 149
Askold, 10
Augustus, Roman Emperor, 107
Aurelius Antoninus, Marcus, 233
Avakkum (Protopope), 48
Avdéev, 152.
Azev, 193, 194

Baader, 92, 286, 324, 331
Babeuf, 421
Bacon, 61
Baer, 291
Bakounine, *see* Bakunin
Bakunin, 148, 149, 153, 154, 334, 341, 346, 347, 349, 350, 351, 360, 374, 393, 398, 399, 400, 401, 403, 404, 405, 407, 417, 418, 420, 423, 430-471
Ballanche, 226
Baranov, 156
Barjatynskii, 121, 239
Batjuškov, 121, 373
Batu Khan, 419
Bauer, 444
Bayer, 215
Beaulieu, *see* Leroy-Beaulieu
Beaumarchais, 386
Beccaria, 70, 83
Bělinskii, 113, 114, 121, 124, 126, 133, 148, 149, 200, 254, 330, 334, 336, 337, 340, 347, 348, 850-378, 381, 382, 384, 387, 393, 397, 398, 399, 400, 401, 402, 405, 409, 410, 427, 431, 432, 434, 451, 453, 456

Běljaev, 333, 344
Běloręckii, 169
Benckendorff, 93, 96, 106, 231
Benediktov, 370
Benjamin Constant, see Constant
Bentham, 83, 95, 386
Berdjaev, 335
Bestužev, 104, 112, 116, 121, 124
Bestužev-Rjumin, 333
Bezobrazov, 171
Bibikov, 71
Biran, 259
Biron, 66, 79
Bismarck, 161, 310, 466
Blackstone, 70, 85
Blanc, 123, 362, 386, 418
Bobrikov, 173
Bodenstein, see Carlstadt
Bodjanskii, 308
Bogolěpov, 172
Bogoljubskii, 23
Boltin, 80, 81, 89, 114, 214, 215, 318, 330
Bonald, 84, 95, 108, 203, 226, 331, 339
Boniface VIII, 63
Borgo, see Pozzo di Borgo
Boris Godunov, Tsar of Russia, 31
Borkheim, 398
Botkin, 340, 347, 348, 350, 359, 367, 378, 434
Brambeus, see Senkovskii
Brandes, 3
Brežnovský, 191
Bruno Bauer, see Bauer
Büchner, 149
Buckle, 217
Budilovič, 333
Buharev, 149
Bulgarin, 311, 369
Bulygin, 174, 175, 178
Bunge, 161
Buraček, 114
Burke, 84
Busenbaum, 286
Butaševič, see Petraševskii
Byron, 96, 115, 125, 317, 318, 386, 390, 391, 392, 393, 397, 399, 402, 406, 407, 424, 427

Čaadaev, P. J., 106, 111, 113, 148, 217, 221-236, 237-240, 254, 257, 265, 273, 283, 284, 318, 319, 321, 322, 328, 334, 337, 338, 339, 347, 350, 353, 368, 382, 386, 392, 393, 394, 412
Čaadaev, M., 221

Cabet, 123, 362
Cafiero, 469
Čaikovskii, 153
Carlstadt, 256
Carlyle, 125, 380, 382, 392
Carnot, 419
Caspar Hauser, 428
Catherine, Tsarevna of Russia, Duchess of Mecklenburg, 67
Catherine I, Tsarina of Russia, 66, 67, 72, 79
Catherine II the Great, Tsarina of Russia, 66-72, 75-81, 82, 83, 86, 110, 115, 116, 131, 134, 138, 144, 385
Cavaignac, 389
Cavour, 343
Čehov, 160
Čelakovský, 308
Čerep-Spiridovič, 315
Čerkezov, 470
Černaev, 310
Černyševskii, 141, 148, 152, 153, 186, 200, 334, 349, 381, 393, 397, 399, 418, 424, 431
Chamberlain, 281
Charlemagne, 18
Charles Frederick, Duke of Holstein-Gottorp, 67
Chateaubriand, 84, 226, 227, 317, 390
Chrysorrhoas, see Joannes Damascenus
Čičerin, 312, 340, 343, 344, 345, 346, 348, 349, 423
Cicero, 69
Cloots, 388
Comte, 149, 203, 206, 208, 210, 217, 366, 367, 369, 386, 387, 392, 393, 395, 397, 432, 447, 448, 463, 464
Condorcet, 78, 202, 204
Congreve, 419
Considérant, 386
Constant, 95, 115, 286
Constantine Nikolaievič, Grand Duke of Russia, 156
Constantine Pavlovič, Grand Duke of Russia, 67, 83, 105, 136
Constantius II, Roman Emperor, 37
Copernicus, 212
Čulkov, 78
Cyril, 283, 308
Czartoryski, 83

Damascenus, see Joannes Damascenus
Danilevskii, 124, 291-293, 334, 383
Darwin, 149, 204, 291
Daškova, 69
Debagorii-Mokrievič, 454

Degaev, 193
Deržavin, 90, 116, 373
Descartes, 61, 203, 210
Desnickii, 70
Destutt de Tracy, 95
Diderot, 69, 70, 74, 85, 186, 397
Dir, 10
Dmitrii Donskoi, 20
Dmitriev-Mamonov, 78, 101, 102
Dobner, 297
Dobroljubov, 141, 148, 349, 381
Dobrovský, 297, 307
Donskoi, see Dmitrii Donskoi
Dostoevskii, F., 107, 113, 121, 124, 131,
    146, 148, 149, 159, 160, 161, 186,
    198, 236, 291, 320, 327, 330, 332,
    335, 350, 367, 368, 370, 379, 382,
    383
Dostoevskii, M., 379, 382, 383
Dragomanov, 157, 159, 303, 387, 435,
    450, 454, 457
Družinin, 148, 348
Dubrovin, 192, 193
Durov, 113

Eckartshausen, 84, 226, 386
Elagin, 239, 253
Elizabeth Alekséevna, see Louisa Maria
Eliseev, 149
Elizabeth, Queen of England, 190
Elizabeth, Tsarina of Russia, 66, 67,
    68, 71, 73, 79
Elysard (pseudonym of Bakunin) 436
Eminov, 78
Engelhardt, 105
Engels, 150, 358, 365, 366, 425, 432,
    459, 461, 462, 465, 469
Epicurus, 233
Eschenmayer, 386
Evdokija, see Lopuhin
Ewers, 215

Faděev, 309
Fénelon, 78
Ferguson, 202
Feuerbach, 123, 149, 150, 186, 207,
    213, 256, 331, 340, 341, 350, 351,
    358, 359, 360, 361, 365, 366, 368,
    369, 376, 386, 387, 392, 393, 400,
    401, 403, 408, 418, 421, 422, 425,
    432, 434, 444, 446, 462
Fichte, 115, 123, 211, 212, 213, 244,
    253, 260, 281, 320, 338, 350, 351,
    353, 356, 358, 360, 361, 376, 400,
    401, 432, 433, 435, 443, 448, 453
Filaret (Mme. Kiréevskii's confessor), 241

Filaret, Metropolitan of Moscow, 93,
    110, 116
Filaret (Patriarch and Co-Tsar), 35, 44,
    67, 195
Fischer, 383
Flerovskii, 166
Fletcher, 51
Fonvizin, D. I., 69, 79
Fonvizin, M. A., 307
Fotii Spasskii, 93, 94, 110, 265
Fourier, 84, 123, 124, 331, 362, 386, 418
Francis I, Emperor of Austria, 82
Frank, 222
Frederick II, the Great, King of Prussia,
    68, 74, 76, 82
Frederick William III, King of Prussia,
    82, 355
Frederick William IV, King of Prussia,
    105, 106, 436

Gagarin, 222, 228, 229, 265, 286
Gai, 299
Galič, 339
Gans, 239
Gapon, 174
Garašanin, 106
Garibaldi, 387
Gävernitz, see Schulze-Gävernitz
Genghis Khan, 419
Gennadii (Archbishop of Novgorod,
    15th century), 44, 45
Gentz, 84, 109, 317
George Sand, see Sand
Geršenzon, 227, 335
Giers, 167
Glinka, S., 354
Glinka, T., 354
Gobineau, 281
Godunov, see Boris
Goethe, 123, 347, 350, 356, 359, 390,
    392, 393, 402, 422
Gogol, 112, 113, 114, 121, 135, 137,
    232, 238, 239, 254, 288, 309, 319,
    330, 350, 352, 364, 365, 367, 368,
    370, 373, 374, 377, 393, 398, 411
Golovin, 128, 183
Golicyn, 94, 286
Gončarov, 121, 146, 350, 369, 370
Goremykin, 181
Gor'kii, 178, 332, 346
Görres, 95, 109, 331
Gradovskii, 344, 349
Granovskii, 112, 216, 239, 249, 254,
    324, 328, 337, 339, 340, 341, 347,
    348, 350, 354, 386, 392, 400, 423,
    436

Greč, 369
Griboedov, 95, 112, 121, 126, 224, 225, 239, 370, 373
Grigor'ev, 200, 334, 335, 379-383
Grigorovič, 121, 135, 137, 147, 350, 370
Grimm, 296
Grote, 208
Grün, 393
Gué, 432, 456
Guillaume, 435
Guyon, 84
Guizot, 123

Habakkuk, see Avakkum
Haller, 317
Hanka, 282, 298, 308, 309, 310
Hardenberg, 95
Hartmann, 281, 463
Hauser, 428
Havliček, 298, 308
Haxthausen, 123, 312, 316, 319, 328, 329, 344
Hegel, 122, 123, 149, 150, 203, 205, 213, 217, 222, 226, 237, 239, 244, 246, 248, 258, 259, 261, 267, 270, 271, 272, 281, 282, 284, 285, 286, 305, 319, 324, 331, 337, 338, 339, 340, 347, 350, 351, 352, 353, 355, 356, 357, 359, 360, 362, 366, 371, 372, 374, 376, 377, 382, 386, 390, 400, 401, 408, 410, 418, 422, 430, 432, 434, 437, 440, 443, 448, 462, 464, 465
Heine, 150, 360
Helena Pavlovna, 136
Helferich, 168
Helvetius, 77
Heraskov, 78
Herberstein, 24, 51
Herder, 71, 72, 76, 116, 202, 211, 215-271, 273, 279, 281, 297, 298, 299, 317, 318, 319, 386
Herwegh, 387, 462
Herzen, 73, 79, 100, 104, 106, 107, 112, 113, 122, 125, 126, 128, 135, 148, 149, 151, 153, 154, 186, 224, 232, 236, 239, 254, 287, 312, 320, 328, 334, 337, 340, 341, 342, 346, 347, 349, 350, 351, 354, 359, 360, 361, 363, 374, 384-429, 431, 432, 433, 434, 435, 445, 446, 450, 453, 454, 456, 457, 458, 460, 464, 468, 470
Herzenstein, 182, 192, 193
Hess, 453
Hilferding, 333

Hmelnickii, 71
Hobbes, 397, 409
Hoffmann, 123, 347, 350
Holbach, 74, 77
Homer, 233, 330
Homjakov, Aleksěi, 113, 148, 235, 238, 239, 241, 247, 249, 253, 254-266, 267, 269, 270, 271, 272, 273, 282-286, 288, 291, 293, 309, 310, 320, 322-324, 326-328, 330, 332-335, 336, 337, 365, 367, 370, 380, 382, 393, 399, 415
Homjakov (Octobrist), 185
Horsey, 51
Houston Chamberlain, see Chamberlain
Hume, 202, 203, 205, 206, 208, 209, 210, 244, 318, 358, 369, 393, 397
Huss, 298
Hutton, 402

Iskander, 387, see also Herzen
Ivan the Terrible, see John IV
Ivan III, 20, 91, 215
Ivan Kalita (Grand Prince 14th century), 20
Ivanov, 153
Ivanov-Razumnik, 351
Iosif (15th-century ecclesiastical reformer), 43, 44
Izmailov, 78

Jacobi, 212
Jakovlev, 385
Jakuškin, 104, 147, 225
Jazykov, 121, 236, 239, 254, 330, 337
Javorskii, 57, 63, 285
Joannes Damascenus, 248, 331
John IV, the Terrible, Tsar of Russia, 20, 25, 26, 28, 42, 44, 50, 51, 58, 67, 188, 275, 330, 349
John V, Tsar of Russia, 28, 67
John VI, Tsar of Russia, 66, 67
Jollos, 192
Joseph II, Emperor of Holy Roman Empire, 76, 82, 294
Jung, J. H., called Stilling, see Jung-Stilling
Jungmann, 298
Jung-Stilling, 84, 92, 226
Jur'evič, see Zahar'in
Jurii (Grand Prince 14th Century), 20

Kačenovskii, 308, 348
Kaisarov, 89
Kalita, see Ivan Kalita
Kankrin, 89

Kant, 123, 203, 205, 206, 208, 210, 211, 212, 213, 244, 246, 247, 253, 256, 258, 259, 260, 318, 338, 349, 400, 401, 432, 433, 435, 443, 448
Kantemir, 73
Karadšič, 299
Karakozov, 153, 405, 452, 466
Karamzin, 85, 88, 90, 101, 115, 116, 120, 214, 215, 216, 237, 332, 345, 348, 349
Karazin, 84, 88, 89, 90, 416
Karlstadt, see Carlstadt
Katkov, 148, 152, 156, 157, 171, 192, 291, 312, 347, 423
Kavelin, 141, 287, 324, 344, 349, 350, 384, 387, 391, 423
Ketčer, 347
Khan, see Genghis, and Batu
Kirěev, 315
Kirěevskii, Ivan, 113, 148, 235, 238-254, 255, 257, 258, 259, 260, 261, 267, 272, 273, 282, 283, 285, 286, 288, 291, 309, 315, 318, 320-330, 333-335, 338, 339, 347, 350, 367, 373, 382, 393
Kirěevskii, Madame, 241
Kirěevskii, Petr, 238, 239, 241, 254, 329
Kirillov, see Petraševskii
Kiselev, 129, 130
Ključevskii, 28
Klopstock, 116, 320
Kock, 350
Kočubei, 83, 85
Kohanovskaja, 330
Kojalovič, 333
Kolcov, 348, 370
Kollár, 297, 298, 299, 306, 307, 308
Köppen, 308
Korf, 144
Korrakov, 79
Košelev, 241, 254, 309, 327, 328, 333
Kossuth, 106
Kostomarov, 302, 303, 308
Kotošihin, 51
Krasinski, 305
Kravčinskii, see Stepniak
Križanič, 51, 299, 307
Kropotkin, 135, 186, 187, 189, 190, 432, 468, 470
Krüdener, 93, 94, 110
Krylov, 121, 373
Küchelbecker, 237, 239
Küchelberg, 104
Kurbskii, 25, 44, 51, 127
Kuropatkin, 167

Lagarde, 281

Laharpe, 83
Lamanskii, 299, 303, 310, 323, 333
Lamennais, 231, 234, 390
Lamettrie, 77
Lamsdorf, 105
Landauer, 435
Lange, 383
Lanskoi, 79
Lascaris, 46
Lassalle, 150, 186, 363, 365, 469
Laveleye, 468
Lavrov, 154, 156, 435, 469
Le Clerc, 80
Ledru-Rollin, 362
Leibnitz, 55, 76
Leont'ev, 160, 333, 334
Leopardi, 386
Leopold (Charles Leopold), Duke of Mecklenburg, 67
Lermontov, 73, 112, 114, 121, 370, 373, 377, 380
Leroux, 362
Leroy-Beaulieu, 17
Lěskov, 146
Lessing, 123, 202, 203, 320
Levitov, 147
Ligne, 79
Littré, 366, 386
Locke, 69, 85
Lomonosov, 65, 73, 114, 215, 216, 232
Lomtatidze, 190
Lopuhin (chief of police), 194
Lopuhin, Evdokija, 67
Lopuhin (freemason), 75, 84
Loris-Melikov, 155, 156, 159, 194
Louis Blanc, see Blanc
Louis XIV, King of France, 59
Louis XV, King of France, 76
Louis XVI, King of France, 360
Louis Philippe, King of the French, 105, 123, 242, 389
Louisa Maria, Princess of Baden (Elizabeth Alekséevna, wife of Alexander I, Tsar of Russia), 92
Lukin, 114
Luther, 256, 284
L'vov, 78, 114

Mably, 74, 76
Makarii, 241, 335
Magnickii, 93, 308
Maikov, Apollon, 124, 147, 330
Maikov, Valerian, 124, 148, 348, 373
Maistre, 84, 108, 117, 203, 225, 227, 317, 331, 337, 390, 395
Malon, 457

Malthus, 202, 204
Manutius, 46
Marat, 407
Marcus Aurelius, see Aurelius
Maria Theodorovna, see Sophia Dorothea, etc.
Maria Theresa, Queen of Hungary and Bohemia, wife of Francis I, Emperor of Holy Roman Empire, 76, 294
Marlinskii, see Bestuzev
Marquart, 11
Martynov, 152, 286
Marx, 150, 186, 203, 207, 213, 217, 320, 358, 363, 364, 365, 366, 403, 414, 418, 425, 432, 434, 435, 450, 455, 458, 459, 461–471
Mazzini, 106, 387, 404
Maxim the Greek, 46, 47, 51
Medicus, 203
Medvěděv, 45
Melikov, see Loris-Melikov
Mel'nikov, 5, 147
Mendelssohn, 211
Menšikov, 53, 59
Menzel, 354, 356
Merežkovskii, 160
Meščerskii, 286
Methodius, 283, 308
Metternich, 92, 96, 106, 111, 133, 193, 229
Mezencev, 154, 160
Michael Theodorovič, Tsar of Russia, 35, 44, 45, 52, 67
Michelet, 239, 386, 412, 417, 421
Mickiewicz, 305, 306, 311
Mihailov, 152
Mihailovskii, 148, 156, 200
Miljukov, A. P., 124, 333
Miljutin, 148
Mill, 149, 386, 427
Minié, 419
Minzes, 435, 454
Mirabeau, 401
Mirskii, see Svjatopolk-Mirskii
Mitrofan, 185
Mogila, 63
Mohammed (Prophet), 233
Möhler, 286
Mokrievič, Debagorii, 454
Moleschott, 149
Momonov, see Dmitriev-Mamonov
Monge, 419
Monomachus, see Vladimir Monomachus
Montalembert, 325

Montesquieu, 69, 70, 74, 83, 85, 86, 95, 202, 386
Mordvinov, 90
Morelly, 74
Müller, 215, 317
Murav'ev Amurskii, 434
Murav'ev-Apostol, Sergii, 104, 433
Murav'ev, Nikita, 98, 104
Muromcev, 179
Musset, 317
Nadeždin, 221, 225, 348, 350, 352, 370
Napoleon I, 85, 91, 93, 97, 117, 178, 254, 271, 279, 319, 360, 389, 401, 443
Napoleon III, 106, 112, 305, 389, 416, 458
Nebuchadnezzar, 48, 297
Nečaev, 153, 407, 433, 435, 454, 457, 462, 467, 468, 470
Nekrasov, 121–138, 146, 350, 370
Nelidov, 132
Nestor, 10, 214, 307
Nettlau, 435
Nicholas I, Tsar of Russia, 67, 79, 82, 88, 105–108, 110–115, 117, 119–122, 125, 126, 128–133, 136, 140, 144, 147, 149, 161, 216, 217, 221, 224, 226; 231, 237, 242, 249, 253, 265, 303, 307, 308, 316, 325, 326, 336, 342, 348, 351, 354, 355, 360, 361, 369, 371, 375, 384, 385, 404, 412, 427, 430, 456
Nicholas II, Tsar of Russia, 67, 157, 170, 173, 186, 190, 191, 192, 315
Niebuhr, 216, 390
Nikita, 67
Nikitenko, 147
Nikon (Patriarch), 46, 47, 48, 49, 54
Nil Sorskii, 44
Novalis, 317
Novgorodcev, 160
Novikov, 75, 89, 98, 330
Novosilcev, 85, 88, 89

Obolenskii, 136
Obradovič, 299
Odoevskii, 104, 123, 239, 339, 346, 366
Ogarev, 340, 349, 360, 361, 386, 387, 396, 404, 407, 413, 428, 429, 432, 434, 435, 457, 461
Oken, 239, 386
Oleg, 10, 11
Orlov, Prince (Dekabrist), 101, 102
Ostrovskii, 113, 121, 146, 330, 381, 382
Overbeck, 317

Ovid, 107
Owen, 84, 417

Pahlen, 158
Paine, 205, 211, 404
Paisii, 301
Palacký, 298, 308, 309, 460
Panaev, 124
Panin, 69
Pascal, 232, 248
Paškov, 151
Passek, Vadim, 387
Paul de Kock, 350
Paul, Saint, 355
Paul, Tsar of Russia, 66, 67, 69, 75, 76, 82, 83, 91, 92, 130, 131, 228, 416
Pavlov, 302, 347, 350, 352, 386
Pavlovna, see Helena Pavlovna
Pečerin, 228, 229
Pečerskii, see Mel'nikov
Pelzel, 297
Perovskaja, 158
Pestalozzi, 83
Pestel, 99, 100–105, 136, 142, 345, 386, 417, 457, 458
Peter I, the Great, Tsar of Russia, 1, 4, 9, 27, 28, 29, 31, 48, 49, 53–81, 86, 91, 103, 110, 116, 118, 168, 190, 214, 216, 230, 232, 236, 240, 245, 249, 262, 264, 285, 290, 316, 322, 331, 336, 337, 343, 344, 368, 374, 412
Peter II, Tsar of Russia, 67, 69, 71
Peter III, Tsar of Russia, 66, 67, 68
Petraševskii and the Petraševcy group, 107, 113, 124, 131, 291, 365, 418
Petrov, 185
Philip II, King of Spain, 359
Photius, see Fotii Spasskii
Photius, Patriarch of Constantinople, 223
Pierre Leroux, see Leroux
Pirogov, 144
Pisarev, 148, 152, 153, 334, 381, 398, 470
Pisemskii, 121, 146, 329
Plato, 69, 91, 157, 207, 208, 226, 250, 426
Plehanov, 180, 186, 334, 467
Pleščeev, 113, 124
Pleve, 173, 193, 194
Pnin, 77, 89
Pobědonoscev, 148, 156, 157, 158, 168, 171, 173, 174, 176, 291, 344
Pogodin, 113, 239, 253, 289, 293, 309, 314, 315, 334, 353
Polěnov, 80

Polevoi, 112, 113, 116, 124, 126, 239, 348, 359
Poležaev, 108, 370
Pomjalovskii, 147
Popov, 78
Porphyrogenitus, 13
Pososkov, 54, 60, 65
Potemkin, 79
Pozzo di Borgo, 221
Preis, 308
Procopius, 13
Prokopovič, see Theophan Prokopovič
Protasov, 111
Proudhon, 337, 340, 351, 362, 386, 392, 416, 419, 430, 432, 434, 446, 448, 453, 458, 462
Puchta, 272
Pugačev, 48, 49, 71, 74, 76, 77, 407, 457, 458, 469
Puriškivic, 192
Puškin, 73, 95, 103, 104, 112, 113, 114, 121, 137, 225, 232, 236, 239, 254, 276, 318, 319, 330, 350, 370, 373, 379, 380, 382, 386, 393, 414
Pypin, 346, 348, 349, 351

Quinet, 387, 401

Radiščev, 76, 77, 78, 79, 80, 82, 83, 84, 85, 88, 89, 177, 186, 200, 338
Radlov, 199, 200, 201, 202
Radstock, 151
Rahmanin, 78
Ranke, 348
Rasputin, 195
Raumer, 239
Raynal, 76
Razin, 31, 469
Razumnik, see Ivanov-Razumnik
Razumovskii, 79
Renan, 449, 456
Rennenkampf, 312
Rěšetnikov, 147
Reutz, 215.
Rieger, 310, 460
Ritter, 239, 348
Rjumin, see Bestužev-Rjumin
Rjurik, 10, 60
Robespierre, 90, 338, 360, 362, 388, 390, 401
Rollin, see Ledru-Rollin
Roman, see Zahar'in
Romanov, House of, 67
Rosenkampf, 85
Rostovcev, 136
Rothe, 263

Rothschild, 426
Rousseau, 74, 76, 77, 85, 86, 117, 202, 249, 257, 317, 318, 319, 338, 390, 392, 402, 421
Rückert, 292
Ruge, 432, 434, 436, 458, 459
Runič, 93
Rylěev, 104, 112, 121, 254, 265, 386
Rysakov, 155

Sabler, 194
Šafařík, 298, 307, 308, 309
Saharov, 171
Saint-Just, 362, 390
Saint-Simon, 84, 123, 124, 231, 331, 362, 380, 386, 392, 418, 422, 436
Saltykov, 113, 123, 124, 146, 365
Samarin, 47, 239, 254, 255, 258, 266, 285–287, 288, 291, 309, 312, 322, 324–328, 337, 345, 367, 384
Sand, 123, 356, 362, 434, 462
Savigny, 203, 272, 348
Savonarola, 46
Ščapov, 49, 302
Ščedrin, see Saltykov
Ščerbatov (historian), 70, 80, 81, 89, 114, 214, 215, 221, 318, 330
Ščerbatova, 221
Schelling, 123, 213, 217, 222, 226, 231, 233, 234, 237, 239, 240, 244, 246, 247, 248, 249, 251, 253, 259, 260, 261, 271, 282, 305, 324, 331, 338, 339, 340, 347, 350, 351, 352, 355, 356, 371, 372, 375, 376, 382, 386, 400, 401, 432, 434, 436, 437, 443
Schiemann, 387, 435
Schiff, 393
Schiller, 123, 136, 202, 320, 347, 350, 359, 363, 386, 402, 435
Schlegel, 226, 235, 260, 272, 317
Schleiermacher, 122, 239–248
Schlosser, 202
Schlözer, 202, 203, 215, 216, 307
Schopenhauer, 149, 210, 211, 213, 259, 281, 392, 398, 427, 433, 453, 463
Schubert, 339
Schulze-Gävernitz, 329
Selivanov, 93
Semevskii, 327
Senkovskii, 311
Šeremetev, 59, 147
Sergii, Archbishop of Finland, 335
Sergius, Grand Duke, 173, 193
Serno-Solov'evič, A. A., 398
Serno-Solov'evič, N. A., 398
Ševčenko, 107, 113, 303, 423

Ševyrev, 239, 276, 286, 298, 309, 337
Shakespeare, 320, 347, 377, 397
Sibirjakov, 136
Silvester (author of Domostroi), 43
Sineus, 10
Šiškov, 115, 116, 237, 238, 307, 308, 323, 330
Skoběev, 65
Skovoroda, 199
Smith, 70, 83, 90, 119, 202
Sočinskii, 107
Socrates, 208, 233
Solncev, 110
Solov'ev, S. M., 344, 349
Solov'ev, Vladmir, 160, 198, 199, 292, 321, 333, 335
Solov'evič, see Serno-Solov'evič
Sophia (Tsarevna, sister of Peter the Great), 29, 58, 67
Sophia, Dorothea Augusta, Princess of Würtemberg (Maria Theodorovna), Tsarina of Russia, 67
Sorskii, see Nil Sorskii
Spasowicz, 348, 349
Spasskii, see Fotii Spasskii
Spencer, 149, 186, 207
Speranskii, 85, 86, 87, 90, 93, 108, 116, 127
Spinoza, 186, 399
Spiridovič, see Čerep-Spiridovič
Srezněvskii, 308
Staël, 115, 116, 226
Stahl, 203, 337
Stankevič, 125, 267, 339, 344, 347, 348, 350, 351, 352, 361, 366, 367, 377, 429, 430, 433, 434
Stasjulevič, 349
Stead, 189
Steffens, 247, 248
Stein, 95, 127
Sten'ka Razin, see Razin
Stepniak, 151, 154, 160
Sterne, 76
Stilling, see Jung-Stilling
Stirner, 150, 207, 212, 213, 256, 261, 326, 331, 365, 392, 393, 401, 425, 432
Stojunin, 144
Stolberg, 317
Stolypin, 181, 185, 187, 189, 193
Storch, 119, 216
Strahov, 200, 322, 383
Strauss, 186, 207, 361, 368, 443, 449
Struve, 160, 172
Stuhr, 239
Štur, 299
Sudeikin, 193

Sumarokov, 77, 89, 114
Sungurov, 125
Süssmilch, 203
Suvarov, 91
Svjatopolk-Mirskii, 173
Swedenborg, 84, 386
Sypjagin, 173, 174

Tatarinova, 93
Tatiščev, 80, 214, 215, 216
Tauler, 84, 227
Tetens, 211
Theodore Aleksěevič, Tsar of Russia, 26, 29, 45, 67
Theodore Ivanovič, Tsar of Russia, 29
Theophan Prokopovič, 61, 62, 63, 66, 285
Theophil, 193
Tihomirov, 160
Tjutčev, 326, 330, 341
Tkačev, 154
Tocqueville, 325
Tolstoi, Aleksěi, 147
Tolstoi, D. A., 157, 158, 193
Tolstoi, Lev N., 3, 4, 73, 121, 144, 146, 151, 159, 186, 187, 190, 199, 200, 233, 354, 382, 383
Tönnies, 332
Towianski, 305
Tracy, see Destutt de Tracy
Tredjakovskii, 114, 214, 215
Trepov, 154
Truvor, 10
Tschadaieff, see Čaadaev
Turgenev, Ivan, 113, 121, 123, 137, 138, 146, 147, 186, 276, 319, 329, 334, 347, 349, 350, 356, 367, 370, 373, 382, 384, 387, 389, 398, 400, 415
Turgenev, Nikolai, 101, 127, 128, 140, 142, 151, 225, 232, 236, 342, 345, 349, 424
Turgot, 116, 202
Tveritinov, 61
Tylor, 207

Uhtomskii, 167, 168
Ulrich von Hutten, 402
Ušinskii, 144, 302
Uspenskii, 124, 147
Utin, 349, 435
Uvarov, 109, 111, 113, 129, 130, 136, 192, 217, 221, 222, 235, 236, 237, 265, 291, 308, 309, 313, 319, 323, 342, 355, 384

Vadim Passek, 387
Valuev, 156, 239, 254, 304
Vasilčikov, 79
Vasilii (Grand Prince, 15th century), 20
Venelin, 301
Venevitinov, 121, 239, 371
Vereščagin, 469
Vico, 202, 206, 207, 358, 386, 392
Vinet, 248
Vissarion, 369, see also Bělinskii
Vjazemskii, 89, 113, 239
Vladimir Monomachus, 23, 40, 43, 109, 420, 421, 426
Vladimir Aleksandrovič, Grand Duke, 193
Vladimir (Saint, 10th century), 38, 39, 275, 319
Vodovozov, 302
Vogt, 149, 361, 386, 387, 392, 393, 396, 432, 434, 448
Voigt, 297
Voltaire, 66, 69, 71, 74, 76, 78, 82, 85, 116, 122, 186, 202, 203, 226, 319, 338, 353, 385, 386, 392, 395, 402, 435
Volynskii, 160
Vyšnegradskii, 161

Wagner, Richard, 281, 434
Weitling, 417
Werder, 348
Witte, 161, 163, 178, 181, 183
Worzel, 396
Wronski, 305

Yxkull, 286

Zagoskin, 114, 116, 324
Zahar'in (boyar), 67
Zahar'in (writer), 78
Zahar'ina, 386, 387
Zasulič, 154
Zavitnevič, 259
Zavodskii, 79
Zorin, 79
Zlatovratskii, 148
Zubatov, 174
Žukovskii, N., 435
Žukovskii, V. A., 105, 120, 136, 147, 238, 239, 373, 374
Zwingli, 256